The Subject of Care

feminist constructions

Series Editors: Hilde Lindemann Nelson
and Sara Ruddick

Feminist Constructions publishes accessible books that send feminist ethics in promising new directions. Feminist ethics has excelled at critique, identifying masculinist bias in social practice and in the moral theory that is used to justify that practice. The series continues the work of critique, but its emphasis falls on construction. Moving beyond critique, the series aims to build a positive body of theory that extends feminist moral understandings.

Recognition, Responsibility, and Rights
    edited by Robin N. Fiore and Hilde Lindemann Nelson

Feminists Doing Ethics
    edited by Peggy DesAutels and Joanne Waugh

Gender Struggles: Practical Approaches to Contemporary Feminism
    edited by Constance L. Mui and Julien S. Murphy

"Sympathy and Solidarity" and Other Essays
    by Sandra Lee Bartky

The Subject of Violence: Arendtean Exercises in Understanding
    by Bat-Ami Bar On

How Can I Be Trusted? A Virtue Theory of Trustworthiness
    by Nancy Nyquist Potter

Moral Contexts
    by Margaret Urban Walker

The Subject of Care: Feminist Perspectives on Dependency
    by Eva Feder Kittay and Ellen K. Feder

Forthcoming books in the series by:

Anita Allen; Amy Baehr; Joan Mason-Grant; and Chris Cuomo

The Subject of Care

Feminist Perspectives on Dependency

Eva Feder Kittay
and Ellen K. Feder

ROWMAN & LITTLEFIELD PUBLISHERS, INC.
Lanham • Boulder • New York • Oxford

ROWMAN & LITTLEFIELD PUBLISHERS, INC.

Published in the United States of America
by Rowman & Littlefield Publishers, Inc.
A Member of the Rowman & Littlefield Publishing Group
4720 Boston Way, Lanham, Maryland 20706
www.rowmanlittlefield.com

PO Box 317
Oxford
OX2 9RU, UK

British Library Cataloguing in Publication Information Available

Library of Congress Cataloging-in-Publication Data

The subject of care : feminist perspectives on dependency / [edited by] Eva Feder Kittay
   and Ellen K. Feder.
      p. cm.—(Feminist constructions)
   ISBN 0-7425-1362-9 (alk. paper) — ISBN 0-7425-1363-7 (pbk.: alk. paper)
   1. Feminism. 2. Child welfare—United States. 3. Mother and child—United
States. 4. Caregivers—Family relationships. 5. Family services—United States.
I. Kittay, Eva Feder.   II. Feder, Ellen K.   III. Series.

HQ1206.S9 2003
305.42—dc21   2002011811

Printed in the United States of America

♾™ The paper used in this publication meets the minimum requirements of American
National Standard for Information Sciences—Permanence of Paper for Printed Library
Materials, ANSI/NISO Z39.48-1992.

To the feminist philosophers who have nurtured, and been nurtured, at Stony Brook

Contents

Acknowledgments

We were ourselves the subjects of care undertaken by the many people who helped us in the preparation of this volume. The project was the inspiration of the editors of the Feminist Constructions series. We want to thank Sara Ruddick and Hilde Lindemann Nelson for their vision, their gentle but persuasive urging, and their support throughout. In the final preparation of the chapters, we were fortunate to have the skillful help of Sarah Miller, John Wright, and Shelley Harshe. Maureen MacGrogan was instrumental in helping us get started on the volume, and we are grateful to her, as well as to Eve DeVaro and her assistant, John Wehmueller, who were always available to address our concerns as they gamely took over the project at Rowman & Littlefield. Also, a thanks to John Calderone, our production editor. Finally, we want to acknowledge the caring forbearance of Jeffrey Kittay and Jennifer Di Toro, which provided us with the time and space in which to complete our work.

Introduction

Ellen K. Feder
Eva Feder Kittay

Simone de Beauvoir, speaking of the limitations of women's freedom and equality, wrote: "Now, what peculiarly signalizes the situation of woman is that she—a free and autonomous being like all human creatures—nevertheless finds herself living in a world where men compel her to assume the status of the Other." Given women's dependence on men—economic, social, legal, political, and for the constitution of her very identity, Beauvoir asked, "How can a human being in woman's situation attain fulfillment. . . . How can independence be recovered in a state of dependency?" What Beauvoir saw "in the state of dependency" are women subjected to men.[1] But women remain subjugated and are hindered in their quest to become subjects by virtue of another dependency, one that remains largely unacknowledged in Beauvoir's ambitious analysis of women's situation: This is the dependence of those for whom women are traditionally obligated to care.

The focus on independence and the assumption that dependency is to be avoided—views so evident in Beauvoir's statement and in much of feminist discourse that followed her—have obscured the importance and the potential value and power of attending to women's traditional role as caregiver. As women have pursued the project of independence that Beauvoir set forth, we have encountered limitations in the conceptions of freedom and equality that are modeled on the lives men have led, conceptions that take for granted the caregiving historically performed by women.[2]

DEPENDENCY AND THE SUBJECT OF CARE

As feminists have begun to devote critical attention to the practice and ethical dimensions of caring labor, they have developed a framework within which to

1

reconsider independence and dependence.[3] Feminists have demonstrated that caregiving is not merely a "natural" activity, an inevitable feature of women's essential nature. It is a thoughtful, intentional work.[4] Furthermore, as a moral activity, it presents an alternative to models of social and political life fixated on interactions between autonomous equal agents.[5] With the revaluation of the practice of care in mind, feminists have begun to identify a moral language to describe (and help guide) the ethical dimension of interactions of unequals, attending both to the inequality between caregiver and the dependent to be cared for and the inequality between those who are not caregivers and those who are.[6] While theoretical prominence has been given to interactions among equals in the canonical works of political and moral philosophy, relations among unequals in fact dominate our social life.

By focusing on the essential labor of care, some feminists have come to see the notion of independence as itself problematic and the fact of dependence as one that has to be taken into account in any full appraisal of women's freedom and equality.[7] A care ethics has furthermore pointed to the undesirability of limiting our understanding of human moral interactions to a model based on such independence. Considerations such as these have indicated how misleading ethical and political theories based on independent actors have been. Women's dilemma, as Beauvoir had it, is that while a woman is a free and autonomous being, she is constrained by a situation that leaves her dependent. Remarking on the difficulties of women attaining full citizenship, Carole Pateman speaks of "Wollstonecraft's dilemma," that is, women's demand to be accorded equal citizenship, while at the same time demanding that their special responsibilities *as women* be recognized.[8] We can perhaps better identify the source of the dilemma in the very impossibility of a project of independence that both relies on and masks the inevitability of human dependency and the work of giving care to dependents.

All persons, in fact, spend a considerable portion of their lives either as dependents, caring for dependents, or in relations where they have responsibility for dependents. In speaking of dependents here, we mean to speak of those persons who are dependent on an other in order to meet essential needs that they are unable to meet themselves because of their youth, severe illness, disability, or frail old age. Persons who are dependent in this sense, we suggest, are "inevitably" so, while other dependencies are not inevitable but are derivative of or constructed by social arrangements.[9] Care of dependents often results in the derivative dependency on, or a vulnerability to, others who provide the resources necessary to sustain both the dependent and those who tend to the dependent. Those who tend to dependents we call "dependency workers." Dependency work may be familial and unpaid or waged labor, but wherever it is found, it is largely carried out by women, and not infrequently by women (and sometimes men) who are marginalized by virtue of race and class. In spite of the time, energy, and resources, both material and emotional, both social and individual, that dependency care requires—in spite of the importance in our lives of the relations we have with those upon whom we have depended and who depend upon us—dependency concerns rarely enter into philosophical and political discussions. The fact of human vulnerability and frailty that dependency underscores must function in our very conceptions of ourselves as subjects and moral agents.[10]

An ethics of care may be one way to understand the moral commitments and relations that arise among the persons unequally positioned in relations of dependency. Yet the harms and vulnerabilities that accrue to those who do dependency work may also reveal a limitation in care ethics and suggest the need to reintegrate care into a paradigm of just moral and political arrangements, but one that acknowledges those dependencies that call for care and support. Such a paradigm is not yet available. Though the unfairness and injustices that result from the current organization of dependency work have important economic bases and legal repercussions, dependency concerns are not highlighted in legal or economic contexts. The costs of caring for dependents are generally borne by individual families and sometimes by individual women, yet the social benefits of such care are distributed throughout society. While familial care robs the workforce of women whose skills and training are lost to the labor force, paid care always seems *too expensive.* And this despite the fact that those paid are paid poorly and generally work without the benefits other workers enjoy in industrialized nations. In law, we see little of the way of recognition of the crucial role of dependency work in our understanding of the public good. In spite of the clear findings that women who have the exclusive responsibility for care of dependents are especially vulnerable to poverty and abuse, recognition of the importance of dependency concerns for women's equality is also absent in public policy.[11]

While Beauvoir's question "How can independence be recovered in the state of dependency?" asked about women's possibility of acting autonomously when they were bound to others in ways that subordinated them, we can reinterpret the question to mean "How can we deal justly with the demands of dependencies that constitute inevitable facts of human existence, so that we avoid domination and subordination with respect to care and dependency?" How, that is, can the consequences of human dependency be equitably borne by all, so that some do not experience themselves as intolerably dependent in order for others to experience themselves as fully independent? The project of this volume, then, is to develop feminist understandings of dependency that will help us reconfigure the way we can think about dependency, and reassess the place dependency occupies in our lives and in a just social order in which we all can find a meaningful sense of freedom grounded in human dependence.

*****

We have arranged the chapters in the collection into five parts. The first part of the volume, "Contesting the 'Independent Man,'" focuses on the terms that shape conceptions of dependence and independence. "Legal and Economic Relations in the Face of Dependency," the second part, takes the critical analysis of dependency offered in part I into the areas of law and economics. The third part of the volume, "Just Social Arrangements and Familial Responsibility for Dependency," looks in detail at the ways in which women have been disadvantaged in practice and excluded in theoretical work by virtue of their responsibilities for dependency care. The analyses in the chapters in the first three parts treat the work of caring without dwelling on distinctions between the needs of different populations of dependents and the particular requirements emerging from these different forms of dependency. The fourth part, "Dependency Care in Cases of Specific Vulnerability," concentrates on the particularity of such needs, even as it underscores the commonalties that are experienced in dependency relations. In the last set of chapters, "Dependency, Subjectivity, and Identity," the notion of dependency leaves the relatively narrow domain of the caring labor that is associated with the fulfillment of basic needs and enters a wider social domain in which our social dependencies become important in the constitution of our identities.

CONTESTING THE "INDEPENDENT MAN"

As the chapters in this part make clear, issues of dependence and independence are more difficult to tease apart than it first appears. On the one hand, what might look to us like unalterable dependencies may be the result of alterable social conditions, as the disability community has powerfully shown.[12] On the other hand, what seems to be independence results from invisible or unacknowledged dependencies on others, or on economic or political institutions and on social understandings of what constitutes dependence and independence. As long as we maintain the fiction of the "normal" moral/political/legal/economic agent as the independent actor, dependency will continue to be seen as a peripheral concern, when it is in fact central to all our lives.

Nancy Fraser and Linda Gordon's landmark chapter, "A Genealogy of *Dependency:* Tracing a Keyword of the U.S. Welfare State," looks at the layers of meaning that the term *dependency* has taken on through Western history. Once a term encompassing notions of subordination across social strata, in its current, and pejorative, use in the phrase *welfare dependency*, dependency is the condition of an "individual." As the condition of an individual, rather than a social position, the dependent is pathologized, feminized, and racialized. "The preeminent stereotype," they note, "is the unmarried teenage mother caught in the 'welfare trap' and rendered dronelike and passive." Opposed to her is the fully enfranchised citizen, the "rational man" who is a full contributor to the economic order and to social life. The ideal of independence and its identification with wage labor goes unquestioned among conservatives and liberals alike.

Iris Marion Young argues in "Autonomy, Welfare Reform, and Meaningful Work" that the fiction of the independent actor appears in contemporary welfare policy in the mandate of "self-sufficiency." Young's analysis, focusing on contemporary discourse shaping welfare policy, identifies a conceptual confusion between self-sufficiency and autonomy. Self-sufficiency, the current goal of social policy, is quixotic and pernicious: it cannot genuinely be achieved and the pretense that it can obfuscates unavoidable dependencies. Autonomy, on the other hand, is a morally desirable attainment.

In "Dependency and Choice: The Two Faces of Eve," Rickie Solinger reminds us that autonomy has not always been seen as desirable for women, even as poor women today are penalized for their "failure" to be "self-sufficient." Solinger reflects on the important relation between *choice* and *dependency*, pointing out that the terms "vibrantly interact with each other . . . and together shape and justify punitive and constraining public policies, including eugenically based definitions of motherhood." By introducing the term *choice*, a word that resonates in the discourse on reproductive rights, Solinger brings to bear crucial connections between welfare debates and social control of women's reproduction. In the past, white middle-class women's status as women relied on their successful assumption of "dependency," but, having assumed this position, a woman was judged incapable of choice—the choice to terminate a pregnancy. Poor women today who are dependent as welfare recipients are excoriated for their independence in making "choices" to have children. Dependency renders one ineligible for the exercise of choice—but the choices that are sanctioned depend on the race and social class of the women: White women are stigmatized for seeking abortion, and black women for having children; white women are criticized for "choosing to work" and black women for "choosing not to work."

All three chapters expose an ideological function of the discourse and social policies concerning "dependency." The remaining chapters investigate the issues raised here at different levels of analysis and at the points in people's lives in which dependency figures.

JUST SOCIAL ARRANGEMENTS AND FAMILIAL RESPONSIBILITY FOR DEPENDENCY

Diemut Grace Bubeck's chapter "Justice and the Labor of Care," undertakes a close analysis of the demands of dependency work. Applying the Marxian concepts of "necessary labor" and exploitation to the care of dependents, she demonstrates first that women's caring is work that belongs under the category of "necessary labor," but, unlike other forms of necessary labor, this work cannot be supplanted by automation or made superfluous by increases in an economy's productive capacity. In limiting care to meeting the basic human needs of one who cannot meet those needs herself, Bubeck's definition of care coincides with Eva Feder Kittay's concept of "dependency work."[13] Like Kittay and Martha Fineman,[14] she argues that the labor of care is such that those who perform it become vulnerable to exploitation. The mechanism of exploitation is one that she identifies as "the circle of care." The circle of care embraces women in an ethic of care. While an ethic of care may be normative for those who are engaged in caring, within that ethic, Bubeck argues, women cannot find redress for the exploitation of their labor. Instead, we need a theory of justice that addresses these concerns. Neither care ethics nor theories of the just state thus far have seriously grappled with the injustices that result from the gendered assignment of caring labor.

Fineman's pioneering work in legal theory on dependency figures in her chapter for this volume, "Masking Dependency: The Political Role of Family Rhetoric," which reinforces points developed by other contributors, especially Bubeck, Young, and Martha McCluskey (see below). The vulnerability to exploitation that Bubeck so decisively demonstrates is addressed by Fineman in her critique of the family's "natural" role in caring for dependents. She argues that "the ideal of family is essential to maintaining the myth that autonomy and independence can be obtained." This myth—operating in public policy, law, and liberal political theory—depends on a family structure that assumes full responsibility for caring for dependents, thus obviating the need for communal support for caring labor.

Many of the preceding chapters have located a source of tension between political theory, especially liberalism, and the requirements of human dependency. In "The Future of Feminist Liberalism," Martha Nussbaum addresses the failure of current liberal theories to address meaningfully questions concerning dependency. This failure, she argues, does not require the rejection of liberalism, but rather a significant recasting of it. Feminist criticism of liberalism suggests changing the conception of the person. Rather than the Kantian conception that guides liberal theories of justice, we need an Aristotelian one that "builds growth and decline into the trajectory of human life." Such a reconceptualization should not, she argues, "disable liberalism." Instead, it can provide an interpretation of liberalism that it is "more attentive to need and its material and institutional conditions." Such a revision would also address the need to refigure the nature of the family and its role in public life.

LEGAL AND ECONOMIC RELATIONS
IN THE FACE OF DEPENDENCY

In this part, Robin West looks at our legal history and finds the power to support those engaged in dependency work in the liberal notion of rights. McCluskey, working within legal theory, and Ofelia Schutte, examining the literature in economic development and Third World feminism, level criticisms at the principles of *neo*liberalism as they become enshrined in law and economic policy. Of special concern is the elevation of free markets over and even at the expense of the well-being of the vulnerable, both domestically and globally.

In "The Right to Care," West argues for a fundamental right to care and a "nested right" of caregivers to what Kittay calls *doulia*. There is no doubt that care is essential; it is indeed necessary for the development of autonomous legal subjects. Caring labor can thus be understood as a "substantial part of adult identity." Despite this, caregiving largely goes unacknowledged, uncompensated, and unprotected. West argues that "in a modern world that purports to value both the care that is requisite of healthy, adult, liberal society, the exclusion of caregiving and caregivers from the protective domain of rights looks downright anomalous." She maintains that there are resources within our legal system that provide the ground for a right to care, a right that would include, among other things, subsidies for care work.

In "Subsidized Lives and the Ideology of Efficiency," McCluskey focuses on precisely this question of compensation for the work of care. Liberal political and economic theory is grounded in a conception of individual autonomy that relegates dependency to the realm of the family. As a consequence, the theory that provides the justification for corporate and capital subsidies as a "public benefit" militates against the provision of what she calls "caretaking subsidies." Yet the distinction between the two forms of subsidy is not based on sound economic principles but on ideology. McCluskey calls for increased scrutiny of the principles of "economic efficiency" that make a "moral hazard" out of subsidizing the work of caring labor here and abroad.

The neoliberal characterization of corporate subsidy as a "necessary price of economic development in a competitive global market," as compared with the characterization of the support of caregivers as an "unnecessary subsidy hindering global economic development," is developed in detail in Schutte's chapter. In "Dependency Work, Women, and the Global Economy," Schutte examines unpaid care work in the United States and the developing world in light of neoliberal economic policies. Neoliberal policies effectively complement the structure of gender relations to marginalize caring labor by relegating it to the private sphere. Within this framework, women who seek to succeed can do so only on the condition that they liberate themselves from caring labor, creating what some feminist economists have characterized as a "care deficit" in developing countries. Dismantling the neoliberal policies of the state, and with it, the social organization of gender that these policies simultaneously conceal and uphold, is, Schutte argues, among the greatest "existential and political challenges we face today."

DEPENDENCY CARE IN CASES OF SPECIFIC VULNERABILITY

As we turn our attention to a number of particular instances of dependency and dependency care, we see ways in which different dependencies interact with the social setting in which they are located, sometimes mitigating or magnifying the extent of dependency and the burdens of dependency work, and sometimes creating a new set of dependencies. As the chapters by Robert Goodin and Diane Gibson and

Eva Feder Kittay acknowledge, the fragilities and incapacities experienced by the elderly and those with severe mental retardation would render an individual dependent regardless of prevailing social conditions. These are clearly "inevitable" dependencies. By contrast, Dorothy Roberts's analysis demonstrates that the poverty, abuse, and neglect that *exacerbate* the dependency of children who wind up in foster care, however, are not inevitable and would be altered in a more just society. Similarly, Feder argues, the particular dependency produced in the medical treatment of children with ambiguous genitalia is not inevitable. The intersexed infant is, of course, as an infant, inevitably dependent. However, the fact that the child is intersexed need not intensify the extent to which the parents become dependent on medical professionals in caring for their child, were intersexuality viewed as a variant of human sexuality instead of as a pathology, and were its very existence not clothed in secrecy. Yet attention to the care of the clearly inevitable dependencies of a frail, infirm old age and severe mental retardation reveals the ways in which the justice or injustice of the social organization of care has a profound effect on the well-being of the cared-for and the caregiver alike.

In "The Decasualization of Eldercare" Goodin and Gibson explore the implications of the increasing "deinstitutionalization" of caregiving for the frail elderly. Traditionally "casual," the labor of care for the elderly has taken place in the family setting alongside the "ordinary activities of daily life." Contemporary society has seen a "decasualization" of this care at the same time that the care for highly dependent individuals has moved from institutional settings into community-based settings. While community-based care for the elderly is seen as more desirable because of the intimacy and integration into community life it can provide, this trend has resulted, Goodin and Gibson argue, in an increased burden on the part of caregivers and a corresponding decrease in the quality of care received. Government policy committed to protecting the vulnerable must assume a public responsibility for the care of highly dependent individuals, as well as support for caregivers.

The extent to which the adequate support of caregivers of highly dependent persons is crucial to protecting those who are highly vulnerable becomes most obvious in the case of people with severe mental retardation. Their extreme vulnerability, which is related to the level of care they require and the level of functioning that they attain, appears to make them unsuitable to assume citizenship or even moral personhood in a society based on liberal principles. As a consequence, the care they receive comes not as an entitlement from claims of justice but from whatever benevolence the society musters on their behalf.

In "When Caring Is Just and Justice Is Caring: Justice and Mental Retardation," Kittay argues that in the case of people with severe cognitive impairments, benevolence is a self-defeating strategy. Charity in this case yields paltry resources, which in turn makes it impossible to compensate caregivers adequately and to give them the dignity that is their due. With a population as vulnerable as the severely mentally retarded, this neglect of the caregiver too easily results in neglectful and abusive treatment of the cared-for, thereby defeating the purpose of the benevolence on which the mentally retarded have to depend. Kittay therefore argues that we need a theory of justice and a theory of personhood that begin with dependency and consequently include all dependents, including those with severe mental retardation.

As Kittay's article indicates, stigmatized groups can experience the fact of dependency in ways that are heightened and complicated by discrimination and exclusion. In "'Doctor's Orders': Parents and Intersexed Children," Ellen Feder examines the special vulnerability experienced by parents of intersexed children. Interviews with parents reveal the unusual degree of parents' isolation made necessary by the secret of their children's difference. It is not, however, some malevolence on the part of physicians that results in difficulties for the parents and the child. It is rather the preservative and conservative nature of what Pierre Bourdieu has called *habitus*, "systems of durable, transposable dispositions . . . which generate and organize practices and representations that can be objectively adapted to their outcomes without presupposing a conscious aiming at ends" that makes sense of the problematic treatment of parents of intersexed children. The habitus that structures the lives of physicians and parents alike embraces a singular norm of gender formation—a norm that is enforced by doctors and sustained by the secrecy that is imposed on parents. This secrecy magnifies parents' vulnerability and results not only in harmful medical intervention, but, Feder argues, in a fragility of the caring relationship between parent and child.

The fragility of the dependency relationship itself is also evidenced, as Roberts shows, in child welfare arrangements in the United States. In her chapter, "Poverty, Race, and the Distortion of Dependency: The Case of Kinship Care," Roberts argues that the administration of kinship foster care in the United States is marked by racism that "distorts the state's approach to the dependency relationship" in the case of poor black families. Families in need are provided with necessary financial support only when familial rights are ceded to the state. This support is provided in direct proportion to the degree of state surveillance to which families are subjected. Roberts argues that widening state support for "kinship care"—where children are placed with relatives in state-managed foster care—marks an increasing intervention into and disruption of black families. Rather than support for the relations of dependency that obtain in black families, Roberts concludes, "the state treats black caregivers as dependent and takes authority over their children."

DEPENDENCY, SUBJECTIVITY, AND IDENTITY

Until this point, the volume has taken the paradigmatic case of dependency to be the case in which an individual who needs to have fundamental needs met and cannot meet these needs herself must depend on another to meet those needs, and a dependency worker who meets those fundamental needs herself develops a derivative dependency on another. Each of the chapters in the concluding part focuses on the ways in which dependency is crucial to our self-understanding, where that self-understanding is effectively tied to our nature as dependent beings. Whether it is our dependency on another for basic care, on interactions with others for a social identity, or on the earth for the materials that make life itself possible, we must take account of the fact of dependency in our very conceptions of the self.

The complex interplay of racism and dependency we find in Roberts's chapter is further elaborated in Elizabeth V. Spelman's chapter, where she shows how racial identities in the United States develop through a kind of dependency work that African Americans do for white Americans. In "'Race' and the Labor of Identity" Spelman underscores the inequality of dependence in the constitution of identity and shows how this inequality is tied to African Americans' participation in what Ivan Illich called "shadow work"—work that is essential but that goes on with little acknowledgment and little, if any, compensation. Among the forms of shadow work that African Americans engage in is the caring labor that is so frequently done by women of all races. The unequal relations that are implicated in shadow work, Spelman argues, are also involved in the inequalities in the dependency upon which racial identity formation is founded.

In "Subjectivity as Responsivity: The Ethical Implications of Dependency," Kelly Oliver continues to show us how the relation of dependency has important consequences beyond the care of a dependent. She reads in Hegel's account of the struggle between lord and bondsman the revelation that subjectivity itself is founded in dependency on the subjectivity of the other. The responsibility entailed by this reliance on "the other"—a responsibility to be open to the needs of the other—is an ethical responsibility, one undertaken for the sake of the other on whom one depends. Indeed, the foundation of ethics itself lies in the conception of the self as fundamentally dependent, and this dependence lies ultimately, as Hegel's bondsman finally realizes, in the earth itself.

This dependence on the earth is foregrounded in the final chapter. In "Dependence on Place, Dependence in Place," Bonnie Mann finds in feminist postmodern conceptions of the sublime, the desire to escape the most fundamental dependency of all, that is, our dependence on our material being and on the natural environment. Instead, Mann wants to allow our dependence on the planet earth for the very air we breathe, and the very liquid that flows through our veins, to figure in an essential way in a revised feminist sublime. Using the moral implications of our relations to others in dependency relations of care, she extracts notions of moral indebtedness that need to reconceive our relation to the earth. From such a reconceptualization may emerge a new relation to the sublime, one that can celebrate rather than seek to escape from our essential in-placement.

The chapters in this collection are but a start of a research project, one that we hope will be advanced by this volume. We cannot continue to build our conceptions of a just society and the good life and to shape our aspirations for freedom and sublime experience without facing human dependency head-on. As Mann so convincingly argues, it is not only the liberation of women, or even the liberation of those who have been discriminated against and subordinated, but the very viability of human existence on earth that is at stake.

NOTES

1. Simone de Beauvoir, *The Second Sex*, trans. H. M. Parshley (New York: Alfred Knopf, 1952), 35.

2. See, for example, Carol Pateman, *The Sexual Contract* (Stanford, Calif.: Stanford University Press, 1989); Martha Albertson Fineman, *The Illusion of Equality* (Chicago: University of Chicago Press, 1991); Nancy Folbre, *The Invisible Heart: Economics and Family Values* (New York: New Press, 2001).

3. Among the many works on this subject, see Carol Gilligan, *In a Different Voice* (Cambridge, Mass.: Harvard University Press, 1982); Carol Gilligan, "Moral Orientation and Moral Development," in *Women and Moral Theory*, ed. Eva Feder Kittay and Diana T. Meyers (Totowa, N.J.: Rowman & Littlefield, 1987), 19–33; Nel Noddings, *Caring: A Feminine Approach to Ethics* (Berkeley: University of California Press, 1984); Marsha Hanen and Kai Nielsen, *Science, Morality and Feminist Theory* (Minneapolis: University of Minnesota Press, 1986); Eva Feder Kittay and Diana T. Meyers, eds., *Women and Moral Theory*; Sara Ruddick, *Maternal Thinking* (Boston, Mass.: Beacon, 1989); Emily Abel and Margaret K. Nelson, eds., *Circles of Care: Work and Identity in Women's Lives* (Albany, N.Y.: SUNY Press, 1990).

4. For example, see Virginia Held, "Non-Contractual Society: A Feminist View," *Canadian Journal of Philosophy*, Supplementary Volume 13 (1987): 111–35; Virginia Held, "Feminism and Moral Theory," in *Women and Moral Theory*, ed. Eva F. Kittay and Diana T. Meyers (Totowa, N.J.: Rowman & Littlefield, 1987), 111–28; Annette C. Baier, "The Need for More than Justice," in *Science, Morality & Feminist Theory*, ed. Marsha Hanen and Kai Nielsen (Alberta, Canada: University of Calgary Press, 1987), 41–56. Ruddick, *Maternal Thinking*.

5. Some works along these lines include Joan Tronto, *Moral Boundaries: A Political Argument for an Ethic of Care* (New York: Routledge, 1993); Susan J. Hekman, *Moral Voices: Moral Selves* (University Park: Pennsylvania State University Press, 1995); Grace Clement, *Care, Autonomy and Justice* (Boulder, Colo.: Westview, 1996); Nancy E. Snow, ed., *In the Company of Others: Perspectives on Community, Family, and Culture* (Totowa, N.J.: Rowman & Littlefield, 1996); Patrice DiQuinzio and Iris Marion Young, eds., *Feminist Ethics & Social Policy* (Bloomington: Indiana University Press, 1997).

6. For instance, Jeffrey Blustein, *Care and Commitment: Taking the Personal Point of View* (New York: Oxford University Press, 1991); Diemut Bubeck, *Care, Gender, and Justice* (Oxford, U.K.: Clarendon Press, 1995); Suzanne Gordon and Patricia Benner, eds. *Caregiving: Readings in Knowledge, Practice, Ethics, and Politics* (Philadelphia: University of Pennsylvania Press, 1996); Peta Bowden, *Caring: Gender-Sensitive Ethics* (New

York: Routledge, 1997); Eva Feder Kittay, *Love's Labor: Essays on Women, Equality and Dependence* (New York: Routledge, 1999).

7. See, especially, Fineman, *The Illusion of Equality*; Martha Albertson Fineman, *The Neutered Mother, the Sexual Family, and Other Twentieth Century Tragedies* (New York: Routledge, 1995); Eva Feder Kittay, "A Review of Political Liberalism," *APA Newsletter* (1994); Eva Feder Kittay, "Taking Dependency Seriously: The Family and Medical Leave Act Considered in Light of the Social Organization of Dependency Work and Gender Equality," *Hypatia* 10, no. 1 (winter 1995): 8–29; Robin West, *Caring for Justice* (New York: New York University Press, 1997); Kittay, *Love's Labor*.

8. Carole Pateman, "The Patriarchal Welfare State," in *Democracy and the Welfare State*, ed. Amy Gutman (Princeton, N.J.: Princeton University Press, 1988).

9. Fineman, *The Neutered Mother, the Sexual Family, and Other Twentieth Century Tragedies*; Kittay, "Taking Dependency Seriously: The Family and Medical Leave Act Considered in Light of the Social Organization of Dependency Work and Gender Equality."

10. Robert Goodin, *Protecting the Vulnerable* (Chicago: University of Chicago Press, 1985); Alasdair MacIntyre, *Dependent Rational Animals: Why Human Beings Need the Virtues* (Chicago: Open Court, 1999).

11. Folbre, *The Invisible Heart*.

12. For example, Len Barton, ed., *Disability and Dependency* (London: Falmer, 1989).

13. Kittay, *Love's Labor*.

14. Fineman, *The Neutered Mother, the Sexual Family, and Other Twentieth Century Tragedies*.

1

CONTESTING THE "INDEPENDENT MAN"

1

A Genealogy of *Dependency*: Tracing a Keyword of the U.S. Welfare State

Nancy Fraser and Linda Gordon

Dependency has become a keyword of U.S. politics. Politicians of diverse views regularly criticize what they term *welfare dependency*. Supreme Court Justice Clarence Thomas spoke for many conservatives in 1980 when he vilified his sister: "She gets mad when the mailman is late with her welfare check. That's how dependent she is. What's worse is that now her kids feel entitled to the check, too. They have no motivation for doing better or getting out of that situation" (quoted in Tumulty 1991). Liberals usually blame the victim less, but they, too, decry welfare dependency. Democratic Senator Daniel P. Moynihan prefigured today's discourse when he began his 1973 book by claiming that "the issue of welfare is the issue of dependency. It is different from poverty. To be poor is an objective condition; to be dependent, a subjective one as well. . . . Being poor is often associated with considerable personal qualities; being dependent rarely so. [Dependency] is an incomplete state in life: normal in the child, abnormal in the adult. In a world where completed men and women stand on their own feet, persons who are dependent— as the buried imagery of the word denotes—hang" (Moynihan 1973, 17). Today, "policy experts" from both major parties agree "that [welfare] dependency is bad for people, that it undermines their motivation to support themselves, and isolates and stigmatizes welfare recipients in a way that over a long period feeds into and accentuates the underclass mindset and condition" (Nathan 1986, 248).

If we can step back from this discourse, however, we can interrogate some of its underlying presuppositions. Why are debates about poverty and inequality in the Unites States now being framed in terms of welfare dependency? How did the receipt of public assistance become associated with dependency, and why are the connotations of that word in this context so negative? What are the gender and racial subtexts of this discourse, and what tacit assumptions underlie it?

We propose to shed some light on these issues by examining welfare-related meanings of the word *dependency*.[1] We analyze *dependency* as a keyword of the

U.S. welfare state and reconstruct its genealogy. By charting some major historical shifts in the usage of this term, we excavate some of the tacit assumptions and connotations that it still carries today but that usually go without saying.

Our approach is inspired in part by the English cultural–materialist critic Raymond Williams (1976). Following Williams and others, we assume that the terms that are used to describe social life are also active forces shaping it.[2] A crucial element of politics, then, is the struggle to define social reality and to interpret people's inchoate aspirations and needs (Fraser 1990). Particular words and expressions often become focal in such struggles, functioning as keywords, sites at which the meaning of social experience is negotiated and contested (Williams 1976). Keywords typically carry unspoken assumptions and connotations that can powerfully influence the discourses they permeate—in part by constituting a body of *doxa*, or taken-for-granted commonsense belief that escapes critical scrutiny (Bourdieu 1977).

We seek to dispel the *doxa* surrounding current U.S. discussions of dependency by reconstructing that term's genealogy. Modifying an approach associated with Michel Foucault (1984), we excavate broad historical shifts in linguistic usage that can rarely be attributed to specific agents. We do *not* present a causal analysis. Rather, by contrasting present meanings of dependency with past meanings, we aim to defamiliarize taken-for-granted beliefs in order to render them susceptible to critique and to illuminate present-day conflicts.

Our approach differs from Foucault's, however, in two crucial respects: we seek to contextualize discursive shifts in relation to broad institutional and social–structural shifts, and we welcome normative political reflection.[3] Our chapter is a collaboration between a philosopher and a historian. We combine historical analysis of linguistic and social–structural changes with conceptual analysis of the discursive construction of social problems, and we leaven the mix with a feminist interest in envisioning emancipatory alternatives.

In what follows, then, we provide a genealogy of *dependency*. We sketch the history of this term and explicate the assumptions and connotations it carries today in U.S. debates about welfare—especially assumptions about human nature, gender roles, the causes of poverty, the nature of citizenship, the sources of entitlement, and what counts as work and as a contribution to society. We contend that unreflective uses of this keyword serve to enshrine certain interpretations of social life as authoritative and to delegitimate or obscure others, generally to the advantage of dominant groups in society and to the disadvantage of subordinate ones. All told, we provide a critique of ideology in the form of a critical political semantics.

Dependency, we argue, is an ideological term. In current U.S. policy discourse it usually refers to the condition of poor women with children who maintain their families with neither a male breadwinner nor an adequate wage and who rely for economic support on a stingy and politically unpopular government program called Aid to Families with Dependent Children (AFDC). Participation in this highly stigmatized program may be demoralizing in many cases, even though it may enable women to leave abusive or unsatisfying relationships without having to give up their children. Still, naming the problems of poor, solo-mother families as *dependency* tends to make them appear to be individual problems, as much moral or psychological as economic. The term carries strong emotive and visual associations and a powerful pejorative charge. In current debates, the expression *welfare dependency* evokes the image of "the welfare mother," often figured as a young, unmarried black woman (perhaps even a teenager) of uncontrolled sexuality. The power of this image is overdetermined, we contend, since it condenses multiple and often contradictory meanings of dependency. Only by disaggregating those different strands, by unpacking the tacit assumptions and evaluative connotations that underlie them, can we begin to understand, and to dislodge, the force of the stereotype.

REGISTERS OF MEANING

In its root meaning, the verb *to depend* refers to a physical relationship in which one thing hangs from another. The more abstract meanings—social, economic, psychological, and political—were originally metaphorical. In current usage, we find four registers in which the meanings of dependency reverberate. The first is an economic register, in which one depends on some other person(s) or institution for subsistence. In a second register, the term denotes a sociolegal status, the lack of a separate legal or public identity, as in the status of married women created by coverture. The third register is political: here dependency means subjection to an external ruling power and may be predicated of a colony or of a subject caste of noncitizen residents. The fourth register we call the moral/psychological; dependency in this sense is an individual character trait like lack of willpower or excessive emotional neediness.

To be sure, not every use of *dependency* fits neatly into one and only one of these registers. Still, by distinguishing them analytically we present a matrix on which to plot the historical adventures of the term. In what follows, we trace the shift from a patriarchal preindustrial usage in which women, however subordinate, shared a condition of dependency with many men to a modern, industrial, male-supremacist usage that constructed a specifically feminine sense of dependency. That usage is now giving way, we contend, to a postindustrial usage in which growing numbers of relatively prosperous women claim the same kind of independence that men do while a more stigmatized but still feminized sense of dependency attaches to groups considered deviant and superfluous. Not just gender but also racializing practices play a major role in these shifts, as do changes in the organization and meaning of labor.

PREINDUSTRIAL *DEPENDENCY*

In preindustrial English usage, the most common meaning of *dependency* was subordination. The economic, sociolegal, and political registers were relatively undifferentiated, reflecting the fusion of various forms of hierarchy in state and society, and the moral/psychological use of the term barely existed. The earliest social definition of the verb *to depend (on)* in the *Oxford English Dictionary* (*OED*) is "to be connected within a relation of subordination." A *dependent*, from at least 1588, was one "who depends on another for support, position, etc.; a retainer, attendant, subordinate, servant." A *dependency* was either a retinue or body of servants or a foreign territorial possession or colony. This family of terms applied widely in a hierarchical social context in which nearly everyone was subordinate to someone else but did not incur individual stigma thereby (Gundersen 1987).

We can appreciate just how common dependency was in preindustrial society by examining its opposite. The term *independence* at first applied primarily to aggregate entities, not to individuals; thus in the seventeenth century a nation or a church congregation could be independent. By the eighteenth century, however, an individual could be said to have an *independency*, meaning an ownership of property, a fortune that made it possible to live without laboring. (This sense of the term, which we would today call economic, survives in our expressions *to be independently wealthy* and *a person of independent means*.) To be dependent, in contrast, was to gain one's livelihood by working for someone else. This of course was the condition of most people, of wage laborers as well as serfs and slaves, of most men as well as most women.[4]

Dependency, therefore, was a normal, as opposed to a deviant, condition, a social relation, as opposed to an individual, trait. Thus, it did not carry any moral opprobrium. Neither English nor U.S. dictionaries report any pejorative uses of the term before the early twentieth century. In fact, some leading preinudstrial definitions were explicitly positive, implying trusting, relying on, counting on another, the predecessors of today's *dependable*.

Nevertheless, *dependency* did mean status inferiority and legal coverture, being a part of a unit headed by someone else who had legal standing. In a world of status hierarchies dominated by great landowners and their retainers, all members of a household other than its "head" were dependents, as were free or servile peasants on an estate. They were, as Peter Laslett put it, "caught up, so to speak, 'subsumed' . . . into the personalities of their fathers and masters" (1971, 21).

Dependency also had what we would today call political consequences. While the term did not mean precisely *unfree*, its context was a social order in which subjection, not citizenship, was the norm. *Independence* connoted unusual privilege and superiority, as in freedom from labor. Thus, throughout most of the European development of representative government, independence in the sense of property ownership was a prerequisite for political rights. When dependents began to claim rights and liberty, they perforce became revolutionaries.

Dependency was not then applied uniquely to characterize the relation of a wife to her husband. Women's dependency, like children's, meant being on a lower rung in a long social ladder; their husbands and fathers were above them but below others. For the agrarian majority, moreover, there was no implication of unilateral economic dependency, because women's and children's labor was recognized as essential to the family economy; the women were economic dependents only in the sense that the men of their class were as well. In general, women's dependency in preindustrial society was less gender-specific than it later became; it was similar in kind to that of subordinate men, only multiplied. But so too were the lives of children, servants, and the elderly overlaid with multiple layers of dependency.

In practice, of course, these preindustrial arrangements did not always provide satisfactorily for the poor. In the fourteenth century new, stronger states began to limit the freedom of movement of the destitute and to codify older informal distinctions between those worthy and unworthy of assistance. When the English Poor Law of 1601 confirmed this latter distinction, it was already shameful to ask for public help. But the culture neither disapproved of dependency nor valorized individual independence. Rather, the aim of the statutes was to return the mobile, uprooted, and excessively "independent" poor to their local parishes or communities and, hence, to enforce their traditional dependencies.

Nevertheless, dependency was not universally approved or uncontested. It was subject, rather, to principled challenges from at least the seventeenth century on, when liberal–individualist political arguments became common. The terms *dependence* and *independence* often figured centrally in political debates in this period, as they did, for example, in the Putney Debates of the English Civil War. Sometimes they even became key signifiers of social crisis, as in the seventeenth-century English controversy about "out-of-doors" servants, hired help who did not reside in the homes of their masters and who were not bound by indentures of similar legal understandings. In the discourse of the time, the anomalous "independence" of these men served as a general figure for social disorder, a lightning rod focusing on diffuse cultural anxieties—much as the anomalous "dependence" of "welfare mothers" does today.

INDUSTRIAL *DEPENDENCY*: THE WORKER AND HIS NEGATIVES

With the rise of industrial capitalism, the semantic geography of dependency shifted significantly. In the eighteenth and nineteenth centuries, *independence,* not *dependence,* figured centrally in political and economic discourse; and its meanings were radically democratized. But if we read the discourse about independence carefully, we see the shadow of a powerful anxiety about dependency.

What in preindustrial society had been a normal and unstigmatized condition became deviant and stigmatized. More precisely, certain dependencies became shameful while others were deemed natural and proper. In particular, as eighteenth- and nineteenth-century political culture intensified gender difference, new, specifically gendered senses of dependency appeared—states considered proper for women but degrading for men. Likewise, emergent racial constructions made some forms of dependency appropriate for the "dark races" but intolerable for "whites." Such differentiated valuations became possible as the term's preindustrial unity fractured. No longer designating only generalized subordination, *dependency* in the industrial era could be sociolegal or political or economic. With these distinctions came another major semantic shift: now *dependency* need not always refer to a social relation; it could also designate an individual character trait. Thus, the moral/psychological register was born.

These redefinitions were greatly influenced by Radical Protestantism. It elaborated a new positive image of individual independence and a critique of sociolegal and political dependency. In the Catholic and the early Protestant traditions, dependence on a master had been modeled on dependence on God. In contrast, to the radicals of the English Civil War, or to Puritans, Quakers, and the Congregationalists in the United States, rejecting dependence on a master was akin to rejecting blasphemy and false gods (Hill 1972). From this perspective, status hierarchies no longer appeared natural or just. Political subjection and sociolegal subsumption were offenses to human dignity, defensible only under special conditions, if supportable at all. These beliefs informed a variety of radical movements throughout the industrial era, including abolition, feminism, and labor organizing, with substantial successes. In the nineteenth century these movements abolished slavery and some of the legal disabilities of women. More thoroughgoing victories were won by white male workers who, in the eighteenth and nineteenth centuries, threw off their sociolegal and political dependency and won civil and electoral rights. In the age of democratic revolutions, the developing new concept of citizenship rested on independence; dependency was deemed antithetical to citizenship.

Changes in the civil and political landscape of dependence and independence were accompanied by even more dramatic changes in the economic register. When white workingmen demanded civil and electoral rights, they claimed to be independent. This entailed reinterpreting the meaning of wage labor so as to divest it of the association with dependency. That in turn required a shift in focus—from the experience of means of labor (e.g., ownership of tools or land, control of skills, and the organization of work) to its remuneration and how that was spent. Radical workingmen, who had earlier rejected wage labor was "wage slavery," claimed a new form of manly independence within it. Their collective pride drew on another aspect of Protestantism, its work ethic, that valorized discipline and labor. Workers sought to reclaim these values within the victorious wage labor system; many of them—women as well as men—created and exercised a new kind of independence in their militance and boldness toward employers. Through their struggles, economic independence came eventually to encompass the ideal of earning a family wage, a wage sufficient to maintain a household and to support a dependent wife and children. Thus, workingmen expanded the meaning of economic independence to include a form of wage labor in addition to property ownership and self-employment.[5]

This shift in the meaning of independence also transformed the meanings of dependency. As wage labor became increasingly normative—and increasingly definitive of independence—it was precisely those excluded from wage labor who appeared to personify dependency. In the new industrial semantics, there emerged three principal icons of dependency, all effectively negatives of the dominant image of "the worker" and each embodying a different aspect of non-independence.

The first icon of industrial dependency was "the pauper," who lived not on wages but on poor relief.[6] In the strenuous new culture of emergent capitalism, the figure of the pauper was like a bad double of the upstanding workingman, threatening the latter should he lag. The image of the pauper was elaborated largely in the emerging new register of dependency discourse—the moral/psychological register. Paupers were not simply poor but degraded, their character corrupted and their will sapped through reliance on charity. To be sure, the moral/psychological condition of pauperism was related to the economic condition of poverty, but the relationship was not simple, but complex. While nineteenth-century charity experts acknowledged that poverty could contribute to pauperization, they also held that character defects could cause poverty (Gordon 1992). Toward the end of the century, as hereditarian (eugenic) thought caught on, the pauper's character defects were given a basis in biology. The pauper's dependency was figured as unlike the serf's in that it was unilateral, not reciprocal. To be a pauper was not to be subordinate within a system of productive labor; it was to be outside such a system altogether.

A second icon of industrial dependency was embodied alternately in the figures of "the colonial native" and "the slave." They, of course, were very much inside the economic system, their labor often fundamental to the development of capital and industry. Whereas the pauper represented the characterological distillation of economic dependency, natives and slaves personified political subjection.[7] Their images as "savage," "childlike," and "submissive" became salient as the old, territorial sense of dependency as a colony became intertwined with a new, racist discourse developed to justify colonialism and slavery.[8] There emerged a drift from an older sense of dependency as a relation of subjection imposed by an imperial power on an indigenous population to a newer sense of dependency as an inherent property or character trait of the people so subjected. In earlier usage, colonials were dependent because they had been conquered; in nineteenth-century imperialist culture, they were conquered because they were dependent. In this new conception, it was the intrinsic, essential dependency of natives and slaves that justified their colonization and enslavement.

The dependency of the native and the slave, like that of the pauper, was elaborated largely in the moral/psychological register. The character traits adduced to justify imperialism and slavery, however, arose less from individual temperament than from the supposed nature of human groups. Racialist thought was the linchpin for this reasoning. By licensing a view of "the Negro" as fundamentally *other*, it provided the extraordinary justificatory power required to rationalize subjection at a time when liberty and equality were being proclaimed inalienable "rights of men"—for example, in that classic rejection of colonial status, the United States' Declaration of Independence. Thus racism helped transform dependency as political subjection into dependency as psychology and forged enduring links between the discourse of dependency and racial oppression.

Like the pauper, the native and the slave were excluded from wage labor and thus were negatives of the image of the worker. They shared that characteristic, if little else, with the third major icon of dependency in the industrial era: the newly invented figure of "the housewife." As we saw, the independence of the white workingman presupposed the ideal of the family wage, a wage sufficient to maintain a household and to support a nonemployed wife and children. Thus, for wage labor to create (white male) independence, white female economic dependence was required. Women were thus transformed "from partners to parasites" (Land 1980, 57; Boydston 1991). But this transformation was by no means universal. In the United States, for example. The family wage ideal held greater sway among whites than among blacks and was at variance with actual practice for all of the poor and the working class. Moreover, both employed and nonemployed wives continued to perform work once considered crucial to a family economy. Since few husbands actually were able to support a family singlehandedly, most families continued to depend on the labor of women and children. Nevertheless, the family wage norm commanded great loyalty in the United States, partly because it was used by the organized working class as an argument for higher wages (Hughes 1925; Breckinridge 1928; Pruette 1934; Gordon 1992).

Several different registers of dependency converged in the figure of the housewife. This figure melded woman's traditional sociolegal and political dependency with her more recent economic dependency in the industrial order. Continuing from preindustrial usage was the assumption that fathers headed households and that other household members were represented by them, as codified in the legal doctrine of coverture. The sociolegal and political dependency of wives enforced their new economic dependency, since under coverture even married women who were wage workers could not legally control their wages. But the connotations of female dependency were altered. Although erstwhile dependent white men gained political rights, most white women remained legally and politically dependent. The result was to feminize—and stigmatize—sociolegal and political dependency, making coverture appear increasingly obnoxious and stimulating agitation for the statutes and court decisions that eventually dismantled it.

Together, then, a series of new personifications of dependency combined to constitute the underside of the workingman's independence. Henceforth, those who aspired to full membership in society would have to distinguish themselves from the pauper, the native, the slave, and the housewife in order to construct their independence. In a social order in which wage labor was becoming hegemonic, it was possible to encapsulate all these distinctions simultaneously in the ideal of the family wage. On the one hand, and most overtly, the ideal of the family wage premised the white workingman's independence on his wife's subordination and economic dependence. But on the other hand, it simultaneously contrasted with counterimages of dependent men—first with degraded male paupers on poor relief and later with racist stereotypes of Negro men unable to dominate Negro women. The family wage, therefore, was a vehicle for elaborating meanings of dependence and independence that were deeply inflected by gender, race, and class.

In this new industrial semantics, white workingmen appeared to be economically independent, but their independence was largely illusory and ideological. Since few actually earned enough to support a family singlehandedly, most depended in fact—if not in word—on their wives' and children's contributions. Equally important, the language of wage labor in capitalism denied workers' dependence on their employers, thereby veiling their status as subordinates in a unit headed by someone else. Thus, hierarchy that had been relatively explicit and visible in the peasant–landlord relation was mystified in the relationship of factory operative to factory owner. There was a sense in which the economic dependency of the white workingman was spirited away through linguistic sleight of hand—somewhat like reducing the number of poor people by lowering the official poverty demarcating line.

By definition, then, economic inequality among white men no longer created dependency. But noneconomic hierarchy among white men was considered unacceptable in the United States. Thus, *dependency* was redefined to refer exclusively to those noneconomic relations of subordination deemed suitable only for people of color and for white women. The result was to differentiate dimensions of dependency that had been fused in preindustrial usage. Whereas all relations of subordination had previously counted as dependency relations, now capital-labor relations were exempted. Sociolegal and political hierarchy appeared to diverge from economic hierarchy, and only the former seemed incompatible with hegemonic views of society. It seemed to follow, moreover, that were sociolegal dependency and political dependency ever to be formally abolished, no social–structural dependency would remain. Any dependency that did persist could only be moral or psychological.

THE RISE OF AMERICAN *WELFARE DEPENDENCY*: 1890–1945

Informed by these general features of industrial-era semantics, a distinctive welfare-related use of *dependency* developed in the United States. Originating in the late-nineteenth-century discourse of pauperism, modified in the Progressive Era, and stabilized in the period of the New Deal, this use of the term was fundamentally ambiguous, slipping easily, and repeatedly, from an economic meaning to a moral/psychological meaning.

The United States was especially hospitable to elaborating dependency as a defect of individual character. Because the country lacked a strong legacy of

feudalism or aristocracy and thus a strong popular sense of reciprocal obligations between lord and man, the older preindustrial meanings of dependency—
as an ordinary, majority condition—were weak and the pejorative meanings
were stronger. In the colonial period, dependency was seen mainly as a voluntary condition, as in indentured servitude. But the American Revolution so valorized independence that it stripped dependency of its voluntarism, emphasized
its powerlessness, and imbued it with stigma. One result was to change the
meaning of women's social and legal dependency, making it distinctly inferior
(Gundersen 1987).

The long American love affair with independence was politically double-
edged. On the one hand, it helped nurture powerful labor and women's movements. On the other hand, the absence of a hierarchical social tradition in which
subordination was understood to be structural, not characterological, facilitated
hostility to public support for the poor. Also influential was the very nature of the
American state, weak and decentralized in comparison to European states
throughout the nineteenth century. All told, the United States proved fertile soil
for the moral/psychological discourse of dependency.

As discussed earlier, the most general definition of economic dependency in
this era was simply non-wage-earning. By the end of the nineteenth century,
however, that definition had divided into two: a "good" household dependency,
predicated of children and wives, and an increasingly "bad" (or at least dubious)
charity dependency, predicated of recipients of relief. Both senses had as their
reference point the ideal of the family wage, and both were eventually incorporated into the discourse of the national state. The good household sense was
elaborated via the census (Folbre 1991) and by the Internal Revenue Service,
which installed the category of dependent as the norm for wives. The already
problematic charity sense became even more pejorative with the development of
public assistance. The old distinction between the deserving and the undeserving poor intensified in the late nineteenth century's Gilded Age. Theoretically,
the undeserving should not be receiving aid, but constant vigilance was required
to ensure they did not slip in, disguising themselves as deserving. Dependence
on assistance became increasingly stigmatized, and it was harder and harder to
rely on relief without being branded a pauper.

Ironically, reformers in the 1890s introduced the word *dependent* into relief
discourse as a substitute for *pauper* precisely in order to destigmatize the receipt
of help. They first applied the word to children, the paradigmatic "innocent" victims of poverty.[9] Then, in the early twentieth century, Progressive Era reformers
began to apply the term to adults, again to rid them of stigma. Only after World
War II did *dependent* become the hegemonic word for a recipient of aid.[10] By
then, however, the term's pejorative connotations were fixed.

The attempt to get rid of stigma by replacing *pauperism* with *dependency*
failed. Talk about economic dependency repeatedly slid into condemnation of
moral/psychological dependency. Even during the Depression of the 1930s,

experts worried that receipt of relief would create "habits of dependence" or, as one charity leader put it, "a belligerent dependency, an attitude of having a right and title to relief" (Brandt 1932, 23–24; Gibbons 1933; Vaile 1934, 26). Because the hard times lasted so long and created so many newly poor people, there was a slight improvement in the status of recipients of aid. But attacks on "chiseling" and "corruption" continued to embarrass those receiving assistance, and many of the neediest welfare beneficiaries accepted public aid only after much hesitation and with great shame, so strong was the stigma of dependency (Bakke 1940a, 1940b).

Most important, the New Deal intensified the dishonor of receiving help by consolidating a two-track welfare system. First-track programs like unemployment and old-age insurance offered aid as an entitlement, without stigma or supervision and hence without dependency. Such programs were constructed to create the misleading appearance that beneficiaries merely got back what they put in. They constructed an honorable status for recipients and are not called welfare even today. Intended at least partially to replace the white workingman's family wage, first-track programs excluded most minorities and white women. In contrast, second-track public assistance programs, among which Aid to Dependent Children (ADC), later Aid to Families with Dependent Children (AFDC), became the biggest and most well-known, continued the private charity tradition of searching out the deserving few among the many chiselers. Funded from general tax revenues instead of from earmarked wage deductions, these programs created the appearance that claimants were getting something for nothing (Fraser and Gordon 1992). They established entirely different conditions for receiving aid: means-testing; morals-testing; moral and household supervision; home visits; extremely low stipends—in short, all the conditions associated with welfare dependency today (Fraser 1987; Gordon 1990; Nelson 1990).[11]

The racial and sexual exclusions of the first-track programs were not accidental. They were designed to win the support of Southern legislators who wanted to keep blacks dependent in another sense, namely, on low wages or sharecropping (Quadagno 1988). Equally deliberate was the construction of the differential in legitimacy between the two tracks of the welfare system. The Social Security Board propagandized for Social Security Old Age Insurance (the program today called just "Social Security") precisely because, at first, it did not seem more earned or more dignified than public assistance. To make Social Security more acceptable, the board worked to stigmatize public assistance, even pressuring states to keep stipends low (Cates 1983).

Most Americans today still distinguish between "welfare" and "nonwelfare" forms of public provision and see only the former as creating dependency. The assumptions underlying these distinctions, however, had to be constructed politically. Old people became privileged (nonwelfare) recipients only through decades of militant organization and lobbying. All programs of public provision, whether they are called welfare or not, shore up some dependencies and discourage others.

Social Security subverted adults' sense of responsibility for their parents, for example. Public assistance programs, by contrast, aimed to buttress the dependence of the poor on low-wage labor, of wives on husbands, of children on their parents.

The conditions of second-track assistance made recipients view their dependence on public assistance as inferior to the supposed independence of wage labor (Milwaukee County Welfare Rights Organization 1972; West 1981; Pope 1989, 73, 144). Wage labor, meanwhile, had become so naturalized that its own inherent supervision could be overlooked; thus one ADC recipient complained, "Welfare life is a difficult experience. . . . When you work, you don't have to report to anyone" (Barnes 1987, vi). Yet the designers of ADC did not initially intend to drive white solo mothers into paid employment. Rather, they wanted to protect the norm of the family wage by making dependence on a male breadwinner continue to seem preferable to dependence on the state (Gordon 1992). Aid to Dependent Children occupied the strategic semantic space where the good household sense of dependency and the bad relief sense of dependency intersected. It enforced at once the positive connotations of the first and the negative connotations of the second.

Thus, the poor solo mother was enshrined as the quintessential *welfare dependent*.[12] That designation has thus become significant not only for what it includes but also for what it excludes and occludes. Although it appears to mean relying on the government for economic support, not all recipients of public funds are equally considered dependent. Hardly anyone today calls recipients of Social Security retirement insurance *dependents*. Similarly, persons receiving unemployment insurance, agricultural loans, and home mortgage assistance are excluded from that categorization, as indeed are defense contractors and the beneficiaries of corporate bailouts and regressive taxation.

POSTINDUSTRIAL SOCIETY AND THE DISAPPEARANCE OF "GOOD" DEPENDENCY

With the transition to a postindustrial phase of capitalism, the semantic map of dependency is being redrawn yet again. Whereas industrial usage had cast some forms of dependency as natural and proper, postindustrial usage figures all forms as avoidable and blameworthy. No longer moderated by any positive countercurrents, the term's pejorative connotations are being strengthened. Industrial usage had recognized some forms of dependency to be rooted in relations of subordination; postindustrial usage, in contrast, focuses more intensely on the traits of individuals. The moral/psychological register is expanding, therefore, and its qualitative character is changing, with new psychological and therapeutic idioms displacing the explicitly racist and misogynous idioms of the industrial era. Yet dependency nonetheless remains feminized and racialized; the new psychological meanings have strong feminine associations, while currents once associated with the native and the slave are increasingly inflecting the discourse about welfare.

One major influence here is the formal abolition of much of the legal and political dependency that was endemic to industrial society. Housewives, paupers,
natives, and the descendants of slaves are no longer formally excluded from most
civil and political rights; neither their subsumption nor their subjection is viewed
as legitimate. Thus, major forms of dependency deemed proper in industrial
usage are now considered objectionable, and postindustrial uses of the term carry
a stronger negative charge.

A second major shift in the geography of postindustrial dependency is affecting the economic register. This is the decentering of the ideal of the family wage,
which had been the gravitational center of industrial usage. The relative deindustrialization of the United States is restructuring the political economy, making the
single-earner family far less viable. The loss of higher paid "male" manufacturing jobs and the massive entry of women into low-wage service work are meanwhile altering the gender composition of employment (Smith 1984). At the same
time, divorce is common and, thanks in large part to the feminist and gay and lesbian liberation movements, changing gender norms are helping to proliferate new
family forms, making the male breadwinner/female homemaker model less attractive to many (Stacey 1987, 1990; Weston 1991). Thus, the family wage ideal
is no longer hegemonic but competes with alternative gender norms, family
forms, and economic arrangements. It no longer goes without saying that a
woman should rely on a man for economic support, nor that mothers should not
also be "workers." Thus, another major form of dependency that was positively
inflected in industrial semantics has become contested if not simply negative.

The combined result of these developments is to increase the stigma of dependency. With all legal and political dependency now illegitimate, and with wives'
economic dependency now contested, there is no longer any self-evidently good
adult dependency in postindustrial society. Rather, all dependency is suspect, and independence is enjoined upon everyone. Independence, however, remains identified
with wage labor. That identification seems even to increase in a context where there
is no longer any "good" adult personification of dependency who can be counter-
posed to "the worker." In this context, the worker tends to become the universal social subject: everyone is expected to "work" and to be "self-supporting." Any adult
not perceived as a worker shoulders a heavier burden of self-justification. Thus, a
norm previously restricted to white workingmen applied increasingly to everyone.
Yet this norm still carries a racial and gender subtext, as it supposes that the worker
has access to a job paying a decent wage and is not also a primary parent.

If one result of these developments is an increase in dependency's negative
connotations, another is its increased individualization. As we saw, talk of dependency as a character trait of individuals was already widespread in the industrial period, diminishing the preindustrial emphasis on relations of subordination.
The importance of individualized dependency tends to be heightened, however,
now that sociolegal and political dependency are officially ended. Absent coverture and Jim Crow, it has become possible to claim that equality of opportunity

exists and that individual merit determines outcomes. As we saw, the groundwork for the view was laid by industrial usage, which redefined dependency so as to exclude capitalist relations of subordination. With capitalist economic dependency already abolished by definition, and with legal and political dependency now abolished by law, postindustrial society appears to some conservatives and liberals to have eliminated every social–structural basis of dependency. Whatever dependency remains, therefore, can be interpreted as the fault of individuals. That interpretation does not go uncontested, to be sure, but the burden of argument has shifted. Now those who would deny that the fault lies in themselves must swim upstream against the prevailing semantic currents. Postindustrial dependency, thus, is increasingly individualized.

WELFARE DEPENDENCY AS POSTINDUSTRIAL PATHOLOGY

The worsening connotations of *welfare dependency* have been nourished by several streams from outside the field of welfare. New postindustrial medical and psychological discourses have associated dependency with pathology. In articles with titles such as "Pharmacist Involvement in a Chemical-Dependency Rehabilitation Program" (Haynes 1988), social scientists began in the 1980s to write about *chemical, alcohol,* and *drug dependency,* all euphemisms for addiction. Because welfare claimants are often—falsely—assumed to be addicts, the pathological connotations of *drug dependency* tend also to infect *welfare dependency,* increasing stigmatization.

A second important postindustrial current is the rise of new psychological meanings of dependency with very strong feminine associations. In the 1950s, social workers influenced by psychiatry began to diagnose dependence as a form of immaturity common among women, particularly among solo mothers (who were often, of course, welfare claimants). "Dependent, irresponsible, and unstable, they respond like small children to the immediate moment," declared the author of a 1954 discussion of out-of-wedlock pregnancy (Young 1954, 87). The problem was that women were supposed to be just dependent enough, and it was easy to tip over into excess in either direction. The norm, moreover, was racially marked, as white women were usually portrayed as erring on the side of excessive dependence, while black women were typically charged with excessive independence.

Psychologized dependency became the target of some of the earliest second-wave feminism. Betty Friedan's 1963 classic, *The Feminine Mystique,* provided a phenomenological account of the housewife's psychological dependency and drew from it a political critique of her social subordination. More recently, however, a burgeoning cultural-feminist, postfeminist, and antifeminist self-help and pop-psychology literature has obfuscated the link between the psychological and the political. In Colette Dowling's 1981 book, *The Cinderella Complex,* women's dependency was hypostatized as a depth-psychological gender structure: "women's hidden fear of independence" or the "wish to be saved." The late 1980s saw a spate of books about "codependency," a supposedly prototypically female syndrome of supporting or "enabling" the dependency of someone else. In a metaphor that reflects the drug hysteria of the period, dependency here, too, is an addiction. Apparently, even if a woman manages herself to escape her gender's predilection to dependency, she is still liable to incur the blame for facilitating the dependency of her husband or children. This completes the vicious circle: the increased stigmatizing of dependency in the culture at large has also deepened contempt for those who care for dependents, reinforcing the traditionally low status of the female helping professions, such as nursing and social work (Sapiro 1990).

The 1980s saw a cultural panic about dependency. In 1980, the American Psychiatric Association codified "Dependent Personality Disorder" (DPD) as an official psychopathology. According to the 1987 edition of the *Diagnostic and Statistical Manual of Mental Disorders* (DSM-III-R), "The essential feature of this disorder is a pervasive pattern of dependent and submissive behavior beginning by early childhood. . . . People with this disorder are unable to make everyday decisions without an excessive amount of advice and reassurance from others, and will even allow others to make most of their important decisions. . . . The disorder is apparently common and is diagnosed more frequently in females" (American Psychiatric Association 1987, 353–54).

The codification of DPD as an official psychopathology represents a new stage in the history of the moral/psychological register. Here the social relations of dependency disappear entirely into the personality of the dependent. Overt moralism also disappears in the apparently neutral, scientific, medicalized formulation. Thus, although the defining traits of the dependent personality match point for point the traits traditionally ascribed to housewives, paupers, natives, and slaves, all links to subordination have vanished. The only remaining trace of those themes is the flat, categorical, and uninterpreted observation that DPD is "diagnosed more frequently in females."

If psychological discourse has further feminized and individualized dependency, other postindustrial developments have further racialized it. The increased stigmatization of welfare dependency followed a general increase in public provision in the United States, the removal of some discriminatory practices that had previously excluded minority women from participation in AFDC, especially in the South, and the transfer of many white women to first-track programs as social-insurance coverage expanded. By the 1970s the figure of the black solo mother had come to epitomize welfare dependency. As a result, the new discourse about welfare draws on older symbolic currents that linked dependency with racist ideologies.

The ground was laid by a long, somewhat contradictory stream of discourse about "the black family," in which African American gender and kinship relations were measured against white middle-class norms and deemed pathological. One supposedly pathological element was "the excessive independence" of black women, an ideologically distorted allusion to long traditions of wage work, educational achievement, and community activism. The 1960s and 1970s discourse about poverty recapitulated traditions of misogyny toward African American women; in Daniel Moynihan's diagnosis, for example, "matriarchal" families had "emasculated" black men and created a "culture of poverty" based on a "tangle of [family] pathology" (Rainwater and Yancey 1967). This discourse placed black AFDC claimants in a double bind: they were pathologically independent with respect to men and pathologically dependent with respect to government.

By the 1980s, however, the racial imagery of dependency had shifted. The black welfare mother that haunted the white imagination ceased to be the powerful matriarch. Now the preeminent stereotype is the unmarried teenage mother caught in the "welfare trap" and rendered dronelike and passive. This new icon of welfare dependency is younger and weaker then the matriarch. She is often evoked in the phrase *children having children,* which can express feminist sympathy or antifeminist contempt, black appeals for parental control or white-racist eugenic anxieties.

Many of these postindustrial discourses coalesced in the early 1990s. Then–Vice President Dan Quayle brought together the pathologized, feminized, and racialized currents in his comment on the May 1992 Los Angeles riot: "Our inner cities are filled with children having children . . . with people who are dependent on drugs and on the narcotic of welfare" (Quayle 1992).

Thus postindustrial culture has called up a new personification of dependency: the black, unmarried, teenaged, welfare-dependent mother. This image has usurped the symbolic space previously occupied by the housewife, the pauper, the native, and the slave, while absorbing and condensing their connotations. Black, female, a pauper, not a worker, a housewife and mother, yet practically a child herself—the new stereotype partakes of virtually every quality that has been coded historically as antithetical to independence. Condensing multiple, often contradictory meanings of dependency, it is a powerful ideological trope that simultaneously organizes diffuse cultural anxieties and dissimulates their social bases.

POSTINDUSTRIAL POLICY AND THE POLITICS OF DEPENDENCY

Despite the worsening economic outlook for many Americans in the last few decades, there has been no cultural revaluation of welfare. Families working harder for less often resent those who appear to them not to be working at all. Apparently lost, at least for now, are the struggles of the 1960s that aimed to recast AFDC as an entitlement in order to promote recipients' independence. Instead, the honorific term *independent* remains firmly centered on wage labor, no matter how impoverished the worker. Welfare dependency, in contrast, has been inflated into a behavioral syndrome and made to seem more contemptible.

Contemporary policy discourse about welfare dependency is thoroughly inflected by these assumptions. It divides into two major streams. The first continues the rhetoric of pauperism and the culture of poverty. It is used in both conservative and liberal, victim-blaming or non-victim-blaming ways, depending on the causal structure of the argument. The contention is that poor, dependent people have something more than lack of money wrong with them. The flaws can be located in biology, psychology, upbringing, neighborhood influence; they can be cast as cause or as effect of poverty, or even as both simultaneously. Conservatives, such as George Gilder (1981) and Lawrence Mead (1986), argue that welfare causes moral/ psychological dependency. Liberals, such as William Julius Wilson (1987) and Christopher Jencks (1992), blame social and economic influences but often agree that claimants' culture and behavior are problematic.

A second stream of thought begins from neoclassical economic premises. It assumes a "rational man" facing choices in which welfare and work are both options. For these policy analysts, the moral/psychological meanings of dependency are present but uninterrogated, assumed to be undesirable. Liberals of this school, such as many of the social scientists associated with the Institute for Research on Poverty at the University of Wisconsin, grant that welfare inevitably has some bad, dependency-creating effects but claim that these are outweighed by other, good effects like improved conditions for children, increased societal stability, and relief of suffering. Conservatives of this school, such as Charles Murray (1984), disagree. The two camps argue above all about the question of incentives. Do AFDC stipends encourage women to have more out-of-wedlock children? Do they discourage them from accepting jobs? Can reducing or withholding stipends serve as a stick to encourage recipients to stay in school, keep their children in school, get married?

Certainly, there are real and significant differences here, but there are also important similarities. Liberals and conservatives of both schools rarely situate the notion of dependency in its historical or economic context; nor do they interrogate it presuppositions. Neither group questions the assumption that independence is an unmitigated good nor its identification with wage labor. Many poverty and welfare analysts equivocate between an official position that *dependency* is a value-neutral term for receipt of (or need for) welfare and a usage that makes it a synonym for *pauperism.*

These assumptions permeate the public sphere. In the current round of alarms about welfare dependency, it is increasingly claimed that "welfare mothers ought to work," a usage that tacitly defines work as wage earning and child raising as nonwork. Here we run up against contradictions in the discourse of dependency: when the subject under consideration is teenage pregnancy, these mothers are cast as children; when the subject is welfare, they become adults who should be self-supporting. It is only in the last decade that welfare experts have reached a consensus on the view that AFDC recipients should be employed. The older view, which underlay the original passage of ADC, was that children need a mother at home—although in practice there was always a class double standard, since full-time maternal domesticity was a privilege that had to be purchased, not an entitlement poor women could claim. However, as wage work among mothers of young children has become more widespread and normative, the last defenders of a welfare program that permitted recipients to concentrate full-time on child raising were silenced

None of the negative imagery about welfare dependency has gone uncontested, of course. From the 1950s through the 1970s, many of these presuppositions were challenged, most directly in the mid-1960s by an organization of women welfare claimants, the National Welfare Rights Organization (NWRO). The women of NWRO cast their relation with the welfare system as active rather than passive, a matter of claiming rights rather than receiving charity. They also insisted that their domestic labor was socially necessary and praiseworthy. Their perspective helped reconstruct the arguments for welfare, spurring poverty lawyers and radical intellectuals to develop a legal and political–theoretical basis for welfare as an entitlement and right. Edward Sparer, a legal strategist for the welfare rights movement, challenged the usual understanding of dependency: "The charge of antiwelfare politicians is that welfare makes the recipient 'dependent.' What this means is that the recipient depends on the welfare check for his [*sic*] material subsistence rather than upon some other source . . . whether that is good or bad depends on whether a better source of income is available. . . . The real problem . . . is something entirely different. The recipient and the applicant traditionally have been dependent on the whim of the caseworker" (Sparer 1970–71, 71). The cure for welfare dependency, then, was welfare rights. Had the NWRO not been greatly weakened by the late 1970s, the revived discourse of pauperism in the 1980s could not have become hegemonic.

Even in the absence of a powerful National Welfare Rights Organization, many AFDC recipients maintained their own oppositional interpretation of welfare dependency. They complained not only of stingy allowances but also of infantilization due to supervision, loss of privacy, and a maze of bureaucratic rules that constrained their decisions about housing, jobs, and even (until the 1960s) sexual relations. In the claimants' view, welfare dependency is a social condition, not a psychological state, a condition they analyze in terms of power relations. It is what a left-wing English dictionary of social welfare calls *enforced dependency,* "the creation of a dependent class" as a result of "enforced reliance . . . for necessary psychological or material resources" (Timms and Timms 1982, 55–56).

This idea of enforced dependency was central to another, related challenge to the dominant discourse. During the period in which NWRO activism was at its height, New Left revisionist historians developed an interpretation of the welfare state as an apparatus of social control. They argued that what apologists portrayed as helping practices were actually modes of domination that created enforced dependency. The New Left critique bore some resemblance to the NWRO critique, but the overlap was only partial. The historians of social control told their story mainly from the perspective of the "helpers" and cast recipients as almost entirely passive. They thereby occluded the agency of actual or potential welfare claimants in articulating needs, demanding rights, and making claims.[13]

Still another contemporary challenge to mainstream uses of *dependency* arose from a New Left school of international political economy. The context was the realization, after the first heady days of postwar decolonization, that politically independent former colonies remained economically dependent. In *dependency theory,* radical theorists of "underdevelopment" used the concept of dependency to analyze the global neocolonial economic order from an antiracist and anti-imperialist perspective. In doing so, they resurrected the old preindustrial meaning of dependency as a subjected territory, seeking thereby to divest the term of its newer moral/psychological accretions and to retrieve the occluded dimensions of subjection and subordination. This usage remains strong in Latin America as well as in U.S. social–scientific literature, where we find articles such as "Institutionalizing Dependency: The Impact of Two Decades of Planned Agricultural Modernization" (Gates 1988).

What all these oppositional discourses share is a rejection of the dominant emphasis on dependency as an individual trait. They seek to shift the focus back to the social relations of subordination. But they do not have much impact on mainstream talk about welfare in the United States today. On the contrary, with economic dependency now a synonym for poverty, and with moral/psychological dependency now a personality disorder, talk of dependency as a social relation of subordination has become increasingly rare. Power and domination tend to disappear.[14]

CONCLUSION

Dependency, once a general-purpose term for all social relations of subordination, is now differentiated into several analytically distinct registers. In the economic register, its meaning has shifted from gaining one's livelihood by working for someone else to relying for support on charity or welfare; wage labor now confers independence. In the sociolegal register, the meaning of dependency as subsumption is unchanged, but its scope of reference and connotations have altered: once a socially approved majority condition, it first became a group-based status deemed proper for some classes of persons but not others and then shifted again to designate (except in the case of children) an anomalous, highly stigmatized status of deviant and incompetent individuals. Likewise, in the political register, dependency's meaning as subjection to an external governing power has remained relatively constant, but its evaluative connotations worsened as individual political rights and national sovereignty became normative. Meanwhile, with the emergence of a newer moral/psychological register, properties once ascribed to social relations came to be posited instead as inherent character traits of individuals or groups, and the connotations here, too, have worsened. This last register now claims an increasingly large proportion of the discourse, as if the social relations of dependency were being absorbed into personality. Symptomatically, erstwhile relational understandings have been hypostatized in a veritable portrait gallery of dependent personalities: first, housewives, paupers, natives, and slaves; then poor, solo, black teenage mothers.

These shifts in the semantics of dependency reflect some major sociohistorical developments. One is the progressive differentiation of the official economy—that which is counted in the domestic national product—as a seemingly autonomous system that dominates social life. Before the rise of capitalism, all forms of work were woven into a net of dependencies, which constituted a single, continuous fabric of social hierarchies. The whole set of relations was constrained by moral understandings, as in the preindustrial idea of a moral economy. In the patriarchal families and communities that characterized the preindustrial period, women were subordinated and their labor often controlled by others, but their labor was visible, understood, and valued. With the emergence of religious and secular individualism, on the one hand, and of industrial capitalism, on the other, a sharp, new dichotomy was constructed in which economic dependency and economic independence were unalterably opposed to one another. A crucial corollary of this dependence/independence dichotomy, and of the hegemony of wage labor in general, was the occlusion and devaluation of women's unwaged domestic and parenting labor.

The genealogy of dependency also expresses the modern emphasis on individual personality. This is the deepest meaning of the spectacular rise of the moral/psychological register, which constructs yet another version of the independence/dependence dichotomy. In the moral/psychological version, social relations are hypostatized as properties of individuals or groups. Fear of dependency, both explicit and implicit, posits an ideal, independent personality in contrast to which those considered dependent are deviant. This contrast bears traces of a sexual division of labor that assigns men primary responsibility as providers or breadwinners and women primary responsibility as caretakers and nurturers and then treats the derivative personality patterns as fundamental. It is as if male breadwinners absorbed into their personalities the independence associated with their ideologically interpreted economic role, whereas the persons of female nurturers became saturated with the dependency of those for whom they care. In this way, the opposition between the independent personality and the dependent personality maps onto a whole series of hierarchical oppositions and dichotomies that are central in modern culture: masculine/feminine, public/private, work/care, success/love, individual/ community, economy/family, and competitive/self-sacrificing.

A genealogy cannot tell us how to respond politically to today's discourse about welfare dependency. It does suggest, however, the limits of any response that presupposes rather than challenges the definition of the problem that is implicit in that expression. An adequate response would need to question our received valuations and definitions of dependence and independence in order to allow new, emancipatory social visions to emerge. Some contemporary welfare-rights activists adopt this strategy, continuing the NWRO tradition. Pat Gowens, for example, elaborates a feminist reinterpretation of dependency:

> The vast majority of mothers of *all classes and all educational levels* "depends" on another income. It may come from child support . . . or from a husband who earns $20,000 while she averages $7,000. But "dependence" more accurately defines dads who count on women's unwaged labor to raise children and care for the home. Surely, "dependence" doesn't define the single mom who does it all: child-rearing, homemaking, and bringing in the money (one way or another). When caregiving is valued and paid, when dependence is not a dirty word, and interdependence is the norm—only then will we make a dent in poverty. (Gowens 1991, 90–91)

NOTES

This chapter originally appeared in *Signs* 19, no. 2 (winter 1994): 309–36. Copyright ©1994 by Nancy Fraser and Linda Gordon. Reprinted with permission.

Nancy Fraser is grateful for research support from the Center for Urban Affairs, Northwestern University; the Newberry Library/National Endowment for the Humanities; and the American Council of Learned Societies. Linda Gordon thanks the University of Wisconsin Graduate School, Vilas Trust, and the Institute for Research on Poverty. We both thank the Rockefeller Foundation Research and Study Center, Bellagio, Italy. We are also grateful for helpful comments from Lisa Brush, Robert Entman, Joel Handler, Dirk Hartog, Barbara Hobson, Allen Hunter, Eva Kittay, Felicia Kornbluh, Jenny Mansbridge, Linda Nicholson, Erik Wright, Eli Zaretsky, and the *Signs* reviewers and editors.

1. Another part of the story, of course, concerns the word *welfare*. In this article, our focus is U.S. political culture and thus North American English usage. Our findings should be of more general interest, however, as some other languages have similar meanings embedded in analogous words. In this article we have of necessity used British sources for the early stages of our genealogy, which spans the sixteenth and seventeenth centuries. We assume that these meanings of *dependency* were brought to "the New World" and were formative for the early stages of U.S. political culture.

2. This stress on the performative, as opposed to the representational, dimension of language is a hallmark of the pragmatics tradition in the philosophy of language. It has been fruitfully adapted for sociocultural analysis by several writes in addition to Williams. See, e.g., Bourdieu 1977, 1990a, 1990b; Scott 1988; Fraser 1989, 1990, 1992; and Butler 1990.

3. The critical literature on Foucault is enormous. For feminist assessments, see Butler 1987; Weedon 1987; the essays in Diamond and Quinby 1988; Alcoff 1990; and Hartsock 1990. For balanced discussions of Foucault's strengths and weaknesses, see Fraser 1989; McCarthy 1991; and Honneth 1992.

4. In preindustrial society, moreover, the reverse dependence of the master upon his men was widely recognized. The historian Christopher Hill evoked that understanding when he characterized the "essence" of feudal society as "the bond of loyalty and dependence between lord and man" (1972, 32). Here *dependence* means interdependence.

5. One might say that this redefinition foregrounded wage labors *as* a new form of property, namely, property in one's own labor power. This conception was premised on what Macpherson (1962) called "possessive individualism," the assumption of an individual's property in his [*sic*] own person. Leading to the construction of wages as an entitlement, this approach was overwhelmingly male. Allen Hunter (personal communication, 1992) describes it as a loss of systemic critique, a sense of independence gained by narrowing the focus to the individual worker and leaving behind aspirations for collective independence from capital.

6. In the sixteenth century the term *pauper* had meant simply a poor person and, in law, one who was allowed to sue or defend in a court without paying costs (*OED*). Two centuries later, it took on a more restricted definition, denoting a new class of persons who subsisted on poor relief instead of wages and who were held to be deviant and blameworthy.

7. Actually, there are many variants within the family of images that personify subjection in the industrial era. Among these are related but not identical stereotypes of the Russian serf, the Caribbean slave, the slave in the United States, and the American Indian. Moreover, there are distinct male and female stereotypes within each of those categories. We simplify here in order to highlight the features that are common to all these images, notably the idea of natural subjection rooted in race. We focus especially on stereotypes that portray African Americans as personifications of dependency because of their historic importance and contemporary resonance in the U.S. language of social welfare.

8. The evolution of the term *native* neatly encapsulates this process. Its original meaning in English, dating from about 1450, was tied to dependency: "one born in bondage; a born thrall," but without racial meaning. Two centuries later it carried the additional meaning of colored or black (*OED*).

9. For example, Warner (1894–1930) uses *dependent* only for children. The same is true of Abbott and Breckinridge (1921, 7) and National Conference of Charities and Correction (1890s-1920s). This usage produced some curious effects because of its intersection with the dependency produced by the normative family. For example, charity experts debated the propriety of "keeping dependent children in their own homes." The children in question were considered dependent because their parent(s) could not support them; yet other children were deemed dependent precisely because their parents did support them.

10. Studies of welfare done in the 1940s still used the word *dependents* only in the sense of those supported by family head; see, e.g., Brown 1940; Howard 1943; Bruno 1948.

11. Starting in the 1960s increasing numbers of black women were able to claim AFDC, but prior to that they were largely excluded. At first, the language of the New Deal followed the precedent of earlier programs in applying the term *dependent* to children. De facto, however, the recipients of ADC were virtually exclusively solo mothers. Between the 1940s and 1960s the term's reference gradually shifted from the children to their mothers.

12. Men on "general relief" are sometimes also included in that designation; their treatment by the welfare system is usually as bad or worse.

13. For a fuller discussion of the social control critique, see Gordon 1990. On needs claims, see Fraser 1990 and Nelson 1990.

14. For an argument that Bill Clinton's neoliberal discourse continues to individualize dependency, see Fraser 1993.

REFERENCES

Abbot, Edith, and Sophonisba P. Breckinridge. 1921. *The Administration of the Aid-to-Mothers Law in Illinois.* Publication no. 82. Washington, D.C.: U.S. Children's Bureau.

Alcoff, Linda. 1990. "Feminist Politics and Foucault: The Limits to a Collaboration." In *Crisis in Continental Philosophy,* ed. Arleen B. Dallery and Charles E. Scott, 69–86. Albany: SUNY Press.

American Psychiatric Association. 1987. *Diagnostic and Statistical Manual of Mental Disorders,* 3d. ed. revised. Washington D.C.: American Psychiatric Association.

Bakke, E. Wight. 1940a. *Citizens without Work: A Study of the Effects of Unemployment upon Workers' Social Relations and Practices.* New Haven, Conn.: Yale University Press.

———. 1940b. *The Unemployed Worker: A Study of the Task of Making a Living without a Job.* New Haven, Conn.: Yale University Press.

Barnes, Annie S. 1987. *Single Parents in Black America: A Study in Culture and Legitimacy.* Bristol, Conn.: Wyndham Hall.

Bourdieu, Pierre. 1977. *Outline of a Theory of Practice.* Cambridge: Cambridge University Press.

———. 1990a. *In Other Words,* trans. Matthew Adamson. Oxford: Polity.

———. 1990b. *The Logic of Practice,* trans. Richard Nice. Stanford, Calif.: Stanford University Press.

Boydston, Jeanne. 1991. *Home and Work: Housework, Wages, and the Ideology of Labor in the Early Republic.* New York: Oxford.

Brandt, Lilian. 1932. *An Impressionistic View of the Winter of 1930–31 in New York City.* New York: Welfare Council of New York City.

Breckinridge, Sophonisba P. 1928. "The House Responsibilities of Women Workers and the 'Equal Wage.'" *Journal of Political Economy* 31: 521–43.

Brown, Josephine Chapin. 1940. *Public Relief, 1929–1939.* New York: Henry Holt.

Bruno, Frank J. 1948. *Trends in Social Work.* New York: Columbia University Press.

Butler, Judith. 1987. "Variations on Sex and Gender: Beauvoir, Wittig and Foucault." In *Feminism as Critique,* ed. Seyla Benhabib and Drucilla Cornell, 128–42. Minneapolis: University of Minnesota Press.

———. 1990. *Gender Trouble: Feminism and the Subversion of Identity.* New York: Routledge.

Cates, Jerry R. 1983. *Insuring Inequality: Administrative Leadership in Social Security, 1935–54.* Ann Arbor: University of Michigan Press.

Diamond, Irene, and Lee Quinby, eds. 1988. *Foucault and Feminism: Reflections on Resistance.* Boston: Northeastern University Press.

Dowling, Colette. 1981. *The Cinderella Complex: Women's Hidden Fear of Independence.* New York: Summit.

Folbre, Nancy. 1991. "The Unproductive Housewife: Her Evolution in Nineteenth-Century Economic Thought." *Signs: Journal of Women in Culture and Society* 16 (no. 3): 463–84.

Foucault, Michel. 1984. "Nietzsche, Genealogy, History." In *The Foucault Reader,* ed. Paul Rabinow, 76–100. New York: Pantheon.

Fraser, Nancy. 1987. "Women, Welfare, and the Politics of Need Interpretation." *Hypatia: A Journal of Feminist Philosophy* 2 (no. 1): 103–21.

———. 1989. *Unruly Practices: Power, Discourse, and Gender in Contemporary Social Theory.* Minneapolis: University of Minnesota Press.

———. 1990. "Struggle over Needs: Outline of a Socialist-Feminist Critical Theory of Late-Capitalist Political Culture." In *Women, the State, and Welfare*, ed. Linda Gordon, 199–225. Madison: University of Wisconsin Press.

———. 1992. "The Uses and Abuses of French Discourse Theories for Feminist Politics." In *Revaluing French Feminism: Critical Essays on Difference, Agency, and Culture*, ed. Nancy Fraser and Sandra Bartky, 177–94. Bloomington: Indiana University Press.

———. 1993. "Clintonism, Welfare, and the Antisocial Wage: The Emergence of a Neoliberal Political Imaginary." *Rethinking Marxism* 6 (no. 1): 1–15.

Fraser, Nancy, and Linda Gordon. 1992. "Contract versus Charity: Why Is There No Social Citizenship in the United States?" *Socialist Review* 22 (no. 3):45–68.

Friedan, Betty. 1963. *The Feminine Mystique*. New York: Norton.

Gates, M. 1988. "Institutionalizing Dependency: The Impact of Two Decades of Planned Agricultural Modernization." *Journal of Developing Areas* 22 (no. 3):293–320.

Gibbons, Mary L. 1933. "Family Life Today and Tomorrow." *Proceedings, National Conference of Catholic Charities* 19: 133–68.

Gilder, George. 1981. *Wealth and Poverty*. New York: Basic.

Gordon, Linda. 1990. "The New Feminist Scholarship on the Welfare State." In *Women, the State, and Welfare*, ed. Linda Gordon, 9–35. Madison: University of Wisconsin Press.

———. 1992. "Social Insurance and Public Assistance: The Influence of Gender in Welfare Thought in the United States, 1890–1935." *American Historical Review* 97 (no. 1): 19–54.

Gowens, Pat. 1991. "Welfare, Learnfare—Unfair! A Letter to My Governor." *Ms.* (September-October), 90–91.

Gundersen, Joan R. 1987. "Independence, Citizenship, and the American Revolution." *Signs* 13 (no. 1): 59–77.

Hartsock, Nancy. 1990. "Foucault on Power: A Theory for Women?" In *Feminism/Postmodernism*, ed. Linda J. Nicholson, 157–75. New York: Routledge.

Haynes, M. 1988. "Pharmacist Involvement in a Chemical-Dependency Rehabilitation Program." *American Journal of Hospital Pharmacy* 45 (no. 10): 2099–2101.

Hill, Christopher. 1972. *The World Turned Upside Down: Radical Ideas during the English Revolution*. New York: Viking.

Honneth, Axel. 1992. *The Critique of Power: Reflective Stages in a Cricial Social Theory*. Cambridge, Mass.: MIT Press.

Howard, Donald S. 1943. *The WPA and Federal Relief Policy*. New York: Russell Sage.

Hughes, Gwendolyn S. 1925. *Mothers in Industry*. New York: New Republic.

Jencks, Christopher. 1992. *Rethinking Social Policy: Race, Poverty, and the Underclass*. Cambridge, Mass.: Harvard University Press.

Land, Hilary. 1980. "The Family Wage." *Feminist Review* 6: 55–77.

Laslett, Peter. 1971. *The World We Have Lost: England before the Industrial Age*. New York: Scribner.

McCarthy, Thomas. 1991. *Ideals and Illusions: On Reconstruction and Deconstruction in Contemporary Critical Theory*. Cambridge, Mass.: MIT Press.

Macpherson, C. B. 1962. *The Political Theory of Possessive Individualism: Hobbes to Locke*. Oxford: Oxford University Press.

Mead, Lawrence. 1986. *Beyond Entitlement: The Social Obligations of Citizenship*. New York: Free Press.

Milwaukee County Welfare Rights Organization. 1972. *Welfare Mothers Speak Out*. New York: Norton.

Moynihan, Daniel P. 1973. *The Politics of a Guaranteed Income: The Nixon Administration and the Family Assistance Plan.* New York: Random House.

Murray, Charles. 1984. *Losing Ground: American Social Policy, 1950–1980.* New York: Basic.

Nathan, Richard P. 1986. "The Underclass—Will It Always Be with Us?" Unpublished paper, quoted by William Julius Wilson, "Social Policy and Minority Groups: What Might Have Been and What Might We See in the Future." In *Divided Opportunities: Minorities, Poverty, and Social Policy,* ed. Gary D. Sandefur and Marta Tienda, 231–52. New York: Plenum.

National Conference of Charities and Correction. 1890s-1920s. *Proceedings.*

Nelson, Barbara J. 1990. "The Origins of the Two-Channel Welfare State: Workmen's Compensation and Mothers' Aid." In *Women, the State, and Welfare,* ed. Linda Gordon, 123–51. Madison: University of Wisconsin Press.

Pope, Jacqueline. 1989. *Biting the Hand That Feeds Them: Organizing Women on Welfare at the Grass Roots Level.* New York: Praeger.

Pruette, Lorine, ed. 1934. *Women Workers through the Depression: A Study of White Collar Employment Made by the American Woman's Association.* New York: Macmillian.

Quadagno, Jill. 1988. "From Old-Age Assistance to Supplemental Social Security Income: The Political Economy of Relief in the South, 1935–1972." In *The Politics of Social Policy in the United States,* ed. Margaret Weir, Ann Shola Orloff, and Theda Skocpol, 235–63. Princeton, N.J.: Princeton University Press.

Quayle, Dan. 1992. "Excerpts from Vice President's Speech on Cities and Poverty." *New York Times,* May 20.

Rainwater, Lee, and William L. Yancey. 1967. *The Moynihan Report and the Politics of Controversy.* Cambridge, Mass.: MIT Press.

Sapiro, Virginia. 1990. "The Gender Basis of American Social Policy." In *Women, the State, and Welfare,* ed. Linda Gordon, 36–54. Madison: University of Wisconsin Press.

Scott, Joan Wallach. 1988. *Gender and the Politics of History.* New York: Columbia University Press.

Smith, Joan. 1984. "The Paradox of Women's Poverty: Wage-earning Women and Economic Transformation." *Signs* 10 (no. 2): 291–310.

Sparer, Edward V. 1971. (c. 1970). "The Right to Welfare." In *The Rights of Americans: What They Are—What They Should Be,* ed. Norman Dorsen, 65–93. New York: Pantheon.

Stacey, Judith. 1987. "Sexism by a Subtler Name? Postindustrial Conditions and Postfeminist Consciousness in the Silicon Valley." *Socialist Review* 96: 7–28.

———. 1990. *Brave New Families: Stories of Domestic Upheaval in Late Twentieth Century America.* New York: Basic.

Timms, Noel, and Rita Timms. 1982. *Dictionary of Social Welfare.* London: Routledge & Kegan Paul.

Tumulty, Karen. 1991. *Los Angeles Times,* July 5.

Vaile, Gertrude. 1934. "Public Relief." In *College Women and the Social Sciences,* ed. Herbert Elmer Mills, 19–40. New York: John Day.

Warner, Amos Griswold. 1894–1930. *American Charities and Social Work.* New York: Thomas Y. Crowell.

Weedon, Chris. 1987. *Feminist Practice and Poststructuralist Theory.* Oxford: Basil Blackwell.

West, Guida. 1981. *The National Welfare Rights Movement: The Social Protest of Poor Women.* New York: Praeger.

Weston, Kath. 1991. *Families We Choose: Lesbians, Gays, Kinship.* New York: Columbia University Press.

Williams, Raymond. 1976. *Keywords: A Vocabulary of Culture and Society.* Oxford: Oxford University Press.

Wilson, William Julius. 1987. *The Truly Disadvantaged: The Inner City, the Underclass, and Public Policy.* Chicago: University of Chicago Press.

Young, Leontine. 1954. *Out of Wedlock.* New York: McGraw Hill.

2

Autonomy, Welfare Reform, and Meaningful Work

Iris Marion Young

On March 3, 1999, I attended a rally in Pittsburgh to mark the second anniversary of the implementation of the Temporary Assistance for Needy Families (TANF) Program in Pennsylvania. Under the provisions of the Personal Responsibility and Work Opportunity Reconciliation Act (PRWORA) of 1996, recipients of TANF are supposed to stop receiving benefits after twenty-four consecutive months. The crowd that stood in the rain listening to music and speeches thus marked the first major turning point in the most radical change in public assistance in the United States in fifty years, which removed the torn safety net that had existed under poor parents.

Most of the speakers at the rally were recipients or former recipients, part of a newly formed organization, the Welfare Justice Project. One African American woman who looked to be in her mid-twenties particularly impressed me. She recalled the years she had been on public assistance with her two small children, and how under the new state program she had been through training as a carpenter's assistant and was now off welfare. She proudly pronounced herself on the road to self-sufficiency and exhorted her fellow recipients and former recipients to work hard to gain their own self-sufficiency. Recipients should demand their rights from the welfare system, including enrollment in training programs like hers, as well as transportation to the programs and child care. The main problem with the welfare system, she declared, was that many case workers were not following the law and neglecting to work out a plan with recipients to gain them skills that will make them self-sufficient. Instead, caseworkers were assigning recipients immediately to unskilled work activities or enrolling them in meaningless "job-readiness" programs.

While the participants at this rally made assertive claims in energetic ways, for the most part they did so within the terms of the legislation that had so radically shifted the conditions of the receipt of public assistance. They seemed to accept the idea that the need to care for their children was not sufficient reason to receive a small monthly check, and that the state had a right to expect that they "earn" that money by a "work activity." They appeared to accept the bargain the law offered them: If you attend programs and go to your work assignments, then you will become self-sufficient. So, soon after a rather large change in policy, whose terms and provisions were controversial and contested before its implementation, there was a surprising consensus among policymakers, service providers, academic researchers, and affected persons that the basic assumptions of welfare policy are correct. Nearly everyone seemed to agree that recipients of public assistance should "work," that having a job is the only meaning of "work," and that the goal of welfare programs is to make people "self-sufficient."

There are critics of contemporary welfare policy, of course. They point to many flaws in the new system that leave poor adults and children unprotected. In the rush to get people off welfare, states may discourage eligible people from accessing benefits, and many do not well track what has happened to recipients who have left the system. Every state now has a more complex system of benefits and services, whose rules are more confusing and change rapidly. Recipients and potential recipients often sit across the desk from social workers who are poorly trained and overworked. Work requirements for receipt of public assistance have called attention to the need for more child-care services, and funding has increased for this purpose, but the welfare of many children is nevertheless often endangered by the system. Child care is rarely available for evening or night hours, when many jobs require working such hours. Most states provide or reimburse child care only for young children, expecting parents to leave their teenagers unsupervised. Reimbursement checks take months to arrive, during which time mothers either forgo food to pay for child care or incur a debt to child-care workers who eventually leave. Formal after-school programs for school-age children are almost nonexistent.[1]

The insistence that welfare recipients get jobs has promoted important new questions and research about the availability of jobs and the level of pay and benefits are required for jobs to pull families out of poverty. Some critics of current welfare policy point out that most recipients of public assistance get off welfare to perform low-skilled jobs that neither pay well nor develop skills so that the workers can move up the economic ladder. If the goal of welfare policy is to make poor families self-sufficient, these critics say, then these wage earners need to have jobs that pay a *living* wage, which some estimate at almost twice the minimum wage if needed to support a family of three.[2] The goal of self-sufficiency is a cruel joke, moreover, these advocates say, if the good jobs are not secure, don't have decent working conditions, and do not carry good health and retirement benefits. These are all important issues, but they nevertheless stay within the basic terms of the new policy consensus, which equates work with having a job and takes self-sufficiency as a norm and condition of responsible adult life.

In this chapter I question this apparent consensus that the purpose of welfare policy is to make people self-sufficient.[3] I argue that the welfare policy's rhetoric of work and self-sufficiency expresses a damaging ideology that operates further to close the universe of discourse about the respect people deserve, the meaning and expectations of work, and aspirations for autonomy. I borrow the phrase "close the universe of discourse" from Herbert Marcuse's *One Dimensional Man*. An important feature of what Marcuse calls "one dimensional society" is that prevailing discourses referring to everyday life, politics, power, and social relations of production and consumption are so framed that they provoke uncritical assent and acceptance by closing off the possibility of mediated reflection. They close off understanding of the concreteness of particular historical circumstances as they may differ from others and represent concepts that might be thought opposed or contradictory as belonging to a harmonious whole.[4]

One of the effects of the new welfare system is to close the universe of discourse about the meanings of autonomy and work. Its rhetoric mystifies the idea of self-sufficiency. I think the widely accepted logic that says that welfare recipients should work at a job and that if they do they will become self-sufficient is an *ideology*: It systematically distorts people's understanding of their social conditions in ways that reinforce unjust relations of economic and social power, at the same time that it inhibits imagining alternatives.

In what follows I distinguish conceptually between the value of autonomy, on the one hand, which ought to be understood as a right, and self-sufficiency, which is a normalizing and impossible ideal. I suggest that one reason that the rhetoric of self-sufficiency commands assent is that it relies on the positive value of autonomy. I argue, furthermore, that welfare practice relies on another positive value, that everyone should make a social contribution, but that it wrongly reduces making a social contribution to having a job.

These ideological elisions, I suggest, have disciplinary consequences not only for recipients of public assistance, but for all workers. By "discipline," I mean drawing bounds around what dominant norms posit as appropriate or acceptable behavior for respectable citizens. I argue that there are several disciplinary consequences to the discourse and practice that require welfare recipients to "work," identify "working" with having a job, and hold up self-sufficiency as the norm of respectability. First, under these conditions it becomes even more difficult than before for people to refuse a job because they find it beneath their dignity. Second, the reduction of work to having a job further obscures unpaid and privatized care work and housework that take place in the home. Third, by narrowing opportunities of people on public assistance to obtain postsecondary training, skill development becomes more of a privilege than before. Fourth, these rhetorical norms of work and self-sufficiency further normalize what I call the "hale and hearty" worker, stigmatizing and disadvantaging the many people whose capabilities mean they should work less or at a slower pace than others. Finally, and perhaps most important, I argue that the disciplines of work and welfare render even more utopian than before a yearning for meaningful work that ought to be a social ideal.

SEDUCTIONS OF SELF-SUFFICIENCY

One of the propositions about which there is wide consensus is that the goal of welfare policy ought to be to make poor people self-sufficient. At the first level, of course, this proposition means nothing other than that the goal of policy is to get recipients to move from welfare receipt to having jobs. In the next section I critically analyze the reduction of work to having a job this goal of policy pre-supposes. Here I am interested in interrogating the connotations of the term *self-sufficiency*. This particular term carries a great deal of resonance, a history, a set of images, and desires not attached to what appear to be equivalent terms such as *employed* or even *independent*. The layers and resonance of the term, I believe, carry ideological force.

Literally speaking, for a person, or more likely a group such as a family or a vil-lage, to be self-sufficient means that he or they can meet his or their material and emotional needs without having to rely on others. A self-sufficient person or group, in this strong sense, might well have much exchange and social contact, but is not forced to have these in order to survive and thrive. In this rugged individu-alist imagination, a person, a family, a community, are all self-sufficient if they can meet their own needs with minimal adjustment to the desires or actions of others.

Historically, such an ideal of self-sufficiency underlies norms of respect that confer full citizenship on persons. Feminist political theory has shown that the concept of the modern liberal or republican citizen is that of the male head of a self-sufficient household. Entrance into the public world of political decision making with other citizens on an equal basis requires that none of the citizens are beholden to any of the others for their livelihood and those of their children. Only then can they be free to speak their mind and be equal in stature. Just as much, the citizen needs to leave behind a private world where material, emotional, and sexual needs are met.[5]

This normative linkage of citizenship with self-sufficiency, in this sense of be-ing able to support oneself without relation to others, was always utopian. In the days of the yeoman farmer or the independent craftsperson or manufacturer, how-ever, it was not laughable to aspire to a condition approximating self-sufficiency. In today's very different economy, perhaps some people can be self-sufficient in the sense of not having to depend on or be answerable to others to meet their needs, but they are few. Most people's livelihood depends on the fortunes and goodwill of a person or organization that employs them. The viability of those employers themselves depends on often distant economic processes. Almost no one can claim to be self-sufficient in the sense of not having his or her well-being heavily conditioned by vast webs of interdependence.

Everyone knows this, of course, and thus the conditions of being considered self-sufficient have shifted from being able to gain a livelihood without having to work for another to gaining a livelihood through wage employment.[6] When welfare rhet-oric invokes self-sufficiency today, it doesn't mean being literally independent from engagement with others to meet one's needs. It means only having a job and therefore, according to the terms of the welfare state, no longer being dependent on public funds. Even though many jobs do not pay enough to meet one's needs, are only part time, are very insecure, and make a person highly dependent on employers and coworkers, these facts are obscured by the language of self-sufficiency.

Despite changed social circumstances that make being self-sufficient nearly impossible for most, the language of self-sufficiency retains the connotation of being able to fend for oneself and one's loved ones, without being forced to seek help from others and without standing in relations with others that one has not chosen. It would be so nice to be left alone, and not have to anticipate the actions of others as they might affect oneself, and not have to be answerable to them for one's own actions. The discourse of self-sufficiency continues to express this utopian desire, which makes it a seductive language.

Some critics of contemporary welfare policy question the equation of self-sufficiency with having a job, any job. They argue that demands and aspirations for self-sufficiency are a hoax unless former state dependents have *good* jobs—jobs that really pay a wage sufficient to support a family in a decent life, which are secure over time, have good health and retirement benefits, and have decent working conditions. Here is how one advocacy group critical of current policy, Women's Association for Women's Alternatives (WAWA), defines what it calls a Self-Sufficiency Standard: "how much income is needed, for a family of a given composition in a given place, to adequately meet its basic needs—without public or private assistance."[7] This concept of a self-sufficiency standard criticizes current ways of measuring poverty, both on account of having too low a standard and in the fact that it does not attend to income security over time for families. The group calculates the wages adults must earn to meet the needs of families at twice the minimum wage or more, depending on the family size and location. If welfare policy were really about combating poverty, such advocates argue, then it would need to be tied more broadly to employment and human capital investment policy to raise wages, expand opportunities for the acquisition of qualifications, and expand the supply of good jobs.

I agree with these critics and think they are raising important issues. I think that it is a mistake to tie them, however, to a rhetoric of self-sufficiency. Taken literally, WAWA's definition of self-sufficiency is absurd. Taken literally, it would seem to imply that those who meet their needs without relying on public assistance or private charity do not depend on individuals or organizations to ensure their subsistence. The definition makes it sound like they just work for themselves. But, of course, workers don't; they depend on the needs and desires of their employers for their subsistence. The rhetoric of self-sufficiency obscures this dependence on employer power. Accepting the language of self-sufficiency means accepting a norm that people should be able to go it alone without aid and support from others. Societies may be obliged to offer aid and support to enable people to meet their standard of self-sufficiency, when such support should cease. The difference between conservatives and liberals then turns on how much support is called for, but they do not disagree that the norm to which everyone is expected to conform eventually is the ability to go it alone without support. In the next section I argue that the rhetoric of self-sufficiency works ideologically because it relies on a value of autonomy. Contrary to the suggestion of this rhetoric, however, the realization of autonomy for most people requires social support, rather than being equivalent to or conditional on being self-sufficient.

AUTONOMY VERSUS SELF-SUFFICIENCY

I have argued that the rhetoric of self-sufficiency invokes an impossible but seductive ideal. My claim is that this rhetoric is ideological: It sets a framework of thought that achieves wider consent but that systematically distorts people's understanding of their social conditions in ways that reinforce unjust relations of economic and social power. Like many others, this ideology is convincing partly because it relies on appeals to real values. I think that the language of self-sufficiency commands the assent even of recipients because it relies on a core value that we ought to affirm: autonomy.

The philosophical literature on the concept of autonomy is vast, and I will not review it here. Much of this literature theorizes autonomy in the sense of *moral* autonomy. Generally deriving from a Kantian approach to moral action, these theories inquire about the conditions that actions, judgments, or persons should satisfy to be considered reflectively rational and free of heteronomous influence: the sway of unquestioned tradition or authority, the irrationalities of impulse or addictive desire, the constraints of threat or fear, and so on. Autonomy as a moral ideal in these senses is a virtue and an achievement that most people fall short of most of the time; it must be cultivated through education and maintained with reflection and deliberation.

For the purposes of this argument, I am concerned with a different meaning of autonomy, which some theorists call *personal* autonomy. This concerns a condition of personal freedom and self-determination. I define such personal autonomy as being able to determine one's own projects and goals, how one will live one's life, without having to answer for those goals to others, and without having to obey the orders of others about how one will live.[8] An autonomous person is not dependent on another to set the direction of her life, and others do not have the right to determine what is good for her. Unlike the virtue of moral autonomy, personal autonomy should be thought of as a condition that a society should respect for all persons. Personal autonomy is conceptually close to liberty; where liberty is about simple noninterference, letting people alone; however, personal autonomy carries the additional meanings of being able to decide one's own goals and their means to fulfillment, and meeting with respect from others in one's right to govern one's life. In a democratic society

of equal citizens everyone ought to be autonomous in this sense; autonomy
should be a right.

What poor people and their advocates hope to gain from embracing the language
of self-sufficiency in welfare discourse, I suggest, is autonomy.[9] For in the United
States welfare receipt deprives people of autonomy in significant ways. The state
says that because you receive aid, its agents can set specific conditions on how you
will live, sometimes even on where you will live. The system too often treats poor
people as though they do not have rights to decide what vocation to pursue, how to
allocate their time between family responsibilities and work outside the home, how
to meet their family responsibilities, and so on. Too often, that is, poor people are
not granted the minimal respect owed to equal citizens.

On the contrary, the rhetoric of self-sufficiency as it resounds in welfare policy
puts conditions on gaining such respect and being autonomous. Just as the old republican notion of citizenship presumed that only heads of self-sufficient families
can participate with others equally in collective self-rule, so a contemporary norm
of citizenship in the sense of deserving equal respect and having equal rights is tied
to the contemporary meaning of self-sufficiency.[10] Those who need help and support from others do not deserve equal respect, nor can they expect to be able to decide how they will conduct their lives. If you are dependent, then those on whom
you depend have some say over the goals you set for yourself and how you will
enact them. Since most people want to be autonomous and they fail to question
this conceptual and practical tie between autonomy and self-sufficiency, they implicitly accept self-sufficiency as a condition of equal respect and autonomy.

But they should not. Equating a right to autonomy and respect with self-
sufficiency in the sense of not having to depend on others for help and being
able to support oneself and one's loved ones puts impossibly demanding conditions on the earning of respect. It establishes a normative hierarchy where
only those with extraordinary material and personal resources or extraordinary
good luck enough to be strongly self-sufficient have a right to full respect.
Linking the value of autonomy to a concept of self-sufficiency, moreover, tends
wrongly to privilege dispositions to be separate from others over the often un-
chosen claims and consequences of personal and social relationships.[11]

The better conceptual and practical link, I suggest, is between autonomy, on the
one hand, and supportive interdependence, on the other. Our social world is too
complex, and it contains too many physical, economic, and emotional hazards really to expect that most people can pursue productive lives most of the time without a wide net of social supports. Some people with disabilities need extra resources, equipment, or personal care in order to function autonomously. People
who do unpaid care work need to be supplied with means of subsistence and comfort. Most people have their capacities enhanced if they have help in learning new
skills or theories and in negotiating the complexities of this society's financial
and bureaucratic relations. Some people are lucky enough to have families,
churches, or unions with commitments to mutual aid and resources enough to en-

sure them private support. Many people are not so lucky, however, and many of these people are not "poor" by government definition.

If we care about enabling autonomous and productive lives for everyone, then we ought to recognize a need for aid and support as the norm, and the ability to fend for oneself as the exception. Everyone should have the right to be autonomous; a condition of the realization of such autonomy for most people, at least at some times in their lives, is that they receive some resources and/or interpersonal support and assistance from others. Certain forms of dependence and interdependence, that is, should be understood as *normal* conditions of being autonomous. Even with a progressive understanding of "self-sufficiency" that refuses to accept low-wage unskilled jobs as making poor people self-sufficient, the ideology of self-sufficiency still makes independence normative for autonomous persons and thereby judges those whom for whatever reason the society finds overly dependent as less worthy.

REDUCTION OF WORK TO A JOB

The rhetoric of welfare reform draws on another proper and widely shared intuition about the terms of social cooperation, which it then twists into the insistence that only those with a paid job are worthy citizens. Ideals of equal citizenship exhort citizens to engage in activities that productively contribute to their own well-being and to that of others. A society cannot continue for long unless its members are willing to contribute to the production of the goods it consumes, to the organization and operation of its institutions, and to the production of cultural works that express its history and meanings. Members of the society who benefit from these cooperative collective activities, and who are able to contribute to the production of these benefits, are rightly condemned when they do not do so. "From each according to his contribution, to each according to his needs" may not be the proper formulation, but some form of reciprocity between citizen rights and citizen responsibilities is a necessary aspect of a just society. Most people wish to live up to this expectation; most people wish to spend at least some of their time *working*, in this sense of devoting their energy and attention to useful activities for which they receive social recognition and affirmation.

Both the rhetoric of welfare reform and the wider economistic ideology on which it draws, however, narrow and distort what it means for a person to contribute to activities of social cooperation. They reduce making a social contribution, or what I am calling "work" in a broad sense, to having a job. I define a *job* as a task assigned by a powerful person for which he or she is willing to pay. It is not hard to show that having a job and making a social contribution may or may not coincide. Does helping to produce a different-tasting toothpaste contribute usefully to the social good? Does spending day after day at an automatic dialing machine and occasionally persuading a consumer to switch long-distance companies expand the general welfare? Do spectators who invest in high-rise office buildings that remain half empty contribute to the social good? Many jobs are arguably socially wasteful, even directly harmful in their effects.

At the same time, many unpaid or poorly paid activities contribute centrally to the social good. Paramount among these is caring for children and other family members, and doing housework for them and oneself. There are many other important activities that contribute to communities that are often not paid or poorly paid: community caretaking and organizing, care of the natural environment, and the production and dissemination of artworks and performances. People who aim to enhance their skills and capacities to contribute to society, moreover, need support to study. They are usually engaged in productive activity by learning, and it is often difficult for people to develop skills and capacities very efficiently if they must worry about their daily bread.

Welfare as we once knew it grudgingly recognized that the responsible care of children and household is work. Aid for Dependent Children (ADC) and Aid to Families with Dependent Children (AFDC) were based on a premise that children of poor parents deserve as much as others to live with and be cared for by their parents, and that public subsistence support may be necessary to enable this. As recently as 1973 a report issued by the Nixon administration's federal Welfare Department justified broader support for AFDC mothers on grounds that they ought to have the option to work at home taking care of their children instead of working outside the home without suffering in poverty.[12]

The old welfare system also grudgingly allowed poor mothers to enroll in college or technical training programs and receive benefits, sometimes for years, while increasing their qualifications. Under the new system, states have the power to set up education and training programs that seriously develop capacities and skills of recipients in specialized fields where there appear to be future opportunities. They are allowed to encourage recipients to obtain post–high school associate, four-year college, or technical degrees. They can work with regional employers and unions to develop apprenticeship programs. Some such programs have indeed been instituted since passage of this law. Such programs are rather expensive to establish and implement, however, and more expensive for each person than the old welfare system was. Effective education and training of this sort, moreover, take years. During all this time recipients are not "working," in the sense of doing a job. States are permitted to design a welfare system that enables recipients to get real training and advanced education, but most do not.

The "work-first" programs most states have chosen to implement make it extremely difficult for recipients seriously to increase their knowledge and skills. Work-first philosophy says that the surest road to "self-sufficiency" is for mothers to go to a job right away, whatever their skill level and whatever the kind of job that may be available. In some states, such as Pennsylvania, a TANF recipient can attend school or a training program for no more than twelve months. Often, even before those twelve months are up, she must attend a training or "job-readiness" program as a condition of receiving benefits. In Illinois the official policy is that recipients can have up to two years for learning English or getting a GED, and up to one year for vocational training, but rarely are recipients allowed to take so long.

Most recipients are expected to spend their time searching for low-paid unskilled work. Some state and local programs run "work activities" in government offices, hospitals, and parks. That is, welfare recipients unable to find employment in the private sector increasingly work for the counties that administer their welfare, picking up garbage and litter, cleaning office buildings, or doing clerical work or child care for the welfare programs. Despite the claims of some that welfare policy should be directed at reducing poverty, not simply at getting people to work, the dominant policy position gives priority to making people do a job, pretty much any job, and the dominant position is that this is both the necessary and the sufficient condition for successful welfare policy.

Leah Vosko reports that the Wisconsin TANF program is encouraging many single mothers to become child-care providers through the market, especially those reaching time limits or who are difficult to place. In the process, state agencies are not strongly enforcing child-care provider training regulations. Thus the activities that these women might perform regarding their own children, which the system will not regard as "work," suddenly become recognized as "work" that they perform for other women's children for pay.[13]

DISCIPLINARY CONSEQUENCES OF THE RHETORIC AND PRACTICE OF WELFARE POLICY

Contemporary welfare policy in the United States makes "work" a condition of welfare receipt, reduces work to a job, and equates having a job with self-sufficiency. I have argued that each of these elements is ideological. An important effect of this welfare ideology, I believe, is that it further disciplines not only welfare recipients, but also many, if not all, working people who have never applied for public assistance. Here I will explain five disciplinary consequences. Welfare rhetoric and policy (a) further closes the possibility that workers can refuse work; (b) makes skill development more a privilege than before; (c) further devalues and obscures care work; (d) normalizes the "hale and hearty" worker; and (e) makes a yearning for meaningful work more utopian.

Cannot Refuse Work

When public officials promote work-first policies, community leaders applaud them, and recipients are forced to accept them, the consequences are an increase in disciplinary exploitation for many. The possibility of saying "no" to an unacceptable job declines. To a large extent, whatever is presented to them as a work opportunity, whatever the nature of the work, the social relations, pay, or working conditions, they must accept. Reports from some public assistance programs have been coming out that cities and counties are sometimes requiring recipients to do dirty or unpleasant work without supplying adequate protective clothing or equipment. Other recipients are supposedly being taught responsible work habits by having to put books in boxes or sort hangers out of boxes.

Whatever small zone of autonomy recipients had under the previous welfare system is even further narrowed to nearly zero on this system. Before, the law would allow a person who met eligibility requirements to receive welfare support when she had chosen not to work at a job she found unacceptable, or when she decided she wanted to try to earn a degree. Her options were limited, but the existence of a "safety net" gave her a little freedom to decide what to do with her life within those limitations. Women from the Welfare Justice Project of Pittsburgh complain that public assistance counselors routinely fail to offer the range of job and training options legally allowable by state law. Often recipients have no choice but to accept the only private or public job offered or lose benefits.

Making jobs a legitimate condition for the receipt of public assistance, however, further closes the universe of discourse about work. Work becomes defined as what an authority says is work. Worries that the low pay and lack of benefits of many jobs will not lift families out of poverty have inspired movements for a "living wage," which have had some policy successes in some cities. Now that working at a task defined by a powerful person, for which that person is willing to pay, has become a condition of accessing most benefits and services, however, there is far too little attention paid to how to improve pay, benefits, and working conditions. Indeed, it is in the interest of many well-placed people to expand the pool of competition for poorly compensated jobs.

Skill Development Becomes More a Privilege

As I have summarized, work-first policies specifically do not encourage recipients of public assistance to increase their education and skills while receiving benefits. Welfare, as we once knew it, did allow recipients to enroll in post–high school technical training or college degree programs. Under the current system, for the most part, if recipients wish to pursue skill development or training, they must do so on their own time, after they have fulfilled their work requirement. Since the objective of welfare policy is to move people off the rolls as soon as possible, recipients are encouraged to take full-time jobs that cut down even more on time for study.

Coupled with the fact that tuition for training programs and university study is rising and grant and loan assistance for low-income people has been declining, this consequence of welfare policy widens the gap separating middle-class people and their children from lower-class people. The society continues to cut off opportunities for relatively disadvantaged people to develop their knowledge and skills at the same time that it heaps worse blame on people for not doing so. Obtaining advanced training has become even more a *class privilege*, rather than an opportunity that ought to be available to anyone. Even less than before can the society claim to promote upward class mobility. If they don't have some money and material support from parents or other private patrons in order to free some of their time, most people simply cannot study.

Further Devalues and Obscures Care Work

Perhaps the most far-reaching consequence of work-first policies is that they effectively abolish any recognition that care work in the home is an important and dignified form of work that deserves social support. Taking care of children and other family members becomes even more devalued than before. The need for care work does not thereby decline, and indeed increases, often due to other public-service cutbacks. The fact that families and communities depend on this unpaid work, however, becomes further obscured, as does the fact that needs may go unmet because mothers are overworked.

This change has occurred in the context of feminist criticisms of confining women to a private sphere and labor market changes that have pulled most mothers into the workforce. Contemporary societal devaluation of care work can be partly attributed to getting only part of the feminist message about women's equality. Feminists criticized a social division of labor that defined women's proper place as performing unpaid work at home for men and children. They rightly criticized practices that excluded women from other opportunities because it was assumed that women are "needed" at home; they rightly argued that the life of the housewife was often isolating, tedious, and lacking in skill development and intellectual stimulation, and that women should have equal opportunities with men in the public world of work.

More than feminism, structural economic changes have transformed the composition of the labor force since the early 1970s. Most mothers of school-age children, regardless of marital status or race, work at a waged job to support or help support their families. To be sure, many work only part-time in order to accommodate their unpaid domestic responsibilities, and many work at jobs that keep them barely above poverty or that would put them in poverty if they did not have another wage earner in the household. Commentators have pointed out that just those overworked, low-income mothers provided primary constituency support for work-first welfare policies. Why should some mothers have the option of staying home to care for their children, even if that option pays very little and subjects them to huge hassles and stigma, when other low-income mothers lack that option? Normalization of the life of the working mother has closed the universe of discourse about unpaid work in the home.

While policymakers and employers have appropriated the feminist discourse of equality in the public world of work for their own purposes and benefit, they have paid scant attention to another side of feminist arguments about housework: that the modern system of wage labor depends on the performance of generally unacknowledged and uncompensated work outside the formal "productive" sector.[14] Public institutions and private employers continue to count on the unpaid performance of care work, housework, organization of consumption, and service access work that is necessary and not organized through the labor market.

Even as their social policies render domestic work increasingly invisible and devalued, all over the world social policy implicitly relies on the assumption that time and energy available for unpaid domestic work are expandable. If funding cuts force the schools to lay off librarians, school officials assume that they can count on parents to volunteer their time for staffing the library. National healthcare systems faced with cost pressures cut back on reimbursement for home health-care services, implicitly assuming that such services will be reformed for no pay by family members. Governments under structural adjustment pressures eliminate food subsidies, thereby increasing the work of those no longer able to afford prepared foods.[15]

Even in the 1970s, feminist calls for wages for housework were considered rather extreme and fringe, but they were uttered. In 1989 Susan Okin made wages for housework a centerpiece of a program of feminist justice.[16] Welfare reform in the United States and elsewhere has made such an idea increasingly unspeakable. This is another way that these reforms have disciplinary implications for all of us, and not only for poor people. Those who might choose to do only unpaid work at home are decreasingly perceived as social contributors and increasingly perceived as exercising luxury privileges. The public philosophy of today says that it is valuable for parents to take care of their children at home, but only if they are wealthy or have a partner with sufficient income to support an unpaid caregiver.[17] No one has a right to expect material support for doing care work. I do not mean to suggest that it is best for children to be cared for at home or that mothers should not have opportunities to work outside their homes. My own feeling is that a judicious combination of flexible job hours, quality time when parents care for and educate their children, and out-of-home child care is best for both children and parents. My point is only that poor mothers and single mothers ought to have as much freedom as others to manage the combination.

Further devaluation of care work widens the class privilege gap in many ways, not only for today's adults, but even more for tomorrow's. For what happens to the children? The harshness of welfare reform that requires single mothers to leave their children for work has brought the need for child care to the attention of legislators, and moves to increase funding for child-care assistance for low-income people have occurred at both federal and state levels. Even with such new sensitivity, the dangers to children and worries for parents caused by the welfare system are frightening. I recently attended a hearing to evaluate how well the TANF program was doing in Pennsylvania, at which I heard a constant stream of horror stories about the need for and lack of ways for mothers on public assistance to make sure their children are safe and well occupied. Child-care subsidies are good only for children under the age of thirteen in Pennsylvania. Teenagers apparently are expected to stay at home unsupervised for many hours of the day or night, during the years when many studies suggest they are most likely to slack on schoolwork or get into trouble with the law. Even some mothers of older children with disabilities are forced to work or attend programs and receive no help with care of their children. The child-care benefits available to mothers of younger children often do not match their needs or are inadequate. Reimbursement checks take months to arrive, during which time mothers either forgo food to pay for child care or incur a debt to child-care workers who eventually leave. Even when child care is subsidized, poor mothers must still pay as much as $50 per week from their own pockets toward child care. Most child-care programs and workers provide services only for daytime hours, forcing some mothers to leave children unattended when the only job available includes evening or night hours. As a consequence of factors such as these, many children are home alone a great deal, or their mothers renege on their jobs or work requirements, for which they are often punished.[18]

Once again, these difficulties of mixing work and family responsibilities are long-standing and familiar to many workers. Welfare reform has only added recipients of public assistance to the ranks of working parents who strain to take financial and emotional responsibility for care of their children at the same time that they submit to workplace demands that make meeting those responsibilities very difficult. The disciplinary consequence of welfare reform in this case, as I see it, is that it further absolves both employers and public services of responsibilities for easing that strain.[19] Also important is that it tends to absolve men from sharing housework and parenting work with women, and it tends to absolve men from putting pressure on their employers to accommodate to family responsibilities.

Normalizing the Hale and Hearty Worker

The welfare rhetoric that associates respect for citizens with self-sufficiency denigrates all persons who depend on the care and support of others for reasons of ability—children, obviously, but also people with disabilities and old people. Requirements that people be "self-sufficient," and the association of self-sufficiency with doing tasks assigned by powerful people according to their specifications, further marginalize those who are not as able to "work" the same long hours, dizzying pace, and highly mobile jobs as can some workers.

I have argued previously that at least all adults of work age have a right to be autonomous: They should be able to make decisions about their lives with real options and have those decisions respected by others. People who need assistance in manipulating buttons and zippers, are unable to walk far, or do not have energy required for working forty hours a week should not be forced to submit to the plans others make for them or be made abjectly dependent on them. Because the dominant ideology associates "working" with activities, hours, and settings that assume the "hale and hearty" body, however, and because independence as autonomy is assigned only to those who fit that paradigm, those unable to meet these standards of ability and/or who need the help of others to participate in public social life are marginalized and lack the full status of respected citizens.

Ironically, another consequence of narrowing the discourse of work and welfare may be a further narrowing of the scope allowed by deviations from the norm of the "hale and hearty" worker. Welfare reform seems to have this effect in a practical way. It narrows what counts as a "disability" that can exempt a person from work requirements in order to receive public assistance, and it allows more discretion for caseworkers to determine if a person can be exempt.[20] It also places a limit on the total percentage of any caseload that can be exempt from work requirements. The practical effect of provisions such as these must be that some people are forced into "work" in situations physically or mentally dangerous to their health, while others drop out of the system and must rely on other resources to meet their needs, or do without. These practices arising from welfare policy contribute to normalizing particular standards of work, thereby endangering some people or making them worse "failures."[21]

When working at institutionally defined wage labor becomes the only seriously recognized manner of earning respect for making a social contribution, and thus the right to autonomy, then anyone who is unable to "work" at that standard is marginalized further. Such normalization is unjust: At the same time that it denigrates "dependent" people, it forces many of those who do not meet its norms into greater dependence than would be necessary under more flexible norms and practices. Almost everyone is able to engage in socially useful activity if they have physical or social supports to accommodate their particular abilities, and if they are able to participate in defining the manner and pace of their work. Old people or people with disabilities ought not in fact be *exempted* from the expectation that they work in the sense of contribute usefully to their own welfare and the welfare of their communities. It is legitimate to expect everyone to do what he or she can to be productive, and being subject to such expectations is better than being discarded as useless. A humane enactment of such expectations not only should understand that there are many ways to make social contributions, not all of which involve having a job, as I argued previously, but also should organize its institutions so that people of differing abilities can nevertheless all make productive contributions.

MEANINGFUL WORK

Plenty of people who never applied for public assistance, of course, feel and act as though they have no choice but to work at a job they find beneath their dignity, meaningless, poorly paying, and with lousy working conditions. Making jobs a legitimate condition for the receipt of public assistance, however, further closes the universe of discourse about work. Work becomes defined simply as what an authority says is work. It becomes even more difficult than before to question the *quality* of jobs. When critics of welfare policy talk about *good* jobs, they refer to important issues like pay and working conditions. Even the most progressive critics, however, have not raised questions about what effect work-first policies have on the quality of the *content* of work: whether the work itself is useful, engages the interest of the worker, develops his or her skills, and takes place in a context of respectful social relations. Welfare rhetoric and its assumptions further narrow the universe of discourse about whether work should be *meaningful*.

The dream of meaningful work is at least as old as ideals of socialism, perhaps as old as humanity. A call for meaningful work is undoubtedly less a political program than an ideal, a limit concept according to which we can criticize existing social arrangements and person situates and take action to improve them. Karl Marx defines meaningful work in a section of the *Economic and Philosophical Manuscripts,* entitled, in my edition, "Alienated Labor versus Truly Human Production." Truly human production would offer to the worker an objectification of her individuality and would give her a sense of efficacious power in the world of things. She would gain satisfaction from knowing that the production satisfies human needs. Producers and consumers would experience one another in social relations of mutuality contributing to a collective creativity.[22]

Now, at least since Louis Althusser, it is no longer possible to read Marx's humanism without seeing metaphysical baggage of a naive conception of human nature, and a romanticism of craft production as the model of work, and so on. I will not review such criticisms here.[23] It seems to me nevertheless that a core ideal of meaningful work can be retained that sheds some of this baggage.[24] Here is what I understand by the concept.

An ideal of meaningful work says that work people do ought to be clearly connected to social uses and should be recognized by others for its contribution to the well-being of persons or their dwelling environments or to the well-being of other creatures and their dwelling environments. Meaningful work may be hard work, and it need not involve sophisticated knowledge, techniques, or organizational skills. It ought to engage a person's interest, intellect, and commitment, however, at least in some of its aspects, and workers ought to be able to take pride in the work when it is well done. It ought to contribute in determinate ways to the development of a person's capacities, either directly in the skills the work requires one to learn, or more indirectly in its requirements for cooperative interaction and organization. It is difficult for work to be meaningful in any of these ways, finally, if the worker is not in some measure *autonomous* in the work. The worker, that is, participates in defining work objectives and the means of their achievement.

In defining meaningful work I have tried to avoid taking either art or science or running a factory as paradigms of work. I am trying to formulate a minimalist ideal, one that I think most people can imagine aspiring to, whatever their current education or skills. Wage work *can* be meaningful in some of the senses discussed previously; some people who work for a wage or salary think their work is meaningful today, and they are probably right. Yet commodification of work puts pressure against its remaining meaningful: because the employer takes over more and more of its definition, divides the labor into relatively meaningless and repetitive bits, adds to the amount and speed of the work, orients production or service to profitable or organizational ends that seem to serve little human purpose, and so on. One need only to talk with formerly autonomous and dedicated physicians undergoing the HMO revolution to learn about transitions from situations where work seemed meaningful to those where its meaning has become questionable.

Earlier, I argued that there are important ways of making a social contribution that are not jobs, such as caring for children and household, community organizing, organizing and working in unpaid producer or service cooperatives, and producing artworks. These sorts of activities can sometimes constitute meaningful work, but the social pressures to narrow the meaning of work to having a job also militate against this association. When a person engages in such unpaid activity, too often it does not receive the social recognition necessary to its counting as a meaningful social contribution. For the persons doing it, it is either privatized labor done because it has to be done or something like a "hobby" from which she or he derives a "leisure time" satisfaction.[25]

Despite the massive cynicism of our age, I do not think that an ideal of meaningful work has lost its appeal in today's society. I think that even today most people yearn for meaningfulness in their work in something like the sense I have defined. Yet more than ever before, it seems to me, dominant ideology and practices tell them that their yearnings are utopian. Many workers have become either monitors of machines or monitored by machines. While they must be more educated than their grandparents were, their work is often tedious, routine, and without a tangible connection between the worker and the organizational outcome of work. Much professional work has become more high-pressured and time-consuming, at the same time that its internal evaluations, teamwork, and reorganization efforts frequently seem pointless to its cubicle dwellers. Some are forced to work sixty hours a week, while others beg for twenty, and job security has decreased over the last two decades. In this context, a "good" job has come to mean one with decent pay and benefits, acceptable working conditions, and opportunities for socializing, but does not refer to the content of the work itself.

I think that contemporary welfare policy and rhetoric contribute to disciplining all workers so that any rebellion against this condition of routine and mindlessness becomes even more unthinkable than before. This system that requires doing a job as a condition of the receipt of public assistance further distances the concept of work from ideas of social need and autonomy. Under this system, work is any task that a welfare authority or private employer assigns a person, and a person gets recognition only for working in that sense. Other possible activities simply are not work. When mothers might be taking care of their kids or helping to build a playground in the neighborhood, they instead pick up trash with a pointed stick or do clerical work for the county TANF program. A welfare system that puts "work first" further contributes to obscuring for all workers the utopian vision of being occupied with a useful and challenging activity that gives one pride and recognition as a contributor to the well-being of living things. Most people's lives today, however, are still largely taken up by their work, and many harbor a hope, in spite of their cynicism, that this work can be interesting and valuable. Sometimes people rightly think their work is valuable, but they are the privileged few, especially if they are not forced to perform it under highly stressed and poorly paid conditions. Advocates of welfare justice should reopen the question of the purposes of work and its meaning, and in this way resist the narrowing of the terms of full citizenship to acceptance of whatever tasks a powerful person assigns.

In this and the other ways I have indicated, this chapter calls on social critics to challenge the prevailing terms of discourse about work, autonomy, and citizenship. We should challenge the notion that the only "real" work is a paid job, and that all workers should be able to meet the same standards of time and stress. We should question norms that afford autonomy only to those deemed self-sufficient and instead insist that being autonomous requires strong social supports for most people for most of their lives. We should challenge the assumption that the only way to make a recognized social contribution is through labor market participation and struggle for ways seriously to value other contributions. And finally, we should be prepared to face the derision of our fellow citizens by envisioning contexts of meaningful work.

NOTES

1. My support for these claims is anecdotal. It derives from a hearing sponsored by the State of Pennsylvania Department of Public Welfare, December 1999, and from interviews with service providers in Chicago helping TANF, particularly from Women Employed, Chicago, Illinois, May 2000. Since state policies and local conditions on child-care availability vary, it is very difficult to know about these matters in a systematic way, and I am not aware of any published systematic studies.

2. Women's Association for Women's Alternatives has helped prepare reports for a number of U.S. states that attempt to estimate the difference between the income a family actually needs to have its needs minimally met, and the minimum wage. The report for Pennsylvania estimates that a single-adult family with two children needs about $26,388 as a minimum, and that working full time at minimum wage will give that family $13,528 after taxes. Betty Mandell reports a similar gap for the Boston area; see Mandell, "Welfare Reform: The War against the Poor," *New Politics* 8, no. 30 (2001): 37–56.

3. Versions of this chapter have been presented at several forums from whose discussions I have received helpful comments: Center for European Studies, Stanford University; Feminist Theory Colloquium, University of Pittsburgh; Gender and Society Workshop, University of Chicago, North American Society for Social Philosophy. I am grateful also to David Alexander, Lisa Brush, Sylvia Bashevkin, Marilyn Friedman, Eva Feder Kittay, Ruth

Lister, Patchen Markell, and Leah Vosko for helpful comments. Michael Reinhard and Shang Ha provided important research assistance.

4. Herbert Marcuse, *One Dimensional Man* (Boston: Beacon, 1964), chapter 4.

5. I have reviewed this argument in another work. See I. M. Young, "Mothers, Citizenship, and Independence: A Critique of Pure Family Values," in *Intersecting Voices: Dilemmas of Gender, Political Philosophy, and Policy* (Princeton, N.J.: Princeton University Press, 1997); the lines of this sort of account first appeared in Susan Moller Okin, *Women in Western Political Thought* (Princeton, N.J.: Princeton University Press, 1979); and Carole Pateman, *The Sexual Contract* (Palo Alto, Calif.: Stanford University Press, 1988). For variations and additions on these analyses, see Anna Yeatman, "Beyond Natural Right: The Conditions for University Citizenship," *Social Concept* 4 (1988): 3–32; Susan James, "The Good-Enough Citizen: Female Citizenship and Independence," in Gisela Bock and Susan James, eds., *Beyond Equality and Difference: Citizenship, Feminist Politics, and Female Subjectivity* (London: Routledge, 1992); Virginia Held, *Feminist Morality* (Chicago: University of Chicago Press, 1993), especially chapter 9.

6. Nancy Fraser and Linda Gordon trace this shift in the meanings of independence and dependence in "A Genealogy of 'Dependency': Tracing a Keyword of the U.S. Welfare State," reprinted in this volume.

7. Women's Association for Women's Alternatives, Summary Report, *The Self-Sufficiency Standard for Pennsylvania*, May 1999, 1.

8. On the distinction between moral autonomy and personal autonomy, see Joel Feinberg, "Autonomy," in John Christman, ed., *The Inner Citadel* (New York: Oxford University Press, 1989); Marilyn Friedman, "Autonomy and Social Relationships: Rethinking the Feminist Critique," in Diana Tietjens Meyers, ed., *Feminists Rethink the Self* (Boulder, Colo.: Westview, 1997), 40–61.

9. John Christman discusses the conditions of autonomy and why welfare policy impedes, rather than encourages, autonomy. See "Autonomy, Independence, and Poverty-Related Welfare Policies," *Public Affairs Quarterly* 12, no. 4 (October 1998): 383–405.

10. In the previously cited paper, "Mothers, Citizenship, and Independence: A Critique of Pure Family Values," I have developed a similar analysis. Janine Brodie has argued that neoliberal restructuring discourse, with its distinction between "good," self-reliant citizens, and "bad," dependent or needy citizens, undermines the deserving status of women (especially single mothers) and thus the claim-making basis of women in the terrain of poverty and social policy. See Brodie, *Politics on the Margins—Restructuring and the Canadian Women's Movement* (Halifax: Fernwood, 1995).

11. Feinberg argues that the value of autonomy should be distinguished from such a notion of separated self; op. cit. A parallel feminist critique of a masculinist privileging of a separated self over a relational self also comes to the conclusion that a value of autonomy should not be tied to self-sufficiency. See, for example, Jennifer Nedelsky, "Relational Autonomy," *Yale Women's Law Journal* 1, no. 1 (1989): 7–36; Diana Tietjens Meyers, *Self, Society, and Personal Choice* (New York: Columbia University Press, 1989); Virginia Held, *Feminist Morality*, especially chapters 8, 9, and 10; Marilyn Friedman discusses how feminist concepts of autonomy are not so far removed from that of several important male philosophers on this point; critique of the association of autonomy with separation and self-sufficiency, she argues, is properly addressed to more popularly held ideas, as in welfare rhetoric. See Friedman, "Autonomy and Social Relationships: Rethinking the Feminist Critique," in Diana Tietjens Meyers, ed., *Feminists Rethink the Self* (Boulder, Colo.:

Westview, 1997); for a somewhat different feminist interpretation of autonomy, see Patricia Huntington, "Towards a Dialectical Concept of Autonomy: Revisiting the Feminist Alliance with Poststructuralism," *Philosophy and Social Criticism* 21, no. 1 (1995): 37–55; papers collected by Catriona Mackenzie and Natalie Stoljar in their volume *Relational Autonomy: Feminist Perspectives on Autonomy, Agency, and the Social Self* (New York: Oxford University Press, 2000) offer important variations on feminist interpretations of the concept of autonomy.

12. Eileen Boris, "The Racialized Gendered State: Constructions of Citizenship in the U.S.," *Social Politics: International Studies in Gender, State, and Society* 2 (summer 1992): 160–80.

13. Leah F. Vosko, "Mandatory 'Marriage' or Obligatory Waged Work: Social Assistance and the Single Mother's Complex Roles in Wisconsin and Ontario," paper presented at a meeting of the International Political Science Association, Quebec, August 2000. Vosko finds that the new public assistance program in the Canadian province of Ontario is similar in many ways to U.S. programs. For another comparison of U.S. and Canadian welfare policies, as well as with those in the U.K., see Sylvia Bashevkin, "Road-Testing the Third Way: Welfare Reform during the Clinton, Cretien, and Blair Years," paper presented at a meeting of the International Political Science Association, Quebec, August 2000.

14. Ruth Lister details the complex ambivalence and interaction of feminist analyses of the value of unpaid domestic work at the same time that feminists insist on women's equal opportunity in the world of paid employment. See Ruth Lister, *Citizenship: Feminist Perspectives* (New York: New York University Press, 1997), chapter 7. Lister argues that policies requiring single mothers to seek paid employment are legitimate, because paid employment is in fact the primary means of achieving social citizenship. In my opinion, such a position does not sufficiently question the equation of paid work with social contribution. Gwendolyn Mink also sets the expectation that single mothers work outside the home in the context of partial public appropriation of feminist discourse. She strongly challenges the trend, however, arguing as I do further on, that caring for one's own children at home is work and ought to be recognized as such. Recent welfare reform further obscures that work, she believes, at the same time that it endangers the well-being of children and other dependent people, because their caregivers can devote less time and energy to their care. See Mink, *Welfare's End* (Ithaca, N.Y.: Cornell University Press, 1998), especially chapter 4. See also Mink, "Aren't Poor Single Mothers Women? Feminists, Welfare Reform, and Welfare Justice," in Gwendolyn Mink, ed., *Whose Welfare?* (Ithaca, N.Y.: Cornell University Press, 1999), 171–88. Dorothy Roberts discusses the implications of this obscuring of women's caregiving work, at the same time that it is made more difficult, in the context of a history of devaluation of and attack on the mothering desires of African American women; see Roberts, "Welfare's Ban on Poor Motherhood," in Mink, ed., *Whose Welfare?* pp. 152–67. Eva Feder Kittay has elaborated a theory of equality that criticizes the way liberal societies obscure the facts of human dependency and the work that must be done to care for dependent people. Such political and social critique is crucially important for setting a context for welfare policy. See Kittay, *Love's Labor* (New York: Routledge, 1997). See also Kittay, "Welfare, Dependency, and a Public Ethic of Care," in Mink, ed., *Whose Welfare?* pp. 189–213.

15. Diane Elson, "Male Bias in Structural Adjustment Policies," in Haleh Afshar and Carolyne Dennis, *Women and Adjustment Policies in the Third World* (New York: St. Martin's, 1993).

16. Okin, *Justice, Gender and the Family* (New York: Basic, 1989).

17. Gwendolyn Mink discusses how being able to take care of children at home has become more of a class privilege. *Welfare's End,* 120–22.

18. See Mandell, op. cit. See also footnote 1.

19. See Women's Committee of One Hundred, "An Immodest Proposal," at www.welfare2002.org/.

20. U.S. Department of Health and Human Services, "State Welfare-to-Work Policies for People with Disabilities: Changes since Welfare Reform" (October 1998).

21. In another work I have discussed the ways that current antidiscrimination law seems unable to challenge the right of employers to define the content and standards of work in ways that exclude people with disabilities. See "Disability and the Definition of Work," in Leslie Francis and Anita Silvers, eds., *Americans with Disabilities: Exploring Implications of the Law for Individuals and Institutions* (New York: Routledge, 2000).

22. Frederic L. Bender, *Karl Marx: The Essential Writings* (Boulder, Colo.: Westview), 124–25.

23. Louis Althusser, "The '1844 Manuscripts' of Karl Marx," and "Marxism and Humanism," both in *For Marx* (New York: Vintage, 1970).

24. For a useful philosophical account of meaningful work, see Norman E. Bowie, "A Kantian Theory of Meaningful Work," *Journal of Business Ethics* 17 (1988): 1083–92. Bowie includes good wages in his definition of meaningful work, which I want to take as a different issue.

25. Claus Offe and Rolf G. Heinze, *Beyond Employment: Time, Work and the Informal Economy,* Alan Brady, trans. (Philadelphia: Temple University Press, 1992); they criticize the reduction of all work to wage work and review experiments in structuring work outside labor markets.

3

Dependency and Choice: The Two Faces of Eve

Rickie Solinger

Beggars can't be choosers.

—Old saw

If people are willing to believe these lies [about welfare mothers], it's partly because they're just special versions of the lies that society tells about all women.

—Johnnie Tillmon, "Welfare Is a Women's Issue," 1972

Dependency—as in "the deep, dark pit of welfare dependency"[1]—is the dirtiest word in the United States today. *Choice*—as in the choice to get an abortion—is not so generally reviled as dependency, though it does spark more violent controversy. These two words—these groaningly laden concepts—*dependency* and *choice*—may be the two most powerful abstractions governing women's lives in the United States. As a matter of course, we use these words separately, to refer to apparently distinct issues: welfare and abortion. But it seems to me that these terms (both their official policy definitions and typical public usage) are actually *coupled.* Together they bind the lives of women in concrete ways and keep women vulnerable to censure and control.

Dependency and choice refer to each other, directly: they are antitheses that depend on each other for meaning—and for the shifting meanings that society has attached to them over time. One reason that it seems useful to clarify this relationship between dependency and choice now is that welfare reformers have very successfully named dependency as the disease of poor women. As a result, poor women are more than ever isolated in this country from others, most consequentially from other women. In the interest of reconciling the history and the concerns of middle-class women and poor women, I want to consider the

61

relationship between these two key concepts and how these terms have been applied to the lives of women, especially mothers, in two different eras of the twentieth century.

OVERVIEW: DEPENDENCY AND CHOICE IN THE 1950s AND 1980s

It is a well-known fact that in our recent past, dependency was considered a normative and positive attribute of some white American women. In the 1950s cultural authorities, including psychiatrists, professors, and judges, insisted in every way they could that dependency was a gender-appropriate status for white, middle-class wives, mothers, and daughters. These authorities urged other authorities—teachers, parents, employers—to enforce female dependency within the school, the family, the workplace. Along with psychologists and sexologists, parenting experts of that era described such women as dependent on men and the family for self-definition and self-preservation. One popular parents' guide, referring to the family responsibilities of white, middle-class women, explained, "A married woman only has two jobs, one to care for her children, the other to keep a man happy."[2] Femininity indexes in the 1950s invited these women to determine whether they were *dependent enough* to claim status as "real women."

Today, of course, the personal trait of dependency is roundly condemned in any adult, especially in poor women tagged as welfare dependents. But whether dependency is generally considered a good thing for white women, as it was in the 1950s, or a bad thing for poor women and many women of color, as it is today, *the core, essential attribute of a person in the state of dependency is the absence of the capacity to make sensible choices.*

Over time, social commentators have been consistent: dependent women can't make good choices. When female dependency was good, in the early postwar decades, Midge Decter wrote that young women were "plagued with choices." And that was bad because "choice breeds restlessness." Choice also, she wrote, could create "a disruption of the natural order" of the lives of young women and cause "grave concern" and "domestic crises."[3] In the 1980s, when female dependency on welfare became the target of public vitriol, Gary Bauer described the source of the problem as women's "reckless choices." If women continued irresponsibly to choose divorce and illegitimacy, he observed, "there will either be no next generation, or [there will be] a next generation that is worse than none at all."[4]

Attaching the epithet "dependent" to womanhood, to groups of women, or to an individual woman has never been enough, of course, to stop women from trying in various ways to control their own lives by making choices. But women tagged as dependent, whether in the 1950s or the 1980s, who exhibited choice-like behavior, were accused of dangerous, pathological behavior. They were routinely described as mentally sick or scammers, or both.

Perhaps the most frequently quoted book from the earlier period, *Modern Woman: The Lost Sex,* defined the "independent woman," that is, again, a white, middle-class woman who made choices for herself against the grain of culturally prescribed femininity, as "a contradiction in terms." This woman debased her essential nature by attempting to rival men.[5] Predictably, instead of improving women's lot, this "masculinization" led women into discontent, frustration, hostility, destructiveness, frigidity, and child rejection. The authors of *Modern Woman* argued that when women attempted to exercise independent judgment and choice, they became neurotic feminists. In the era of glorified and mandated female dependence, the desire to exercise choice was said to reflect and intensify women's mental illness. The authors suggested mass psychotherapy for women in the United States. Only professional treatment, they argued, could revitalize the natural dependency of American women and their femininity.

Many nominally dependent girls and women in the 1950s made decisions for themselves, of course. For example, many made choices when they found themselves pregnant in difficult circumstances.[6] Millions throughout the decade sought and got illegal abortions or "therapeutic" hospital abortions.[7] But Mary Romm, a psychoanalyst, sounding much like the authors of *Modern Woman: The Lost Sex,* claimed in a 1954 book on therapeutic abortion that "the very fact that a pregnant woman cannot tolerate a pregnancy is an indication that the pre-pregnant personality of this woman was immature and in that sense can be labeled as psychopathological. The problem centers around unresolved oedipal situations. Exaggerated narcissism is present in all cases."[8] In short, any woman who chose to have an abortion demonstrated by that choice that she was sick.

Smaller numbers of white, mostly middle-class, unmarried girls and women found ways to have and keep their children, resisting the intense pressure in those days for this group to relinquish their babies for adoption.[9] Such a person was sure to be condemned for that choice and found, because of it, to be mentally unstable.[10] Many experts on unwed pregnancy in the 1950s believed that all white, unmarried women who got pregnant suffered from neurosis. But they held apart a special classification for the ones who chose to keep their babies: psychosis. Again, a dependent female who exercised what looked like reproductive choice revealed the mark of bad sense, bad choice, and pathology. None of these females escaped the censure of experts—physicians, psychologists, and social workers, often lawyers and judges, frequently journalists—who expressed their discomfort with the specter of dependent women making choices.

In the 1950s, work was another area in which white women who made choices were marked as ill or abnormal. In fact, in the 1950s, women defined specifically as working "by choice," instead of from necessity, were "empirically associated" with causing serious social problems, such as juvenile delinquency and divorce. One of many studies designed to measure the (bad) effects of mothers working in the postwar era was called, "Employment Status of Mothers and Some Aspects of Mental Illness." The author's findings were complicated, but in the end he concluded, "if women become employed [that is, choose to work] in order to express neurotic pressures from within their own personalities, then employment of the mother may lead to a breakdown in the quality of family interaction."[11]

Today the choice to get an abortion, to become a single mother, or to take a job has become so normal for so many women in the United States that the association of choice and mental illness in our recent past may seem outlandish, or simply quaint. But many women who confronted difficult reproductive or employment issues personally in the 1950s remember how inconsistent and even dangerous it was to mix "choice" with "dependency" in those days.

By the 1980s, the capacity of many women to make sensible reproductive and employment choices was recognized, as dependency ceased to modify the life status of every female. Women who were poor in the Reagan era, however, were not generally considered able to make sensible choices or to choose without opprobrium, particularly if they were welfare recipients and therefore *dependent*. When this kind of woman exhibited choice-like behavior (for example, getting pregnant, staying pregnant, staying home to take care of her children), she was accused of irresponsible behavior or worse.[12]

Stereotypes associated with the behavior of "welfare mothers" are based on a belief in the incompatibility of dependency and sensible or good choices. More pointedly, the stereotypes explicitly connect dependency and bad choices or scamming. For example, women who receive welfare benefits have been accused of having babies for the sole purpose of making themselves eligible for benefits or for additional benefits. This charge clearly reflects a judgment that such women don't—and can't—make good choices. The same is true for claims that welfare dependents spend their checks on luxuries while letting their children go hungry, or that they typically stay on welfare for generations, or that they prefer to laze about rather than get a job. By the middle 1970s, many middle-class women may have achieved the status of choice makers, but poor women generally remained trapped by a label of dependency that, by definition, excluded them from that status.

Ironically, as many middle-class women sloughed off a number of the trappings of "dependency," most of them did not look back to consider the situation of other women still entrapped. But whether a woman was "privately" dependent on her husband in the 1950s or "publicly" dependent on welfare in the 1980s—and exercised what looked like choice—her behavior stimulated cultural judgments and public policies designed to stamp out choice and legislation enabling the state to punish her for making choices. In the earlier period, when the behavior of white, middle-class women was at issue, sanctions took forms such as antiabortion statutes and prosecutions, the adoption mandate, and misogynistic psychiatric diagnoses and treatment. Later, as poor women of color were targeted, "family caps," welfare time limits, and public denouncements were sanctions of choice.

Many women who attained the status of choice makers in the 1970s and 1980s experienced this achievement as an individual accomplishment. They ignored or slighted the impact of mass movements and economic shifts that relieved them of full dependency status. Women who felt they chose, or personally earned, this new status had some reasonable grounds for defining themselves as independent actors. If a person recognized as having the capacity to make sensible choices cannot be classified as a dependent, then many women who began to make important choices for themselves in the 1970s and 1980s could justifiably claim independence. After all, the experience of making choices in the life-defining realms of sex and employment supported many women's belief that they were operating in the world on a basis more like men. In addition, the consumerist notion of "choice"—that which individuals may exercise freely and independently in the marketplace, when they have the resources to do so—supported many women's belief that being able to make choices about their own lives was a hallmark and proof of independence.[13] This last point rang especially true as larger numbers of women, both married and single, took on paying jobs and began to earn the money that made their choices possible.[14]

Many men and women in the United States today are so focused on the association of dependency and welfare—and on the assumptions about dependent women making bad choices that characterize welfare reform rhetoric and law— that it is difficult to remember how radically definitions and valuations of female dependency have changed since the early postwar decades. So it must be stressed that between 1950 and 1980, Americans did dramatically alter their attitudes regarding the nature of dependency, regarding who we define as dependent, whose dependency we find acceptable, and who in our society has the capacity to make sensible choices in their own behalf.

In this chapter, I consider the case of shifting attitudes toward working mothers to demonstrate the nature of these changes and to raise questions about the consequences. This case shows clearly that in our recent past, female dependency was widely considered normative and healthy, and female choice was pathologized. By the 1980s, dependency was associated with pathology, while choice was considerably normalized, though restricted to women defined by some measure as independent. It is important to note that whichever model of dependency and choice was ascendant, dependency and choice were in a fixed, antithetical relation to each other. And this relationship between dependency and choice created fertile grounds for justifying the regulation of women's behavior, including the punishment of women who resisted regulation or could not meet its conditions.

DEPENDENCY AND CHOICE IN THE 1950s: PATHOLOGY AT WORK

Defining women's roles in the 1950s has been a special challenge for writers of women's history in the Unites States, partly because so many people—including many historians themselves—"remember" the decade through the great, iconic women of that time: TV matrons. And the television moms, such as June Cleaver and Harriet Nelson, were always the same, always at home, always lovingly available to their children and husbands. Recently historians have gone some distance toward showing that, for real women, the 1950s were a much more complicated era.[15] They have asked questions about which women actually were housewives and only housewives after World War II. They have considered the ways in which real women experienced their domestic roles and meshed them with roles outside their homes. Historians have questioned why cultural authorities then exhorted women so often and so threateningly to be first and foremost "good mothers" and "good wives." They have documented the lives of women whose experiences in the 1950s were "nonconforming," for example, the women who streamed into the paid workforce, joined unions, organized and marched for civil rights and against the bomb, and got illegal abortions. They have uncovered aspects of American culture in the 1950s that encouraged women to resist culturally mandated feminine roles and supported the idea that women could make— and ought to make—significant contributions to society as mothers and as workers, at the same time.

Two very striking features of the 1950s especially stand out. First, the number of married women, with children living at home, who took paying jobs escalated rapidly in the 1950s. By the end of the decade, 39 percent of all women with school-aged children were in the labor force. Second, the responses to this phenomenon—white mothers at work—were deeply ambivalent and often hostile.[16] Americans had just recently experienced crisis-driven, "artificially high" levels of female workforce participation during World War II. The number of working mothers with children under the age of eighteen doubled between 1941 and 1945. But when it became clear that lots of white mothers were in the workforce to stay, Americans did not simply embrace wage-earning for this group. Early in the postwar era, the results of one large poll measuring attitudes toward women working revealed the public's resistance: three-quarters of the sample believed that "an employer should fire a competent woman whose husband could support her, in preference to an inefficient man who had a family to maintain."[17]

Social commentators and ordinary people talked endlessly about the meaning and the impact of white mothers working. Most were especially worried about the dangers that might befall children, husbands, whole families, and communities if these mothers continued to slight or abandon their domestic stations for paying work. In 1955, for example, *Ladies Home Journal* warned "the American woman" that "her children will hate her if she works."[18]

Articles in the popular press, academic studies, cocktail conversation, cartoons, and books devoted to the subject of white mothers working often had at their heart a concern about preserving the traditional and antithetical relationship between female dependency and choice. Typically and meaningfully, these various discussions distinguished mothers who *chose to work* from women who had *no choice* but to work. The first group got almost all of the attention. Commentators usually ignored the lives of poor and minority mothers who were much more likely to be employed than the white, middle-class mothers whose jobs caused so much concern.

Discussion about white mothers working took place, of course, in an era when psychiatrists, psychologists, child-rearing experts, and others were intent on educating the public about the pathologies associated with womanhood and mother-hood *generally*. White, middle-class mothers who seemed to have pushed aside their dependent role came in for harsh evaluations. The influential family thera-pist Nathan Ackerman described the modern family as under the sway of the "dramatized" mother, a woman whose aggressiveness masked the sadness and fear she felt now that it seemed she could no longer "depend safely on the man" of the family.[19] Other therapists observed "hostile onslaughts of these aggressive women" in their offices, often dragging along their "confused, tense," and dis-turbed children for treatment.[20] Such bad mothers were "ambitious and control-ling"[21] and "dominated by a vengeful competitive attitude toward males and by a strong wish to be a man."[22]

Employed white mothers were widely considered a subgroup of this reviled cat-egory of aggressive women. This was so despite—and because of—the fact that during the 1950s so many mothers with children between six and seventeen years old were working outside their houses. As the *Saturday Evening Post* editorialized, "With one woman of three in the United States working full or part time outside the home, you'd think the public would accept this as a necessary part of our mod-ern, superproductive life." But, the editorial went on, "a lot of people don't accept" working mothers.[23] "The Tangled Case of the Working Mother," a 1961 essay in the *New York Times Magazine,* classified this type as "so suspect in our culture that any new study appearing to link her working with delinquency, school failure, or emotional disturbance in her young, is almost certain . . . to make headlines."[24] Studies also regularly associated these employed mothers with fathers dethroned and pushed, as Ackerman put it, into the shadows—and with feminine dependency denied.

Given this climate, white mothers—especially those associated with the en-grossing category of "middle class" in the postwar years—who were deciding whether to take jobs were counseled to make that choice very carefully. They were urged to plumb their motivations with virtually impossible thoroughness. A *New York Times Magazine* feature called "Mother's Dilemma: To Work or Not?"[25] listed the questions such a mother should ask herself before seeking employment: "Do I need the money and for what? Do I make my decisions as a team member of the family? Do I consider husband and children too? Have I balanced the pos-sible cost of financing, training, the physical exertion, and the time factor against the end result of a work experience that may or may not be satisfying and stimu-lating?" The implication here and elsewhere was that most of these mothers jumped into jobs willy-nilly, and many ended up making poor, selfish, and dam-aging choices.

In the late 1940s and into the 1950s, academic researchers took up the task of proving that too many women were, indeed, making bad choices when they went out to work. The dozens of studies designed to measure the impact of mothers' employment were constructed on a racially specific base of doubt. Over and over, researchers reflected public skepticism as they fielded studies aiming to uncover the contradictions that resulted when natural dependents (that is, white mothers) chose to work. Studies tested whether mothers who worked, and their daughters, ended up with diminished femininity, whether the woman's mothering skills were weakened by working, and whether children whose mothers worked were more likely to get in trouble or do poorly in school.

These postwar studies, based on the responses of white, middle-class samples, with all other demographic groups carefully screened out, often yielded uncertain results. No matter what the data appeared to show, however, the researchers underscored continuing worries about the relationship between white maternal employment, juvenile delinquency, and other forms of personal and family "functional disorganization." Many of the studies did pinpoint trouble spots. A sympathetic researcher, who believed that daughters of white working mothers could be inspired by their mothers' efforts, admitted that all the girls with working mothers in her study scored below normal on the Index of Traditional Femininity.[26] Another study examined the "adjustment" to families of 302 Missouri girls between the ages of thirteen and eighteen. It found that "girls whose mothers are employed are, on the average, more poorly adjusted to family life than are those whose mothers do not work and . . . there is greater feeling of lack of love, understanding, and interest between many parents and their daughters if the mother works . . . [and] also . . . greater lack of cooperation and appreciation of the part of the girls in the homes of employed mothers."

In the late 1950s, the Harvard-based researchers Eleanor and Sheldon Glueck looked at how one influential profession assessed working mothers and family problems. In "Working Mothers and Delinquency," the Gluecks observed,

> Psychiatrists . . . view with alarm the growing excursions of young [white] mothers into factory and shop. They are convinced that the economic gain to the family is far too high a price to pay for the loss of emotional stability of the children. They point to the child's repeated traumatic experiences when again and again his mother, the major source and symbol of his security and love, goes off and leaves him yearningly unsatisfied. . . . They speculate that beneath the ostensible economic reason for the mother's leaving the family roof there may be in many cases the deeper motivation of a wish to escape maternal responsibility or a pathologic drive to compete with men.[27]

Like others, psychiatrists linked the harm that befell children of white working mothers to the sick or bad wishes/drives/*choices* of these women. The implication of this and many of the postwar studies was that white mothers, children, and whole families would be healthier, albeit a bit less economically flush, if the mother accepted dependency and eschewed choice.

To be sure, other prominent experts in the postwar era spoke up in defense of white, working mothers and tried valiantly to uncouple the subjects of maternal employment and women's pathological choices. But even the defenders of women's choice to work often ended up cautioning women about the dangers or disappointments of choice. A prominent guidebook for modern middle-class women explained, "We are concerned mainly with the woman who has been brought up to feel that she is free, that she has a choice, yet who becomes discouraged and baffled by her actual life . . . because it often seems as though she had no real choice, as though in the end it always boiled down to the one bitter choice: do you want to be an aggressive careerist or a dull housewife."[28]

Psychologist Stella Chess was one of the few mental health experts of the era who attempted to rehabilitate all mothers, in part by downplaying the problematic, choice, and by suggesting that families exist in complex contexts. Mothers, Chess argued, are only one element of this context. They can't be saddled with the responsibility for everything that goes wrong in the family, whether they are employed or not. "In analyzing child behavior problems," Chess wrote in a 1964 response to the hundreds of mother-blaming books and articles published in the postwar period, "diagnosticians must refrain from automatically assuming that the child's problems stem from the mother's attitude and behavior toward him, and explore other possible influences such as developmental history, socioeconomic circumstances, family and health and educational background."[29]

But between 1945 and 1965, the most high-profile pronouncements about the wages of previously fully dependent, white mothers going to work were censorious. In this vein, psychiatrist Leo Bartemeier announced in a 1955 *McCall's* article, "Is a Working Mother a Threat to the Home?": "Until children are at least six, motherhood is a 24-hour job and one that no one can do for you. A mother who runs out on her children to work—except in cases of absolute necessity—betrays a deep dissatisfaction with motherhood or with her marriage. Chances are, she is driven by sick, competitive feelings toward men, or some other personality problem. She does a grave disservice to her children, although the harm may not show up for years."[30]

Other experts, however, were most concerned about the harm that showed up immediately, in the form of juvenile delinquency. Harvard's Eleanor Maccoby referred to "the positive correlation assumed [to exist] between mothers' employment and juvenile delinquency," and remarked that "it is not uncommon to find a judge in a juvenile court delivering a strong reprimand to a working mother and urging her to stay at home."[31] James H. B. Brossard, the author of one of the most influential child development texts of the era, told this vivid story about child neglect in his widely used and cited volume: "Ernestine had a part in her school play. Her working mother rushed there in time to see her daughter appear on the stage displaying an atrocious color combination and stockings with two holes showing. Shortly afterwards, the mother withdrew from employment. In her letter to her employer, she wrote that 'every growing child needs a mother in the home.'"[32]

The author of the 1955 *McCall's* article, Elizabeth Pope, began her consideration of the threat posed by white, working mothers by naming the force that led many mothers into the workforce: "the seduction of a weekly pay check."[33] The Gluecks used related language in 1957, similarly associating the "choice" to work with illicit temptation and will-less women lacking the capacity to exercise good judgment: "Basically," they wrote, "the time is ripe for a reassessment of the entire situation. As more and more *enticements* in the way of financial gain, *excitement*, and independence from the husband are offered married women to *lure* them from their domestic duties, the problem is becoming more widespread and acute"[34] (italics added).

Susan Hartmann is undoubtedly correct in labeling the postwar decades a period of transition regarding women's employment.[35] And periods of transition are often marked by a surgence of conservatism, that is, aggressive resistance to change. Between 1945 and 1965, while millions of mothers of school-age children in the United States were accepting paid employment, many Americans did not adjust gracefully to the change. During these postwar decades, hefty cultural resources were devoted to disseminating and enforcing messages about the natural dependency of Mother and the pathological essence of her efforts to undermine or slough off that status.

Considerable cultural resources were also—wittingly or unwittingly—devoted to foregrounding the mostly white, mostly middle-income women who went to work "by choice" against other women, often poor and African American, who were defined, when they were noticed at all, as having *no choice* but to work. The work lives of these two groups were often dependent on each other, of course. As Mirra Komarovsky put it, "Back of a career mother, there often stands another woman," one she described as "a person of inferior skills."[36]

DEPENDENCY, NO CHOICE, AND BAD CHOICE: SHIFTING THE FOREGROUND

The almost exclusive focus in the mass media and academic studies on the white mother's work dilemma came close to eclipsing the situation of "the mother [who] is compelled to work."[37] This was the mother "forced by grim economic necessity to go to the factory or to clean offices while leaving young children in the care of an adolescent daughter. . . ." This was the mother "whose every earned penny must be spent in the corner grocery and who returns from her job to do the washing and the cooking and the cleaning for the family."[38] As one researcher put it in 1955, "The overwhelming majority of [such mothers] can't afford to choose."[39] For these women, work was a given. And so was their dependency, defined by their race, gender, and class "inferiority" and by their typical status as low-paid domestic service workers. These women were defined as dependents even though they worked day in and day out to support their families.[40] While the bad choices of white, economically better-off mothers justified public excoriation, the choiceless status of poor mothers of color justified workplace and other forms of exploitation. White women were perceived as thrusting themselves into the workforce because they were psychologically disturbed, while African American and other women of color were described as fully alienated from the civilized complexities of psychology. For a poor woman, survival issues, some claimed, "superseded attention to her own psychological dilemmas," if, indeed, she had such dilemmas at all.[41]

This perspective was, of course, congruent with prevailing racial distinctions in the realm of sexual misbehavior. Sexually misbehaving white females in the postwar era were diagnosed as psychologically disturbed (because they made the bad choice to engage in nonmarital sexual relations), while African American females were described as sexually impelled by earthy, biologically determined forces that overtook them in the absence of psyche.[42]

Until the Moynihan Report was published in 1965,[43] the employment behavior of African American women was not usually associated with pathology.[44] Social commentators did not believe that poor minority women were capable of making the bad choices that were the hallmark of pathology in that era. (It is possible that it wasn't until after 1960—when the rates of domestic service jobs held by African American women began to decline dramatically as other employment opportunities opened up,[45] and white employers had less absolute control over these women—that mainstream commentators began to associate African American women's work lives with bad choices and pathology.) But even before the Moynihan Report, experts *were* worried about the social consequences, if not the psychological causes, of maternal employment for minorities. Experts' concern about what would happen to small African American children whose mothers worked rarely included references to toddlers developing unhealthy anxiety levels and separation traumas.[46] Concerns were more likely to center on the substitute care that relatives could give to these youngsters with working mothers, which was "not likely to be adequate."[47]

After approximately 1965, the *choicelessness* associated with the work and other life experiences of women of color began a process of mutation. Academics and social commentators in the popular media referred less often to these women as having no choice. Now African American women—poor women of color, generally—were accused, as white women had been, of making bad choices. This shift from "no choice" to "bad choices" in the case of women of color was occurring, in zero-sum fashion, as middle-class, white women were beginning to win rights to make sensible and depathologized choices for themselves about work, contraception, and abortion. Now poor women of color replaced middle-class working mothers in the foreground of public discussion and concern.

When policymakers and commentators accused poor women of color of making bad choices, the charge was complex. Often it referred to the fact that these women were unemployed. Just as often, it referred to the fact that they had jobs while African American men did not. But once women of color were associated with making bad choices, the charges spread to cover all the important areas of their lives: work, sex, marriage, family, and motherhood. In 1965, the Moynihan Report enumerated the consequences of these bad choices: African American women were making a mistake by taking jobs and status from black men; they were making a consequential mistake by presiding over families constructed, non-normatively, as matriarchies. They were making bad choices when they didn't marry and had babies anyway. All these mistakes and bad choices inexorably led African American women (and other poor women of color) deep into welfare dependency.

"Culture of poverty" theory, introduced most prominently by anthropologist Oscar Lewis in *La Vida: A Puerto Rican Family in the Culture of Poverty, San Juan and New York,* a book published one year after Moynihan's report on the black family, provided a richly narrative and decidedly unpsychological explanation for the charge that poor women made bad choices.[48] In the somewhat liberalized political climate of the 1960s, Lewis intended to render "the poor" as legitimate, interesting subjects whose lives were battered by poverty. He wanted to show that poverty itself generated a way of life that constituted a unique culture of poverty. This was a liberal, innovative perspective because "the poor" had previously been constructed as lacking culture.

Despite this intention, however, policy analysts and others read accounts of the culture of poverty as evidence that the folkways of the poor were crude and irresponsibly self-indulgent. The inescapable moral of culture of poverty analysis was that the poor became economically disadvantaged because they misbehaved perpetually. Their disorganized hedonism—constructed of bad choices—was both a mark of poverty and what chained them to poverty, generation after generation. Analysts denied or diminished the roles of racism, colonialism, substandard housing, education, medical care, and job opportunities in creating and sustaining poverty. Poverty and the culture it allegedly spawned—the culture of dependency—were seen as the offspring of individual and group irresponsibility or poor choices.

This interpretation of the culture of poverty theory was successfully popularized at the height of the civil rights movement. For some, the culture of poverty theory functioned as a justification for resisting institutionalized, racial equality. Many politicians, policymakers, academics, and others used Lewis's work to justify the position that it was deeply problematic to mount public policy initiatives to ameliorate the lives of the poor. After all, the culturally determined bad choices of poor people themselves caused their lives of endemic, enduring poverty and dependency. This adaptation and application of the culture of poverty theory was particularly unfair in the case of African American women, who by the mid-1960s were, in very large numbers, making significant and sensible choices in their own interests, even within the context of a violently racist society. These choices included a mass exodus from domestic service jobs as soon as they had other opportunities (in 1960, 39.3 percent of African American women workers were domestics; in 1990 2.2 percent[49]) and a mass participation in the civil rights movement.[50] Nevertheless, the fact that so many African American mothers remained poor in the United States sustained the popularity of the culture of poverty theory, locking it into the heart of conservative politics for the rest of the twentieth century. It helped consign poor women of color to a status defined by the combination of "bad choices" and "dependency."

In the first two postwar decades, the lives of most mothers were constrained by the culturally mandated association of mothers and dependency and by the related alienation of women from sensible decision making. But the different experiences of white, middle-class women and poor women of color within these constraints demonstrate a key aspect of the relationship between sexism, racism, and class oppression. When cultural, political, and legal authorities have taken the right to deny all women independence and access to self-determining decision making, these authorities have also been able to treat different groups of women differently, depending on the variables of race and class.

In the earlier period, white, middle-class women were excoriated for violating the conditions of dependency when they "chose" to work for wages. But those with jobs were more likely to achieve diagnoses of "deviance" as bad choice makers than they were to achieve "independence" in the 1950s. On the other hand, social commentators rendered the work lives of mothers of color invisible. Although these mothers were much more likely than white mothers to work for wages, they did not achieve the status of "independence" either. Social commentators claimed that these mothers worked because their poverty gave them "no choice." This claim obscured the racist and sexist standpoint of commentators. It also justified the proposition that mothers of color were essentially dependent, no matter whether or how much they worked outside the home. This was so because, in the United States, the woman constrained from making choices is the same woman who cannot make a good choice. In either case, forced alienation from choice is the fundamental condition of adult "dependency."

THE DEATH OF REPUBLICAN MOTHERHOOD: DISCONNECTING DEPENDENCY AND CHOICE

Between the late 1960s and 1980, American culture experienced a phenomenon that can be called "the death of Republican Motherhood."[51] During this period, the United States underwent a traumatic and very public shattering of what had been widely considered a relatively stable, if racialized, set of concepts defining "mother." Over the course of this scant decade and a half, the landscape became littered with new kinds of mothers. Many mothers in new roles made strong claims that they defined their motherhood status for themselves by virtue of newly normalized choice. Many others, though, were defined by cultural commentators as occupying a status shaped by the older category: bad choice. All of these mothers' statuses, however, were associated with mothers making choices, often about the relationship between motherhood and work. The American public struggled in this period to reconcile or reject the validity of this association.

During the 1970s, formerly disgraced unwed mothers became simply "single mothers." Legions aimed to become supermoms, with high-powered careers and a passel of kids. Mothers became murderers of unborn babies, welfare dependents with too many kids, welfare queens, and heads of households in unprecedented numbers. They became mommy track mothers, American mothers of third world babies, earthmothers, militant stay-at-home moms, technologically assisted mothers, feminist mothers, lesbian mothers. They became mothers who should put their children in day care because, experts warned, they were unequipped to be good mothers. Alternatively, they were tagged as mothers who selfishly and neglectfully stuck their children in day care.

Not too far into this period, motherhood had become "a very uncertain assignment" in the United States, with no single language or set of criteria to describe its status or to evaluate women who held it.[52] In 1977, one young woman attending a meeting on the family at Tulane University was reported in the *New York Times* as plaintively asking the panel of experts before her, "I just want to get married and have a child. Is that still okay?" At the same time, other women were deeply engaged in "the fight . . . to win agreement that working women can also be mothers."[53] Still others, of course, were becoming poor, single mothers and facing the charge that nonworking, poor women could not afford to be mothers and should refrain from having children. But most important, all of these mothers were associated with making choices—often called *lifestyle choices*— whether they were rich or poor, white or not. Now choice seemed normalized for mothers; in fact it was an integral part of becoming a mother in the first place. This was an early and powerful impression created by *Roe v. Wade* and by the liberatory promises of the civil rights movement and women's movement.[54]

By the early 1970s, in fact, many women appeared to be choosing their motherhood circumstances from a menu of options. Contraception and abortion were available to millions of women. Single mothers became heads of households in explosive numbers.[55] Welfare eligibility and benefits expanded, stimulating the claim that, in response, poor mothers were illegitimately "choosing" motherhood.[56] And mothers entered the labor force in unprecedented numbers. During the 1970s, three of five people entering the workforce were women. And just as dramatic, between 1950 and 1980, the labor force participation of women went from 35 percent to 52 percent.[57] Many Americans watched the behavior of mothers with alarm. While most would not have put it this way at the time, in retrospect it seems as though some of that alarm had to do with the ways in which women were constructing lives for themselves that ignored or denied the 1950s relationship between dependency and choice. Gary Bauer described the great problem these women represented for policymakers as a matter of figuring out "how to get the genie of personal indulgence back into the bottle of legal restraints."[58]

Many Americans in the late 1970s and 1980s expressed their disapproval of women submitting to personal indulgences by supporting "dependency advocates"—spokespersons who repudiated the "rights" and "choice" gains of the 1960s and early 1970s and advocated overturning them. Others remained silent as these advocates attacked women for behaving as if they were no longer dependents. "Dependency advocates" focused efforts in many policy arenas that affected the lives of girls and women. Some focused on recriminalizing and repathologizing abortion. Others were interested in constraining and punishing teenagers who got pregnant. Still others stressed the importance of defeating the Equal Rights Amendment. Perhaps the most extensive and ultimately most successful effort of "dependency advocates" was in the area of women and work.

In 1978, Sheila Kammerman of the Columbia University School of Social Work remarked that "underlying all United States policy today affecting families . . . is a pervasive ambivalence about women working."[59] Politicians, policymakers, and conservative commentators in the Reagan era drew on that ambivalence to blunt the impact of feminist- and civil rights-driven guarantees for women workers. They also focused on reforging the link between dependency and pathologized choices that many women had recently broken. This part was a cynical effort. Many who worked hardest to resuscitate the definition of unemployed, poor mothers as dependents making bad choices had generally been hostile to the needs of employed mothers and had participated in efforts to limit their achievements. During Reagan's presidency, these efforts included failing to insist that employers comply with Title VII of the Civil Rights Act of 1964 and providing only weak enforcement of the affirmative action order that prohibited federal contract funds from going to employers who discriminated in employment policies and practices. Yet even as they withheld support for women workers in the 1980s, conservatives used the burgeoning rates of employment among mothers with young children to make the case that the poverty and unemployment of mothers on welfare were their own fault.

REVITALIZING DEPENDENCY, REPATHOLOGIZING CHOICE

Politicians and policymakers used two key strategies in the 1980s to revitalize dependency, this time as a degraded, not normative, condition of (some) women. First, policymakers set about repathologizing "choice-like behavior" for poor, unemployed, single mothers. Second, policymakers constructed an effective policy apparatus to punish poor, unemployed mothers whose receipt of welfare "proved" that they had made bad choices.

Efforts to repathologize choice were central to redefining dependency as a degraded status. But the argument was different now from what it had been thirty years before. In the 1950s, (white) women were supposed to be dependent. Their independent choices were inconsistent with dependency and therefore were very likely to reflect poor decision making and carry bad consequences. In the 1980s, politicians and others claimed that dependent women (of color) got that way, not because of their gender, but because of their bad choices in the face of "opportunity" and "guaranteed equal rights." Those engaged in revitalizing dependency insisted that the choices a woman made while she was dependent were likely to be bad, as well, because dependency was still inconsistent with sensible choices.

By 1980, poor, unemployed, single mothers of young children were extremely vulnerable to the charge that they were welfare dependents because they had made bad choices. Few Americans who were not on welfare calculated the impact of factors beyond the control of these women that pushed them to accept public assistance. These factors included the lack of appropriate jobs that paid a living wage for women in their situation and the lack of affordable day care, coupled with the fact that welfare benefits grew in the early 1970s faster than wages.[60]

Nevertheless, in the 1980s, after the real value of the welfare check began to plummet, conservative politicians and public policy experts attacked poor mothers with vigor, claiming that their receipt of welfare benefits—their welfare dependency—was built on choices that reflected irresponsibility, even depravity. Lawrence Mead, a politics professor at New York University and a major spokesman for this position, drew a thick bottom line in defining "welfare mothers" during a congressional hearing in the mid-1980s. "I wanted to comment," he said, "on the presumption that the poor are like the rest of us." This, Mead argued, was a misconception. Unlike "us," the poor are "remarkably unresponsive to . . . economic incentives." He found their behavior "a mystery," but suggested an interpretive key: welfare recipients were "semi-socialized." Unable to make sensible choices, they became wholly dependent on welfare.[61]

The purpose of policy, Mead argued, is "not to expand the freedom of . . . recipients. It is, in fact, to constrict their freedom in necessary ways."[62] In other words, poor women could not and should not exercise choice. Mead and others in the policy arena were emphatic: when poor, unemployed women made unconstrained choices for themselves, the consequences were awful. Gary Bauer admitted in a 1986 report to President Reagan that he could cite no statistical evidence to prove that these unemployed women decided to have babies in order to collect welfare. "[A]nd yet," he claimed, even the "most casual observer of public assistance programs" could perceive this motivation.[63] Revitalizing this thirty-year-old charge—that dependent women were schemers who debased their bodies and degraded motherhood for public money—depended on convincing the citizenry that dependent women were deliberate malfeasants or compulsive miscreants. Either way, their choice to have babies and to stay home with them was constructed as pathological. Many argued that compounding this bad choice was another, though less bad choice: the unnatural decision to give birth to babies who would not have proper fathers.[64]

Basically, these charges against poor, unemployed mothers made sense to many Americans because these women did not have paying jobs.[65] After all, following the legalization of abortion, *the single motherhood of women with decent jobs was far less morally or otherwise problematic for most Americans.*[66] Economic dependency, caused by bad choices and leading to more of the same, was now seen as the core problem of poor, unemployed mothers, not racism or sexism or the effects of deindustrialization, or even the absence of a husband, all of which exercised powerful constraints on the opportunities of poor women.[67] Lawrence Mead, Gary Bauer, and Charles Murray met a warm reception in Washington after 1980, when they claimed that eradicating dependency involved aborting the bad choices of poor women, including their choices to have too many children.

While increasing the military budget, granting corporate tax relief, and investing in the private sector, the Reagan administration aimed to "break the cycle of dependency" by reducing the number of choices a poor, unemployed mother could make. For example, the administration eliminated CETA and diminished appropriations for the Vocational Education Act, which had provided jobs and training options for poor mothers. The U.S. Civil Rights Commission noted early in the Reagan era that "Federal support for employment and training programs has decreased dramatically, and therefore, special efforts will be needed to provide alternate sources of skills training for poor women unable to gain access to currently available resources. If not, they may find themselves trapped in poverty in spite of their best efforts to avoid or overcome their dependency."[68]

The administration also crafted policies that eliminated a significant amount of public housing stock, raised rents, and reduced federal subsidies for new construction and rehabilitation of dilapidated housing stock. It slashed fuel assistance programs for low-income households and made obtaining free legal representation much more difficult for poor women. Very significantly, the administration cut allocations for child-care programs at the same time that 36 percent of low-income women and 45 percent of single mothers said they would work if child care were available. For example, Title XX of the Social Services block grant, a major source of child-care funding, was cut 21 percent in 1981.[69] Finally, Reagan's policies continued the process of reducing the real value of the average AFDC check—between 1970 and 1985, the real value of these benefits declined 33 percent—and began aggressively pushing mothers with young and younger children into the workforce.[70]

As housing, employment and training options, and day-care programs were liquidated or hobbled in the 1980s, the administration also focused on policy initiatives that would directly punish unemployed, poor mothers for the double-barreled bad choice they were accused of making: having a baby and not having a job. (In this climate, Lawrence Mead suggested that "Congress might wish to consider differentiating between married and unmarried mothers, the latter to face more immediate work obligations."[71]) Typically, punishments targeted the reproductive capacity of these mothers and aimed to make any additional bad choices (babies) impossible, at least until the woman got a job, and maybe forever.

Hilmar G. Moore, the chairman of the Texas Human Resources Board and the mayor of Richmond, pushed in 1980 for a policy in Texas mandating sterilization of mothers on welfare.[72] Policymakers in other states designed programs for paying indigent women to put their babies up for adoption, for establishing "family caps," and then for paying recipients to use Norplant, a long-acting contraceptive.[73]

All of these proposals were predicated on the belief that the dependency of an un-employed, poor woman canceled out her right to have a baby. Because so many women made the "bad choice" to have a baby despite these strictures (Mead and others were calling this phenomenon "the plague of illegitimacy"), public policies were needed to constrain their fertility effectively. The point was not only to reduce the number of welfare dependents, but also to punish women who persisted in be-having as if pregnancy were a legitimate choice for poor women without jobs.

The results of Reagan-era policies were very quickly grim. Between 1980 and 1984, the incomes of the bottom one-fifth of American families, a quintile that in-cluded 43 percent of African American families, dropped by 9 percent. At the same time, income rose 9 percent for the top quintile, a segment that took in only 7 percent of African American families.[74] The Congressional Research Service reported that 557,000 people became poor because of cutbacks in social programs that Congress approved at the request of President Reagan during the first years of his administration. This was in addition to the 1.6 million people who became poor in 1982 due to the economic recession.[75] In these same years, the percent-age of children who were living in poverty rose from 16 percent to 20 percent, a development that brought the number of children in the United States living in households subsisting at or near poverty levels to one in four.[76]

Colorado Representative Patricia Schroeder reflected on the Reagan admin-istration's cruel treatment of the mothers of these poor children. "I think," she said, "one of the toughest things that's gone on [recently] . . . was the cutting off of the life raft we had thrown to those kind [*sic*] of women." Poor mothers had been "so excited," according to Schroeder, to have educational and occu-pational training options available to them. Now those were gone. "And I don't think there's anything crueler or more dangerous in a society than to say, 'Here is the life raft,' they climb up and, just as they're ready to enjoy it, you push them back off and say, 'Whoops, not yet. We decided we don't have room for you this time.'"[77]

This politics of reviling and punishing poor mothers for being unemployed, while at the same time making it more difficult for them to receive the education and training necessary to secure family-sustaining jobs, was a hallmark of the Reagan years. President Reagan, himself, complained that people unhappy with this policy paradox were simply "sob sisters" unwilling to face reality.[78]

President Reagan's epithet—"sob sisters"—perfectly captured the conserva-tives' firm determination in the 1980s to clarify welfare as an issue associated with weak women. Opponents of tough (masculine) Reagan policy were cast as emotional, irrational partisans, wallowing in expensive and destructive sentimen-tality. Also, Reagan administration attacks on "sob sisters" (welfare mothers and others who spoke out in support of these women's needs) were calculated to sal-vage traditional gender and race ideologies that had been battered by a generation of liberatory legislative, judicial, and policy innovations and mass movements.[79]

Having lost significant battles in the effort to maintain male supremacy and white supremacy in the generation between 1954 and 1980, Reagan-aligned politicians and policymakers were waging one of their fiercest battles over considerably diminished terrain: the definition of poor women. Many entered this battle as though the fight to constrain the misbehavior of unemployed, poor mothers was the last great legitimate effort of government and as though winning this battle was crucial to restoring the health of American society.

The conservatives' struggle to define and constrain poor, unemployed mothers was characterized throughout the 1980s by desperate determination and distortion, not unlike what characterized the reactionary struggles in the United States against school integration and legal abortion. This determination stemmed in part from so many traditional features of women's roles having already been effaced.[80] Between 1960 and 1970, for example, the number of female-headed families increased ten times as rapidly as the number of two-parent families. In 1971, 2.1 million single mothers were employed outside the home; twenty years later, 5.8 million were. By 1980, mothers going out to work, full- or part-time, had become so normative for women of every class, married and single, that President Carter designated the day before Labor day as Working Mother's Day.[81] Still, conservatives such as Gary Bauer held out hope that the phenomenon of white mothers working for pay was a temporary aberration caused by "bad economic policy in Washington." He imagined that "with the breaking of inflation, a gradual decline of interest rates, and the return of stability and predictability to the economy," many of these mothers might go back home.

Reagan-era policies defining and constraining poor, unemployed mothers effectively masked the role of large economic forces in creating and sustaining the poverty of these women. Conservative policy advocates ignored problems such as that a minimum wage–no benefits service job could not support a mother and child above the poverty level and that real wages had been declining for American workers since 1973. They did not link the decline in high-paying manufacturing jobs, the increase in low-paying service jobs, poverty policies that forbade poor people to accumulate savings, or the sharp increase in uneven income distribution to the hard time that many mothers had escaping poverty. The only significant cause of women's poverty, now called with a nasty edge *dependency,* was the bad choices of women whose choice making needed to be proscribed.

DEPENDENCY AND CHOICE: UNDERWRITING PARADOXES WE CAN LIVE WITH

The extraordinary success of welfare "reformers" in the 1980s and 1990s—culminating with President Clinton and congressional Democrats and Republicans all joining to enact the Personal Responsibility Act in August 1996—reflects the completion of the process of reinstitutionalizing "female dependency" and reaffirming the relationship between dependency and women making bad choices. In addition to welfare "reform," another measure of the long-term success of policymakers in this domain is how effective dependency and choice have been in

resolving potentially very troubling policy paradoxes regarding the lives of re-
sourceless women.

For the past two decades, many congressional and state politicians have
worked hard to ensure that few poor women would have abortions paid for with
public funds. At the same time, many of the same politicians have overseen cuts
in welfare benefits, including child-care subsidies, and have worked to impose
"family caps" and stimulate public censure of "excessively fertile" women. Many
Americans have had a hard time understanding how these apparently contradictory policy initiatives can simultaneously serve our national interests. Some feminists and others have adopted the slogan "Life begins at conception and ends at
birth" to express their frustration with the impact of these contradictory policies.
But for an *explanation* of how politicians—and a large segment of the American
public—resolve the apparent contradiction or live comfortably with the paradox,
one may look at the revitalized relationship between dependency and choice. Today many Americans are convinced that poor women as dependents do not and
cannot make good choices. This conviction tends to be applied categorically,
whether a poor woman chooses to get an abortion that she does not have the
money to pay for herself or whether she chooses to have a baby while she is poor.
Adapting the perspective of Mary Romm, the 1950s psychoanalyst, policymakers insist that these pregnancy and motherhood choices of poor, dependent
women, *whatever the choices are,* "are immature and in that sense can be labeled
as pathological." In short, when poor women appear to exercise choice regarding
pregnancy and motherhood, they are blamed and blocked and finally excoriated
as bad mothers.

Pregnant teenagers, of course, face similar policy paradoxes. Many of the same
politicians and policymakers determined to block this group's access to sex education and safe, effective contraception also champion parental consent laws to
constrain the abortion choices of teenagers. And these are often the same folks
who lament teenage pregnancy and lambaste poor, teenage mothers. Again, many
Americans live comfortably with apparently contradictory policies that are resolved not by a real belief that dependent girls will stop having sex, but by the
conviction that they can be stopped from making choices.

The role that the dependency/choice antithesis plays in making sense of these
paradoxical policies illustrates the powerful relationship between welfare politics and reproductive politics today. Far from simply referring to the separate
arenas of welfare and abortion, dependency and choice vibrantly interact with
each other, depend on each other for meaning, and together shape and justify
punitive and constraining public policies, including eugenically based definitions of motherhood.

Dependency, and its association with bad choices, shapes dangerous terrain for
women today, just as these concepts did in the past. Today the foregrounded target is the poor, unemployed mother, rather than the white, middle-class mother of
the postwar years, but both groups of mothers have suffered substantially because
of the kinds of policies these terms have always mandated. We must remember

that the protracted struggle for women's rights in this country had at its heart women's determination to disassociate themselves from "dependency" and establish their right to make motherhood and employment decisions on their own behalf. Women struggled for these goals because of the ways in which they had been constrained and tainted by "dependency" and "bad choice." Remembering women's efforts to change these conditions of their lives may stimulate contemporary, female choice makers to feel less comfortable with the slurs regarding dependency and bad choices that are attached to vulnerable women today.

But if women, particularly poor women, are finally to be disassociated from "dependency" and "bad choices," the task will require more than sharpening the memories of female choice makers. The task will require, at least, the emergence of a vibrant justice movement that unrelentingly demands the conditions of human dignity and independence for all women, including all mothers, in this country. These claims might be made using the same language, and with the same intentions, that the "founding fathers" used in behalf of "free white men" in 1776.

NOTES

This chapter originally appeared in *Whose Welfare?* edited by Gwendolyn Mink (Ithaca, N.Y.: Cornell University Press, 1999). Copyright ©1998 by *Social Justice*. Reprinted by permission of the publisher, Cornell University Press.

1. Senator Orrin Hatch, *Women in Transition,* Hearing before the Committee on Labor and Human Resources, U.S. Senate, 98th Congress, 1st session, An Examination of Problems Faced by Women in Transition from Work without Pay to Economic Self-Sufficiency, November 8, 1983 (Washington, D.C.: U.S. Government Printing Office, 1984), 2.

2. David Goodman, *A Parent's Guide to the Emotional Needs of Children* (New York: Hawthorne, 1959), 35.

3. Midge Decter, "Women at Work," *Commentary Magazine* (March 1961): 243–50.

4. Gary L. Bauer, *The Family: Preserving America's Future* (Washington, D.C.: U.S. Department of Education, 12 December 1986), 1.

5. Ferdinand Lundberg and Marynia Farnham, *Modern Woman: The Lost Sex* (New York: Grosset and Dunlap, 1947).

6. In this era, unwanted pregnancy itself was often considered a sick choice. See, for example, Stephen Fleck, "Pregnancy as a Symptom of Adolescent Maladjustment," *International Journal of Social Psychiatry* 2 (autumn 1956): 118–31.

7. Rickie Solinger, "A Complete Disaster: Abortion and the Politics of Hospital Abortion Committees, 1950–1970," *Feminist Studies* 19 (summer 1993): 241–68.

8. Mary Romm, in Harold Rosen, *Therapeutic Abortion* (New York: Julian Press, 1954).

9. Rickie Solinger, *Wake Up Little Susie: Single Pregnancy and Race before* Roe v. Wade (New York: Routledge, 1993), chapter 5.

10. See, for example, Henry Meyer, Wyatt Jones, and Edgar F. Borgatta, "The Decision by Unmarried Mothers to Keep or Surrender Their Babies," *Marriage and Family Living* 18 (April 1956): 5–6.

11. Lawrence J. Sharp, "Employment Status of Mothers and Some Aspects of Mental Illness," *American Sociological Review* 25 (October 1960): 714–17.

12. Rickie Solinger, "Poisonous Choice," in Molly Ladd Taylor and Lauri Umansky, eds., *Bad Mothers* (New York: New York University Press, 1997).

13. See Solinger, "Poisonous Choice."

14. By 1972, among white married women who lived with their husbands, 40.5 percent were employed; among black women in the same situation, 51.9 percent worked. Just a generation earlier, in 1941, only about one of ten married women was in the workforce. *Economic Problems of Women,* Part 3, Hearings before the Joint Economic Committee, Congress of the United States, 93d Congress, 1st session (Washington, D.C.: U.S. Government Printing Office, 1973), 548.

15. Most important, see Joanne Meyerowitz, ed., *Not June Cleaver: Women and Gender in Postwar America, 1945–1960* (Philadelphia: Temple University Press, 1994).

16. Susan M. Hartmann in "Women's Employment and the Domestic Ideal in the Early Cold War Years" and Joanne Meyerowitz in "Beyond the Feminine Mystique: A Reassessment of Postwar Mass Culture, 1946–1958," both in *Not June Cleaver,* demonstrate that hostility toward working mothers was not ubiquitous. Nevertheless, responses to the swell of mothers in the workforce *were* often hostile.

17. *Womanpower: A Statement by the National Manpower Council with Chapters by the Council Staff* (New York: Columbia University Press, 1957).

18. Agnes Meyer, "Children in Trouble," *Ladies Home Journal* 72 (March 1955): 205.

19. Nathan W. Ackerman, *The Psychodynamics of Family Life: Diagnosis and Treatment of Family Relationships* (New York: Basic, 1958), 178–79.

20. Dorothy McGriff, "Working with a Group of Authoritative Mothers," *Social Work* 5 (January 1960): 63–68.

21. Charles Wener, Marion W. Handlon, and Ann M. Garner, "Patterns of Mothering in Psychosomatic Disorders," *Merrill Palmer Quarterly* 6 (April 1960): 165–70.

22. Herbert S. Strean, "Treatment of Mothers and Sons in the Absence of the Father," *Social Work* 6 (July 1961): 29–35.

23. "Is It Too Late to Send Working Mothers Back to the Kitchen?" editorial in the *Saturday Evening Post* (24 January 1959): 10.

24. Dorothy Barclay, "The Tangled Case of the Working Mother," *New York Times Magazine* (14 May 1961): 75. Also see, for example, *Womanpower*: "This impact of married women's working on the welfare of their children has probably received more widespread attention than any other issue growing out of the increasing employment of women. . . . Many observers have been quick to attribute the reported rise in juvenile delinquency to the absence of working mothers from the home," 54.

25. Helen F. Southard, "Mother's Dilemma: To Work or Not?" *New York Times Magazine* (17 July 1960): 39.

26. Elizabeth Douvan, "Employment and the Adolescent," in F. Ivan Nye and Lois Wladis Hoffman, eds., *The Employed Mother in America* (Chicago: Rand McNally, 1963), 142–64.

27. Sheldon Glueck and Eleanor Glueck, "Working Mothers and Delinquency," *Mental Hygiene* 41 (1957): 327–52.

28. Sidonie M. Gruenberg and Hilda Sidney Krech, *The Many Lives of Modern Woman: A Guide to Happiness in Her Complex Roles* (Garden City, N.Y.: Doubleday, 1952), 30.

29. Stella Chess, "Mal de Mere," *American Journal of Orthopsychiatry* 34 (July 1964): 613–14.

30. Elizabeth Pope, "Is a Working Mother a Threat to the Home?" *McCall's* (July 1955): 29.

31. Eleanor E. Maccoby, "Children and Working Mothers," *Children* 5 (1958): 83–89.

32. James H. B. Brossard, *The Sociology of Child Development* (New York: Harper and Brothers, 1948), 383.

33. Pope, "Is a Working Mother a Threat?" 29.

34. Glueck and Glueck, "Working Mothers and Delinquency," 350.

35. Hartmann, "Women's Employment and the Domestic Ideal," 84.

36. Mirra Komarovsky, *Women in the Modern World: Their Education and Their Dilemmas* (Boston: Little, Brown, 1953), 191.

37. *Womanpower,* 340.

38. Komarovsky, *Women in the Modern World,* 189.

39. Pope, "Is a Working Mother a Threat?" quoting Marie Jahoda, associate director of the New York University Research Center for Human Relations, 73.

40. In 1960, 39.3 percent of African American women workers were employed in domestic service jobs; 23 percent worked in service jobs outside private households. Teresa Amott and Julie Matthaei, *Race, Gender, and Work: A Multi-Cultural Economic History of Women in the United States* (Boston: South End Press, 1996), table 6-1, 158.

41. Alva Myrdal and Viola Klein, *Women's Two Roles: Home and Work* (London: Routledge and Kegan Paul, 1956), 151.

42. See Solinger, *Wake Up Little Susie.*

43. Daniel Patrick Moynihan, *The Negro Family: The Case for National Action* (Washington D.C.: Government Printing Office, 1965).

44. See Franklin E. Frazier, *The Negro Family in the United States* (Chicago: University of Chicago Press, 1939), for an earlier and equally influential treatment of black family dilemmas and "pathologies." This study, in fact, provided the basis of Moynihan's later work.

45. Amott and Matthaei show that "between 1930 and 1960 the share of Black women employed in manufacturing jobs almost doubled, while the share in clerical and sales jobs grew eightfold. These changes finally allowed Black women to move out of private household service, which employed 42 percent of Black women workers in 1950, 39 percent in 1960, and 18 percent in 1970." *Race, Gender, and Work,* 173.

46. See, for example, Lois Meek Stolz, "Effects of Maternal Employment: Evidence from Research," *Child Development* 31 (December 1960): 749–82.

47. "Conference Discussion: Working Mothers and the Development of Children," in *Work in the Lives of Married Women* (New York: Columbia University Press, 1958), 186.

48. Oscar Lewis, *La Vida: A Puerto Rican Family in the Culture of Poverty, San Juan and New York* (New York: Random House, 1966).

49. See note 44.

50. See Paula Giddings, *When and Where I Enter: The Impact of Black Women on Race and Sex in America* (New York: William Morrow, 1984), part III.

51. I deal with this subject in depth in the final chapter of a manuscript in progress, "The Cost of Choice: How Choice Trumped Women's Rights after *Roe v. Wade.*"

52. C. Christian Beels, "The Case of the Vanishing Mommy," *New York Times,* 4 July 1976, VI, 28.

53. Jon Nordheimer, "The Family in Transition: A Challenge from Within," *New York Times,* 27 November 1977, I.

54. See Solinger, "Poisonous Choice."

55. Between 1960 and 1977, the number of one-parent families grew twice as fast as the number of two-parent families. Jean Y. Jones, *The American Family: Problems and Federal Policies* (Washington, D.C.: Congressional Research Service, Library of Congress, 1977), 6.

56. Between 1960 and 1970, the value of welfare benefits increased 75 percent. Harriet Ross and Isabel Sawhill, *Time of Transition: The Growth of Families Headed by Women* (Washington, D.C.: Urban Institute, 1975), 98.

57. *Economic Problems of Women,* 1982, 4.

58. Gary Bauer, *The Family: Preserving America's Future,* 4.

59. White House Conference on the Family, 1978, 182.

60. In 1975, the prospects looked good for poor women. Two policy analysts found, "Overall, the picture is one of the more favorable income and benefit statuses for female-headed families in many jurisdictions, and of increasing favor for those families as (1) welfare benefits grow faster than earnings, and (2) female-headed families continue to experience broader categorical eligibility for cash and in-kind programs, and lower tax rates in those programs than husband-wife families." Ross and Sawhill, *Time of Transition,* 101. Mimi Abramovitz notes that "between 1960 and 1970, the average earnings of workers rose by 48 percent, while the average AFDC benefits jumped 78 percent. In the early 1970s, the AFDC grant exceeded the minimum wage in many high-benefit states." *Under Attack, Fighting Back: Women and Welfare in the United States* (New York: Monthly Review Press, 1996), 76.

61. *Workfare vs. Welfare,* Hearing before the Subcommittee on Trade, Productivity, and Economic Growth of the Joint Economic Committee, U.S. Congress, 99th Congress, 2d Session, April 23, 1986 (Washington, D.C.: Government Printing Office), 98.

62. *Workfare vs. Welfare,* Hearing before the Subcommittee on Trade, Productivity, and Economic Growth, 39.

63. Bauer, *The Family,* 24.

64. See, for example, Anthony Brandt, "The Right to Be a Mother," *McCall's* (March 1984): 146.

65. In "The Patriarchal Welfare State," Carol Pateman argues that paid employment has replaced military service as "the key to [male] citizenship." In the 1980s, employment—or economic solvency—was becoming key to female citizenship as well. In *Democracy and the Welfare State,* ed. Amy Gutmann (Princeton: Princeton University Press, 1988), 237.

66. See Solinger, "Poisonous Choice."

67. The U.S. Civil Rights Commission asserted in 1983, "Poor women do participate in the laborforce. . . . The problem is they are often unable to find work, must work part-time, or the jobs do not pay a wage adequate to support a family." *A Growing Crisis: Disadvantaged Women and Their Children* (Washington, D.C.: U.S. Civil Rights Commission, May 1983).

68. *A Growing Crisis,* 35.

69. *Problems of Working Women,* Hearing before the Joint Economic Committee, U.S. Congress, 98th Congress, 2d Session, April 3, 1984 (Washington, D.C.: Government Printing Office), 97; *Barriers to Self-Sufficiency for Single Female Heads of Families,* Hearings before a Subcommittee of the Committee on Governmental Operations, U.S. House of Representatives, 99th Congress, 1st Session, July 9–10, 1985 (Washington, D.C.: Government Printing Office), 179.

70. *Poverty and Hunger in the Black Family,* Hearing before the Select Committee on Hunger, U.S. House of Representatives, 99th Congress, 1st Session, September 26, 1985 (Washington, D.C.: Government Printing Office), 6.

71. *Barriers to Self-Sufficiency,* 509.

72. *New York Times,* 28 February 1980, 16.

73. See, for example, Isabel Wilkerson, "Wisconsin Welfare Plan: To Reward the Married," *New York Times,* 12 February 1991, 16; also see Carol Sanger, "M is for the Many Things," *Southern California Review of Law and Women's Studies* 1 (1992).

74. *Poverty and Hunger in the Black Family, 15.*

75. *New York Times,* 26 July 1984, 19.

76. *New York Times,* 29 April 1983, 12.

77. *Economic Status of Women,* 1982, 33.

78. *New York Times*, 3 March 1982, 26.

79. See Gwendolyn Mink, "Welfare Reform in Historical Perspective," *Connecticut Law Review* (spring 1994): 882.

80. See Ross and Sawhill, 5.

81. "Single Mothers Struggle with Tiny Paychecks and Little Help," *New York Times,* 31 March 1992, 1; *New York Times,* 30 August 1980, 44; *Economic Problems of Women,* 1982, 4.

II

LEGAL AND ECONOMIC RELATIONS
IN THE FACE OF DEPENDENCY

4

The Right to Care

Robin West

Do individuals have a fundamental *right,* in liberal societies that protect individual rights, to care for their dependents? And if they do, does that right imply a "nested" right to some measure of state, social, or community support for caregiving labor, so that caregiving does not impoverish the caregiver, leaving her, and her dependents, unduly vulnerable? To use Eva Kittay's term for the social support needed to ensure a caregiver's well-being, do caregivers have a right to *doulia*?[1] Caregiving is obviously crucial labor, both to the cared-for individual and to the society and species of which the individual is a part: Without minimal care in infancy, none of us would survive, and without decent care during our extended childhoods, none of us would flourish. It is also crucial to the survival of political liberalism, no matter how that ideal is defined. Without care, and a lot of it, we would have virtually no chance of becoming either the autonomous individuals honored by liberal philosophers, and protected, at least in theory, by liberal rights, or the responsible, civic-minded political actors, committed to and interested in the common good and the public square, so valued by modern civic republicans.[2] Nor would we become the productive, or creative, or iconoclastic, artists, musicians, artisans, and freethinkers, so esteemed by libertarians, or the reliable producers or consumers of wealth so valued by liberal economists. Without care, we would not become liberal individuals, wealth-maximizing entrepreneurs, iconoclastic thinkers, or public-spirited communitarians, in any of the exalted senses of those phrases intended by our contemporary, liberal philosophers. Without the provision of care in infancy, childhood, and old age, the species would simply die out, as would liberalism, along with all else we collectively cherish.

Furthermore, while virtually all of us receive care for a substantial portion of our childhood, most of us, even in liberal societies that obsessively honor and reward heroic individualism, will spend a good part of our adult lives providing care to dependents, either infants, children, or the aged, and sometimes all three simultaneously. For many of us, this caregiving labor (and its fruits) is the central adventure of a lifetime; it is what gives life its point, provides it with meaning, and returns to those who give it some measure of security and emotional sustenance. For even more of us, whether or not we *like* it and regardless of how we regard it, caregiving labor, for children and the aged, is the work we will do that creates the relationships, families, and communities within which our lives are made pleasurable and connected to something larger than ourselves. Thus, caring labor is not only essential to the survival and flourishing of the individual cared for and vital to the well-being of the community. It is also a substantial part of adult identity.

It is also clear, however, that in a market-oriented, social world, caregiving labor leaves the caregiver profoundly vulnerable, and when the caregiver is vulnerable, so are the dependents for whom she cares. In part because of our patriarchic history, and the embeddedness of that history in our current markets, caregiving labor, largely done by women, is either totally unpaid or poorly underpaid labor. A woman caring for her own dependents is not compensated for the work she is doing, and a woman caring for the dependents of others is at best poorly compensated. Even caregivers who are also employed in some additional salaried or wage-earning work, however, will feel the brunt of this history. Employers, for the most part, are neither expected to nor required to accommodate caregiving obligations. As a consequence, caregiving employees will be adversely affected by this history of nonaccommodation: absences related to caregiving exigencies, for example, may lead to loss of pay or termination of the employment, part-time employment lacks benefits crucial to the well-being of oneself and one's dependents, and in salaried work, shortened work hours due to the necessities of caregiving will disparately affect income, benefits, and opportunities for advancement.

Thus, caregivers who lack support, or *doulia*, run the risk of serious impoverishment. Furthermore, without assistance, a caregiver may be politically disempowered as well: She will have neither time nor resolve to immerse herself in affairs of state. Likewise, while giving care, a caregiver is also largely precluded by the demands of her dependents from participation in the community's shared culture: As Harriet Beecher Stowe once remarked, in explaining why *Uncle Tom's Cabin* was not a better book, it is hard to produce high quality art when there are children's needs to which one *must*—and will—attend.[3] As essential as care is to the nurturance and maturation of individuals who will themselves, possibly, become liberal individuals and responsible, public-spirited, republican citizens, so the provision of care—the doing of care labor—seems to be strikingly incompatible with those very identities, at least as our current work world is now constructed. Putting it a little differently, whoever does the caregiving work in a liberal society, if that work is done without support, will be, for that very reason, disabled from participating as a liberal equal in the larger society of which she is a member. Whatever class of persons does the caregiving work will likewise be precluded as a class from that equal liberal citizenship.

We are left, then, with this problem: Caregiving labor is an essential, foundational, precondition of liberal society, but the market and political economy long associated with liberalism leave those who provide the care vulnerable and leave the class of persons who provide it—generally, women—disproportionately, or unequally so. It would be fair to surmise, given this state of affairs, that in a liberal world that depends crucially upon caregiving labor, and employs rights to assure the conditions of liberalism, that rights to care, as well as rights to the *doulia*, or support, that would protect the caregiver would be given a very high priority. Nevertheless, and without a doubt, the traditional liberal answer to the question posed herein has been a resounding "no." Rights, in liberal societies, protect individuals' autonomy, will, choices, plans of life, contracts, property, and conscience. Women give birth to and then provide care to children who mature into those rights-bearing autonomous adult individuals and then often provide the care for those adults when they have reached an age such that they yet again require full-time caregiving assistance. But no regime of rights protects caregivers or caregiving labor. Rights have never been viewed, within liberalism, as a source of support for caregivers.

This is not to say that liberal rights in toto have been of no use to women, or even of no use to women who are, have been, or might become caregivers. Rather, rights, in contemporary liberal societies, have helped women no less than men, when women, whether or not they are caregivers, acting as individuals, have sought to limit state involvement in their individualistic and atomistic lives. Thus, women, like men, enjoy rights of autonomy, conscience, speech, movement, association, contract, property, and religion. Women also, like men, now enjoy "nondiscrimination" rights: rights not to be irrationally categorized, or classified, by the state, and, within limited conditions, by private entities as well, according to unrealistic, stereotypical notions of women's nature—a stereotype generally garnered from their caregiving role.[4] Thus women cannot be irrationally precluded from jury duty, military service, employment opportunities, or political office solely by virtue of being women, on the specious grounds that because they are women, their caring nature or their caregiving obligations per se incapacitate them for such service, labor, or public role. Women have *rights* not to be so precluded, and even not to be so precluded on precisely that ground: that is, a woman has a right not to be stereotypically presumed to be a caregiver, and if she is a caregiver, she has a right not to be stereotypically presumed to have certain traits, such as an inability to engage in market wage labor or fulfill political, civic roles, because of her caregiving work.[5] Furthermore, in almost all contemporary liberal societies, so-called privacy rights typically protect women who, acting individualistically, decide *not to be* caregivers or to limit their caregiving obligations: thus, rights now guarantee many, perhaps most, women in liberal societies with nonconsensual pregnancies the freedom to abort the pregnancy (though only if they can pay for the procedure) and more broadly, the right to use contraception so as to prevent pregnancy.[6] And lastly, and as I will discuss in a little more detail further on, caregivers who are parents, including women, at least so long as they are in financially secure and relatively traditional families, have very limited, negative "parental rights," rooted in norms of familial autonomy, to make decisions regarding their children's education and upbringing, and to make those decisions free of state interference (although, again, not a positive right to actually *obtain* high-quality public education, health care, or any other material assistance requisite to that upbringing). Thus, and as the Court has recently reconfirmed, parents, including mothers, in traditional and independent families, have negative rights to keep intermeddling states, bureaucrats, departments of education, social workers, grandmothers, grandfathers, and other unwanted relatives and strangers out of the privacy of their home and away from their children, should the parents, acting as parents, deem it in the best interest of their children to do so.[7] Parents may, for example, to take a final example, "homeschool" their children, and in any language they choose, without state interference.[8] They have a "right" to do so and have had such a right for almost one hundred years.

But neither nondiscrimination rights not to be precluded from public life on the basis of false generalities regarding the nature of caregiving work, privacy rights not to become a caregiver if one chooses not to, nor parental rights to be free of excessive interference by the state in the raising and educating of one's children have ever been extended to include, or interpreted so as to imply, a right to material support from the state for the caregiving labor itself. Caregivers—whether or not they choose to become such, whether or not they are parents, and whether they are men or women—enjoy no rights *of support*. There is no right to the doulia of which Eva Kittay speaks. Caregivers do not have rights to either the financial or the in-kind assistance that would guarantee them some measure of security in their caregiving work. Nor do they have rights to help with the work itself, which would in turn free them to participate in political and cultural life.

In a modern liberal world that purports to value both the care that is a requisite of healthy, adult, liberal society and gender equality, the exclusion of caregiving and caregivers from the protective domain of rights looks downright anomalous. When viewed in light of other protections for caregiving and family autonomy, the omission requires justification. For roughly the first two centuries of liberal theory and politics, the exclusion of caregiving and caregivers from the protective embrace of rights, and hence from liberalism, was justified explicitly by reference to the differences between male and female nature, and the ill-suitedness of women for the realms of life from which caregiving seemed to preclude them.[9] The modern liberal account of the exclusion is harder to construct, but it presumably rests not on the imperatives of "women's nature," but rather, perhaps, on a reliance on "women's choice." What caregivers *should* do, on this constructed vision, in a post–welfare reform *and* post–formal equality liberal world, is raise children with the economic support of a husband, even if that means she risks becoming economically dependent upon him and vulnerable to his exploitation or abuse. But, it is important to realize, women are by no means *required* to do so. A woman can, after all, choose not to become a caregiver at all—she has that right. Just as important, she has the choice to be a caregiver and raise her children outside of marriage. Consequently, if a woman "chooses" to raise her children outside of traditional marriage, then her impoverishment and struggle to parent without social supports by virtue of that choice were just that—her choice—and therefore her own responsibility. Thus, so long as women are free to choose to become or not to become mothers, and free to choose whether to do so within or outside of marriage, then their relative impoverishment and lack of support should they choose to do so outside of marriage, once they are immersed in caregiving labor, are simply of no moment, even if the exclusion does seem to differentially create hardships for women. To paternalistically protect women from the consequences of their own choices—choices available, after all, at least in theory, to either sex—would do nothing but interfere with women's autonomy. No one, so might go the argument, after all, is *forced* to mother, and no one is forced to mother outside of marriage—at least so long as adoption is an available option for the fruits of nonconsensual pregnancies, and abortion is legal. Women are not conscripted into involuntary, nonmarital mothering. That the decision to mother, when voluntarily made, has economic consequences—that it has "opportunity costs"—does not in any fundamental way distinguish it from any other chosen lifestyle: The decision to mother might well diminish one's life's earnings, but so might the decision to sail around the world. So long as both are freely chosen, there is no greater reason to support the former than the latter with a regime of rights.

Thus, within contemporary liberalism, the tension between liberal individualism and formal equality, on the one hand, and the demands of caregiving, on the other, is resolved by reference to women's choice, rather than to women's nature—a woman might choose to mother within a traditional marriage, she might choose not to mother at all, or she might choose to mother outside of marriage. If caregiving is chosen rather than imposed, and open to all rather than only to women, then the anomaly noted previously—that egalitarian liberalism requires cared-for individuals, but caregivers are rendered unequal by a social structure that refuses any rights of support for caregiving labor—more or less disappears. After all, this state of affairs is chosen; it is the cumulative result of individual choices. It is no longer the result of "stereotype," or social pressure, or traditional gender-role indoctrination. Choices that impoverish us—so long as they are free—do not make us unequal. They just represent our freely preferred styles of life. If I choose not to work very hard and play a lot of pickup basketball or sail around the world instead, I can hardly complain that I am not supported by the state in my leisure, or even that I am "impoverished"; likewise, if I choose to mother outside of marriage, I can hardly complain that if the state denies me income supports, I am thereby "impoverished." A choice is a choice is a choice. Liberalism protects our choices through a regime of rights. It is not required to protect us from the consequences—and particularly the economic consequences—of those choices.

This more contemporary-sounding justification for the exclusion of caregiving, however—we might call it the "women's choice" justification—is surely as strained and unacceptable as its nineteenth-century, "women's nature" counterpart. First, of course, not all abortions are legal, and for many poor or geographically isolated women facing nonconsensual and unwanted pregnancies, they are in practice unobtainable. Furthermore, for many women and girls, motherhood is in no meaningful sense a choice at all: Women are still quite routinely implicitly pressured, and still oftentimes explicitly trained, to embrace careers of dependent domesticity. But as important, whether chosen or not, once embarked upon, pregnancy, childbirth, and caregiving potentially impoverish the caregiver whether or not motherhood is consensually chosen, for a reason that quite sharply distinguishes it from other "chosen" paths of life: As Kittay so carefully argues, caregivers, because of both moral and emotional imperatives, are unlikely, either as individuals or as a group, to use traditional levers of economic struggle to remedy the risks of impoverishment and diminished opportunities brought on by this labor. Unpaid caregiving is not work that caregivers simply abandon, or should simply abandon, when an equal or more rewarding opportunity presents itself. It is not, in other words, nor should it be, regarded as *"employment at will,"* to use the legal term of art for wage labor that is nonunionized, typically undercompensated, and unprotected, but that is theoretically justified by the fact that the autonomous, "at will" employee, no less than the "at will" employer, can terminate the employment at any time, should a better opportunity come along. Caregivers, like "employees-at-will," are undercompensated and unprotected, but unlike employees-at-will, they enjoy no such "autonomy" freeing them to leave the job at any point (and thereby exert some pressure, by virtue of their legal freedom to walk off the job, to improve working conditions). Rather, caregivers virtually *by definition* are emotionally and ethically committed to the work of caring for their dependents. They don't unionize, walk off the job, or strike for better working conditions. They don't individualistically keep an eye out for the better entrepreneurial opportunity just around the corner. They don't, in short, commodify their labor. Quite the contrary. Consequently, caregivers receive all the vulnerability but none of the solace and certainly none of the security from the "at will" aspect of their employment. Their "autonomy" does not protect them. If caregiving is not to impoverish or diminish the opportunities of those who engage in it, they need familial, community, or state support, whether or not the decision to embark on the caregiving path was voluntarily taken.

And caregivers continue to have no rights to support, just as the public will to provide that support is eroding, both nationally and globally, and just as the need for it increases. To be sure, even in the United States, where such support has historically been miserly compared with other wealthy industrialized democracies, Congress and state legislatures have been moved, from time to time, to provide

some level of support for caregiving labor. In the early part of the twentieth century, state legislatures passed legislation protecting, first, war widows, and then
eventually all widows, with dependent children.[10] At midcentury, with Depression-
era memories still fresh, that legislation was expanded into an entitlement to economic assistance provided to all poor mothers without husbands, regardless of
whether or not widowed.[11] This is even the case for the Family and Medical Leave
Act of 1993,[12] which essentially protects (some) caregivers from losing their jobs
after giving birth to newborns, taking on the care of an adopted child, or faced with
a family health crisis demanding their care and time, but makes no provision for
paid leaves. But in all of these cases, the assistance provided by these bits of legislation has been regarded as, in effect, state-sponsored charity; as fulfilling, at
most, a state's or a community's duty to provide assistance to its weaker citizens.
That assistance is decidedly not perceived as the provision of a level of support to
which citizens doing vital work are entitled *as a matter of right*. Likewise, when
the state withdraws support, as the U.S. Congress did in the 1996 Personal Responsibility and Work Opportunity Reconciliation Act,[13] which effectively ended
the federal guarantee of support for poor women with dependent children, it is
viewed as, at worst, a breach of a moral obligation or perhaps an unwise matter of
policy. It is most assuredly not viewed as an infringement of anyone's civil, individual, human, or constitutional rights.

What have feminists made of this enduring refusal of liberal theory and liberal societies to construct, recognize, or embrace rights of care? Two related
lines of analysis have emerged. First, over the last twenty years, a number of
feminists in a range of disciplines, including Martha Fineman in law[14] and Eva
Kittay in philosophy,[15] have argued that the incompatibility of caregiving labor
on the one hand, and liberal rights on the other, implies neither the peculiar il-
liberalism of women's nature, nor even (or only) the need for greater reproductive choice, but rather, the inadequacies of liberal theory itself. Liberalism, not
women, according to this now quite fully developed "dependency critique," is
what is flawed. Liberalism, and the rights culture it has fostered, fails to even acknowledge, much less address, the brute facts of human dependency, the societal as well as individual need for extensive caregiving labor that that fact of dependency demands of us, the disproportionately female labor that constitutes
"dependency work," the inequalities that gendered division of labor fosters, and
the inhumane consequences for children, as well as women, of the false view of
human nature on which liberal regard and solicitude for robust individualism
rests. What we should conclude from this incompatibility is not that women are
distinctively illiberal, according to Fineman, Kittay, and other dependency critics, or that the human relations within the private sphere must by definition be
beyond the state's reach, or even that women must be free not to be caregivers.
Rather, what we should conclude is that liberalism, and the legal institutions that
rest on it, are just plain starkly inhumane: They do not well serve the human
community. Because they exclude from consideration the nature of our extended

dependency upon others in infancy and old age both, they do not accurately reflect our humanity, and because they do not accurately reflect our humanity, they cannot adequately serve our human and social needs.

Other feminists and women's studies scholars, including notably Carol Gilligan in psychology[16] and Nel Noddings in philosophy,[17] have argued that the apparent incapacity of liberalism to embrace dependency work reflects an even larger incongruence: The ethic of rights, Gilligan and Noddings argue, has been constructed in a way that is not just hostile to, but diametrically antithetical to, an ethic of caregiving. If so, then it is not at all surprising that rights have not been reconfigured so as to protect the vulnerabilities to which caregiving leads: The modes of thought to construct the former are radically at odds with the modes of being central to the doing of the latter. Liberal rights fail to protect caregivers, in essence, because the "rights mentality" is at war with caring labor. Like the dependency critique developed by Fineman and Kittay, then, the ethical critique suggested in the work of Gilligan and Noddings (and others) seemingly concludes that liberalism and the rights at its core are in some fundamental way incompatible with the work of caregiving. According to both of these lines of analysis, the exclusion of caregivers—overwhelmingly women—from liberalism's domain is structural, and even definitional. It will not be overcome by insisting on the formal equality of women to men, or the equal availability to all of previously gendered roles, either in the world of wage work or domestic labor. Caregivers will continue to be excluded, regardless of whether or not women are welcomed to liberalism's domain, and regardless of whether it is women or men doing the caregiving work.

What has not been systematically explored, to date, in either the liberal and constitutional literature on rights, or the philosophical writing on the ethic of care, is the possibility of constructing liberal rights so as to protect the interests, needs, material security, and aspirations of caregivers. Liberalism has unquestionably, to date, been hostile to caregivers and caregiving labor, but it may be unduly pessimistic to assume, on that ground alone, that liberalism is monolithically and even definitionally configured so as to exclude the natures of caregivers or the work they do. Liberalism, and rights, may prove more malleable than that. It is not, at any rate, obvious that a generous and reconfigured liberalism, understood as a philosophical guide to political choice, is dependent upon a false and counterexperiential account of human nature. Perhaps what we ought to conclude, from the inhumane failure of the liberal rights tradition, to date, to extend protective rights to the needs of caregivers, is that liberalism needs to be amended. At any rate, it seems to me that the most "natural" conclusion to draw from both Gilligan and Noddings's demonstration of our rights culture's failure to acknowledge the ethical dimension of care, and Fineman's and Kittay's critique of liberalism's failure to protect the caregiving labor required by our human condition, is that liberalism ought be expanded so as to embrace a right to care—and that it ought to do so, furthermore, with all deliberate speed.

CONSTRUCTING LIBERAL RIGHTS TO CARE

Rights, in liberal constitutional democracies, are widely understood as imperative constraints upon or guides for representative politics, justified by some aspect of our universally shared human nature. Thus, the consequence of having a
right is that the state *must* either take, or not take, some action: Rights are imperatives that states must heed, not suggestions. We have the rights we have in
a liberal society, however, because of our understanding of *who we are* and who
we ideally wish to be. We have various autonomy rights, for example, which
means that the state must refrain from actions that infringe upon our autonomy,
because we believe, rightly or wrongly, that our nature is such that we flourish
when left free to decide matters of conscience, religion, or belief, for ourselves.
We also have various property rights, which means that the state must protect
our property from infringement and may not itself confiscate it without compensation, because we believe, rightly or wrongly, that our nature is such that we
are made secure and thus better off through private ownership of possessions.
We have privacy rights, because we believe that we need a sphere of untram-
meled privacy, or intimacy, in order to thrive; we have contract rights, because
we believe we are creatures who benefit from unregulated bargains; we have
nondiscrimination rights, because we believe we have a shared nature that belies
stereotyped differences. All of these rights, presumably, either stay or guide the
state's hand, and all of them, by virtue of doing so, presumably, benefit us both
collectively and individually, even where and when our representative lawmakers, speaking for a temporal majority of us, believe otherwise. And they do so,
finally, because they protect some sphere of life (such as personal intimacy or
economic markets) or some activity (such as expression or religious worship)
or some source of identity (such as ethnicity or sexual orientation) that we have
come to believe is essential for our ability to flourish.

Why, though, and when, are rights necessary? Why won't standard politics
protect those spheres of life necessary for flourishing? Essentially, rights are necessary, in liberal societies, when, for some reason, the sphere of life, service, freedom, activity, or identity that is protected by the right, and so necessary to flourishing, might nevertheless be systematically undervalued, underappreciated, or
underprotected by standard political processes. Thus, we enjoy rights of expression, rather than simply whatever expressive freedoms are from time to time
granted by the state, because we suspect that without the right, expressive freedom will be unduly curtailed—temporal political passions will silence the voice
of dissenters, and although there may be palpable short-term gains from that censorship, in the long run, we believe, we would all lose by the silencing. We enjoy
a right to vote, or to be free of enslavement, because we suspect that without such
a right, conditions might impel a political repeal of such freedoms. We enjoy
rights to privacy likewise because we fear the censorial hand of an oppressively
judgmental state moved by temporal and impassioned moral majorities more than

we fear the consequences of private immorality. In some liberal societies (not this one), there exist rights to a living wage, to labor, to shelter, and to food, and again, these "welfare rights," where they exist, are justified, in part, by the awareness that the standard tools of political or economic reform will not readily yield them: There is no economic or political imperative forcing the employer's or the state's hand. But here as elsewhere, we construct and then enjoy rights when we come to understand, in what Bruce Ackerman calls a "constitutional moment,"[18] that we must have them in order to thrive and that the political process is unlikely to confer them.

There are (at least) two further reasons we sometimes construct antimajoritarian rights, according to standard liberal theory, worth mentioning here. First, at least sometimes in the United States and elsewhere, we construct rights when we have reason to believe that a particular practice or activity, if unchecked, will have a severe and adverse affect on a subgroup that has historically been subordinated. Thus, we have rights of nondiscrimination in employment, housing, and public accommodations, in part, because we believe that those private markets will adversely impact upon racial minorities, even where such discriminatory practices would be inefficient as well as unfair, and we have rights against de jure laws that delineate between us on the basis of race because of a similar suspicion regarding our political processes. And lastly, here and elsewhere, at least on occasion, we construct rights to underscore our most fundamental and most shared intergenerational values. The panoply of rights we protect expresses our social self-understanding, and more specifically, it expresses a self-understanding meant to endure even in times of its political neglect. It is not surprising, then, that the construction of a right requires intergenerational cooperation. The need for the right is most visible when the practice it would protect is most vulnerable, and when the political will to actually create it is accordingly lacking.

Does this widely shared, and I think, noncontroversial understanding of the various rationales for rights suggest a basis for a right to give care and a right to the doulia needed to support it? I think so. Clearly, our nature is such that we thrive when cared for. Our nature is also such that our period of infantile need is extended over time, and likewise is our period of caregiving labor. We flourish both individually and communally when decent care is provided, and we suffer when it is not. The better the care for infants and children, the more they will thrive, and the more likely they will mature to become liberal and equal citizens who can themselves provide care, as well as fulfill responsibilities of citizenship in a liberal society. The better the care we receive during our declining years, the less likely we are to feel cheated out of the rewards for years of labor. The better the care that is provided in cases of disease and disability, the greater the sense of comfort that we will not be abandoned, should we find ourselves critically ill or disabled. And, the more demanding and consuming is the care, the harder it is to provide without support.

Furthermore, we have very good reason to think that standard political and economic tools will not generate market or political protections for this labor or for those who provide it. Caregivers do not, as a rule, willy-nilly abandon infants or dependents, even under very harsh conditions. A pressing moral imperative to perform the work uninterruptedly once it is undertaken, together with the emotional attachment of caregiver and cared-for that results from caregiving labor, strongly suggest that the work will be less supported than it should be in democratic, market economies. There is no political will or need to support caregiving labor if it is going to be performed in any event, and no organizational ability to confront that lack of will with some set of non-negotiable "caregivers' demands," so long as caregivers continue to provide the services regardless of whether those "demands" are met, enduring either impoverishment or dependency as the cost of doing so. We therefore have good reason to believe that familial and economic institutions, if unchecked, will continue to undercompensate caregiving labor, and that women will be adversely impacted, as a group, by that practice. For this utterly unexceptional reason, deeply familiar to liberal theorists, we need rights of care, then, to protect caregivers against the pendulum swings of public support and neglect for their work.

Likewise, we need rights of care to protect women and men from the inegalitarian consequences of that neglect, just as we need rights of nondiscrimination to protect potential employees from the adverse consequences of irrational racism or sexism, and lastly, we need a right of care and a right to supported caregiving labor to better express our self-understanding as a species for whom caregiving is a central life activity. Thus, all three rationales for rights—the dysfunction of political and economic processes for protecting caregiving labor; the inegalitarian consequences for a historically subordinated group of not doing so, and our self-understanding that successful caregiving is indispensable to a liberal state, as well as to a full conception of persons—point in the direction of care and doulia rights. Whether we are presently in a "constitutional moment" that might support the creation of such a right is, of course, an open question: We may now be in a period when the political will to support caregiving labor in any way other than through traditional family structures is at an all-time low. But we are also in a period when the need for such a right is increasingly vividly clear to many people who historically have had no sense of it whatsoever: men, because of feminist advances and rising feminist consciousness, are actually *doing* caregiving labor and consequently experiencing some of the risks of that work.[19] Women and men who are caring for dependents know they need support, and they also increasingly know that complete economic dependency upon a marital partner in an unequal economic relationship is not a viable long-term solution. A right to support for caregiving labor might, then, express that quite fundamental shift in our collective and social self-understanding.

CONSTITUTIONAL AUTHORITY FOR A RIGHT TO CARE

Does the U.S. Constitution authorize recognition of a right to care, and of the doulia necessary to protect it? The document, of course, nowhere speaks of a "right to care," but that silence is clearly not determinative: The Constitution doesn't speak of a "right to privacy," or of the "separation of powers," or of an "exclusionary rule," or of a "right to parent" either. Of greater consequence than the document's silence is the Supreme Court's interpretations and actions, and here, the story is somewhat more complicated. On the one hand, and perhaps needless to say, the Court has never made mention of a right to care. Nor has the Court *ever* interpreted the Constitution as requiring even minimal state obligations to provide material support for poor people, or for that matter for anyone. Further, in the pivotal 1989 case *DeShaney v. Winnebago County Department of Social Services*, the Court stated flatly, albeit in dicta, that the Constitution across the board excludes even a hint of such positive state obligations or positive individual or citizen rights.[20] There is no sign, finally, that the Court will change course either now or in the near future, even should the Court become a somewhat more liberal institution than its recent and current personnel permit it to be.

On the other hand, it is not at all hard to find, in the Court's two centuries of constitutional interpretation, authority for the existence of a right to care. During the first half of the twentieth century, in a wave of libertarian judicial activism, the Supreme Court interpreted the Fourteenth Amendment's notoriously vague and open-ended "due-process clause," which simply denies states the power to deprive citizens of "life, liberty, or property without due process of law," as implicitly protecting not only these "procedural rights" to some sort of process, as the language of the clause most transparently suggests, but also a panoply of *unenumerated*, substantive rights—or, as they came to be called, "fundamental" rights—against pernicious legislation.[21] The Court, in that activist and libertarian era, went on to hold that the fundamental, unenumerated rights protected by the so-called substantive prong of the due-process clause include not just fundamental rights to contract and property, to be enjoyed free of interfering state regulation, but also the rights of parents to educate and raise their children as they saw fit, free of state interference.[22] At that time, the activist Court spoke confidently of the centrality of both the institution of the family *and* the importance of caregiving and child raising to adult life, and the need to somehow acknowledge that centrality in our foundational political institutions, and it was quite willing to use its powers of constitutional interpretation and the open-ended "liberty" phrase in the Fourteenth Amendment to do so. Thus, the Court "freely" interpreted the "liberty" protected by the due-process clause against unwise legislation, as incorporating the liberty to educate and raise children in a manner chosen by the parents. It accordingly found a number of laws, including laws requiring English-language instruction and mandatory public education, to be unconstitutional.

Although those cases are now viewed as important primarily for the claim that the due-process clause protects substantive, unenumerated, fundamental rights against pernicious legislation—rather than protecting only the right to not be summarily deprived of property or liberty without "legal process"—their particular holdings regarding parental rights continue to be good law. Just this past term, the Court reinvoked the "parents' rights" line of authority, while striking a state law that apparently gave judges wide latitude in awarding visitation rights to grandparents, over the objections of parents.[23] The antiactivist Rehnquist Court did so, furthermore, unambiguously, under the so-called substantive prong of the liberty clause, using the 1930s parents' rights cases as precedential authority. Parents' rights, and more generally parents' rights jurisprudence, are alive and well, even in the hands of a strict constructionist, originalist, and relatively conservative Supreme Court.

And, at least arguably, these parents' rights cases provide some precedential support for the notion that the Constitution can be read as requiring the state to guarantee that parenting, or caring, be effective, and to do so through the provision of doulia. Clearly, the parents' rights as originally envisioned in the first part of the century by the Supreme Court were regarded as individual, and indeed patriarchal, rights, which were generally justified by, and in sync with, the states' and community's interest in maintaining strong traditional families that would in turn produce robust healthy citizens—and *not* justified by the community's interest in an ethic of doulia more broadly conceived. Nevertheless, rights evolve, as our understanding of their ethical roots evolves. Parents' rights today might profitably be viewed as justified by the states' and community's interest in ensuring the well-being of all caregivers. We now realize that not only children in traditional families, but all of us at various points in our lives, require intense full-time care, and that not only traditional mothers in nuclear families, but again many or perhaps all of us at some point, will be called upon to provide that care. Our understanding, in other words, of the community's interest, that both bolsters and grounds this right, has deepened, and so then might our understanding of the contours of the right itself.[24] To put the argument in classic, analogic form, surely, if state legislation permitting visitation by grandparents against the will of the parents so interferes with a parent's right and responsibility to parent as to be unconstitutional, then social institutions or laws that impoverish caregivers, and so interfere with a caregiver's ability to provide care, ought be under a constitutional cloud as well. That those social institutions continue to adversely impact women likewise leads support to the conclusion that since the 1970s, the Court has at least been constitutionally concerned, as the Court a century ago most assuredly was not, with conditions that systematically disadvantage women. Putting the point metaphorically, one might say that the old "family rights" cases from the first half of the twentieth century, particularly if intertwined with the Court's equality jurisprudence from the second half, imply the groundwork, or the roots, of a twenty-first-century constitutional right of care. The recognized rights of parents to provide for, raise, and educate their children, when combined with a premise of equality (rather than with the premise of patriarchy quite explicitly embraced by the early-twentieth-century Court) strongly suggest the existence of a fundamental right to care, a core right, furthermore, to which parental rights of authority might properly be viewed as "merely" penumbral.

Of course, this constructed, precedential argument for a presently existing constitutional right to care is (*in one sense* of what it means to "do" constitutional law, or what it means to say what our current constitutional law "is") baldly counterhistorical, even wildly so. After all, instead of looking at what could happen to the family rights cases of the 1930s, just look at what *did* happen, and what did not: The "family rights" or "parents' rights" first articulated in the 1930s never developed, in the Court's jurisprudence, into a right to care; they never even took the first baby step. Rather, the Court's first major expansion of the parent's rights precedents came in 1964, in *Griswold v. Connecticut*,[25] when the Court reasoned from the old "parents' rights" logic, to a more general right of marital "privacy," which in turn encompassed a right of married persons to contraception. This was followed a short time later with *Eisenstadt v. Baird*,[26] which importantly extended the logic of *Griswold* to single people, thus obliterating the connection—albeit tenuous—still recognized in *Griswold* between the family rights logic of the early cases and the institution of marriage. The Court next decided *Roe v. Wade*,[27] which established a right to an abortion, and did so using exactly the same line of cases. In all of these 1960s and 1970s "reproductive rights" cases, the Court relied heavily on its parents' rights decisions of a half century earlier, first for the general proposition that the Fourteenth Amendment's due-process clause contains within it substantive, unenumerated, fundamental rights that cannot be constitutionally infringed upon by legislation, and second, for the more specific proposition that the "right to privacy" within which to make decisions whether or not to have children is one such right. Thus, the right to raise one's family, and particularly the right to educate one's children, free of interference from the state—first put forward in the 1920s and 1930s—was invoked, in the 1960s and 1970s, as the precedential support for the mid- and late-century right to purchase and use contraception, and then the right to purchase an abortion.[28] Rather than a right to care, in other words, the right to parent became essentially the right *not* to parent, or put more crudely, but possibly more accurately, the right to have heterosexual sex without reproductive consequences. It became a negative and quite limited right to be free of state involvement in matters pertaining to reproductive freedom.

Such a privacy right, or liberty right, to "heterosexual sex without babies," as its critics might put it, has been unquestionably of great importance in securing fundamental rights of privacy and liberty for women. But nevertheless, the "privacy jurisprudence" developed by the Court has proven to be a mixed blessing for caregivers. Once parents' rights to rear children are transformed into a privacy right to be free of parental or caring obligations, it is much harder to argue that these same rights can or should embrace a robust right to care, much less a right to doulia: Indeed, arguably, by freeing women *not* to parent, or to parent only "at will," the Court's privacy jurisprudence *undercuts*, rather than supports, such a claim. I think it's fair to say that the Fourteenth Amendment due-process "right to parent," as the Court's decision during this term regarding the constitutional limits on grandparents' visitation permitted by states attests, *in the Court's collective consciousness*, now consists of, at most, on the one hand, a negative right to use contraception or procure abortions (within limits) free of state interference, and on the other hand, an autonomy right of parents to be free of either state or third-party interference in their decisions regarding their children's upbringing, should they freely decide to have them. Some of the language of the decisions, particularly the early decisions, supports the idea of a right to care. But the case law the Court has developed from that early language by no means unambiguously implies the existence of such a right, and the language of the later cases, particularly taken in conjunction with the Court's insistence in other contexts that the Constitution consists solely of negative rights, seriously undermines it.

So where does this history of judicial interpretation leave the constitutional status of a right to care? To summarize so far: The Constitution nowhere mentions a right to care, but it does guarantee that "life, liberty or property" cannot be taken away without due process of law, and the Court has, for a hundred years now, and as recently as last term, affirmed that that right consists of not just rights to be protected by legal process, but also of fundamental unenumerated rights that cannot be infringed upon by pernicious legislation. Furthermore, the Court has consistently interpreted those fundamental, unenumerated rights as including a "right to parent." The Court *could* conceivably expand, or reinterpret, such a right as protecting a more general, as well as more generous, "right to care"; this would surely be no more or less "activist" than its construction of rights to contraception and abortion services. It has not, however, done so, and it is extremely unlikely that it will do so in the foreseeable future; indeed, at least the current Court is increasingly disinclined to interpret fundamental rights as including *any* positive right against a state, or imposing any positive duty upon a state. A blanket prohibition of positive rights leaves little room for a judicially recognized right to care.

However, it would be a grave mistake to imply from even a confident prediction that the Supreme Court will not, in the foreseeable future, interpret the Constitution as protecting a right to care, that we do not have one. There are several reasons not to read too much into predictions about what the Court will or won't do, when specifying the case for or against a constitutional right. First, of course, predictions can always be wrong; the Court's interpretation of the Constitution evolves, and evolves to fit a changing social self-identity. That the Court has never located in the Fourteenth Amendment, or any other constitutional source, authority for a right to care does not mean that it could not do so in the future, and should it do so, such a right would be no less constitutionally "authorized" than the right to integrated schooling, the right to be read one's Miranda warnings, the right to procure first-term abortions, or the right to raise one's children free of the meddling interference of unwelcome grandparents, none of which is mentioned in the Constitution, but all of which are now recognized as constitutionally mandated rights. And at least arguably, such an evolution would be a seemingly *more* natural, not less natural, extension of the parental rights cases that eventually became the cornerstone of our reproductive freedom jurisprudence. The early parental rights cases, after all, relied heavily on the importance of parenting to adult life, which would also be one of the cornerstones of the modern right to care. The privacy and reproductive freedom cases, by contrast, obviously suggest very much the opposite, although they manage to judiciously avoid saying as much.

The second reason we should not read too much into the Court's failure to construct a right to care is simply that we should be careful not to overstate the Court's institutional role in our constitutional system of government, or its generative role in our system of constitutional meanings. The U.S. Constitution is not the only source of constitutional authority, and the U.S. Constitution is not the only constitution with which courts grapple. States have constitutions as well, and many of them contain language that could readily suggest a right to care, and without the history of hostile judicial interpretation to weigh it down. Furthermore, the Supreme Court is not the only arbiter, even assuming it is the final arbiter, of constitutional wisdom, even in the federal system. State courts, state legislators, Congress, the executive branches at both the state and federal level, and, most important, citizens, all have constitutional obligations and responsibilities, including the responsibility to interpret both state and federal constitutions. This is particularly important in the context of a right to care. A right to care, if it exists, is unquestionably a positive, as well as negative, right: If it exists, it requires states and legislatures and Congress to do something, not just refrain from doing the impermissible.[29] If a right to care can fairly be implied from our constitutional history, it will fall to state and federal legislators, not to courts, to enact legislation to give it meaning. Thus, it is legislators, not courts, that need to be convinced of the existence of such rights, as it is legislators, not courts, that ought to legislate on the basis of it.

But last, and most important, we should not overstate the importance of the judicially interpreted Constitution, or mistake it for "the" meaning of the Constitution, because to do so misstates and misunderstands the function of constitutionalism itself. If we have a constitutional right to care, then we have it regardless of whether or not the Supreme Court has yet recognized it—this is the consequence of "taking rights seriously," to use Ronald Dworkin's fecund phrase.[30] If we have a right, we have it because such a right is morally justified and because it is a part of the way we have come to "constitute" ourselves as a people, as in part—but only in part—evidenced by our constitutional documents, and by our evolving and interpretive constitutional law. To enact laws pursuant to such a right, and to refrain from passing laws that would violate such a right, are legislative tasks and responsibilities. Such legislation, prompted by the imperative dimension of a right, is neither conditioned upon nor triggered by any judicial pronouncement regarding the status of the right. It is conditioned upon—and triggered by—political will.

LIBERAL, CRITICAL, AND CONSERVATIVE OBJECTIONS

Let me conclude by cataloging and then briefly responding to the most salient objections, or worries, that might be posited to a constructed right to care, by liberal legal and constitutional theorists, critical legal scholars, and conservative legal thinkers, respectively. Liberal legalists might pose three related objections. First, it might be objected that a positive right to support for caregiving labor flies in the face of now conventional understandings of liberal, constitutional rights, at least as that tradition has been understood in the United States. U.S. constitutional rights, whatever might be the case elsewhere, are now widely understood to be necessarily "negative": Rights give us a shield of protection against an overly intrusive state, but they do not entitle us to any sort of positive state action. A state that overlegislates, or irrationally legislates, runs the risk of running afoul of constitutional understandings, and a court might accordingly strike the errant legislation as unconstitutional. A state that underlegislates—that passively or irrationally refuses to enact law—might be in breach of moral or political duties, but it has not breached any constitutional obligations or infringed upon any constitutional rights. Even a state that failed to legislate against violently criminal activity, thus leaving citizens at the mercy of undeterred private violence, according to the current Supreme Court, would breach no right—we do not have a right, as the Court famously claimed ten years ago, to a police force or to any other governmental service.[31] The Constitution does not require the state to do anything on behalf of our rights; it only forbids the state from acting in certain ways. We have rights only to keep the state out of our affairs where it has no business meddling. We do not have rights to state services, protection, or provisions. A right to support for caregiving labor would unquestionably be a positive right; it would require the state to support the work of caregiving with either financial assistance, assistance in kind, or some combination. As such, it is antithetical to our constitutional scheme.

Relatedly, it might be objected, rights, as understood in the liberal constitutional tradition, are functionally protected by the courts, through adjudication, against recalcitrant legislators and pernicious legislation; they do not and should not compel or guide legislation. Thus, we have a right to free expression, and what that means, pragmatically, is that a law that infringes upon it will be struck by a court as unconstitutional; it does not mean that legislators are constitutionally bound to pass legislation that will protect the conditions for the free interchange of ideas. Rights are shields against unconstitutional state action; they do not provide protection against unconstitutional social conditions, which then must be rectified through legal action. We do not have "rights," against "society," to be protected by laws passed by legislators so as to protect those rights; rather, we have "rights" against the "state," and against the pernicious and overreaching laws it passes, to be protected, in turn, by court action. Rights constrain states or sovereigns. They do not *guide* them.

And lastly, rights, conventionally understood in liberal legal discourse, protect our robust, autonomous, heroically independent, and fiercely individualistic selves. They do not nor should not protect our dependent, relational, communitarian, duty-bound selves; in fact, if anything, rights exist precisely so as to ensure that such relational duties and dependencies do not overburden us. Rights protect our freedoms to think whatever we think, express ourselves as we wish, worship whom we please, own property, and enter into contracts according to our own rights. A right to care and a right to supported caregiving, from a conventional, liberal-constitutional perspective, are virtually oxymoronic. Rights protect our freedom to differentiate, divorce from, and distance ourselves from others: I have a right to privacy in my home, to school my children as I wish, to utter hateful utterances or absorb pornographic images, to lock my door and keep my neighbors at arm's length, and to secure my possessions, views, and entitlements from the prying eyes of states, communities, and others. Rights of free speech and rights to be free of arbitrary arrest might protect the panhandler against state harassment when he stands on the street and asks for change, but far more clearly, rights unambiguously protect my right to avert my eyes from his and keep my wallet in my pocket as I walk by. They protect my freedom *not* to teach my children lessons in civic obligation. They protect my freedom *not* to provide blood, kidneys, or reproductive services to anyone, notably including my dependents. They protect my right to "bowl alone" if I wish, and more generally, they protect my right to be "left alone." Rights limit our obligations, they do not create obligations, and they assuredly do not protect us within relationships created through those obligations, or more specifically protect us against the exploitative potential created by our obligatory commitments. They do not protect our vulnerability brought on us by virtue of our human dependencies or our communitarian interdependencies. We are, from a liberal perspective, essentially, autonomous and independent selves who thrive when "left alone" to explore our individuality apart from the constraining and distorting influences of others. A right to care is oxymoronic, then, because it protects us in our weakness, rather than promoting, celebrating, and protecting our individualistic strength.

A quite different set of objections might be posed by radical legal scholars, and particularly critical legal scholars influenced by the "rights critique"[32] developed in American and English law schools during the 1980s and 1990s. There are basically two such objections, I think, both of which are at heart strategic, or pragmatic, rather than theoretical. The first such objection goes to the danger of "co-optation." Even if rights are not necessarily negative or individualistic, the

Robin West

tendency to cast them as such in capitalist and liberal societies is overwhelming, and in light of that history, any attempt to construct a positive and nonindividualistic right is likely to be worse than futile. A right, then, even if initially posed, or desired, as a positive and communitarian right can be easily transformed through judicial interpretive processes into a negative right, often used against the very group that urged the right's construction. Thus, a positive right to be free of white racism, for example, which would clearly require the state to act so as to address the problem and consequences of white racism, becomes, instead, in the hands of judicial interpreters, a negative right to be free of discriminatory, racially motivated state legislation, and eventually a "right" to color-blind legislation, and finally a right *of whites* to be free of the burdens of affirmative action. Similarly, a "right," say, to meaningful political participation becomes a right to be free of state censorship, and then eventually a right to influence, even with vast and disproportionate wealth, political processes, and outcomes. A "right to work," urged as a positive citizenship right in the post–Civil War era, becomes a negative "antipaternalism" right to set terms of employment contracts that are free of state efforts to raise minimum wages or impose maximum hours constraints. This list could be extended quite easily; there are plenty of reasons to be legitimately worried that in capitalist societies rights tend to backfire against progressive causes. The co-optation danger, in this context, is that a right to care, even if crafted as a positive right to material support in caregiving labor, might quickly become nothing more than a negative right to either stay home and raise one's children oneself or to hire a nanny of one's choice, free of regulatory constraints such as mandated labor conditions, social security payments, or minimum-wage laws. The right to care could in rather short order become a rhetorical justification for policies that could well make life harder rather than easier for caregivers.

The second worry prompted by the rights critique is that a right to care, even if secured, would benefit only a few and would further legitimate the continuing structural injustices that plague our contemporary world. A right not to be discriminated against by the state on the basis of race, for example, does more than simply fail to address the problems created by white racism in the private sphere: It exacerbates them, and it exacerbates them by legitimating them. It falsely suggests that the problem of racism is one of state racism and then falsely promises that by forbidding it, it has addressed every legitimate problem of justice suffered by nonwhites. The harms caused by private white racism are thereby erased, minimized, or perversely valorized. Likewise, a right to purchase an abortion does more than simply fail to address the real reproductive health problems of poor women; it suggests, wrongly, that the primary constraint on reproductive freedom is moralistic legislation, rather than poverty, and then promises, cruelly, that a right to purchase an abortion is all that women facing unwanted pregnancies have a right to expect abortion from a just state. Likewise here, a right to supported caregiving would do more than simply fail to address the material needs of poor people. It would suggest wrongly that the only problem of poverty that is a problem of justice is the inability to provide adequate care without support. It would then promise, again cruelly, that a right to such support is all that is needed to rectify the injustices of poverty.

Finally, we can readily fashion the outlines of a conservative, traditionalist objection. A right to supported care, even if required by justice, might be disastrous for the human community it supposedly serves. Dependents, caregivers, and those who support them might all be better off within the confines of traditionally understood marital compacts: The caregiver—generally but not necessarily a woman—cares for dependents, and her husband, or spouse, supports her. She is dependent upon and therefore subservient to his benign authority. In a well-functioning family unit, no right is necessary to protect the position of caregivers, while actually providing a right is worse than unnecessary: It holds out incentives that would encourage, or at least not discourage, child raising outside of marriage. Children raised outside of marriage face higher risks of poverty, criminality, learning disabilities and low education rates, and a host of additional social disabilities. What we need to do to address these social ills is attack their cause, and their cause is the flight from marriage, stability, and responsibility that married life entails. A caregiver's right to social or state support would perversely worsen the conditions it set out to address.

RESPONSES

Let me take these objections in order—liberal, critical, and conservative. First, on the negativity and atomism of rights, the negativity of rights even in U.S. constitutional law is easily overstated. Any number of positive rights have in fact been recognized, at one time or another, by the Supreme Court, including not just the rights of criminal defendants to a court-appointed lawyer and the right to Miranda warnings, but also the right of all of us to vote.[33] Outside of the United States, it is quite clear that liberal societies can and do honor, recognize, and in some cases constitutionalize positive rights and do not noticeably sacrifice their liberality by doing so.[34] Furthermore, at the center of a Hobbesian and Lockean understanding of the liberal state, surely a theoretical cornerstone of American constitutionalism, is a distinctly positive right: the right to protection, by the state, against private violence, and a positive duty of the state sovereign to provide that protection. Notwithstanding the Court's logic in *DeShaney*, individuals, so said Hobbes, give up the right of self-help and self-defense in the state of nature when entering the civil compact, and what they get in exchange for that concession is the right, clearly positive, to enjoy the protection of the sovereign against private aggression. The U.S. Constitution both explicitly recognizes and even expands this positive, Hobbesian right to protection: The Fourteenth Amendment, passed in part to assure that freed slaves would be protected against white violence and vengeance, guarantees not only protection of the law, but equal protection of the law. The Supreme Court and liberal constitutional commentators are simply wrong to insist that the American constitution is one of "negative" rights only.

To be sure, a right to protection against private violence is not the same thing as a right to supported caregiving. Nevertheless, neither the existence of, nor the case for the latter, is undercut by its positivity. Positivity is by no means either a necessary feature of the rights protected by liberalism or a compelling, structural feature of American constitutionalism. Furthermore, if we were to recognize a positive right to protection against private violence and exploitation as at the heart of our constitutional scheme of government—and again, concededly, we currently do not—we could, possibly, envision a quite different set of penumbra rights emanating from that core, just as we now envision penumbral, unenumerated rights emanating from our core, negative right to be left alone. A right to the equal protection of the law against private violence, for example, if recognized as guaranteeing a positive right to protection against violence (as its roots in the antilynching campaigns of the amendment period suggest it should be) and not just a nondiscrimination right to equal, even if inadequate, protection, might not just more clearly impose duties of protection on states, but might also project a "gravitational pull" on the meaning of other phrases, to use a popular constitutional metaphor. The phrase most likely impacted by such a pull would surely be the substantive prong of the due-process clause. If that prong does indeed imply substantive, unenumerated rights, and if those rights might be positive in character, and if we are right to be constitutionally concerned about societal conditions that reinforce gendered inequality, then the case for a "penumbral," unenumerated right to care looks quite solid indeed.

Relatedly, there is nothing about a right, and at the end of the day nothing about American constitutionalism, that suggests that rights are *only* what courts are inclined to protect. Rather, the insistence of some American liberal constitutionalists that courts, and not legislators, enforce rights, and that rights therefore provide protection only against states and state action, rather than against private or social wrongs, seems deeply mistaken. The constitutionalists' focus on judicial control of the creation of rights, for example, flies in the face of powerful and general jurisprudential understandings of rights, which in turn ground rights in entitlements and expectations individuals hold vis-à-vis and against social equals, to be protected by law, not just entitlements and expectations individuals hold vis-à-vis states.[35] There is similarly nothing in the United States' constitutional tradition to suggest such a narrow and cramped understanding. Most assuredly, judicial review, and, therefore, judicial supremacy regarding constitutional interpretation, is unquestionably a part of our tradition. The Court gets the last word. It doesn't follow, however, from the Supreme Court's authority as the final arbiter of constitutional meaning that it is the exclusive interpreter: As mentioned, legislators, executives, and citizens all have constitutional obligations, and such obligations logically entail the necessity of constitutional interpretation as well. Nor does it follow from judicial supremacy that courts, and only courts, are constitutionally obligated to protect and take action to protect the rights of citizens. Legislators, too, take an oath to uphold the constitution; legislators, too, are required to do so.

Nor is there anything intrinsic to the rights tradition that weds it to a falsely atomistic conception of our nature. Rights and the liberal tradition that fosters them have changed, sometimes dramatically, to reflect changing understandings of our nature, no less than changing circumstances: We now accord rights to classes of people routinely denied them at the birth of liberal theory, and we have done so explicitly on the basis of changing understandings of the universality of fundamental attributes. We have created rights to reproductive decision making, although in the past reproduction was relegated to fate rather than to choice, and we have done so because of our belief that autonomy regarding reproduction better suits our nature. We have created rights of nondiscrimination, and we have vastly expanded the scope of our rights of free expression, well beyond anything that could conceivably have been intended by the framers, and we have done so largely because of changing accounts of who and what we are. There is no reason that liberal theory, and the rights it supports, could not transform itself so as to meet the "dependency critique." One way to do so, although there could well be others, would be to fashion liberal rights of care and, in so doing, both protect and acknowledge the caring labor that makes liberalism and all else possible.

And what of the critics' worries of co-optation and legitimation? Rights are indeed often co-opted, and negative rights do tend to legitimate the injustice that they either insulate or fail to address. But we should be careful not to throw the baby out with the bath water. That rights can be co-opted does not distinguish them from other legal or political tools of progressive reform, and that they legitimate what they fail to address might simply be a cost worth absorbing or a risk worth taking. While a right to care might legitimate the poverty it leaves untouched, it touches quite a lot. Furthermore, abandoning rights, as the critics would apparently have us do, and attempts to improve social conditions through rights, carries its own strategic costs and they are substantial: Rights, should progressives abandon the project of constructed, describing, and defending rights, would then become the sole province of the libertarian and conservative right. The end result of a world in which progressives, but not others, have abandoned rights, is dystopic, in the extreme: It is a world in which we have rights to property, guns, privacy, contract, and employment at will, but no rights to a clean environment, a decent education, support in caregiving labor, a good job, protection against violence, exploitation, or subordination, shelter, food, or a living wage. There are powerful forces afoot in our contemporary globalized Zeitgeist to produce just such a dystopic world. But feminists, progressives, and leftists shouldn't embrace it, or unwittingly support such a paradigm shift, because of a too-ready acquiescent fear that liberal rights are too dangerous a means of establishing social progress. Rights wedded without dissent to a market-economic vision of a night-watchman state is the risk incurred by doing so.

And finally, would a right to care only exacerbate social ills currently caused by child raising outside of marriage? There is no space here to rehearse the long-standing debates over welfare policy, much of which centers on this question. However, it is worth noting that marriage itself might look very different—and more appealing—if it were itself nested within, and justified by, a fundamental right to care, rather than a right to privacy or even a right to parent. If individuals have a right to provide care without being made unduly vulnerable by virtue of doing so—a right to doulia—a marriage, ideally, both could and should be understood as meeting the right by providing the support. For marriage to actually be a form of doulia, however, rather than a form of exploitation, the institution of marriage would have to be reconceived, and the various panoply of laws that regulate marriage would have to be modified to reflect that new direction. Some reforms toward this reconstruction would be modest. The income produced in the labor market by one partner, for example, could be required, by law, to be given to both partners. The future needs of the caregiving partner could be fully recognized and protected through equalizing the social security entitlements of both partners. Fathers could be expected or required—not just permitted—to take extended leaves from work to provide hands-on support for caregivers upon the birth or adoption of a child . . . and so on. More fundamentally, and more drastically, laws aimed at protecting women and caregivers within marriages from abuse and exploitation would have to be strengthened, and with the goal of protecting the caregivers' rights—an understanding, it's worth noting, diametrically contrary to the current Court's understanding of congressional attempts to address domestic violence. Were marriage to be so understood, and the laws sustaining it reformed to reflect that understanding, it would itself constitute a form of doulia and would satisfy any right to doulia a caregiver within a marriage might have.

Were marriage to be so constructed, or reconstructed, would the existence of a right to doulia nevertheless create an undesirable incentive to avoid marriage altogether? Again, wouldn't this simply exacerbate the social ills caused by out-of-wedlock births, and really for no good reason, were marriage to be reformed so as to make it a more desirable form of doulia? There are two responses. First, it is altogether possible that the social ills of poverty, higher infant mortality rates, lower birth weights, less and lower quality education, poorer nutrition, higher rates of criminality, higher rates of incarceration, and greater health risks, all suffered by children of single mothers, and all lamented by social conservatives, are "caused" less (if at all) by the marital status of the single mother than by the lack of the right to supported care proposed here: The impoverished single mother, after all, currently lacks both a husband and a right to doulia. But more important, there is no reason to think that a right to doulia would create perverse incentives to pursue viable, healthy marriages. The claim that it would, I think, both understates the value of marriage and overstates the worth of the doulia right: Marriage supplies warmth and companionship, the sharing of daily responsibilities and decisions, as well as support, while the doulia right is only to the latter.

The right proposed here—a right to doulia, or supported caregiving—would mean that the single mother would be guaranteed a level of material, financial support, of in-kind assistance, and of help with the caregiving itself, so as to assure that she can provide adequate care without endangering herself and her dependents. Even if we accept *arguendo* the conservative's judgment that marriage is the best institutional context within which to care for dependents, there is no reason to think that such a right would supplant marriage. If it is truly the case that marriage—understood as available to all, regardless of sexual orientation—really is a better way, emotionally, morally, and financially, to live one's adult life, a right to doulia surely constitutes no threat to it. Nor is there any reason to think that such a right would or should supplant public efforts to encourage marital lifestyles as a socially preferred means of assuring adequate care. It would mean, however, that our priorities would shift. Our rights would, as they should, expand so as to protect that which makes social life possible—caregiving—while our policies, such as our current policy preference for marriage, would reflect our current sense of the best means of providing care. It would mean that women, along with their dependents, who cannot or choose not to raise children or care for elderly or disabled dependents' marriages, but nevertheless care for dependents, are not punished for doing so. Children and their mothers, and more generally dependents and their caregivers, both inside and outside of marriage, would enjoy public support, rather than contempt or neglect, and they would enjoy that public support because they have a right to it, not because from time to time and under limited circumstances they spark our pity. It would mean that we would no longer perceive caregivers in need as contemptible, or at best pitiful, and above all, as lacking rights. It would mean that we would quit blinding ourselves—quite *willfully* blinding ourselves, because we all know better—to the necessity and importance of the work they do. We would quit viewing caregivers—when we view them at all—as nothing but a burden; as nothing but dependent upon us.

NOTES

1. Eva Feder Kittay, *Love's Labor: Essays on Women, Equality, and Dependency* (New York: Routledge, 1999), 68. Kittay states the principle of *doulia* in this way: "Just as we have required care to survive and thrive, so we need to provide conditions that allow others—including those who do the work of caring—to receive the care they need to survive and thrive."

The word *doulia* is Kittay's improvisation of the Greek word *doula*, which designates a postpartum helper assigned to assist a new mother as she takes charge of her newborn infant. *Doulia,* then, designates the "arrangement by which service is passed on so that those who become needy by virtue of tending to those in need can be cared for as well." Kittay goes on to explain *doulia*'s ethic as being rooted in an extended, social reciprocity: "*Doulia* is part of an ethic that is captured in the colloquial phrase 'what goes around comes around.' If someone helps another in her need, someone, in turn, will help the helper when she is needy—whether the neediness derives from her position as caregiver or from circumstances that pertain to health or age." Kittay, at 107 (footnotes omitted).

2. Linda MacClain, "Care as a Public Value: Linking Responsibility, Resources, and Republicanism," *Chicago-Kent Law Review* 76, no. 3 (2001): 1673.

3. Tillie Olsen, *Silences* (New York: Delacorte, 1978), 204–05.

4. Mary Becker et al., *Cases and Materials on Feminist Jurisprudence: Taking Women Seriously* (St. Paul, Minn.: West Publishing, 1994), chapters. 2, 9–11.

5. See, e.g., *Virginia Military Inst. v. U.S.*, 508 U.S. 946 (1993); International Union, *UAW v. Johnson Controls, Inc.*, 499 U.S. 187 (1991); *Price Waterhouse v. Hopkins*, 490 U.S. 228 (1989); *California Savings and Loan Ass'n v. Guerra*, 479 U.S. 272 (1987); *Wimberly v. Labor and Indus. Relations Comm'n of Mo.*, 479 U.S. 511 (1987); *Rostker v. Goldberg*, 453 U.S. 57 (1981); *Orr v. Orr*, 440 U.S. 268 (1979); *Personnel Adm'r of Mass. v. Feeney*, 442 U.S. 256 (1979); *Craig v. Boren*, 429 U.S. 190 (1976); *Geduldig v. Aiello*, 417 U.S. 484 (1974); *Frontiero v. Richardson*, 411 U.S. 677 (1973); *Reed v. Reed*, 404 U.S. 71 (1971).

6. See *Planned Parenthood of Southeastern Pa. v. Casey*, 505 U.S. 833 (1992); *Roe v. Wade*, 410 U.S. 113 (1973); *Eisenstadt v. Baird*, 405 U.S. 438 (1972); *Griswold v. Conn.*, 381 U.S. 479 (1965).

7. See *Troxel v. Granville*, 530 U.S. 120 S. Ct. 2054 (2000). As Jill Hasday has recently argued, the situation is very different for single mothers dependent on state assistance, who must tolerate, as a condition of receiving that assistance, considerable inference with their decision-making authority within their families by a wide range of social-service providers. See Jill Elaine Hasday, "Parenthood Divided: A Legal History of the Bifurcated Law of Parental Relations," *Georgetown Law Journal* 90, no. 2 (2002): 299.

8. See *Meyer v. Nebraska*, 262 U.S. 390, 399 (1923).

9. See *Bradwell v. Illinois*, 83 U.S. (16 Wall.) 130 (1873), for a classic example of how this understanding infected the Supreme Court's interpretation of the Constitution.

10. See Becker, supra note 4, at 888. See also Kittay, supra note 1, at 124–31.

11. See Social Security Act, chapter 531, §§ 401–06, 49 Stat. 620, 627–29 (1935). See also Becker, supra note 4, at 888; Sylvia A. Law, "Women, Work, Welfare, and the Preservation of Patriarchy," *University of Pennsylvania Law Review* 131 (1983): 1249, 1254–61.

12. Family and Medical Leave Act of 1993, Pub. L. No. 103-3, 107 Stat. 6 (codified as amended in scattered sections of 2 U.S.C., 5 U.S.C., and 29 U.S.C.).

13. Personal Responsibility and Work Opportunity Reconciliation Act of 1996, Pub. L. No. 104-193, 100 Stat. 2105 (codified as amended in scattered sections of 7 U.S.C., 8 U.S.C., 21 U.S.C., 25 U.S.C., and 42 U.S.C.).

14. Martha A. Fineman, *The Neutered Mother: The Sexual Family and Other Twentieth Century Tragedies* (New York: Routledge, 1995).

15. Kittay, supra note 1.

16. Carol Gilligan, *In a Different Voice: Psychological Theory and Women's Development* (Cambridge, Mass.: Harvard University Press, 1982).

17. Nel Noddings, *Caring: A Feminine Approach to Ethics and Moral Education* (Berkeley: University of California Press, 1984).

18. Bruce A. Ackerman, *We the People* (Cambridge, Mass.: Belknap Press of Harvard University Press, 1991).

19. And, of course, businesses are increasingly dependent on noncaregiving female labor and may be starting to see the advantages of a gender-integrated workforce. All who profit from those businesses—owners, managers, employees, and customers and consumers—have a stake in facilitating the participation of women in them and therefore of strengthening the position of caregivers, both male and female, so as to better enable that participation.

20. See *DeShaney v. Winnebago County Department of Social Services*, 489 U.S. 189 (1989). In *DeShaney*, a four-year-old boy and his mother sued the Winnebago County Department of Social Services for failing to adequately protect him against the abusive violence of his father, which was so severe as to leave him profoundly brain-damaged. The Court held that the plaintiffs had failed to show that the county's social services department was sufficiently involved in the boy's case so as to pass the requisite level of "state action" needed to trigger constitutional guarantees; the Constitution protects us against the actions of states, not private parties.

The Court then went on to claim, although it was not necessary to the "state action" holding, that the Constitution is one of "negative liberties" only, and that for that reason as well, the state had no affirmative obligation to protect Michael DeShaney against private violence. Even if the state of Wisconsin had no police force, the Court claimed, there would be no violation of Michael's or anyone else's constitutional rights to liberty—the Constitution provides only negative rights of protection against excessive state action, not positive rights to some minimal degree of state support or protection.

21. See, generally, Paul Brest and Sanford Levinson, *Processes of Constitutional Decisionmaking: Cases and Materials,* 3d ed. (Boston: Little, Brown, 1992), chapters 9, 11; Geoffrey R. Stone et al., *Constitutional Law,* 3d ed. (Boston: Little, Brown, 1996), chapter 6; *Lochner v. New York*, 198 U.S. 45 (1905); *Hammer v. Dagenhart*, 247 U.S. 251 (1918); *A.L.A. Schechter Poultry Corp. v. United States*, 295 U.S. 495 (1935); *Carter v. Carter Coal Co.*, 298 U.S. 238 (1936).

22. See, e.g., *Prince v. Massachusetts*, 321 U.S. 158, 166 (1943); *Pierce v. Society of the Sisters of the Holy Names of Jesus and Mary,* 268 U.S. 510, 534 (1925); *Meyer v. Nebraska*, 262 U.S. 390, 399 (1923).

23. See *Troxel v. Granville*, 530 U.S. 120 S. Ct. 2054 (2000).

24. The Supreme Judicial Court of Massachusetts' notoriously antimaternalist and antiparentalist reasoning in *Upton v. JWP Businessland* throws even the limited understanding of the social interest in parenting in doubt. In *Upton v. JWP Businessland,* the Court held that it was not a violation of public policy for Businessland to discharge Joanna Upton, an at-will employee, because she was a single mother unwilling to work newly imposed long hours because of her need to care for her young son. See *Upton v. JWP Businessland*, 425 Mass. 756, 757, 682 N.E.2d 1357 (1997). A right to care, if one can be defended, highlights that case's flaws.

25. 381 U.S. 479 (1965).

26. 405 U.S. 438 (1972).

27. 410 U.S. 113 (1973).

28. Again, it is important to note that the right established in *Roe, Casey,* and the later "reproductive rights" cases is not the right to have an abortion; it is the right to contract for abortion services, free of undue state interference. It is not a right to the funding necessary to obtain an abortion.

29. It should be noted that other countries embracing a rights tradition, as well as international organizations such as the United Nations, enumerate and attempt to protect

positive rights. The United States' hostility to the possibility of protecting positive rights through constitutional mechanisms can fairly be described as extreme. See generally, Robin West, "Revitalizing Rights," in *Rights*, Robin West, ed. (Burlington: Ashgate, Dartmouth, 2001).

30. Ronald Dworkin, *Taking Rights Seriously* (Cambridge, Mass.: Harvard University Press, 1977).

31. DeShaney, supra note 27, at 195–96.

32. See Morton J. Horwitz, "Rights," *Harvard Civil Rights-Civil Liberties Law Review* 23 (1988): 393; Mark V. Tushnet "An Essay on Rights," *Texas Law Review* 62 (1984): 1363.

33. See Susan Bandes, "The Negative Constitution: A Critique," *Michigan Law Review* 88 (1990): 2271.

34. See Mary Ann Glendon, "Rights in Twentieth Century Constitutions," *University of Chicago Law Review* 59 (1992): 519.

35. See Richard S. Markovits, "Legitimate Legal Argument and Internally-Right Answers to Legal-Rights Questions," *Chicago-Kent Law Review* 74 (1999): 415, 426–27.

5

Subsidized Lives and the Ideology of Efficiency

Martha T. McCluskey

We all live subsidized lives.

—Martha Albertson Fineman[1]

[T]he habits of self-reliance and individual responsibility . . . are and must be constitutive of the entire American political order.

—William J. Bennett and John J. DiIulio, Jr.[2]

How can feminists bring caretaking from the margins to the center of society? Legal scholar Martha Fineman argues that to better recognize and reward dependent care, we must rethink the three basic institutions of state, market, and family.[3]

In the dominant liberal political theory, autonomy is the key to both a free state and a free market; dependency is relegated to the family. Fineman builds on a substantial body of feminist work challenging this myth of autonomy by explaining that dependency is a universal and inevitable part of the human condition: Everyone experiences dependency as a child, and most experience varying degrees of dependency at least sometime in their adult lives because of advanced age or illness.[4] Fineman advocates restructuring the relationship between the state and market to acknowledge that dependency and dependent care are integral to a well-functioning state and market. In particular, she argues that the state and market should play a major role in supporting the needs of caretakers and their dependents, for example, through comprehensive public funding for dependent care and through workplace accommodations for family-based caretaking needs.[5]

But at the beginning of the twenty-first century, political and economic changes are moving in the opposite direction, pushing the family and its caretaking labor further toward the margins of the market and state. Welfare state systems that took steps toward spreading responsibility for dependent care from the family to the state and market now face attack and retrenchment. This is a time of strong political movement toward privatizing responsibility for caretaking as a problem of individual families, and of women in particular within those families.

For example, in the United States, the federal welfare reform legislation enacted in 1996 requires mothers in poverty to substitute market labor or unpaid "workfare" for government support for child care. In many developed nations, increased pressure for labor market "flexibility" in a competitive global market often requires working-class and middle-class parents to bend their family lives to accommodate lower pay, longer hours, fewer benefits and protections, and less stable employment. Around the world, reduced government spending on social services and public infrastructure means families—caretakers—put more time and money into procuring or providing transportation, education, health care, recreation, and dependent care. This movement away from social support for human needs appears to many to be the inevitable result of a newly integrated global economy.

Two strands of right-wing ideology have helped widen the chasm between feminist visions of collective responsibility for caretaking and the current political reality. First, many feminist critics have recognized how state and market support for caretaking has been undermined by neoconservative ideology, which defends a hierarchical and patriarchal vision of caretaking at the margins of state and market, relegated to unpaid or underpaid women in families headed by men. For example, George Gilder argues that welfare support for mothers tends to "destroy the key role and authority of the father."[6] Gilder complains that the father "can no longer feel manly in his own home. . . . In the welfare culture, money becomes not something earned by men through hard work, but a right conferred on women by the state."[7]

A second, and perhaps stronger, ideological barrier to broader public support for caretaking comes from neoliberal ideology, which defends the "free market" and "economic efficiency" as pillars of state and society. Like neoconservativism's overtly gendered vision, neoliberalism's superficially gender-neutral doctrine keeps caretakers and their dependents—most women—from securing their fair share of support from the state and market.

Fineman asserts that "we all live subsidized lives."[8] At one level, this statement recognizes the importance and universality of dependent care. None of us are self-made; all have depended on others—especially mothers—to give us birth, to nurture and teach us in the myriad ways required to become functional human beings. All will need to depend on others at some point in our lives to perform the mundane tasks of daily living, as well as to reach larger goals. At another level, we all live subsidized—and subsidizing—lives because we all receive benefits and costs from a wide range of resources we did not directly produce or purchase: whether in the form of government aid, inheritance, tax breaks, private charity, infrastructure, the natural environment, or the generations of labor and wisdom that went into shaping the political, social, and economic institutions that frame our lives.

From this foundation of subsidized lives, Fineman questions why some subsidies are stigmatized while others are hidden or rewarded.[9] In this chapter, I aim to follow up on her question by exploring how neoliberal ideology, which pervades contemporary policy, scholarship, and culture, makes ubiquitous subsidies take on drastically different meanings.

Neoliberalism incorporates and promotes the neoclassical version of economics as a matter of scientific fact, divorced from politics or ideology. Neoclassical economics teaches that scarce resources mean we cannot have it all, but that impartial cost–benefit calculations tell us how to make the most of what we have. The question of which subsidies are public rights and which subsidies are public wrongs thereby appears to become a question of economics, not politics—of principle or fact, not power. Neoliberal ideology transforms the privatization of caretaking from a moral, divine, or biological imperative (in the view of neo-conservatives and the religious right) to an economic imperative.

Feminists—including Fineman—have gone far to expose the biases underlying the seemingly neutral liberal principles in the context of equality theory. But as "efficiency" goals eclipse "equality" goals, feminists' critical scrutiny needs to turn toward "economic efficiency" principles.

FROM "SPECIAL" TREATMENT TO "REDISTRIBUTIVE" TREATMENT

In an earlier book, Fineman broke new ground by explaining how the illusion of *equality* serves to shift family resources away from caretaking women in divorce.[10] The neoliberal illusion of *efficiency* similarly serves to shift state and market resources away from caretaking women in work and citizenship. The opposition between efficiency and redistribution—or between economic growth and social equity—is a central strategy through which public subsidies to support caretaking needs are constructed as antithetical to state, market, and family, while public subsidies to support (nonhuman) capital and corporate needs are constructed as essential to state, market, and family.

In neoclassical economic theory, "efficient" policies are those that increase the overall size of the economic "pie," while "redistributive" policies are those that change the size of different slices within the "pie." This opposition between wealth creation and wealth division forms the dominant framework for analysis of law and policy today. Liberals and conservatives disagree on the relative weight that should be given to each side of this opposition, but scholars and policymakers across the mainstream political spectrum typically assume that these two choices frame the debate.

Just as contemporary public policy analysis presents two competing choices, efficiency versus redistribution, traditional equality analysis similarly presents two competing choices, equal treatment versus special (or different) treatment. Within both of these analytical frames, one choice tends to appear objective, the other subjective; one choice tends to appear neutral, the other preferential. This article argues that for both frameworks, that appearance is false. By framing the choices this way, both dichotomies mask inherent biases and baseline moral judgments that devalue caretaking labor.

To bring caretaking from the margins to the center, feminists have challenged the supposedly neutral framework of equality law within which support for women's particular needs—such as the demands of caretaking—is constructed as a "special" accommodation outside the scope of "normal" equal treatment.[11] Similarly, to bring caretaking from the margins to the center in the neoliberal age, feminists must challenge the supposedly neutral free-market framework within which women's particular needs—especially those of caretaking—are constructed as "redistributive" subsidies outside the scope of a normally efficient market.

The efficiency/redistribution framework has become a primary means of differentiating among various forms of public support. Public support for caretaking falls squarely on the redistributive side of the line, in the conventional wisdom. For example, many characterize the former Aid to Families with Dependent Children (AFDC), the target of recent federal welfare reform, as redistributing money from taxpayers to single parents (or unemployed couples) in poverty.[12] Similarly, many describe the Family and Medical Leave Act as redistributing resources from employers to workers by giving some employees a right to twelve weeks unpaid leave from their jobs for dependent care or serious illness.[13]

But by framing collective responsibility for caretaking as a policy choice in favor of redistribution over efficiency—fairness over growth—neoclassical economic theory implicitly devalues this choice. By definition, efficiency is about promoting overall gain (maximizing aggregate resources); redistribution is about benefiting some at the expense of others (moving resources around). Efficiency, in other words, is defined as furthering the public interest; redistribution as furthering particular interests. Even if these redistributive goals deserve public support, compared to efficiency goals they will always seem parochial and problematic.

Since an efficient distribution of resources, by definition, maximizes overall gain, a redistribution of resources that deviates from this efficient division will risk reducing overall gain. According to the neoclassical framework, then, redistribution poses tough trade-offs. Scarce resources limit the benefits that can be achieved by redividing the pie in pursuit of fairness.

Following this reasoning, the dominant economic theory teaches that redistributive policies driven by good intentions (such as subsidizing caretakers) will have unintended consequences that hurt both their beneficiaries and others. For example, mainstream economists warn that redistributive subsidies may provide some people with a temporarily bigger slice of the pie, but at the risk of shrinking the overall pie—thereby diminishing that slice over the long run and hurting the beneficiaries of the redistribution, as well as others.[14]

Many feminists have criticized the equal treatment/special treatment framework for presenting a bad choice for women with caretaking responsibilities, arguing that either way women lose.[15] Under this framework, women can either be "equal," at the cost of ignoring gender differences (social or biological) such as the particular demands of pregnancy or caretaking, or women can be "different," at the cost of perpetuating pregnancy or caretaking needs as inherently deviant and dependent on "special" protection. For example, the "normal career track" requires freedom from caretaking demands; but the "mommy track" channels workers with caretaking responsibilities into a separate and subordinate path that is likely to lead to lower pay and greater job insecurity.[16] Many commentators insist that we cannot have it both ways: Women must either demonstrate equality and independence by forsaking "special" protections, or else accept (or even celebrate) subordination and insecurity as the price of difference.[17]

Though superficially neutral, the efficiency/redistribution dichotomy presents a similarly skewed choice for feminism in general and caretaking responsibilities in particular. Either way, most caretakers (and most women) lose. Feminists can choose efficiency, which involves directing public assistance away from caretaking in order to support economic growth. Or, feminists can choose redistribution, which involves taking public assistance away from economic growth in order to support caretaking—with the predicted result that many caretakers (and society as a whole) will face greater economic insecurity in the long run. According to free-market theory, the economic reality of scarce resources dictates that we cannot have it both ways. If feminists insist on "rights" to redistributive subsidies, they must accept the hidden costs of these subsidies.

Examples of the purported costs of redistributive policies are legion. In the prevailing story told by welfare-reform advocates, the former federal AFDC program ended up hurting the families it aimed to subsidize.[18] This view asserts that AFDC created a cycle of dependency by providing an alternative to wage work (or wage-working husbands) for single mothers, thereby encouraging women and families in poverty to forgo productive labor market (or marriage) opportunities that supposedly would have improved their lives in the long run. For example, California governor Pete Wilson argued that "while the welfare system was begun with the best of intentions, it has begun a downward spiral of permanent dependency and suffocating hopelessness . . . it is stifling and degrading to the very people it claims to help."[19]

Similarly, according to predominant wisdom, redistributive subsidies aimed at helping working- or middle-class caretakers also end up hurting their intended beneficiaries. For example, many argue that the employer-based subsidy for family care (unpaid work leave) mandated by the Family and Medical Leave Act induces employers to limit jobs and wages for workers with caretaking needs.[20] In addition, the neoclassical framework predicts that by diverting employers' resources from production to redistribution, we will sacrifice economic growth and competitiveness—thus leading to fewer jobs and higher consumer prices in the long run. For example, Massachusetts business lobbyists warned that state businesses would be at a competitive disadvantage if the state enacted legislation requiring employers to provide paid family leave.[21] Western European countries are often cited as a warning of such trade-offs: with more generous protections for workers and families comes high unemployment and slow economies,[22] so the conventional story goes, although the evidence of this link is tenuous.[23]

The primacy of efficiency over redistribution is the core principle of the neoliberal consensus that drives contemporary policymaking in the United States and much of the world. As a *Wall Street Journal* article approvingly noted, the choice of efficiency over redistribution now has bipartisan support.[24] The article quotes the 1992 Democratic Party platform to show how far that party has turned away from the redistributive goals of its past: "above all, instead of dividing the economic pie, [the "new" Democratic party] focuses on making the pie grow."[25] Similarly, the 1996 national Democratic Party platform singled out welfare as an example of the failures of redistribution and highlighted reforms replacing welfare with wage work as an example of the party's embrace of the opposite course of wealth production.[26] After President Clinton's 1996 reelection, the head of the Democratic Leadership Council attributed Clinton's continued success to his ability to "reconnect the Democratic Party with its real tradition . . . of economic growth and opportunity, not redistribution."[27]

To defend public support for caretaking, feminists must challenge not simply this prevailing choice of efficiency over redistribution, but also the framework that makes redistribution seem so costly. That is, we must show that efficiency is not only the *wrong* goal, but an *illusory* goal—just as Fineman and other feminists have showed that a neutral concept of equality is illusory.[28] As with the equal treatment/special treatment dilemma, feminists can escape the bad choices of the efficiency/redistribution dilemma by showing that this framework rests on biased norms and double standards.

WHOSE EFFICIENCY?

Feminists have explained how seemingly neutral ideas of equality in liberal theory in fact incorporate gendered norms. Women's reproductive or caretaking needs are different and in need of special treatment only if one assumes as the norm a person without these needs—such as a stereotypical man.[29] Any analysis of sameness or difference necessarily requires a standard of comparison.[30] It is the implicit standard of a traditional man that makes the choice of equal or different treatment so costly for women—and so beneficial for men.[31] Traditional men can be both equal *and* different—having it both ways—because equal treatment is defined to privilege their specific needs not as differences but as unstated norms.[32]

For example, the lawsuit challenging the male-only admittance policy of the Virginia Military Institute raised the question of whether women should have equal treatment, by being given the opportunity to join a public military-style school featuring a stereotypically masculine adversative model of education,—or whether women would be best served through different treatment, by being offered a separate, less well-endowed, and less well-connected school featuring a more nurturing approach.[33] Men who conformed to the dominant stereotype, however, had no such dilemma: They had a prestigious and prosperous publicly supported school geared to their particular "differences." This contrasting set of choices, one tough and one easy, is neither neutral nor natural. It is the result of gendered power: the political decision to devote public resources to promote a specific ideal of masculinity.

In short, ostensibly neutral ideals of equality necessarily incorporate assumptions about *whose* particular differences are taken as the standard for comparison. Feminists accordingly ask the questions: equal to *whom*, according to *what* standard? Similarly, the ostensibly neutral ideal of efficiency always incorporates assumptions about *whose* particular interests are taken as the standard for determining society's well-being. Feminists should ask the questions: efficient for *whom*, according to *what* standards? Distributive ideals are integral to—not opposed to—efficiency ideals, just as value judgments about difference are inherent in ideals of equality.

The current neoliberal view of efficiency rests on the biased assumption that certain *capital and corporate* interests are necessarily in the *public* interest— because these interests are the standard by which economic growth is measured. In contrast, this view of efficiency generally assumes caretakers' interests are *private* or *special* interests—because these interests are defined as a deviation from that standard of economic growth. Because the needs of elite capital and corporate interests are presumed to stand for the needs of society as a whole, these interests can have it both ways. They can be both subsidized and efficient at the same time.

The current economic orthodoxy embraces this double standard as an economic fact. Though "what's good for General Motors is good for America" is a joke, its message is often taken seriously. By presuming that our existing economic structure generally reflects an efficient free market that maximizes overall growth, this orthodoxy reaches the circular conclusion that those whom the existing market benefits most are those who benefit society the most—and therefore those who should get the most social support. For example, economist Gordon Tullock writes approvingly that "most economists would agree that taking funds from the poor and giving them to the well-off would accelerate growth" and that such a policy would, in theory, make the poor better off.[34] Such views continue to support the trickle-down policies that gained prominence in the Reagan years.

For example, former president George H. W. Bush attempted to enact a capital gains tax cut that would have provided 80 percent of its benefits to individuals earning more than $100,000 a year.[35] Nonetheless, Bush explained that his proposal would benefit the majority of Americans because it would "make us more successful in the increasingly competitive international marketplace, creating more jobs and better living standards for Americans."[36] According to Republican leaders supporting the proposal, tax breaks for wealthy investors are about "creating wealth," not "redistributing wealth."[37]

Similarly, neoliberal economic reforms have emphasized fiscal austerity policies, which redirect taxpayer funds from social welfare programs and public infrastructure to deficit-cutting and debt repayment—thereby increasing security for wealthy bondholders.[38] International Monetary Fund (IMF) deputy director Stanley Fischer justified the harsh effects of such policies on developing nations by explaining that "fiscal tightening is almost always the key to stabilization" necessary to attract foreign capital for economic growth.[39] In the 2000 U.S. presidential campaign, Democratic candidate Al Gore adopted the position that the federal budget surplus should be used for debt reduction, rather than for substantial expansions in social welfare programs.[40] President Clinton rationalized the Democrats' decision to emphasize fiscal restraint as a means of enhancing economic growth: "The less money we tie up in publicly held debt, the more money we free up for private-sector investment."[41]

In addition to fiscal austerity, neoliberal policies have promoted monetary austerity, privatization, and liberalization of constraints on international finance and trade, all of which directly benefit wealthy capital owners.[42] Although these policies typically result in greater insecurity for most people, they are justified on the theory that in the long run gains to wealthy multinational investors will spread to others. For example, one analyst explained that the IMF's "structural adjustment" reforms, which impose neoliberal policies on developing countries as a condition of assistance, aim to "change the relative prices of capital and labor" so that international capital gets higher returns and freedom, and labor gets lower wages and fewer rights—on the theory that this will benefit society on the whole through "a great increase in the use of labor."[43]

But a standard of justice that measures public benefits according to the specific interests of the wealthiest capital holders is no more likely to benefit the average caretaker and her family than is a standard of equality that measures women according to the specific needs of the stereotypical noncaretaking man. Indeed, advocates acknowledge that the success of structural adjustment policies depends on the "creative response" of women's "domestic management."[44] That is, neoliberal policymakers assume that family caretakers will act as "shock-absorbers," coping with reduced public services and reduced wage income by working more (in both unpaid and paid jobs) and by consuming less.[45]

The double standard that holds that increased public support for capital, not caretakers, will promote the long-term public good rests on ideological faith— and political power—more than on economic evidence. First, evidence of supposed aggregate growth resulting from supposed efficiency-oriented policies is weak. IMF researchers have admitted that the economic evidence of improved economic growth from neoliberal structural adjustment policies in developing nations is uncertain.[46] One analysis of the annual average rate of growth of GDP per capital for fifty-six countries shows that in all regions of the world except for Asia, growth *declined* in the period of capital liberalization (1973–1992) compared to the prior period of currency and trade controls (1950–1973).[47]

Second, the "aggregate growth" promoted by neoliberal policies fails to benefit most people. In the United States, for example, the majority of society has gained little from the supposed economic booms of the 1980s and 1990s: the top 1 percent of wealth holders received 62 percent of the total gain in marketable wealth between 1983 and 1989, while the "bottom" 80 percent of Americans received only 1 percent of this growth.[48] Considering financial wealth only (rather than total net worth), the majority of society *lost* ground from 1983 to 1989: This period of "trickle down" growth left the "bottom" 80 percent with 3 percent *less* financial wealth.[49]

While growth-oriented policies favoring wealthy investors may produce jobs, more jobs do not necessarily translate into improved living standards for the majority, especially for caretakers—because more jobs can simply mean more work for less gain. Income inequality rose more in the Clinton economic recovery years of 1993 and 1994 than during the entire previous decade of Reaganomics.[50] In the mid-1990s, median family income was less than it was in 1986.[51] After inflation, private-sector workers' compensation per hour was less in 1995 than in 1992.[52] From 1967 to 1997, the annual income of the poorest 20 percent in the United States declined 2.4 percent and that of the middle 20 percent declined 0.7 percent, while the income of the richest 5 percent gained 20.4 percent.[53] Even though, since 1996, average wages have increased compared to the early 1990s, these gains from economic expansion have still left U.S. workers with lower average earnings (adjusted for inflation) than in 1973.[54]

Moreover, many Americans have buttressed their stagnant or declining income by working longer hours—a change that is especially burdensome for caretakers. Americans worked for wages 138 hours a year more, on average, in 1987 than in 1969.[55] This growth in work hours has continued. In 1996, Americans' wage work hours averaged 45 hours a year more than in 1989;[56] middle-class married couples increased their annual hours of work outside the home by more than three weeks a year during this same period.[57] It took approximately 500 more hours of wage work to make the average U.S. family income in 1997 than in 1977.[58]

Furthermore, rising perceptions of job insecurity may make it harder for workers to bargain for accommodations for family responsibilities.[59] From 1979 to 1990, 24 percent of workers in large corporations reported that they feared job layoffs; by 1995 and 1996, that percentage increased to 46 percent.[60] High inequality and the precariousness of middle-class status contributed to many Americans' decision to increase work hours rather than leisure or family time during recent periods of economic growth.[61]

This trend toward lower wages, longer hours, and increased income inequality extends worldwide. The IMF's structural adjustment policies appear to have produced few trickle-down benefits to the average caretaker and her family. Indeed, much evidence suggests that most women and their dependents have paid an enormous price. These policies have often led to increased prices for basic consumer goods, in part because of reduced subsidies for domestic agriculture, reduced public infrastructure spending, increased dependence on imported goods, and collapsing currency prices.[62] For example, after neoliberal austerity policies were imposed on Peru in 1990, consumer prices in Lima were higher than in New York, while average earnings plummeted.[63] And in 1992, it took the equivalent of nine months of an average worker's pay to buy a winter coat in Russia.[64]

In addition, neoliberal policies have led to dramatic declines in public sanitation, public health, education, and infrastructure in many countries.[65] For example, Mozambique, a model of compliance with investor-friendly neoliberal policies promoted by the IMF, spends twice as much on interest payments to foreign creditors as it does on health services.[66] For large portions of the world's population, these effects have contributed to catastrophic increases in disease[67] and malnutrition,[68] resulting in depressed standards of living[69] and life expectancy.[70]

Although neoliberals tend to argue that this disastrous global economic situation would be even worse without the recent shift in support from human needs to capital needs, any truth to that argument may be attributable to contingent— and gendered—political power, not to inviolable economic principle. President Clinton, for example, backed away from spending on social programs when Federal Reserve Chairman Alan Greenspan threatened to raise interest rates.[71] Similarly, threats of capital withdrawal have impeded many nations from sticking to their goals of maintaining social service spending. For example, as one reporter explains, "Every few weeks a team of economists from the International Monetary Fund shows up in Moscow to determine if [Russian Prime Minister Primakov] has put together what they politely term a 'realistic' budget."[72] For another example, Moody's Investor Services downgraded Sweden's debt rating in 1995, pressuring the government to cut child allowances and unemployment benefits.[73]

But if political and legal institutions were restructured to give more control to the average caretaker and less to elite capital interests, governments might have more bargaining power with which to make social spending less costly. Imagine, for example, the different economic choices that might be available if the law required the Federal Reserve's committee for setting monetary policy to meet openly and to include the same number of child-care workers and welfare recipients as bankers, or if the IMF's governance structure gave a significant voice to women and their dependents in developing countries. Or, imagine the different political choices that might be possible if major campaign finance reforms in the United States allowed presidents and congressional members to seek election without catering primarily to corporate and capital interests.

Even if we accept the neoliberal credo that aggregate growth—efficiency—is good for its own sake (regardless of whether the majority shares in that gain), we are still left with the question of *whose* growth should count in measuring that aggregate gain. Conventional measurements of economic growth, such as Gross Domestic Product (GDP), are biased against caretaking. For example, GDP counts as growth an increase in health-care expenses due to a rise in cancer cases from corporate pollution.[74] In contrast, GDP does not count as growth an improvement in a family's health, leisure, and happiness when a mother has more time free from wage work to take her child to the park after school, instead of leaving the child alone in front of the television. Nor would GDP include as growth the family's gain from visiting a free public park instead of paying for a private recreational facility. If unpaid household labor and caretaking were included in the conventional standards for measuring economic growth, subsidies for a range of caretaking activities disproportionately performed by women could suddenly be transformed from costly redistribution into productive growth.[75]

WHOSE MORAL HAZARD?

In sum, the dominant efficiency/redistribution framework incorporates a double standard that exaggerates the public benefits of corporate and capital subsidies compared to caretaking subsidies. In addition, this framework perpetuates a double standard that exaggerates the public costs of caretaking subsidies compared to corporate and capital subsidies. In particular, the prevailing ideology of efficiency provides a purportedly value-neutral economic justification for complaints about welfare dependency.

According to neoclassical economics, to fully account for the costs and benefits of any given subsidy, we need to consider the inevitable incentive effects. That is, subsidies may change, as well as support, behavior. That incentive effect underlies the problem economists term moral hazard—the tendency of those who receive protection against a certain cost to take less care to avoid that cost than they would otherwise. Neoclassical economic theory explains that moral hazard is inefficient: It hurts society in the long run by driving up overall costs.

In the recent debate over federal welfare reform, the pervasive demands for "personal responsibility" have focused both explicitly and implicitly on moral hazard. For example, Heritage Foundation commentators explained that "[t]he key problem is that welfare programs present a 'moral hazard' problem . . . when welfare benefits are tied, directly or indirectly, to such behaviors as low work effort, divorce, and illegitimacy, welfare strongly promotes an increase in those behaviors."[76]

This Heritage Foundation report emphasizes the public harm resulting from welfare's moral hazard: "[T]he more that is spent, the more people in apparent need of aid who appear. The taxpayer is trapped in a cycle in which spending generates illegitimacy and dependency, which in turn generate demands for even greater spending."[77] Critics of other subsidies for caretakers have also stressed moral hazard problems. For example, conservatives have warned that federal subsidies for day-care expenses will create financial incentives to remove children from unpaid family home care into "institutional" settings.[78]

But the supposed harms of moral hazard are social constructions, based on gendered values, not economic truths. The idea behind the "moral hazard" concept is simply that we tend to get more of something when it is subsidized. Whether or not that increase is good or bad depends on a baseline norm: a value judgment about the appropriateness of having more of whatever is subsidized.

Consider the boom in corporate subsidies that has accompanied the recent decline in government social spending and welfare support. To encourage businesses to relocate or remain in their area, state and local governments have shelled out a conservatively estimated $50 billion a year in the 1990s for business tax breaks, grants, loans, and services, along with plentiful protection from regulation.[79] In a similar global trend, many nations offer generous subsidy packages to cultivate business development that otherwise might not be feasible.[80]

Subsidies to attract business present a classic example of moral hazard. To maintain or increase local jobs, governments protect businesses from some of the risks of providing those local jobs. For example, in 1997 Pennsylvania subsidized a European shipbuilding corporation in hopes of keeping alive an otherwise dying local industry that provided high-paying local shipbuilding jobs.[81] But the more governments "insure" businesses against the costs of job creation, the more costly—and uncertain—job creation becomes for governments. These subsidies encourage businesses to seek greater profit not through improved productivity or innovation, but by moving (or threatening to move) to jurisdictions that offer better protections, generating a cycle of escalating demands for ever-greater government handouts.

This moral hazard from corporate welfare is rarely labeled or condemned as such. Although criticism of government bidding wars is beginning to get more attention in the mainstream media, the dominant political position appears to accept these bad incentives as a price worth paying.[82] For example, a *Time* magazine series on corporate welfare concluded that "it's not much of a debate; the mayors cave" when faced with never-ending demands for corporate subsidies as the price of local jobs.[83] The public costs of collective support for corporate relocation are widely discounted—in contrast to the presumed public costs of collective support for caretaking.

This double standard for moral hazard rests on several problematic normative assumptions that should be examined and challenged more openly. First, the incentive effects of corporate subsidies are often constructed as inherently desirable, ignoring any harmful effects. In the dominant rush to improve the "business climate," the general assumption tends to be that it is *good* if business subsidies produce more business than otherwise possible under existing economic and

legal conditions. In contrast, dominant politics often assumes it is *bad* that welfare or child-care subsidies produce more child care—or children—in families
that are not self-sustaining under existing legal and market arrangements. This
logic values profits and jobs over children and caretaking.

But, of course, the effects of more business or even more jobs are not necessarily beneficial to society. Corporate subsidies that succeed in attracting business may
produce costs to society through lost funding for investments in public infrastructure and social services, environmental damage, higher taxes, higher government
debt costs, decreased productivity, or a decline in political legitimacy. A Minnesota
study, for example, reported that corporate subsidies in that state diverted $100 mil-
lion a year from education funds.[84] In addition, the supposed benefits from increased jobs may be illusory: Jobs may be transferred, or even eliminated, rather
than increased; or anticipated jobs may be low-paying, unsafe, or temporary.

Just as the supposed economic and social benefits of subsidies to attract private
business can be viewed as costly moral hazards, the supposed moral hazards of
caretaking subsidies can be constructed as social and economic benefits—
depending in part on one's values about gender, race, class, and sexuality. Martha
Fineman's work powerfully advances the feminist view that making it easier for
women (or men) to care (and to better care) for children outside patriarchal, economically privileged families is *good* for society.[85] For example, the so-called
moral hazard from caretaking subsidies means more healthy, happy, and productive
parents and children among the large numbers of families that do not fit the traditional stereotype. This supposed moral hazard also means less dependence by caretakers and children on abusive or unloving breadwinners and less dependence of
caretakers and children on unsafe, unhealthy, or unsatisfying jobs. As Deborah
Stone argues, some behavior changes induced by protective subsidies should be
viewed as positive "moral opportunities," instead of as negative "moral hazards."[86]

A second way in which biased norms, not impartial science, create the double
standard for moral hazard is through a selective rejection of economic efficiency
goals. When it comes to social spending or labor regulation, advocates for an improved business climate typically invoke neoclassical economics to stress the
need to substitute tough-minded cost–benefit calculations for soft-hearted sympathy for dependents or their caretakers. The predominant view purports to make
economic efficiency and individual responsibility the overarching principles.
When it comes to fostering support for corporate subsidies, however, pro-
business advocates often argue for the primacy of spiritual ideals and social connection over economic calculations and individual autonomy.

For example, Connecticut legislators recently voted overwhelmingly in favor of
a record $374 million subsidy to encourage relocation of the Patriots football team
to Hartford.[87] Supporters discounted evidence that the net economic benefits for
the state were meager at best. A consultant hired to evaluate the deal defended his
favorable report against criticisms of poor accounting by emphasizing "that many
of the benefits are intangible" and that "the elected officials approved this project

on more than just the numbers. . . . It wasn't just a fiscal benefits driver."[88] Political leaders backing the deal stressed that it "galvanized everyone in the community"[89] and could boost community "confidence,"[90] "vibrancy," and status, benefits that are "hard to measure in dollars."[91]

Similarly, when business leaders lobbied county legislators for a $60 million subsidy for the Buffalo Bills football team, they sidestepped a critic's efforts to investigate the costs and benefits of the deal like a "smart business decision." [92] Instead, advocates presented a report emphasizing that the benefits of the Bills are "not merely economic" but of a "spiritual character," providing a "powerful unifying force" to the community.[93] A gendered double standard underlies the view that state subsidies for football teams do not create a "cycle of dependency" in need of public restraint, but instead exemplify beneficial community interdependence in need of public nurturing.

Third, the special treatment for moral hazard from corporate subsidies is frequently justified on the ground that these costs are inevitable. As one news report concluded, "Unfortunately, the subsidy game won't end anytime soon. That being the case, most communities cannot afford to sit on the sidelines."[94] In fact, corporations seeking subsidies do not portray the subsidies as inefficient market disruptions, but instead as the kind of rational self-interest maximizing that grounds efficient markets. Defending Intel Corporation's invitation to states to bid for subsidies for a new computer-chip plant in 1993, an executive explained, "We're going to build where Intel gets the best deal."[95] Similarly, after admitting the intractability of moral hazard problems from IMF bailouts (which subsidize international investors), IMF Deputy Director Stanley Fischer advised that "we should remind ourselves that moral hazard is something to be lived with and controlled rather than fully eliminated" because there are no better alternatives for dealing with international debt crises.[96]

That is, neoliberal ideology presents corporate moral hazard as a *necessary price* of economic development in a competitive global market, while the caretakers' moral hazard is an *unnecessary subsidy* hindering competitive global economic development. This difference stems from power differences—shaped by legal and political structures—rather than from natural or neutral market forces. Because neoliberal policies tend to increase capital mobility, to restrict local power to regulate business, and to reduce collective sources of support for families, workers, and communities, these policies tend to make states, workers, and families more dependent on corporate and capital interests. Legal and political impediments to alternative routes toward economic development (such as support for local businesses, wage hikes, unionization, public jobs, public support for caretakers, as well as stricter antitrust laws) protect national and multinational corporate investors from seeking support on terms more favorable to taxpayers, workers, or families.

Finally, another bias distorts discussion of supposedly harmful incentives from caretaking subsidies: the failure to recognize that moral hazard runs both ways, because caretaking subsidies run both ways. That is, *reducing* collective support for caretakers will *increase* moral hazard by *increasing* the subsidies provided by caretakers to the rest of society. Martha Fineman insightfully casts caretakers as *subsidizers* as well as the subsidized: The market and the state depend on their unpaid or underpaid labor.[97] Welfare reform policies that require caretakers to assume increased personal responsibility will therefore increase subsidies by caretakers to society in general. These policies make caretakers shoulder more of the costs of the dependent care from which society benefits.

These subsidies by caretakers to others create incentives for costly behavioral changes—a typical moral hazard scenario. For example, replacing "welfare" with "workfare" for single parents in poverty increases subsidies to employers. Workfare requirements (and other welfare limits) increase the supply of low-cost workers, which in turn depresses wages and job security for competing workers. As employers increase their dependence on workfare (and former welfare recipients) to reduce their labor costs, more workers will increasingly need to supplement their wages (and offset increased costs and longer working hours) with unpaid and underpaid caretaking labor, taxpayer assistance, or charity. In a cycle of dependency, employers and shareholders increasingly may seek profit not through the hard work of innovation and other efficient improvements, but through wage reductions and increased labor "flexibility" (along with taxpayer and charitable subsidies) that redistribute and add to the costs of caretaking for workers (and communities).

In another example, welfare reform policies aimed at discouraging the supposed moral hazards of single motherhood and illegitimacy could instead be viewed as *increasing* moral hazard among heterosexual men seeking families. Conservative welfare critics often worry that many men will have difficulty attracting or retaining wives and children if they have to compete with other sources of support available to mothers. George Gilder, for example, asserts that "nothing is so destructive" to men's values, emotional well-being, productivity, and sexual potency than the knowledge that his wife and children may not need him as a financial provider.[98] By adopting policies that skew public support for caretaking to "traditional" families, the state subsidizes some heterosexual men, so that they do not have to make as much effort as they otherwise would to satisfy their wives and children (appropriating conservative welfare critics' logic). These subsidies lead to what could be construed as a cycle of dependency, in which men increasingly seek to retain marriageability or fatherhood through state regulation and state subsidies rather than by taking personal responsibility for their needs.

Finally, on a global scale, neoliberal policies—enforced by the IMF, World Bank, and international economic agreements—often increase moral hazard by shifting the costs of social programs from the state and the market to the family. Martha Fineman describes caretakers' unpaid or underpaid labor as a societal debt used to support market and state institutions.[99] Following her reasoning, collective support for caretakers is an obligation owed in payment for this debt.[100] In this view, neoliberal fiscal austerity policies that reduce social support for care-takers result in a default on debt payments.

This caretaking "debt default" in effect requires caretakers to subsidize inter-national investors. When the IMF's structural adjustment policies pressure na-tions to cut social spending to reduce government deficits, an intended effect is to divert more government resources from social welfare programs to payments to international creditors such as commercial banks. The caretaking debt default that typically results from deficit-reduction policies provides international in-vestors with higher returns for less risk by decreasing trade deficits, decreasing inflation, and supporting currency value.

But these subsidies by caretakers to international financiers create moral haz-ard problems. Policymakers often use neoliberal fiscal austerity programs to bail out lenders whose original loans have failed to achieve expected economic results.[101] If governments alter their fiscal policies to protect international cred-itors against economic difficulties that threaten investment returns or debt re-payment, then international lenders may be less careful in making loans. As a result, we now face the possibility of a cycle of dependency in which interna-tional investors are becoming less self-sufficient, seeking profits through in-creased cost-shifting to unpaid caretakers rather than through prudent investing—arguably contributing to a global race to the bottom that increases overall costs.

International institutions like the World Trade Organization (WTO) were formed to prevent the destructive competition that can result from protectionist national subsidies. In orthodox economic trade theory, competition produces in-centives for nations to subsidize their own industries, even though those subsidies leave most nations and multinational corporations worse off in the end—a classic prisoner's dilemma problem. According to dominant economic theory, therefore, international cooperation and regulation are necessary to ensure "fair competition" and "free" trade.

Taking seriously Fineman's analysis of caretaking labor as a hidden subsidy, perhaps we should reorient the IMF, WTO, and other international institutions so that they work to prevent nations from pursuing economic gain through a destruc-tive competition to increase subsidies from caretakers. That is, social welfare cuts could be viewed as anticompetitive "dumping" or unfair protectionism in violation of free-trade policy. "Antidumping" provisions in international free-trade agree-ments address the problem that government subsidies or protections may allow ex-porters to increase market share and to undermine foreign competitors by selling products at prices below "normal value." Following this reasoning, the unpaid la-bor of caretakers can be viewed as a subsidy to local producers who may then of-fer exports in foreign markets below "normal value"[102]—thereby pressuring com-petitors to similarly seek political and economic environments that shift costs to caretakers. Current economic orthodoxy makes such an argument seem far-fetched, but that shows the importance of feminist attempts to expand discussion about the gendered values implicit in the failure to recognize the social and economic value of dependent care.

DEPENDENCE ON WHOM?

The revival of rhetoric stressing the virtues of independence in fact serves to promote new (or renewed) dependence and control. Welfare reform is one wave in a powerful contemporary movement to make the state (and its citizens), along with most families (and their caretakers), increasingly subordinate to—and dependent on—a market structured in the interests of a wealthy minority.

This movement aims to construct collective support for caretaking as a major threat to society: The welfare state becomes the pejorative "nanny state." For instance, a Cato Institute report used the title "The Advancing Nanny State" to portray child-care subsidies as a great danger to family and market.[103] An editorial in the *Investors' Business Daily* explains that the opposite of the Founders' vision of civil liberty is "a nanny state with growing bureaucracy, swarms of regulations, ever-growing taxes and coercive rules to force citizens to do just what big-government types want."[104]

The "nanny state" slur is revealing for how it represents the nemesis of political and economic autonomy. This term ridicules the usurpation of a traditional class, as well as gender order: It implies that nannies are women and domestic servants, not leaders of a free society. This image suggests that making caretaking central to the state threatens not just to give women authority in state and market, but to give "servants" authority in those spheres. By insinuating that "nanny" should be removed from state to home, welfare state critics evoke an image of a return to a patriarchal estate, where freedom, responsibility, and self-reliance mean that those who work—whether in the market or the family—leave the governing to their masters.

The rise of the neoliberal ideology of "efficiency" appears to have elevated "economics" over politics, "market" over state. While this ideology imagines a strong state as a stereotypical "nanny," infantilizing her charges through excessive control or attachment, it appears to imagine a strong market as a stereotypical "daddy," whose discipline and distance lead to self-reliant growth. But the neoliberal movement to make the supposed free-market master of state and family is fundamentally about redistributing power within the market, state, and family. Free-market ideology turns moral questions of "rights" and "fairness," which should be open to public debate, into questions of "economic efficiency," relegated to technical cost–benefit calculation and removed from democratic control.

Where this economic ideology governs, it is not enough to make caretaking subsidies *fair* or *right*; we must go further to challenge the rules that make fairness costly and so-called efficiency neutral and necessary. By examining the double standard for public support for caretaking versus public support for capital and corporate interests, we can better see how supposed principles of efficiency inextricably depend on moral and political assumptions about the *fair* distribution of resources. The question for debate should not be whether subsidies for caretakers are economically efficient, but *for whom*, and according to *what standard* of economic well-being.

Furthermore, the debate should focus on the institutional arrangements that threaten to make caretaking subsidies such a costly choice for most governments. In the guise of promoting efficiency, neoliberal policies are succeeding in redistributing political and economic power so that corporate and capital subsidies appear to be an economic necessity in a global market. At the same time, these policies are establishing structures that make caretaking subsidies appear to be an unaffordable luxury that most nations must sacrifice in favor of support for capital interests. But law and politics, not neutral economics, determine who must accept tough trade-offs due to limited resources and who can reject such limits as "inefficient" or illegal constraints on "free trade," "property rights," or "competitiveness."

The promise of Martha Fineman's vision of expansive public support for caretaking should not be clouded by the difficulty of getting from here to there. Challenging the supposed economic barriers to caretaking subsidies imposed by the dominant free-market ideology is a crucial step along the way. By opposing the neoliberal ideology that is shifting costs to so many, feminists can open up new possibilities for democracy and fairness that will help transcend differences of family, race, geography, and gender.

NOTES

This chapter originally appeared in *American University Journal of Gender, Social Policy and the Law* 8, no. 115 (2000): 121–49. Copyright © 2000 by *American University Journal of Gender, Social Policy, and the Law*. Reprinted by permission of the publisher, *American University Journal of Gender, Social Policy, and the Law*.

1. Fineman, "Cracking the Foundational Myths: Independence, Autonomy and Self Sufficiency," *American University Journal of Gender, Social Policy, and Law* 8, no. 1 (2000): 13, 22.

2. "What Good Is Government?" *Commentary* 104 (1997): 25, 31.

3. See Martha Fineman, "Foundational Myths," 13–15.

4. Fineman, "Foundational Myths," 18.

5. Fineman, "Foundational Myths," 26–27.

6. George Gilder, "The Coming Welfare Crisis," *Heritage Foundation Policy Review* 11 (1980): 25, 26.

7. Gilder, "The Coming Welfare Crisis," 26–27.

8. Fineman, "Foundational Myths," 23.

9. Fineman, "Foundational Myths," 23.

10. Martha Albertson Fineman, *The Illusion of Equality: The Rhetoric and Reality of Divorce Reform* (Chicago: University of Chicago Press, 1991).

11. See, e.g., Lucinda M. Finley, "Transcending Equality Theory: A Way Out of the Maternity in the Workplace Debate," *Columbia Law Review* 86 (1986): 1118; Christine A. Littleton, "Reconstructing Sexual Equality," *California Law Review* 75 (1987): 1279.

12. See, e.g., Anne L. Alstott, "Tax Policy and Feminism: Competing Goals and Institutional Choices," *Columbia Law Review* 96 (1996): 2001, 2077.

13. See, e.g., Thomas F. Cotter, "Legal Pragmatism and the Law & Economics Movement," *Georgia Law Journal* 84 (1996): 2071, 2112.

14. See, e.g., Gordon Tullock, "The Reality of Redistribution," in *Poverty & Inequality: Economics of Income Redistribution,* ed. Jon Neill (Kalamazoo, Mich.: W. E. Upjohn Institute for Employment Research, 1997), 127–30.

15. See, e.g., Catharine MacKinnon, *Toward a Feminist Theory of the State* (Cambridge, Mass.: Harvard University Press, 1989), 221; Littleton, "Reconstructing Sexual Equality," 251–52; Finley, "Transcending Equality Theory," 1158.

16. See Kathryn Abrams, "The Constitution of Women," *Alabama Law Review* 48 (1997): 861, 870 (using the "mommy track" as an example of the problems with a "differences" approach to equality).

17. See, e.g., "Interview by Mary Tillotson with Suzanne Fields," CNN & Company, Cable News Network (Transcript #479) (December 1, 1994) (arguing against protections from sexual harassment and date rape on the ground that women cannot assert equality and victimization at the same time).

18. See Thomas J. Duesterberg, "Reforming the Welfare State," *Society* 35 (1998): 44.

19. See Pete Wilson and Chuck Poochigan, "California's Gains in Welfare Reform Are Merely a Start," *Fresno Bee,* July 1, 1997, B5(N).

20. See, e.g., Maria O'Brien Hylton, "'Parental' Leaves and Poor Women: Paying the Price for Time Off," *University of Pittsburgh Law Review* 52 (1991): 475, 493.

21. Diane E. Lewis, "Mass Advocates Hail Clinton Family-Leave Plan," *Boston Globe,* May 25, 1999, D2(N).

22. See Sylvia Nasar, "Where Joblessness Is a Way of Making a Living," *New York Times,* May 9, 1999, 5(N).

23. See, e.g., Rebecca Blank, "Does a Larger Social Safety Net Mean Less Economic Flexibility?" in *Working under Different Rules,* ed. Richard B. Freeman (New York: Russell Sage, 1994), 157, 178 (finding that differences among nations in family leave and day-care policies affected family behavior, but that other factors caused higher European unemployment rates in the 1980s and 1990s).

24. Gerald F. Seib and Alan Murrey, "Changed Party: Democrats' Platform Shows How Different They Are from 1972," *Wall Street Journal,* July 15, 1992, A1(N) (speculating that the policy change may be due to increased fund-raising demands).

25. Gerald F. Seib and Alan Murrey, "Changed Party," A1.

26. See Position Paper, "Platform Committee to the 1996 Democratic National Convention," August 28, 1996, available in 1996 Westlaw 490886, at *41.

27. Joel Bleifuss, "Whose Party Is It?" *In These Times,* February 3, 1997, 12 (quoting Al From, in a speech for the Democratic Leadership Council's annual policy forum).

28. See Martha Albertson Fineman, *The Neutered Mother, the Sexual Family and Other Twentieth Century Tragedies* (New York: Routledge, 1995), 189–90; Martha Minow, *Making All the Difference* (Ithaca, N.Y.: Cornell University Press, 1990), 111.

29. See Finley, "Transcending Equality Theory," 1156 (explaining how maternity leave becomes "special" in a pejorative sense "only because it is not something men need").

30. Minow, *Making All the Difference*, 3–4.

31. See MacKinnon, *Feminism Unmodified* (Cambridge, Mass.: Harvard University Press, 1987), 34.

32. MacKinnon, *Feminism Unmodified*, 39.

33. See *United States v. Virginia*, 116 S. Ct. 2264, 2272-73 (1996) (holding that Virginia's policy of excluding women from admission to the Virginia Military Institute was unconstitutional sex discrimination, even though the state established a new women-only institute).

34. Tullock, "The Reality of Redistribution," 129–30.

35. See Jeffrey H. Birnbaum, "Vote, Key Victory for Bush, Increases the Likelihood of Tax-Cut Law in 1989," *Wall Street Journal*, September 29, 1989, available at Westlaw, 1989 WL-WSJ 467839.

36. Birnbaum, "Vote, Key Victory for Bush" (quoting Bush).

37. Birnbaum, "Vote, Key Victory for Bush (quoting House Republican leader and Illinois congressperson Robert Michel).

38. See Doug Henwood, "Sloth and Discipline," *Left Business Observer* 88 (1999): 1, 7 (explaining that money for debt paydown comes disproportionately from low- and middle-income taxpayers and is paid to mainly upper-income bondholders).

39. See Stanley Fischer, "Structural Adjustment Lessons from the 1980s," in *Structural Adjustment: Retrospect and Prospect,* ed. Daniel M. Schydlowsky (Westport, Conn.: Praeger, 1995), 23.

40. See Robert B. Reich, "Is Scrooge a Democrat Now?" *The American Prospect* 11, June 19–July 3, 2000, 96 (criticizing Gore's position).

41. See "Economy: The Clinton Budget: President's Budget Offers Broad Package of Tax Incentives and Spending Increases," *Wall Street Journal*, February 2, 1999, A2(N) (quoting President Clinton).

42. See Robin Hahnel, *Panic Rules: Everything You Need to Know about the Global Economy* (Cambridge, Mass.: South End, 1999), 52.

43. See James H. Weaver, "What Is Structural Adjustment?" in *Structural Adjustment: Retrospect and Prospect,* ed. Daniel M. Schydlowsky (Westport, Conn.: Praeger, 1995), 23.

44. See Mariarosa Dalla Costa, "Introduction," in *Paying the Price: Women and the Politics of International Economic Strategy*, ed. Mariarosa Dalla Costa and Giovanna F. Dalla Costa (Atlantic Highlands, N.J.: Zed Books, 1995), 7–8.

45. See Janine Brodie, "Shifting the Boundaries: Gender and the Politics of Restructuring," in *The Strategic Silence: Gender and Economic Policy,* ed. Isabella Bakker (Atlantic Highlands, N.J.: Zed Books, 1994), 46, 50.

46. See Moshin Khan, "The Macroeconomic Effects of Fund Supported Adjustment Programs," *IMF Staff Papers* 37 (1990): 196, 222 (stating that "it is often found that [structural adjustment] programs are associated with a rise in inflation and a fall in the growth rate"). A 1997 internal IMF review reported lower economic growth during the period of 1991–95 for countries participating in its Enhanced Structural Adjustment Facility, designed to foster "sustainable economic growth," than in nonparticipating developing countries. IMF, "The ESAF at Ten Years: Economic Adjustment and Reform in Low-Income Countries" (IMF Occasional Paper, no. 156, December 1997).

47. Robin Hahnel, "Capitalist Globalism in Crisis: Part IV: What to Want and What to Fear from Globalization," *Z Magazine* 12 (March 1999): 52, 53 (citing figures from Angus

Maddison, *Monitoring the World Economy 1820–1992*, Appendix D, 193–206 (Paris: Development Centre of the Organisation for Economic Co-Operation and Development, 1995).

48. See Edward N. Wolff, *Top Heavy* (New York: Twentieth Century Fund, 1995), 12–13.

49. Wolff, *Top Heavy,* 12–13.

50. See Paul A. Gigot, "Potomac Watch: Clintonomics: Tastes Great, Less Filling," *Wall Street Journal,* June 7, 1996, A12(N) (quoting Larry Lindsey, Federal Reserve governor).

51. Gigot, "Potomac Watch," A12(N) (reporting data from White House statistics).

52. Gigot, "Potomac Watch," A12(N) (quoting Martin Felstein).

53. See Doug Henwood, "Playing the Numbers: Proposal to Adjust Consumer Price Index," *The Nation,* March 29, 1991, 4 (citing inflation adjusted figures).

54. In 1998, hourly wages for average workers were 6.2 percent below 1973 levels (adjusting for inflation); weekly wages were 12 percent below 1973 levels. Chuck Collins, Betsy Leondar-Wright, and Holly Sklar, *Shifting Fortunes* 27 (Boston: United for a Fair Economy, 1999). In contrast, non–farm business productivity rose almost 33 percent from 1973 to the late 1990s. Id. See also Lawrence Mishel, Jared Bernstein, and John Schmitt, *The State of Working America, 1998–99* (Ithaca, N.Y.: Cornell University Press, 1999), 119–218 (presenting data on changes in wage levels and structures over the last several decades).

55. Juliet Schor, "Worktime in Contemporary Context: Amending the Fair Labor Standards Act," *Chicago-Kent Law Review* 70 (1994): 157, 158.

56. Mishel et al., *The State of Working America,* 122.

57. Mishel et al., *The State of Working America,* 17–18.

58. Doug Henwood, "Work Detail" (graphic), *Left Business Observer* 86, November 18, 1998, 1(N).

59. See "Champion of Working Moms: Pediatrician T. Berry Brazelton Sees a Hardening of Attitudes against the Needs of Parents," *Los Angeles Times,* November 6, 1995, D2(3)(N) (interviewing a child-development expert who explained that recent trends of downsizing and layoffs make it harder for parents, especially women, to get employers to accommodate family needs).

60. Mark Weisbrot, "Globalization for Whom," *Cornell International Law Journal* 31 (1999): 631, 635–36 (quoting the *Hearing Before the Comm. on Banking, Housing and Urban Affairs,* 105th Congress 36 [1997] [statement of Alan Greenspan, chairman, Board of Governors of the Federal Reserve System]).

61. See Phineas Baxandall and Marc Breslow, "Does Inequality Cause Overwork?" in *Real World Macro,* 16th ed., ed. Marc Breslow, Ellen Frank, John Miller, Abby Scher, and the Dollars & Sense Collective (Cambridge, Mass.: Dollars & Sense, 1999), 25.

62. See Nicole Wendt, "50th Anniversary of the World Bank and the IMF Prompts Criticism," *International Finance and Development Book,* ed. Enrique Carrasco, at www.uiowa.edu/ifdebook/ebook/contents/part2-II.shtml, part B(5) at 6.

63. Michel Chossudovsky, *The Globalisation of Poverty* (Atlantic Highlands, N.J.: Zed Books, 1991), 191.

64. Chossudovsky, *The Globalisation of Poverty,* 227.

65. See Chossudovsky, *The Globalisation of Poverty,* 101–258 (describing case studies of social impact of neoliberal policy in Somalia, Rwanda, India, Bangladesh, Vietnam, Brazil, Peru, Bolivia, Russia, and the former Yugoslavia).

66. Michael Holman and Quentin Peel, "Too Much to Bear," *Financial Times* (London), June 12, 1999, 12(N).

67. Chossudovsky, *The Globalisation of Poverty,* 72 (reporting a resurgence of formerly controlled communicable diseases in sub-Saharan Africa, Latin America, and India, arguably caused or exacerbated by declines in urban sanitation and other forms of public health spending as a result of structural adjustment programs).

68. Chossudovsky, *The Globalisation of Poverty,* 192, 203, table 10.4 (describing policies leading to increased malnutrition in Peru from 1975 to 1985); id., at 129 (describing how IMF policies increased famine in India).

69. Chossudovsky, *The Globalisation of Poverty,* 26 (concluding that "[i]n both the South and the East, the compression of living standards since the early 1980s has been considerably greater than that experienced by the rich countries during the 1930s").

70. For example, Russia's life expectancy for men declined from 65.6 to 57 in five years. Robin Hahnel, "Capitalist Globalism in Crisis: Boom and Bust," *Z Magazine* 11 (December 1998): 46, 48.

71. See Jacob Schlesinger, "The Clinton Budget: Keynes Mutiny: Why Is the Economist Passe, with So Much of the World in Recession?" *Wall Street Journal,* February 2, 1999, 1(N) (explaining that Greenspan makes it clear that he would "punish higher deficits with higher rates—a major factor in keeping the Clinton administration's spending desires in check").

72. David E. Sanger, "Markets Are Freer Than Politicians," *New York Times,* February 21, 1999, 5(N).

73. Chossudovsky, *The Globalisation of Poverty,* 18.

74. See Marc Breslow, "Is the U.S. Making Progress?" in *Real World Macro* 6 (criticizing current standards for calculating GDP).

75. See Marjorie W. Williams, "Gender, Productivity and Macro-Economic Policies in the Context of Structural Adjustment and Change," in *The Strategic Silence: Gender and Economic Policy,* 81–82 (discussing how gender-biased measurements of macroeconomic growth give misleading support for diverting government subsidies from social spending that benefits women to subsidies for corporations); Kathleen Cloud and Nancy Garrett, "Counting Women's Work," *Real World Macro,* 12–13 (discussing alternative calculations of economic growth that recognize women's unpaid household labor).

76. See Robert Rector and William Lauber, "America's Failed $5.4 Trillion War on Poverty," Executive Summary, *Heritage Foundation Reports* 3 (1995).

77. Rector and Lauber, "America's Failed $5.4 Trillion War on Poverty," 3.

78. "Day Care Crazy," *Investors' Business Daily,* December 19, 1997, editorial, A26(N).

79. See Neil DeMause, "Corporations Jump from Town to Town in Search of the Best Public Subsidy," *In These Times,* May 31, 1998, 11, 12(N). This is more than annual expenditures for welfare and food stamps—and does not include even greater federal spending on corporate subsidies.

80. See William Greider, *One World, Ready or Not: The Manic Logic of Global Capitalism* (New York: Simon & Schuster, 1997), 82.

81. See Donald L. Barlett and James B. Steele, "States at War," *Time,* November 9, 1998, 44.

82. See also infra text accompanying notes 151–155 (describing the perception that corporate subsidies are now a normal part of doing business).

83. See Donald L. Barlett and James B. Steele, "Five Ways Out," *Time,* November 30, 1998, 66.

84. DeMause, "Corporations Jump from Town to Town," 12.

85. See Fineman, *Neutered Mother*, 125.

86. Deborah Stone, "Beyond Moral Hazard: Insurance as Moral Opportunity," *Connecticut Insurance Law Journal* 6 (2000): 11.

87. See Tom Puleo and Christopher Keating, "State: We'll Take It by Overwhelming Margin, Legislature Approves Patriots Package; Excitement of Deal Overtakes Doubters," *Hartford Courant,* December 16, 1998, A1(N) (reporting cost estimate from the legislature's Office of Fiscal Analysis).

88. See Glenn Cheney, "KPMG Called Offsides on New England Patriots Study," *Accounting Today,* February 22–March 14, 1999, 5, 37 (quoting Ronald D. Burton, of consulting firm KPMG Peat Marwick).

89. "All Things Considered: Controversy over the Deal the State of Connecticut Has Proposed to Bring the New England Patriots to Hartford" (NPR radio broadcast, December 4, 1998) [hereinafter "Controversy"] (quoting Connecticut Speaker of the House Tom Ritter).

90. Paul Frisman, "Patriot Games," *Connecticut Law Tribune,* March 15, 1999 (quoting supporter and real estate attorney Michael J. Cacace).

91. See "Controversy" (quoting Kevin Sullivan, Democratic president of the State Senate, who promoted the benefits of "activity and vibrancy").

92. See Margaret Hammersley, "Report Calls Bills an Intrinsic Part of Life" in *WNY, Buffalo News,* June 6, 1997, 1C (reporting that legislator Albert DeBenedetti, D-Buffalo, put himself at odds with Democratic leadership by emphasizing the need to consider possible costs of the subsidy).

93. See Hammersley, "Report Calls Bills an Intrinsic Part of Life" (quoting the report of a business task force of the Greater Buffalo Partnership, presented to the Erie County Legislature).

94. Tony Cox, "Only the Real Stars Should Get Business Subsidies," *Arkansas Democrat-Gazette,* August 23, 1998, BM5 (NW edition)(N).

95. See Donald L. Barlett and James B. Steele, "States at War," 48 (noting that the company received over a third of a billion dollars in aid from the highest bidder, Sandoval County, New Mexico).

96. Stanley Fischer, "On the Need for an International Lender of Last Resort," www.imf.org/external/np/speeches/1999/010399.HTM (June 9, 1999).

97. Fineman, *Cracking the Foundational Myths,* 17.

98. See Gilder, "The Coming Welfare Crisis," 26.

99. Fineman, *Cracking the Foundational Myths,* 21.

100. See Fineman, *Cracking the Foundational Myths,* 19.

101. Wendt, "50th Anniversary of the World Bank and the IMF Prompts Criticism," Part Two, II (B)(5) (discussing critics' claims that, through IMF and World Bank mandates for reduced social spending, the poor bear the burdens resulting from failed commercial bank loans meant to improve the economy).

102. See Bernard Hoekman and Michel Kostecki, *The Political Economy of the World Trading System: From GATT to WTO* (New York: Oxford University Press, 1995), 173.

103. See Suzanne Fields, "Viewpoint: Beware PM Day Care," *The Commercial Appeal,* November 2, 1997, B6 (favorably discussing the Cato report).

104. Editorial, "What the Founders Can Teach Us," *Investors Business Daily,* July 2, 1998, A28(N).

6

Dependency Work, Women, and the Global Economy

Ofelia Schutte

For women concerned with equality, the unequal division of labor between women and men has been a source of long-standing concern. While there are many ramifications of this problem—including the access to and retention of women in male-dominated professions, the issue of equal pay for equal work, and the equal access to all levels of education and professional training for women and men—perhaps the most recalcitrant form of division of labor is that pertaining to what scholars have called "dependency work." As defined by Eva Kittay, dependency work is "the work of caring for those who are inevitably dependent."[1] Although dependency work may be paid or unpaid, when done without pay the dependency worker's charge is usually a member of that person's family to whom a familial obligation is felt (an elderly parent, a child, a seriously disabled family member). "As long as an individual is responsible for the care of another who is dependent on her, I call that person a dependency worker," states Kittay.[2] This terminology highlights the fact that dependency work is work, regardless of whether it is also motivated by love, duty, feelings of responsibility or gratitude, or any other emotional or moral attitude binding the relationship between the worker and her charge.

In this chapter, I focus on unpaid dependency work and the larger genus to which unpaid dependency work belongs, namely, unpaid care work. Unpaid care work involves caring for others even if they are not, strictly speaking, dependents; for example, preparing meals for healthy adult members of the household. I look at unpaid dependency work and care work in the context of familiar (United States) and unfamiliar (developing world) locations. Because of the statistical nature of some of the data collected on a global scale regarding unpaid care work, I use gender as the principal category of analysis. My analysis nevertheless presupposes that race, ethnicity, class, and other factors constitute important variables relevant to a discussion of women's work. For this reason, I include a critique of neoliberal economic policies and their impact, especially on women's lives in developing countries.[3]

The concept of neoliberalism is not often explicitly referred to in U.S. politics, although it is a familiar concept in Latin America and elsewhere around the world. According to the French theorist Pierre Bourdieu, neoliberalism may be described as a "utopia" of capitalist market forces. Bourdieu calls it a utopia whose politics are "aimed at *putting into question all collective structures* capable of obstructing the logic of the pure market."[4] He notes that this utopia "generates a potent belief," a faith in "free trade" not subject to disconfirmation in reality.[5] Critics of neoliberalism claim that its logic of economic gain fails to take into account the long-term affects and social costs of short-term profit making. For example, Bourdieu calls attention to the hard-won workers' rights protected by the state, whose weakening and elimination are goals of neoliberal policy.[6] Neoliberalism's philosophical roots go back to classic liberalism, which views the state as operating in the interest of trade.[7] This classic concept of liberalism contrasts sharply with the liberalism embraced by many liberals in the United States today. The latter tend to endorse a second concept of liberalism, which looks at the state as a protector of citizens' rights in social matters such as health, education, and employment rights.[8] In other words, by shifting priorities from the domain of collective rights and entitlements to that of free trade, neoliberalism is aimed at dismantling the social gains resulting from the second understanding of liberalism, one of whose historical by-products was the so-called welfare state. In the course of this chapter, I address what is at stake for women in developing countries given the global implementation of neoliberal policies.

Although I take economic issues and their political consequences as a major focus, the point of departure for my critique is ethical and existential. I am concerned with how different economic circumstances affect the life choices available to women who are existentially "thrown" into dependency work and unpaid care work situations. What type of society and social programs would help these women control their dependency work situation rather than be controlled by it? How does the neoliberal program aimed at satisfying the wealth-accruing dreams of abstract man affect the ordinary lives of concrete women? How is the distribution of chores and caregiving activities affected by the neoliberal utopia? What is the relationship, if any, between the distribution of caregiving and the distribution of wealth? Because of a personal family situation dealing with my mother's illness, I have had to face situations in which the life projects of one person may be interrupted (or even destroyed) by the needs of another. This has led me to reflect on principles of fairness and equity in the domestic and public sectors that can be used to prevent women's lives from being limited unreasonably by unavoidable caregiving activities.

I argue that the West holds conflicting values when it promotes ideals of personal independence for women at the same time that it supports neoliberal policies of structural adjustment that require the trimming down of social services (including child care), education, and health benefits to the world's population. Beginning with a look at dependency work in the context of domestic gender relations and the invisibility of women's unpaid care work, I examine feminist criticisms of economic models that leave out the contributions of unpaid care workers. This critique is followed by a contextual analysis of unpaid care workers and dependency work in the light of increasing inequalities resulting from the neoliberal economic policies ruling contemporary globalization processes throughout the world. From a materialist economic standpoint, it is not factually possible to cut back programs that assist women in their caregiving tasks while at the same time claiming to grant more freedom to these same women. Unless other factors were to intervene—such as the elimination of poverty or the shifting of caregiving duties to men—the cancellation of programs that assist women caregivers contradicts the goal of female independence from patriarchal constraints.

Since most of the world's women are burdened with the special tasks of dependency care and unpaid care work, the mandated budget cuts in social services, health, and education necessarily lead to the transfer of additional chores to the household. Under neoliberal cutbacks women are more hard-pressed than usual to provide services to their families such as adequately feeding the members of the household and caring for the sick, young, and elderly. Unpaid care work and dependency work are largely differentiated by gender both in this country and abroad. This means that women spend much energy and time servicing others' needs. As a result, a woman may experience a drastic reduction of the time available to pursue her own education, paid work initiatives, health-care management, leisure, and other objectives.

Before assessing how the large (macro) economic theories and policies affect women, it is necessary to identify unpaid care work as productive work and to determine what proportions of time women and men spend, respectively, in unpaid work in the home. Unless this work, which is largely performed by women, is identified and measured, it is not possible to calculate its impact on the economy or on the way unpaid care workers are affected by various economic policies. Feminist economists interested in the proportion of time women and men spend on care arrangements have classified unpaid dependency work (as understood by Kittay) under the category of "unpaid care work." The United Nations Development Fund for Women (UNIFEM) has recently published its first biennial report assessing women's economic and political progress since the mid-1980s. This report offers the following definition of "unpaid care work":

> The word "unpaid" differentiates this care from paid care provided by employees in the public and NGO sectors and employees and self-employed persons in the private sector. The word "care" indicates that the services provided nurture other people. The word "work" indicates that these activities are costly in time and energy and are undertaken as obligations (contractual or social).[9]

UNIFEM's report cautions that the term *care* used in its terminology may be misleading insofar as care may be extracted unwillingly from the care worker and that, given the vulnerability of the charge, there is no guarantee that the charge will not be abused in this work. Nevertheless, the category "unpaid care work" is used to signal the fact that "interpersonal attention" to someone's needs is at stake and that such attention ought to be seen as an important part of the fabric of a well-functioning society.[10]

Because of its social and human importance, unpaid care work should not be taken for granted. Nevertheless, it seems that precisely because society cannot get along without it and because enough people (primarily women) end up doing it as an inescapable task, insufficient attention is given to the burden this type of work can have on the overall quality of women's lives. The reason unpaid dependency work and other unpaid care work can be such a burdensome task for women is that, as mentioned earlier, the amount of time this type of work requires can severely limit the kind and scope of other activities a woman may perform in her adult life. In addition, unpaid dependency work limits a woman's mobility insofar as the charge's movements are limited to a specific area and the care worker must oversee her charge. If the charge is confined to bed, for example, the dependency worker may be restricted to spaces within listening distance from the bed (so as to be able to hear the charge's call) or to spaces close enough to the bedside to monitor her charge periodically.

If the dependency worker lacks control over the use of her time and if she is restricted in space to the general area or the specific location where the caregiving responsibilities take place, a significant disruption of her normal development as an individual occurs. It is estimated that women in developing countries with an average of three children must stay out of the labor force for a minimum of three to four years and as many as ten to twelve years if they cannot afford or find satisfactory child care.[11] Restrictions of time and space and absence from the workforce (if she wanted or needed a job) are not the sole constraints affecting the dependency worker. Her sleep may be interrupted throughout the night because she must tend to her charge, and she may be more subject to depression and other psychological disorders on account of the stress produced by her inescapable task. Conversely, she may develop a stoic attitude toward life in order to protect herself from her feelings of frustration over the many other opportunities she is missing. Another form of defense against the frustration of inescapable care work is becoming moralistic and losing the capacity to empathize strongly with others, except to endorse the self-sacrifice of other women toward similar ends. Economically, dependency work tends to be a costly task for women who depend on a working wage, given the fact that the time spent on unpaid care work will disenfranchise them from the income they could have secured had they been free to engage in paid employment. One study in the United States found that people caring for elderly relatives "on average lost more than half a million dollars in lost wages, social security and pension benefits over their lifetimes."[12]

Another study showed that elderly caregivers who felt stressed caring for their disabled spouses had over a 60 percent higher risk of dying than others of the same age who either were not caring for a disabled spouse or did not experience a stressful caring situation.[13]

Clearly, dependency work is an emotionally and economically costly activity for those who engage in it, regardless of any feeling of satisfaction they may derive from caring for the dependent or from "doing the right thing" (as perceived by self and others). Available data from various countries, in both the developed and developing parts of the world, show that in the 1990s the proportions of time spent by women and men at home on unpaid care work (a category larger than, but closely related to, dependency work) were roughly 70 percent for women and 30 percent for men.[14] The greater the percentage of time spent on unpaid care work, the greater the economic disadvantage for the dependency worker in today's market economy. Even outside employment does not prevent women, as much as it does men, from devoting extra hours to unpaid care work. A 1995 study in Mexico, for example, found that 90.5 percent of women who were "economically active" outside the home, as compared with 62.4 percent of men, also engaged in unpaid care work in the home.[15] In one study in Nicaragua from the early 1990s, men spent only eight hours per week while women spent forty hours per week on unpaid care work in the home. But this sample of women was already spending thirty-seven hours per week on paid work outside the home, whereas the men were doing paid work for forty-seven hours each week. Adding these figures shows that the women in the study spent a total of seventy-seven hours per week on both activities combined, while men's combined total was fifty-five hours per week.[16] They worked more than twenty hours per week more than the men. This suggests that women's tasks were undervalorized since the discrepancy in the distribution of work according to gender seems highly inequitable. The extra burden on women's time came from doing the bulk of the unpaid domestic work. Depending on country or region or cultural origin, this work is considered primarily or exclusively "women's work."

IDENTIFYING AND MEASURING UNPAID CARE WORK

In order to situate the question of the impact of unpaid dependency work in the context of global and transnational discussions of women in the global economy, I need to shift the analysis from "unpaid dependency work" to the larger category of "unpaid care work." Feminist economists monitoring the impact of globalization processes on women are using the latter category; this facilitates the collection of systematic data. Sometimes I use the terms *unpaid dependency work* and *unpaid care work* interchangeably, however, on the assumption that the care work being referred to is dependency work and as a reminder that our point of entry into this discussion was motivated by my interest in the ethics of unpaid dependency work.

I address two features of the larger problem of unpaid care work. First is the question of whether and how such work is measured in the standard economic theories that guide the planning of globalization processes today. In addition, I discuss how cultural differences affect the recognition of unpaid care work and related strategies used to demand fairness for women caregivers. Second is the nature of the neoliberal globalization processes and goals that affect the status of women involved in unpaid care work. Efforts to improve the status of women in their respective countries are correlated—among other factors such as girls' and women's access to good education and health services—with improved conditions for care work, both paid and unpaid.

There are at least two considerations affecting the measurement of women's unpaid care work. For the work to be measured, it has to be visible. It needs to be identifiable by a particular category or name. So much of women's unpaid care work has been "invisible," both to society and to those compiling economic data, that simply identifying it and beginning to count it on a worldwide basis represents a not insignificant achievement. Feminist economists are at the forefront of this endeavor.[17] Addressing the omission of gender analysis in both macroeconomic and microeconomic theories, feminist economists demonstrate the need to consider gender differences in consumption and production as well as the impact on women of abstract theoretical categories that fail to recognize or address gender difference. For example, Lorraine Corner points out that if microeconomic theory works with the category of the individual units of goods and services that are produced or consumed in the market domain, it will not measure the things women produce and consume in the household outside of the market.[18] According to these methodological assumptions, the things women produce and consume in the household are not thought to pertain to the domain of economic theory.

Corner identifies such "boundary blinkers" in theory as "a failure to correctly specify the 'base population' for the measurement of economic activity."[19] She notes that the economic activity of women is discounted or undercounted. Moreover, if, for example, women are spending their time and energy in the household making sure their children are healthy, this work is invisible because it is not part of the marketed system of health care. The transfer of value from the household to the market domain is not acknowledged because economic theory is only looking at what gets produced in the market or "monetized" domain.[20] The invisibility of women's unpaid care work is thus discounted twice. First, the activity is not considered productive in and of itself. Second, if public services in health and education are cut, for example, and these activities by default are forced to revert back to the home, the activities' cost to women who would otherwise be free to do something else with their time is not counted. Thus, what may appear to be a savings regarding public expenses at no cost to anyone fails to show the extra costs these activities represent to women, who are not compensated for this work.[21] In short, "economics presents an inaccurate and incomplete picture of the micro-level consequences of macro-level policies" because its methodology does

not acknowledge the domestic activities outside the market or the "transfers over
time between the household and the market."[22] This methodological definition of
what constitutes the field's appropriate domain, she claims, results in a significant
gender bias because as it happens women are doing the larger proportion of unpaid work in the home.[23]

CULTURAL DIFFERENCES IN RECOGNIZING UNPAID CARE WORK

So far, following the suggestions of feminist economists, I have defined unpaid care work, and I have also referred to data reporting that women do a
larger proportion of this work not only in the United States but throughout the
world. There are significant differences, however, in the ways women in different locations undertake and analyze the meaning of unpaid care work. Economic conditions and cultural traditions and habits are some of the principal
differentiators of women within and across countries. Poor women and women
in low-income households, both in developed and developing countries, tend
to be affected negatively by current economic policies in global capitalism
with respect to unpaid care work. But, as some scholars have shown, the types
of justification women have offered on behalf of a more equitable plan for taking care of dependents is not uniform throughout all cultures. Western feminists have appealed largely to the principle of equality to protest the unequal
division of labor by sex in unpaid care work. Compensation for unpaid care
work is sought on the basis of the inequality this extra burden places on
women (particularly poor women).[24] In contrast, Caribbean women have appealed largely to the importance of work done in family nurturance and maintenance and in caring for the sick and disabled. Compensation has been sought
on the basis of the value of the work performed and the absence of anyone else
to perform it.[25]

In recent years, a third approach (capable of including the other two perspectives) highlights the asymmetrical proportions of time spent on unpaid care
activities according to gender in a context in which control over how an individual spends her time is a basic indicator of the quality of life for that person.[26]
It is then argued that global development policies ought to be raising the quality of people's lives (including women's lives), not undermining it. This last approach is promising in terms of its potential for raising everyone's consciousness on feminist and economic justice issues, since assessing the proportions of
time allocation a person spends in different activities is a universal factor applicable to everyone's lived experience. This information is useful to individuals, families, employers, agencies, policymakers, health professionals, educa-
tors, the state, and economic planners. It is an important question for any
society to know who is performing the unpaid work of socializing children and
caring for dependents in the home, what is the economic value and cost of this

work, and what principles of fairness ought to govern the practices of these socially necessary and humanly significant activities.

Implicit in the reevaluation of unpaid care work and dependency work is the extent to which women can set the unpaid care work aside and enter the paid labor force. When this happens, different cultural justifications may be observed of women's move from the home to the paid labor domain. Anthropologist Helen Safa, a specialist in Caribbean studies, notes that in the developed world when women entered the labor force, the rationality of treating women as individuals comparable to men in the workplace overtook the prior ideology of protecting women's traditional functions in the domain of the home.[27] In contrast, Safa claims that in Latin America and the Caribbean "gender differences continue to be emphasized over individual rights, with women seen primarily as housewives and mothers and men primarily as breadwinners."[28] Given the economic policies established in the 1980s, there have been cuts in social services in both regions, shifting the weight of the costs in question to individual families. Safa argues that the way these cuts have been assumed in Latin America and the Caribbean as they impact women and families, however, is different from their impact in the United States. She observes that in the United States, the social services were more developed than in the Caribbean.[29] As the reductions in services affected families, more women entered the workforce. However, with the diminishing opportunities for good jobs, women and men have faced unemployment or temporary low-wage employment. Safa points out that in these conditions, the justification in the United States for including more women in the workforce as well as for assisting unemployed women and female heads of household continues to be the principle of equality and equal opportunities.[30] The situation Safa describes regarding the emphasis on equal opportunity and individualism in the United States as compared with Latin American and Caribbean countries reveals the strong influence of liberal feminism in this country.

In contrast, Safa notes that in the Caribbean region, the "redistributive state" was weak prior to the structural adjustment policies that required the cutbacks in social services. Some workers' benefits had been gained, as elsewhere in the world, on the assumption that men are the heads of families. These gains included "social security, public education and health, and minimum wage laws."[31] Many Caribbean countries were hit hard as a result of structural adjustment policies and related cuts and services since the mid-1980s, a situation that affected not only the household political economy Safa has studied but the entire cultural domain.[32] As the family income and buying power diminished, women tried to enter the workforce in larger numbers. Safa points out that when Caribbean women organized to obtain basic needs from the society and the state, their demands were phrased in terms of the support needed for child care and other domestic needs, not "in terms of gender equality."[33] She interprets the former emphasis as a continued affirmation of women's family-oriented gender identities, particularly as mothers. Thus the persistence of the distinction between the domain of the home and that of the public, in Safa's analysis, is supported in large part by the action of women themselves.[34]

Safa is calling attention to the fact that in Latin America and the Caribbean, women's collective demands on behalf of the survival needs of the household and family have been overwhelmingly dominant over demands for gender equality in the workplace. In part I think this may be explained as a result of the enormous survival crisis affecting the poor and low-income population of this vast region. Not all demands for justice are equal in times of crisis. In the critical circumstances Latin American and Caribbean women have faced, it is understandable that they have demanded justice for caregiving needs from the state as an expression of their culturally accepted, gender-normative voices. This makes sense if the culture does not reward any other strong standpoints from which women may speak and be heard as a powerful social force. It can be argued that, politically speaking, a conservative public and government are more likely to accede to women's demands if the demand is phrased as an extension of the maternal function. But as a feminist who is a native Latin American, I believe feminists must consider and propose alternatives to the use of this discourse. Although this discourse understandably is built out of a reference to women's nourishing maternal experiences, it may lock women into a predominantly (one could essay, essentialist) maternal role, to which are assigned the inescapable responsibilities of care work. When this happens, the culture's gender standards may enable women—or, more likely, some of the women in the total female population—to seek individual solutions for care work if they are unable to take on such responsibilities. But the culture, the state, and society are not likely to deliver collective solutions applicable to all women. It is the failure of collective options for the relief of women's unpaid care work that motivates my inquiry.[35] Without the notion of the right to a balanced individual development for every person, whether male or female, it is not easy to free women as a collective group from the cultural burden of having to be ultimately accountable for the care work.[36]

Another view of the situation of women as unpaid care and dependency workers in developing countries is offered by Akwilina Kayumba, a physician in Dar Es Salaam, Tanzania.[37] At a recent conference on development ethics in that city, Dr. Kayumba argued that the AIDS epidemic in sub-Saharan Africa and in Tanzania creates special burdens for women, who are identified by tradition and culture as the primary caregivers for diseased and dying family members.[38] Lack of resources for clinics and state-supported infrastructure means that sick persons will require everyday care at home until death takes place. As long as someone is ill in the family, the woman's caregiving duties do not end. (Here we need to consider the additional factor that in the case of HIV/AIDS more than one family member and the caregiver herself may become infected.) Against the traditional gender division of caregiving according to gender, Kayumba holds a gender-inclusive view of care. She calls attention to the fact that a man as well as a woman can do the work required in caring for dependents, including the sick and the dying.

Kayumba suggests that one of the reasons women are specifically designated as caregivers (apart from views that assign this role to them as their natural destiny) is that given the disparity in men's and women's earned income, a man, having the higher income, is pressured not to give up his job. If one of the couple must stay at home, the task falls on the one with the lower income-earning capacity (usually the woman). But the force of tradition is such that even if the man were unemployed the task often falls on the woman. How can Tanzanian girls and women escape from these inevitable chores and become both contributing family members and productive members of their society in highly needed professional fields? Kayumba notes that education is essential but also public awareness of the importance of women's contributions in both the domestic and public spheres. She argues that women need "flexibility" in their domestic schedules so they can offer their best both to their families and to society (through professional training, community leadership, and paid employment). If men support the concept of the need for flexibility in their partners' schedules and are willing to commit some of their time to dependency work, Kayumba argues, families will emerge stronger for it.

Kayumba's position with regard to the redistribution of unpaid care work in the home is in keeping with the ideas promoted by feminists engaged in international development work. From her standpoint regarding the need to reshape gender roles in the family, globalization processes may be perceived as contributing to women's educational and economic opportunities. This is indeed the line taken by the human rights–oriented wing of the United Nations development programs, for whom women's rights are central to human rights. But I should note that this is still very much an ideal, not an accomplished fact.[39] In reality, the neoliberal policy directing globalization processes is focused on economic profit, not on human rights or women's rights. Of course, human rights may come into play if they are seen as positively instrumental to business growth.

Kayumba is right on target regarding the need to have a much more flexible view of the genders with respect to caregiving work and women's contributions to science, culture, and community. This is, indeed, the valuable focus of her contribution. Our feminist analysis must proceed further, however. For what happens, for example, if men do not voluntarily take on caregiving activities? It is reasonable to assume that social programs and opportunities would need to be made available to women so that they can move on with their lives and not be burdened by a totality of caregiving tasks. Again, the question of the collective as distinguished from the individual solutions for women caregivers needs to be asked. From this larger perspective it seems that hopes for improvement in the quality of women's lives are best supported under conditions in which the state public health sector and other social services (under scrutiny to avoid corruption) are funded adequately so that the domestic sector is not impacted adversely by health-related dependency work.

THE ECONOMIC REALITIES OF
ADJUSTMENT AND GLOBALIZATION

The human concerns for equity in unpaid care work that we have discussed so far run into one major structural obstacle for their implementation. This obstacle is the neoliberal economic policy accepted by countries as a condition of international trade. To understand the difficulties in which women, particularly poor women, are trapped today, it is necessary to mention the structure and operating goals of the neoliberal state and its economic expansion through accelerated globalization processes. The conditions of trade are so strictly defined by international agreements that they can undermine the politics of representation and the principle of popular sovereignty, which form the basis of modern democracy. As mentioned earlier, neoliberalism is presumably blind to gender issues. The question is, once the gender issues are identified and their relevance can no longer be ignored, *can neoliberalism be induced to change its direction and admit the concerns of social justice?*

According to Gayatri Spivak, neoliberalism is a "world economic system that, in the name of Development, and now, 'sustainable development,' removes all barriers between itself and fragile national economies, so that any possibility of social redistribution is severely damaged."[40] In what follows I use feminist analyses of neoliberalism, with the understanding that I am using this material to criticize neoliberal policy beyond the extent of criticism found in some of the sources quoted (in particular, Corner and UNIFEM). There are degrees of feminist criticisms of neoliberalism, with Spivak's position on one radical end and the position of reform-oriented scholars on the other. My objective here is to explain how this system works particularly as it affects women in developing countries. The implementation of this system has exacerbated the conditions of unpaid care work.

As applied to developing countries, the two major components of macroeconomic theory guiding neoliberalism are stabilization and structural adjustment policy.[41] "Both stabilization and structural adjustment have emphasized a reduced role for government and increasing reliance on market forces for resource allocation. Specific measures include privatisation of government agencies and instrumentalities, contracting out publicly-provided services to the private sector, and deregulation of markets."[42] International agencies, principally the International Monetary Fund (IMF) and the World Bank, have been key players in the pressure to get developing nations to comply with these economic policies. As Corner points out, "an IMF stabilization program has usually been a prerequisite for a World Bank Structural Adjustment Loan."[43] For example, in Latin America, the large foreign debts most countries were facing in the 1980s meant that with high interest rates servicing the debts, the burden of paying the interest on the debt led to a crisis situation in the national economies. The only feasible way out for most countries (since no other alternative was available under a capitalist system) was to institute the IMF- and World Bank–mandated stabilization and structural adjustment policies.

The creditors from the North chose this route as the major prerequisite for allowing future credit to indebted developing countries.[44] One of the most peculiar aspects of neoliberalism is its aggressive stance against anything it associates with a socialist idea of the redistribution of wealth and resources. In the United States, neoliberalism (though not necessarily under this name) also militates against "liberal" programs of social entitlement such as welfare and state-controlled social security. Neoliberalism is fiercely anticommunist and anti-socialist and, to a considerable extent, antiliberal (as "liberal" is used rhetorically in U.S. political campaigns). Neoliberalism's aggressive pursuit of privatization defends the interest of private wealth, making inequality a premise of development. In pursuit of business deals international trade agreements can be used to override national laws. In this context, hard-won democratic rights in various countries can be overturned. For example, if the protection of wildlife is considered an obstacle to trade, the protection is superseded by the trade agreement. Neoliberalism reveals how little power citizens have to control policy in their respective countries, not to mention the world at large. As a result, neoliberalism generates a flurry of political activity at the grassroots levels, as people feel increasingly distant from and frustrated with the macropolitics enacted by their national governments. Some of these grassroots movements are actually quite empowering to women and ethnic minorities. Yet, at the same time, neoliberal political forces try to appropriate the popular discontent with government and aim it at the dismantling (whether gradual or drastic) of state-funded programs.

While it cannot be doubted that neoliberal policies have addressed some ineffective national economic programs in need of reform, the problem is that simultaneously they have swept away important social entitlements for working people throughout the world. The welfare state was dismantled much as the Soviet Union was (although the two were not equivalent). The private market has stepped in to redesign the education, health, and social services sectors under a "for profit" business agenda. In the United States, the cuts have been more gradual and less severe than in developing nations. Nevertheless, some noticeable cuts in recent years have been the withdrawal of funding for public radio and television, large cuts in state-funded public education, enlarged class sizes in public schools and universities, more part-time and temporary work and fewer tenured and tenure-track positions at the nation's colleges and universities, welfare reform, continued opposition to a universal health insurance coverage, disqualification of immigrants from some health services, and reduction in Medicaid reimbursement for paid care workers. On the other side of the equation, trends show the granting of franchises to companies such as Coca-Cola to sell their products in the nation's schools in exchange for private contributions to the public school budget (as a response to diminished public funding), renewed efforts to transfer support from public to private and religious schools, renewed efforts to increase military spending, and increased patrol and fortification of U.S. borders to prevent the entry of illegal immigrants from developing countries. Migration from regions where downsizing and privatization have led to more unemployment or to drastic cuts in wage earnings, in turn, increases the proportion of new immigrants among the poor in developed countries. One account of the racism and other difficulties facing many new immigrants in the United States describes "global restructuring" as supporting "the channeling and entrapment of migrant women and women of color in exploitative, low-wage service work."[45] Migration is largely a consequence of the entrenched poverty in developing countries, which neoliberal policies have not remedied.[46] In fact, the gap between the rich and the poor has increased since the mid-1980s when these economic policies began to be implemented. For example, as of 1998, the world's two hundred wealthiest people had assets higher than the total combined income of 41 percent of the total global population.[47]

The conjunction of neoliberal economic policies with the liberalization of markets and technologies on a global scale leads to the acceleration of market expansion throughout the world. Feminist economists point out that although "international trade, investment and migration are not new phenomena," what makes the last two decades different is "the acceleration of speed and scope of movements of real and financial capital" as a result of (a) "the removal of state controls on trade and investment" and (b) "new information and communication technologies."[48] With the removal of state controls, businesses can relocate their production at different sites in various parts of the world based on their profits and convenience. The private sectors of each country are combining their forces to form a global private sector, and more aspects of life are commercialized as markets continue to expand.[49] In sum, "the result has been the rapid growth of output and employment in some parts of the world, but at the cost of growing inequality within and between countries."[50]

Needless to say, a large part of the jobs developed as a result of neoliberal policies are low-paying, temporary, or part-time jobs with no long-term security for employees and often with few or no benefits. Free-trade zones have mushroomed in many developing countries where the cheap labor of local residents is used. Workers' rights are dismantled in both developed and developing countries as plants are shut down and the labor is relocated according to piecework produced or assembled wherever business finds cheaper production costs. Poor and developing countries compete with each other to see which one can offer the lowest cost to outside business investors. This competition drives down the cost of labor internationally given the fact that no matter how low the wages might be for some people, there are worse-off people elsewhere who will work at a still lower wage. The drive for cheap production costs also produces large tolls on environmental protection throughout the world. The mobility of capital across national borders keeps the pressure on workers to sacrifice their expectations for good contracts and benefits, at the same time that labor organizing in the free-trade zones is often punished or banned. By abolishing national restrictions to trade and withdrawing credit for future development from any national government that fails to conform to neoliberal policies, the capitalist private sector appears to have locked in this system for generations to come. The system is in. The cost is enormous. "There is persistent malnutrition for millions of people."[51] Among other problems, approximately "one hundred thirty million children have no access to primary education" and "in sub-Saharan Africa incomes are actually lower than they were 30 years ago."[52] The world's ecosystem and nonhuman species are taking a toll as the business sectors are given more opportunities to drive down their costs even if it means more environmental damage and lack of enforcement for wildlife protection.

For the world's women, particularly women in low-income and poor households in developing countries, there are mixed results. In part, this is because despite the uniform and relentless trio of stabilization, adjustment, and liberalization of markets, these policies are applied in different places and circumstances, sometimes with better results than others. Local conditions affect the pace as well as the impact of these policies. In general, however, some broad claims are reiterated in much of the literature sensitive to women's rights. On the one hand, new job opportunities have been created (though on the lower, temporary end of the workforce and for women with some degree of education). There are also new as well as ongoing opportunities for women's social movements, though it is still a long road before adequate political representation is reached. On the other, the neoliberal cuts mean more unpaid care work and dependency work for women in the domestic sector. There is also little help from the state and, for the world's poor, little or no reliable health care, limited reproductive rights for women, and, given the scarcity of resources for poor families, the vulnerability that being born female brings to any girl. Experience tells us that, if in a pinch, families will invest their limited resources on boys rather than girls because boys still have the chance of making more money than girls over a lifetime. It is clear to those of us who think along gender lines that these global and local economic changes have specific gender effects, especially when one observes the gendered patterns of economic dislocation and employment.[53]

The neoliberal discourse promotes the independence of individuals without thinking through the consequences of neoliberal policies on women and girls. The politicians promoting neoliberal programs (often called "reforms") interpellate the public in terms of the people's national identity as "Americans," "Mexicans," and so on. Gender difference is not often invoked in the process of interpellation except in cases in which conservative notions of gender difference and gender normativity (the woman as loyal wife and mother) are part of the party's platform. The independence of "Americans" or "individuals" is invoked even as the public support of health services and social welfare is cut out. Existentially speaking, the rhetoric of shame replaces the sense of entitlement as befitting the position of beneficiaries or recipients of social services. Attention to the structural causes of individual need is diverted to the promotion of privatizing the state enterprises, as if privatization as such would help solve every social problem.

But whose independence do such policies favor? They favor the independence of those who have had an affluent life and whose best interests are served in the accelerated accumulation of wealth. In comparison, the independence of large numbers of women who have no access to wealth is made a more distant possibility by neoliberal policies. Rather than making such women more independent, the neoliberal reforms force them more sharply into situations of time scarcity from which they may not easily exit. Alternatively, time scarcity may force paid and unpaid workers to lower the quality of their input, thereby indirectly lowering the standard of living of all those affected by their reduced involvement.

I am assuming that a life of independence is facilitated by a significant disposable portion of leisure time for a person to pursue her own aims. This is usually depicted in the media as a middle-class expectation, but outside of the particular class context, leisure time is a legitimate aspiration for everyone regardless of age, race, gender, disability, or class. In addition, in the absence of understandable physical restrictions, a life of independence requires mobility and the assumption that usually a person will not be confined during her leisure time to the same site or sites that constitute her (paid or unpaid) workplace. Western ideals of personal independence are incompatible with budget cuts aimed at reducing social services despite the efforts of politicians and planners to present the image of budget cuts as economically empowering to individuals. What is more consistent with neoliberal economics as the latter affects the majority of the world's women is the conservative ideology of "family values" advocating the restriction of a woman's reproductive freedom and her subordination to the needs of a heterosexual household. The rise of religious fundamentalisms and their specific forms of gender normativity are not surprising during an era marked by neoliberal economic policy, much as the rise of Protestantism was associated with the early and middle stages of capitalism. In Latin America, for example, the new fundamentalisms have largely attracted displaced people and migrants who feel a need for security in uncertain living conditions, whereas the traditional churches minister to more stable and established communities. Although neoliberalism can use top-level women executives and highly educated women, it also needs a reserve "army" of women who are willing to do the unpaid care work in order to hold down the demand for good jobs (since these are relatively few in number in comparison to part-time and temporary jobs). As demonstrated throughout the chapter, neoliberalism also makes use of this large reserve of female labor to shift its resources to projects and goals other than a strong public support of health, education, and social services for the population.

While there is justification for a radical critique of the neoliberal project and its allied agencies,[54] another route of criticism is to point out specific aspects requiring modification. In this regard, UNIFEM offers an articulate effort to slow down neoliberalism until it is reformed and adjusted in view of women's needs.[55] It is also possible for single individuals to offer suggestions for monitoring the effects of neoliberal policies in the interest of generating public discussion of these issues. One recommendation is to monitor the impact of adjustment policies particularly on women in low-income urban and rural households, women employed in the public sector, and rural women.[56] In addition, continual attention needs to be given to identifying the income gaps across and within nations.[57] Reform-oriented critics point out the challenge of expanding the new opportunities that have emerged for educated women while also criticizing the fact that the majority of the world's women are still exploited by low-income labor and unpaid care work.

As to the question of whether women who join the low-paying end of the workforce are better off in such jobs or without them, Safa maintains that they are still exploited at work. Nevertheless she believes that as long as a woman brings home an additional wage and does not simply replace the income of another family worker, she has the capacity to negotiate a better status in the home.[58] This adds up to a gain in the domestic sector but not in the market sector, at least initially. With respect to the quality of paid care work available in the case that some of the burden gets shifted from the family to the public or private sectors, UNIFEM notes that paid care work is likely to get worse because the new economic climate puts pressure on paid work to remain competitive and competitiveness is measured only in terms of short-term goals. Even so, the report recommends that the only solution to relieve women of the special burden of unpaid care work is to distribute the responsibilities for care work among all four sectors of the economy: the domestic, NGO, private, and public sectors.[59] This presupposes that the care gap by gender at home needs to be balanced as well.

What these observations entail is a normative call for redirecting structural adjustment policies to more complex ends. It is not clear to me that the reductionist character of structural adjustment economic analysis is fit to accept feminist arguments. Still, feminist economists warn of an emerging "care deficit" given that so much of a burden is placed on the home by neoliberal policies that this will result in men, women, and children gradually failing to take care of themselves.[60] Similarly the report theorizes a "depletion of human capabilities" when human needs are subordinated universally to market profits and women in the domestic sector are left primarily responsible for attending to people's needs.[61]

THE GOALS OF NEOLIBERAL GLOBALIZING ECONOMIES

The goals of the neoliberal economy are such that they seem to be at odds with the interests and needs of those who do unpaid care work as illustrated above. If this is the case, is there some justification for the neoliberal economy that would offset the extra burdens placed on women as unpaid care workers? Some have argued that although women who do unpaid care work are affected negatively by the neoliberal global economy, other women, primarily literate women, benefit from new employment opportunities.[62] Given the trends to cut jobs and to limit salary increases in the state sector, it is also reasonable to assume that women in households connected to the private, business sectors of the economy are more

likely to gain from neoliberalism than women whose personal or household income depends on the state-funded sector.[63]

The issue of whether neoliberalism has a positive effect on some sectors of the
female population is complicated by the massive migrations it also fosters due to
the large inequalities in economic opportunities between developed and developing countries. Migration is also exacerbated by the factor of capital mobility that,
in a world economy in which capital can move freely across national borders,
makes it possible for businesses to abandon established sites of production and
regroup production in another area. As Spivak astutely notes, the female immigrant (woman of color) in the developed world is placed in competition against
her counterpart in the Third World country of origin as cheap labor for capital's
profit.[64] And, Spivak adds, the one in the country of origin will win this competition since the cost of employing female labor in a developing country's "free-
trade zones," for example, is far less than it is to hire immigrant labor in the
United States or Britain. In raising the question of which women will benefit from
neoliberalism, the global economy and its use of female labor in various contexts
in different parts of the world must be considered. It does appear to be the consensus of several feminist economic studies that while women who do unpaid
care labor, including dependency work, tend to lose—often significantly—from
the all-pervasive global neoliberal economy, those women in low-income sectors
in developing countries who are willing to break ties with care work and join the
workforce—even at low-paying, temporary jobs—may derive some benefit.
Stated differently, a woman who has had a sufficient education may take advantage of economic opportunities as long as she either remains free from care obligations or is able to benefit from substitute care arrangements and resources.

It is clear, however, that the relative and partial progress such women experience is only temporary as long as their job opportunities are both low-paying and
temporary. While the neoliberal economy creates jobs, these tend to have no long-
term security. Unless she is educated in marketable skills, a woman may move
from one job to another without finding any substantive economic security. As
she ages, the possibility that she will become less marketable in a competitive
economy is not likely to make her a winner.[65]

A PLEA FOR ETHICAL BALANCE

Neoliberalism offers a temporary package of short-term benefits for women
who abandon unpaid care work. This is a temporary benefit not only because of
the temporary contracts favored in the neoliberal market but also in relation to
the "timelessness" characterizing unpaid care work (as a recurring inescapable
family obligation). Nevertheless, unpaid care work and its timelessness are necessary and important to the social and moral fabric of society. There is a large
long-term cost to society if unpaid care work is totally abandoned and if economic pressure to perform in the labor force depletes workers from time to care

for others or for themselves. But there is also a large long-term loss if women by virtue of their acculturated gender roles are tied predominantly to unpaid care work and cannot assume leadership roles in paid work and in community projects in a society.

The solution to the problem is for the public sector to take on its share of the timelessness of care work, providing stable (not temporary) social security, including health care, for a country's residents and citizens. This means the dismantling of the neoliberal policies on the state and the market as currently practiced. Likewise, men need to take on their share of the timelessness of unpaid care work. This means the dismantling of gender relations that presuppose a strong division of labor between men and women regarding unpaid care work. In this sense, what Julia Kristeva named "women's time" will be redistributed and given a place concretely in men's lives and in the public domain.[66] These changes, if effective, will manifest a transformation of the sociosymbolic order. To achieve this redistribution of care is therefore one of the greatest existential and political challenges we face today if our interest is to emancipate women and transform the ruling sociosymbolic order.

NOTES

1. Eva Kittay, *Love's Labor: Essays On Women, Equality, and Dependency* (New York: Routledge, 1999), ix.

2. Kittay, *Love's Labor*, 32.

3. It should be emphasized that because of women's differential economic and educational status, among other factors, women in developing countries do not constitute a homogeneous group. My intention is not to generalize about women's diverse situations without qualification. As will become clear toward the end of this chapter, the impact of economic policies on women around the world varies according to different conditions and circumstances. Still, in cases where a large proportion of women are affected by conditions of social or economic disadvantage, attention needs to be placed on their generalizable needs. Where large global trends are discussed, I cannot help but generalize, although I have attempted as much as possible to qualify the references.

4. Pierre Bourdieu, *Acts of Resistance: Against the Tyranny of the Market*, trans. Richard Nice (New York: New Press, 2000), 96.

5. Bourdieu, *Acts of Resistance*, 100.

6. Bourdieu, *Acts of Resistance*, 97–99.

7. Maurice Cranston, "Liberalism," in *The Encyclopedia of Philosophy*, vol. 4 (New York: Macmillan, 1967), 458–61.

8. Cranston, "Liberalism."

9. UNIFEM Biennial Report, *Progress of the World's Women 2000* (New York: United Nations Development Fund for Women, 2000), 24.

10. UNIFEM, *Progress*, 24.

11. Lorraine Corner, *Women, Men and Economics: The Gender-Differentiated Impact of Macroeconomics* (New York: United Nations Development Fund for Women, 1996), 36.

12. UNIFEM, *Progress,* 103.

13. Richard Schulz and Scott R. Beach, "Caregiving as a Risk Factor for Mortality: The Caregiver Health Effects Study," *Journal of the American Medical Association* 282, no. 23 (December 15, 1999): 2215–19.

14. UNIFEM, *Progress,* 101.

15. UNIFEM, *Progress,* 102.

16. Cynthia Chavez Metoyer, *Women and the State in Post-Sandinista Nicaragua* (Boulder, Colo.: Lynne Rienner, 2000), 87.

17. I have referred primarily to Lorraine Corner on this specific point. For the larger view of feminist economics, see the International Association for Feminist Economics' journal, *Feminist Economics,* ed. Diana Strassman (London: Routledge Journals, 1995–present). The UNIFEM Biennial Report, *Progress of the World's Women 2000,* cited in this chapter as a source of feminist economic scholarship and data, is collaboratively produced, with more than thirty staff and advisers listed. Its bibliography and references list more than 230 entries. For a recent sample of feminist economics, see Lourdes Bene-ría, "Globalization, Gender, and the Davos Man," *Feminist Economics* 5, no. 3 (1999): 61–83. A version of this paper was presented at a plenary session at the National Women's Studies Association in Boston (June 2000).

18. Corner, *Women, Men,* 20–21.

19. Corner, *Women, Men,* 21.

20. Corner, *Women, Men,* 21.

21. Corner, *Women, Men,* 21.

22. Corner, *Women, Men,* 21.

23. Corner also observes that when unpaid work in the home is measured, it should be borne in mind that some activities are carried on simultaneously whereas others have a distinct beginning, end, and single-minded attention span. She suggests that much of women's work is of the simultaneous kind while men's work at home is more likely to fit more into separate and distinct activities. See Corner, *Women, Men,* 26.

24. For example, Kittay's work, *Love's Labor,* develops a model of justice for caregivers strongly based on principles of equality. Kittay calls for a "truly inclusive" equality that takes fully into account the concerns related to dependency and dependency work. See Kittay, *Love's Labor,* 19.

25. For example, Safa and Morrissey highlight women's gendered contributions and responsibilities. See Helen Safa, *The Myth of the Male Breadwinner: Women and Industrialization in the Caribbean* (Boulder, Colo.: Westview, 1995). Marietta Morrissey, "Explaining the Caribbean Family: Gender Ideologies and Gender Relations," in *Caribbean Portraits: Essays on Gender Ideologies and Identities,* ed. Christine Barrow (Kingston, Jamaica: Ian Randle Publishers, 1998), 78–79.

26. UNIFEM's *Progress of the World's Women* offers this approach.

27. Safa, *Myth,* 45–46.

28. Safa, *Myth,* 57.

29. Safa, *Myth,* 45–46. Safa's research sample is primarily focused on the Dominican Republic, Puerto Rico, and Cuba. Of these three, the Dominican Republic is more typical of Caribbean economies, since Puerto Rico is part of the U.S. system and Cuba has maintained a socialist system despite many difficulties.

30. Safa, *Myth,* 46, 58.

31. Safa, *Myth,* 57.

32. Honor Ford-Smith, "Ring Ding in a Tight Corner: Sistren, Collective Democracy, and the Organization of Cultural Production," in *Feminist Genealogies, Colonial Legacies,*

Democratic Futures, ed. M. Jacqui Alexander and Chandra Talpade Mohanty (New York: Routledge, 1997): 213–58.

33. Safa, *Myth*, 58.

34. In Safa's view, even if women speak out of a traditional gender identity, their action can be transformative. In voicing their demands to the state and society, women strengthen their sense of agency and modify their traditional homebound roles.

35. As mentioned earlier, I became aware of the enormous responsibility of this work when my mother became ill some years ago. This situation has forced me to address issues I did not foresee in previous work. See Ofelia Schutte, *Cultural Identity and Social Liberation in Latin American Thought* (Albany, N.Y.: SUNY Press, 1993).

36. In a review of several Caribbean studies on the family, sociologist Marietta Morrissey complements Safa's analysis in several respects. Morrissey underscores women's strong commitment to their families, whether as wage earners or unpaid care workers. She emphasizes that the effects of racism and colonialism in the Caribbean keep black men from fulfilling the breadwinner ideal reserved for white men. She notes that when economic difficulties including those caused by budget cuts impact families, women seek wage labor outside the home. Relatives and neighbors often help with child care. (These circumstances assume that there will be relatives and neighbors available to handle some of the caring tasks.) Morrissey depicts women-headed households as a manifestation of women's strengths in providing for themselves and their children under difficult circumstances. She urges women to organize politically to ask the state "to protect women and children" (Morrissey, "Caribbean Family," 88). The demand for recognition of women's needs is made in the name of protecting families, not in the name of equality. Still, Morrissey attains a strong critical standpoint of existing power structures when she supports the view that the lack of resources available for women and other vulnerable groups reveals these groups' lack of political power (Morrissey, "Caribbean Family," 87). In her view poverty is reversible if the political will exists to pressure the state to do something about it.

37. Akwilina Kayumba, "The Role of Women in Taking Care of the Sick Family Members in This Era of HIV/AIDS," *The Journal of Social Philosophy* 31, no. 4 (December 2000).

38. The following comments are taken from Kayumba's conference presentation. Her revised paper appeared in *The Journal of Social Philosophy* 31, no. 4 (December 2000).

39. UNIFEM, *Progress*, 6.

40. Gayatri Spivak, *A Critique of Postcolonial Reason: Toward A History of the Vanishing Present* (Cambridge, Mass.: Harvard University Press, 1999), 357. Spivak's observation reinforces the comments cited earlier by Boudreau. In addition, her observation draws attention to the fact that neoliberalism retakes the neoclassical view of the state as serving in the interest of trade, not the main twentieth-century view of the liberal state as a guarantor of social programs for equal opportunity.

41. Corner, *Women, Men*, 42.

42. Corner, *Women, Men*, 42.

43. Corner, *Women, Men*, 42.

44. I do not discuss here the case of Cuba due to its complexity. I only note in passing that a large part of the rationale for the U.S. trade embargo against the island is that the Cuban government has refused to liberalize and privatize markets as expected or required by the neoliberal structural adjustment policies.

45. Grace Chang, *Disposable Domestics: Immigrant Women Workers in the Global Economy* (Cambridge, Mass.: South End, 2000), 146.

158 *Ofelia Schutte*

46. The poorer the country, it appears that the more fragile its prospects. For the case of Nicaragua, see Chavez Metoyer, *Women and the State*.

47. UNIFEM, *Progress*, 30.

48. UNIFEM, *Progress*, 29.

49. UNIFEM, *Progress*, 29.

50. UNIFEM, *Progress*, 29.

51. UNIFEM, *Progress*, 29.

52. Mary Robinson, "Mary Robinson Speaks to Fulbrighters," *Fulbright Association Newsletter* 21, no. 4 (1999): 6–7. See also Meredith Turshen, "The Ecological Crisis in Tanzania," in *Dangerous Intersections: Feminist Perspectives on Population, Environment, and Development*, ed. J. Silliman and Y. King (Cambridge, Mass.: South End, 1999), 100. Patricia Bifani, "El impacto de los programas de ajuste estructural en las mujeres africanas," in *Globalización y género*, ed. Paloma de Villota (Madrid: Editorial Síntesis, 1999), 319–42.

53. The United Nations' yearly *Human Development Report* now tracks information by gender as well as other variables.

54. Spivak, *Critique*, 357–412.

55. UNIFEM, *Progress*, 145–54.

56. Carmen de la Cruz, "Globalización de la Economía y Justicia Económica," in *Globalización y género,* ed. Paloma de Villota (Madrid: Editorial Síntesis, 1999), 86.

57. Cruz, "Globalización," 86, 81.

58. Safa, *Myth*, 171–72.

59. UNIFEM, *Progress*, 32.

60. UNIFEM, *Progress*, 32.

61. UNIFEM, *Progress*, 26–27.

62. Cf. Corner, *Women, Men*, 48–51.

63. Corner, *Women, Men*, 50.

64. Spivak, *Critique*, 377.

65. Cf. Chavez Metoyer, *Women*, 82–83.

66. Julia Kristeva, "Women's Time," in *The Portable Kristeva*, ed. Kelly Oliver (New York: Columbia University Press, 1997), 349–69.

III

JUST SOCIAL ARRANGEMENTS AND FAMILIAL RESPONSIBILITY FOR DEPENDENCY

7

Justice and the Labor of Care

Diemut Grace Bubeck

Women's work—especially women's unpaid work in the domestic sphere, but by extension also a lot of women's paid work—is best understood not as production, as in the materialist tradition, but as care. I define care as an activity or practice aimed at the meeting of needs in others. As such, it is fundamentally other-directed and beneficial to others, while involving an investment of the carer's time and energy. In this last respect, it is like material production, or any type of work, and can be regarded as a burden, as much as work can. In its other-directed and other-beneficial aspect, however, it is very unlike any of the work that is usually discussed, and it involves very different virtues and values for those engaged in such care, as well as a particular urgency and motivation in those receptive to the demands of need. As I shall argue, the reasons why women do most or all of the caring that needs to be done in any society, and why women are exploited as carers, are manifold. There are material and social constraints, but also, and more interestingly, reasons deriving from the peculiar logic that care as an other-directed practice exhibits: Given the skills and virtues of attentiveness and responsiveness to others that are required in any good carer, it makes those who care vulnerable to exploitation in a very specific way.[1] It is thus this new understanding of women's work as care that allows us also to understand how it is that women are exploited, hence unjustly treated.

NECESSARY LABOR AND THE ABUNDANCE SOLUTION

Karl Marx, impressed by the rapid development of machinery in the nineteenth century and by ever-increasing automation of production, believed in the possibility of relative, if not, complete abundance. Although increased productivity could not abolish the constraints imposed on humans by our needs, it could reduce or

160

even abolish the time we have to spend working toward the satisfaction of those needs—what Marx referred to as "necessary labor," thus freeing us for other, truly free activities. But some necessary labor does not lend itself to being mechanized or automated. In this chapter I look at a part of necessary labor that Marx obviously overlooked, namely, that part of necessary labor that is overwhelmingly performed by women—"women's work." By women's work, I mean housework (that is, the cleaning and tidying of the household unit, the preparation of meals and the work related to it such as washing and cleaning up, and so on), child care (that is, looking after children and attending to their needs whenever required), and caring work (that is, looking after members of the household or extended family if required by sickness, physical or mental disability, or frailty).

Am I right in saying that such traditional women's work is necessary labor? This can certainly be disputed. First, it might be said that there is so much variation across societies and time with regard to what is seen to "need doing" that such activities, arbitrary as they are, could not possibly count as necessary labor. But while the amount of such work may be historically variable and while it may be disputed whether, say, a house has to be cleaned every day or a clearly disabled infant should be cared for,[2] it seems nevertheless clear that some amount of this work has to be done. Insofar as our nature is such that we need livable surroundings, food that needs preparing and clothes that need washing, that we need to be looked after as children, and that we need others to care for us if we are sick, frail, or disabled, women's work is certainly part of that work that is intended by the notion of necessary labor, even if it was not intended by Marx. Furthermore, historical and cultural variations in the amount and kind of necessary labor performed are, of course, part of the development of productive forces over time and space, and as such very much part of Marx's own thought about work, whether necessary or not.

Second, it might be said that necessary labor allows us to "maintain and reproduce" *ourselves*, that is, meet our own needs, while women's work is typically and to a large extent geared toward meeting other people's needs. Now it is true that a lot of women's work is work that we could not do ourselves if we were in need of its benefits—children could not bring themselves up, nor would somebody who is bedridden be able to care for herself—but it is nevertheless work that needs to be done. Moreover, it is work that needs to be done because human nature makes us thus dependent at various points in our lives. The fact, therefore, that not all necessary labor can be performed by ourselves to meet our own needs does not introduce a serious problem with regard to the conception of necessary labor.[3] It merely illustrates the fact that human nature forces not only us, but also others, to engage in certain activities that need doing because our needs have to be met.

Marx presumed that the constraints posed by necessary labor would be eliminated by increased productivity and consequent abundance. He believed this to be "the abundance solution" to the problem for human freedom posed by necessary labor. Assuming, then, that women's work is part of necessary labor, is it amenable to the abundance solution, too? The answer is: Some of it is, but a lot of it is not. More specifically, housework may be, but child care and caring work are not. Remember that abundance was to be possible through increases in productivity through automation—but only housework is the kind of work where automation of some or even all of its component activities is possible. Thus in Western industrialized countries, in contrast with less-developed countries, a lot of the work that used to be done by women in the home has been taken over by industrial and hence increasingly automated production, thus relieving modern housewives in the industrialized countries of considerable amounts of work; there is no reason in principle why it would not be amenable to even further reductions.[4]

The solution to the necessary labor of child care and caring work, by contrast, cannot possibly lie in increasing automation. Thus imagine a society in which sick, old-aged, and disabled people are put into fully automated hospitals and asylums, and where children are brought up by robots. While such a society can be imagined, it would certainly strike most of us as a society not worth living in. In fact, a society in which caring and child rearing are done by machines or robots is a nightmare vision, a dystopia to avoid, rather than a utopia to aim for.

Care, in contrast to housework, consists of interactive kinds of activities that essentially involve social contact between people. This does not imply that considerations of efficiency cannot be applied to those activities. Time can certainly be wasted in those activities that constitute caring and the raising of children. There is, nevertheless, an intrinsic relation between the time spent and the "good" that is produced, which does not apply to the other kinds of necessary labor. The time spent in child care or caring activities cannot be reduced to zero without these activities losing their character and without our giving up the whole purpose served by our engaging in them. Completely automated "care" for the needy is an abandonment of people to machines. It ceases to be care. Furthermore, children who grow up without any human contact (or animal contact, for that matter, remembering the few "wolf children" we have evidence of) do not survive infancy: In bringing up children, we cannot be replaced. Care, then, is the kind of work that not only needs to be done, but that people need to do. It involves human beings, carers, and those cared for as human beings, communicating and interacting with each other, and it requires the exercise of our most distinctive capacities: language and thought and a complex emotional life that allows us to empathize with and understand others and meet their very individual needs.

That part of women's work that is care, then, points up the limited scope (or even the complete wrongheadedness) of the abundance solution to the necessary labor problem. If care is necessary labor, then certain parts of necessary labor cannot be abolished without letting society die out and abandoning people in need, nor can they necessarily be reduced because machines and robots cannot replace people's efforts in care. The automation of care presents us instead with the dystopic nightmare vision of robotized "care" and "parenting." Abundance achieved through automation, therefore, could only seem to Marx to be a solution to the necessary labor problem because he failed to notice—because he failed to think about women's work—the different nature of a lot of the necessary labor that women perform.

THE DEFINITION OF CARE AS AN ACTIVITY

Caring can refer to an emotional state or to an activity or to a combination of the two.[5] This dual reference of "care" is reflected in the literature on care. Thus Noddings has argued that it is the emotional-cum-moral state of "engrossment" in another person's reality that is basic to care,[6] while Parker, on the other hand, has discussed caring as an activity comprising the tasks of "tending."[7] Graham, by contrast, refuses to settle for either aspect by discussing caring as indivisibly both activity and emotion, when she analyzes it as a "labor of love."[8]

The *Oxford English Dictionary* defines *caring for* as "providing for" and "looking after." Presumably, this definition excludes inanimate entities as recipients of care, but it is still rather wide in that it includes under the description of "providing for" activities such as earning money in order to pay for one's parents' stay in a sheltered home for the frail elderly or in order to pay alimony for the children living with the divorced mother. A son could thus "care for" his parents and a father for his children without ever interacting with them or without ever even seeing those he cares for. More typically, however, under the description of "looking after," caring involves some interaction between the carer and the cared for, such as in child care where those caring for children spend a lot of time with them, partly because children's safety has to be guaranteed, but more important, because children need interaction with others and help in various ways. Caring may also involve various forms of physical "tending," whether that is the washing of a frail elderly person, the dressing of a child, or the relaxing massage given by a practitioner.[9] Caring may, however, just be the listening and talking to a distressed friend who needs the company and sympathy of another person in this situation.

In contrast to these rather wide definitions, I would like to offer a more restrictive definition of care as an activity. I shall use *caring* in the following sense:

> Caring for is the meeting of the needs of one person by another person where face-to-face interaction between carer and cared for is a crucial element of the overall activity and where the need is of such a nature that it cannot possibly be met by the person in need herself.[10]

I use the concepts of "carer" and "cared for" to refer to the two positions or roles that the activity of care establishes, that is, that of the person who does the caring and that of the person who is the recipient of the other person's care, respectively.

These may be temporary roles that are interchangeable, as between friends, or relatively fixed roles, as between caring professional and client. Some roles are not interchangeable at all, as, for example, the roles of parent and infant or young child, although, of course, a grown-up child can become a long-term carer for her frail elderly parent, and these roles in turn may be relatively fixed. Also, in some forms of care that have to be provided over extended periods of time, such as child care or the care of disabled or elderly people, the permanently required role or position of the "carer" can be filled by more than one person: both parents, other members of their family, as well as paid carers, may share in the care of children. It is worth stressing, then, that as such, the concepts of "carer" and "cared for" can refer to both fixed and flexible, momentary and long-term, shared and "singly occupied" roles or positions and should not be taken to refer to relatively long-term, socially fixed roles or positions only.

The first qualification of the definition makes interaction between carer and cared for a central element. Consider that a lot of activities, notably all services and, even more widely, all activities productive of use-values—and this could include most paid work in the various sectors of the economy—could be described as at least mediately "meeting needs." Unless there were need in a wide sense, translated into market demand, most of these activities would not be performed, and their performance leads, via a market transaction and the consumption of the use-value, to the meeting of such need. But, presumably, nobody would think it adequate to describe the production of a car as "caring," so obviously the "meeting of needs" has to be qualified appropriately. Now the most typical cases of care, as illustrated previously, seem to involve interaction between carer and cared for, although the interaction may not cover the whole activity or set of activities that is or are described as caring. Take the following examples: cooking her favorite dish for a sick child, arranging an appointment with a physiotherapist for an elderly person who is hard of hearing, or inquiring into possibilities of help for one's partner who is depressed. None of these activities involves interaction with the cared for except at the time when they are asked what they want or informed of or presented with the result of these activities, but I would still want to count them as care. There are other activities that are even more questionably described as "caring," such as washing one's children's clothes, putting the rubbish in the bin (for one's frail neighbor), and cleaning one's sick father's flat. Now insofar as these activities could not be performed by the persons for whom they are done, hence insofar as they meet a need that could not be met by the cared for themselves, they would still qualify as care. There would then be a further question, however, as to whether, for example, the baker cannot be said to care for the frail elderly person, too, since he produced what meets her need and she could not have done so herself. The only way to exclude such counterexamples, it seems to me, is to make face-to-face interaction a crucial element of the activity. This may leave some cases undecided or questionable, but I do not think this matters as long as the central idea and the typical cases are clear, and the most typical cases do involve face-to-face interaction in various ways.

The second qualification of the definition—that care meets a need that cannot possibly be met by the person in need herself—is meant to restrict substantially what counts as care. By *not possibly*, I mean to exclude two sorts of activities. The first consists of basic human needs that a healthy, able-bodied adult is nevertheless capable of meeting herself at least in principle. If others meet those needs for her, they provide a service, but do not care for her. Thus the housewife cooking a meal for her husband is providing a service, while her cooking the same meal for an infant would be care. The second type consists of what we might call socially caused needs (and also wants, desires, and interests), where the person in need could do whatever she has to do to satisfy the need (want, desire, interest) herself if she had learned how to do so or if she made up her mind to do them or if she had chosen a different occupation. In our modern societies there are various things we need that we cannot produce or provide ourselves, not because in principle we are not capable of doing so, but because of the very advanced social division of labor or specialization. The interdependency produced by such diversification of occupations, skills, and knowledge is socially caused, but not strictly, that is, humanly necessary. Caring, by contrast, meets needs that neither derive from the social division of labor nor are satisfiable by the person in need, but that are absolute in that they make those in need necessarily depend on others. Thus a child cannot bring herself up, nor can a bedridden person provide food for herself, nor can somebody in need of talking a problem over with somebody talk to herself.

The idea underlying this second qualification is that throughout the lives of all human beings there are times when we do need others to care for us in various ways, especially at the beginning and the end of our lives, but also whenever we are faced with needs that we cannot possibly meet ourselves. Care, then, is a response to a particular subset of basic human needs, in other words, those that make us dependent on others.

Another distinction, one between care and activities or acts that are expressions of love, friendship, or consideration may further elucidate my definition of care. Such activities—for example, making a cup of tea for one's partner who has just returned from a long day's work, cooking a friend's favorite dish, doing various kinds of favors—may be thought to be care. They are only care in the sense I am putting forward if they do meet a need that the person in need could not meet herself. It is often true, especially in the private sphere of the home, that activities are often both care and activities expressive of love. This may lead one to think that care has to be an expression of love, in other words, that my definition lacks this element and is the worse for it. I think, however, that there are good reasons for keeping the meeting of a particular type of need and the expression of love distinct, while acknowledging that they may often coincide (especially in the private sphere). First, care does not require the existence of an emotional bond between carer and cared for. Second, activities and acts expressive of an emotional bond are not necessarily care according to my definition: They may be and often are services, that is, satisfy needs, wants, or interest that the person could have satisfied herself. What confuses the distinction quite considerably, unfortunately, is the fact that women themselves often think of those they provide care and services for as more helpless and needy than they in fact are, especially if they are male: "My husband/son (who is twenty-five!) doesn't even know how to boil an egg, so how could I not be there to cook breakfast for him?" Since care has been mystified in so many ways, it is all the more important to be clear about what exactly care is and what it is that women do and why they do it. Both distinctions, that between care and activities expressive of love, and that between care and services, will hopefully contribute to more clarity.

The difficulty in delineating care from other types of activities derives from the fact that the definition of care I have given is a *functional* definition. Hence whether a particular activity counts as care or as a service is not dependent on the activity itself, but on the function it has, that is, on whether it meets a certain type of need.[11] Furthermore, whether such activities are expressive of emotional bonds is also immaterial for definitional purposes—although it is, of course, important in real life—since it is the function of the activity that qualifies it as care. The definition thus hinges crucially on the concept of a "need [that] cannot possibly be met by the person in need herself," and it is this focus on the meeting of needs through certain activities that anchors care firmly in the material world of burdens and benefits. I cannot develop a fully fledged theory of need in this context and hence can only refer the reader to a commonsense understanding of our shared human condition, that is, of the fact that human beings have needs at various points in our lives, both physical and emotional, that we cannot meet ourselves. The needs of children and frail elderly, sick, or disabled persons and of persons in need of emotional support are obvious instances, and responses to these needs form the core of activities that are care as I have defined it.

Let me conclude this section with some of the strengths of my definition. First, it is immediately obvious from this definition why care cannot be "rationalized away" like other kinds of work in Marx's utopia of abundance: If care is the meeting of the needs of one person by another person and involves face-to-face interaction, it follows that carers could not be *replaced* by machines, or that they would be replaceable only to the extent that some of the activities they engage in as part of their caring can also be carried out by machines (washing machines, dishwasher, vacuum cleaner) or can be "socialized" (provided by the market, for example, baby food, baby clothes, "meals on wheels"). Second, the definition captures what is common to different forms of care, in contrast to, for example, social policy literature where *care* usually means most forms of care except child care.[12] Social policy literature in Britain may be seen to reflect the bias implicit in welfare state policies: While help may be given with, or the state may even take on, care of ill or elderly or disabled people, it is still implicitly assumed that child care will be provided by the parents, that is, usually the mother. Child care is thus separated out from most other forms of care, and this separation is reflected in the social policy literature. It does not, however, make any theoretical or conceptual sense to do so, and my own definition was developed so as to enable me to point to the commonalities between these different forms of care and also, by doing this, point to all the work hidden from the public eye that women do. Third, then, as will emerge from my argument, my definition of care forms the basis of a materialist account of women's work as care that, in turn, allows me to tell a new "story" of women's exploitation as carers. It thus focuses the discussion on a type of activity that has traditionally not been discussed in political theory, but that sorely needs discussion because it raises questions of social justice. More specifically, care is largely performed by women, it is mostly performed unpaid, and it makes those who perform it, women, dependent on others, men.

THE MATERIAL CONDITIONS OF CARE

The definition of *care* that I have given in the last section has several immediate corollaries. We can begin by noticing that there is a sense in which one does not care for oneself, but rather one "takes care of oneself." This usage may reflect a subtle distinction that is made between the kind of morally serious and involved activity that is focused on others, "caring for," and a more superficial kind of activity or even only protective attitude that one can endorse to one's own benefit and that of others, "taking care of." Once we admit the distinction, however, it is clear that "caring for" is the obvious candidate for referring to those activities that benefit others and for which we in turn depend on others.

If it is true that one cannot care for oneself, then it follows that care has an irreducibly social nature. As such, it can be, and has been, taken as a paradigm case of social interaction.[13] If caring is done *for* others, it follows, furthermore, that it benefits people other than the carer herself. Unlike exchange or contracts, the usual paradigms in liberal social and political theory,[14] caring is not mutually beneficial, but is an asymmetrical transaction of material benefits. While the carer gives her time and energy, attention and skill, the cared for's needs are met. This asymmetry holds for all cases of care that are neither paid, reciprocated, nor remunerated in other ways. Hence, unless the carer is remunerated in some way (in kind or paid), or the care she gives is reciprocated, she incurs a material net burden. While caring can be a very empowering and rewarding thing to do, it is nevertheless, and may equally well feel like, a burden.

I want to suggest that caring is a burden in the same sense in which work is a burden, and since it is commonly accepted that work is a burden, care will have to be recognized as a burden as well.[15] There is a narrow sense of work according to which activities have to be heavy and/or unpleasant toil before they qualify as work. One of the most common usages of "work," by contrast, refers to all paid activities as work. Is work in this wider sense a burden, and if so, in what sense? Clearly, not all work is literally a burden, as would seem obvious considering the "work" of a philosopher, artist, or gardener. The point, however, is that all work can become a burden any time for those engaged in it. First, it can impose a strain on people, for example, the strains resulting from heavy physical work; mindless, repetitive work; or heavy responsibility. There are, however, other strains, such as those of work that is intellectually demanding, risky, or involves interactions with and accommodations of other people's demands. Many of these sorts of strains are shared by caring as well. Hence insofar as work is burdensome because it imposes various strains in various combinations, care is burdensome, too, since it is no different from other types of work in this respect. In fact, it is these strains that make pay necessary. Presumably, most people would not incur the burden of these strains without their work also being a source of material benefits. Second, work is burdensome—as is care—insofar as it has to be done whether or not we happen to feel like doing it. In fact, unpaid care is more like paid work in this respect than most other unpaid activities that people engage in: It imposes demands on the carer that the carer does not necessarily have a choice about meeting. If an infant cries, or an incontinent patient has wet her bed, the infant and patient need attention, whether or not the carer feels like giving it to them. Care, then, is a burden in two important senses in which work is burdensome.

There is also an important difference between work and care, however, since care is not remunerated. Hence unremunerated or unreciprocated care is a material net burden, and further transactions are necessary to produce a situation in which burdens and benefits are in balance for the carer. As we shall see later, it is this characteristic of care that makes those who tend to take it on vulnerable to exploitation. Since caring takes place as a response to certain types of needs— that is, needs the person in need cannot possibly meet herself—caring involves a one-sided dependency of the person in need of care on the prospective carer. Their relationship is not one between equals or of equal bargaining strength since the carer has the power to withhold care and the cared-for's needs have to be met. This power differential is irreducible since the needs to be met cannot be met by those in need themselves: I cannot talk to myself if I need to talk a problem over with somebody—in the best case, a person close and dear to me; in the worst case, a helpline worker—nor can children bring themselves up, nor can a frail ninety-year-old or a mentally disabled person survive without support by others. Again, this situation does not exemplify the usual assumptions made in liberal social and political theory, where people are typically conceived of as (ideally) autonomous, independent agents in control of their choices and their life plans.[16]

The nonprovision of care, therefore, can involve serious harm or even death, and it is in the power of those who are in a position to care to let such harm happen by not caring (or not caring adequately) or to prevent it.[17] In the case of need, then, inaction or the refusal to act are sufficient conditions for harm being incurred by the person in need. This aspect makes situations of need comparable to "emergency" situations of houses on fire or people drowning, which are usually the only type of situations discussed in the literature where inaction will result in harm, and action, conversely, has a peculiarly urgent quality. Cases of need, however, and the meeting of needs, are not chance cases where supererogatory actions are called for, but very mundane and everyday cases of being there and doing things for others who need us. They are not exceptional like emergency situations, but part of each of our lives. The reason, I suspect, why they have not been discussed in the literature until very recently is because the meeting of needs has been and still is mostly done by socially invisible actors, namely, women.[18]

Given the importance of care for those in need and, especially, the harmfulness of inaction or inappropriate care, the most important cognitive capacities, attitudes, and skills (and corresponding virtues) in carers are attentiveness and receptivity, responsiveness, and the ability to respond in the right way to the cared-for and her needs.[19] The best illustration of attentiveness is the heightened attention in parents, even when asleep, to any noise indicating distress in their baby. Receptivity refers more generally to an attitude or a "mode of consciousness" that, in Noddings's description, "attempts to grasp or to receive a reality rather than to impose it."[20] Thus unless a need is perceived to exist, care will not be a response, and the perception of need requires a person's openness to the signs or demands of need. Responsiveness, then, refers to the willingness and ability to respond to such perceived need. Last but not least, the ability to respond in the right way may involve considerable experience and knowledge in the carer: A parent not only has to realize that her baby is not doing well, she also has to know what to do in order to meet a need the baby (or, for example, the confused elderly person) may not even be able to express adequately.

Receptivity and responsiveness to the needs of others, that is, those cared for, imply that in a good carer the power she has over the person cared for is counteracted by her openness toward the cared for, which means that she reacts to a perceived need as a demand on her to care. Consequently, the power balance between carer and cared for undergoes a characteristic reversal in favor of the cared for. Thus women often describe their lives as full-time mothers of small babies as "dictated" by the rhythm of the needs of their babies, by their sleeping and waking periods.[21] Being "on call" as a doctor or nurse in a hospital is an example of such availability in a more formal setting: It institutionalizes receptivity and responsiveness and thus makes doctors and nurses available to patients. This reversal of the power balance may also explain many women's feelings of utter powerlessness and anger vis-à-vis their children or those of nurses vis-à-vis their patients (especially if the latter abuse the system)—feelings that would be difficult to understand if we looked only at the dependency resulting from need and the corresponding power in the carer. In an important sense, therefore, a person having the skills, attitudes, and virtues predisposing her to care is not really "her own woman" to the extent that she takes on, or is simply faced with, long-term caring roles. She is other-directed and heteronomous, hence not the autonomous agent that political and moral theory would have her be.[22] At any point in her life, caring responsibilities may impose themselves on her in a way that is not only not under her control, but that may also render her "life plans" unrealizable in the form so far envisaged.[23]

Perhaps most important, since caring as an activity done by people is situated in time and space and hence in particular social contexts, it is the social context that determines where, when, and by and for whom caring is done, and under what conditions. More specifically, the provision of care can be public, semipublic, or private. Public and semipublic care are provided by paid professionals, often in public or semipublic institutions such as hospitals, homes for elderly or disabled people, health centers, and private practices, while private care is provided unpaid and in the private sphere.[24] It is this latter form, that of unpaid care, which is of specific interest to my argument for two reasons: first, because the bulk of unpaid care is done by women, and second, because it is their performance of unpaid care that makes women vulnerable to exploitation.

Take the example of child care as a typical case of full-time care, that is, where a carer has to be available and potentially involved in caring tasks all the time, in a society divided into public and private spheres. Assume furthermore, as is the case in Great Britain, that child care is not provided publicly so that parents have the choice between buying child care on the market or engaging in it themselves.[25] In such a situation, any parent who cannot afford to buy child care is reduced to a more or less exclusively private person, since she has to be available all the time. This in turn means she will not be able to go out to work.[26] Moreover, since child care does not produce any material benefit for the carer, the carer will have to depend on her husband or partner, her family, or the state for her survival. Full-time carers are thus full-time burdened without receiving any material benefits for their care; their lives are dictated by the needs of others while their own livelihood and well-being are dependent on others. On top of all this, they are virtually excluded from participation in the public sphere. With regard to the balance of material benefits and burdens, as well as more general considerations of self-interest, then, full-time care in societies where the main source of income of most people is waged work is the kind of activity no self-interested individual in her right mind would ever choose to do. Why, then, is it done at all, why do women do it, and why is it mostly women who do it?

One answer to these questions is to point to the economic pressure on women to become full-time carers, or, more euphemistically, the economic rationality of women "choosing" to stay at home as carers, where they have a choice at all. Given that they are in most cases the poorer earners, their withdrawal from the labor market, combined with their husband's continued and/or increased participation in it, allows maximization of household unit income.[27] Now while this explanation seems to make (some) women's continuing role as full-time carers intelligible, it cannot be the whole story since it confounds economic rationality with gender specificity. First, there is evidence from "cross-class" families and from families with employed wives and unemployed husbands that men do not seem to "choose" to become full-time carers in situations where it would make economic sense for them to do so.[28] Second, given that men in comparable situations seem to rank self-interest higher than household rationality, why is it that women do not? Why is it, in other words, that women take on the role of unpaid carers, regardless of whether it is in their self-interest or not? And why, we may further ask, that even in situations where both men and women engage in waged work, is it still women who typically do most or more of the unpaid caring?[29] In order to answer this question, we have to look at additional aspects of care.

THE PSYCHOLOGY OF CARE

The psychological aspects of caring stand in curious contrast to its material conditions. While involving a material net loss, caring is also often one of the most meaningful and rewarding kinds of activity that anyone could engage in. Witness Noddings in her description of caring:

> I am also aided in meeting the burdens of caring by the reciprocal efforts of the cared-for. When my infant wriggles with delight as I bathe or feed him, I am aware of no burden but only a special delight of my own. . . . Many of the "demands" of caring are not felt as demands. They are, rather, the occasions that offer most of what makes life worth living.[30]

Caring, from this perspective, is a mutual giving and taking, a labor of love and rewarding in itself, even if it does not generate any material returns for the carer. The gratitude in the eyes or words of the cared-for, their well-being and happiness, may constitute more of a reward for the carer than any material benefits ever could.[31]

Caring, moreover, can be an extremely empowering kind of activity and is certainly less alienating than a lot of the paid work that women are offered as an alternative or other unpaid services that women are expected to do. Helping others, looking after them and their welfare, meeting their needs, is one of the most important, if not *the* most important, sources of empowerment for many women. The power a carer feels, however, is subjective, a positive sense of ability and energy,[32] and it is this sense of power that underlies the peculiar logic of care whereby the more one gives, the more one is given in return.[33] Women are very susceptible to this kind of power: Women's self-respect and feelings of self-worth do not necessarily depend so much on any of the public indicators of power such as success, powerful positions, or control of material resources, but often on their being needed by and being able to help others.

Note also that this subjective empowerment deriving from "making others well and happy" is not linked in any straightforward way to the very considerable power and influence a carer has over the cared-for's welfare and it may also be felt side by side with feelings of powerlessness. Thus an overprotective mother may think she is not powerful enough really to care for her children (because their well-being does not entirely depend on her), but doing the best she can for them by meeting all their needs (in a way that keeps them dependent on her and that is not in their best interest). The empowerment as well as the powerlessness she may feel contrast with her power over her children's welfare and her abuse of this power, neither of which she may even be aware of.

Note, furthermore, that the empowerment deriving from care is not as such specific to care. We may feel empowered in the same sense of ability and energy by engaging in other activities that are rewarding in themselves. What is specific to care, however, is its essentially other-directed and other-beneficial nature and the fact that the sense of empowerment derives from exactly those features: It is *because* and to the extent that a carer can make others happy and well that she feels powerful. There is, however, another side to the psychology of caring that contrasts with the positive and glowing picture that presents the "best-case scenario" of the psychological aspects of care. There is a corresponding "worst-case scenario." A carer can easily feel exhausted by the seemingly or often actually never-ending demands of others, by the fact that her efforts are directed toward looking after others' well-being, or worse still, that she may feel used by those she cares for, like cheap labor or even like a servant or slave. She may, in fact, not have a life of her own because her life is filled with caring for others. She may feel completely out of control and powerless because she is at the constant beck and call of others. Because of the peculiar skills and virtues of receptivity and responsiveness that caring involves, a carer can be extremely vulnerable to others' demands. And because care *is* asymmetrical in that, unless it is paid, it implies benefiting others and burdening oneself. The worst-case scenario of the psychology of caring thus reflects the material asymmetry noted previously, while the best-case scenario with which I started off at the beginning of this section stands in contradiction to it. Most carers will experience instances of both the best- and the worst-case scenario and will usually find themselves somewhere in-between the two.[34]

How caring is experienced, whether it comes easily or not so easily to people, furthermore depends to some extent on how this activity fits in with their conceptions of themselves and the structures of their personalities. An individual who sees herself as defined in relation to others, as part of a network of relationships, will be more predisposed to relate to others, perceive their needs, and respond to them than a person who sees herself as separate from others and basically defined by the projects she engages in, the positions she holds, the power or money she has.[35] These differences in self-conception and identity have been found to be gendered: It is women who tend to have the former and men who tend to have the latter type of self-conception. The differences themselves have been explained by reference to the fact that it is women who mother.[36] I cannot discuss the details of this account here, however. What is important to note for the purposes of my own argument is that if this account is valid, it provides an important and very fitting part of the microexplanation of why it is that women continue to do most of the caring.

There is one further and crucially important factor that systematically influences the experience of carers. One implication of the best-case scenario is that carers will probably not experience an acute conflict between meeting the needs of others by caring and meeting their own needs, while the worst-case scenario will probably involve awareness of such a conflict and may also involve resentment of the fact that carers cannot meet their own needs as they perceive them. Now to the extent that women are raised to be *selfless* carers, they are taught the denial of their own needs because this will make them less likely to be aware of a possible conflict between meeting their own needs and those of others. This means that their experience as carers will be systematically biased toward the best-case scenario. Even more dramatically, if their needs structure can be changed in such a way that the meeting of the needs of others will also meet their own needs—for example, their need to feel empowered and important by being indispensable or their need to engage in meaningful activities—the problem of a conflict of needs will not even arise and their experience will not even be in danger of approaching the worst-case scenario. The difference in self-conception between a relationally and nonrelationally defined self may be seen to imply such different needs structures as well. These considerations, if valid, imply that women's awareness of their own needs—supposing we know what these are—may be fundamental to their experience as carers, and that the tradition of raising girls to become selfless wives, mothers, and daughters may have done much harm in preventing women from being aware of their own needs.[37] It is important to stress, however, as several authors do, that women's perception of their own needs will be systematically distorted in a society where their prescribed role is that of caring for others and servicing their needs.[38]

By identifying their own needs with those of others, Jean Baker Miller suggests, women may be able to be happy with their caring and servicing lives, but they are not able to develop themselves and their own potential to the full.[39] Nor, we might add, do they necessarily make the best sort of carers: Not only are they in danger of making children too dependent on them, but they will also not be able to perceive needs in others correctly that they have had to deny in themselves.[40] Moreover, as the existence of both best- and worst-case scenarios in caring testifies, it may not always be possible to identify one's own needs successfully with those of others and at points it may just be obvious that one's own needs conflict with the needs of others. The selfless and self-fulfilled carer, in other words, is a dangerous fiction that is imposed on women at their own cost.

THE CIRCLE OF CARE—THE EXPLOITATION OF WOMEN AS CARERS

A story about women's exploitation must be able to point to the mechanism whereby women are exploited, since there is so much variability in women's material lives that generalizations about their material status—hence their exploitation status—are problematic, if not downright impossible. That exploitative mechanism is the "circle of care," an interlocking set of constraints and practices that channels women into doing the bulk of care that needs to be done in any society. It forms a nexus of material practice and corresponding psychology and ideology that it has proven hard for women to escape and for men to enter. Women's actual work as carers is reinforced by their gender identity, by the strong sense of empowerment and self-realization that they draw from it, and by their ethic of care, which compels them to care where they feel needed. The fact, on the other hand, that it is still mostly women and not men who do the caring continuously works to reproduce and develop women's skills and knowledge as carers and thereby to increase their openness and readiness to respond to needs. Both attention and skills are improved by the actual caring of women and predispose them toward further caring, while men's lacking involvement keeps them inattentive to the demands of those in need and to the need to respond by caring. Thus if men's preferred response to need continues to be the provision of material resources, in correspondence with their roles as breadwinners, they continue to get around actual care and fail to develop the skills needed to care well.

The circle of care represents women's part in the sexual division of labor in our societies. It is the social institution of the sexual division of labor that constructs women as carers and thus systematically "extracts surplus labor" in the form of unpaid care from them. The circle of care works more subtly and on many levels, social and individual, situational and psychological, conscious and unconscious. In my story, women may care for reasons completely unrelated to their husbands: Usually, care is a response to a perceived need, that is, is motivated both from within the carer and by the situation she is in, and it is precisely for this reason that women who are open to the demands of need cannot easily stop caring. Force, in my story, is exerted mostly more indirectly by all the social norms and institutions that channel women into care, including their self-conception and ethics, but not at the point where they actually engage in care, and even if there is force at this point, it is more likely to be exerted by the social services or the family at large rather than, or as well as, the husband by himself.

Who benefits from women's exploitation as carers? The beneficiaries in my story are men in general (as well as women who have opted out from caring): Given that so much care needs to be done in any society, and that there is no particular reason why some rather than others should do it, all those who do not do it benefit from the fact that others have taken it upon themselves to do it.[41] Given, moreover, that most of this care is performed unpaid, hence that those who perform it incur a material net burden while at the same time freeing others to pursue materially more beneficial types of activities (income-generating, as well as leisure), it is clear that noncarers are materially better off than carers. Hence noncarers are "extracting surplus labor"—unpaid labor that does not benefit those who perform it—from the carers, hence benefit from the exploitation of carers.[42]

The story of the exploitation of women as carers, then, avoids the problem of the variability in women's particular material conditions by focusing on the mechanism whereby care is "extracted" from carers. This mechanism also explains the continuing material inequality between men and women by reference to two facts:

(1) the fact that most care is unpaid, hence a material net burden for those who care; and (2) the fact that the shouldering of that burden by women frees men to pursue materially more beneficial types of activities, notably income-generating ones.[43] Note, however, that the women do not have to be poor to be exploited as carers, since the notion of exploitation is relative, although it is also true that women are poorer than men, especially with respect to both material resources *and* time—a fact that becomes especially visible after divorce.[44] Thus even though there is variability in women's material lives, as well as a general difficulty to determine their exploitation status—and some women escape exploitation altogether by refusing to care—the exploitative mechanism is in place as long as the sexual division of labor with regard to care persists, that is, as long as the circle of care exists. This, in turn, means that even if not all women are exploited all of the time, women in general are exploited in this specific way, and therefore each woman is highly vulnerable to being actually exploited qua carer.

Two more clarifications may be necessary to complete the picture. First, I do not mean to claim that women are *only* exploited as carers. They may be exploited as wage workers as well, for example, but I do mean to claim that women's exploitation as carers is the main form of exploitation that applies specifically to women. Second, I should add a note about unpaid work that women do that, according to my definition, is not care, but a service. According to this definition, a lot of work that women do for their husbands or adult children cannot be counted as care because it does not meet a need that those in need could not possibly meet themselves. Given that such work is a service and not care, how does it fit into the exploitation story, if at all? In response to this question, I need to point to what we might call the centripetal tendency of the circle of care: While the circle of care is most centrally about care as I have defined it, it also "pulls in" other types of work, notably other unpaid work that is a service according to my definition. The reasons why such work is performed are several, but are crucially related to the specific features of the circle of care. Once the sexual division of labor with regard to care is established—once the circle of care is functioning—differentiation between men and women is established in various ways. Women typically acquire the other-directed and other-beneficial virtues and skills that are required in any good carer, notably a readiness to respond to the demands of need. Given that these virtues and skills open women up to the demands of others, it becomes difficult to restrict responses to care only, since both care and services meet needs and since it is sometimes difficult to establish whether a need is absolute, that is, cannot be met by the person in need herself, or a need that can be thus met. Also, given this care-based gender differentiation, women's self-conception, fulfillment, and happiness are often dependent on being important or even irreplaceable for others, hence will tend to make them want to "do things for others" regardless of whether they are really needed or whether they are merely providing a service. Furthermore, the social roles of "wife," "mother," "daughter," and especially that of "housewife" include both care and services, and once women have adopted those roles, they will understand them as including both and will encounter social pressure if they do not conform. Lastly, femininity is characterized by both care and services for others, by "being there for others," and although it is easier to refuse to conform to the stereotype as far as services are concerned, the confusion nevertheless remains and may be deeply internalized.

All these factors, then, contribute to the widening of the circle of care to include unpaid services as well, but at the heart of the circle of care remains women's performance of care, and it is women's performance of care, not of services, that poses the most difficult problem as far as the abolition of women's exploitation as carers is concerned.

OUTLOOK: CONCLUSIONS AND OPENINGS

What are we to make of this diagnosis? Further conclusions, but also, as always, new openings, suggest themselves at the practical level of thinking about women's exploitation as carers. At the practical level, there is a solution to the exploitation dilemma, which consists of the systematic prevention of the type of situation where carers find themselves trapped by such dilemmas. The exploitation of carers can thus be abolished.

Given, as I have argued previously, the irreconcilable tension between considerations of care and considerations about the exploitation of carers captured in the exploitation dilemma, and given that there is no solution to the dilemma within the ethic of care, the solution has to lie in the application or social realization of considerations of justice. Now, one possible solution—which, since it is obviously silly, I mention only to make a certain point about care—would be to abolish the ethic of care altogether by reeducating carers into fighters so as to deliver them from their vulnerability to exploitation as carers. I take it, however, that this solution is not desirable and that the ethic of care is here to stay. To begin with, care as a practice is bound to continue since there will always be needs that persons other than those in need have to meet. Care as necessary labor, in other words, cannot be abolished precisely because it is necessary labor and will always have to be performed in any human society, whether this is "officially" recognized or not. Furthermore, given the need for, and practice of, care, there will always be people who endorse an ethic of care—assuming that it is the most likely and the most fitting ethic to hold for those who engage in caring, as well as the most beneficial ethic for those cared for. In other words, it is not only necessary that care continue to be performed, but it is also desirable that the ethic of care continue to be held by people. Given, however, that people who hold the ethic of care are vulnerable to exploitation because they do not have the moral resources to prevent their own exploitation, and that social justice demands that nobody be exploited, another solution to the problem will have to be found.

It might be thought, conversely, that the answer to the problem is simply that everybody should care, hence that fighters be reeducated into carers. This, to me, seems an excellent idea for various reasons, not least because the abolition of the moral division of labor would make men and thus societies more humane and livable. The exploitation problem, however, would not be solved by this change either, since it would merely end up making everybody vulnerable to exploitation. While this might be preferable to a situation where only some, mostly women, are vulnerable to exploitation, given that it abolishes the gendered aspect of the moral division of labor and thus spreads the risk of being exploited more evenly, it does not abolish the exploitation of carers as such. The actual burden of care might still be rather uneven because some are faced with more demands on their care than others, simply in virtue of the chance distribution of people with needs that make heavy demands on carers and the uneven distribution of patterns of relatedness. Hence exploitation dilemmas may still arise, and the reeducation of fighters into carers, while spreading the burden of care as well as the risk of exploitation more evenly, does not present a solution to the exploitation problem, although it certainly represents an important and desirable change.

In order to get closer to the solution, then, we have to look again at the situation that gives rise to the exploitation dilemma. The crucial aspect in this situation is the fact that not caring results in harm. If it did not, the carer could freely decide not to care and would therefore not be vulnerable to exploitation. Accordingly, if a carer had systematic access to care provided by others—"third parties"—the dilemma would not arise and exploitation would cease to be the systematic result of carers' endorsing an ethic of care. However, such access cannot be provided privately, either unpaid or via the market, without raising further problems about the uneven provision of such access and the exploitation of badly paid carers. Unpaid care is not always available, especially in the age of the nuclear family where other members of the family who might have helped live too far away. Reliance on the unpaid care of others, at any rate, just passes the problem of exploitation on to other unpaid carers. Leaving the problem to the private market will result in further injustice, as this creates a new class of badly paid carers who work for those who can afford to "buy themselves out" of their caring burden. The more inequality there is in society, the more likely this pattern is to occur. The badly paid carers in turn will not be able to afford to pay for care, hence have to care themselves, and so will those who cannot afford to pay for care. These two groups thus clearly remain vulnerable to exploitation as carers. Hence private provision of care does not solve the problem, since it merely shifts the problem of exploitation to other vulnerable groups in society. The only possible conclusion, therefore, is that a just society has to take it upon itself to provide care for carers to take up as and when they are in danger of becoming overburdened. The practical solution to the exploitation dilemma thus is the systematic social provision of care to replace that of carers where needed. The solution requires, however, that carers' exploitation is seen as a problem of social justice.

This solution recommends itself on various grounds. First, it allows people to endorse an ethic of care because it is safe for them to do so.[45] This seems to me very important not only because, as I point out earlier, the need for care is permanent—because care is necessary labor—but also because a society in which people can endorse and act according to an ethic of care will be a much more humane society. Second, given that it implies the conception of the exploitation dilemma as a *social* problem, it allows further questions to be asked and observations to be made about the distribution of the burden of care at the social level. I point to various such avenues in what follows.

First, it allows us to ask whether the sexual division of labor that makes women provide most of the unpaid care is justified itself, even if the problem of the exploitation of carers can be solved. Thus note that, although I have developed this solution in general terms, that is, for carers in general, it is a solution that will mainly benefit women, given the sexual division of labor. It thus contingently solves the problem of women's exploitation because it solves the problem of carers' exploitation, but it does not address the further question of who should care in the first place. While it takes the exploitative sting out of the ethic of care and therefore out of the sexual division of labor between carers and fighters, it does not provide an answer to the following further question: Even if it is safe to care, is there not something objectionable for some to get away without caring, especially if the universal distribution of care is in itself desirable and probably immensely beneficial? This question can now be posed clearly and, furthermore, more distinctly because it is unrelated to the question of women's oppression. As I argued previously, the abolition of the moral division of labor that goes hand in hand with the sexual division of labor, while in itself not a solution to the exploitation problem, may be an important part of an overall aim for change because it demands from men equally what women have always been expected to provide. The focus of the problem to be solved, in this aim, is correspondingly shifted away from women and onto men: Instead of asking ourselves whether women care too much, we will ask ourselves why is it that men do not care enough?

Second, focusing on the social distribution of care provides an answer to the problem of how women could be freed from their "slavish relationship" to women's work. The answer is that the sexual division of labor has to be understood as a social institution that can be changed, rather than as a natural given. It is this different understanding that will allow, first, the analysis of the mechanisms that enforce the division of labor and, second, conscious social decisions about how to change it. The liberation of women from their "slavish relationship" to care thus implies, most important, the realization that this relationship is socially constructed in the first place, and this in turn implies reflection on the distribution of care at a social level.

Third, the further question can be posed to what extent care should be understood as a private responsibility, and to what extent it should be seen as a public and social responsibility. It is unsatisfactory to conceive of care as work that has to be provided privately, by the family, and more specifically, whose provision it is the duty of the head of the household to ensure. Thus the focus is on the husband and head of household, rather than on men in general, as those who benefit from women's exploitation, and the general implication is that heads of households should do more caring themselves. As I argue earlier, however, a redistribution of care between men and women is by itself no solution to the exploitation of carers. The crucial theoretical move in the solution to the problem, by contrast, is from the microlevel of individual caring relations and provision, such as in households, to the social level. If this theoretical shift is made, it then becomes possible to ask at what level the responsibility for care lies, and to see the fact that it is the very relegation of the responsibility for care to the private sphere, combined with the sexual division of labor, that enables women's exploitation in their own homes.

Fourth, different scenarios of the distribution or provision of care, at both the public and private level, can be thought out, analyzed, and evaluated. Some models may recommend themselves more than others, not only on the grounds that they are less exploitative of carers, but also on other grounds, such as that they provide a way of abolishing instead of reinforcing the sexual division of labor, that they encourage the learning of caring skills, or that they are less exploitative of large families' care for many more children or individual carers' unwavering endorsement of the ethic of care and thus provision of care in the face of huge demands on their care. I sketch three such scenarios to indicate what kind of discussion I have in mind.

First, we might imagine a society where the burden of care is socially recognized as an important task in society and distributed equally to all able members of society. This would certainly abolish exploitation, but it would also require that no care be provided privately, based on patterns of relatedness or willingness to pay, since such private provision—as I have argued previously—would invariably be uneven and thus disturb the intended equal distribution. Care, to adopt Marxist terminology, would thus be completely socialized. But would anybody want this extreme form of reorganization not only of care, but of all social life as we know it, given that nobody could be allowed simply to care for their friend, partner, or child on the basis of their relation to them? Would it be feasible at all, given that no one can prevent people from liking and caring about and for each other?[46] Hence whatever may be said in favor of this scenario, its disadvantages certainly outweigh its attractiveness in "neatly" solving the problem of carers' exploitation.

Second, as mentioned briefly already, we might think about leaving the private distribution of care along patterns of relatedness (and, to some extent, proximity) undisturbed, but with the state providing systematic backup care to private carers as and when needed. This would equally tackle the problem of the exploitation of carers, but would leave the gendered division of care and morality intact. It might also turn out to be extremely expensive if backup care is to be well paid and resources for it have to be raised through taxation. Such a traditional state provision solution thus may well be too expensive, as well as not radical enough.

Third, then, is a more imaginative scenario: Rather than follow the welfare state model of social provision, one might conceive of care as part of a citizen's obligation to contribute her share to one of the most important functions, if not the most important function, any self-governing society has—namely, to ensure the well-being of its members. Citizenship would be redefined to comprise care as much as, or even more importantly than, defense as every citizen's obligation. (Why should killing and destroying, or preparing to kill and destroy, be more honorable and worthy a citizen's contribution to her society than caring?) The obligation would be men's and women's equally and would be discharged by their contributing a certain share of their lifetime to what we might call a "caring service." Such a universal caring service may be a better way of providing backup care for private carers for a number of reasons: It makes care more visible; it gives care the central place and social recognition that has been denied it for so long; it is a "school for carers" for both men and women and may thus have an important role reeducating fighters into carers by fostering the skills and virtues of care in everybody; it abolishes the gendered division of labor and morality; and it may be cheaper than the state provision envisaged in the second scenario.

I cannot pursue this discussion any further, but the point of it should be clear: My presentation of women's work as care and specifically of the exploitation dilemma enables this kind of discussion in a new way because it directs the view to both private and public, individual and social provision of care and the effects such patterns of provision will have. Hopefully, much more discussion at this policy level will take place in the wake of the more theoretical arguments concerning care.

Last, but not least, the problem of the exploitation of carers and therefore that of the exploitation of women forces itself onto the social justice agenda by being posed as a social problem. It has not been part of this agenda, because, until recently, women's oppression and exploitation have not been seen as problems of social justice;[47] as long as care is considered a quintessentially private activity, it seems to lie beyond the scope of any theory of social justice. But whether and to what extent care is considered a public or private responsibility is itself at issue, especially if the relegation of care to the private sphere has such grave consequences. It would seem, therefore, not only that the ethic of care is in need of being complemented by considerations of social justice, but also that the theorization of social justice is in need of being complemented by a theory of care and of women's exploitation as carers.

NOTES

This chapter is compiled from different sections of Diemut Grace Bubeck's *Care, Gender, and Justice*. The editors, together with Sarah C. Miller, edited and did minor rewriting to fashion the selections into a freestanding article. We want to express our gratitude to Sarah Miller for her careful selections of relevant portions. We also are grateful to Diemut Grace Bubeck for allowing us to take these liberties with her work.

1. Exploitation is the extraction of (unpaid or otherwise unremunerated) labor from those who are exploited to the benefit of the exploiter. In the specific case of interest here, it is the extraction of unpaid labor from women by and to the benefit of men.

2. Consider, for example, the ancient Greek practice of infanticide.

3. Marx, in fact, did at least sometimes remember that the "reproduction of labor power" included generational reproduction, hence that necessary labor did not exclusively benefit the worker himself.

4. See A. Bebel, *Women under Socialism* (New York: Schocken, 1971), but also R. Schwartz Cowan, *More Work for Mother* (New York: Basic, 1983).

5. This dual reference could in principle be distinguished by using *caring about* to refer to the emotional state and *caring for* to refer to the activity, but there is no agreement in the literature about the usage of these terms. Thus the distinction between *caring about* and *caring for* had been used to make various and very different conceptual distinctions; it has also been used to distinguish between different types of objects of caring (see J. C. Tronto, "Women and Caring: What Can Feminists Learn about Morality from Caring?" in *Gender/Body/Knowledge,* ed. A. M. Jaggar and S. R. Bordo (New Brunswick, N.J.: Rutgers University Press, 1989), as well as between different components of care (B. Fisher and J. Tronto, "Toward a Feminist Theory of Caring," in *Circles of Care: Work and Identity in Women's Lives,* ed. E. K. Abel and M. K. Nelson (Albany, N.Y.: State University of New York Press, 1990). I shall therefore not use the two terms to make any of these distinctions.

6. N. Noddings, *Caring: A Feminine Approach to Ethics and Moral Education* (Berkeley: University of California Press, 1984); see also M. Mayeroff, *On Caring* (New York: Harper & Row, 1971).

7. R. Parker, "Tending and Social Policy," in *A New Look at the Personal Social Services,* Discussion Paper no. 4, ed. E. M. Goldberg and A. Hatch (London: Policy Studies Institute, 1981), 17. Noddings suggests at some point that the activity of caring "might properly be called care-taking," hence seemingly brackets out caring as an activity from her discussion of caring altogether on the grounds that it is caring as an attitude or emotion that "gives meaning to the caretaking." See Noddings, *Caring,* 22.

8. H. Graham, "Caring: A Labor of Love," in *A Labor of Love: Women, Work and Caring,* ed. J. Finch and D. Groves (London: Routledge & Kegan Paul, 1983), passim; see also J. C. Tronto, *Moral Boundaries: A Political Argument for an Ethic of Care* (London: Routledge, 1993), 104.

9. See Parker's definition of caring as "tending" in the context of a discussion of care for elderly people (Parker, "Tending," 1981).

10. Cf. Parker, "Tending," 17; C. Thomas, "De-Constructing Concepts of Care," *Sociology* 27 (1993); C. Ungerson, "The Language of Care: Crossing the Boundaries," in *Gender and Caring: Work and Welfare in Britain and Scandinavia,* ed. C. Ungerson (Hemel and Hempstead: Harvester Wheatsheaf, 1990); Tronto, *Moral Boundaries,* 105.

11. Hence the definition crosscuts the commonsense distinction between housework and care that I started off with. This does not mean the distinction has become meaningless; it simply means that caring can involve activities usually described as housework.

12. Some feminist authors in the social policy area avoid this bias (e.g., Thomas, "De-Constructing Concepts"; C. Ungerson, "Introduction," in *Gender and Caring: Work and*

Welfare in Britain and Scandinavia, ed. C. Ungerson [Hemel and Hempstead: Harvester Wheatsheaf, 1990]; Ungerson, "The Language of Care"; and H. Graham, "The Concepts of Caring in Feminist Research: The Case of Domestic Service," *Sociology* 25 [1991]). Other feminists, however, have raised doubts about the possibility of speaking meaningfully about care in general—e.g., S. Ruddick, *Maternal Thinking: Toward a Politics of Peace* (London: Women's Press, 1989), 46–47. (But see also S. Ruddick, "The Rationality of Care," in *Women, Militarism, and War*, ed. J. B. Elshtain and S. Tobias [Savage, Md.: Rowman & Littlefield, 1990], where it does seem to be implied that it is possible to generalize over various forms of care.)

13. See V. Held, "Non-Contractual Society: A Feminist View," in *Science, Morality and Feminist Theory*, ed. M. Hanen and K. Nielsen, *Canadian Journal of Philosophy* Supplement (Calgary: University of Calgary Press, 1987); V. Held, *Feminist Morality: Transforming Culture, Society, and Politics* (Chicago: University of Chicago Press, 1993); A. C. Baier, "The Need for More Than Justice," in Hanen and Nielsen, eds., *Science, Morality*. Caring can model more social relationships than mothering. (S. L. Hoagland, "Some Concerns about Nel Noddings' Caring," *Hypatia* 5, no. 1 [1990]: 109–14.)

14. See, e.g., R. Nozick, *Anarchy, State and Utopia* (Oxford: Blackwell, 1974); and C. Pateman, *The Sexual Contract* (Cambridge: Polity, 1988), for a critique of contract theories.

15. I also think that care actually is work, but rather than try to establish this claim, I will simply point out the respects in which care is similar to work, and thus similarly a burden. Richard Norman helped me clarify my argument about care being a burden.

16. To some extent, the fiction of people's autonomy and equal power—as opposed to dependency on others and equal powerlessness—is socially (and theoretically, see, e.g., R. Dworkin, "What Is Equality? Part I: Equality of Welfare; Part II: Equality of Resources," *Philosophy and Public Affairs* 10, no. 3 [1981]: 185–246) maintained and perpetuated through the institution of insurance policies, which turn people in need into people *entitled to* care, i.e., with the power to command care. This institution, however, is accessible only to those able to enter contracts and endowed with material resources—that is, adults with a more than basic income. Hence, on the face of it, given that it is a "solution" only for some, it cannot possibly be a just solution. Moreover, it does not solve, or even address, every human being's utter and absolute dependency at the outset of our lives, nor can it possibly cater for all the various needs that people have and that make them dependent on others, notably emotional ones. Note that this point is not about limits to people's autonomy, such as social context and individual development that can be overcome in ideal circumstances; it is about absolute limits to anybody's autonomy. It is these absolute limits that lack recognition, let alone positive endorsement, in the liberal ideal of autonomy. (See Held, *Feminist Morality*, for an argument in a similar direction.)

17. Those who are "in a position to care" are not necessarily the long-term carers of long-term dependents: If I see a crying child in the street, I am in a position to care, even if this child is a stranger. As noted earlier, the roles of carer and cared-for are not necessarily fixed.

18. R. Goodin's *Protecting the Vulnerable: A Reanalysis of Our Social Responsibilities* (Chicago: University of Chicago Press, 1985) is a noteworthy exception. Yet it is also no acknowledgment of the needs that make *any* human being dependent on others, since his stress lies on created or, at best, grown relations of dependency, while the focus of a theory of care lies on inevitable dependency.

19. See J. C. Tronto, "Reflection on Gender, Morality, and Power: Caring and the Moral Problems of Otherness," in *Gender, Care and Justice in Feminist Political Theory*, ed.

J. C. Tronto et al., compiled by S. Sevenhuijsen (Utrecht: Anna Maria van Schuurman Centrum, Graduate School for Advanced Research in Women's Studies, Working Paper, 1991), 8; Tronto, *Moral Boundaries*, chapter 5; Noddings, *Caring*, 16, 19, 22, 30–35, 122–23 and passim; Ruddick, *Maternal Thinking*.

20. Noddings, *Caring*, 22.

21. See K. Gieve, "And Not to Count the Cost," in *Balancing Acts*, ed. K. Gieve (London: Virago, 1989), 43 ff.

22. Held makes a similar point in Held, "Non-Contractual Society," 103–1; see also Held, *Feminist Morality*.

23. Kymlicka, in his discussion of the ethic of care, realizes the problem of "heteronomy" in care, but shies away from its implications. See W. Kymlicka, *Contemporary Political Philosophy* (Oxford: Oxford University Press, 1990), 280–81.

24. By *public*, I refer here to state-provided care; by semipublic, to private-sector care, that is, to care provided either by professionals as self-employed workers or by professionals employed by commercial or voluntary organizations. This slightly awkward terminology is forced by the fact that there is a third kind of care, which is unpaid and provided in the "private sphere" of people's homes, usually by people related to those they care for, either as kin or as friends or neighbors. See S. M. Okin, *Justice, Gender, and the Family* (New York: Basic, 1991), on the ambiguity of the public/private distinction that forces such terminology.

25. There are two further alternatives, which are, however, both not very common: One could try to arrange for others to provide child care unpaid, either on the basis of exchange, as in child-care groups, or on the basis of kinship relations. While child-care groups are difficult to organize and maintain, members of the family are often not easily available in a society based on nuclear family units or "defective" family units, where only one adult is a full member of the unit. Where extended families are more common, as in some ethnic minority communities, unpaid child care is more easily available.

26. She might take on home work, but home work is even worse paid than typical "women's jobs." See S. Allen and C. Wolkowitz, *Homeworking: Myths and Realities* (Basingstoke: MacMillan Education, 1987).

27. See, e.g., Becker's 'New Home Economics' in G. Becker, *A Treatise on the Family* (Cambridge, Mass.: Harvard University Press, 1981).

28. See S. McRae, *Cross-Class Families* (Oxford: Clarendon, 1986), and L. Morris, *The Workings of the Household* (Cambridge: Polity, 1990).

29. See the data from time budget studies; Hartmann and Pleck provide a useful discussion and overview. Time budget studies are not necessarily reliable indicators of the performance of care, however, because they mainly aim at measuring time spent on housework. Thus some definitions of housework exclude child care, while others include it, but do typically not include other types of care. Some housework tasks, however, will be caring activities according to my definition. It may be argued, therefore, that the amount of housework women do as compared with men is a good indicator of how much care they do as compared with men. This argument is further supported by the fact that both care and housework are traditionally and stereotypically "women's work." H. Hartman, "The Family as the Locus of Gender, Class and Political Struggle: The Example of Housework," in *Feminism and Methodology*, ed. S. Harding (Bloomington and Milton Keynes: Indiana University Press and Open University Press, 1987); J. H. Pleck, *Working Wives/Working Husbands* (Beverly Hills, Calif.: Sage, in cooperation with the National Council on Family Relations, 1985).

30. Noddings, *Caring*, 52.

31. For an argument that the language of "economic man" is particularly inappropriate to caring relationships, see Held, "Non-Contractual Society," and Held, *Feminist Morality*.

32. See Gilligan, reporting McClelland's research on the meaning of power, where men interpret power as "assertion and aggression," while women "portray acts of nurturance as acts of strength." C. Gilligan, *In a Different Voice* (Cambridge, Mass.: Harvard University Press, 1982), 167–68.

33. See Y. Alibhai, "Particularity, Gilligan, and the Two-Levels View: A Reply," *Ethics* 100 (1989): 35; see also Gilligan's more extensive discussion of interdependence in C. Gilligan, "Prologue: Adolescent Development Reconsidered," in *Mapping the Moral Domain: A Contribution of Women's Thinking to Psychology and Education*, ed. C. Gilligan, J. V. Ward, and J. M. Taylor, with B. Bardige (Cambridge, Mass.: Harvard University Graduate School of Education, 1988), 16; and Noddings, *Caring*, 52.

34. See C. Ungerson, *Policy Is Personal: Sex, Gender and Informal Care* (London: Tavistock, 1987).

35. See Gilligan, *Different Voice*; N. Chodorow, *The Reproduction of Mothering* (Berkeley: University of California Press, 1978).

36. See Chodorow, *Reproduction*.

37. See J. B. Miller, *Toward a New Psychology of Women* (Harmondsworth: Pelican, 1988).

38. See, for example, Miller, *Toward*, esp. 18–19.

39. See Miller, *Toward*. For the distorting effects of care on women themselves, their relationships, and the nature of their care, see L. A. Blum, M. Homiak, J. Housman, and N. Scheman, "Altruism and Women's Oppression," in *Women and Philosophy*, ed. C. Gould and M. Wartofsky (Totowa, N.J.: Rowman & Allanheld, 1976); also B. Houston, "Prolegomena to Future Caring," in *Who Cares? Theory, Research and Educational Implications of the Ethics of Care*, ed. M. M. Brabeck (New York: Praeger, 1989).

40. See A. Miller, *Banished Knowledge* (London: Virago, 1990).

41. Delphy's earlier work is more structural than Delphy and Leonard's, and there is at least one earlier paper where Delphy takes a more structural line in answer to the question of who benefits from women's exploitation and the exploitation of ethnic minorities. C. Delphy, "Our Friends and Ourselves," in *Close to Home* (London: Hutchinson, 1984), especially 144 ff.

42. There is a slight complication in this exploitation story compared with more traditional ones: The *immediate* beneficiaries of care—those whose needs are met—are third parties, but not exploiters. This is unlike the more traditional case of exploitation, where the benefit from the work of the exploited accrues to the exploiter. The exploiters, in the case of care, then, are those persons whose time is freed by not having to care.

43. If *time* were focused on more explicitly as a material resource, the difference would be even more obvious. Noncarers gain both time and thus the opportunity to engage in activities that will increase their potential to generate material resources in the future (education; skill and knowledge enhancement through work).

44. On "vulnerability by marriage," see L. Weitzman, *The Divorce Revolution: The Unexpected Social and Economic Consequences for Women and Children in America* (New York: Free Press, 1985); also Okin, *Justice, Gender*.

45. Brecht's play *The Good Person of Szechuan* deals with a structurally very similar problem: The one morally good person in a morally corrupt society ends up having to double up as her wicked (male) cousin in order to put to a halt the typically self-destructive situation she

finds herself in. (Interestingly enough, the cousin starts appearing only at the point where the good person has to make provisions for her baby to be born.) Brecht thus didactically leads his audience to the conclusion that the world needs changing so that it is safe to be good: a move from the individual to the social level exactly parallel to the one I am proposing.

46. This last point, ironically enough, is parallel to Nozick's Wilt Chamberlain argument that nobody can prevent capitalist acts from occurring spontaneously (Nozick, *Anarchy*, 160–62).

47. See Okin, *Justice, Gender*.

8

The Future of Feminist Liberalism

Martha C. Nussbaum

Giribala, at the age of fourteen, then started off to make her home with her husband. Her mother put into a bundle the pots and pans that she would be needing. Watching her doing that, Aulchand remarked, "Put in some rice and lentils too. I've got a job at the house of the *babu*. Must report to work the moment I get back. . . ."

Giribala picked up the bundle of rice, lentils, and cooking oil and left her village, walking a few steps behind him. He walked ahead, and from time to time asked her to walk faster, as the afternoon was starting to fade.

—Mahasweta Devi, "Giribala," 1982[1]

It will be seen how in place of the *wealth* and *poverty* of political economy come the *rich human being* and *rich human need*. The rich human being is . . . the human being *in need of* a totality of human life-activities.

—Marx, *Economic and Philosophical Manuscripts of 1844*

LIBERALISM AND FEMINISM

During the 1950s and 1960s, it was widely believed that political philosophy had come to a stop. The normative tradition of theorizing about justice that extended, in Western thought, from Plato through Sidgwick and T. H. Green was condemned as "nonsense" by those under the sway of positivism, since it pursued neither conceptual analysis nor empirical factual inquiry. Young American philosophers were discouraged from pursuing projects in this area, unless they confined themselves to analyzing the function of moral and political language.

By now, all this has dramatically changed. Theorizing about justice is one of the most fertile areas of work for young philosophers, and there is virtually no department that would condemn all such work as soft and unphilosophical. Two distinct sources of creativity in this area must be credited with the shift, and it is the tense relationship between them that I wish to consider.

On the one hand, writers in the tradition of Kantian liberalism must surely be given much of the credit for the turn back to substantive political philosophy. John Rawls and Jürgen Habermas, in particular, have become central points of reference, and both must surely be counted as among the most distinguished philosophers of our century.

On the other hand, the most creative movement in the revival of theorizing about justice, I would argue, has been feminist philosophy, which has put new questions on the agenda of moral, political, and legal thought and has pursued those questions with a prophetic sense of urgency that can be lacking in our sometimes all-too-detached profession. Important though issues of gender justice are now agreed to be, they were simply not addressed in most major works of political philosophy in the Western tradition; or, as in the case of Rousseau, they were addressed in a perverse and unhelpful manner. Plato and John Stuart Mill are major exceptions; Mill's *The Subjection of Women* is still one of the major works in the subject, alongside the writings of Mary Wollstonecraft and other feminist women who wrote philosophy before the late-twentieth-century feminist movement.[2] But systematic investigation of justice in the family, of domestic violence and child abuse, of sexual harassment and full workplace equality—all these awaited the modern feminist movement and have been illuminated by its insights.[3]

As the names of Wollstonecraft and Mill indicate, liberalism and feminism have not always been at odds in our philosophical tradition.[4] Even today, some of our most influential feminist philosophers are liberals.[5] But, on the whole, liberalism has not fared well in feminist circles. Leading feminists have denounced liberalism as a theoretical approach with insufficient radical potential to expose the roots of women's subordination or to articulate principles for a society of gender justice.[6]

I have argued in the past that some of these feminist criticisms are based on a misunderstanding of the deepest and most appealing liberal conceptions, and that other criticisms, while based on an adequate understanding, should themselves be rejected in favor of liberal conceptions by those who seek full justice for the world's women.[7] Here I shall not return to those arguments. Instead, I investigate two areas of political thought in which liberalism, even in its strongest forms, has not yet given satisfactory answers to deep problems exposed by feminist thinkers. [8] These areas are the need for care in times of extreme dependency, and the political role of the family. I argue that the failure of current liberal theories to solve these problems does not mean that we should reject liberalism; it does mean, however, that we need to recast it in some major ways. I'll conclude that a form of liberalism based on ideas of human functioning and capability can carry us further than we have been able to go so far.

NEED AND DEPENDENCY

All theories of justice and morality based on the idea of a social contract adopt a fictional hypothesis that appears innocent, but that ultimately has problematic consequences. This is the fiction of competent adulthood. Whatever differences there are among the different founders of that tradition, all accept the basic Lockean conception of a contract among parties who, in the state of nature, are "free, equal, and independent."[9] Thus for Kant, persons are characterized by both freedom and equality, and the social contract is defined as an agreement among persons so characterized. Contemporary contractarians explicitly adopt this hypothesis. For David Gauthier, people of unusual need are "not party to the moral relationships grounded by a contractarian theory."[10] Similarly, the citizens in Rawls's Well Ordered Society are "fully cooperating members of society over a complete life."[11]

Life, of course, is not like that. Real people begin their lives as helpless infants and remain in a state of extreme, asymmetrical dependency, both physical and mental, for anywhere from ten to twenty years. At the other end of life, those who are lucky enough to live on into old age are likely to encounter another period of extreme dependency, either physical or mental or both, which may itself continue in some form for as much as twenty years. During the middle years of life, many of us encounter periods of extreme dependency, some of which involve our mental powers and some our bodily powers only, but all of which may put us in need of daily, even hourly, care by others. Finally, and centrally, there are many citizens who never have the physical and/or mental powers requisite for independence. These citizens are dependent in different ways. Some have high intellectual capabilities, but are unable to give and receive love and friendship; some are capable of love, but unable to learn basic intellectual skills. Some have substantial emotional and intellectual capabilities, but in a form or at a level that requires special care. These lifelong states of asymmetrical dependency are in many respects isomorphic to the states of infants and the elderly.

In short, any real society is a caregiving and care-receiving society and must therefore discover ways of coping with these facts of human neediness and dependency that are compatible with the self-respect of the recipients and do not exploit the caregivers. This is a central issue for feminism since, in every part of the world, women do a large part of this work, usually without pay, and often without recognition that it is work. They are often thereby handicapped in other functions of life.[12]

It must be said at the outset that in this particular area a Kantian starting point is likely to give bad guidance. For Kant, human dignity and our moral capacity, dignity's source, are radically separate from the natural world. Morality certainly has the task of providing for human neediness, but the idea that we are at bottom split beings, both rational persons and animal dwellers in the world of nature, never ceases to influence Kant's way of thinking about how these deliberations about our needs will go.

What's wrong with the split? Quite a lot. First, it ignores the fact that our dignity is just the dignity of a certain sort of animal. It is the animal sort of dignity, and that very sort of dignity could not be possessed by a being who was not mortal and vulnerable, just as the beauty of a cherry tree in bloom could not be possessed by a diamond. If it makes sense to think of God as having dignity (I'm not sure—magnificence and awe-inspiringness seem more appropriate attributes), it is emphatically not dignity of that type.[13] Second, the split wrongly denies that animality can itself have a dignity; thus it leads us to slight aspects of our own lives that have worth and to distort our relation to the other animals.[14] Third, it makes us think of the core of ourselves as self-sufficient, not in need of the gifts of fortune; in so thinking we greatly distort the nature of our own morality and rationality, which are thoroughly material and animal themselves; we learn to ignore the fact that disease, old age, and accident can impede the moral and rational functions, just as much as the other animal functions. Fourth, it makes us think of ourselves as atemporal. We forget that the usual human life cycle brings with it periods of extreme dependency, in which our functioning is very similar to that enjoyed by the mentally or physically handicapped throughout their lives.

It is important to notice that the split goes wrong in both directions: It suggests, as I have said, that our rationality is independent of our vulnerable animality; and it also suggests that animality, and nonhuman animals, lack intelligence, are just brutish and "dumb." Both implications of the split should, of course, be called into question: In nature we find a rich continuum of types of intelligence and of practical capacities of many types; we cannot understand ourselves well without situating ourselves within that continuum.[15]

Political thought in the Kantian social-contract tradition (to stick with the part of the tradition I find deepest and most appealing) suffers from the conception of the person with which it begins. Rawls's contracting parties are fully aware of their need for material goods. Here Rawls diverges from Kant, building need into the foundations of the theory.[16] But he does so only to a degree, for the parties are imagined throughout as competent contracting adults, roughly similar in need, and capable of a level of social cooperation that makes them able to make a contract with others. Such a hypothesis seems required by the very idea of a contract for mutual advantage.

In so conceiving of persons, Rawls explicitly omits from the situation of basic political choice the more extreme forms of need and dependency human beings may experience. His very concept of social cooperation is based on the idea of reciprocity between rough equals, and has no explicit place for relations of extreme dependency. Thus, for example, Rawls refuses to grant that we have any duties of justice to animals, on the grounds that they are not capable of reciprocity (TJ, 17, 504–05); they are owed "compassion and humanity," but "[t]hey are outside the scope of the theory of justice, and it does not seem possible to extend the contract doctrine so as to include them in a natural way" (TJ, 512). This makes a large difference to his theory of political distribution. For his account of the primary goods, introduced, as it is, as an account of the needs of citizens who are characterized by the two moral powers and by the capacity to be "fully cooperating," has no place for the need of many real people for the kind of care we give to people who are not independent.[17]

Now, of course, Rawls is perfectly aware that his theory focuses on some cases and leaves others to one side. He insists that although the need for care for people who are not independent is "a pressing practical question," it may reasonably be postponed to the legislative stage, after basic political institutions are designed:

> So let's add that all citizens are fully cooperating members of society over the course of a complete life. This means that everyone has sufficient intellectual powers to play a normal part in society, and no one suffers from unusual needs that are especially difficult to fulfill, for example, unusual and costly medical requirements. Of course, care for those with such requirements is a pressing practical question. But at this initial stage, the fundamental problem of social justice arises between those who are full and active and morally conscientious participants in society, and directly or indirectly associated together throughout a complete life. Therefore, it is sensible to lay aside certain difficult complications. If we can work out a theory that covers the fundamental case, we can try to extend it to other cases later. (DL, 546)

This reply seems inadequate. Care for children, the elderly, and the mentally and physically handicapped is a major part of the work that needs to be done in any society, and in most societies it is a source of great injustice. Any theory of justice needs to think about the problem from the beginning, in the design of the most basic level of institutions, and particularly in its theory of the primary goods.[18]

More generally, variations and asymmetries in physical need are simply not isolated or easily isolatable cases; they are a pervasive fact of human life: Pregnant or lactating women need more nutrients than nonpregnant persons; children need more protein than adults; and the very young and very old need more care than others in most areas of their lives. Even within the clearly recognized terrain of the "fully cooperating," then, the theory of primary goods seems flawed if it does not take such variations into account in measuring who is and is not the least well off, rather than, as the theory recommends, determining that status by income and wealth alone.[19] Amartya Sen has used the example of a person in a wheelchair, who will certainly need more resources to be fully mobile than will a person whose limbs work well.[20] With the same amount of income and wealth, this person will actually be much worse off than someone whose limbs work well.[21] Rawls can't consistently exclude this person, who surely has the mental and moral powers. But even if he should exclude these physical disabilities, as some of his remarks suggest,[22] the problem of variation in need is pervasive. So even in order to take account of the physical needs of nondisabled citizens—which the theory seems bound, even on its own terms, to take account of[23]—Rawls will need a way of measuring well-being that does not rely on income and wealth alone, but looks at the abilities of citizens to engage in a wide range of human activities.

Thomas Scanlon confronts these problems facing a Kantian contract doctrine much more directly than does Rawls. I am unable here to discuss the subtleties of his view, which in any case is a moral and not a political contract doctrine, and which does not employ a hypothetical initial contract situation as does Rawls's theory. But, taking cognizance of the problem posed for such a theory by people with various handicaps, and by nonhuman animals, he concludes that we may recognize facts of extreme dependency in such a doctrine in one of two ways. Either we may persist in our pursuit of the contract doctrine and say that the contracting parties are also trustees for those who are incapable of participating in that process; or we may say that the contract doctrine offers an account of only one part of morality: We will need a different account to cope with the facts of extreme dependency.[24] Applied to the Rawlsian project of selecting principles of justice that will form the basic structure of society,[25] this would mean that we either take the parties in the Original Position to be trustees for the interests of all dependent members of society, as they currently are trustees for future generations—or else we should grant that the Original Position is not a complete device for designing political justice, and that other approaches are also required.

The first solution seems unsatisfactory. To make the "fully cooperating" trustees in a hypothetical original situation slights the dignity of physically and mentally handicapped people, suggesting that they are worthy of respect in the design of basic political institutions only on account of some relationship in which they stand to so-called fully cooperating people. The bargain, after all, is a bargain for mutual advantage, and it assumes a rough equality among its participants; the dependents enter the bargain not because they are equipped to participate in such a bargain, but only because a contracting party cares about their interests. Furthermore, the move also means making the "fully cooperating" trustees for their own infancy and senility and perhaps other stages of their own lives. Gauthier puts the problem most starkly, when he says that the elderly have paid for their care by earlier periods of productive activity, but the handicapped have not.[26] In other words, for the contractarian only productivity justifies, ultimately, a claim to support, and the elderly get support only because at one time they were not elderly. Animality and human neediness, all on their own, cannot justify a claim to support. Rawls's theory, though more subtle than Gauthier's, still suffers from something like this problem. To require of the parties that they split their thinking in this way, conceiving of themselves as made up of two parts, the rational and the animal, is to force into their thinking a Kantian splitting that may well prejudice their thinking about the dignity of animality in themselves. Are we not in effect saying that animality gets support only in virtue of its contingent link to "fully cooperating" adulthood? And doesn't this slight the dignity and worth that needy human animals surely possess even when they are not fully cooperating? Surely, if it is not necessary to require such split thinking, we should avoid it.

Thus I prefer the second solution: The contract doctrine does not provide a complete ethical theory. But this reply, which would be fine for Scanlon, because he is doing ethical theory, employs no hypothetical initial situation, makes no claims to completeness, and creates large problems for the contract doctrine in the area of political theory. Any approach to the design of basic political institutions must aim at a certain degree of completeness and finality, as Rawls's doctrine explicitly does.[27] We are designing the basic structure of society, those institutions that influence all citizens' life-chances pervasively and from the start. So it is not open to us to say: We have done one part of that task, but, of course, other parts, equally basic, based on completely different principles, will come along later. If we leave for another day not only our relations to the nonhuman animals, but also the needs entailed by our own animality, that would leave huge areas of political justice up for grabs and would entail the recognition of much indeterminacy in the account of basic justice as so far worked out.

What, then, can be done to give the problem of care and dependency sufficient prominence in a theory of justice? The first thing we might try, one that has been suggested by Eva Kittay in her fine book, is to add the need for care during periods of extreme and asymmetrical dependency to the Rawlsian list of primary goods, thinking of care as among the basic needs of citizens.[28]

This suggestion, if we adopt it, would lead us to make another modification, for care is hardly a commodity, like income and wealth, to be measured by the sheer amount of it citizens have. Thus adding care to the list would cause us to notice that Rawls's list of primary goods is already quite heterogeneous in its structure. Some of its members are thing-like items such as income and wealth; but some are already more like human capabilities to function in various ways: the liberties, opportunities, and powers, and also the social basis of self-respect. Along with this suggestion, we might propose understanding the entire list of primary goods as a list not of things, but of basic capabilities.[29] This change would not only enable us to deal better with people's needs for various types of love and care as elements of the list, but would also answer the point that Sen has repeatedly made all along about the unreliability of income and wealth as indices of well-being. The well-being of citizens will now be measured not by the sheer amount of income and wealth they have, but by the degree to which they have the various capabilities on the list. One may be well-off in terms of income and wealth and yet unable to function well in the workplace, because of burdens of caregiving at home.[30]

If we accepted these two changes, we would surely add a third, highly relevant to our thoughts about infancy and old age. We would add other capability-like items to the list of basic goods: for example, the social basis of health, and the social basis of imagination and emotional well-being.[31]

Suppose, then, we do make these three changes in the list of primary goods: We add care in times of extreme dependency to the list of primary goods; we reconfigure the list as a list of capabilities; and we add other pertinent items to the list as well. Have we done enough to salvage the contract doctrine as a way of generating basic political principles? I believe that there is still room for doubt. Consider the role of primary goods in Rawls's theory. The account of primary goods is introduced in connection with the Kantian political conception of the person, as an account of what citizens characterized by the two moral powers need.[32] Thus, we have attributed basic importance to care only from the point of view of our own current independence. It is good to be cared for only because care subserves moral personality, understood in a Kantian way as conceptually quite distinct from need and animality. This seems like another more subtle way of making our animality subserve our humanity, where humanity is understood to exclude animality. The idea is that because we are dignified beings capable of political reciprocity, therefore we had better provide for times when we are not that, so we can get back to being that as quickly as possible. I think that this is a dubious enough way to think about illnesses in the prime of life; but it surely leads us in the direction of a contemptuous attitude toward infancy and childhood, and, a particular danger in our society, toward elderly disability. Finally, it leads us strongly in the direction of not fully valuing those with lifelong mental disabilities: Somehow or other, care for them is supposed to be valuable only for the sake of what it does for the "fully cooperating." They are, it would seem, being used as means for someone else's ends, and their full humanity is still being denied.

So I believe that we need to delve deeper, redesigning the political conception of the person, bringing the rational and the animal into a more intimate relation with one another, and acknowledging that there are many types of dignity in the world, including the dignity of mentally disabled children and adults, the dignity of the senile demented elderly, and the dignity of babies at the breast. We want the picture of the parties who design political institutions to build these facts in from the start. The kind of reciprocity in which we humanly engage has its periods of symmetry, but also, of necessity, its periods of more or less extreme asymmetry—and this is part of our lives that we bring into our situation as parties who design just institutions. And this may well mean that the theory cannot be a contractarian theory at all.

Such a conclusion should be reached with caution. Rawls's theory has often been wrongly criticized, because critics have not noticed that his model of the person in the Original Position is complex: His account of the person is not simply the account of the rationality of the parties, but that account *combined with* the account of the veil of ignorance, which is a complex way of modeling benevolence. Thus it is incorrect to say that he has not included concern for others in the conception of the person that forms the foundation of his theory—as he has noted, discussing Schopenhauer's similar critique of

Kant.[33] What this mistake shows us is that the contract doctrine has many ways of modeling the person; so we should not rule out the possibility that some device may be found through which a doctrine basically contractarian in spirit could model need and animality, just as it has modeled benevolence.[34] There is, however, some reason to doubt that this can be done. For any such model would still involve a split of just the sort I've objected to, one that makes our rationality trustee, in effect, for our animality. And that, as I've argued, is inadequate for the kind of dignity and centrality we want to give to the problems of asymmetrical need.

Thus, while not denying that some determined contractarian might possibly solve this problem, I think it best to proceed as if it has not been solved. When we add to our worries the fact that Rawls's contract doctrine uses a political concept of the person at a number of different points, most of them not in association with the complex model of the original position, we have even more reason to want the political concept of the person to be one that does justice to temporality and need.

So I believe we need to adopt a political conception of the person that is more Aristotelian than Kantian,[35] one that sees the person from the start as both capable and needy—"in need of a rich plurality of life-activities," to use Marx's phrase, whose availability will be the measure of well-being. Such a conception of the person, which builds growth and decline into the trajectory of human life, will put us on the road to thinking well about what society should design. We don't have to contract for what we need by producing; we have a claim to support in the dignity of our human need itself. Since this is not just an Aristotelian idea, but one that corresponds to human experience, there is good reason to think that it can command a political consensus in a pluralistic society. If we begin with this conception of the person and with a suitable list of the central capabilities as primary goods, we can begin designing institutions by asking what it would take to get citizens up to an acceptable level on all these capabilities.

In *Women and Human Development* I therefore propose that the idea of central human capabilities be used as the analogue of Rawlsian primary goods, and that the guiding political conception of the person should be an Aristotelian/Marxian conception of the human being as in need of a rich plurality of life-activities, to be shaped by both practical reason and affiliation. I argue that these interlocking conceptions can form the core of a political conception that is a form of political liberalism, close to Rawls's in many ways. The core of the political conceptions is endorsed for political purposes only, giving citizens a great deal of space to pursue their own comprehensive conceptions of value, whether secular or religious. Yet more room for a reasonable pluralism in conceptions of the good is secured by insisting that the appropriate political goal is capability only: Citizens should be given the option, in each area, of functioning in accordance with a given capability or not so functioning.

To secure a capability to a citizen, it is not enough to create a sphere of noninterference; the public conception must design the material and institutional environment so that it provides the requisite affirmative support for all the relevant capabilities.[36] Thus care for physical and mental dependency needs will enter into the conception at many points, as part of what is required to secure to citizens one of the capabilities on the list.[37]

My solution to these problems lies, then, squarely within the liberal tradition. But Kittay suggests that we should go further, departing from that tradition altogether. She holds that Western political theory must be radically reconfigured to put the fact of dependency at its heart. The fact, she says, that we are all "some mother's child," existing in intertwined relations of dependency, should be the guiding image for political thought.[38] Such a care-based theory, she thinks, will be likely to be very different from any liberal theory, since the liberal tradition is deeply committed to goals of independence and liberty. Although Kittay supplies few details to clarify the practical meaning of the difference, I think her idea is that the care-based theory would support a type of politics that provides comprehensive support for need throughout all citizens' lives, as in some familiar ideals of the welfare state—but a welfare state in which liberty is far less important than security and well-being.

Kittay is not altogether consistent on this point. At times she herself uses classic liberal arguments, saying that we need to remember that caregivers have their own lives to lead and to support policies that give them more choices.[39] But, on the whole, she rejects, in the abstract, solutions that emphasize freedom as a central political goal. The concrete measures she favors do not seem to have such sweeping antiliberal implications. The restoration and expansion of Aid to Families with Dependent Children; expansion of the Family and Medical Leave Act of 1993; various educational measures promoting the dignity of the disabled, through a judicious combination of "mainstreaming" and separate education[40]—all these are familiar liberal policies, which can be combined with an emphasis on choice and liberty as important social goals. Kittay's most controversial proposal, that of a direct non-means-tested payment to those who care for family dependents at home—clearly has, or could have, a liberal rationale: that of ensuring that these people are seen as active, dignified workers, rather than passive noncontributors.

Indeed, if we adopt all the changes I have proposed, we will still have a theory that is basically liberal. For theories that take their start from an idea of human capability and functioning emphasize the importance of giving all citizens the chance to develop the full range of human powers, at whatever level their condition allows, and to enjoy the sort of liberty and independence their condition allows. Would we do better to reject this theory in favor of Kittay's idea, rejecting independence as a major social goal and conceiving of the state as a universal mother? To be sure, nobody is ever self-sufficient; the independence we enjoy is always both temporary and partial, and it is good to be reminded of that fact by a theory that also stresses the importance of care in times of dependency. But is being "some mother's child" a sufficient image for the citizen in a just society? I think we need a lot more: liberty and opportunity, the chance to form a plan of life, the chance to learn and imagine on one's own.

These goals are as important for the mentally handicapped as they are for others, though much more difficult to achieve. Although Kittay's daughter Sesha will never live on her own (and although Kittay is right to say that independence should not be seen as a necessary condition of dignity for all mentally disabled people),[41] many others do aspire to hold a job, and vote, and tell their own story. Michael Bérubé ends his compelling account of his son's life with the hope that Jamie, too, will write a book about himself, as two adults with Down syndrome recently have.[42] One day Jamie's kindergarten teacher went round the room, asking the children what they wanted to be when they grew up. They said the usual things: basketball star, ballet dancer, fireman. The teacher wasn't sure Jamie would understand the question, so she asked it very clearly. Jamie just said, "Big." And his literal answer, said the teacher, taught them all something about the question. Bérubé, too, wants, simply, a society in which his son will be able to be "big": healthy, educated, loving, active, seen as a particular person with something distinctive to contribute, rather than as "a retarded child."

For that to happen, his dependencies must be understood and supported. But so, too, must his need to be distinct and an individual, and at this point Bérubé refers sympathetically to Rawls. He argues that the idea at the heart of the Individuals With Disabilities Education Act (IDEA)—the idea that every child has the right to an "appropriate education" in the "least restrictive environment" possible, based on an "Individualized Education Plan"—is a profoundly liberal idea, an idea about individuality and freedom. One of the most important kinds of support mentally disabled children need is the support required to be free-choosing adults, each in his or her own way. Insofar as Kittay suggests that we downplay or marginalize such liberal notions in favor of a conception of the state that makes it the parental supporter of its so-called children's needs, I think she goes too far, misconceiving what justice would be for both the disabled and the elderly. Even for Sesha, who will never vote or write, doesn't a full human life involve a kind of freedom and individuality, namely, a space in which to exchange love and enjoy light and sound, free from confinement and mockery?

So I believe that the problem we have investigated shows us that liberal theory needs to question some of its most traditional starting points—questioning, in the process, the Kantian notion of the person. But that does not disable liberalism; it just challenges us all to produce a new form of liberalism, more attentive to need and its material and institutional conditions. The liberal ideas of freedom and of the human need for various types of liberty of action are precious ideas that feminist philosophers, it seems to me, should cherish and further develop, creating theories that make it possible for all citizens to have the support they need for the full development of their human capabilities.

JUSTICE IN THE FAMILY

The most difficult problem liberal theory faces in the area of women's equality is the problem of the family.[43] On the one hand, the family is among the most significant arenas in which people pursue their own conceptions of the good and transmit them to the next generation. This fact suggests that a liberal society should give people considerable latitude to form families as they choose. On the other hand, the family is one of the most nonvoluntary and pervasively influential of social institutions, and one of the most notorious homes of sex hierarchy, denial of equal opportunity, and sex-based violence and humiliation. These facts suggest that a society committed to equal justice for all citizens, and to securing for all citizens the social bases of liberty, opportunity, and self-respect, must constrain the family in the name of justice. Most liberal theories (Mill being the honorable exception) have simply neglected this problem or have treated the family as a "private" sphere into which political justice should not meddle.[44] As Catharine MacKinnon has observed, the public–private distinction has typically functioned to protect *male* privacy, and not female privacy, and thence the unlimited sway of men over women in a protected domain; thus liberal rhetoric about the sanctity of privacy should strike us as "an injury got up as a gift."[45] Rawls from the first has denied that the family is a space exempt from the claims of justice, by asserting that it is part of society's basic structure, ergo one of those institutions to which principles of justice would apply.[46] But, having granted this, he then has to solve one of the most difficult of problems: how to render this institution compatible with justice.[47]

In "The Idea of Public Reason Revisited,"[48] Rawls has finally addressed the problem. He makes two claims, which are difficult to render consistent. On the one hand, he asserts that the family forms part of society's basic structure (788). At the same time, however, he claims that the two principles of justice, while they apply directly to the basic structure, do not "apply directly to the internal life of families" (788–89). In fact, he continues, the principles apply to families in just the way that they apply to society's many voluntary associations, such as churches and universities (789). That is, the principles supply external constraints on what the associations can do, but they do not regulate their internal workings. A university, for example, cannot violate basic provisions of the criminal law, or of political justice more generally; but it may assign functions in accordance with its own criteria, whatever they are. So, too, with the family: The principles of justice do supply real constraints, by specifying the basic rights of equal citizens. The family cannot violate these rights. "The equal rights of women and the basic rights of their children as future citizens are inalienable and protect them wherever they are. Gender distinctions limiting those rights and liberties are excluded" (791). And yet, citizens are not required to raise their children in accordance with liberal principles; we may have to allow for some traditional gendered division of labor in families, "provided it is fully voluntary and does not result from or lead to injustice" (792)—words that are honorable, but difficult to apply to reality.[49]

In practical terms, Rawls thinks that we cannot make rules for the division of labor in families, or penalize those who don't comply. But at the legislative stage we can introduce laws that protect women's full equality as citizens—for example, divorce laws of the sort favored by Susan Okin: "It seems intolerably unjust that a husband may depart the family taking his earning power with him and leaving his wife and children far less advantaged than before. . . . A society that permits this does not care about women, much less about their equality, or even about their children, who are its future" (793).[50]

These proposals raise three large questions. First of all, if the family is part of the basic structure, how can it also be a voluntary institution, analogous to a church or a university?[51] The institutions of the basic structure are those whose influence is pervasive and present from the start of a human life. The family is such an institution; universities and churches (except as extensions of families) are not. For adult women, membership in a family may be voluntary (though this is not always clear), and Rawls's protection of their exit options may suffice to ensure their full equality. But children are simply hostages to the family in which they grow up, and their participation in its gendered structure is by no means voluntary. Granted, it is not terribly clear what it would mean to apply the principles of justice to the family *as part of the basic structure,* for surely the principles apply to the basic structure taken as a whole, and this does not entail that they apply piecemeal to every institution that forms part of the basic structure.[52] And yet the fact that the family is part of the basic structure, and universities, and so on, are not, ought to make *some* difference in the way in which the principles apply; Rawls ought to have given us some account of that difference.

Second, Rawls does not acknowledge the parochial character of the Western nuclear family. Surprisingly, he still seems to regard some such unit as having a quasi-natural status and as characterized by what he continues to call "natural affections"; although he has broadened his account to include nontraditional nuclear groupings, such as same-sex couples, he nowhere acknowledges the parochial character of the whole idea of raising children in a nuclear family. Village groups, extended families, women's collectives, kibbutzim, these and other groups have been involved in raising children; the contracting parties, not knowing where they are in place and time, should not give preference to a Western bourgeois form over other possible forms. They should look at the issues of justice with an open mind, giving favor to those groupings that seem most capable of rearing children, compatibly with other requirements of justice.

Third, Rawls does not recognize the extent to which, in all modern societies, the "family" is a creation of state action, enjoying a very different status from that of a church or a university. People associate in many different ways, live together, love each other, have children. Which of these will get the name "family" is a legal and political matter, never one to be decided simply by the parties themselves. The state constitutes the family structure through its laws, defining which groups of people can count as families, defining the privileges and rights of family members, defining what marriage and divorce are, what legitimacy and parental responsibility are, and so forth. This difference makes a difference: The state is present in the family from the start, in a way that is less clearly the case with the religious body or the university; it is the state that says what this thing *is* and controls how one becomes a member of it.[53]

To see this more clearly, let us consider the rituals that define a person as a member of an association: in the (private) university, matriculation (and, later, the granting of a degree); in a religious body, baptism, conversion, or some analogous entrance rite; in the family, marriage. Now it is evident that the state has some connection with university matriculation/graduation and with religious baptism/conversion: It polices these rites on the outside, by defining the institution as enjoying tax-free status, by preventing the use of cruelty or other illegalities in the ritual, and so forth. But marriage is from the start a public, state-administered rite. There are state laws defining it, which restrict entry into that privileged domain. The state does not police marriage on the outside; it marries people. Other similar people who don't meet the state's test cannot count as married, even if they satisfy all private and even religious criteria for marriage. (Thus, same-sex couples whose unions have been solemnized by some religious body still are not married, because the state has not granted them a license.) All human associations are shaped by laws and institutions, which either favor or disfavor them, and structure them in various ways. But the family is shaped by law in a yet deeper and more thoroughgoing way, in the sense that its very definition is legal and political; individuals may call themselves "a family" if they wish, but they only get to be one, in the sense that is socially significant and that yields a wide range of social recognitions and benefits,[54] if they satisfy legal tests. In short, the political sphere cannot avoid directly shaping the family structure, by recognizing some and not other groupings as families. Rawls tends to treat the family as an organization that has an extrapolitical existence and to ask how far the state may interfere with it. If, instead, he had recognized the foundational character of the state's presence in the family, he might have granted that it makes good sense for principles of justice to recognize and favor any units, traditional or nontraditional, that perform the functions associated with family in ways that are compatible with political justice.

My feeling is that in this delicate area Rawls has been too ready to recognize what are, in effect, group rights: the right of families, conceived of as pre-political, to protection against state action. Put another way, his distinction between external and internal regulation re-creates the problematic features of the very distinction he

questions, the distinction between the public and the private sphere. If we really acknowledge the equal worth of all citizens and the profound vulnerability of children
in families, we should, I believe, conceive of the entire issue in a subtly different
way: by thinking how we may balance adult freedom of association, and other important interests in pursuing one's own conception of the good, against the liberties
and opportunities of children as future citizens.

Once again, beginning from citizens' needs for a wide range of human capabilities puts the problem on a subtly different footing from the start and enables
us to move forward. No group gets special privileges qua group. But all persons
deserve support for a wide range of capabilities—prominently including not only
the capabilities of freedom of religion and freedom of association, but also the capability to form relationships of affection and care.[55]

If we proceed in this way and recognize in addition that there is no group that exists "by nature" and that the family is more a state creation than most other associations, then the natural question will be: What forms of state action, and what forms
of privilege given to certain groupings, will best protect the liberties and opportunities of women and children, within limits set by the protection of adult freedom
of association and other important liberties? In posing this question, we do not
assume that any one affiliative grouping is prior or central in promoting those
capabilities. People have needs for love and care, for reproduction, for sexual expression; children have needs for love, support, and education; and people also enjoy a wide range of associational liberties. But at this point I believe we need to look
and see how different groupings of persons do in promoting these capabilities. In
some nations—for example, India—women's collectives play a valuable role in
giving women love and friendship, in caring for children, and in fostering the other
capabilities. Conventional families often do less well. Sometimes a women's collective appears to be more truly a child's family than is its nuclear home, as when,
as often happens, women's collectives protect children from sexual abuse or
arrange for children at risk of abuse or child marriage to be protected through state-
run schools. There need not even be a presumption that all the functions we now
associate with family will be bundled under a single institution. Thus France has
acted wisely, I believe, when it asks why the definition of household for the purposes of inheritance should be at all the same as the account of who gets to adopt
and raise children. Brothers and sisters who live in the same house may be a household for the former purpose, but not for the latter.[56] My approach would urge that
such decisions be contextual, asking how, in the given history and circumstances,
public policy can best promote the claims of the human capabilities. The only thing
that stops state intervention is the person and the various liberties and rights of the
person, including associative liberties, the right to be free from unwarranted search
and seizure, and so forth. The family has no power to stop this intervention on its
own, as though it were a mystical unity over and above the lives of its members.

Similarly, my approach urges us to question whether the distinctions relied
upon by Rawls's current position—distinctions between external and internal

regulation, and between state action and inaction, are really coherent. Laws governing marriage, divorce, compulsory education, inheritance—all are as internal as anything can be in the family. Nor should the criminal justice system know a distinction between inside and outside, in the definition and ranking of criminal offenses: It should treat rape as rape, battery as battery, coercion as coercion, wherever they occur. To let things take their status quo antecourse is to choose a course of action, not to be completely neutral. In short, the state's interest in protecting the dignity, integrity, and well-being of each citizen never simply leads to external constraints on the family structure, whatever appearances may be; it always leads to positive constructing of the family institution. This constructing should be done in ways that are compatible with political justice.[57]

In practical terms, my approach in terms of the promotion of capabilities and Rawls's approach, which views the two principles of justice as supplying external constraints on the family, will give many of the same answers. Laws against marital rape, laws protecting marital consent, laws mandating compulsory education, laws banning child marriage and child labor, laws ensuring an appropriate material recognition of the wife's economic contribution to the family, laws providing child care to support working mothers, laws promoting the nutrition and health of girl children—all these laws, I think, we would support as appropriate expressions of state concern for citizens and future citizens. But the grounds on which we will support them will be subtly different. Rawls sees the laws as supplying external constraints on something that has its own form, the way laws constrain a university or a church; I see them as contributing to the constitution of an institution that is in the most direct sense a part of the basic structure of society.

Furthermore, my approach, like Rawls's, would permit the state to give conventional family groupings certain special privileges and protections, just as it gives religious bodies certain privileges and protections. It will probably do so in many cases, since the family does promote the rearing of children, as well as serving other needs of citizens. Thus parents may be given certain limited kinds of deference in making choices regarding their children. And tax breaks for family units are not ruled out, insofar as these units promote human capabilities. But for me, the reason the state will choose such policies is to protect the central capabilities of individuals; the definition of family, and the policies chosen, should be chosen with this aim in view. Rawls does not ask how "family" should be defined, nor does he make it clear on what basis it should have special privileges, although the state's interest in its future citizens would appear to be one such basis.[58]

Most important of all, because Rawls takes the family as given, he does not ask what my approach urges us to ask at all times: What other affective and associational ties deserve public protection and support? It is not at all clear, then, what role nontraditional affective groupings such as Indian women's collectives, or French Pacts of Civil Solidarity, could play in his account of society's basic structure. And yet he proceeds as if, at the level of the Original Position, the account is historically neutral, not biased in favor of the status quo in any given place and time. In my approach, at that basic level we have only the capabilities to consider,[59] and we may consider any institutional grouping that can promote them. At a later, more concrete level—corresponding to Rawls's constitutional and legislative stages—such inquiries will rightly become contextual, although even at that point this will not mean that the traditional form of a practice will have exclusive privileges.

Notice, then, that my approach leaves for fine-tuned contextual judgment certain matters that Kantian liberalism wishes to settle in a definite way before launching into the currents of history, including the all-important question what forms of human organization shall be favored for the care and education of children. I urge that these questions be left to the contextual deliberation of citizens, in the light of their history and their current problems, and in the light of the capability list, which remains relatively constant over time. Such an approach will strike the Rawlsian as dangerously "intuitionistic," and yet we should not purchase definiteness at the price of falsehood, by stating or implying that a parochial grouping is ahistorical and universal.[60]

Again, my approach would forbid certain types of interference with the family structure that Rawls's approach would also forbid. For me as for Rawls, it is wrong for the state to mandate the equal division of domestic labor or equal decision making in the household. But again, the reasons for this shared conclusion will differ. Rawls judges that it is wrong to interfere with the internal workings of a particular institution, deemed to exist apart from the state—whereas I judge simply that there are associational liberties of individuals, and liberties of speech, that should always be protected for citizens, no matter where they occur. (Rawls might have reached a result similar to the one he does reach by relying on the priority of liberty; but, significantly, he does not use that argument.) It just seems an intolerable infringement of liberty for the state to get involved in dictating how people do their dishes. But for me, dubious conduct gets less prima facie protection if it is in the family than if it is in a purely voluntary association, since the family (for children at any rate) is a nonvoluntary institution that influences citizens' life-chances pervasively and from the start.

In a wide range of areas, our approaches will support different choices of public policy. In my approach, the central capabilities always supply a compelling interest for purposes of government action. Thus it will be all right to render dowry illegal in India (as has been done), given the compelling evidence that the dowry system is a major source of women's capability failure.[61] I believe that Rawls would have a difficult time justifying this law—because he is thinking of the family as pre-political and dowry as one of the choices it makes in its pre-political state. For me, by contrast, the family is constituted by laws and institutions, and one of the questions to be asked is whether dowry-giving is one of the things it should be in the business of doing. Permitting dowry is not neutral state inaction toward an autonomous private entity; it is another (alternative) way of constituting a part of the public sphere. Again, interference with traditional decision-making patterns in the family will be much easier to justify on my approach than on Rawls's. Consider the Mahila Samakhya project in Andhra Pradesh, in southern India. This project, funded and run by the national government, is explicitly aimed at increasing women's confidence and initiative, and empowering them in their dealings with employers, government officials, and husbands, and extending a wide range of life options to their female children. There is no doubt at all that the government is attempting to reconstruct the family by altering social norms and perceptions. No community and no individual is forced to join, and this is a reservation I would support. Nonetheless, it seems likely that there is more in the way of endorsing a particular conception of family governance than Rawls would consider acceptable. Apart from the content of the teaching, the very existence of the women's collectives as a focus for women's affective lives transforms the family profoundly, making it no longer the sole source of personal affiliation. It seems likely that Rawls would oppose government support for such collectives on that account, thinking of it as the endorsement of one conception of the good over another—for much the same reason that he has opposed government support for music and the arts. For me, the fact that women's capabilities are in a perilous state, together with the fact that empowerment programs have succeeded in giving them greater control over their material and political environment, gives government a compelling interest in introducing such programs.

Or consider governmental programs that focus on giving women access to credit and economic self-sufficiency, together with education in confidence and leadership.[62] (Such programs are common in developing countries; at least some such programs are governmental.) I surmise that for Rawls such programs would be an impermissible interference by government into the family structure. The very idea that government would support an all-women's bank, for example, would be highly suspect. For me, while I think it's very important for a program like this to be noncoercive, it seems quite all right for government to act in ways that aim at changing social norms that shape the family and at promoting capabilities in those who lack them. For after all, and this is the crux of the matter, government is already in the business of constructing an institution that is part of the basic structure of society. It had better do this job well.

The largest difference in the two approaches will be in the treatment of female children. It is here, especially, that my approach recognizes the pervasive and non-voluntary nature of family membership and gives the state broad latitude in shaping perception and behavior to promote the development of female children to full adult capability in the major areas. This means not only abolishing child marriage and (where practically possible) child labor and (where practically possible) mandating compulsory primary and secondary education for all children. Rawls would presumably also favor these changes. It also means encouraging the public perception that women are suited for many different roles in life, something that Rawls is likely to see as too much promoting of a definite conception of the good. Thus the content of public education should include information about options for women and about resistance to women's inequality.[63] In addition to regular schooling, the Indian government also supports residential programs for young girls who are at risk for child marriage, to remove them from home and give them education and job training. Rawls would be likely to see this as too much state intervention, even if the mothers consent to the girls going away; after all, government is saying, "I will support you if you leave this dangerous structure." My approach judges that the protection of girls' capabilities warrants an interventionist strategy.

Rawls's approach to the family and mine are very close. Both of us take our bearings from the idea of the dignity and worth of humanity, and the idea that no human being shall be used as a mere means for the ends of others. Both of us define the person as the basis of distribution; both of us see an important role for liberties of association and self-definition; both of us recognize the intrinsic value of love and care. But Rawls, while rejecting the public–private distinction, remains halfhearted in that rejection. I have tried to show how an approach through the central capabilities would capture the value of family love and care, while nonetheless rejecting more consistently a distinction that has disfigured the lives of girls and women through the ages.[64]

A LIBERAL FUTURE?

Liberal political thought has not yet realized its full potential. In two areas crucial to women's equality, there are basic problems with liberal doctrines as so far developed. These difficulties give us good reason to try out new liberal alternatives; one that deserves a hearing is a neo-Aristotelian liberalism based on an idea of human capabilities as central political goals.

It seems clear that a theory basically liberal in spirit can meet the problems of need and dependency. The difficulties pertaining to the family raise more troubling issues, for they seem to threaten the very project of a political liberalism, an approach committed both to respecting each person as an end and to respecting the fact of reasonable pluralism among comprehensive views of life. There is no doubt that some of the major comprehensive views of what gives life meaning are dead set against the kind of revisionary treatment of family structure that my approach sees required by political justice. Extending the privileges of marriage to previously unrecognized couples is at least on our political agenda; radical rethinking of the institutions of marriage and family will be much more difficult to achieve, although nations such as France and India have been able to go further. It is no accident that in a sphere that is the home both of intimate self-definition and also of egregious wrongdoing the search for liberal justice should encounter difficulties, for liberal justice is committed both to protecting spheres of self-definition and to ending the wrongful tyranny of some people over others.

But the failure to have a fully satisfactory solution to these difficulties is not a failure of liberal justice, because the liberal is right. Self-definition is important, and it is also important to end wrongful tyranny. The tension that results from these twin principles is at the heart of liberalism, but it is a valuable and fruitful tension, not one that shows confusion or moral failure. In general, tension within a theory does not necessarily show that it is defective; it may simply show that it is in touch with the difficulty of life. And that, I believe, is the case here. Reflection on the tension ought to lead us, over time, to figure out how to design a society that balances these competing values as well as they can be balanced, and to provide institutional protections for women and children who currently suffer from unresolved conflicts between them.

This effort would do well to begin by imagining and studying the many ways in which groups of people of many different types have managed, in different places at different times, to care for one another and to raise children with both love and justice.

APPENDIX: THE CENTRAL HUMAN CAPABILITIES (AS IN *WOMEN AND HUMAN DEVELOPMENT,* 2000)

1. Life. Being able to live to the end of a human life of normal length; not dying prematurely or before one's life is so reduced as to be not worth living.
2. Bodily Health. Being able to have good health, including reproductive health; to be adequately nourished; to have adequate shelter.
3. Bodily Integrity. Being able to move freely from place to place; to be secure against violent assault, including sexual assault and domestic violence; having opportunities for sexual satisfaction and for choice in matters of reproduction.
4. Senses, Imagination, and Thought. Being able to use the senses, to imagine, think, and reason—and to do these things in a "truly human" way, a way informed and cultivated by an adequate education, including, but by no means limited to, literacy and basic mathematical and scientific training. Being able to use imagination and thought in connection with experiencing and producing works and events of one's own choice, religious, literary, musical, and so forth. Being able to use one's mind in ways protected by guarantees of freedom of expression with respect to both political and artistic speech, and freedom of religious exercise. Being able to have pleasurable experiences and to avoid nonbeneficial pain.
5. Emotions. Being able to have attachments to things and people outside ourselves; to love those who love and care for us, to grieve at their absence; in general, to love, to grieve, to experience longing, gratitude, and justified anger. Not having one's emotional development blighted by fear and anxiety. (Supporting this capability means supporting forms of human association that can be shown to be crucial in their development.)

6. Practical Reason. Being able to form a conception of the good and to engage in critical reflection about the planning of one's life. (This entails protection for the liberty of conscience and religious observance.)

7. Affiliation.

A. Being able to live with and toward others, to recognize and show concern for other human beings, to engage in various forms of social interaction; to be able to imagine the situation of another. (Protecting this capability means protecting institutions that constitute and nourish such forms of affiliation, and also protecting the freedom of assembly and political speech.)

B. Having the social bases of self-respect and nonhumiliation; being able to be treated as a dignified being whose worth is equal to that of others. This entails provisions of nondiscrimination on the basis of race, sex, sexual orientation, ethnicity, caste, religion, and national origin.

8. Other Species. Being able to live with concern for and in relation to animals, plants, and the world of nature.

9. Play. Being able to laugh, to play, to enjoy recreational activities.

10. Control over One's Environment.

A. Political. Being able to participate effectively in political choices that govern one's life; having the right of political participation, protections of free speech and association.

B. Material. Being able to hold property (both land and movable goods) and having property rights on an equal basis with others; having the right to seek employment on an equal basis with others; having the freedom from unwarranted search and seizure. In work, being able to work as a human being, exercising practical reason and entering into meaningful relationships of mutual recognition with other workers.

NOTES

I am grateful to Ann Cudd, John Deigh, Dolores Dooley, Chad Flanders, Jill Hasday, Eva Kittay, Charles Larmore, Peter Cicchino, Thomas Scanlon, David Strauss, and Cass Sunstein for comments on a previous draft and to Geof Sayre McCord, Tom Hill, Jr., and other members of the Research Triangle Ethics discussion group for extremely helpful discussion of these issues. This chapter is dedicated to the memory of Peter Cicchino, gifted law professor, feminist, and courageous social activist, who died of cancer on July 8, 2000, at the age of thirty-nine. I discuss Peter's views about Aristotle in the section titled "Need and Dependency."

This chapter originally appeared in *Proceedings and Addresses of the American Philosophical Association*, vol. 74, no. 2 (Newark, Del.: American Philosophical Association, 2000), 47–79. Copyright © 2000 by the American Philosophical Association. Reprinted by permission of the publisher, the American Philosophical Association.

1. Translated from the Bengali by Kalpana Bardhan, in *Of Women, Outcastes, Peasants, and Rebels* (Berkeley: University of California Press, 1990). The story (originally published

in 1982) concerns Giribala's arranged marriage to a man both improvident and corrupt, who eventually sells two of their daughters into prostitution to get spending money for himself. The story ends as Giribala leaves with the two remaining children. Its final sentence: "She just kept walking."

2. John Stuart Mill, *The Subjection of Women* (1869), ed. Susan M. Okin (Indianapolis, Ind.: Hackett, 1988); Mary Wollstonecraft, *A Vindication of the Rights of Woman* (1792) (London and New York: Penguin, 1992). Seventeenth-century feminists Mary Astell and Damaris Lady Masham are helpfully discussed in Margaret Atherton, "Cartesian Reason and Gendered Reason," in *A Mind of One's Own: Feminist Essays on Reason and Objectivity*, ed. Louise M. Antony and Charlotte Witt (Boulder, Colo.: Westview, 1993). Harriet Taylor (Mill)'s *The Enfranchisement of Women* (1851) is an important contribution to the nineteenth-century debate; see edition in John Stuart Mill and Harriet Taylor Mill, *Essays on Sex Equality*, ed. Alice S. Rossi (Chicago: University of Chicago Press, 1970); for a good treatment of the Mills' views on these issues, see Gail Tulloch, *Mill and Sexual Equality* (Hemel Hempstead, Hertfordshire and Boulder, Colo.: Harvester Wheatsheaf and Lynne Rienner, 1989). Another prominent woman in Utilitarian circles was Anna Doyle Wheeler, who coauthored with economist William Thompson the *Appeal of One-Half the Human Race, Women, against the Pretensions of the Other Half, Men, to Retain Them in Political and Thence in Civil and Domestic Slavery* (London: Longmans, 1825); on her writings, see Dolores Dooley, *Equality in Community: Sexual Equality in the Writings of William Thompson and Anna Doyle Wheeler* (Cork, Ireland: Cork University Press, 1996). On nineteenth-century feminist thought about domestic violence and marital rape, see Jill Elaine Hasday, "Contest and Consent: A Legal History of Marital Rape," *California Law Review* 88 (2000). Many other examples could be added. From a very different philosophical tradition, a major influence on modern feminism has been Simone de Beauvoir, *The Second Sex*, trans. H. Parshley (New York: Bantam, 1953); much of her work is compatible with liberalism.

3. Again, however, one should remember that these themes were central in nineteenth-century feminism as well; see, for example, Hasday (previous n. 3), and Reva B. Siegel, "'The Rule of Love': Wife Beating as Prerogative and Privacy," *Yale Law Journal* 105 (1996): 2117–2207.

4. See also the works of Harriet Taylor and Anna Doyle Wheeler, cited in n. 3 earlier.

5. Barbara Herman, Onora O'Neill, Sharon Lloyd, and the late Jean Hampton (all students of John Rawls) write feminist philosophy in the Kantian liberal tradition. See Herman, "Could It Be Worth Thinking about Kant on Sex and Marriage?" in *A Mind of One's Own* (previous n. 3), 49–68; O'Neill, "Justice, Gender, and International Boundaries," in *The Quality of Life*, ed. M. Nussbaum and A. Sen (Oxford: Clarendon, 1993), 303–35; Lloyd, "Family Justice and Social Justice," *Pacific Philosophical Quarterly* 75 (1994): 353–71; Hampton, "Feminist Contractarianism," in *A Mind of One's Own* (previous n. 3), 227–56, and "The Case for Feminism" and "Hampton's Reply" in *The Liberation Debate*, ed. M. Leahy and D. Cohn-Sherbok (London: Routledge, 1996), 3–24, 41–45; in this same category see also the first feminist critique of Rawls, in Jane English, "Justice between Generations," *Philosophical Studies* 31 (1977): 91–104. Susan Moller Okin, surely one of the most influential contemporary feminists, is, though a critic of Rawls, clearly in the liberal tradition and a particular admirer of Mill; see *Women in Western Political Thought* (Princeton, N.J.: Princeton University Press, 1978); "Justice and Gender," *Philosophy and Public Affairs* 16 (1987): 42–72; "Reason and Feeling in Thinking about

Justice," *Ethics* 99 (1989a): 229–49; *Justice, Gender, and the Family* (New York: Basic, 1989); "Political Liberalism, Justice, and Gender," *Ethics* 105: 23–43; *Is Multicultural-ism Bad for Women?* (Princeton, N.J.: Princeton University Press, 1999). Two other lib-eral feminists whose views lie closer to those of Mill (and T. H. Green 1994) than to any other earlier figure in the tradition are Elizabeth Anderson and Candace Vogler; see An-derson, *Value in Ethics and Economics* (Cambridge, Mass.: Harvard University Press, 1993); and "John Stuart Mill and Experiments in Living," *Ethics* 102 (1991): 4–26; Vogler, *John Stuart Mill's Deliberative Landscape*, Garland Dissertation Series, ed. R. Nozick (2000); and "Philosophical Feminism, Feminist Philosophy," *Philosophical Top-ics* 23 (1995): 295–319. The work of Jürgen Habermas has been a major influence on the writings of Seyla Benhabib, whom I think it would be correct to count as a liberal femi-nist; see *Situating the Self: Gender, Community, and Postmodernism in Contemporary Ethics* (New York: Routledge, 1992); an anthology of feminist writing in the Haber-masian tradition is *Feminists Read Habermas*, ed. Johanna Meehan (New York: Rout-ledge, 1995). Another feminist prominently influenced by Habermas, Iris Young, is prob-ably not correctly classified as a liberal; see "The Ideal of Community and the Politics of Difference," in *Feminism and Postmodernism*, ed. Linda Nicholson (New York: Routledge, 1990); and *Justice and the Politics of Difference* (Princeton, N.J.: Princeton University Press, 1990); and *Throwing Like a Girl and Other Essays in Feminist Philos-ophy and Social Theory* (Bloomington: Indiana University Press, 1990). Finally, on the continent, a prominent liberal feminist influenced by both Rawls and Habermas, as well as by the work of Okin and other liberal feminists, is Herlinde Pauer-Studer, *Das Andere der Gerechtigkeit: Moraltheorie im Kontext der Geschlechterdifferenz* (Berlin: Akademie Verlag, 1996). In India (though the word *liberal* would be avoided, since there it means "libertarian") most prominent feminist political thinkers are liberal social-democrats of some type; see Bina Agarwal, *A Field of One's Own: Gender and Land Rights in South Asia* (Cambridge: Cambridge University Press, 1994), and "'Bargaining' and Gender Relations: Within and beyond the Household," *Feminist Economics* 3 (1997): 1–51; Zoya Hasan, "In-troduction" and essay, "Minority Identity, State Policy and the Political Process" (59–73), in Hasan, ed., *Forging Identities: Gender, Communities, and the State in India* (Boulder, Colo.: Westview, 1994); Roop Rekha Verma, "Femininity, Equality, and Personhood," in *Women, Culture, and Development*, ed. M. Nussbaum and J. Glover (Oxford: Clarendon, 1995), 433–43; and one should, of course, include in this category the feminist writings of Amartya Sen, discussed in both text and notes further on. Once again, this list is very incomplete.

    6. Some influential such critiques have been Alison Jaggar, *Feminist Politics and Human Nature* (Totowa, N.J.: Rowman & Allanheld, 1983; reprint, 1988), especially 27–50, 173–206; Carole Pateman, *The Problem of Political Obligation: A Critique of Liberal Theory* (Berkeley: University of California Press, 1979), and *The Sexual Contract* (Stanford, Calif.: Stanford University Press, 1988); Nancy C. M. Hartsock, *Money, Sex, and Power* (Boston: Northeastern University Press, 1983); Catharine MacKinnon, *Toward a Feminist Theory of the State* (Cambridge, Mass.: Harvard University Press, 1989), especially chapters 3 and 8, and *Feminism Unmodified* (Cambridge, Mass.: Harvard University Press, 1987), es-pecially chapters 2 and 8. In "The Feminist Critique" I argue that MacKinnon's primary tar-get is a type of neutralist liberalism that is quite common in legal circles, but that her critique can be met by the strongest forms of contemporary liberal philosophy, including, on some topics, at least, the views of Rawls. See the section titled "Justice in the Family" for her valu-able critique of liberalism on the public–private distinction.

7. "The Feminist Critique of Liberalism," chapter 2 of *Sex and Social Justice* (New York: Oxford University Press, 1999), 55–80; also published as a Lindley Lecture, 1997, University of Kansas Press.

8. In "Rawls and Feminism," in *The Cambridge Companion to Rawls*, ed. Samuel Freeman (Cambridge: Cambridge University Press, 2000), I argue that liberal views have not yet provided an adequate account of global justice, and that global justice is a central feminist issue because women in poorer nations are especially likely to be deprived of basic human goods, including education, health, bodily integrity, and life. Securing to women the basic necessary conditions of a decent life is the central theme of my *Women and Human Development: The Capabilities Approach* (Cambridge: Cambridge University Press, 2000), hereafter WHD; thinking globally about the need for redistribution of wealth from richer to poorer nations is the central concern of *The Cosmopolitan Tradition* (the Castle Lectures at Yale University, 2000, and under contract to Yale University Press).

9. Locke, *Second Treatise on Government*, chapter 8.

10. David Gauthier, *Morals by Agreement* (New York: Oxford University Press, 1986), 18, speaking of all "persons who decrease th[e] average level" of well-being in a society.

11. In the subsequent discussion I refer to the following works of Rawls: *A Theory of Justice* (Cambridge, Mass.: Harvard University Press, 1971), hereafter TJ; *Political Liberalism*, expanded paperback edition (New York: Columbia University Press, 1996), hereafter PL; the Dewey Lectures, "Kantian Constructivism in Moral Theory," *The Journal of Philosophy* 77 (1980): 515–71. References to citizens as "fully cooperating" occur frequently in DL and PL, for example, DL, 546; PL, 183.

12. This is a major theme in recent feminist work; see especially Eva Kittay, *Love's Labor: Essays on Women, Equality, and Dependency* (New York: Routledge, 1999); Nancy Folbre, "Care and the Global Economy," background paper prepared for the *Human Development Report 1999*, United Nations Development Programme (New York: Oxford University Press, 1999), and, based largely on Folbre, chapter 3, of *Human Development Report 1999*; Joan Williams, *Unbending Gender: Why Family and Work Conflict and What to Do about It* (New York: Oxford University Press, 2000); Mona Harrington, *Care and Equality* (New York: Knopf, 1999). Earlier influential work in this area includes: Martha A. Fineman, *The Illusion of Equality* (Chicago: University of Chicago Press, 1991), and *The Neutered Mother, the Sexual Family and Other Twentieth Century Tragedies* (New York: Routledge, 1995); Sarah Ruddick, *Maternal Thinking* (New York: Beacon, 1989); Joan Tronto, *Moral Boundaries: A Political Argument for an Ethic of Care* (New York: Routledge, 1993); Virginia Held, *Feminist Morality: Transforming Culture, Society, and Politics* (Chicago: University of Chicago Press, 1993); Robin West, *Caring for Justice* (New York: New York University Press, 1997). For an excellent collection of articles from diverse feminist perspectives, see *Justice and Care: Essential Readings in Feminist Ethics*, ed. Virginia Held (Boulder, Colo.: Westview, 1995).

13. This problem is exacerbated, of course, by Kant's focus on some aspects of our humanity and not on others as what particularly constitutes its worth and dignity.

14. For one particularly valuable treatment of this theme, see James Rachels, *Created from Animals: The Moral Implications of Darwinism* (New York: Oxford University Press, 1990). Two wonderful pictures of the animal sort of dignity: Barbara Smuts, untitled reply to J. M. Coetzee, in *The Lives of Animals*, ed. Amy Gutmann (Princeton, N.J.: Princeton University Press, 1999), and, my favorite, George Pitcher, *The Dogs Who Came to Stay* (New York: G. Putnam, 1995). I discuss the implications of recognizing the dignity of

nonhuman animals in a review article about Steven M. Wise's *Rattling the Cage: Toward Legal Rights for Animals* (Cambridge, Mass.: Perseus, 2000), forthcoming in the *Harvard Law Review*. See also Alasdair MacIntyre, *Dependent Rational Animals: Why Human Beings Need the Virtues* (Peru, Ill.: Open Court, 1999).

15. See, especially, Rachels and MacIntyre (previous n. 15).

16. I do not mean to deny that Kant gives need an important role in his theory; for just one good treatment of this aspect of Kant's thought, see Allen Wood, *Kant's Ethical Theory* (Cambridge: Cambridge University Press, 1999). What I mean is that whereas for Kant personality and animality are conceptually independent, and personality is not itself understood in terms of need, for Rawls these two elements are more thoroughly integrated, and the person is understood from the first as in need of material and other goods.

17. As Eva Kittay has argued in an excellent discussion (*Love's Labor*, 88–99, and see also "Human Dependency and Rawlsian Equality," in *Feminists Rethink the Self*, ed. Diana T. Meyers [Boulder, Colo.: Westview, 1997], 219–66), there are five places in Rawls's theory where he fails to confront facts of asymmetrical neediness that might naturally have been confronted. (1) His account of the "circumstances of justice" assumes a rough equality between persons, such that none could dominate all the others; thus we are not invited to consider relations of justice that might obtain between an adult and her infants or her senile demented parents. (2) Rawls's idealization of citizens as "fully cooperating," etc., puts to one side the large facts about extreme neediness I have just mentioned. (3) His conception of social cooperation, again, is based on the idea of reciprocity between equals and has no explicit place for relations of extreme dependency. (4) His account of the primary goods, introduced, as it is, as an account of the needs of citizens who are characterized by the two moral powers and by the capacity to be "fully cooperating," has no place for the need of many real people for the kind of care we give to people who are not independent. And (5) his account of citizens' freedom as involving the concept of being a self-authenticating source of valid claims (e.g., PL, 32) fails to make a place for any freedom that might be enjoyed by someone who is not independent in that sense.

18. See Kittay, *Love's Labor*, 77: "Dependency must be faced from the beginning of any project in egalitarian theory that hopes to include all persons within its scope." For a remarkable narrative of a particular life that shows exactly how many social structures play a part in the life of a mentally handicapped child from the very beginning, see Michael Bérubé, *Life As We Know It: A Father, a Family, and an Exceptional Child* (New York: Vintage, 1996).

19. This point has been repeatedly made by Amartya Sen in recommending an approach based on capability and functioning over the Rawlsian approach to primary goods; for the classic original statement, see Sen, "Equality of What?" in Sen, *Choice, Welfare, and Measurement* (Oxford: Basil Blackwell, 1982), 353–69; other good accounts of the approach are in Sen, "Capability and Well-Being," in *The Quality of Life*, ed. M. Nussbaum and A. Sen (Oxford: Clarendon, 1993), 30–53; "Gender Inequality and Theories of Justice," in *Women, Culture and Development*, ed. M. Nussbaum and J. Glover (Oxford: Clarendon, 1995), and *Inequality Reexamined* (New York: Russell Sage, 1992), especially chapters 1, 3, and 5.

20. Sen, "Equality of What?"

21. Two further problems not raised by Sen: First, even if we were to give more income and wealth to the person in a wheelchair, this would not solve the problem, for making this person mobile requires public action (construction of wheelchair ramps, accessible busses, etc.) that individuals cannot achieve on their own. Second, even if the

person in the wheelchair were equally well off with regard to economic well-being, there is a separate issue of dignity and self-respect. By measuring relative social positions by income and wealth alone, Rawls ignores the possibility that a group may be reasonably well-off economically, but suffer grave disabilities with regard to the social bases of self-respect. One might argue that gays and lesbians in our society are in precisely that position, but certainly the physically and mentally handicapped will be in that position, unless society makes a major and fundamental commitment to inclusion and respect.

22. At times, as in the passage from the DL cited in the previous text, Rawls suggests leaving aside all severe or expensive physical illness, as well as mental disability; see also PL, 272, n. 10. At other times (e.g., PL, 302), he treats possession of the two moral powers as a sufficient, as well as a necessary, condition of fully cooperating status.

23. Rawls proposes taking account of it at the legislative stage (see PL, 183–86), but given the pervasive role of political institutions in shaping the life chances of such citizens from the very beginning of a human life, this seems an inadequate reply. The concrete strategems adopted to address issues of disability (laws mandating wheelchair ramps, laws such as the Individuals with Disabilities Education Act) could well be left until this stage; but the fact that citizens experience such needs for care must be recognized from the start, and a commitment made to address these concerns.

24. Scanlon, *What We Owe to Each Other* (Cambridge, Mass.: Harvard University Press, 1999), 177–87. I am very grateful to Scanlon for correspondence that makes the complexity of his approach to these cases clear. Because this is a chapter about the basic structure of a political conception, I shall hope to take up his views elsewhere.

25. Once again, it is very important to stress the fact that this is Rawls's project, not Scanlon's, and that Scanlon does not recommend applying it in this way.

26. *Morals by Agreement*, 18, n. 30.

27. See, for example, TJ, 135, where finality is a formal condition on political principles, and 175–78, in the argument for the two principles where it is made clear that the agreement "is final and made in perpetuity" and that "there is no second chance" (176). Rawls's opposition to intuitionism focuses on this issue; see, for example, TJ, 35–36.

28. Kittay, *Love's Labor*, 102–03.

29. Like Sen, I defend this idea, in WHD, chapter 1; unlike Sen, I propose an actual list of the central capabilities, analogous to primary goods. WHD, chapter 1, discusses in detail the relationship of my approach to Rawls's.

30. On this point, see especially Williams, *Unbending Gender* (previous n. 13).

31. See my discussion of this point in WHD, chapter 1.

32. In TJ primary goods were characterized as all-purpose means to the pursuit of one's own conception of the good, whatever it is; in DL and PL, the interpretation shifts, and Rawls acknowledges that they are means with regard to the Kantian political conception of the person; see PL, 187–90.

33. I discuss this issue in detail in "Rawls and Feminism," with respect to both Rawls's text and the most prominent feminist critiques. See, for example, Seyla Benhabib, "The Generalized and the Concrete Other," in *Situating the Self*, 148–77; Marilyn Friedman, *What Are Friends For? Feminist Perspectives on Personal Relationships and Moral Theory* (Ithaca, N.Y.: Cornell University Press, 1993).

34. I owe this point to Geof Sayre-McCord, who pointed out that I myself have criticized feminists who don't see the Veil of Ignorance as part of the model of the person; see "Rawls and Feminism."

35. As Peter Cicchino eloquently put this point, Aristotle's conception is not deductive or a priori; it respects widely held views about human reality, but takes experience as its source and guide. Second, it takes seriously the materiality of human beings—their need for food, shelter, friendship, care, what might be called their basic dependency. Third, it is epistemologically modest—it does not claim to have the exactitude of mathematics, but rather is content to look for "such precision as accords with the subject-matter" (Cicchino, "Building of Foundational Myths: Feminism and the Recovery of 'Human Nature': A Response to Martha Fineman," April 15, 1999).

36. In that way my view is close to the type of liberalism defended (against Lockean contractarianism) by T. H. Green, though my form is not perfectionistic, but is, rather, a form of political liberalism. I have found very illuminating the discussion of the liberal tradition in John Deigh, "Liberalism and Freedom," forthcoming in *Social and Political Philosophy: Contemporary Perspectives*, ed. James Sterba (London: Routledge, 2001).

37. I attach the current version of the capabilities list as an appendix. The view is further debated in a symposium on my political philosophy in *Ethics* (Fall 2000); see in particular the paper by Richard Arneson, which takes me up on the question of capability and functioning, arguing that a more robust perfectionism that makes actual functioning the goal is required in areas such as health. I dispute this, defending my form of political liberalism, in "Aristotle, Politics, and Human Capabilities: A Response to Antony, Arneson, Charlesworth, and Mulgan," *Ethics* 111 (2000): 102–40.

38. Kittay, *Love's Labor*, chapter 1, part 3, on political strategies, is entitled "Some Mother's Child."

39. For passages that focus on the need of the individual for choice and independence, see, for example, 34–35, 53, 98, and 192, n. 32.

40. Kittay, *Love's Labor*, chapter 5.

41. See Kittay, *Love's Labor*, chapter 6, a beautiful and lucid account of her daughter's life.

42. Bérubé, *Life as We Know It*, 264: "For I have no sweeter dream than to imagine— aesthetically and ethically and parentally—that Jamie will someday be his own advocate, his own author, his own best representative." The book he mentions is Mitchell Levitz and Jason Kingsley, *Count Us In: Growing Up with Down Syndrome* (New York: Harcourt Brace, 1994).

43. The ideas in this section are developed at greater length in WHD, chapter 4.

44. Or, as in the case of Rousseau (see my remarks in the section titled "Liberalism and Feminism") and Hegel (if one should call either of them liberals), they have treated the topic in a rather unhelpful way.

45. MacKinnon, "Privacy v. Equality: Beyond Roe v. Wade," in *Feminism Unmodified*, 100; cf. *Feminist Theory of the State*, 191 (previous n. 7).

46. The development of Rawls's ideas about the family is traced in detail in my "Rawls and Feminism." For the family as part of the basic structure, see, for example, TJ, 4, 462; PL, 258. At this point already, Rawls alludes to problems of justice within the family, thinking of inequalities of opportunities between children because of unequal parental treatment; see TJ, 74, 301, and especially 511: "Is the family to be abolished then? Taken all by itself and given a certain primacy, the idea of equality of opportunity inclines in this direction."

47. The most influential critique of Rawls on this point is that of Susan Okin, in "Justice and Gender," and *Justice, Gender, and the Family* (previous n. 6).

48. Rawls, "The Idea of Public Reason Revisited," *University of Chicago Law Review* 64 (1997): 765–807, now reprinted in Rawls, *The Law of Peoples* (Cambridge, Mass.: Harvard University Press, 1999), 129–80; my page references are to the *Law Review* version.

49. Rawls understands the fact that it is chosen on the basis of one's religion as a sufficient condition of *voluntariness*, in background conditions that are fair (792 and note 68); he notes that the question needs a fuller discussion.

50. See the related defense of the Rawlsian position in Lloyd (previous note 6).

51. On this tension, see also G. A. Cohen, "Where the Action Is: On the Site of Distributive Justice," *Philosophy and Public Affairs* 26 (1997): 3–30.

52. See the good comments on this point in Lloyd (previous note 6).

53. See Martha Minow, "All in the Family and in All Families: Membership, Loving, and Owing," in *Sex, Preference, and Family: Essays on Law and Nature*, ed. D. Estlund and M. Nussbaum (New York: Oxford University Press, 1997), 249–76, with many fascinating examples of how the Immigration and Naturalization Service (INS) uses definitions of "family" to restrict immigration; Frances Olsen, "The Family and the Market: A Study of Ideology and Legal Reform," *Harvard Law Review* 96 (1983): 1497–1577; and Olsen, "The Myth of State Intervention in the Family," *University of Michigan Journal of Law Reform* 18 (1985): 1497–1577.

54. In *Baehr v. Lewin*, 852 P.2d 44 (Hawaii SC 1993), the Hawaii Supreme Court gave the following list of the political and social benefits of marriage:

1. A variety of state income tax advantages, including deductions, credits, rates, exemptions, and estimates;
2. Public assistance from and exemptions relating to the Department of Human Services;
3. Control, division, acquisition, and disposition of community property;
4. Rights relating to dower, courtesy, and inheritance;
5. Rights to notice, protection, benefits, and inheritance under the Uniform Probate Code;
6. Award of child custody and support payments in divorce proceedings;
7. The right to spousal support;
8. The right to enter into premarital agreements;
9. The right to file a nonsupport action;
10. Post-divorce rights relating to support and property division;
11. The benefit of the spousal privilege and confidential marital communications;
12. The benefit of the exemption of real property from attachment or execution;
13. The right to bring a wrongful death action.

And this list is far from complete; to get even close, we need to add: the right of next of kin in hospital visitation and decisions about medical treatment and burial; immigration advantages; and many other discounts and privileges available to married couples on a local basis. Finally, there are issues in the area of the "social bases of self-respect," to use Rawls's excellent phrase: public recognition of one's union as on a par with, having a dignity equal to that of, others is a major social good.

55. This is the approach that I develop more fully in WHD, chapter 4.

56. See the good discussion in Michael Warner, *The Trouble with Normal: Sex, Politics, and the Ethics of Queer Life* (New York: Free Press, 1999); and Claudia Card, "Against Marriage and Motherhood," *Hypatia* 11, no. 3 (summer 1996): 1–23.

57. Similarly, one should question standard distinctions between state action and inaction in this sphere; the state is acting as much when it supports conventional heterosexual marriage as when it extends similar privileges to nontraditional groups.

58. Many comparisons become difficult to make at this point, because my approach has no sequence analogous to the Rawlsian four-stage sequence.

59. At their most general level the capabilities are taken to be neutral across time as well as place, though their more concrete specifications (literacy, for example, as a concrete specification of an educational capability) are held to be relatively time-specific.

60. See further remarks on this issue in WHD, chapters 3 and 4.

61. For relevant background information focusing on India, see WHD, introduction and chapters 1 and 4.

62. Again, these programs are described in WHD, especially the introduction.

63. In WHD, chapter 3, I discuss *Wisconsin v. Yoder*, where Amish parents won the right to remove their children from two years of required public education. I consider this case a very hard case for my approach, and I recommend a balancing approach (based on the Religious Freedom Restoration Act of 1993) that would surely not satisfy the Rawlsian's demand for principles that are final, fully general, and ordered in advance.

64. For related observations about the public–private distinction, see my "Is Privacy Good for Women? What the Indian Constitutional Tradition Can Teach Us about Sex Equality," *The Boston Review* 25 (April/May 2000): 42–47; a longer article on the same topic is forthcoming as "Sex Equality, Liberty, and Privacy: A Comparative Approach to the Feminist Critique," in *Constitutional Ideas and Political Practices: Fifty Years of the Republic*, ed. E. Sridharan, R. Sudarshan, and Z. Hasan, eds. (Delhi: Oxford University Press, forthcoming).

9

Masking Dependency: The Political Role of Family Rhetoric

Martha L. A. Fineman

INTRODUCTION

In this chapter, I want to explore the schizophrenic nature of the interaction between social ideals and empirical observations concerning dependency. I am particularly interested in the family as a social and political construct that facilitates this interaction. Specifically, I argue that continued adherence to an unrealistic and unrepresentative set of assumptions about the family affects the way we perceive and attempt to solve persistent problems of poverty and social welfare. In the normative conclusions that are generated and reiterated in political and popular discussions about family, we assess the "justice" of particular policies addressing societal problems with reference to concepts such as the individual and dependency.

Images of the traditional family pervade contemporary political and legal discourse. Rhetoric about this family's form and function ignores or obscures the nature and extent of individual dependency. It also masks the costs of necessary caretaking of dependents, costs that are disproportionately assumed by women. Dependency should be understood to be both inevitable and universal. My argument that in a just society there must be a fundamental obligation for the community to provide for its weaker members is built upon this proposition. Of necessity, fulfilling that collective obligation in a society that has historically appropriated, rather than economically rewarded, caretaking labor will have some redistributive (or market correcting) consequences when those who currently care for dependents at substantial cost to themselves are finally compensated.

The ideal of family is essential to maintaining the myth that autonomy and independence can be attained. Our society mythologizes concepts such as "independence" and "autonomy" despite the concrete indications surrounding us that these ideals are, in fact, unrealizable and unrealistic. Those members of society who openly manifest the reality of dependency—either as dependents or caretakers in

215

need of economic subsidy—are rendered deviants. Unable to mask dependency by retreating to contrived social institutions like the family, single-mother caretakers in particular are stigmatized and subjected to epithets and scorn for embodying a dependency that society would rather deny.[1]

Inconspicuously complementing the myth of individual autonomy are assumptions about the context in which individuals exist in our society, particularly the assumption that we belong to or aspire to belong to families. A traditional family is typically imagined: a husband and wife—formally married and living together—with their biological children. The husband performs as the head of the household, providing economic support and discipline for the dependent wife and children, who correspondingly owe him duties of obedience and respect. This assumed archetypal family provides the normative expectations for the institution of the family.

This vision of the family is perceived as facilitating individual identity and development. It is touted as the site for intimate connection, the place for individuals to retreat when seeking to satisfy human needs.[2] We desire to be part of a family because we experience it as a psychological conglomerate of nurture and support and/or an emotional proving ground for individual self-development. Other socially supported functions assigned to the family are associated with its role as an economic unit. The "household" is the relevant demographic measure in a variety of economic contexts.[3] The family also has had a historic monopoly on "legitimate" reproduction.[4] Children born outside of the traditional (marriage-based) family are labeled "illegitimate" or deemed "bastards."[5] In addition to its psychological and functional dimensions, the family also serves as a powerful ideological symbol with political implications. It is the intimate unit in policy and legal discussions that is exclusively designated as what is normatively desirable.

The continued resort to the traditional family as a cultural icon and political anchor is puzzling given the changes in society over the past several decades. In particular, women's rejection of the hierarchical family[6]; the dissolution of the conceptual lines that had been drawn at the turn of the century between the domestic or "private" sphere and the market/political or "public" sphere[7]; and the increased participation of women in the paid workforce[8] (with their consequential shouldering of dual responsibilities) challenge the vitality and desirability of the traditional family. We seem to ignore these changes with our continued resort to the traditional family unit.

Altered expectations and aspirations about equality and economic opportunity have been the impetus for many individual women to change the ways they practice mothering. On a societal level, these changes have generated reconsideration of the meaning and implications of motherhood. This process of cultural and social rethinking presents a challenge to the dominance of the traditional family model. The rather rapid acceptance (and embrace) of possibly viable and desirable alternatives by certain subsets of society seems to have struck terror in the hearts of many, women and men alike. In some quarters, change is perceived as inherently destabilizing. Groups who view change as inherently destabilizing often also tend to consider the family to be a foundational institution essential to civilization.[9] Its instability is perceived, therefore, as the equivalent of a threat to society.

Policymakers and lawmakers scramble to understand and to address the implications of change for the family. Reflecting the deep divisions within society on these issues, some seek to impose sanctions and incentives to suppress the emerging social realities or to make them conform to the old ideal.[10] Others take a more pragmatic track and, conceding that change is inevitable, explore the ways in which laws might be refashioned to accommodate the new social realities and their undesirable material consequences.

The current incoherence between family reality and the images of family in law exposes the dominant ideology and its role in policy formation. Refusing to address and to assess the continued viability of ideological assumptions, politicians and pundits resort to condemnation and to repressive policy suggestions. This pattern of reaction to changing family behavior should raise questions about the responsive capabilities of our lawmaking institutions.

FAMILY, LAW, AND LEGITIMACY

Law performs an important societal function when it monitors or disciplines transformations and transitions in society, imposing conceptual order on the chaos generated by the perception of change. Widespread changes in behavior or rejection of existing social institutions by a significant segment of society should be the impetus for a collective reconsideration of the continued viability of the old normative system. If, instead, change becomes the occasion for retrenchment and repression, inspiring mean-spirited and dangerous polemics that are passed off as politics, the legitimacy of the entire legal system will eventually be undermined.

Reconsideration of basic social institutions does not take place without constraints, of course. Widely held and insistently reinforced beliefs of what is natural, normal, and desirable affect how we approach change. Ideologies that reference collectively held conceptions tame radical initiatives and impulses. In legal reform, the fundamental and initial debate is always about the underlying cultural and social constructs.[11] As components of the dominant ideological structure in which later discussions about policy take place, these constructs direct the progression of reform. Nevertheless, when there are such fundamental shifts in family formation and functioning as we now experience, it is foolish and shortsighted to rely exclusively on antiquated visions and ignore the emerging social realities.

Family

Historically, the American family has been our most explicitly gendered institution.[12] The family has been justified and valorized as an institution for its perceived role in reproducing and transmitting norms of social behavior to all its members, but most particularly to the young. It continues to be gendered in its operations and expectations, as well as in the values that it represents. Concurrently, the complementary legal roles of Husband–Father, Wife–Mother, and Child–Adult are formulated in the context of the relationship between the state and the legally contrived institution of the "official" family. Dependency, "naturally" assigned to the family, is privatized. It is not anticipated in the ideology that either the market or the state will directly contribute to or assist in the necessary caretaking—that is done in the privacy of the family. The ideology of the private family mandates that the unit nurture its members and provide for them economically. The burdens of economic support and caretaking—costs of intrafamily dependency—are allocated within the family based on the perceived family roles its members play.[13] This assignment of burdens within the family operates in an inherently unequal manner; the uncompensated tasks of caretaking are placed with women while men pursue careers that provide economically for the family but also enhance their individual career or work prospects. This division of family labor, perpetuating historic gendered family roles, has been understood as just and "natural," rather than manufactured or contrived.[14]

As appealing as this traditional model may be to some, it is essential to note that even had the world once been so simple, things have changed. An examination of the current statistics on intimate associations reveals that domestic arrangements that do not conform to the traditional family unit are on the rise.[15] More and more individuals are living alone than in decades past.[16] Divorce rates hover around 50 percent, and never-married motherhood is on the rise, even among middle-class, educated women.[17] Couples choose not to become parents in larger numbers than prior generations.[18] Furthermore, even in conforming families (married with children), the traditional roles have broken down. Many women work outside of the home either in a full- or part-time capacity, and some are as deeply committed to career and job advancement as their husbands.[19]

Looking at family reality, however, involves more than just a reference to these empirical changes. The statistics have normative as well as empirical implications. The fact that the United States has a multiplicity of ethnic, religious, and cultural traditions supports the argument that we should develop a pluralistic social model inclusive of diverse family practices. For example, in recent years some people have begun to question the received wisdom as to what should constitute the core or central family connection.[20] Marriage has historically been considered the fundamental building block of society. In the words of Chief Justice Morrison R. Waite over a century ago: "Marriage, while from its very nature a sacred obligation, is . . . a civil contract, and usually regulated by law. Upon [marriage] society may be said to be built, and out of its fruits spring social relations and social obligations and duties, with which government is necessarily required to deal."[21]

Some people continue to insist that legitimate families can only be built upon the foundation of a traditional marital tie. Others emphasize the biological connection and minimize the importance of legal relations in favor of kinship structures that form affiliations transcending current formal definitions of the family.[22] For others, the preference is for an affectional family, a unit composed of those with whom we choose to connect but who may not be "related" to us by either blood or marriage.[23] Family affiliations are expressed in different kinds of affiliational acts. Some are sexually based,[24] as with marriage. Some are forged biologically, as through parenthood. Others are more relational, such as those based on nurturing or caretaking[25] or those developed through affection and acceptance of interdependence.[26]

Each of the alternative conceptions of the central or core family connection assumes certain things about what is appropriate and desirable. Each family form carries within its confines the possibility of exclusion and stigma that attaches to nonconforming relationships. Each model, in defining itself, defines the parameters of what is natural or appropriate. The converse of the created ideal may become defined as deviant or pathological. Such a process has attended the dominance of our official and, often, legal adherence to the unitary, heterogeneous patriarchal family.[27] The dominant ideological construction of the family assumes only one appropriate model of family formation, heterosexual marriage.

This model controls the political process in which the state, through its institutions and designated actors, wields the symbolic power of this normative structure in order to justify a parsimonious distribution of economic and social subsidies to nontraditional families.[28] This is occurring in the context of the current debate about the family in the United States. Our debates focus on family form, not function. We are concerned with the legal status and living arrangements of parents; increasingly we impose punitive measures on those who deviate from the traditional model. A discussion of what societal role the family plays—its relationship to the obligations of the state—has not taken place. We deal in platitudes rather than assess what functions we want from the family (whatever its form). Nor do we engage in realistic explorations of how family functions might be successfully performed by nontraditional family units if they were adequately assisted by public subsidies and support now reserved for the nuclear family.

The Family in Politics

In spite of alternative visions and nonconforming behavior, the politically normative family remains intact: the heterosexual, formally married couple and their biological children. Intimate groups that do not conform to this model historically have been labeled "deviant" and subjected to explicit state regulation and control justified by their nonconformity.[29] The level of state intervention, control, and punishment is being raised currently. For example, the rhetoric directed at unmarried and/or poor women has moved in the space of a few months from that of the disapproving patriarch to that of the ranting, righteous witch hunter. Given a patina of academic respectability by the likes of Charles Murray,[30] and led by the careening crusading of Newt Gingrich,[31] the descriptive terms and accusations directed at the most defenseless people in our society stigmatize and dehumanize them.[32] We reject a humane social "contract"—one based on the spirit of collective responsibility and an appreciation of the generalized interdependence among all members of society—in favor of a public, ritualistic washing of the federal hands and the devolution of responsibility to states. Many of the states, however, have already declared their intention to pass the problem further down the line, eventually laying the burden on the poor themselves.[33] We have witnessed the creation of explicit punitive and mean-spirited government measures disguised as "reforms."[34]

The idealized family has become the panacea for all social ills in contemporary policy discussions. The institution of marriage is seriously offered as the uniquely appropriate form for social policy, and systems of proposed disincentives to keep unmarried women from reproducing are debated by a multiplicity of predominantly male politicians in various halls of power. Women who do not conform—either by refusing to marry or to participate in paternity proceedings—are faced with threats that their children will be placed in orphanages or that restrictive measures and conditions will be attached to their societal subsidies.[35] They are punished by cuts in their meager pubic assistance awards if they have additional children,[36] refuse to (or cannot) name the father of their children,[37] are unable to ensure that their children attend school,[38] or fail to get vaccinations for their children.[39] Draconian incentive systems are proposed to tie them to a world of wage work or make work[40]; all of this in a system that refuses to consider mothering to be work.[41]

What have these women done to "deserve" such harsh words and punitive measures? In large part it is the stigma of being poor.[42] But more than poverty is at issue. The broad general target is unmarried women with children, and the attacks on these mothers are the opening salvo of a reactionary plan to discipline women who do not conform to the roles they are assigned within the traditional scheme of the family. This is why all women, whether they are mothers or not, should be concerned with the current debate about poverty. Although the welfare debate seemingly stigmatizes only one form of mothering as pathological, political rhetoric reinforces, re-creates, and reiterates several fundamental premises about families that will be used against all women. Paramount among these is, of course, the strong preference for formally celebrated heterosexual marriage that functions as a reproductive unit and is thus the "core" upon which all else is founded. This preference places responsible reproduction (indeed, responsible sexuality) solely within the context of the traditional family—a context in which legal consequences are clear and decisions will be considered and controlled. Motherhood outside this family unit will be punished and stigmatized. Non-mothers will also be disciplined, pressured, and pitied.[43] Attacks on birth control and abortion can be viewed as extolling the inevitability and naturalness of motherhood.

THE FAMILY IN LAW

The Sexual Organization of Family Intimacy

Our conception of the family as an entity is built around a core unit, the married couple. The basic family relationship is founded on the sexual affiliation or conjugation of two heterosexual adults. This heterosexual unit continues to be considered as presumptively appropriate and it retains viability as the essential family connection. Even contemporary critics of the institution are typically revisionists, viewing marriage to be merely in need of some updating and structural reformulation. In fact, arguments that other sexual affiliations—such as nonmarital cohabitation or same-sex relationships—deserve the same privileges afforded to marriage, far from challenging the privileged status of marriage, reinforce it by inscribing onto it the attributes of normalcy, desirability, and privilege.

The Egalitarian Organization of the Family

As a result of reform movements of the 1970s and 1980s, certain aspects of the law reflect a gender-neutral family ideal.[44] Our linguistic model is now one of an egalitarian family, based on the marital "partnership" of husband and wife. Gone from our formal, official discourse is the hierarchical organization of the common-law marriage described so graphically by Blackstone under the doctrines of "unity" and "merger."[45]

Female subservience is no longer assumed by formal legal rules,[46] nor is women's inherent incompetence in the business and market world seriously asserted and used as a basis for exclusion by courts and legislatures. Wives and mothers are held equally responsible for the economic well-being of their families[47] and no longer presumed by virtue of their sex to be the preferred parent in custody disputes.[48] Many legal disabilities for nonmarital children have been removed.[49] There is less stigma to divorce with the ascendancy of "no-fault" philosophy whereby marriages are terminated because of "irreconcilable differences" rather than the culpable conduct of one spouse.

Rhetorical changes in law and legislation, however, do not reflect "real" changes, nor can they compel such changes. In considering the empirical data on the operation of the family, the inescapable conclusion—rhetoric aside—is that gender divisions persist. Women continue to bear the "burdens of intimacy"—the "costs" of "inevitable dependency"—in our society.[50] As a definitional note, "burden" is not the same as oppression. I use the term to signal clearly that there are costs associated with the caretaking tasks that women typically perform in our society. These labors may provide joy, but they are also burdensome and have material costs and consequences that go uncompensated within the private family. Not to recognize these labors as "burdens" ignores the costs to women. If such labor remains invisible, the fact that it goes uncompensated is condoned.

A second definitional point is that it is important to differentiate between various forms of dependency. I am interested in two specific dependencies. The first I label "inevitable dependency." It is inevitable in that it flows from the status and situation of being a child and often accompanies aging, illness, or disability. This type of dependency is biological and developmental in nature. It is universal. In this sense dependency will always be (and always has been) with us as a society and as individuals. In the current welfare debate the paradigmatic inevitable dependent is the child, considered to be "worthy" or "deserving" of help. The second, complementary form of dependency, however, is more problematic for policymakers. Those who care for inevitable dependents are often themselves dependent—a derivative dependency that stems from their roles as caretakers and the need for resources that their duties generate. This type of dependency is not inevitable, nor is it universal. It is socially defined and assigned, and that assignment is gendered.

Noting that the costs of caretaking associated with these dependencies continue to be allocated to women should not be understood as an argument about essentialism. The allocation is accomplished and reinforced by the culture and ideology of the family. Nonetheless, because something is a social construct does not mean it will be easy to change. In fact, change is difficult because of the tenacity of the potent traditional ideology of the family in American culture.

In discussing the family, we seem caught in a variety of conceptual traps. Abstract notions of equality have become the measure for early feminist efforts to reform the family. Emphasizing equality shifted the focus on relationships between men and women and husbands and wives and led to the articulation of a reform goal in which existing gendered roles within the confines of the traditionally populated family unit would be reorganized.[51] Rather than challenging the basic structure, early reformers merely expected that fathers would perform more household duties as modern mothers spent more time and energy on market endeavors. Under this view marital partners, fulfilling egalitarian impulses, would simply rework their relationship into a nonhierarchical form. The marital tie, nonetheless, would continue to serve as the anchor defining and giving content to their relationship, while defining other family associations.

This approach to family reform influenced and informed the legal changes made during the past several decades—the refashioning of the "egalitarian family" from the structure of its common-law hulk.[52] The grand aspirations for equality are manifested in terms we now use to discuss family relationships—we substitute "partnership" for marriage; "shared parenting" for mothering and fathering; "interdependency" and "contribution" for need and obligatory domestic labor. Unfortunately, this focus on equality has severe practical and theoretical limitations.[53] Reformers naively assumed that sharing could and would happen. With the egalitarian aspiration ensconced in law, women would be freed to develop their careers and men would be unconstrained in choosing nurturing over other endeavors. Such assumptions, viewing the husband and wife as the basic family unit, are unrealistic in a society with a divorce rate hovering at 50 percent and never-married motherhood on the rise.[54]

These statistics indicate that the time has come to admit that the gendered notion of the role-defined and mutually dependent marital couple no longer serves as an adequate concept. We must begin to rethink the institution of the contemporary family in a way that is responsive to emerging realities. We must begin to think of family policy in terms of the functions we want the family to perform and to leave behind our obsession with form. We should establish a system of sanctions and rewards that reflects the functions society should protect and encourage through social and economic subsidies. Our meager and sporadic family policies fail to facilitate or to support families as they struggle to fulfill their expectations and responsibilities. Unlike other industrialized democracies we have no well-defined notion of collective responsibility for inevitable dependency—lacking are basic income guarantees, comprehensive publicly assisted day care, universal health care coverage, and other societal structures and institutions to help shoulder caretaking burdens. In fact, recent welfare reforms resort to the privatized solutions of marriage or child support as the answer for myriad societal problems, including child poverty.

The Public Role of the Private Family

In attempting to analyze the tenacity of the sexually affiliated or marriage-based notion of family, we must consider the structural position of the family. In this assessment, we must surrender our preoccupation with the roles of individuals within the family and concentrate on the institution in relation to the state. The relevant questions are: What is the role of the family as a social institution? How does it interact with the state and how does this interaction reflect the ideological underpinnings of the structure? It is important in this regard to remember that the family is first and foremost a social institution. As such it is defined and given social content by significant systems of belief or knowledge with coercive potential exceeding that of law. In this regard, the family as an institution embedded in social understanding should be understood as resistant to redefinition.[55]

THE FAMILY IN SOCIETY

Within the variety of extralegal cultural and social systems that shape our beliefs about families there are certain core concepts or "metanarratives"[56] that predominate and affect law, as well as shape and influence reform. Two interrelated metanarratives about the American family direct current social policy and limit possible policy initiatives that would help functioning, nontraditional families. The first is that family has a "natural" form—husband, wife and child (the nuclear family)—built around a foundational sexual affiliation reinforced by reproductive biology. This natural family purportedly predates the state; it is also viewed as a complement to the state, essential to the state's very existence.

The second metanarrative is that of the private family—a unit entitled to protection from the state. Freedom from state intervention is conferred as a "reward" for fulfilling societal and political expectations that the family is the natural repository for inevitable dependency. The private family is the social institution that is relied upon to raise children and care for the ill, the needy, and the dependent. Ideally it performs these tasks as a self-contained and self-sufficient unit without demanding public resources to do so. In the societal division of labor among institutions, the private family bears the burden of dependency, not the public state. Resort to the state is considered a failure. By according to the private family responsibility for inevitable dependency, society directs dependency away from the state and privatizes it.

As with individual autonomy and self-sufficiency the notion of the private family has important ideological and political currency. As an ideological construct, the private family masks the universal and inevitable nature of dependency and allows the public and government officials to frame rhetoric in terms idealizing capitalistic individualism, independence, self-sufficiency, and autonomy. Significantly, the ideals of self-sufficiency and autonomy operate on two levels: they construct the ideal family as well as the ideal individual within our culture. Applying the ideal of self-sufficiency and autonomy to the private family is as unrealistic as applying it to individuals. Private families receive many hidden direct and indirect subsidies through tax, inheritance, marriage, and other laws. Employer contributions to health and life insurance policies are not counted as income (and hence are not taxed as income)[57]; interspousal transfers are not taxed as gifts[58]; imputed income—domestic labor—is not included as income although the wage earner benefits from it.[59] (Meanwhile, the home-worker receives neither compensation nor pension benefits for her tasks.) Middle-class deductions, such as that for interest paid on mortgage debt[60] or certain child-care expenses,[61] are considered appropriate even though they remove income from the taxable pool.

One rallying cry in favor of welfare caps was that welfare recipients should not receive extra benefits if they had additional children when private families qualified for no such subsidy. Missing from the attack was the realization that for each additional child, private families receive a tax deduction worth considerably more than the pittance typically given to welfare mothers who have more children.

The two metanarratives—that of the natural family and that of the private family—are composed of interdependent assumptions that reinforce one another on an ideological level and perversely interact with one another. The result is the continuation of gender inequality. The tasks assigned the private family mandate that burdens or costs associated with dependency be allocated among family members, and this allocation is gendered. In other words, our perception of the family as a social institution facilitates the continuation of gendered role divisions and frustrates the egalitarian ideal.

Disciplining Deviant Women

The very definition of single motherhood as an independent and significant social problem, as well as the nature and direction of suggested remedies for the "crisis," show the strength of the natural and private family concepts in tandem. Under the ideal system, private families need economic resources, and their members need nurture. The head of the household "naturally" supplies his family's economic needs; his wife, the adult "naturally" dependent on her husband's economic provisions for her household work, supplies the caretaking. The reform objective for single-mother families—whether divorced or never married—is to reconstitute the natural family; this is to be achieved by bringing (back) the male to properly privatize dependency. Strikingly central to all family and welfare reforms is the image of male as head of the household. Widespread single motherhood has made it impossible to continue to respond to dependency within the confines of our family ideology. Single motherhood presents strong evidence that the nuclear family paradigm has failed; it illustrates that the private-natural family is no longer viable as the sole, or even primary, institutional response to dependency.[62]

In constructing the problems presented by, as well as the solutions for, both the never-married mother and the divorced mother, the absence of a male is assumed central. The male presence in the form of economic support is induced by conferring "rights" over children. The vision is that male discipline and control can make the family whole in some mystical sense. The economically viable male becomes a vehicle for social policy: "he" is the universal answer, the means offered for resolving the problems of poverty and despair. Consequently, it is hoped that conducting paternity proceedings and forcing fathers to pay child support will alleviate poverty. Both divorce and welfare reforms attempt to reconstitute the natural family, by bringing the father into the picture through an economic and disciplinary connection reminiscent of the traditional male role in the hierarchical private family.[63] Patriarchy is thus reasserted and modified to meet new social realities.

Further consideration of the circumstances in which the private-natural family fails will illuminate the previous abstractions. The current economic circumstances make it unlikely that marriage will resolve the problems of most poor women and children. Unemployment, "downsizing," and the change from a manufacturing to a service economy have eroded the wage scale for many men.[64] In addition, the flight of businesses to suburbs makes finding jobs harder for urban workers who are unable to make the commute.

Even if economic patterns do not create insurmountable obstacles to using marriage as the solution for poverty, significant changes in the way we define family behaviors and aspirations will have an impact. One set of difficulties is presented by the widespread acceptance of the egalitarian family among elites. The second set of problems is found in the sense of crisis surrounding the increased number of women—from all classes and races, resulting from either our high divorce rate or because they never married in the first place—who become single mothers.[65]

As an articulated ideal, the egalitarian family is imposed on existing couple-based family units, and it generates tensions insofar as one goal to be attained by the partners is equality in the marketplace. Equality as an ideal has developed in a society that rewards and values market work, and feminist theory has reflected this. Mothering and other family work is to be "managed" so women are free to develop their careers. Attempts to achieve equality in the public sphere, particularly in the market, however, leave the two-parent family as an institution potentially without available caretakers.[66]

The never-married or divorced single-mother case presents a version of the same dilemma. Without a designated "partner," if the mother devotes her time to market work in order to support her child no one will be available to perform her caretaker role. If she fulfills her culturally assigned obligations by sacrificing her career to bear the burdens of dependency, as a single mother without a wage earner to support her, she will starve unless she goes begging to the state. In any event her family has not dealt with its dependencies privately.

Both of these situations reveal the latent gender implications embedded in the private family. The task assigned the private family—its societal role as the private repository of inevitable dependency—mandates two parents and some form of role differentiation and division. Given these demands, the family will assume the traditional natural form almost inevitably. This family seems destined to be gendered and unequal.

Of course, the rhetorical resolution for the potential dilemma that there will be no caretaker in the egalitarian coupled family has been to "share" caretaking. Rhetoric aside, empirical information indicates that sharing is not taking place. The figures are overwhelming; little has changed in terms of who does domestic labor, and this is typically true regardless whether or not both partners work.[67] Hence, women must either give up the hope for equality or hire other women at (typically) meager wages to carry the burdens of dependency for them. In either case, some woman's labor is appropriated for necessary caretaking and un- or undercompensated even within the charade of the egalitarian marriage.[68]

In instances where it is necessary to compromise one spouse's career for caretaking, economic incentives guide the choice between marital partners. Equality fictions in the family may abound, but continuing market inequalities typically ensure that when there is a need for a family member to accommodate caretaking by forgoing market time, the efficient caretaker will be the lesser earner, usually the woman.[69] In addition to this economic channeling, centuries of social and cultural conditioning shape the way women understand and exercise their "choices" in defining their family role.[70] Family failures with regard to children, evidenced in even minor deviations from an unattainable ideal, are most likely placed at a mother's feet.[71] Working mothers elicit fears that generations of children will be abandoned to neglect and the horrors of day-care regimentation and abuse.

In the case of single mothers—whether divorced or never married—the inadequacies of the private family are incapable of resolution by pretenses toward equality within the nuclear unit. These families are beyond that paradigm and are consequentially stigmatized and demonized. Single-mother families are consistently designated "deviant" and "pathological."[72] Ignoring evidence indicating that poverty, not family form, causes harms, policymakers identify single mothers as the cause of crime, poverty, and societal decadence.[73]

On a policy level, the rhetoric currently surrounding never-married mothers tragically obscures the magnitude and dimensions of the economic deprivations that make it difficult for any women outside of the patriarchical family (and many within it) to raise their children.[74] Rather than addressing the needs of existing caretakers, legislators compete to concoct disincentives for single motherhood to punish women for reproducing and incentives designed to push mothers to create a nuclear family.

A Claim for Justice

When a woman becomes a mother she performs a valuable societal function. She is reproducing to the benefit of the state, the workforce, and the family. The significance of her task historically has been the justification for subjecting her as "mother" to state power. She is supervised and judged according to standards that do not apply to other citizens. The behavior of mothers is regulated through the companion normative systems of law and family ideology. If mothers are found wanting, they may be punished. This is particularly true for poor and single mothers, but all women as mothers risk intervention and subjugation based on their status. State-imposed supervision and control of mothers, and the corresponding sacrifice of privacy, should form the basis for an entitlement to justice by mothers—a claim for the resources to perform the tasks society demands of them.

Of course, my conclusion is not so simple to implement. Our societal sense of what constitutes "justice" for families as social entities, as well as our conclusions about what is "just" in the face of interfamilial conflicts, are formulated in the context of existing, historically legitimized power relations. Our definition and acceptance of the nuclear family as a legal and, perhaps, to a somewhat lesser extent, a social institution, and the acceptance of assigned roles to individual family members reflect the contemporary (and temporal) resolution of struggles for power and dominance.[75]

Conversely, our experience of "power" is filtered through our perception of "justice." Justice legitimizes and condones what might otherwise be viewed as inappropriate coercive maintenance of certain traditional family forms and expressions of individual power within families. Society's sense of justice currently allows some politicians to condemn alternatives to the preferred family arrangement as deviant and to propose subjecting them to exercises of state power that would not typically be condoned if directed toward traditional entities. Intrusion and supervision are justified because of the deviation from state norms. At the same time, families that are in conformity with state standards are empowered. We perceive that their conformity has justly earned them a right to protection and privacy.

Justice, as a normative conclusion, reflects a particular ideological position. A particular ideology is tested through the interaction of power (or institutions of power, such as law) and prevalent concepts of "justice." For this reason, it is artificial and inappropriate to separate the concept of justice from that of power or ideology.[76] Appreciating these grand theoretical concepts and understanding their implications in society mandate appreciating and understanding the way they affect and influence each other.

In the context of policy development regarding single mothers, the law as "power" and the reform rhetoric as "justice" (or justification) intersect and reinforce each other to portray nonconforming social behavior as behavior in need of punishment, supervision, regulation, containment, and control. Disciplining women is understood to be necessary and appropriate. Traditional family structures and individual roles are perceived as necessary and therefore "neutral" and "just." Unequal allocations of major societal resources (including both cultural and economic capital) to subsidize existing nuclear families are justified by the dominant family ideology.

The subsidized nuclear family unit, mischaracterized as "self-sufficient" and "independent," is held out as the ideal norm. The subsequent apparently successful performance of this class of families furthers the ideology of the independent family and masks or distorts the universal and extensive nature of dependency in society. Their subsidized existence solidifies the notion that successful families manage dependency without resorting to the state.

Challenges to the justness of formulating and implementing state family policy around a model that conforms neither to the way in which a great number of Americans live their lives, nor to the dictates of its own rhetoric, have not been successful.[77] In fact, deviant intimate entities—those families that are poor (or fail to conform to the nuclear model)—are relegated to a separate, stigmatized set of subsidies, increasingly punitive in nature and in implementation. These dependent families are vilified in public discourse and provided with "incentives" to replicate the ideal model.

One concrete manifestation of the injustice of our policies is found in the highly pronounced gendered poverty gap in the United States. American women are much more likely to be poor than are American men.[78] A recent study indicates that American women are 41 percent more likely to live in poverty than are American men.[79] By contrast, poverty is more "equally" experienced in countries like the Netherlands and Italy.[80] Marriage equalizes the ratio—poor couples share meager resources, but one prominent factor lifting women to the level of males who are better off is the availability of government benefits. In the Netherlands, for example, there is a low overall poverty rate, and an almost nonexistent gender poverty gap, due to the generous welfare system.[81]

The approach in this country must change and those women who are caretakers must be given a right to resources to enable them to perform the tasks we demand of them. The concept of justice must be reformulated so that punitive and mean-spirited laws designed to discipline women and children into patriarchy are seen as inappropriate. Transforming justice requires an attack on the underlying ideology that valorizes the nuclear family. A reformulated vision of justice would relate to the empirical needs of society, accepting and accommodating the inevitability of dependency and recognizing the claim of caretakers for resources necessary to accomplish their nurturing tasks.

For too long and for too great an extent, family policy in this country has been fashioned to further the nuclear family ideal. Policy based on the traditional family unit fosters the assumption that the maintenance of intimacy (including everything from contraception to responsibility for the day-to-day care of children) is primarily a "private" task.

It is essential for feminists to point out consistently that without substantial rethinking of the concepts underlying patriarchy—such as that of the private-natural family—the condition of women is unlikely to improve significantly. Without such rethinking it will be a bleak future for women and those inevitable dependents for whom we care.

NOTES

I would like to thank Sara Velazquez and Susannah J. Braffman for their invaluable assistance on the final draft of this chapter. This chapter reflects many themes set forth in Martha Albertson Fineman, *The Neutered Mother, The Sexual Family and Other Twentieth Century Tragedies* (New York: Routledge, 1995).

This chapter originally appeared in *Virginia Law Review* 81, no. 8 (November 1995): 2181–215. Copyright © 1995 by Virginia Law Review Association. Reprinted by permission of the publisher, Virginia Law Review Association.

1. See infra Part II.B.

2. Long ago, in *Maynard v. Hill*, 125 U.S. 190 (1888), the U.S. Supreme Court characterized marriage as "the most important relation in life" (Ibid., 205), and as "the foundation of the family and of society, without which there would be neither civilization nor progress" (Ibid., 211). In *Meyer v. Nebraska*, 262 U.S. 390 (1923), the Court recognized that the right "to marry, establish a home and bring up children" is a central part of the liberty protected by the due process clause (Ibid., 399).

3. We see this, for example, in census figures where a person living alone is designated a household. See Terry Lugaila, U.S. Department of Commerce, Series P-23, No. 181, "Households, Families, and Children: A 30-Year Perspective" (Washington: U.S. Department of Commerce, 1992), 14. In contrast, a family is defined as a "group of two or more persons related by birth, marriage or adoption residing together" (Ibid.). It is interesting to note that this bureaucratic definition fully incorporates all of the types of families that many American politicians are attempting to marginalize. For a multicultural economic

study of households, past and present, see generally Gary S. Becker, *A Treatise on the Family* (enlarged ed. 1991).

4. In *Lester v. Lester*, 87 N.Y.S.2d 517 (N.Y. Fam. Ct. 1949), Justice Panken stated:

> Man enters a marital relationship to perpetuate the species. The family is the result of marital re-
> lationship. It is the institution which determines in a large measure the environmental influences,
> cultural backgrounds, and even economic status of its members. It is the foundation upon which
> society rests and is the basis for the family and all of its benefits. (Ibid., 520)

See also June Carbone, "Income Sharing: Redefining the Family in Terms of Community," *Hous. Law Review* 31 (1994): 359, 398 (recognizing the historical "insistence on the traditional family as the sole permissible locus of childrearing").

5. Some of these stigmatizing terms are currently used in the political debates over welfare reform. See Fineman, *Neutered Mother, Sexual Family*, chapter 5.

6. This trend is evinced by the growing number of women who will never marry. See
Arthur J. Norton and Louisa F. Miller, "Marriage, Divorce, and Remarriage in the 1990s"
(Washington, D.C.: Bureau of the Census, U.S. Department of Commerce, 1992), 1–4
(indicating a significant drop in the number of women who ever marry). For example, from
1975–1990, the number of women aged twenty to twenty-four who ever married dropped
from 63 percent to 38 percent; for ages twenty-five to twenty-nine, the percentage dropped
from 87 percent to 69 percent; for ages thirty to thirty-four, from 93 percent to 82 percent;
and for ages thirty-five to thirty-nine, from 96 percent to 89 percent) (Ibid., 3).

7. For enlightening discussions of the public/private sphere, see Nancy F. Cott, *The
Bonds of Womanhood: "Woman's Spheres" in New England, 1780–1835* (New Haven,
Conn.: Yale University Press, 1977); Frances E. Olsen, "The Family and The Market: A
Study of Ideology and Legal Reform," *Harvard Law Review* 96 (1983): 1497; Nadine
Taub and Elizabeth M. Schnieder, "Women's Subordination and the Role of Law,"
reprinted in *The Politics of Law: A Progressive Critique*, ed. David Kairys, 2d ed. (New
York: Pantheon, 1990), 150; see also Sylvia A. Law, "Rethinking Sex and the Constitution," *University of Pennsylvania Law Review* 132 (1984): 955 (describing women's subservience to men both in the workplace and the domestic sphere and arguing that to
achieve a "stronger constitutional concept of sex-based equality" an acknowledgment of
biological differences between men and women is in order).

8. See generally Carbone, note 4 (discussing societal and economic pressures on women
to marry and surveying studies demonstrating that as more women have entered the job
market, marriage rates have gone down); Reva B. Siegel, "Home as Work: The First
Women's Rights Claims Concerning Wives' Household Labor, 1850–1880," *Yale Law
Journal* 103 (1994): 1073 (detailing the move toward increased female labor participation).

9. Diana Hochstedt Butler quotes a Republican presidential hopeful as saying: "'Almost every problem we have in this society can be attributed to the breakdown of the marriage-based, two parent family'" (Diana Hochstedt Butler, "Romanticizing the Family,"
Baltimore Sun, May 26, 1995, 19A). The Religious Right similarly embraces this belief in
the need to return to traditional family values as a response to societal problems. They
have most recently demonstrated this through their support of the "Contract with the
American Family" (Ibid.).

Ralph Reed, executive director of the Christian Coalition and sponsor of the "Contract with
the American Family," also attributes problems in society to cultural changes. He has stated:

What ails America isn't just its budget is out of balance, or just that its taxes are too high, or just that it isn't creating enough jobs. . . . It's the culture, it's values, it's a coarsening of the cultural environment. It's a break-up of the family, and these are the things that we want to see addressed. (*MacNeil/Lehrer Newshour* [PBS television broadcast, September 11, 1995])

10. Charles Murray, Newt Gingrich, and the Republican Contract with America urge that if mothers cannot care for their children, primarily because they are poor, the children should be removed from them and placed in orphanages. See, e.g., Charles Murray, "The Coming White Underclass," *Wall Street Journal*, October 29, 1993, A14; Dennis B. Roddy, "The War on Welfare; Legislators Sing the Praises of Orphanages, Foster Homes, with Little Mention of the Cost," *Pittsburgh Post-Gazette*, January 29, 1995, A1.

Generally, advocates for children, professional and nonprofessional, are appalled at this suggestion. See Jenny Dean, "The Modern Orphan," *St. Petersburg Times*, January 29, 1995, 1A ("[Children's advocacy groups] were outraged by the notion that mothers would have to give up their children simply because they were poor"). Dean describes orphanages such as The Children's Home and Boys' Town in Florida as places "where children end up after they have failed in foster families" (Ibid.). What these children need, according to child welfare experts, is a "safe, stable family" (Ibid.); see also Lynn Benson, "Dysfunctional Speaker?" *Star Tribune*, February 4, 1995, 16A (reader letter) (urging that it is wrong to remove children from their homes only because their parents are poor). Some in the media, holding a similar view, have investigated the past and current history of orphanages and children's homes in this country. See, e.g., Rachel L. Jones, "Talk of Orphanages Collides with Grim Realities," *Pittsburgh Post-Gazette*, December 25, 1994, A10. Jones describes a child at the New England Home for Little Wanderers, where "the majority [of children] must be medicated to cope with reality" (Ibid.). Jones's research has convinced her that the "cozy, poignant, drug-free, bruise-free fantasy of orphanages" is outdated (Ibid.). She quotes the executive director of the New England Home for Little Wanderers expressing his agreement: "If they do exist, I have no idea where" (Ibid.). Jones also interviewed Nan Dale, executive director of Children's Village in Dobbs Ferry, New York, who stated: "In no way am I saying that a group home is better than a family. . . . But we're being pushed to send kids back into horrifying situations in the name of family preservation." Dale continued: "The orphanage talk is just the government reneging on its promise to every citizen that it will provide a safe, decent place to raise their kids. It's the easy way out" (Ibid.); see also John Milne, "Home for Youths Teaches an Ethic of Love, Albeit at a Heftier Annual Cost," *Boston Globe*, December 18, 1994, 85. Milne describes some success stories at the Good-Will Hinckley Home, which cares for approximately eighty-nine children. The costs there are $24,000 per year per child. Milne notes that at this time, 460,000 children are being cared for outside the home, up from 300,000 in 1987 (Ibid.). Dennis Roddy describes the success story of one child who was taken from the South Bronx and placed in an institution. The child became a high-school football star and was expected to graduate from college in the near future (Roddy, supra, A1). The institution is considered to be moderately priced, but the price tag for the success—well worth it, of course—was $200,000 (five years in the institution for $173,000 and foster care at $10,945 per year) (Ibid.). This is roughly six times the national average of $1,584 paid annually for Aid to Families with Dependent Children (AFDC) (Ibid.). But see Brian R. Foltz, "Don't Look Only at Short-Term Costs of Caring for At-Risk Children," *Pittsburgh Post-Gazette*, February 19, 1995, E2 (arguing that even at $200,000, successful prevention is a bargain).

A Time/CNN survey found, however, that 72 percent of respondents (including two out of three Republicans) oppose orphanages (Milne, supra, 85). Fred Taylor, executive director of the nonprofit For Love of Children (FLOC), presents a historic view of orphanages in the District of Columbia (Fred Taylor, "Boys' Town? D.C. Can Do Better," *Washington Post*, February 19, 1995, C8). From 1948 to 1973, the number of children at Junior Village grew from 30 to over 900, "sometimes three to a bed" (Ibid.). This expansion was largely the result of welfare reform that between 1962 and 1965 dropped 4,000 women and children from the District of Columbia's welfare rolls and caused the population of Junior Village to quadruple to over 900. Taylor notes that "the adult survivors of that experience speak with intense anger and regret of those lost years" (Ibid.). He goes on to present another, more humane approach to the admittedly difficult problems we face with our nation's children, recommending building family and community with the "better use of both government and untapped community resources" (Ibid.).

11. One indication of this is the *New York Times* analysis that blamed Sweden's current fiscal difficulties on its expansive welfare structure (Richard W. Stevenson, "A Deficit Reigns in Sweden's Welfare State," *New York Times*, February 2, 1995, A1). This subtly biased article reflects that even a liberal paper may view more socialistic governments negatively. The article cast reported Swedish budgetary problems as vindication of anti-big government attitudes, capitalism, and the puritan work ethic. But see Erik Rhodes, "Sweden's Social Policies Put Us to Shame," *New York Times*, February 10, 1995, A28 (letter to the editor) (criticizing Stevenson's article as an unfair portrayal of the Swedish welfare system and the Swedes themselves).

12. For a discussion of the historically gendered nature of the family with respect to child custody, see Martha L. Fineman and Anne Opie, "The Uses of Social Science Data in Legal Policymaking: Custody Determinations at Divorce," *Wisconsin Law Review* (1987): 107, 111–12.

13. The state will provide assistance if the family falls below the governmentally defined standards of self-sufficiency and independence that are part of the family ideology in our culture.

14. See, e.g., David Popenoe, "Parental Adrogny; Sex Differences in Parenting," *Society* (September 1993): 5, 9 ("It should be recognized, of course, that the parenting of young infants is not a 'natural' activity for males").

15. See Lugaila, note 3. In 1960, the census counted 53 million households; in 1990 the figure was 93 million (Ibid., 15). (The term *household* refers to one or more people who live together. Nonfamily households are those in which the person lives alone or with one or more unrelated people.) In 1960 married couples comprised 75 percent of the family households; in 1990, the figure was down to 56 percent. Conversely, the number of nonfamily households rose from 15 percent in 1960 to 29 percent in 1990 (Ibid.); see also Constance Sorrentino, "The Changing Family in International Perspective," *Monthly Lab. Review* (March 1990): 41 (documenting a decline in the size of families and a move away from the nuclear family form).

16. In 1960, 4.3 percent of men and 8.7 percent of women lived alone (Lugaila, note 3, at 15). By 1990, those numbers had increased to 9.7 percent and 14.9 percent, respectively (Ibid.); see also "How We're Changing: Demographic State of the Nation: 1993," Special Studies Series, P-23, No. 184 (Washington, D.C.: Bureau of the Census, U.S. Department of Commerce, February 1993) (stating that single-person households comprised approximately one-quarter of all households in 1989).

17. The Bureau of the Census estimates that half of all marriages entered into since 1970 could end in divorce, with the majority of the parties remarrying (Lugaila, note 3, 8). Approximately 25 percent of families were single-parent families in 1990 (Ibid., 36). In 1960, 8.0 percent of children lived with only their mother, 1.1 percent lived with only their father, and 3.2 percent had some other type of living arrangement (Ibid.). By 1990 these figures were 21.6 percent (mothers), 3.1 percent (fathers), and 2.7 percent (other) (Ibid.). The number of white single-parent families increased from 7.1 percent to 19.2 percent; the number of African-American single-parent families increased from 21.9 percent to 54.8 percent (Ibid., 37). In 1990, 22 percent of white single-parent families had a never-married parent; for African-American families the number was 53 percent, and for Hispanics, 37 percent (Ibid., 21). For data on the growing numbers of educated, middle-class single mothers, see infra note 54.

18. Households comprised of married couples living with their children declined from 44.2 percent in 1960 to 26.3 percent in 1990, and other families with children increased from 4.4 percent to 8.3 percent. See Lugaila, note 3, 15. The percentage of married couples without children remained approximately the same at around 30 percent (Ibid.).

19. In 1990, in approximately 70 percent of two-parent families with children, both parents worked (Lugaila, note 3, 42). In 27.5 percent of the families, both parents worked full-time; in 30 percent the husband worked full-time, the wife less than year-round full-time; in 21 percent the wife worked only in the home; and in 21 percent the husband worked less than full-time (Ibid., 43).

20. See, e.g., Tamar Lewin, "Poll of Teen-Agers: Battle of the Sexes on Roles in Family," *New York Times*, July 11, 1994, A1, B7 (relating results of a survey finding that over half of teenage girls polled would consider single parenthood, and an overwhelming number were more committed to having a successful career than making a marriage).

21. *Reynolds v. United States*, 98 U.S. 145, 165 (1878); see also *Loving v. Virginia*, 388 U.S. 1, 12 (1967) [quoting *Skinner v. Oklahoma*, 316 U.S. 535, 541 (1942) ("Marriage is one of the 'basic rights of man,' [*sic*] fundamental to our very existence and survival")]. The foundational role of marriage was eulogized by Judge Robert Bork: "The reason for protecting the family and the institution of marriage is not merely that they are fundamental to our society but that our entire tradition is to encourage, support, and respect them" (*Franz v. United States*, 712 F.2d 1428, 1438 [D.C. Cir. 1983] [Bork, J., concurring in part and dissenting in part]). More recently, Justice O'Connor, ruling that states could not prevent prison inmates from marrying while incarcerated, echoed this thought:

> Marriages . . . are expressions of emotional support and public commitment. These elements are an important and significant aspect of the marital relationship. In addition, many religions recognize marriage as having spiritual significance; . . . the commitment of marriage may be an exercise of religious faith as well as an expression of personal dedication. . . . Marital status often is a precondition to the receipt of government benefits (e.g., Social Security benefits), property rights (e.g., tenancy by the entirety, inheritance rights), and other, less tangible benefits (e.g., legitimation of children born out of wedlock). (*Turner v. Safley*, 482 U.S. 78, 95–96 [1987])

22. See, e.g., Carol B. Stack, *All Our Kin: Strategies for Survival in a Black Community* (New York: Harper and Row, 1974) (explaining the difference between kin and blood relationships among poor urban African Americans); Patricia Hill Collins, "The Meaning of Motherhood in Black Culture and Black Mother/Daughter Relationships," *Sage* (fall 1987): 3 (discussing the role of family networks in African American child-rearing).

23. See, e.g., Frances K. Goldscheider and Linda J. Waite, *New Families, No Families? The Transformation of the American Home* (Berkeley: University of California Press,

1991), 16–19, 67–72 (charting the rise in "nonfamily" living by young adults since the 1950s and its effect on family structure); Amy Swerdlow, Renata Bridenthal, Joan Kelly, and Phyllis Vine, *Families in Flux*, rev. ed. (New York: Feminist Press at The City University of New York, 1989) (exploring alternative family structures); Kath Weston, *Families We Choose: Lesbians, Gays, Kinship* (New York: Columbia University Press, 1991); Mary P. Treuthart, "Adopting a More Realistic Definition of 'Family,'" *Gonz. Law Review* 26 (1990–1991): 91, 97 (asserting that "many people subscribe to a broader definition of family than the definitions utilized by most courts and legislatures").

24. See note, "Looking for a Family Resemblance: The Limits of the Functional Approach to the Legal Definition of Family," *Harvard Law Review* 104 (1991): 1640 (hereinafter "Looking for a Family Resemblance") (discussing problems with the functional conception of family as applied to homosexual couples and other nontraditional families); see also Craig A. Bowman and Blake M. Cornish, note, "A More Perfect Union: A Legal and Social Analysis of Domestic Partnership Ordinances," *Columbia Law Review* 104 (1992): 1164, 1186–95 (discussing recent proposals for legally recognized domestic partnership agreements). But see generally Nancy D. Polikoff, "We Will Get What We Ask For: Why Legalizing Gay and Lesbian Marriage Will Not 'Dismantle the Legal Structure of Gender in Every Marriage,'" *Virginia Law Review* 79 (1993): 1535 (arguing against gay and lesbian demands for access to marriage because of the need to challenge the assumptions inherent in the institution of marriage and family).

25. See, e.g., Katharine T. Bartlett, "Rethinking Parenthood as an Exclusive Status: The Need for Legal Alternatives When the Premise of the Nuclear Family Has Failed," *Virginia Law Review* 70 (1984): 879, 944 (criticizing continued reluctance of the law to recognize psychological parent–child relationships that arise outside the nuclear family); Kris Franklin, note, "'A Family Like Any Other Family': Alternative Methods of Defining Family in Law," *New York University Review of Law and Social Change* 18 (1990–1991): 1027, 1062–64 (advocating reformulation of legal definition of parenthood to reflect existing pluralities of family types); "Looking for a Family Resemblance," note 24, 1640 (asserting that "the traditional nuclear family is rapidly becoming an American anachronism").

26. For an interesting example of this practice, see Sherry R. Anderson and Patricia Hopkins, *The Feminine Face of God: The Unfolding of the Sacred in Women* (New York: Bantam, 1991), 211–13 (describing Maya Angelou's practice of choosing sisters by making an agreement with the chosen sister, discussing the new bond with family members, and forging a family commitment).

27. One of the most entrenched notions about marriage is that it is reserved exclusively for a commitment between one man and one woman. Most state statutes, explicitly or implicitly, limit marriage to "a male and a female." E.g., Ariz. Rev. Stat. Ann. sec. 25–125 (1991); Fla. Stat. Ann. sec. 741.04 (West 1986); Ga. Code Ann. sec. 19-3-30 (1991); Idaho Code sec. 32-201 (Supp. 1995) (effective January 1, 1996); Utah Code Ann. sec. 30-1-2(5) (1995). For a brief period in 1993, many gay and lesbian couples hoped this would change when the Hawaii Supreme Court held that strict scrutiny analysis would be applied to the question of whether the state's male/female marriage requirement constituted sex-based discrimination against homosexuals by prohibiting exercise of their civil right to marry. *Baehr v. Lewin*, 852 P.2d 44 (Haw. 1993). To uphold the statute, on remand, the state would be required to demonstrate that the sex-based classification was justified by compelling state interests (Ibid., 67). Responding to this ruling, the Hawaii legislature quickly amended the law to require that marriage be a union "only

between a man and a woman." Haw. Rev. Stat. sec. 572–71 (Supp. 1994). The legislature made the following findings:

> SECTION 1. Legislative findings and purpose. The legislature finds that Hawaii's marriage licensing laws were originally and are presently intended to apply only to male-female couples, not same-sex couples. This determination is one of policy. Any change in these laws must come from either the legislature or a constitutional convention, not the judiciary. The Hawaii supreme court's recent plurality opinion in *Baehr v. Lewin*, 74 Haw. 530, 852 P.2d 44 (1993), effaces the recognized tradition of marriage in this State and, in so doing, impermissibly negates the constitutionally mandated role of the legislature as a co-equal, coordinate branch of government. (1994 Haw. Sess. Laws, Act 217, sec. 1)

28. In contrast, married people receive favorable treatment through estate and gift tax laws. 26 U.S.C. 2056, 2523 (1988). But see David J. Roberts and Mark J. Sullivan, "The Federal Income Tax: Where Are the Family Values?," *Tax Notes* 57 (October 26, 1992): 547, 548–50 (outlining sections of the tax laws that penalize certain married people).

29. See Fineman, *Neutered Mother, Sexual Family*, chapter 5.

30. When Charles Murray first began his crusade, many people, including feminists and politicians, dismissed him as ultraconservative, too radical even for the ultra-right. Today his punitive ideas are being adopted by Congress and the states. He is one of the most vicious commentators on the increased rates of single motherhood, blaming it for all the ills of society: "Illegitimacy is the single most important social problem of our time—more important than crime, drugs, poverty, illiteracy, welfare or homelessness because it drives everything else" (Murray, note 10, A14). In this article, Murray urged that aid to unmarried mothers be terminated; then if the community fails to come to their aid, the children could be placed into orphanages (Ibid.). For a more extensive discussion of the demonization of single mothers and a critique of the characterization of them as the cause of all current social ills, see Fineman, *Neutered Mother, Sexual Family*, chapter 5.

31. According to one published report, House Speaker Newt Gingrich's verbal attacks are carefully calculated (Rupert Cornwell, "Newt Inflates His Word Power," *Independent* (London), February 4, 1995, 10). In 1990 Gingrich's staff circulated a handbook called *Language, A Key Mechanism of Control*, which suggests, on the one hand, words that should be used, and, on the other hand, words that should be avoided (Ibid.). Half of the entries are "optimistic positive governing words"; the other half are "contrasting words." Contrasting words include terms such as "'pathetic,'" "'sick,'" "'liberal,'" "'traitor,'" and "'hypocrisy,'" to be used in describing "'an opponent, his record, his proposals and his party'" (Ibid.) (quoting Newt Gingrich, *Language, A Key Mechanism of Control*). To describe spending cuts, Frank Luntz, Newt Gingrich's pollster, suggests targeting "'bureaucrats,'" not "'programmes'"; "'charities are OK; orphanages are not'" (Ibid.).

32. The image of the "Welfare Queen" is just one example of this distortion. Others include the assertion that the typical woman on welfare has numerous children, primarily to receive benefits. In reality, the birth rate for these women is essentially the same as for the typical American family. See Mimi Abramovitz and Fred Newdom, "Women on Welfare—Myths and Realities, Resource: Women, Work and Welfare" (The Women's Resource Center of New York, Inc., New York, New York) *Newsletter*, January 1995, 8 (stating that "the typical welfare family is comprised of a mother and two children, slightly less than the size of the average family in the United States"). Studies demonstrate that the birth rate among women on welfare is unrelated to the amount of assistance available.

In 1994, seventy-six leading researchers concluded that AFDC is not a principal factor affecting out-of-wedlock births.

> Most research examining the effect of higher welfare benefits on out-of-wedlock childbearing and teen pregnancy finds that benefit levels have no significant effect on the likelihood that black women and girls will have children outside of marriage and either no significant effect, or only a small effect, on the likelihood that whites will have such births. . . . The evidence suggests that welfare has not played a major role in the rise in out of wedlock births. (Mark Greenberg, Center for Law and Social Policy, "Contract with Disaster, The Impact on States of the Personal Responsibility Act" [November 1994], 4 [quoting "Welfare and Out of Wedlock Births: A Research Summary" (June 23, 1994)])

Another myth contributing to the anger and hostility of the middle class toward welfare recipients is that welfare is a significant part of the budget. Actually, AFDC accounts for approximately 1 percent of the federal budget (Marlene Andrejco, "A New Contract Is Needed That Will Favor the Poor and Combat Poverty," *Pittsburgh Post-Gazette*, May 11, 1995, A18).

We further demonize these women by promoting the idea that they are lazy and do not want to work. Not true. The fact is that both the states and the federal government have tried many work programs in the past, most of which have failed through no fault of the welfare participants. For example, Christopher Jencks and Kathryn Edin note:

> The essence of the so-called "welfare trap" is not that welfare warps women's personalities or makes them pathologically dependent, though that may occasionally happen. The essence of the "trap" is that while welfare pays badly, low-wage jobs pay even worse. Most welfare mothers are quite willing to work if they end up with significantly more disposable income as a result. But they are not willing to work if working will leave them as poor as they were when they stayed home. (Christopher Jencks and Kathryn Edin, "The Real Welfare Problem," *American Prospect* 1, no. 31 [1990]: 43–44)

See also Mimi Abramovitz, "Why Welfare Reform Is a Sham," *The Nation*, September 26, 1988, 221, 246 (stating that although California officials acknowledged that graduates of a training program, to stay off welfare, needed to earn a minimum of $11.00 per hour, they were averaging only $6.50 per hour). A 1986 study of work programs revealed that low wages forced 43 percent of Massachusetts training graduates back onto welfare (Joan Walsh, "Take This Job or Shove It," *Mother Jones*, September 1988, 30, 32); see also Jason DeParle, "Welfare Mothers Find Jobs Are Easier to Get than Hold," *New York Times*, October 24, 1994, A1, A14 (noting that many mothers on welfare who get jobs have a hard time keeping them because of low pay, lack of training, harsh working conditions, and other problems including lack of social skills, child care, health insurance, and resentful boyfriends; consequently, at Project Match in Chicago 46 percent lost their jobs within six months and 73 percent within a year); Isabel Wilkerson, "An Intimate Look at Welfare: Women Who've Been There," *New York Times*, February 17, 1995, A1, A18 (discussing difficulties women encounter with welfare and working).

33. See, e.g., Eric Lipton, "Officials Ask: What Price More Spending Authority?" *Washington Post*, February 20, 1995, D1, D4 (discussing local reactions to block grant proposals); Isabel V. Sawhill and Demetra S. Nightingale, "Real Reform or a Shift of Responsibilities?" *Washington Post*, February 20, 1995, A29 (discussing emphasis on block grants in lieu of true reform of welfare programs).

34. E.g., N.J. Stat. Ann. sec. 44:10-3.5 (West 1993) (eliminating incremental increase in AFDC benefits for birth of additional child); Ga. Code Ann. sec. 49-4-115 (1994) (same); see also Madeline Henley, "The Creation and Perpetuation of the Mother/Body Myth: Judicial and Legislative Enlistment of Norplant," *Buffalo Law Review* 41 (1993): 703, 751–52 (discussing welfare reforms in New Jersey, Wisconsin, California, and other states). Virginia plans to require AFDC recipients to work and intends to eliminate increases in benefits for additional births, although in Virginia "a mother with two children [now only receives] $285 a month, not including food stamps. . . . [and] $61 more for each additional child up to five" (Peter Baker, "Virginia Jumps at Chance to Shake Up Welfare," *Washington Post*, February 22, 1994, B1, B2). Colorado, Florida, Iowa, Vermont and Wisconsin have received federal waivers from the Department of Health and Human Services to cut off AFDC benefits after a set period (Ibid., B1). New Jersey's family cap program has also been approved (Ibid.). See also Tenn. Code Ann. sec. 71-5-133 (Supp. 1994) (requiring that all AFDC recipients be provided written information regarding availability of Norplant when they apply or are recertified for benefits).

Many of these and other reforms have been incorporated into The Personal Responsibility Act, H.R. 4, 104th Cong., 1st Sess. (1995). Among other things, this bill would amend the Social Security Act to deny assistance to children born to young women under 18 years of age, limit the amount of money that can be spent on the poor regardless of need (block grants), cut over $18 billion from food assistance programs—including food stamps, Women, Infants, and Children Program (WIC), and school lunch/breakfast programs—over the next four years, and end the entitlement status of these programs. When the state runs out of money, people will be placed on waiting lists and will be denied benefits no matter how destitute they are. See Center on Social Welfare Policy and Law, "Ways and Means Committee Backs Block Grants," *Welfare Reform (?) News*, March 1995, 1–4 (hereinafter *Welfare Reform (?) News*). (One assumes that it is at this stage that children will be removed from their homes and placed in orphanages.)

The Senate's plan for welfare reform, passed on September 19, 1995, includes similar provisions eliminating the federal guarantee of assistance to poor families, and substituting unlimited federal support with block grants to the states. Unlike the House bill, however, the Senate bill would give the states the discretion to deny assistance to children born to unmarried, teen-age mothers and to additional children born while the mother is on welfare. Further, the Senate bill, unlike the House bill, requires states to maintain a set spending level ("A Quandary for Clinton: Most Democrats Back a Bill of Lesser Evils," *New York Times*, September 20, 1995, A1, B9).

Although the Senate bill may appear less harsh than the House bill, critics emphasize that it will nonetheless have a devastating impact on poor families. See "The Stampede to Harsh Welfare," *New York Times*, September 20, 1995, A20 (outlining the detrimental effects the Senate bill will have on the poor, and concluding that although the Senate plan may "look better" than the House plan, "it is neither humane, nor reasonable").

35. In some states, women receiving benefits are required to present evidence from paternity proceedings as a condition of receiving their benefits. For example, Wis. Stat. Ann. sec. 49.19(4)(h)(1)(a) (West 1987), makes full cooperation in paternity determinations of "nonmarital" children a condition of eligibility for receiving assistance. Pursuant to Wis. Stat. Ann. sec. 49.19(4)(h)(2) (West 1987), failure to cooperate will disqualify the caretaker for assistance, and "protective payments" for the child will be paid to "a person other than the person charged with the care of the dependent child." Wisconsin law also requires

the state attorney to file an action for paternity within six months of receiving notice that no father is named on the birth certificate of a child, if paternity has not been adjudicated already, regardless of the wishes of the mother. Wis. Stat. Ann. sec. 767.45(6m) (West 1993); see also Cal. Welf. and Inst. Code sec. 11477(b) (West 1991) (requiring aid recipients to cooperate in establishing paternity).

At this time federal law provides for "good cause" refusal to name the father. 42 U.S.C. sec. 602(a)(26)(B)(ii) (1988). "Good cause" is based on the needs of the child and exists only when the child will suffer physical or emotional harm or the mother will suffer such harm that she will be unable to care adequately for the child. 45 C.F.R. 232.42(a)(1)(i)–(iv) (1994). For an extremely punitive application of this standard, see *Waller v. Carlton County Human Servs. Department*, No. C6-89-1116, 1989 WL 145393 (Minn. Ct. App. 1989) (holding "good cause" standard was unsatisfied when woman's account of rape could not be corroborated after she failed to report the rape to police because she feared harm to herself and her child). Women who have named as fathers men whose subsequent blood tests have proved them not to be the father and women who do not know the name or location of the father also have been subjected to severe scrutiny and questioning by state agencies. For example, in *Allen v. Eichler*, 1990 WL 58223 (Del. Super. Ct. 1990), after several men whom the plaintiff had named as the possible father were excluded by blood tests or could not be found, the agency demanded a calendar on which the plaintiff had supposedly written the names of sexual partners. When she refused, she was deemed uncooperative, and her benefits were cut (Ibid., *Neutered Mother, Sexual Family*, 1). One of the provisions of the Personal Responsibility Act reduces AFDC benefits until paternity is established, even when the mother is cooperating fully; if the mother does not cooperate at all, she will be denied aid entirely (*Welfare Reform (?) News*, note 34, 3).

36. See note 34.

37. See note 35.

38. Many states are turning to programs, like Learnfare, which penalize aid recipients, under some circumstances, if they fail to attend school. See, e.g., Fla. Stat. Ann. sec. 409.933 (West 1995); Wis. Stat. Ann. sec. 49.50(7)(g), (h) (West Supp. 1994). These programs, however, can be problematic. A 1990 audit of the Wisconsin Learnfare program found that 84 percent of the orders imposing sanctions were overturned by an administrative judge "because of errors in record-keeping by either the schools or the welfare agency" (Paul Taylor, "Welfare Policy's 'New Paternalism' Uses Benefits to Alter Recipients' Behavior," *Washington Post*, June 8, 1991, A3).

39. See, e.g., Colo. Rev. Stat. sec. 26-2-507 (1)(a)–(b) (Supp. 1994); Virginia Code Ann. sec. 63.1-105.2 (Michie 1995).

40. Many states have imposed "Workfare" programs that require aid recipients to work or participate in job training in order to receive benefits; failure to comply risks the termination of benefits. See, e.g., Conn. Gen. Stat. Ann. sec. 17b-682 (West Supp. 1995); Fla. Stat. Ann. sec. 409.924 (West Supp. 1995); Ind. Code Ann. sec. 12-20-11-1 (Burns 1995); Ohio Rev. Code Ann. sec. 5101.84 (Anderson Supp. 1994); Wis. Stat. Ann. sec. 49.27(5) (West Supp. 1994).

41. Even under the best conditions mothering is work, of course. It is work that is not incorporated into the gross national product, however, and for that reason is often overlooked by various policymakers. For the poor, particularly AFDC recipients, motherhood is even more work in our suspicious and demeaning welfare system. Lines are long and forms and formalities profuse. See generally William H. Simon, "Legality, Bureaucracy,

and Class in the Welfare System," *Yale Law Journal* 92 (1983): 1198 (arguing that the mechanism used to provide aid to the poor is impersonal and formalized).

42. This phenomenon is detailed in Fineman, *Neutered Mother, Sexual Family*, chapter 5.

43. See, e.g., Anne Raver, "Great Expectations: Coping with the Pressure to Reproduce in Our Baby Boom Society," *Newsday*, March 4, 1989, pt. II, p. 1; Paula Voel, "Choosing to Be Childless: So What if They Don't Harbor the Nesting Instinct? These Women Are Content with Their Lives," October 20, 1993, Lifestyles 9.

44. For further discussion of this point as it relates to reform of divorce and property division laws, see Martha L. Fineman, "Implementing Equality: Ideology, Contradiction and Social Change: A Study of Rhetoric and Results in the Regulation of the Consequences of Divorce," *Wisconsin Law Review* (1983): 789, 851–52.

45. 1 William Blackstone, Commentaries, 442–44.

46. See *Craig v. Boren*, 429 U.S. 190, 197 (1976) (adopting an intermediate level of review for the examination of sex-based classifications, requiring that such classifications serve "important governmental objectives and . . . be substantially related to the achievement of those objectives").

47. See *Orr v. Orr*, 440 U.S. 268 (1979) (invalidating, on equal protection grounds, a Louisiana statute providing that only husbands could be held responsible for alimony payments).

48. Courts have rejected the tender years doctrine and other gender-based presumptions and now invoke the best interests of the child as the controlling factor in custody determinations. See, e.g., *Johnson v. Johnson*, 564 P.2d 71 (Alaska 1977), cert. denied, 434 U.S. 1048 (1978); In Re Marriage of Bowen, 219 N.W. 2d 683 (Iowa 1974); *State ex rel. Watts v. Watts*, 350 N.Y.S. 2d 285 (1973).

49. See *Gomez v. Perez*, 409 U.S. 535, 538 (1973) (holding that "a State may not invidiously discriminate against illegitimate children by denying them substantial benefits accorded children generally").

50. Studies indicate that across cultures mothers still perform the vast bulk of child care and housework. See "Report of the International Labor Organization," September 6, 1992 (presenting results of a global survey on the distribution of housework and family responsibilities between men and women, which reveals that women still do the vast majority of the work despite the existence in some countries of shared-responsibility laws); see also David Briscoe, "'All Work and No Pay' World," *Times*, September 8, 1992 (discussing report prepared by the International Labor Organization finding that, worldwide, women work more for less pay than men); Anna Quindlen, "Abhors a Vacuum," *New York Times*, September 9, 1992, A21 (same); "Women Work Harder but Paid Less," Xinhau News Agency, September 6, 1992 (same). For further discussion of the unequal distribution of household responsibilities between men and women, see Janice Drakich, "In Search of the Better Parent: The Social Construction of Ideologies of Fatherhood," *Canadian Journal of Women and Law* 3 (1989): 69, 83–87 (reviewing a 1988 study showing that employed women still spend twice as much time with child care and housework as do their husbands, and demonstrating that contrary to popular anecdotal information, fathers today are actually participating in child care only slightly more than they did in 1967); "Project, Law Firms and Lawyers with Children: An Empirical Analysis of Family/Work Conflict," *Stanford Law Review* 34 (1982): 1263 (demonstrating that law firms and law students expect females to be more involved with parenting than with working and contending that structural reform is needed to correct this imbalance); Mary Jo Bane, Laura Lain, Lydia O'Donnell, C. Anne Steuve, and Barbara

Wells, *Monthly Labor Review* (October 1979): 50, 52–53 (claiming that mothers are more likely to pass up work opportunities to raise children); Victor R. Fuchs, "Sex Differences in Economic Well-Being," *Science* 232 (1986): 459 (chronicling the effect that gender and motherhood continue to have on the wages and employment opportunities of women). But see Bureau of the Census, U.S. Department of Commerce, "How We're Changing: Demographic State of the Nation: 1994," Special Studies Series P-23, No. 187 (Washington, D.C.: Bureau of the Census, U.S. Department of Commerce, 1994), 2 (reporting that more fathers are becoming primary caregivers as more women return to work).

For a contrasting opinion, see Nancy R. Gibbs, "Bringing Up Father," *Time*, June 28, 1993, 53. She asserts that even those men who wish to be more involved are frequently stymied by work requirements and women's intransigence. Bosses do not want men to take paternity leave; women do not want them to do child care unless they do it "their" way.

51. Susan Moller Okin seems to be ascribing to this view when she says:

> Only children who are equally mothered and fathered can develop fully the psychological and moral capacities that currently seem to be unevenly distributed between the sexes. Only when men participate equally in what have been principally women's realms of meeting the daily material and psychological needs of those close to them . . . will members of both sexes be able to develop a more complete human personality. (Susan Moller Okin, *Justice, Gender, and the Family* [New York: Basic, 1989], 107)

52. This vision of reform was particularly narrow in its consideration of only some family actors in its reconstituted vision. The roles of husband and wife were restructured in regard to child care and vaguely described household domestic tasks; little thought, however seems to have been given to the demands on domestic time and labor spent caring for the elderly, the ill, or the disabled. The egalitarian family was structured on the basis of sexual affiliation—the assumed inevitability of heterosexual pairing and its association with reproductive destiny were expressed in family form. No one argued over who would care for grandma in developing the rhetoric of the "new man" in the reconstructed family story.

The social assignment of dependency is even more pronounced (and less challenged) when it comes to care for the elderly or ill. Daughters (or daughters-in-law) are those to whom elderly parents look for expected accommodations. See, e.g., Hilde Lindemann Nelson and James Lindemann Nelson, "Frail Parents, Robust Duties," *Utah Law Review* (1992): 747.

53. Failing to recognize the gendered nature of the world, early feminists mistakenly believed that formal equality would rectify past discrimination. See, e.g., Wendy W. Williams, "The Equality Crisis: Some Reflections," *Women's Rights Law Report* 7 (1982): 175. Unfortunately this was not, and could not, be true. To be successful, any theory seeking to change women's lives and their relationship to mainstream culture, i.e., patriarchal culture, must be gendered. It must be centered around women and their experiences, which are gendered. Women's experience is not neutral and cannot be theorized as such. See Martha Albertson Fineman, *The Illusion of Equality: The Rhetoric and Reality of Divorce Reform* (Chicago: University of Chicago Press, 1991).

54. Recent Census figures show an increase in never-married motherhood. See Amara Bachu, Bureau of the Census, U.S. Department of Commerce, Pub. No. P20-470, "Fertility of American Women: June 1992" (Washington, D.C.: Bureau of the Census, U.S. Department of Commerce, 1993), xix. A survey of unmarried women from eighteen to forty-four years of age showed an increase in never-married motherhood from 15 percent in 1982 to

24 percent in 1992 (Ibid.). The rate of births by unmarried women with at least one year of college education increased from 5.5 percent to 11.3 percent (Ibid.). For women in professional or managerial positions, it rose from 3.1 percent to 8.3 percent (Ibid.).

The media has paid a great deal of attention to the increase in out-of-wedlock births. See, e.g., Joan Beck, "Nation Must Stem the Tide of Births Out of Wedlock," *New Orleans Times–Picayune*, March 6, 1993, B7; Richard Cohen, "Judging Single Mothers," *Washington Post*, July 16, 1993, A19; Jason DeParle, "Big Rise in Births Outside Wedlock," *New York Times*, July 14, 1993, A1; Carol Lawson, "'Who Is My Daddy?' Can Be Answered in Different Ways" and Anne Lamott, "When Going It Alone Turns Out to Be Not So Alone at All," combined articles featured in "Single but Mothers by Choice," *New York Times*, August 5, 1993, C1; Katha Pollitt, "Bothered and Bewildered," *New York Times*, July 22, 1993, A23; Richard Whitmire, "Number of Never-Married Moms Stretches across Income Lines," Gannett News Service, July 13, 1993. And, of course, we all recall the Quayle debacle over Murphy Brown. "'Hollywood thinks it's cute to glamorize illegitimacy,' Quayle told reporters. . . . 'Hollywood doesn't get it'" (John E. Yang and Ann Devroy, "Quayle: 'Hollywood Doesn't Get It': Administration Struggles to Explain Attack on TV's Murphy Brown," *Washington Post*, May 21, 1992, A1); see also Barbara Dafoe Whitehead, "Dan Quayle Was Right," *Atlantic*, April 1993, 47 (arguing that children who do not live with both of their biological parents are disadvantaged). This view, however, is far from universally accepted:

> Before Democrats embrace the view that marriage is the best antidote to poverty, educational failure and psychological distress, they might consult the two-parent families devastated by layoffs in the steel, defense, timber and auto industries—families whose children now exhibit most of the emotional and cognitive problems generally blamed on divorce. (Stephanie Coontz, "Dan Quayle Is Still Wrong: Why the Two Parent Paradigm Is No Guarantor of Happiness," *Washington Post*, May 11, 1993, C5)

Interestingly, it was this increase in nonmarital births among white women that seems to have been the proverbial "last straw" for those in power. As Charles Murray has said: "The brutal truth is that American society as a whole could survive when illegitimacy became epidemic within a comparatively small ethnic minority. It cannot survive the same epidemic among whites" (Murray, note 10, A14).

55. Individual understandings about family are shaped by societal forces and manifest those forces. So, although one may "choose" to live outside of the conventional norms, one does not escape them entirely. No one is exempt from the implications of the culture in which she lives—culture influences our actions, our aspirations, our politics, and what we envision as possibilities.

56. Fineman states:

> Essentially a modernist concept, a meta- or public narrative is understood to be the story or "narrative" which legitimates and controls knowledge in the Western world. The modernist attempts to characterize the world as ultimately unrepresentable, while relying on a form of narrative presentation that is familiar or recognizable and which offers the reader or listener a degree of comfort. (Martha Albertson Fineman, "Our Sacred Institution: The Ideal of the Family in American Law and Society," *Utah Law Review* [1993] 387, 387n2

"The notion of the metanarrative assumes some sort of hierarchy of cultural representations and cultural values. Since the Enlightenment, for example, the central western metanarrative has been that of progress, reason, and revolution, a public narrative of Darwinian evolution and class struggle" (Fineman, *Neutered Mother, Sexual Family*, 169n14). Metanarratives are normative and aid in the formation of collective identities by encouraging a linear and narrow interpretation of history (Ibid.).

For example, a single metanarrative has established public law adjudication as the paradigm for all adjudication, whether the question implicates common law, statutory construction, or constitutional interpretation. For a critique of an approach that relies on the same principles to analyze common law, statutory construction, and constitutional interpretation, see Melvin Aron Eisenberg, *The Nature of the Common Law* (Cambridge, Mass.: Harvard University Press, 1988), 8–13. In contrast, postmodern theories rely on "local, interlocking language games" to replace the idea of overarching structures. Jennifer Wicke, "Postmodern Identity and the Legal Subject," *University of Colorado Law Review* 62 (1991): 455, 462; see generally Fredric Jameson, *Postmodernism, or, The Cultural Logic of Late Capitalism* (Durham: Duke University Press, 1991); Willem van Reijen and Dick Veerman, "An Interview with Jean-Francois Lyotard," *Theory, Culture and Society* 5 (1988): 277, 301–02 (discussing the abandonment of the metanarrative). Postmodernists reject metanarratives, viewing culture and society as a complex interaction without any single exclusive or overpowering identity. See David Kolb, *The Critique of Pure Modernity: Hegel, Heidegger and After* (Chicago: University of Chicago Press, 1986), chapter 12 (claiming that metanarratives are increasingly irrelevant); Richard M. Thomas, "Milton and Mass Culture: Toward a Postmodernist Theory of Tolerance," *University of Colorado Law Review* 62 (1991): 525, 525–30 (summarizing the debate regarding the metanarrative); see also Roberto M. Unger, *Law in Modern Society: Toward a Criticism of Social Theory* (New York: Free Press, 1976), 37–43, 134–37 (describing the difficulty of finding a universal truth that links humankind).

57. I.R.C. sec. 105 (1988 and Supp. 1994).

58. I.R.C. sec. 2523 (1988 and Supp. 1994).

59. See William A. Klein and Joseph Bankman, *Federal Income Taxation*, 10th ed. (Boston: Little, Brown, 1994), 120–22.

60. I.R.C. sec. 163(h)(3) (1988).

61. I.R.C. sec. 21 (1988).

62. Although the private-natural family is not the only possible response to dependency, punitive and harsh measures designed to stigmatize those who deviate from the failed norm seem preferred by many policymakers. See Martha L. Fineman, "Images of Mothers in Poverty Discourses," *Duke Law Journal* (1991): 274 (hereinafter Fineman, "Images") (linking patriarchal ideology to discourses which use single-mother status as a primary indicator of poverty); Martha Albertson Fineman, "Intimacy Outside of the Natural Family: The Limits of Privacy," *Connecticut Law Review* 23 (1991): 955 (arguing that the state justifies invasions of poor women's privacy on the basis of their perceived deviancy).

63. Equality imagery has taken hold in this area. The argument is that fathers as equal parents are equally obligated to be with and care for children, but (the myth grows) they fail to do so because mothers have superior rights over children. According to this view, if law gives fathers more rights over children, they will pay child support for those children. Some have attempted to assess whether more rights actually translate into more support. See, e.g., Eleanor E. Maccoby and Robert H. Mnookin, *Dividing the Child: Social and Legal Dilemmas of Custody* (Cambridge, Mass.: Harvard University Press, 1992), 251–57 (examining the correlation between compliance with child support obligations and various other factors

and finding that the more contact a father has with his child, the greater the chance of compliance); see also Martha Albertson Fineman, "Legal Stories, Change, and Incentives—Reinforcing the Law of the Father," *New York Law School Law Review* 37 (1992): 227 (arguing against reliance on legal incentives to encourage men to use birth control).

64. See, e.g., Thomas B. Edsall, "Age of Irritation: The New, Bitter Politics of Fear," *Washington Post*, November 28, 1993, C1, C4; Barbara Vobejda, "Education Is No Protection from Wage Squeeze, Report Says," *Washington Post*, September 4, 1994, A20.

65. See note 54 and accompanying text.

66. The solution may be to hire caretakers, but this may come with its own set of problems, as the Zoe Baird and Kimba Woods incidents indicated for professional moms. See Thomas L. Friedman, "Clinton Concedes He Erred on Baird Nomination," *New York Times*, January 23, 1993, A1; Ruth Marcus, "Babysitter Problems Sink Second Clinton Prospect: Wood Withdraws from Consideration as Attorney General," *Washington Post*, February 6, 1993, A1.

67. See note 50 and accompanying text.

68. See generally Ann Laquer Estin, "Maintenance, Alimony, and the Rehabilitation of Family Care," *North Carolina Law Review* 71 (1993): 721, 776 ("Caregiving remains invisible . . . because the law construes family care as matter of love and obligation, not . . . personal choice or arm's-length bargaining"); Siegel, note 8, 1214 ("Today . . . it is women who perform the work of the family, women who seek to escape the work, and women who eke out a living performing the work—for other women"); Joyce Davis, "Enhanced Earning Capacity/Human Capital: The Reluctance to Call It Property" (unpublished manuscript, on file with the Virginia Law Review Association), 16–17.

69. See Estin, note 68, 780 (stating that most caregiving costs fall disproportionately on women); Cynthia Starnes, "Applications of a Contemporary Partnership Model for Divorce," *Brigham Young University Journal of Public Law* 8 (1993): 107 (advocating the replacement of current no-fault divorce laws with a broad application of partnership principles so that women are compensated fairly as caretakers); J. Thomas Oldham, "Putting Asunder in the 1990s," *California Law Review* 80 (1992): 1091 (reviewing *Divorce Reform at the Crossroads* [ed. Stephen D. Sugarman and Herma Hill Kay, 1990]).

70. See Carbone, note 8, 363–72.

71. Cf. Barbara Stark, "Divorce Law, Feminism, and Psychoanalysis: In Dreams Begin Responsibilities," *UCLA Law Review* 38 (1991): 1483, 1507 (maintaining that the woman is often blamed for divorce because her domestic role burdens her with preserving the marriage).

72. See Fineman, *Neutered Mother, Sexual Family*, chapter 5.

73. This language is used to describe both types of single mothers, although it is most viciously directed at never-married mothers. See Fineman, "Images," note 62, 280–82.

74. A great deal of evidence indicates that reliance on the private solution of child support is inadequate. Of the 10 million women living with children under twenty-one years of age whose father is not living in the household, only 58 percent were awarded child support payments. See Lugaila, note 3, 40. Slightly more than half of these women received the full amount of payments due (Ibid., 41). In 1991, 35.6 percent of single mothers fell below the poverty line. Mwangi S. Kimenyi and John Mukum Mbaku, "Female Headship, Feminization of Poverty and Welfare," *S. Economics Journal* 62 (1995): 44, 44. Of the 4.2 million women never awarded child support, 64 percent wanted child support. Gordon H. Lester, Bureau of the Census, U.S. Department of Commerce, Consumer Income Series

P-60, No. 173, "Child Support and Alimony: 1989," (Washington, D.C.: Bureau of the Census, U.S. Department of Commerce, 1991), 10. Furthermore, there is significant doubt as to whether the current reforms are effective measures for increasing child support payments from absent fathers. The reforms are hindered by the failure of many states to enforce child support obligations. Family Welfare Reform Act: Hearings on H.R. 1720 Before the Subcomm. on Pub. Assistance and Unemployment Compensation of the House Comm. on Ways and Means, 100th Cong., 1st Sess 134-43 (1987) (statement of Robert C. Harris, associate deputy director, family support administrator, Office of Child Support Enforcement, U.S. Department of Health and Human Services). Moreover, delays in institution of wage withholding and approval of federal funding have contributed to a low rate of payment collection under the reforms (Ibid., 162–72) (statement of G. Diane Dodson, Special Counsel for Family Law and Policy, Women's Legal Defense Fund).

75. The model for family formation and operation historically was patriarchal. Although pure patriarchy is no longer a dominant mode of social organization, the basic tenets remain fundamentally ingrained in the way we define families and understand intimacy.

76. The inseparability of power from justice is generalizable to other subject areas. A major premise adhered to by the Law and Society tradition is that all events, concepts, and concerns must be understood in the contexts in which they operate. Feminists, in particular, have highlighted the significance of the ideological medium in which legal concepts operate. See, e.g., *Women in Law: Explorations in Law, Family and Sexuality*, ed. Julia Brophy and Carol Smart (London: Routledge and Kegan Paul, 1985); Martha Albertson Fineman, "Feminist Theory in Law: The Difference It Makes," *Columbia Journal of Gender and Law* 2 (1992): 1; Deborah L. Rhode, "The 'No-Problem' Problem: Feminist Challenges and Cultural Change," *Yale Law Journal* 100 (1991): 1731; Reva Siegel, "Reasoning from the Body: A Historical Perspective on Abortion Regulation and Questions of Equal Protection," *Stanford Law Review* 44 (1992): 261; see also Carol Sanger, "Seasoned to the Use," *Michigan Law Review* 87 (1989): 1338, 1357–65 (reviewing Scott Turow, *Presumed Innocent* [1987] and Sue Miller, *The Good Mother* [1986]) (describing how both novels demonstrate that American society perceives, and law accepts, motherhood and sexuality as incompatible).

77. The historic construct of the family in its relationship to the state also has implications for what is considered "just" in individual contexts.

78. See Lynne M. Casper, Sara S. McLanahan, and Irwin Garfinkel, "The Gender-Poverty Gap: What We Can Learn from Other Countries," *American Social Review* 59 (1994): 594 (indicating the existence of a poverty gap between men and women in America and contrasting this gap to that found in other countries).

79. Ibid., 598.

80. Ibid.

81. Ibid., 602. The Netherlands has a relatively high income floor, and no citizen is allowed to fall beneath it, regardless of work history. Sweden takes a different track, encouraging mothers to work. In Sweden, women's high employment rates substantially reduce the gender poverty gap (Ibid., 600).

IV

DEPENDENCY CARE IN CASES OF SPECIFIC VULNERABILITY

10

The Decasualization of Eldercare

Robert E. Goodin and Diane Gibson

"**P**rotecting the vulnerable" is a succinct way of characterizing many of our strongest social responsibilities. When others are helpless, they need to be helped; when others are vulnerable, they need to be protected; and when others' interests are especially sensitive to your actions and choices, then (other things being equal) you have a particularly strong responsibility to provide the needed assistance and protection.[1] That model arguably applies even to the most impersonal of business relations, to contracts and such like. But it is a model that finds particular resonance in personal relations, among family and friends, dependents and their carers.

Those two pairs are not necessarily the same, of course. Caring labor can be (and increasingly is) performed on a commercial basis. But, historically, it has been first and foremost a family concern; and, philosophically, that is for good reason. There are certain highly valued qualities associated with the sort of care provided casually by families and friends that cannot be easily replicated in the commercial sphere. In the language of vulnerabilities, "care in the community" used to address vulnerabilities that the market leaves largely untouched.

That has changed, however, under the influence of pressures from two sides. On the one side, increasingly dependent people are being thrust into the community sector. Thus, the needs being catered for in the community sector are increasingly such that they can decreasingly benefit from the peculiar virtues of community care. On the other side, community carers are themselves increasingly unable to provide that peculiar sort of care anyway. Having increasingly to fit unpaid caring labor in alongside the demands of paid labor, carers are decreasingly able to provide precisely the sort of care that used most to differentiate community from more institutionalized forms of care.

We illustrate those themes by particular reference to care for the frail elderly, by way of a particular example. But, presumably, the same conclusions would apply to community care for dependents quite generally. Deinstitutionalization across the board is thrusting ever more dependent people of all sorts into community care, at the same time as community carers are less and less able to cater to their needs in the casual ways that used to be the highly valued hallmarks of care in the community.

THE WORLD WE HAVE LOST

Until relatively recently, eldercare was a pretty casual affair. Most elders were cared for by others with whom they shared a house: equally elderly (and sometimes more frail) partners or unmarried or even married children and their families. Most elders living alone had children nearby, who almost invariably called in on them on a weekly, often daily, basis.[2] The care and assistance provided to elders in such circumstances were typically provided as incidental asides to the ordinary activities of daily life.

That is not to say that traditional carers were any less assiduous, or that their caring burdens were any less arduous. Certainly, it is not to suggest that these traditional carers were any less attentive to the needs and concerns of those for whom they cared. Instead, it is just to say that "caregiving" was not traditionally seen as the principal basis of the relationship, nor would "caregiving" have been the primary way in which participants would themselves have described the activities going on within it.[3] Caregiving of the traditional sort was casual, in the sense of being ancillary to something else in the relationship and the activities emanating from it.

In recent times, there has been a striking "decasualization" of care for the elderly. This is represented most fully, of course, in the professionalization of caregiving in institutionalized and semi-institutionalized settings: nursing homes, hostels, retirement communities, and so on. It is represented, too, by the professionalization of the helping professions. Doctors and nurses, caseworkers, and other professionals are increasingly taking over tasks that once would have fallen to family and friends. But the decasualization of care is evident in changing patterns of care within the community as well.

One aspect of that is the increasing demands on carers, traditionally and still almost invariably women, to juggle the time demands of paid employment and unpaid caregiving. As available time contracts, attention is increasingly concentrated; instead of letting "what you need to do for Grandmother" come about casually, as an ancillary adjunct to other things you happen to be doing with her, you increasingly compartmentalize them and perform them deliberately in the strictly limited time available for the task. Something important, we suggest, is lost in the process. Our discussion of "two kinds of care" strives to show what.

Another aspect of the decasualization of care in the community has to do with the nature of the dependencies that it is being asked to accommodate. Ever more dependent people are being cared for in the community; and the more dependent the person is, the more intensively carers have to attend to that person's needs. It may still be best, both from the point of view of carers and of care recipients, for those dependents' needs to be the responsibility of intimates, rather than institutions.[4] But cozily casual care of highly dependent people is simply not an option, in the community or elsewhere. That brute fact must be taken into account, both in deciding what sorts of needs we expect to be cared for in the community and in deciding what sorts of supports we are going to provide for carers undertaking those tasks in the community.

TWO KINDS OF CARE

The form of care with which we are all most familiar is, inevitably, that of young children. We have all been on the receiving end of it, in our own day; and a great majority of us have had experience of providing it, in turn. There are, however, special features of that case that make it inadequate as the basis of a general model of care.

One reason, of course, has to do with the progressive nature of childhood and the tutelary role of caregivers vis-à-vis care recipients in such circumstances. Parents are supposed to tell-cum-teach their children what to do. There would be something wrong with people who did not adopt a suitably parental-cum-paternalistic stance toward children in their charge. All that is far harder to justify vis-à-vis dependents who are not of tender years or infirm minds. Even in the case of elders with moderately advanced dementia, we ought not ride roughshod over such evaluative capacities as they still retain.[5] That is all the more true as regards dependents whose frailties are limited to the more purely physical.

Another reason, connected to the first, is that other sorts of dependents—the elderly and the disabled—typically can reasonably aspire to "independent living" of a sort that young children cannot.[6] Of course, even infants can be left in a safely structured environment (a crib or playpen) for a time; they can amuse themselves and benefit from the experience. But as children grow older, caring is usually best done from more of a distance. They need to learn to do things for themselves, with carers serving increasingly just as backstops and supports.

Reflecting upon what "care in the community" for the elderly and the disabled ought involve, we suggest that that model of caring for older children at a distance might serve as a better model. With very many of the elderly and the disabled (as with most older children), hands-on caring time is much less important than simply "being there" in the background: on call, if help is needed, but waiting to be called, rather than imposing or intruding.

THE CONCEPT OF CARE

"Care" is at one and the same time an attitude ("caring about") and an action ("taking care").[7] Typically, the latter proceeds from the former, the attitude prompting the action.[8] That is the way the feminist "ethic of care" is supposed to work, for example.[9] But the two are separable, certainly in principle and occasionally in practice as well. Nursing, one of the quintessentially "caring professions," is said to be best practiced by practitioners who do not *wholly* subsume and internalize the perspective of their patients.[10]

"Cares" are burdens. A "life full of cares" is full of worries and of woes. Being "careful" is being attentive to those concerns; being "careless" is being neglectful of them; being "care free" is being impervious to them, in an almost childlike fashion.

"Caring labor" is labor, and "dependency work" work, with all that that implies.[11] It is an effort, in the first instance. It is productive, in the second. Yet we know altogether too little about the "production function" associated with caring labor and its consequences. The outputs are just too intangible, the causal chains just too complex and intertwined.

Here we offer speculations and some policy prescriptions that would seem to follow if those speculations are correct. But while those speculations are not without substantiation, they remain largely speculative and the conclusions correspondingly tentative.

CLAUSTROPHOBIC CARING

Nel Noddings elaborates in the following terms her ideal caring relationship by reference to the example of teachers and students:

> the kind of caring ideally required of teachers [is] . . . to establish a deep, lasting, time-consuming personal relationship with every student. What I must do is to be totally nonselectively present to the student—to each student—as he addresses me. The time interval may be brief but the encounter is total.[12]

This full-bore sort of caring is what we shall dub "claustrophobic caring." The "encounter is total"; the carer fully apprehends and absorbs the perspective of the cared-for; the cared-for is in danger of being left with no independent perspective, it having been totally absorbed in course of the encounter.

Such complete openness to the perspective of the Other may well be ideal in relations among equals.[13] But in the context of dependency relationships, particularly, that seems far from ideal. The dependent's own independent voice is readily extinguished or rendered dispensable, insofar as the carer can credibly claim to apprehend fully the dependent's perspective. And that is objectionable for two reasons: first, of course, because the claim may actually be incorrect; but second, and more important, because it deprives the dependent of any powers of *agency* in the relationship. That may be true, and objectionable, even among a society of equals[14] where each is capable, at least in theory, of presenting one's point of view, but it would be particularly objectionable for people in positions of dependency, whose autonomy and agency are already precarious and who would rightly resent even more powerfully further diminutions of them.

Thus it is not surprising that writers on nursing ethics resist Noddings's "total encounter" model of caring. Far better, they say, to leave the patients some independent space.[15] So, too, say the elderly. One of the earliest and strongest findings to emerge out of surveys of the elderly is their strong preference for living independently in their own homes, for as long as possible.[16] And so, too, say the disabled. One of the strongest demands of the disability rights movement is for people with disabilities to enjoy the maximum possible control over their own lives.[17]

CASUAL CARING: CARE AS AN ESSENTIAL BY-PRODUCT

Time-use studies standardly distinguish between "primary" and "secondary activities," things that are done incidentally with and at the same time as the primary activity. Examples are talking to the kids while cooking or listening to the radio while driving. Studies suggest that perhaps half the time (perhaps more) that parents spend caring for children is as an activity of this "secondary" sort.[18] There are good reasons, which we shall now elaborate, for thinking that its being "incidental" in this way might contribute importantly to the quality of the care being provided.

Jon Elster speculates that there are certain things that, by their nature, are "essentially by-products." They cannot be obtained by being directly, intentionally pursued; instead, they can be produced only indirectly or unintentionally, as a by-product of doing something else. Falling asleep is one example: The harder you concentrate on falling asleep, the more wakeful you become; you can trick yourself into sleep only by focusing your mind on something else, like counting sheep. Another example is Tocqueville's claim that whether or not it is any good as a way of establishing guilt or innocence, the jury system provides wonderful training in the skills of democratic citizenship. True though that may be, it would be counterproductive of that goal to tell jurors that that (rather than establishing guilt or innocence) was what they were in the jury room to do.[19]

Caring labor, in its fullest flowering, is importantly akin to that. Of course, it is perfectly possible to take care of someone even if you do not care in the least for them or about them; surly college scouts have done so for snooty Oxbridge undergraduates for countless generations. But there is a distinctive kind of care that can only be provided by someone who genuinely does care, and what gives such caring behavior its distinctive quality is precisely the presumption that it proceeds almost automatically from the caring attitude. You see what the other you care about needs, and you do it—"without thinking twice," as the saying goes.

That is not to say that people who care cannot cogitate on what the other really needs, on how they might best help, and so on. Caring labor might involve (indeed, often requires) serious consideration and careful planning. The point is merely that deliberately "forming an intention to help" is alien to a caring relationship of this deeper sort. That background intention is ever-present. It does not have to be conjured up. And helping behavior is a by-product of that standing background intention.

Similar help—identical performances—might be provided by other people from other motives. The same cake can be baked for love or for money. (Imagine a baker popping an extra cake into his ordinarily commercial oven for his own child's birthday.) But it is essential to the nature of the one as an act of love that it was done as an automatic by-product of that attitude.

In other cases, caring behaviors are not so obviously reducible to "the byproduct of an attitude" of care. Paid carers who internalize their roles might equally "casually" and automatically perform caring services for their clients. What matters here is the casualness of the performance—the absence of any felt need to reflect on the question of "why should I"—that characterizes casual caring of this sort. Caring that is the essential by-product of a commercial contract, duly internalized, can be just as casual as any other.

THE CHANGING NATURE OF CARE IN THE COMMUNITY

Our thesis for the remainder of this chapter is twofold. First, we argue that the comparative advantage of community-based care lies in its greater capacity to provide care of the sort that we will characterize, variously, as "care at a distance," "casual care," or "independence-respecting care," all of which we regard as allied, but not identical, notions. It is far more difficult, and correspondingly less common, for institution-based care to be organized in such ways.

Second, we argue that the caring responsibilities that are being displaced into the community are increasingly of a sort that decreasingly benefit from that comparative advantage. That is to say, the caring responsibilities now being displaced into the community are increasingly for people whose dependencies are such that they require far more than the sort of casual "care at a distance" that is the forte of community-based arrangements. Among highly dependent populations, care simply cannot be independence-respecting, in any substantial measure.

Personalized care might still be preferred to impersonal forms of care, and care by intimates rather than care by strangers might be preferred for that reason, even (or perhaps especially) for highly dependent people—be they infants, severely disabled people, or the infirm elderly. But the *kind* of care that is being provided to them is no longer the kind of care that is the peculiar forte of community-based arrangements. The proposition that there is a distinctive form of care that can much better be provided in the community than in institutional settings simply fails to apply, in those cases.

That is to say, there is one less reason for us to impose on community carers, when it comes to highly dependent care recipients. There is also all the more reason for state-provided services to relieve—permanently or temporarily, persistently or intermittently—community-based carers for highly dependent people.

WHO OUGHT TO BE CARED FOR IN THE COMMUNITY?

Clearly, there is no simple answer to the question. Who should be cared for in the community—who would benefit from the peculiar advantages of that form of care, and who needs more than it can offer? The answer to each question depends on idiosyncratic circumstances that can never be captured in any standardized needs assessment. Still, those standardized catalogs tell us something of importance for determining the general outlines of policy, even if they do not tell us everything that assessment teams ought to take into account in determining where any given client ought to go.

The story those standardized needs-assessment inventories tell is inevitably a mixed one. By those standards, inevitably, there will be some people in institutions who need not be and there will be others who are not in institutions who apparently ought to be. U.S. estimates suggest that circa the late 1980s, more than 15 percent of nursing home residents could be cared for at lower levels of care.[20] On the other hand, some 3.5 percent of people aged sixty-five and over living in the community need active or standby help with one or more of the "Activities of Daily Living"; and if we were to include people who were cognitively impaired as well, that might exceed 6 percent.[21]

In Australia, too, highly dependent people are increasingly cared for in the community. Over the decade 1988–1998, the proportion of the total population with a severe or profound handicap being cared for in nursing homes or hostels dropped from 21 percent to 15 percent; and the proportion living in the community, either alone or with others, increased correspondingly (to 85 percent). A relatively larger proportion of the "old old" reside in health establishments. But even among the group aged eighty years and over who have a severe or profound handicap, fully half of them are still being cared for in the community (55 percent, up from 50 percent ten years before).[22]

The burden borne by these community carers is often considerable. Australian data again show that over half of people who are identified as "primary carers" for people with one or more disabilities in core activity areas (mobility, self-care, and communication) spend forty hours a week or more in caring labor. The percentage varies somewhat with the age of the carer, with older carers devoting relatively more time to those tasks than younger ones. But even among carers who are themselves of prime working age (ages 25–44), fully 37 percent of them report spending forty hours or more in unpaid caring labor.[23]

HOW OUGHT THE COMMUNITY CARE FOR ELDERS?

There are increasing pressures on community care, coming from two sides. On the one side, it is under pressure from increasing labor force participation, particularly of women who have traditionally done most of the caring labor on an unpaid basis.[24] The fewer people there are outside the paid labor force, the fewer people there are available (and the fewer hours the others have available) to do unpaid caring labor.

Some sorts of labor force participation are more of a hindrance to unpaid caring labor than others, of course. Participation in the paid labor force is more consistent with the provision of care on a casual basis, first, if it is flexible in its timing. Then carers can still be "on call" when needed by care recipients. Second, paid employment is more consistent with unpaid caring labor the more limited it is in its hours. It is not strictly necessary for the paid labor to be literally part time, but at the very least must not involve such a heavy time commitment as to occupy virtually all the hours that might conceivably be used for unpaid caring labor.

On the other side, home care is under increasing pressure from the nature of the dependent populations being cared for in the community and from the shrinkage of social support networks. Nearly 40 percent of Australians who are serving as "primary carers" for people with profound or severe handicaps in the community report that they have no "fall-back cover," no one who could take over caring responsibilities from them, if necessary.[25]

Government provision of services or subsidies can, of course, go some way toward making up for all that. Evidence from the United States seems to show that generous home-care programs increase the likelihood that unmarried persons will live independently rather than (being forced to) live in shared housing or a nursing home or hostel.[26] But it seems unlikely that government support will ever be more than a marginal supplement. On average, the Australian Home and Community Care scheme, for example, provides merely one and a half hours of home help per month to each person aged sixty-five and over who has a profound or severe handicap, and under half an hour a month in assistance with personal care or home nursing.[27] This is against a background in which more than half the clients of those services need "some help" (just under a tenth need "total help") dressing, and a fifth need "some help" with eating and with mobility.[28]

CONCLUSION: THE DECASUALIZATION OF CARE

"Casual labor," by definitions dear to the keepers of the official national accounts, is intermittent and incidental. Caring labor can be casual in just that way, providing a little help here and there on the side. For certain sorts of people, such casual caring is ideally suited to their needs. They are the sorts of people for whom care in the community, with its greater capacity for such casual care at a distance, is ideally tailored.

Increasingly, however, what we see is the "decasualization" of community-based care. More and more of the needs to which it is expected to respond require responses of a far more than casual sort. And as caring tasks become more intensive, community carers themselves grow increasingly dependent upon public support of various sorts, if only to provide occasional respite from their caring burdens. That is one of the more important new tasks incumbent upon public policy organized around principles of "protecting the vulnerable."

Equally, policy genuinely guided by principles of "protecting the vulnerable" ought to be prepared to take public responsibility for highly dependent populations who have in recent years increasingly been forced back into the community, whatever their own or their carers' preferences in the matter. Whatever rationale there might once have been for automatically assuming the desirability of ever more community care is to be desired has increasingly been eroded, as those being cared for in the community have become increasingly dependent people who are less and less capable of benefiting from the peculiar qualities that community care might have to offer.

Let us not be mistaken. Ours is not an argument against community care, *tout court*. Neither do we deny that a great many highly dependent people have always been cared for in the community; and most of them have been cared for very well indeed, even where their dependency levels are such that they require much more than the "casual" sort of care that is the peculiar province of the community sector.

Our positive argument can be summarized in these two propositions. First, there ought to be adequate institutional alternatives for highly dependent people who cannot cope, or who cannot be coped with, in the community. Second, there ought to be adequate institutional supports (home help, respite services, etc.) for community carers under pressure from twin demands, caring for increasingly dependent dependents at the same time as increasingly needing to work in paid labor.

NOTES

We are grateful to Eva Kittay for prompting this chapter and for her comments on earlier drafts of it and to Nancy Folbre for incisive discussions. The views represented are those of theauthors alone and do not reflect those of their advisers or employers.

1. Robert E. Goodin, *Protecting the Vulnerable* (Chicago: University of Chicago Press, 1985).

2. That was the pattern in early postwar England, anyway, judging from Peter Townsend, *The Family Life of Older People* (Harmondsworth, Mddx.: Penguin, 1957), 44, 49. Townsend reports just over half of people aged sixty-five or over sharing the same dwelling as one of their children and another 38 percent having at least one of their children within a five-minute walk away (44) and that fully 78 percent of his elderly Bethnal Green respondents saw at least one of their children daily, and fully 97 percent saw one of them at least weekly

(49). Whether it had any long historical precedent in preindustrial times (as social scientists had long presumed) has been very much an open question, since the publication of Peter Laslett, ed., *Household and Family in Past Time* (Cambridge: Cambridge University Press, 1972); Laslett's introductory essay, "The History of the Family," 1–102, at 58–73, discusses the lack of any evidence of "generational depth" in households anywhere outside Japan, and in personal discussions (February 2000) Laslett tells us of evidence of considerable geographic mobility in preindustrial England, from which he would infer that many elderly would not have had children remaining in the same town or village, even.

3. That is partly because "caregiving" is itself something of a neologism. But even reverting to older locutions, people would ordinarily have spoken of "going over to help Grandmother" (usually, with a specific task), in revealing contrast to the way the same people would have talked about "taking care of the kids."

4. Eva Feder Kittay speaks eloquently on that point in *Love's Labor* (New York: Routledge, 1999), chapter 6.

5. Agnieszka Jaworska, "Respecting the Margins of Agency: Alzheimer's Patients and the Capacity to Value," *Philosophy & Public Affairs* 28, no. 2 (spring 1999): 105–38.

6. Jenny Morris, *Independent Lives: Community Care & Disabled People* (London: Macmillan, 1993). Jane Lakey, *Caring about Independence: Disabled People & the Independent Living Fund*, PSI Research Report 768 (London: Policy Studies Institute, 1994).

7. As in the title essay in Harry G. Frankfurt, *The Importance of What We Care About* (Cambridge: Cambridge University Press, 1988); Jeffrey Blustein, *Care and Commitment* (New York: Oxford University Press, 1991); Joan C. Tronto, *Moral Boundaries: A Political Argument for an Ethic of Care* (New York: Routledge, 1993), especially chapter 4.

8. Thus, "caring labor" is typically said to be a subspecies of "emotional labor"; see Susan Himmelweit, "Caring Labor," *Annals of the American Academy of Political and Social Sciences* 561 (January 1999): 27–38.

9. Carol Gilligan, *In a Different Voice: Psychological Theory and Women's Development* (Cambridge, Mass.: Harvard University Press, 1982). Nel Noddings, *Caring: A Feminine Approach to Ethics & Moral Education* (Berkeley: University of California Press, 1984). Joan C. Tronto, "Beyond Gender Difference to a Theory of Care," *Signs* 12 (1987): 644–63, and *Moral Boundaries*, Special Issue of *Hypatia* 10, no. 2 (spring 1995), especially Virginia Held, "The Meshing of Care and Justice," 128–32; Joan C. Tronto, "Care as a Basis for Radical Political Judgments," 141–49; and Annette Baier, "A Note on Justice, Care & Immigration Policy," 150–52. Clare Ungerson, *Policy Is Personal: Sex, Gender and Informal Care* (London: Tavistock, 1987). Carol Thomas, "De-Constructing Concepts of Care," *Sociology* 27 (1993): 649–69. Moira Gatens, ed., *Feminist Ethics* (Aldershot: Dartmouth, 2000).

10. Helga Kuhse, *Caring: Nurses, Women & Ethics* (Oxford: Blackwell, 1997), chapter 7. Cf. S. F. Fry, "The Role of Caring in a Theory of Nursing Ethics," *Hypatia* 4, no. 2 (summer 1989): 88–103.

11. Kittay, *Love's Labor*, especially chapter 2. Himmelweit, "Caring Labor."

12. Nel Noddings, *Caring: A Feminine Approach to Ethics & Moral Education* (Berkeley: University of California Press, 1984), 179–80.

13. Seyla Benhabib, "The Generalized and the Concrete Other," *Situating the Self* (Oxford: Polity, 1992), 148–77.

14. It might thus be an objection to the model proposed by I. M. Young, *Intersecting Voices* (Princeton, N.J.: Princeton University Press, 1997), chapter 2.

15. Kuhse, *Caring* 149.

16. Townsend, *The Family Life of Older People.*

17. Morris, *Independent Lives.*

18. W. Keith Bryant and Cathleen D. Zick, "An Examination of Parent–Child Shared Time," *Journal of Marriage & the Family* 58 (1996): 227–37; Australian Bureau of Statistics, *How Australians Use Their Time,* Catalogue No. 4153.0 (Canberra: ABS, 1994), 8, 15; John Robinson and Geoffrey Godbey, *Time for Life: The Surprising Ways Americans Use Their Time* (University Park: Pennsylvania State University Press, 1997), 107. These are quite probably underestimates: coding categories are activity-oriented; respondents are unlikely to have reported themselves to be "looking after the kids" when they were simply "on call" or "within earshot" but not actively engaged in child care. See Cathleen D. Zick and W. Keith Bryant, "A New Look at Parents' Time Spent in Child Care: Primary and Secondary Time Use," *Social Science Research* 25 (1996): 1–21.

19. Jon Elster, "States That Are Essentially By-Products," *Sour Grapes* (Cambridge: Cambridge University Press, 1983), chapter 2.

20. W. D. Spector, J. Reschovsky, and J. D. Cohen, "Appropriate Placement of Nursing Home Residents in Lower Levels of Care," *Milbank Quarterly* 74, no. 1 (1996): 139–60.

21. R. Stone and C. M. Murtaugh, "The Elderly Population with Chronic Functional Disability: Implications for Home Care Eligibility," *The Gerontologist* 30, no. 4 (1990): 491–96. W. D. Spector, "Cognitive Impairment and Disruptive Behaviors among Elderly Persons Living in the Community: Implications for Targeting Long-Term Care," *The Gerontologist* 31, no. 1 (1991): 51–59.

22. Diane Gibson, Bella Holmes, and Zhibin Liu, "Aged Care," *Australia's Welfare 1999: Services & Assistance* (Canberra: Australian Institute of Health & Welfare, 1999), 165–214, at 171.

23. Gibson, Holmes, and Liu, "Aged Care," 174.

24. Australian statistics are again illustrative; see, e.g., Peter Saunders, "Changing Work Patterns and the Community Services Workforce," *Australia's Welfare 1999*, 38–87.

25. Diane Gibson, Elizabeth Butkus, Anne Jenkins, Sushma Mathur, and Zhibin Liu, *The Respite Care Needs of Australians,* Respite Review Supporting Paper 1 (Canberra: Australian Institute of Health and Welfare, 1996).

26. L. E. Pezzin, P. Kemper, and J. Reschovsky, "Does Publicly Provided Home Care Substitute for Family Care? Experimental Evidence with Endogenous Living Arrangements," *Journal of Human Resources* 31, no. 3 (1996): 650–76; P. Kemper and L. E. Pezzin, "The Effect of Public Provision of Home Care on Living and Care Arrangements: Evidence from the Channeling Experiment," *Alternatives for Ensuring Long-Term Care*, ed. R. Eisen and F. Sloan (Amsterdam: Kluwer, 1996), 125–46.

27. Gibson, Holmes, and Liu, "Aged Care," 186.

28. Gibson, Holmes, and Liu, "Aged Care," 204.

11

When Caring Is Just and Justice Is Caring: Justice and Mental Retardation

Eva Feder Kittay

"Praise to you, Lord God, king of the universe, who varies the forms of thy creatures." So begins an ancient Hebrew prayer which is to be recited upon encountering an individual with "deformities."

—Wolf Wolfensberger, *The Principles of Normalization in Human Services*

When speaking of a person labeled "profoundly mentally retarded" emphasize "profound."

—David Hingsburger, *First Contact: Charting Inner Space*

INTERJECTING VOICE

Among the various human forms alluded to in the Hebrew prayer, mental retardation appears to be one of the most difficult to celebrate.[1] It is the disability that other disabled persons do not want attributed to them. It is the disability for which prospective parents are most likely to use selective abortion (Wertz 2000). And it is the disability that prompted one of the most illustrious U.S. Supreme Court justices to endorse forced sterilization, because "three generations of imbeciles are enough."[2] The mentally retarded have at times been objects of pity, compassion, or abuse by their caretakers and society at large. But they have rarely been seen as subjects, as citizens, as persons with equal entitlement to fulfillment.

Mental retardation comes to the public's attention in sensational stories that expose appalling forms of abuse. We encountered the horror decades ago in *Look* magazine's photo exposé "Christmas in Purgatory" and, more recently, in the heavily illustrated article in the *New York Times Magazine* showing conditions at Hidalgo in Guadalajara, Mexico, one of many "Global Willowbrooks"

(Winerip 2000); or closer to home, the *Washington Post*'s coverage of the unexplained and uninvestigated deaths of mentally retarded people living in the city-funded group homes of the nation's capital (Vobejda 2000). And we gasp at the inhumanity of those entrusted with the care of extremely vulnerable people. We wonder: How can this happen? How is it that we allow this to occur?

Although we occasionally hear of these extreme cases of abuse, the victimization of severely intellectually disabled persons is more pervasive than these isolated examples suggest. Many individuals with mental retardation, especially when it is severe or profound or compounded by other disabilities, have been unaffected by the important strides made by other people with disabilities. Advocates of disability rights have insisted that the independence and productivity that are essential to being considered equal citizens in a liberal society are no less attainable for the disabled than for the nondisabled. They have argued that their impairments are only disabling in an environment that is hostile to their differences and that has been constructed to exclude them. Yet, the impairment of mental retardation is not easily addressed by physical changes in the environment. Although a significant number of mentally disabled persons have been moved out of large state institutions into smaller, community-based facilities or independent apartments and are employed in supportive environments, most will need to be financially supported or to subsist on very low salaries. Of all disabled people, the severely mentally retarded have least benefited from the inclusion fought for by the disability community (Ferguson 1994).

Perhaps this should not be surprising. The movement for the rights and inclusion of people with disabilities has followed a blueprint developed by persons of color, women, and gays and lesbians. All of these attempts by the marginalized to be recognized and fully enfranchised demanded that the practice of liberalism be consistent with its tenets of universal equality and freedom. All the formerly excluded have insisted on no longer being silenced, on having their voices heard. But for many with severe mental retardation, such a demand for voice appears futile. Even though other movements of inclusion have challenged the liberalism that they nonetheless invoked, the inclusion of people with mental retardation may well be liberalism's limit case, just as it is a limiting case for the demands of many in the disability community. Liberalism invokes a notion of political participation in which one makes one's voice heard. It depends on a conception of the person as independent, rational, and capable of self-sufficiency. And it holds to a conception of society as an association of such independent equals. Yet many with severe retardation cannot ever hope to be equal in these terms. Some, at least, may never be able to be independent or capable of participating in rational deliberation.

Those who speak do so in a language not recognized—and even demeaned—by those who speak in the language of the public sphere. Without a claim to cognitive parity, even those who can speak are not recognized as authors or agents in their own right. Those who cannot speak must depend on others to speak for them. Those who can speak find that their voice is given no authority. Perhaps there is no more disabling disablement.

To be heard, to be recognized, to have her needs and wants reckoned along with those of others, the mentally retarded individual requires an advocate—a role that has voice at its center. It is in the role of an advocate for my daughter, Sesha, that I enter into the field of "disability criticism." I have wondered not only how and where I fit into this discourse; I have also considered how I interject my daughter into this critical discourse, into any public discourse. To do so, I must first tell the reader about her, for she cannot speak for herself.

How do I describe Sesha? In speaking not only about her, but for her, I have already begun by describing her in the negative—as one who cannot speak for herself. Yet this lack is a synecdoche for all that she is unable to do: feed herself, dress herself, toilet herself, walk, talk, read, write, draw, say Mama or Papa. I would have preferred to start by speaking of her capabilities: the hugs and kisses she can give, her boundless enjoyment of the sensuous feel of water, or her abiding and profound appreciation of music. When asked about my daughter, I want to tell people that she is a beautiful, loving, joyful young woman. But then I need to tell them what she cannot be, given her profound cognitive limitations, her cerebral palsy, and her seizure disorders. When people ask how old my daughter is I always hesitate, wondering whether to give her chronological age and speak of her as a lovely and intense thirty-year-old woman, or to speak of the indeterminate age that reflects her level of functioning and her total dependence. The positive set of responses is truer to who she is. Her limitations describe the face she shows to those who don't know her, but they also convey the ways she cannot make her own way in the world. Knowing her capabilities, one gets a glimpse into the richness of her life and the remarkable quality of her very being.

Nonetheless, the limitations shape her life and those of her family, so we all must address them if we are to make it possible for her beauty to flourish. Conversely, only by considering her in the fullness of her joys and capacities can we view her impairments in light of her life, her interests, her happiness—and not as projections of her "able" parents or of an able-biased society. An exclusive focus on her limitations would set her outside liberal definitions of personhood and citizenship that are fixated on intellect, independence, and productivity. These values throw into question her entitlement to the resources she needs for her full development and her flourishing.

ADVOCATING FOR THE CARED-FOR
BY ADVOCATING FOR THE CARER

Foremost among her needs is the need for care. If she is to flourish, she needs good caring care—and lots of it. *Care* is a multifaceted term. It is a labor, an attitude, and a virtue. As labor, it is the work of maintaining ourselves and others when we are in a condition of need. It is most noticed in its absence, most needed when it can be least reciprocated. As an attitude, caring denotes a positive, affective bond and investment in another's well-being. The labor can be done without the appropriate attitude. Yet without the attitude of care, the open responsiveness to another that is so essential to understanding what another requires is not possible. That is, the labor unaccompanied by the attitude of care cannot be good care (see Kittay 1999).

Good caring is cultivated as a virtue by some who can provide it for intimates and strangers alike. More frequently it is elicited when we are in an affectionate relationship with another. But even here, consistency of care, maintaining care even when it is difficult and disadvantageous to us, requires the cultivation of the virtue. Care as a virtue is a disposition manifested in caring behavior (the labor and attitude), in which "a shift takes place from the interest in our life situation to the situation of the other, the one in need of care" (Gastmans, Dierckx de Casterlé, and Schotsmans 1998, 53).

Since my daughter requires constant and attentive care, and because such care (the labor) requires devoted and caring caregivers (the attitude), to advocate for my daughter without also advocating for those who are entrusted with her well-being is at once unjust and uncaring toward the caregiver. It also fails to accomplish its original aim of assuring a good and fulfilling life for my daughter. This is so despite the fact that the interests of my daughter and those of her caregivers (whether me or others) are not always aligned, and that the interests of her paid caregivers are not infrequently at odds with those of her familial caregivers.

To give voice to one who cannot speak, whose very agency appears so attenuated, means to pay the utmost heed to what I have called elsewhere the "dependency relation": the relation between one who gives care and one who is dependent upon caregivers for her most basic life functions ("the charge"), a dependency that, while always socially shaped, is grounded in the inevitable circumstances of the human animal (see Kittay 1999).[3]

As a worker (elsewhere I speak of the "dependency worker"), the caregiver is vulnerable to exploitation. But because of the special demands of caregiving and because of the traditional assignment of this work to women or servants, dependency workers are more subject to exploitation than most. When paid, dependency work is rarely well paid. When done by family members, it is, as a rule, unpaid. Paid dependency workers are frequently drawn from classes or groups who are themselves relatively powerless within the society at large and who occupy a social status lower than that of their charge. As a result, even though the charge may be totally dependent on the dependency worker for the satisfaction of fundamental needs, the dependency worker may be vulnerable to those whose interests it serves to have the charge cared for, as well as to the actions of her charge.

Conversely, given the dependency of the charge, or her physical or mental incapacity, the trust invested in the dependency worker not to abuse her power over the charge is enormous. The more stigmatized the condition that gives rise to the dependency and the more excluded and unvoiced the dependent is, the greater the opportunity and latitude for the dependency worker to violate that trust. It is conceivable that sheer coercion and policing could guarantee that a dependency worker charged with the care of a highly vulnerable person will not violate her trust and abuse her power over her charge. But the vigilance required makes such a means ineffectual in all but the most oppressive social conditions. More commonly, the emotional bond that forms between the caregiver and her charge secures the moral obligation to meet the needs of one who is vulnerable to your actions (Goodin 1985). The caregiver who has cultivated the virtue of care comes to view the interest of the charge as part of her own well-being. In the absence of some bonding or some attitudinal commitment, the care may be indifferent or even disastrously poor. Those who advocate for vulnerable persons may ask what conditions would encourage an attitude of care in the caregiver—all the while respecting the caregiver's own needs and desires.

Because good caregiving is inherently other-directed, the agency of the good caregiver is not easily accommodated by the picture of the agent under liberalism, the rationally self-interested actor. Because the severely and profoundly mentally retarded are so dependent on the caregiver to exhibit other-directed behavior, the relationship between the two falls outside of conventional understandings of relationships between equals within liberalism.

The advocate for the severely retarded person needs to look beyond liberalism, while still respecting the values of autonomy and liberty propounded by liberal theory. She must seek conditions that are just to the caregiver as well as conducive to good care and justice for the charge. To advocate for caregivers is to insist that significant resources be set aside to pay for the services of caregivers, to provide them with the same benefits as other workers, to invest in training and the building of skills that will enable those who give care to help their charges develop all their capabilities.

But why, a skeptic may ask, should we invest such resources (presumably public resources if they are to benefit all affected individuals) for the sake of a population that will never be able to reciprocate, whose material contributions will never match the outlay? We can demand such reciprocity from the subject of traditional theories of liberal justice, but it makes little sense in the case of persons whose mental capabilities are very seriously limited. Charity or benevolence may motivate us to contribute to the care of such people, but is there any case to be made for the injustice of doing otherwise? Simply allowing those who cannot care for themselves to go unfed and unattended seems indecent. But do we have any duty to provide for their flourishing? We need therefore to ask what is due to the retarded, why it is due to them, and what is due to those who care for persons as dependent and vulnerable as my daughter and others like her.

THE TRADITION OF PERSONHOOD

William Wordsworth, speaking of his poem "The Idiot Boy," wrote of the "loathing and disgust" evoked by a person with mental retardation, and remarked that this is the consequence of a "want of comprehensiveness of thinking and feeling," a "false delicacy" (De Selincourt 1935, 295–96). Perhaps there will be a time when we can rid people of the "false delicacy" and broaden the measure of thinking and feeling to embrace a capacious concept of personhood. But it was not so in Wordsworth's time, and it is not so now and here. Beauty may charm and physical prowess may awe, but intellect rules supreme.

The intellect not only provides access to power and material goods. From Aristotle to Rawls, it is by virtue of our intellect, our powers of rational deliberation, that humans acquire a unique moral status as well. For Aristotle, the possession of the deliberative faculty and ability to act from rational deliberation was the sine qua non for citizenship, an ability he attributed only to free men, not women and not slaves. The ascendance of humans' rational capacities as the defining mark not only of citizenship but of personhood itself is illustrated by John Locke's definition of a person as "a thinking intelligent being, that has reason and reflection, and can consider itself as itself, the same thinking thing, in different times and places" (1987, 1.27.11). Persons, in turn, become the bearers of rights, the only signers of the social contract, the only actors in our morality plays, the only players to whom the rules of justice pertain, and so, the only ones for whom citizenship and justice are defined.

Kant understood the dignity of humans to derive from their ability to assume duty through a law they themselves author. The capacity that elevates humans to the status of moral agents, he thought, is the rationality by which we judge if we can universalize maxims we choose for our own actions. Rational agency, he maintained, not our mere species membership, gives us the dignity of moral beings. Because we are capable of autonomy, of rationally determining what our duty is, we are due the respect of an end-in-itself, of an inhabitant of the kingdom of ends.

Kant's is a tradition that has endured; it finds especially influential expression today in the theory of justice advanced by John Rawls. Let us linger for a moment on Rawls, for his is the reigning theory of liberalism. Rawls understands justice to be due to those who enter with others into an association based on fair terms of cooperation. Those who are fully cooperating throughout their lives are the free and equal citizens of the well-ordered society. It is they who partake of both the benefits and burdens of social cooperation. Two moral powers, maintains Rawls, can be attributed to citizens who are both rational in recognizing and pursuing their own conception of the good (the first moral power) and reasonable in recognizing the fairness of others also pursuing their own ends (the second moral power). It is the business of a just society to provide its citizens with the means to express these moral powers, that is, to pursue the good life as they see it and to allow others to pursue the good life as they see it. With Rawls's theory of justice, free and equal agents in a fair procedure deliberate and choose the principles by which "primary goods" (the goods we require whatever our conception of the good is) are distributed through the basic institutions of society (Rawls 1980, 526). These goods presume and are determined by a conception of the person as possessing two moral powers, that is, as being both reasonable and rational.

Where in this moral universe—an in a social/political world so represented—is there room for those whose rational, reasonable, and reasoning capacities are impaired, perhaps severely? A conception of the primary goods is not tailored to their lives. It is not clear that their moral powers are adequately captured in this picture of moral life, or that this conception of the moral powers is adequate to provide them with the protection, care, and resources they require to flourish (see Kittay 1999). Can moral citizenship be granted to those lacking such powers, powers presumed in the citizen who is "fully functioning throughout a life"? (Rawls 1980, 546). What moral status does my daughter then have? If she has no place at the table of equal deliberators, of free and equal moral agents, of free and equal citizens, does justice apply to her?[4]

If traditional theories in the Western moral and political tradition are correct in their exclusion, then we have to wonder: When the heart cries "Injustice" upon encountering pictures of the mentally retarded tied to their beds, where one attendant cares for over one hundred entirely dependent residents (as in the "asylum" in Guadalajara), is this merely a misunderstanding of the term *justice*? When we read Nancy Scheper-Hughes's (1992) vivid and sympathetic account of the abject lives of sugarcane workers of northeastern Brazil, of the numbed misery of the mothers who allow their weak (and doubtless impaired) infants to "return to Jesus" by failing to feed them, and believe that unjust circumstances compel these mothers to participate in a moral wrong (albeit one for which they are not the prime culprits)—are we merely foisting sentimental middle-class values on those who cannot afford them? And is there any ground for the accusation that the United States—the wealthiest nation in the history of the world—is unjust for not providing appropriate resources to families who lack means to properly care for their developmentally disabled child? Wealthy parents might, of course, choose to lavish care on their "deviant" family members, just as those with resources can lavishly spend on the many things for which there is no public support. Similarly, a family who has resources to care for a child with Down syndrome might refuse prenatal testing and selective abortion. But should any family expect public support for such a child when an abortion would have been an inexpensive way to prevent such a birth? Are there any claims from justice to extend public provisions for families to lighten the extra demands of raising a child with cognitive deficits so severe that no education or habilitation will turn that child into a future taxpayer?

In the above discussion, we began thinking of the individual with intellectual disabilities, but we soon find ourselves including the family of which she is a part and her caregivers in our consideration. Earlier I spoke of caregivers as if they were different from the family and directed us to the vulnerability of the paid caregiver. But all caregivers, familial or paid, become derivatively dependent when they turn their time, attention, and concerns to a dependent other. And the greater the dependency of their charge, the greater their derivative dependency. Elsewhere

I argue that not only are dependents effectively left out of the social contract, but dependency workers are implicitly excluded as well (Kittay 1999). Even as they advocate for their charge or other dependent kin, their own voice and the needs that arise from their role as caregivers come to be eclipsed. I asked above whether assistance to those who are dependent because of their permanent mental incapacity should expect support at the expense of the public. The same question could be asked of those who provide their care—even though the latter are surely capable of the full functioning that Rawls (1972, 1992) speaks of as requisite to membership in the community of equals. We can ask whether parents or kin who assume the role of caregiver should have claims on the larger society to support them in their efforts to provide care. If, for all the effort and care in raising a child with disabilities into adulthood, there is no payback (conventionally understood) to the society at large, can we still insist that there be a state interest in helping families with the additional burdens of caring for a developmentally disabled child? Is there a state interest in assuring families that their vulnerable child will be well cared for when the family is no longer able or willing to do so?

THE CONSTRUCTION OF DISABILITY, THE ADA, AND MENTAL RETARDATION

The enactment of the 1990 Americans with Disabilities Act (ADA) is an affirmation of the citizenship and the justice due to all disabled persons. That act, however, does not try to establish the ground for affirming the personhood or citizenship of disabled Americans. It assumes it. Its point is to make discrimination based on disability illegal. Modeled on other antidiscrimination legislation, its approach is largely a negative one, stipulating that obstacles not be placed in the way of an individual's opportunity to participate in the social cooperation constitutive of citizenship.

As Anita Silvers (1998) argues, in the case of disability, a purely negative right not to be interfered with actually mandates positive action, such as the building of ramps and the modification of toilet facilities. Such positive action is largely compensatory, since the physiosocial environment might have been built so as not to exclude persons with differing abilities. Silvers makes the case that this approach supports the social model of disability rather than the medical model. The medical model locates the source of disability in the individual: the individual is defective and needs fixing; the social model locates the source of the disability in the social situation: the social situation requires fixing, not the individual. The supposition, endorsed by Silvers and adopted in some of the language of the ADA itself, is that once the barriers to full participation are removed, the disabled will be able to be as productive, self-sustaining, and independent as the abled.

The focus on physical disabilities has given much plausibility to the arguments of the disability community that disadvantage, and the disability that results from a physiological impairment, is itself a consequence of an environment built to accommodate certain capacities but not others. Such analysis of disability is especially applicable to physical disabilities, but may have some limited applicability to persons with a mild retardation as well. As a number of disability theorists and advocates have argued, it is only a consequence of our technologically advanced environment that we need to have skills that depend on very developed and trained cognitive capacities, skills beyond the capacities of mildly retarded persons. In an agrarian community, the mental abilities of a mildly retarded person may be quite sufficient to allow such an individual to live a reasonably independent and productive existence—a life that is viewed as normal. Even if this is true of very mildly retarded adults, there is no accommodation that transforms as severe a case of retardation as that of my daughter, Sesha, into a condition that is not profoundly disabling. The cognitive impairments of the severely and profoundly retarded are not merely contingently disabling. Unlike many disabilities, hers are not simply social constructions. Someone such as my daughter could not survive, much less thrive, without constant and vigilant attention, without someone performing for her nearly all the tasks of daily living, as well as providing for her—and her caregiver—the material resources required for her existence and flourishing.

We might say, however, that in the case of developmental disabilities, especially severe ones, though the disability itself is not socially constructed, the view that mental retardation is a "problem" rather than a possible outcome of human physiology *is*. Those who have developmental disabilities require more supports than those without these impairments. However, they also provide different and rich opportunities for relationships and experiencing new ways of seeing the world (see Cushing and Lewis n.d.; Bogdan and Taylor 1992; and Hingsburger 2000). Constructed only as a problem, Sesha and other developmentally disabled persons appear to have no claim to the aids and supports that they need to live and live well. According to some theories she is not a citizen of this or any country.[5] Must she and those who share her disabilities then be consigned to live off the scraps of a gratuitous and uncertain generosity?

AN ALTERNATIVE CONCEPTION OF PERSONHOOD

In a recent essay, I contrast the lives of those shattered by inappropriate institutions and social neglect with that of Sesha. I evoke a morning in my kitchen when Sesha, accompanied by her caregiver, is having breakfast, and I sneak in to give her a kiss:

> Sesha, as always, is delighted to see me. Anxious to give me one of her distinctive kisses she tries to grab my hair to pull me to her mouth. Yet at the same time my kisses tickle her and make her giggle too hard to concentrate on dropping the jam-covered toast before going after my hair. I can, the sticky toast, the hair-pulling and the raspberry jam-covered mouth. In this charming dance, Sesha and I experience some of our most joyful moments—laughing, ducking, grabbing, kissing. (Kittay 2000b)

They are "small" pleasures, to be sure, but pleasures that provide so much of life's meaning and worth that they permit the deep sorrows of Sesha's limitations to recede into a distant place in the mind; they are small joys, but are so profound that they even make me question that very sorrow. It is a pleasure both Sesha and I would have been denied if we could not share our lives together.

Because we as a family have been able to keep Sesha in our home and community, those who have made contact with her and have learned to see her as we who love her do have gained new perspectives on what it means to be a person. Seeing Sesha in her interactions with those who care for—and about—her reveals that being a person has little to do with rationality and everything to do with *relationships*—to our world and to those in it.

If personhood is limited to those who possess certain intellectual capacities and to those who are productive, then my daughter would not be a person. But my daughter is a person. She is, after all, my daughter. How can she be anything but a person? If traditional conceptions of personhood are not capacious enough to include Sesha and those who share her impairments, we need a new definition. I propose that being a person means having the capacity to be in certain relationships with other persons, to sustain contact with other persons, to shape one's own world and the world of others, and to have a life that another person can conceive of as an imaginative possibility for him- or herself (see Diamond 1991). It is a definition that brings our relationships (real and imaginative) with others to the center of any conception of personhood. We do not become a person without the engagement of other persons—their care, as well as their recognition of the uniqueness and the connectedness of our human agency,[6] and the distinctiveness of our particularly human relations to others and of the world we fashion.[7]

The shaping of one's own world is a gift that each individual possesses and that some make more use of than others. Sesha, in spite of all her limitations, makes ample use of this gift. To be with Sesha is to enter her orbit, to gain a glimpse of the world as she constructs it. Even those who are still more limited than Sesha have this capacity. It requires an openness to experience it. In one who can scarcely move a muscle, a glint in the eye at a strain of familiar music establishes personhood. A slight upturn of the lip in a profoundly and multiply disabled individual when a favorite caregiver comes along, or a look of joy in response to the scent of a perfume—all these establish personhood. We know that there is a person before us when we see, as David Hingsburger (2000, 24) says, that there is "someone home": that the seemingly vacuous look is not vacant at all; that an individual's inability to articulate a "language" as publicly defined does not indicate a lack of anything to say. To fail to recognize that capacity is to deny an individual's personhood. When we do so, we cut ourselves off from those who enlarge our relational possibilities, and we lessen ourselves as persons.

Keeping Sesha at home would not have been possible without an extensive and costly support system. Without these neither Sesha, nor her family, nor those who have come to know her would have come to realize the person she is. Her very personhood would have been denied; ours would have been diminished. But this sort of care is not cost-effective; it cannot be supported by a minimal budget grudgingly set aside for the mentally disabled. The costs can never be recuperated by Sesha's future earnings, and whatever costs might be saved are saved at the expense of those of us who undertake her care.

The view that community placement has as its goal the independence and productivity of the disabled operates with a concept of personhood quite different from the one I invoke here. It is one that depends on "rationality" and on the ability to partake in reciprocal cooperative arrangements. This independence and productivity can be justified as ultimately cost-effective because it turns persons who are dependent on others for support into self-supporting individuals. Cost-effectiveness then becomes part and parcel of the rationale for court decisions based on the ADA. So when it is not cost-effective to promote "independence" and "productivity"—if it would be more costly to promote these than to continue state support—then a way of life that is more self-determining, even when it is desired by the individual and recommended by state-appointed professionals, can be scrapped.

Disabled persons have fought hard for the right to live independently, to have access to work that suits their talents and temperaments, to be included among the "productive" and contributing members of society. They have insisted on their dignity, a dignity that refuses to be an object of pity and charity. They have argued that modifications and accommodations they may require to function independently and be productive should be classed with other antidiscrimination legislation, not glossed as exceptionalism or "special needs." And they have argued that treating disabled people as full citizens will ultimately reduce costs to the wider society, costs incurred by limiting the disabled to a debilitating dependency. Claims for inclusion, full dignity, and citizenship ought to apply in the case of a person with the sorts of dependencies, disabilities, and capabilities of Sesha as well as those who can be independent and productive. Is there a way to reconcile the needs of someone as inevitably dependent as Sesha with the concerns and analyses of those who have argued that both disability and the apparent dependency of disabled people are socially constructed?

Perhaps a way of including the severely intellectually impaired person and bestowing the dignity of citizenship is to interpret what it means to live independently, to be employed, and to be productive, in very broad terms. So, for example, if Sesha, in her adulthood, were to live in an apartment or group home with around-the-clock attendants, we would call this "independent living." If she can be made to partake in one tiny step in an assembly line production, and she is given some material compensation, we would call this "working" and being "productive"—whether or not this activity has any meaning for her.[8] To so stretch these concepts both empties them of meaning and undermines the possibility that dignity is compatible with life-long dependency. It means that when a disabled person requires attendants to help her dress, assist her mobility, or monitor a medical disability–related condition in order to be "independent," we mask a genuine dependency.

But who in any complex society is not dependent on others, for the production of our food, for our mobility, for a multitude of tasks that make it possible for each of us to function in our work and daily living? Many of these dependencies are hidden, as when we fail to think about our dependence on those who grow our food. Other dependencies are hypervisible, such as the dependence that results from certain disabilities or the dependence on state support of poor, single mothers who cannot simultaneously be employed (at minimum wage) and care for young or disabled children. But dependence that goes unacknowledged is still not independence.

Independence, except in some particular actions and functions, is a fiction, regardless of our disabilities, and the pernicious effects of this fiction are encouraged when we hide the ways in which our needs are met in relations of dependencies. On the other hand, this fiction turns those whose dependence cannot be masked into pariahs, or makes them objects of distain or pity. It causes us to refuse assistance when it is needed. It encourages us to either deny that assistance to others when they require it or to be givers of care because we fear having to receive care ourselves. In acknowledging dependency we respect the fact that as individuals our dependency relations are constitutive of who we are and that, as a society, we are inextricably dependent on one another. I suggest that it is perferable to refuse the contractarian basis for the distribution of benefits and burdens (that only those who assume their share of society's burdens are do a fair share of the benefits) and with it the myth of independence and an overemphasis on rationality. In acknowledging dependency we can borrow from what is best in Marx: that benefits and burdens are to be assigned by need and capability, respectively (cf. Nussbaum 2000).

Behind the ADA and the prohibition of discrimination is the deeper concept that physical or mental impairments should not result in lives devoid of the satisfactions for which we all yearn and which make life worth living. The satisfaction of those yearnings may take forms that are distinctive, but the disabled person—even when profoundly mentally retarded—is as entitled to them as the nondisabled. The principle that the disabled are as entitled as the nondisabled should not be held hostage to a notion that a disabled person must become "productive" or live "independently" if "suitably assisted," or that it is less costly to place an individual in a community rather than an institution.

SUPPORTING THE CAREGIVER—JUSTLY

The appalling conditions found in the global Willowbrooks, of which the psychiatric hospital in Mexico is only one example, are part of the history we thought we left behind when we moved large numbers of institutional residents into group homes. But the mistreatment, which largely had been attributed to the systemic inadequacies of what Goffman (1961) had called "total institutions," has resurfaced in group homes. The headline in the *Washington Post* announcing the criminal conduct of those who run many of the group homes in Washington, D.C., and the callousness and indifference of some of the staff, testify to the persistent nature of the problem of good care for the mentally retarded. And this case is only one among many (see Ohlemacher 2000; Tully 1999; and Boo 1999).

In "a society which defines and confines all meaning and worth in terms of production, profit, and pervasive greed," writes James Trent in his history of mental retardation, the intellectually disabled will be exploited (1994, 277). In such a society, their caretakers will also be exploited and will have the opportunity to become victimizers as well as victims. The change from institution to group home can help, but the form of the residence will not alter the poor care its residents receive if the caregivers are as abject as their charges. In such a society, care will be minimal, and callous caretakers will be inevitable.

Family Dependency Work

The home may not always be "a haven in a heartless world," but for the very vulnerable, connections with family members are often the only shield against the slings and arrows of an uncaring society. Family members are often, but not only (and not always), those whose ties are biological or legal, but are those "who by birth, adoption, marriage, or declared commitment share a deep personal connection and are mutually entitled to receive and obligated to provide support of various kinds to the extent possible, especially in times of need" (Levine 1990)

In the United States as well as in most other nations, state support for families who want to keep their family member home is far too limited and tends to be means-tested, providing relief only for families who are below a certain income. As one researcher states, "when programs are limited in scope and size, returning a person with disabilities to the community may be a euphemism for returning the child to the mother" (Nemzoff 1992, 20). Affluent as well as poor families find themselves overwhelmed with medical and caretaking responsibilities. The Kelso family, the father a CEO and the mother an activist for disabled people, made the front page of newspapers across the country when they abandoned their multiply disabled and medically fragile young son in a hospital during the Christmas holidays, when relief caregivers were in very short supply (Jacobs 1999).[9]

Given the circumstances families face, it is hardly a wonder that when families decide to place their child in residential care, there is an estrangement—an estrangement that comes with the relief of a burden too heavy to bear.[10] In group homes within the community there is a better likelihood that the protective connections will be retained, but not for individuals whose families have already lost touch. When families disappear from the scene, there are few who provide the oversight to assure that residents are not neglected or abused. The weight of the burden that causes the estrangement is less a function of the impairment per se than of the larger society's failure to help the family in its efforts to care for its disabled relative.

Although familial caregivers are as capable of neglect and abuse as strangers paid to care,[11] affective bonds that normally form between family members offer important defenses against the harmful behavior, especially when supports are available to ease hardships. It would seem that expenditures that aided mothers, fathers, grandmothers, and other family members who do the dependency work or continue to assume dependency responsibilities even when their relative is in residential care would be especially well spent.

Paid Dependency Workers

If unpaid familial caregivers need assistance in maintaining their relationship to their mentally disabled family member and keeping ties alive for the long haul, caregivers who do their work for pay need support in forming the bonds in the first place. Earlier I argued that abusive behavior by those who are charged with providing care is facilitated not only by the social devaluation of persons with mental disabilities, but also by the devaluation of the caregivers themselves. If we want to remove the prejudice and lack of understanding that blights the lives of people with mental retardation, we can begin by treating their caregivers as if their work mattered (because it does) and as if they mattered (because they do). To do this we need to provide caregivers with conditions that allow them to do their work well and receive just compensation. They need appropriate training, the opportunity to grow in their work, a voice in the care of their charges, compensation that matches the intensity of their labor, and encouragement in their sympathetic and empathic responses to their charges (see Bogdan and Taylor 1992).

I have argued elsewhere that when thinking about the care of dependents, we cannot employ the usual model of reciprocal cooperation, of the equal sharing of benefits and burdens (Kittay 1999). Those who are dependent (at least when, and to what extent, they are) cannot reciprocate the care that they receive. In our dependence, we cannot pay back our caregivers and compensate them for their labor. Another must do so. I have called this form of reciprocation *doulia,* after the doula, the contemporary postpartum caregiver who cares for the mother so that the mother can care for her new infant. I have called for a public conception of doulia, by which the larger society supports those who care for the "inevitably dependent" (dependent because of age, infirmity, or severe disability). I conceive of this as a principle of justice, in fact, a principle of justice that embraces those excluded by the contractual model of reciprocation. We need a principle of doulia for a caring that is justly compensated, and a justice that is caring.

JUST CARING AND CARING JUSTICE

At the beginning of this article, I proposed that advocating for severely and profoundly mentally retarded persons required simultaneously advocating for their caregivers: that such a project was not only just and caring, but was the only way to advocate effectively for the initial group. I have maintained that liberal conceptions of justice have excluded both those with severe developmental disabilities and those who are their caregivers. With a principle of doulia, we have seen how we can reconfigure justice so that the labor of caregiving is counted and rewarded as part of a broader idea of reciprocal social cooperation. Such an idea reflects the view that any society, and surely any decent society, has the care of dependents as one of its central functions.

With one stroke, dependents—be they small children or incapacitated adults, be the impairments physical or mental—become an integral part of any social organization. To presume that they stand outside of justice, that they are not entitled, that—for reasons of their impairments and dependence—they lack rights, seems odd indeed if the point and purpose of such principles (if not the sole one) is a social order that secures the ability to care for dependents.

Inevitable dependencies, the dependencies of our early years, old age, disability, and illness, however, have been privatized, so that we have come to discount them and the integral part of social life they in fact constitute. Doing so permits us to avoid our collective responsibility to maintain dependents. We forget the extent to which we need social organization to assure that should we become dependent, we will have the assistance we need, and to assure that should we have to care for dependents, we ourselves will not come to bear the full burden and become unable to meet our own needs. Not all of us will remain in a state of dependency as profound as that of my daughter. But any of us could become so—an illness or an accident could make us so. From the vantage point of our socially constructed independence, we might think, "Oh, but should that happen, I would rather be dead." From the vantage point of my daughter, that is wasteful of what life has to offer, a failure to appreciate the gifts of being.

Within the reigning liberal understanding of justice, we must continue to think of those with severe or profound cognitive disabilities as exceptional, as those who can never be citizens, whom we will care for out of compassion (or pity?), and who have no rights associated with their needs. If we meet their needs, it is out of a gratuitous kindness, a kindness they have no right to demand. As "exceptions" then, those with profound developmental and cognitive impairments are vulnerable to the vicissitudes, indignities, and stigma of being passive recipients of charity.

However, it may be that calling for charity and benevolence is sufficient for protecting this portion of the disabled population from neglect and abuse, that it is unnecessary to overhaul long-standing treatments of justice because they exclude the retarded. Can't we argue from benevolence and charity that the mentally retarded should not be neglected and abused? Indeed, to invoke "the stigma of being passive recipients of charity" and to speak, as I did earlier, of generosity as uncertain and gratuitous may be prejudicing the case and may be mere rhetoric. Is charity really inadequate? Why insist on a full-blown notion of personhood or citizenship to cover those whom so many have so long viewed as falling short, as inappropriate subjects for justice?

Let us concede, for the sake of argument, that the severely retarded do not have claims to citizenship and may not even be persons. Still, they should not be harmed, because doing so diminishes those in the larger society who would do the harm or allow the harm. Just as cruelty to animals may be immoral not because of what it does to the animal, but because of what it does to those who inflict the cruelty, so we should not be cruel to the mentally retarded. Is this not sufficient to protect the severely retarded from neglect and abuse?

If such thinking is the basis for providing aid, the aid will, of necessity, be a low priority in any public distribution of resources. It will tend to be minimal, except in cases in which individual acts of generosity surface. But if such support is minimal, those who do the dependency work for this population will, as is now the case, be only minimally rewarded for their labors. The respect they gain for their work will be similarly minimal. The low pay and lack of respect will encourage the conditions that breed the neglect and abuse that calls for charity and benevolence were intended to counter.

For nonhuman animals it may be sufficient to invoke the principle that harm inflicted on them is wrong because of what it does to those who do the injury. Nonhuman animals can fend for themselves, if they are not harmed or interfered with by humans. But the fate of human beings who are impaired is intimately tied in with other humans—especially those who provide care. Not being harmed is only part of what we require when we are dependent, and the lack of care—the full-blown sort, not the labor mechanically carried out—is equivalent to harm. How the care is bestowed makes all the difference between the potential for harm and spirit-sustaining aid.

Care is a costly morality: costly in the personal and emotional resources it demands and in the time it consumes (time that cannot be devoted to investing in a career or advancing oneself materially). When care is not adequately supported, either the cost of care is borne by the caregiver alone or the charge fails to receive adequate care—or both suffer. If the retarded person should be treated with charity and benevolence because she should not be harmed, then she must be treated with an enlarged concept of justice—a justice large enough to embrace her and her (familial and nonfamilial) caregivers—that gives a right to care and support for care. Only then can the most vulnerable of disabled people hope to be safe and able to develop and flourish as persons in a just and caring society.

To stigmatize dependency, ignore its frequency, and valorize only a particular segment of human possibility is to shirk our collective responsibility to take care of one another and to ensure that we are well taken care of by someone for whom our well-being matters deeply. Looking at justice through a lens of social constructionism that only sees dependence as constructed and fails to see independence as still more constructed will only reinstate prejudices against disability. This time the prejudice falls most heavily on the shoulders of the severely and profoundly mentally retarded, who are the most vulnerable and whose enormous dependencies cannot be nullified by environmental modifications. But we exclude them from justice at a cost. That cost is the denial of the dependent animals we are. It is a condition no amount of rationality can alter.

Although care seems to have less in common with rights and justice than with virtues and benevolence, the virtue and kind hand of care requires a just setting in which to blossom. In a context of condescending pity (toward the mentally impaired dependent) and exploitative demands (toward the dependency worker), the inequality between dependent and dependency worker too easily fosters domination rather than caring. In a society ruled by the conceptions of liberalism, where rights are "trump cards," charity and benevolence can never replace the guarantees of human dignity that entitlements of justice provide. In the end, this may be the great achievement of liberalism. It is one that we cannot forgo, no matter how much we challenge liberalism in our hope for a more progressive, a more inclusive, and a more caring political vision than it now provides. Justice that is caring begins with an acknowledgment of our dependency and seeks to organize society so that our well-being is not inversely related to our need for care or to care; such justice makes caring itself a mode of just action.

CODA—AN ACKNOWLEDGMENT

For my daughter dependence of the most profound sort will be part of her normal existence. But such dependence does not preclude a certain form of mutual dependence. I depend on her as well. Sesha and her well-being are essential to my own. Her smile chases away the trivial distractions of the day. Her embrace grounds me in what is important and precious. Watching her grow and develop skills and take pride in her accomplishments nurtures me as much as my own work. In another place I've written: "It's perhaps self-delusional to say that I am as dependent on her as she is on me, but perhaps not. Others could take care of her and even love her— in fact, I must think that she will continue to thrive with or without me. But without her, I would wither" (Kittay 2000b). Writing that passage, acknowledging that I was even more dependent on her than she on me, was itself a moment of discovery.

Although my daughter can never be "productive" or pay back to society anything of material value, still her contributions are great. Her sweetness radiates and enriches the lives of everyone she touches, those who allow themselves to be touched by her. Without her abundant and exuberant love, the world would be a more dismal place. I am only beginning to fill volumes with what I have learned from her.

NOTES

This chapter originally appeared in *Public Culture: Society for Transnational Cultural Studies* (Special Issue: The Critical Limits of Embodiment) 13, no. 3 (fall 2001): 557–79. Copyright © 2001 by Eva Feder Kittay. Reprinted with permission.

1. A word about the term *mental retardation*. In speaking of mental retardation, some speak of mental disabilities, or cognitive or intellectual disabilities, or developmental disabilities, or being mentally challenged. I reject the last term as condescending. Although

only mental retardation captures precisely the population I address, I vary the terms with a sensitivity to their over- or underinclusiveness.

2. With this remark, Justice Oliver Wendell Holmes justified upholding the state's right to determine that Carrie Bell, a "feeble-minded woman" residing in a state institution, should be sterilized (*Buck v. Bell,* 274 U.S. 208 [1927).

3. Macintyre (1999) and Nussbaum (2000) tie our dependency to our continuity with other animals.

4. Rawls, in fact, does not seem to think that the individual who is permanently impaired in such a way that he or she cannot fully participate in social cooperation throughout a life is not a citizen. See my discussion of this point in Kittay 1999, 105n. 178.

5. See Sachs 1999 for a report on the hurdles put in the way of persons with mental retardation and other mental disabilities by changes in the immigration law that took effect in 1994.

6. See Becker 2000 for an account of the good of agency and the ADA.

7. I take species membership to be central to our understanding of personhood, as does Diamond (1991). The kiss I share with another human is distinctively human. I argue that to reduce what makes us persons to a set of defined characteristics is a mistake. See Kittay 2000a.

8. These are all interpretations that I have, in fact, heard applied to very severely retarded adults.

9. Manning 2000 places the Kelso case into the context of others raising children with serious medical and mental disabilities.

10. Reported in discussion with the director of Sullivan County Diagnostic Center in Sullivan County, New York.

11. See Bonner and Rimer 2000 for a report on Johnny Paul Penry, a retarded man and convicted rapist and murderer in Texas, who suffered abuse at the hands of his mother.

REFERENCES

Becker, Lawrence C. 2000. The Good of Agency. In *Americans with Disabilities: Exploring Implications of Law for Individuals and Institutions,* edited by Leslie Pickering Francis and Anita Silvers. New York: Routledge.

Bogdan, Robert, and Steven J. Taylor. 1992. "The Social Construction of Humanness." In *Interpreting Disability: A Qualitative Reader,* edited by Philip M. Ferguson, Diane L. Ferguson, and Steven J. Taylor. New York: Teachers College Press.

Bonner, Raymond, and Sara Rimer. 2000. "Mentally Retarded Man Facing Texas Execution Draws Wide Attention." *New York Times,* November 12, A1.

Boo, Katherine. 1999. "Invisible Lives: Troubled System for the Retarded." *Washington Post,* December 5, A1, 3.

Cushing, Pamela, and Tanya Lewis. N.d. "Negotiating Mutuality and Agency in Care-giving Relationships with Women with Intellectual Disabilities." Unpublished manuscript.

DeSelincourt, Ernest, ed. 1935. *The Early Letters of William and Dorothy Wordsworth (1787–1805),* 295–96. Oxford: Clarendon. Quoted in James W. Trent, *The Invention of the Feeble Mind* (Berkeley: University of California Press, 1995), 9.

Diamond, Cora. 1991. The Importance of Being Human. In *Human beings,* edited by David Cockburn, Cambridge: Cambridge University Press.

Ferguson, Philip M. 1994. *Abandoned to their fate: Social policy and Practices toward Severely Retarded People in America,* Philadelphia: Temple University Press.

Gastmans, Chris, Bernadette Dierckx de Casterlé, and Paul Schotsmans. 1998. Nursing Considered as Moral Practice: A Philosophical-Ethical Interpretation of Nursing. *Kennedy Institute of Ethics Journal* 8: 43–69.

Goffman, Erving. 1961. *Asylum: Essays on the Social Situation of Mental Patients and Other Inmates.* New York: Anchor.

Goodin, Robert. 1985. *Protecting the Vulneruble: A Reanalysis of Our Social Responsibilities.* Chicago: University of Chicago Press.

Hingsburger, David. 2000. *First Contact: Charting Inner Space.* Quebec: Diverse City.

Jacobs, Andrew. 1999. "Pennsylvania Couple Accused of Abandoning Disabled Son." *New York Times,* December 31, Al.

Kittay, Eva F. 1999. *Love's Labor: Essays on Equality, Women, and Dependency.* New York: Routledge.

———. 2000a. "Relationality, Impairment and Peter Singer on the Fate of Severely Impaired Infants." *APA Newsletter on Philosophy and Medicine* 99: 253–56.

———. 2000b. "At Home with My Daughter." In *Americans with Disabilities,* edited by Leslie Pickering Francis and Anita Silvers. New York: Routledge.

Levine, Carol. 1990. "AIDS and Changing Concepts of the Family." *The Milbunk Quarterly* 68: 33–57.

Locke, John. 1987. *An Essay Concerning Human Understanding.* Edited and foreword by Peter H. Nidditch. New York: Oxford University Press.

Macintyre, Alisdair. 1999. *Dependent Rational Animals.* Peru, Ill.: Carus.

Manning, Anita. 2000. "Quietly Overwhelmed." *USA Today,* January 17, Al.

Nemzoff, Ruth, E. 1992. "Changing Perceptions of Mothers of Children with Developmental Disabilities 1960–1992: A Critical Review." Working Paper, Working Paper Series. Center on Research on Women: Wellesley College, Wellesley, Mass.

Nussbaum, Martha C. 2000. "The Future of Feminist Liberalism." Presidential address given at the annual meeting of the American Philosophical Association, Central Division, Chicago, April 22.

Ohlemacher, Stephen. 2000. "Retarded Patients Lack Protection, Study Finds." *Cleveland Plain Dealer,* January 8, 1A.

Rawls, John. 1972. *A Theory of Justice.* Cambridge: Harvard University Press.

———. 1980. "Kantian Constructivism in Moral Theory: The Dewey Lectures, 1980." *Journal of Philosophy* 77: 515–72.

———. 1992. *Political Liberalism.* New York: Columbia University Press.

Sachs, Susan. 1999. "An I.N.S. Hurdle for the Disabled: Promised Exemptions Elude Many Would-Be Citizens." *New York Times,* February 18, B1.

Scheper-Hughes, Nancy. 1992. *Death without Weeping: The Violence of Everyday Life in Brazil.* Berkeley: University of California Press.

Silvers, Anita, David Wasserman, and Mary Mahowald. 1998. *Disability, Difference, Discrimination.* Lanham, MD.: Rowman & Littlefield.

Trent, James W. 1995. *The Invention of the Feeble Mind.* Berkeley: University of California Press.

Tully, Tracy. 1999. "Retarded are Found Living in Squalor." *New York Daily News,* July 12, A7.

Vobejda, Barbara. 2000. "City Wards Face Daily Indignities: Documents Illustrate the Suffering of Mentally Retarded in D.C. System." *Washington Post*, February 15, A1.

Wertz, Dorothy. 2000. "Drawing the Line." In *The Ethics of Prenatal Testing and Selective Abortion: A Report From the Hastings Center*, edited by Adrienne Asch and Eric Parens. Philadelphia: Temple University Press.

Winerip, Michael. 2000. "The Global Willowbrook." *New York Times Magazine*, January 16, 58–67.

12

Poverty, Race, and the Distortion of Dependency: The Case of Kinship Care

Dorothy E. Roberts

INTRODUCTION

The inevitable dependency of children requires financial support of children and those who care for them. Law and public policy in the United States assume that caregiving is primarily a private matter. For example, parents are supposed to bear the costs of caring for their children. Martha Fineman,[1] Eva Feder Kittay,[2] and other feminist scholars have shown that relying on private arrangements for inevitable dependencies has negative consequences for women.[3] The nuclear family norm gives women the responsibility of caregiving, while denying them adequate government support and vilifying those who do not depend on husbands. Mothers who are unable to rely on a male breadwinner or their own income to raise their children must pay a high price for state support. The U.S. welfare state provides stingy benefits to poor mothers, who are stigmatized and encumbered by behavioral regulations.[4] Mothers must waive privacy rights as a condition of receiving public aid.[5] The law permits bureaucratic surveillance of clients to determine their eligibility based on both means- and morals-testing, to check their conformance to behavioral mandates, and to guarantee that they are spending benefits properly. The Personal Responsibility and Work Opportunity Reconciliation Act of 1996 (PRWORA)[6] converted welfare from a federal entitlement to a means for states to influence poor mothers' work, marital, and child-bearing decisions.[7]

Less explored by feminist legal scholars is the role of the public child welfare system in caregiving by poor mothers. The child welfare system intervenes when parents are alleged to have abused or neglected their children.[8] State child protective agencies may provide services to these families while keeping them intact or after removing children from the home to be placed in foster care. Although fewer families are involved with child protective services than with the welfare system, the number of children in state custody is alarming. There are more than a half-million children in foster care.[9] The vast majority of these children are poor.[10] Not only is child maltreatment highly correlated with poverty,[11] but child neglect is also defined and interpreted in a way that subjects greater numbers of poor families to state surveillance and intervention.[12] Black children are grossly overrepresented in child welfare caseloads: Nearly half of all children in foster care nationwide are black, although black children are less than 20 percent of the nation's youth.[13] The child welfare system, then, is a significant means of public support of poor children, especially poor black children. It is important for theorists interested in dependency to explore critically the child welfare system's treatment of dependency relationships in the families under state supervision.

The consequences for families involved in the child welfare system are even more devastating than the burdens attached to receiving welfare. Involvement in the child welfare system entails intensive supervision by child protection agencies, which often includes losing legal custody of children to the state. This state intrusion is typically viewed as necessary to protect maltreated children from parental harm. But many parents become involved in the child welfare system because it is the only way to receive needed financial support for their children. I argue in this chapter that transferring parental authority to the state is the price poor black mothers must often pay for state recognition of their children's dependency. Valuing the dependency relationship between black children and their mothers would require providing the resources mothers need to care properly for their children. Racism, however, helps to distort the state's approach to the dependency relationship. The history of African enslavement and a long-standing mythology about black maternal unfitness reinforce the view of black mothers as themselves dependent. The dependency of black children on their mothers, moreover, is treated as a source of intergenerational depravity. Instead of acknowledging and respecting the dependency relationship between black children and their mothers, the state takes authority of the children as a condition of financial support.

In this chapter, I focus on kinship foster care as an example of the distortion of dependency that requires relinquishing legal custody of children to gain access to necessary public resources. Kinship foster care replaces a traditional, private African American family arrangement with a similar structure that is regulated by state child welfare agencies. I examine the consequences for dependency relationships of transforming kinship care from a predominantly private family network to a widely used source of public foster care. Although formal kinship care provides needed financial support for caregiving, it requires making children state wards, and the amount of state payments is correlated to the level of state supervision of caregivers. Incorporating kinship care into the child welfare system often harms families by disrupting, rather than preserving, ties among kin. I contend that the government's failure to respect dependency relationships in these kin networks stems from the child welfare system's more general failure to recognize the social context of dependency and to provide state support for caregiving. The onerous price exacted from poor black families for public assistance demonstrates the need for fundamental change in our philosophy of dependency and caregiving.

THE TRANSFORMATION OF KINSHIP CARE

Kinship care is one response to children's dependency. Mothers have long relied on relatives and neighbors to help them care for their children. Black women in particular share a rich tradition of women-centered, communal child care.[14] These cooperative networks have included members of the extended family (grandmothers, sisters, aunts, and cousins) as well as nonblood kin and neighbors.[15] Their relationship with children ranges from daily assistance to long-term care or informal adoption. Carol Stack's classic research in the "Flats," for example, revealed that many children there moved back and forth between households of close female relatives.[16] Three or more women related to a child formed a cooperative domestic network, taking turns assuming parental responsibility toward the child.

Kinship care historically had a double-edged relationship to the child welfare system. Child rearing by relatives was often a response to poverty and other hardships that made it difficult for parents to raise children by themselves.[17] Indeed, for a century black families had no recourse to the formal child welfare system. blacks were virtually excluded from openly segregated child welfare services until the end of World War II.[18] The late-nineteenth-century orphanages established to rescue destitute immigrant children refused to accept blacks. The few "colored orphan asylums" were woefully inferior and overcrowded. Black people relied primarily on extended family networks and community resources such as churches, women's clubs, and benevolent societies to take care of children whose parents were unable to meet their needs.[19]

Kinship care continued in more recent decades as an informal safety net for struggling black families. By temporarily moving children to the care of kin, parents could avoid either voluntarily relinquishing them to the state or running the risk of coercive state intervention.[20] Kinship care, then, served as a family-preserving alternative to foster care. Skyrocketing female incarceration rates, cutbacks in social services, the AIDS epidemic, and maternal substance abuse led to a resurgence in caregiving by relatives, especially grandmothers, in the late 1980s.[21] Between 1980 and 1990, the number of children living with grandparents increased by 44 percent.[22] By 1994, nearly four million children lived in grandparent-headed households.[23] Almost half of children being raised by grandparents were black.[24]

Kinship care, on the other hand, also invited state intrusion. The black community's cultural tradition of sharing parenting responsibilities among kin has been mistaken as parental neglect.[25] Because mothers who depend on kinship care do not fit the middle-class norm of a primary caregiver supported by her husband and paid child care, they seem to have abrogated their duty toward their children.[26] Ironically, Illinois, a state that now relies heavily on kinship foster care, considered children who lived with relatives other than their parents to be neglected less than a decade ago.[27]

While state child welfare agencies used to consider private kinship care neglectful, they now increasingly turn to relatives to place neglected and abused children. As a matter of definition, private kinship care is arranged by families without child welfare agency involvement; kinship foster care, meanwhile, is provided to children who are in the legal custody of the state.[28] Between 1986 and 1990, the proportion of foster children living with relatives grew from 18 percent to 31 percent in twenty-five states.[29] By 1997, there were at least as many relative caregivers as traditional foster parents in California, Illinois, and New York.[30] An exploding foster care population combined with a shortage of licensed nonrelative foster homes made relatives an attractive placement option.[31] The passage of federal law encouraging family preservation and court decisions guaranteeing relatives the opportunity to serve as foster care providers also facilitated this development.[32] In the landmark decision *Miller v. Youakim*, for example, the U.S. Supreme Court held that otherwise eligible relatives could not be denied foster parent certification and the same financial support as nonkin providers.[33]

Just as private kinship care has been especially prevalent among black families, most children placed in kinship foster care are black.[34] This is both because of the overrepresentation of black children in the foster care population and because agencies are more likely to turn to relatives in the case of black children than with other children. Kinship care is the main type of out-of-home placement for black children in New York City, Chicago, and Philadelphia.[35] In fact, almost all—90 percent—of relative caregivers in Chicago are black.[36]

Compared to nonkin foster care, kinship foster care has many advantages for children. It usually preserves family, community, and cultural ties. For most people, staying in the extended family is in and of itself a benefit for children. Children are more likely to maintain contact with their parents and to remain with siblings if they are living with relatives than if they are placed in nonrelative foster care.[37] It is likely that children are already familiar with the kin caregiver, so the placement avoids that trauma of moving in with strangers.[38] Kinship foster care usually allows children to stay in their communities and to continue the cultural traditions their parents observe. Kinship foster care is more stable: Children living with relatives are less likely to be moved to multiple placements while in substitute care.[39] There is also evidence that children are better cared for by relatives than by strangers: More children in kinship foster care reported that they felt loved and happy, and fewer are abused while in state custody.[40]

Kinship foster care, then, is a chief state response to the dependency of poor black children: it provides financial support for relatives' caregiving. Public assistance is especially significant, because kinship caregivers tend to have limited means and have substantially lower incomes than traditional foster parents.[41] Although federal child welfare policy promotes kinship foster care, it gives states wide latitude in creating the system of financial support for kin caregivers.[42] The level of state support for kinship caregivers is directly correlated with the level of state intrusion into their lives: the higher the payment, the greater the intensity of state supervision. The two principal sources of public financial assistance for relatives are Temporary Assistance to Needy Families (TANF) and foster care benefits.[43] All states offer TANF benefits to relatives caring for children, as they do to other needy families.[44] Foster care stipends, however, are much larger than TANF benefits, and they are multiplied by each child in the home, instead of the marginal increase per child under TANF.[45] A relative caring for several children might receive two to four times as much in foster care payments as she would in welfare benefits.[46]

This difference in levels of support reflects the government's perverse willingness to give more financial aid to children in state custody than to children in the custody of their parents. Relatives can take advantage of the higher benefit level of foster care only by becoming involved in the child protection system. As Jill Duerr Berrick, director of the Berkeley Center for Social Services Research, observes, "This disparity spawns concerns that the foster care payment system may act as an incentive for a troubled family to seek a formal agency-supervised placement with kin rather than sharing child-rearing responsibilities informally with the same relatives."[47] In addition to a stipend, kin foster parents are entitled to Medicaid, clothing allowances, and other assistance to meet the children's needs. Moreover, child welfare agencies make available services that address the parents' problems, such as drug treatment, mental health counseling, and housing assistance, only to families under their supervision.

The amount of kinship foster care payments, in turn, depends on whether or not the kin caregiver is licensed by the state child welfare agency. Most states require relatives to meet the same licensing requirements as nonrelative foster parents to receive foster care payments.[48] The licensing process involves another layer of intrusion into relatives' lives. The agency inspects relatives' homes, including sleeping arrangements, the number of bedrooms, and square footage, and investigates relatives' backgrounds to check for compliance with strict licensing requirements.[49] If relatives are not licensed, they are paid less than licensed foster parents. In some states, unlicensed kin caregivers receive only the TANF child-only benefit; in others, they receive a lower foster care payment.[50]

Finally, several states have implemented an intermediate arrangement called subsidized guardianship. Guardianship gives legal custody to relative caretakers, thus permitting children to stay with relatives on a long-term basis while avoiding the need to terminate parental rights to "free" children for adoption.[51] It addresses the situation of children in kinship foster care who have little chance of either being adopted by the relative or being reunited with their parents. Kin caregivers often reject adoption as both unnecessary for and disruptive of family ties. Many have already made a lifetime commitment to the children in their care, while terminating parental rights to permit adoption would create an adversarial relationship with relatives.[52] Guardians are given a level of state support that reflects the extent of their authority over the children in their care; they typically receive stipends that are less than foster care stipends, but more than TANF benefits.[53]

Thus, families involved in kinship care must exchange a degree of autonomy and independence in child rearing that is in proportion to the amount of financial support they receive from the government. The price of the highest amount of aid—foster care benefits—is relinquishing custody of children to the state and submitting to foster care regulations and supervision by the child welfare system.

THE PRICE OF STATE SUPPORT

Making kinship care part of the child welfare system has a dramatic impact on the relationships of family members and on their relationship to the state. Foster care assistance is only available to state wards. The family must therefore transfer legal custody of the children to the state child welfare agency. In addition, relatives must be approved by the child welfare agency to care for children in its custody. The kin network is transformed from a "natural family" to a "foster family." In *Smith v. Organization of Foster Families for Equality and Reform*,[54] the U.S. Supreme Court upheld limitations on the rights of foster parents on the grounds that a foster family has "its source in state law and contractual arrangements."[55] In the case of kinship care, the extended family exchanges its autonomy over child raising for financial support and services needed to raise its children. Instead of respecting the dependency relations between children and their mothers or kin caregivers, the state appropriates that relationship.

Relatives may become foster parents when the family seeks assistance from child welfare agencies or when agencies seek relatives to provide foster care for children removed from their parents. Increasingly, parents "voluntarily" place their children in foster care to gain access to financial assistance and services needed for caregiving. The number of children in private kinship care has decreased since 1994, while the number in kinship foster care has increased,[56] suggesting that many black extended families are turning to the child welfare system for support.

When a parent turns a child over to foster care, it is rarely truly voluntary. In some cases, desperate parents reluctantly approach the child welfare agency only when they can find no other source of government support. The parents may be too ill or stressed out to care for their children, or their children may need services they cannot afford. The AIDS epidemic has caused an explosion of poor minority mothers who need state assistance for both reasons. Other parents agree to short-term placement or surrender custody as a way of avoiding abuse or neglect proceedings. Some parents believe it is better to voluntarily place their child in foster care for a brief period than to risk child protective authorities taking the child for a long time. Giving up custody to the state has become the price of public support for poor and low-income children. The state then provides to foster parents the very services it denied to the parents. Respite care, for example, is often subsidized by the state for foster parents—but not parents—of children with serious mental health problems.[57]

Parents who turn to child protective services for help often find themselves in an adversarial relationship. Once child welfare agencies have custody of children, they take control of child rearing and place conditions on parents' involvement. Parents have no say over where their children are placed or in important decisions about their children's health, education, and religious and cultural upbringing or even how often they can see them. The child welfare agency may require parents to complete training courses and therapy sessions as a condition of reunification. Most devastating, it may refuse to return children when parents are ready to take them back.[58]

Kinship foster care also requires waiver of protections against state intrusion in family life. Thus, although the children are cared for by kin, it is the state that has authority over them. The parents and kin caregivers must submit to surveillance by caseworkers and requirements that the agency prescribes. Kin foster parents must comply with agency rules specifying the type of home and care they provide, and they must allow periodic visits by caseworkers to check compliance. They must give the agency access to personal information and may have to undergo psychological evaluations. The child may be represented by a guardian ad litem, adding another outsider who has a voice in family affairs.[59] The family also runs the risk that the agency will move the children to another foster home if the relatives fail to comply with agency demands.

Kinship foster care not only gives insufficient support to families, but it often affirmatively harms them. One of the most perplexing discoveries from recent empirical research is that children placed with relatives remain in state custody longer.[60] According to University of Chicago social work professor James P. Gleeson, "[s]tudies in several states have demonstrated lower return home and lower adoption rates for children in formal kinship care than for those in nonrelative care."[61] Although researchers have no definitive explanation, the increased time spent in foster care may result from the inadequacy of reunification and other services provided to families involved in kinship care. The incentives for families themselves to prefer children to remain longer with kin foster caregivers probably also plays a role in delaying reunification. Parents whose children are living with relatives rather than strangers may be less anxious to regain custody because the entire family is comfortable with the living arrangement and because the higher level of financial support foster care provides is needed.[62] Total family income may drop precipitously if children leave grandmother's care to return home. In California, children in kinship homes receiving foster care benefits were half as likely to be reunited with their parents after four years as were children in kinship homes receiving lower welfare benefits.[63] This financial disparity appears to have the greatest impact on black families: "African American children in kinship homes supported by the foster care subsidy remained in care approximately twice as long as all other children."[64] All of these reasons suggest that kinship foster care imposes powerful incentives on poor black families and caseworkers to keep children in state custody. Even with inadequate services and loss of family autonomy, kinship foster care offers the only avenue for needed public support for many children.

Kinship care, which historically kept black families together, sometimes disrupts family relationships when incorporated in the public child welfare system. Madeleine Kurtz, a clinical professor at New York University School of Law, argues that because traditional foster care rules are based on the nuclear family model, they "frustrate the extent to which children might be maintained by extended family."[65] Kurtz presents a case from the New York child welfare system to show that kinship foster care encourages the unnecessary severance of family ties. Nora became the kinship foster caregiver for her infant granddaughter, Evelyn, who was born exposed to crack cocaine.[66] When Evelyn was three years old, the agency obtained an order terminating Nora's daughter's parental rights and Evelyn became a ward of the state. Ending the mother's legal status meant that Nora was only a foster parent—an employee of the state hired to take care of Evelyn; she was no longer Evelyn's legal grandmother.[67] The family lost all of the protections against state disruption that kinship bonds ordinarily afford. So when the agency determined that Nora had a drinking problem and was not an appropriate adoptive parent for Evelyn, it had virtually complete discretion to move Evelyn to a more suitable family.[68] As Kurtz puts it, because Nora had broken the agency's rules, the agency was permitted to "fire a bad foster parent and find a better home for its foster child."[69] No longer a grandmother or a foster parent, Nora—and the rest of Evelyn's family—lacked standing to challenge the agency's plan for Evelyn. Transforming a private kinship care arrangement into a formal one put the family at a disadvantage in its relationship to the state. If Nora had never become a foster parent, her alleged drinking problem could not so easily have justified the destruction of her bonds with her granddaughter.

The transformation of kinship care from a private to a state-run arrangement devalues relatives' caregiving and suppresses the historical strengths of this family form. Social scientists have remarked at the success of black kin networks in meeting the challenges of raising children under conditions of poverty and racial discrimination.[70] Some have called for policymakers to "affirm a black family kinship system that was historically strong, intact, resilient and adaptive."[71] Yet research shows that many caseworkers devalue the important role that kin traditionally have had in helping to raise children.[72] A study of caseworkers serving children in kinship care in Illinois, for example, revealed that caseworkers failed to involve kin caregivers or the rest of the extended family in making long-term plans for the children.[73] According to the study's authors, "permanency plans appear to be made primarily by child welfare caseworkers, their supervisors, and other service providers rather than by the persons who will have to live with the consequences of these decisions."[74] They attributed the lack of involvement by kin both to the bureaucratic nature of child welfare practice and to caseworkers' lack of understanding of kin participation in child rearing as a cultural strength of

African American families.[75] To a large extent, the suppression of kin involvement in decision making is an inherent feature of foster care because it requires relinquishing legal custody of children.

The child welfare system also devalues relative caregivers in its distribution of services. Agencies tend to devote fewer resources to reunification of children in kinship foster care with their parents.[76] Caseworkers have less contact with relatives and the children in their care and are less likely to offer them services.[77] A lawsuit filed in 1986 by the Legal Aid Society on behalf of children in kinship foster care in New York City charged that the child welfare agency delayed paying relatives their stipends and issuing children their Medicaid cards and failed to provide families with necessities such as beds, clothes, and school supplies.[78]

It seems that some agencies view placing children with relatives as a way of cutting costs. Perhaps they believe that children need fewer services if they are being cared for by a grandmother or an aunt. But many kinship caregivers come from poor or low-income families like the grandchildren, nieces, and nephews placed in their homes. They are more likely to be single females and to have less income, more health problems, and more children to take care of than do nonrelative foster parents.[79] Kinship caregivers are therefore in *greater* need of state assistance. Because black children are the most likely to be placed with relatives, these policies systematically provide inferior financial support and services for black children in state custody.[80]

DEPENDENCY AND RACIAL INJUSTICE

Kinship foster care devalues the dependency relationship between black children and their caregivers by providing them with inferior support and by requiring caregivers to relinquish custody of children as a condition of receiving support. Far from respecting dependency relationships in these families, the state bypasses these relationships by treating black caregivers as themselves dependent and by taking direct authority over their children. This distortion of dependency reflects and perpetuates the historical subordination of black people in the United States. The view of black parents as dependent originated in the regime of chattel slavery. Slave law installed white masters as the head of an extended plantation family that included their slaves. The plantation family ruled by white men was considered the best institution to transmit moral values to uncivilized Africans.[81] Courts reasoned that the slave owners' moral authority over the family was ordained by divine imperative. Slaves, on the other hand, had no legal authority over their children.

Legal scholar Peggy Cooper Davis powerfully reveals that a critical aspect of slave masters' control of their slaves was the restriction of slaves' capacity to educate and socialize their children.[82] In this way, whites attempted to prevent slaves from constructing their own system of morals and from acting according to their own chosen values. Slaveholders proclaimed their moral authority by reinforcing the message of parental helplessness, frequently whipping adult slaves in front of their children. The sale of children apart from their parents was another brutal incarnation of this power.

Stereotypes about black people continue to paint them as dependent and in need of white supervision. Particularly relevant is a popular mythology that portrays black women as bad mothers. Three prominent images of black mothers cast them as pathological: the careless black mother, the matriarch, and the welfare queen. These images reflect traits black women are supposed to have that are detrimental to their children. It is believed that black women neglect their children because they do not care enough about them, create a fatherless family structure that provides inadequate supervision of their children, and teach their children an attitude of dependence on government handouts.

The ideal black mother figure, Mammy, selflessly nurtured her master's children, but not her own. Mammy, while caring for her master's children, remained under the constant supervision of her white mistress. She had no real authority over either the white children she raised or the black children she bore. In contrast, whites portrayed slave mothers as negligent and unable to care for their own children. A contemporary image of the careless black mother who harms her children is the pregnant crack addict. Despite similar rates of substance abuse during pregnancy by white and black women, the media erroneously suggested that the problem was most prevalent among blacks.[83] The pregnant crack addict was portrayed as a black woman who put her love for crack above her love for her children. Modern social pundits have also held black mothers responsible for the disintegration of the black family. Stereotypes about deviant black mothers and absent black fathers together form a picture of dysfunctional black families.

Another contemporary image of black mothers is the welfare queen, the lazy mother who refuses to work and breeds children to fatten her monthly check from the government. It is assumed that these mothers cannot be trusted to spend their benefits for the care of their children instead of wasting them on drugs, fancy clothes, and entertainment for themselves. The state therefore supervises them to ensure that benefits are devoted to their children's welfare. Contemporary poverty rhetoric blames poor black mothers for perpetuating welfare dependency by transmitting a deviant lifestyle to their children.[84] Part of the impetus for welfare reform was the sense that payments to black mothers merely encourage this transgenerational pathology. Welfare reform discourse also paid little attention to the relationship between poor black mothers and their children, rarely questioning the impact of compelling these women to leave their young children to find low-paid jobs. This belief that poor black mothers have nothing beneficial to impart to their children helps to legitimate the state's distortion of the dependency relationship.

The continuity of these derogatory maternal stereotypes over centuries suggests that they have a real impact on the state's relationship to black families. All of these myths about black mothers cast them as dependent, devalue their care-giving role, and confirm the need for state supervision of their children. Thus, racism supports the state's distortion of dependency that requires relinquishing authority over children in exchange for public support.

THE FLAWED PHILOSOPHY OF CHILD WELFARE

The distortion of dependency in kinship foster care also stems from a flawed philosophy of child welfare. The state justifies its intrusion into families that receive public support through the child welfare system on the grounds that it is necessary to protect children. Parents referred to child protective services have maltreated their children and must be rehabilitated to ensure it is safe to return their children to them. Foster parents must be carefully regulated to guarantee that they are using subsidies for the benefit of the state wards in their care. Harvard law professor Elizabeth Bartholet, for example, begrudges relatives the stipends they receive to care for foster children, especially if, in the case of subsidized guardianship, they are not "subject to the state supervision that goes with foster parenting."[85] She questions relatives' motives: "For extended family members at the poverty level, as many relatives of victims of maltreatment will be, these stipends may make it worthwhile to agree to foster whether or not they have any capacity or motivation to parent."[86] The transformation of kinship care, however, shows that many families must relinquish custody of children to the state and submit to government supervision because of their poverty more than their maltreatment.

The price the child welfare system exacts for its support stems from an underlying philosophy that ignores the social context of dependency. The child welfare system is built upon the presumption that children's basic needs for sustenance and development will and can be met solely by parents.[87] The state intervenes to provide special institutionalized services—primarily placing children in foster care—only when parents fail to fulfill their caregiving obligations. The child protection approach is inextricably tied to our society's refusal to see a collective responsibility for children's welfare. It is a society willing to pay billions of dollars a year on maintaining poor children as state wards outside their homes, but only a fraction of that on child welfare services to intact families.

This approach to child welfare is defective in three related ways. First, it places all responsibility for taking care of children on their parents, without taking into account the economic, political, and social constraints that prevent many parents from doing so. Most single mothers, for example, face numerous barriers to providing for their children, including a segregated job market, inadequate wages, and a dearth of affordable child care.[88] The child welfare system hides the systemic reasons for families' hardships by laying the blame on individual parents' failings. "The underlying philosophy of the present child welfare system is that *all* families *should* be able to function adequately with-

out the assistance of society," explain Andrew Billingsley and Jeanne Giovannoni, "and that failure to perform the parental role without such assistance is
indicative of individual pathology."[89]

A second defect is that child protection is activated only when families are already in crisis. Respecting the dependency relation between children and their
caregivers would require state intervention that supports families, preserving
family ties and preventing child maltreatment. The role of government under the
current system is limited to rescuing children who have been mistreated by defi-
cient parents, rather than ensuring the health and welfare of all families. Duncan
Lindsey calls this the "residual approach" to child welfare because state intervention is treated as a last resort to be invoked only after the family has exhausted
all resources at its disposal. "[T]he child welfare agency becomes the site of
triage, a battlefront hospital where casualties are sorted and only the most seriously wounded receive attention," Lindsey writes. "But because the damage to
children is so great by the time they enter the system, the number who survive
and benefit is minimal."[90]

Finally, because the system perceives the resulting harm to children as parental
rather than societal failures, state intervention to protect children is punitive in nature. The state's solutions to children's deprivation involve intrusive meddling by
social workers, behavioral requirements, and temporary or permanent removal of
children from their homes. Child protection proceedings are more akin to criminal trials than to most civil adjudications because they pit individuals against the
state and issue moral condemnation of parents.[91]

The child welfare system has become less service-oriented in recent
decades, focusing more on placing children in foster care than on providing
families with needed support. In the last thirty years, as the number of black
children in the child welfare system increased, the number of children receiving child welfare services dropped dramatically, while the foster care population skyrocketed. Between 1977 and 1994, there was a 60 percent decline in
the number of children receiving services in their homes.[92] These seemingly
contradictory observations reflect the transformation of the child welfare system from a social service system that tried (albeit inadequately) to help needy
families to a child protection system that investigates allegations of abuse and
neglect.[93] Black families, who dominate foster care caseloads, are the main casualties of this shift away from service provision toward coercive state intervention, which includes the requirement to relinquish custody of children as a
condition of financial assistance.

CONCLUSION

Kinship foster care illustrates the state's distortion of dependency that requires
forfeiting authority over children to gain access to necessary public resources.

The child welfare system provides foster care only to state wards and gives higher benefits to foster parents. As a result, families involved in kinship foster care must relinquish custody of children and submit to government supervision to receive needed support. Promoted as a way of keeping black families together, this system exacts a high price for state assistance that may include tearing families apart. Instead of acknowledging and respecting the dependency relationships in poor black families, the state treats black caregivers as dependent and takes authority over their children. In this way, the child welfare system reinforces the racist view of African Americans as dependent and in need of white supervision.

The transformation of kinship care from a private family arrangement to a type of public foster care reflects a deeper flaw in the philosophy underlying the child welfare system—the assumption that parents are solely responsible for the care of children and that their inability to provide for them warrants coercive state intervention. The onerous price the child welfare system demands for needed benefits and services demonstrates the need for more generous state support of caregiving.

NOTES

1. See Martha Albertson Fineman, *The Neutered Mother, the Sexual Family, and Other Twentieth Century Tragedies* (New York: Routledge, 1995).

2. See Eva Feder Kittay, *Love's Labor: Essays on Women, Equality, and Dependency* (New York: Routledge, 1999).

3. See, e.g., Nancy Fraser and Linda Gordon, "A Genealogy of 'Dependency': Tracing a Keyword of the U.S. Welfare State," in Nancy Fraser, *Justice Interruptus: Critical Reflections on the "Postsocialist" Condition* (New York: Routledge, 1997), 121 (explaining how relationships of dependency were removed from the market and attached to disfavored and excluded groups).

4. See Gwendolyn Mink, *Welfare's End* (Ithaca, N.Y.: Cornell University Press, 1998), 62–63; Lucy A. Williams, "The Ideology of Division: Behavior Modification Welfare Reform Proposals," *Yale Law Journal* 102 (1992). For historical accounts of the welfare system's regulation of poor mothers, see Mimi Abramovitz, *Regulating the Lives of Women: Social Welfare Policy from Colonial Times to the Present* (Boston: South End, 1998); Linda Gordon, *Pitied but Not Entitled: Single Mothers and the History of Welfare, 1890–1935* (New York: Free Press, 1994); Gwendolyn Mink, *The Wages of Motherhood: Inequality in the Welfare State, 1917–1942* (Ithaca, N.Y.: Cornell University Press, 1995).

5. See Dorothy Roberts, *Killing the Black Body: Race, Reproduction, and the Meaning of Liberty* (New York: Pantheon, 1997), 226–29.

6. Pub. L. No. 104-193, 110 Stat. 2105 (1996).

7. See Francis Fox Piven, "Welfare and Work," in *Whose Welfare?* ed. Gwendolyn Mink (Ithaca, N.Y.: Cornell University Press, 1999), 83; Dorothy Roberts, "Welfare's Ban on Poor Motherhood," in *Whose Welfare?* 152.

8. See, generally, Richard P. Barth et al., *From Child Abuse to Permanency Planning: Child Welfare Services Pathways and Placements* (New York: Aldine de Gruyter, 1994).

9. See Admin. for Children and Families, U.S. Department of Health and Human Services, *The AFCARS Report: Current Estimates as of October 2000*, 1, at www.acf. dhhs.gov/programs/cb/stats/tarreport/rpt10004/ar1000.pdf.

10. See Leroy H. Pelton, *For Reasons of Poverty: A Critical Analysis of the Public Child Welfare System in the United States* (New York: Praeger, 1989), 38–42; Duncan Lindsey, *The Welfare of Children* (New York: Oxford, 1994), 139–55.

11. See Andrea J. Sedlak and Diane D. Broadhurst, U.S. Department of Health and Human Services, "Third National Incidence Study of Child Abuse and Neglect," Final Report 5-4 to 5-8 (1996); Kristine E. Nelson et al., "Chronic Child Neglect in Perspective," *Social Work* 38 (1993): 661.

12. See Renny Golden, *Disposable Children: America's Child Welfare System* (Belmont, Calif.: Wadsworth, 1997); Pelton, *For Reasons of Poverty*, 39–42; Annette R. Appell, "Protecting Children or Punishing Mothers: Gender, Race, and Class in the Child Protection System," *South Carolina Law Review* 48 (1997): 577, 584–85.

13. Admin. for Children and Families, 2.

14. See Patricia Hill Collins, *Black Feminist Thought* (New York: Routledge, 1991), 119–23.

15. See Robert B. Hill, *Informal Adoption among Black Families* (Washington, D.C.: National Urban League, 1977), 29–37; Andrew Billingsley, *Climbing Jacob's Ladder: The Enduring Legacy of African-American Families* (New York: Simon & Schuster, 1992), 30–31.

16. See Carol B. Stack, *All Our Kin: Strategies for Survival in a Black Community* (New York: Harper & Row, 1974).

17. See Elmer P. Martin and Joanne Mitchell Martin, *The Black Extended Family* (Chicago: University of Chicago Press, 1978), 39–43.

18. See Nina Bernstein, *The Lost Children of Wilder: The Epic Struggle to Change Foster Care* (New York: Pantheon, 2001); Andrew Billingsley and Jeanne M. Giovannoni, *Children of the Storm: Black Children and American Child Welfare* (New York: Harcourt, 1972), 34–38; David Rosner and Gerald Markowitz, "Race, Foster Care, and the Politics of Abandonment in New York City," *American Journal of Public Health* 87 (1997): 1844.

19. Billingsley and Giovannoni, *Children of the Storm*, 45–59.

20. See Maria Scannapieco and Sondra Jackson, "Kinship Care: The African American Response to Family Preservation," *Social Work* 41 (1996): 190–94.

21. See Scannapieco and Jackson, "Kinship Care," 192–93; Rob Geen, "In the Interest of Children: Rethinking Federal and State Policies Affecting Kinship Care," *Policy and Practice* (March 2000): 19, 21; Beth McLeod, "Parents the Second Time Around," *San Francisco Examiner*, May 17, 1996, 3(P).

22. See McLeod, "Parents the Second Time Around," 3(P).

23. See Arlene F. Saluter, Bureau of the Census, U.S. Department of Commerce, Pub. No. 20-484, *Marital Status and Living Arrangements: March 1994* (1996), xi.

24. See Charisse Nelson, "The New Nuclear Family: Grandparenting in the Nineties," *Black Child* (July 31, 1997): 9.

25. See Carol B. Stack, "Cultural Perspectives on Child Welfare," *New York University Review of Law and Social Change* 12 (1983–84): 539, 541.

26. See Appell, "Protecting Children," 585–86.

27. Mark Testa, Remarks at Conference on Assessing the Impact of the Adoption and Safe Families Act and Families of Color: Early Observations and Recommendations, sponsored by Child Welfare League of America, Inc., Chicago, Ill. (November 14, 2000).

28. Marianne Takas, "Kinship Care and Family Preservation: Options for States in Legal and Policy Development," 1994 A.B.A. Center on Children and the Law 3 (final rev. ed.).

29. Annie Woodley Brown and Barbara Bailey-Etta, "An Out-of-Home Care System in Crisis: Implications for African American Children in the Child Welfare System," *Child Welfare* 76 (1997): 65, 76.

30. James P. Gleeson et al., "Understanding the Complexity of Practice in Kinship Foster Care," *Child Welfare* 76 (1997): 801–02.

31. See Geen, "In the Interest of Children," 21; Jill Duerr Berrick, "When Children Cannot Remain Home: Foster Family Care and Kinship Care," *Future Child* 8 (1998): 72, 74.

32. Madeleine L. Kurtz, "The Purchase of Families into Foster Care: Two Case Studies and the Lessons They Teach," *Connecticut Law Reveiw* 26 (1994): 1453, 1454; Geen, "In the Interest of Children," 21–22; Gleeson et al., "Understanding the Complexity," 424–25.

33. 440 U.S. 125, 145-46 (1979).

34. See Scannapieco and Jackson, "Kinship Care," 193–94.

35. See Scannapieco and Jackson, "Kinship Care," 193; Sarah Karp, "Adoption Surge: DCFS Policy Spells Pressure for Black Families," *Chicago Reporter* (October 1999): 1, 10.

36. See Karp, "Adoption Surge," 10.

37. See Mark Testa, "Kinship Foster Care in Illinois," *Child Welfare Research Review* 2, ed. Richard P. Barth et al. (1997): 101, 124; Jill D. Berrick et al., "A Comparison of Kinship Foster Homes and Foster Family Homes: Implications for Kinship Foster Care as Family Preservation," *Children and Youth Services Review* 16 (1994): 33, 36; Marla Gottlieb Zwas, "Kinship Foster Care: A Relatively Permanent Solution," *Fordham Urban Law Journal* 20 (1993): 343, 354.

38. See James P. Gleeson and Lynn C. Craig, "Kinship Care in Child Welfare: An Analysis of States' Policies," *Children and Youth Services Review* 16 (1994): 7, 10; Gayle Hafner, "Protections Extended to Foster Children in 'Kinship Care,'" *Youth L. News* (July–August 1991): 8–9.

39. See Berrick et al., "A Comparison of Kinship Foster Homes," 59; Mark E. Courtney and Barbara Needell, "Outcomes of Kinship Care: Lessons from California," ed. Richard P. Barth et al., *Child Welfare Research Review* 2 (1997): 130, 142–43; Alfreda P. Iglehart, "Kinship Foster Care: Placement, Service, and Outcome Issues," *Children and Youth Services Review* 16 (1994): 107, 112.

40. See Susan J. Zuravin et al., "Child Maltreatment in Family Foster Care: Foster Home Correlates," ed. Richard P. Barth et al., *Child Welfare Research Review* 2 (1997): 189, 196; Berrick, "When Children Cannot Remain Home," 80.

41. See Berrick, "When Children Cannot Remain Home," 77, 78, and table 2.

42. See Geen, "In the Interest of Children," 21.

43. Laurie Hanson and Irene Opsahl, "Kinship Caregiving: Law and Policy," *Clearinghouse Review* 30 (1996): 481, 483.

44. Geen, "In the Interest of Children," 21.

45. Hanson and Opsahl, "Kinship Caregiving," 483.

46. Randi Mandelbaum, "Trying to Fit Square Pegs into Round Holes: The Need for a New Funding Scheme for Kinship Caregivers," *Fordham Urban Law Journal* 22 (1995): 907, 915–16; Zwas, "Kinship Foster Care," 365; Note, "The Policy of Penalty in Kinship Care," *Harvard Literary Review* 112 (1999): 1047, 1052–53.

47. Berrick, "When Children Cannot Remain Home," 75–76.

48. See Geen, "In the Interest of Children," 23.

49. See Note, "The Policy of Penalty," 1052.

50. See Geen, "In the Interest of Children," 23; Berrick, "When Children Cannot Remain Home," 76 and table 1.

51. See Gleeson et al., "Understanding the Complexity," 814; Berrick, "When Children Cannot Remain Home," 82–83.

52. See Berrick, "When Children Cannot Remain Home," 82.

53. See Note, "The Policy of Penalty," 1063.

54. 431 U.S. 816 (1977).

55. 431 U.S. 845 (1977).

56. See Geen, "In the Interest of Children," 21.

57. See Geen, "In the Interest of Children, 13–14.

58. See Katherine C. Pearson, "Cooperate or We'll Take Your Child: The Parents' Fictional Voluntary Separation Decision and a Proposal for Change," *Tennessee Law Review.* 65 (1998): 835, 848–49.

59. Hanson and Opsahl, "Kinship Caregiving," 498.

60. See, e.g., Berrick et al., "A Comparison of Kinship Foster Homes," 38; Scannapieco and Jackson, "Kinship Care," 486; Courtney and Needell, "Outcomes of Kinship Care," 137; Testa, "Kinship Foster Care," 112.

61. Gleeson, supra note 31, 430.

62. See supra notes 41, 51, and accompanying text.

63. See Berrick, "When Children Cannot Remain Home," 82.

64. See Berrick, "When Children Cannot Remain Home," 82.

65. Kurtz, "The Purchase of Families," 1457. For a similar argument that the foster care system was not designed to meet the needs of kinship caregivers, see Mandelbaum, "Trying to Fit Square Pegs."

66. See Kurtz, "The Purchase of Families," 1499–1500.

67. See Kurtz, "The Purchase of Families," 1502.

68. See Kurtz, "The Purchase of Families," 1503.

69. See Kurtz, "The Purchase of Families," 1507.

70. See supra notes 15–17.

71. Scannapieco and Jackson, "Kinship Care," 194 (quoting Sadye M. L. Logan et al., *Social Work Practice with Black Families* [1990], 71); see also Ramona Denby and Nolan Rindfleisch, "African Americans' Foster Parenting Experiences: Research Findings and Implications for Policy and Practice," *Children and Youth Services Review* 18 (1996): 523, 545 (discussing the importance of building on African American foster parents' strengths, including family orientation, religious obligation, community responsibility, and the interconnection of family, religion, and community).

72. See Gleeson et al., "Understanding the Complexity," 819; Denby and Rindfleisch, "African Americans' Foster Parenting Experiences," 545.

73. See Gleeson et al., "Understanding the Complexity," 818–19.

74. See Gleeson et al., "Understanding the Complexity," 818.

75. See Gleeson et al., "Understanding the Complexity," 818–19.

76. See Kurtz, "The Purchase of Families," 1472 (citing *Task Force on Permanency Planning for Foster Children, Kinship Foster Care: The Double Edged Dilemma* [1990]).

77. See Gebel, supra note 46; Berrick et al., "A Comparison of Kinship Foster Homes," 58; Gleeson et al., "Understanding the Complexity," 803.

78. See Zwas, "Kinship Foster Care," 355–56.

79. See Gleeson, supra note 31, 442; Gleeson et al., "Understanding the Complexity," 803; Berrick et al., "A Comparison of Kinship Foster Homes," 36, 57.

80. See Gleeson, supra note 31, 442.

81. Orlando Patterson, *Slavery and Social Death: A Comparative Study* (Cambridge, Mass.: Harvard University Press, 1982), 189–90.

82. Peggy Cooper Davis, *Neglected Stories: The Constitution and Family Values* (New York: Hill & Wang, 1997), 81–166.

83. Roberts, *Killing the Black Body*, 154–59.

84. Martha L. Fineman, "Images of Mothers in Poverty Discourses," *Duke Law Journal* (1991): 274; Dorothy E. Roberts, "The Value of Black Mothers' Work," *Connecticut Law Review* 26 (1994): 871, 873–74.

85. Id. at 28.

86. Id. at 92.

87. See Billingsley and Giovannoni, *Children of the Storm*, 4.

88. See Fineman, *The Neutered Mother*, 102–11; Mink, *Welfare's End*, 119.

89. Billingsley and Giovannoni, *Children of the Storm*, viii.

90. See Lindsey, *The Welfare of Children*, 4–5; see also Billingsley and Giovannoni, *Children of the Storm*, 5.

91. The U.S. Supreme Court recognized similarities between proceedings to terminate parental rights and criminal trials. See *Lassiter v. Department of Social Services*, 452 U.S. 18 (1981) (holding that parents have a due-process right to counsel in complex proceedings to terminate parental rights); *Santosky v. Kramer*, 455 U.S. 745 (1982) (holding that termination of parental rights must be justified by clear and convincing evidence).

92. See Children's Bureau, U.S. Department of Health and Human Services, *National Study of Protective, Preventive and Reunification Services Delivered to Children and Their Families* (1997), at www.acf.dhhs.gov/programs/cb/stats/studies/97natstudy/natstudy.htm.

93. See, generally, Barbara J. Nelson, *Making an Issue of Child Abuse: Political Agenda Setting for Social Problems* (Chicago: University of Chicago Press, 1984).

13

Doctor's Orders: Parents and Intersexed Children

Ellen K. Feder

Between May of 2000 and August of 2001, I spoke with parents of "intersexed" children, children born with genitals that are neither clearly male nor clearly female. Routine protocols for "managing" these children include corrective genital surgery and gender reassignment. Since 1995, when intersexed adults first spoke publicly about the debilitating physical and emotional effects of these protocols, a growing body of work testifies to the pain and suffering wrought not only by the incisions and scars left by genital surgeries in infancy and early childhood, but by the secrets and silence maintained by doctors and families.[1]

I sought out these parents—through Internet bulletin boards and personal contacts—because I could find no information that addressed the experience of *parents* of intersexed children. This was striking, I thought: Parents are charged with making the difficult decisions associated with genital surgery and changing gender assignment, and yet there was next to no research available on their experience. Moreover, there are effectively no resources or support available for parents of intersexed infants. The absence of support is even more remarkable when one considers the abundance of resources now available for parents with children born with other congenital problems. Parents and family members are urged to seek help, to join or form support groups. Their children have access to other children like themselves. By contrast, parents of intersexed children are not given the opportunity to meet other parents who have faced similar dilemmas; they are not offered the opportunity to consult mental health professionals with expertise in intersex or even gender development. When they are not urged to keep the "truth" about their children to themselves, they are led to believe that the intersex condition has been "corrected," and that their children will grow up to be "normal" girls or boys.

In reviewing the literature on intersex, it becomes clear that parents' isolation and the striking failure to take account of their experience are not unfortunate effects of the treatment protocol; they are, rather, *essential components of that treat-*

ment. The appearance of ambiguous genitalia in a newborn differs markedly from the host of other conditions—from congenital heart defects to cleft palate—that traditionally warrant surgical intervention. Ambiguous genitalia simply do not constitute a "medical emergency." Doctors agree that in most cases of intersex, early surgical intervention is not necessary for the child's functioning. They also concede that early surgical intervention can result—like any surgery—in harm. With few exceptions, however, doctors continue to perform these surgeries, and defend their practices—which include the failure to secure informed consent from parents—as sound, and even as necessary.

Parents' treatment in cases such as these is striking for the instrumental fashion in which they are regarded by doctors. One doctor with whom I spoke related what he understood as his job when it came to talking to parents of intersexed infants: "I needed to lead them to the right decision."[2] Certain details of a child's condition, and particularly details that might, in the doctors' judgment, interfere with the successful rearing of the child in his or her assigned sex, should, he claimed, be withheld as part of the treatment protocol. The doctor's revelation might be jarring; common sense and fundamental bioethical principles alike dictate that parents must be fully apprised of their child's condition, provided with the understanding that can make truly informed consent to treatment possible. The routine withholding of information in the case of parents of intersexed infants highlights the acute vulnerability of parents—the vulnerability that makes their treatment as what Kant would characterize as "mere means" possible.

In her book *Love's Labor*, Eva Kittay calls attention to the disadvantageous situation of those she calls "dependency workers," those who care for the "inevitably dependent." Parents of young children are dependency workers, as are those whose professional lives are dedicated to the care of the elderly or those with profound disabilities. Dependency workers who care for the vulnerable, are, as Kittay explains, themselves vulnerable by virtue of a "secondary," or "derivative dependency."[3] The secondary dependency of parents is not always apparent in an individualist culture in which parents' sovereignty over themselves and their children is presumed and valued. I would argue that the situation of parents of intersexed children is not different from that of any parent as far as the issue of dependency is concerned; theirs is an extreme variant of the vulnerability all parents face.

In the first part of this chapter, I explore Kittay's analysis of dependency and dependency work as it relates to parents of intersexed children. In attending to the stories of parents, we must attend also to the story of the medical conceptualization of intersex itself. Part II reviews the cursory treatment of parents in the medical literature, and specifically the work that was guided by the dominating influence of psychologist John Money. Despite the fact that Money's reputation has been irrevocably damaged by the revelation of the deception he engineered in the now infamous "case of John/Joan," the protocols of intersex management that everywhere bear his mark retain a powerful and enduring authority. To explain this authority, and its function in parents' relationship to their intersexed children, I turn in the third part to the work of Pierre Bourdieu. It might seem odd to pair the work of Kittay, a liberal feminist who works in the tradition of analytic philosophy, with the work of Bourdieu, a theorist firmly grounded in the Continental tradition. I argue, however, that Bourdieu's conception of *habitus*, and in particular, the preservative and conservative nature of *habitus*, provides a powerful descriptive account that makes sense of the treatment of parents of intersexed children as dependency workers. Bourdieu's account, I conclude, complements Kittay's normative analysis and furthermore demonstrates the radical implications of her work for change.

What follows is taken from a transcript of the first interview I conducted for this project.

I. "RUBY": A MOTHER'S STORY[4]

The first was born in 1961. Doctors thought she was a boy. Her clitoris was enlarged, her labia fused. She was given a male name. But she became sick almost immediately. She couldn't breastfeed, she lost weight, and on New Year's Eve we took her to the ER. The doctors thought she was going to die, but one doctor knew about pediatric endocrinology, and transferred her to the children's hospital in the city. They diagnosed her with CAH[5] and explained that she was female. She had no testicles, but a uterus and ovaries.

At three months, she hemorrhaged; her urethra was connected to her vagina. She had surgery, and they performed a clitorectomy at the same time. She had another surgery when she was two.

The same thing happened with my second daughter. Everyone thought, "This one's the boy," but I knew. I just knew it was a girl, but we gave her a boy's name. When we brought her home, she became very sick. So I insisted that I be sent to the children's hospital again. She was kept in the hospital for a long time, because the doctors thought that any talk about a son would upset my older daughter. At three months she had the clitorectomy. This was a female, and she needed to look like a female. They did leave tissue, but she had a series of infections and she had more surgeries—five by the time she was five years old. She has almost no clitoris left, and massive scarring.

My daughters received medical care throughout their childhood. Once a month, sometimes more, we drove a whole day to get to the hospital. Fifteen hours there and fifteen hours back, with two active children in the backseat. And at the hospital I would have to fight the doctors. They would conduct a study on the salt levels, and make my children sick, and I had to yell at them to stop. The doctors almost gave up on my younger daughter, and I took over a lot of her care. I had to dilate her urethra, and it was so hard. I did cultures for the doctors, too. I grew the bacteria, and the doctors would tell me what antibiotics to give her. I was the one who had to coordinate her care, and I was determined that my daughter not die because her mom didn't fight for her.

We were lucky to be part of these studies, though. As my daughters got older, they started to complain about the examinations. But somebody before my first child was born allowed these doctors—many doctors—to examine their child, to figure out what all this was about. My younger daughter is angry with me as an adult. She felt that she was raped, medically raped. And she's right. And I know how she feels. When you have a baby, you lose your right to modesty, and everyone is looking everywhere. But it was necessary, in my mind, just like when I gave birth. I told my daughters I wish we didn't have to do this. How would you feel having seventeen doctors look at you all at once? But it wasn't just that I felt a responsibility. This was a teaching hospital, and their treatment was being subsidized.

No one wanted to talk about the gender issues, how my daughters wouldn't play with their dolls. Both girls are gay. No one wanted to talk about that. Their father didn't want to deal with the gender issues at all, and his family thought that we had turned two little boys into girls. We divorced in 1976.

I had pastors who told me that they didn't know how to pray for me. And I told them I know how you can pray for me. You imagine a God who is bigger than all of these problems and you ask Him to help me.

As infants and young children, humans are dependent. We need others—most often our parents—to commit themselves to the work of providing what we cannot secure for ourselves. Children who are ill or medically fragile are not exceptions in this respect; their needs magnify the needs—for preservative love, fostering growth, and training for social acceptance[6]—that are common to all children. As the needs of these children are magnified, so, too, are the corresponding demands upon parents with ill or medically fragile children. Those engaged in the practices of mothering will recognize the love that motivates Ruby's determination that her "daughter not die because her mom didn't fight for her." While Ruby's efforts can be seen as heroic, it is difficult to imagine mothers and fathers who would not want to do everything in their power to save the lives of their children. Ruby's explanation to her daughters of the need to consent to invasive examinations reveals both an attempt to foster moral growth and to teach a difficult lesson in training for social acceptance: Other parents sacrificed their children's comfort so that doctors could help you, she tells them, and now we are obliged to do the same. And in life there are times that you must "go along to get along." Sometimes there's no choice.

In providing care to a dependent other, dependency workers are themselves dependent on others to provide the resources they need to do their work as caregivers. All parents require assistance from a host of individuals and institutions to secure what their children need in the way of education, health care, and social security. Parents' own needs, too, must be met in order to enable them to attend properly to their charges. Precisely because Ruby's situation will not permit her to take such support for granted, what Kittay calls the "secondary" or "derivative dependency"—an aspect of the situation of all dependency workers—is especially visible in her case.

The early withdrawal of familial support, first by her in-laws who believed she had robbed them of a grandson two times over, and then by her husband, who failed in so many ways to stand by his wife, meant that the help upon which most mothers in some form rely was largely withheld. The constraints on Ruby's access to the medical care necessary to maintain her children's health demonstrate her dependency on the individual physicians who managed the clinical studies in which her children were enrolled. So long as Ruby's daughters remained subjects of the studies conducted by the hospital, their care would be generously subsidized. Refusal to consent to experimental treatments or yet another examination of her children's genitals would have put Ruby and her family at considerable financial, and thereby medical, risk. Caught in a bind of financial and medical exigency, Ruby could not really be understood to have a choice in the matter. To refuse a medical intervention would have been, in effect, to risk her children's lives. This was a risk she would assume only at those times when she clearly perceived that an intervention itself posed the worse threat. That a mother would be faced with such a dilemma starkly underscores the special vulnerability that accompanies secondary dependency.

Dependency Work and the "Transparent Self"

As a parent, Ruby made decisions on behalf of her young children. Such is the responsibility of the dependency worker who, as in the case of parents of young children, must act to meet the needs of one who cannot meet them for herself. Kittay proposes the conception of a "transparent self" to describe the distinctive connection a dependency worker must maintain in order to engage meaningfully in the work of caring for a dependent other. A "transparent self" is a "self through whom the needs of another are discerned, a self that, when it looks to gauge its own needs, sees first the needs of another."[7] While the achievement of a perfect "transparency" is not possible, Kittay advances the concept as a regulatory ideal to describe the attunement to the needs of another that is necessary for the successful performance of dependency work.

In thinking about the standard cases of mothering, attunement to the needs of a child appears to take two primary forms. In the first, a mother can attend to the dependent child in ways that are sensitive to expressions of need a child can express only imperfectly. For example, a mother can use attentive interpretive skills to discern whether an infant is crying because she is wet, hungry, or wants to be held. In the second, she can use what could be termed the "everyday social knowledge" she has as an adult to anticipate the needs a child cannot. Such needs would include skills required in social interaction with peers and adults, or toilet training. In addition, however, there is an array of needs to which a child may be subject, and for the satisfaction of which the mother will herself require extensive assistance. While a mother might be able to discern a child's discomfort in the common case of an earache, for example, she may not be able to discern the specific cause of the pain. Though the child may be able to express pain or discomfort, she cannot communicate what she needs to treat her medical condition; "everyday social knowledge" does not usually provide such professional and technical information.

Where, as in the case of an earache or other medical problem, the two primary forms of attunement are not finally effective in meeting the needs of her charge, the mother must depend on doctors' "expert knowledge" both to understand and to respond to the needs of her child. Cases such as Ruby's are complicated, I want to argue, by the fact that the "expert knowledge" she is offered as definitive of what her children "need" may not itself be attuned or sensitive to the genuine needs of her children.

In the paradigm case of a dependency relationship as Kittay sees it, three aspects define the labor of the dependency worker:

> It is the work of tending to others in their state of vulnerability—*care*. The labor either sustains ties among intimates or itself creates intimacy and trust—*connection*. And affectional ties—*concern*—generally sustain the connection, even when the work involves an economic exchange. For the dependency worker, the well-being and thriving of the charge is the primary focus of the work. In short, the well-being of the charge is the responsibility of the dependency worker.[8]

To all appearances, Ruby both understands and assumes her responsibilities in just the way Kittay here describes. There can be no question that Ruby cares deeply about her daughters, or that her concern for their well-being could be described as anything less than fierce. In the paradigm case of a dependency relationship, connection cannot but be understood as a necessary corollary of care and concern. And yet, the connection between Ruby and her daughters, and particularly her younger daughter, is attenuated. If it is not for lack of care or concern that the connection between mother and daughters is strained, it seems that the effects of the repeated experience of violation her daughters suffered nevertheless eroded the trust essential to a relationship between a dependency worker and her charge. It was not Ruby who performed surgery or conducted the exams. But it was Ruby who, willing or not, witting or not, sanctioned these actions. The tragic paradox of Ruby's situation is precisely this: Her caring and concerned attempts to fulfill her responsibility for what Kittay calls the "well-being of her charge" led her to consent to actions that resulted in harm to her charge, and eventually, to an erosion of her connection to her charge.

Ruby fulfilled her responsibility to her daughters the best way she knew how. Her "knowing how," however, was tainted by the flawed "expert knowledge" on which she had to depend. The possibility of effecting harm in an effort to do right by one's charge is a risk, certainly, for any dependency worker. In this sense, Ruby's situation exemplifies the sometimes perilous nature of dependency work. Ruby's marked dependence on, and vulnerability to, her children's doctors magnifies an essential relationship not immediately apparent in examinations of dependency relationships, namely, the relationship of the dependency worker to the third party Kittay calls a "provider."[9] A provider is a person or persons responsible for the supply or regulation of some significant external resources. A provider may be the head of a household, who supplies financial support necessary to the maintenance of a child or other dependent. In Ruby's case, the provider who figures most prominently in her life and that of her children is the hospital medical team managing her daughters' care. Even as a provider enables a dependency worker to do her work by supplying necessary resources, a provider may also limit the autonomy of a dependency worker by exploiting her dependency to carry out some other agenda. The relationship between a provider and a dependency worker, like that between a dependency worker and her charge, then, is characterized fundamentally by inequality.[10] Ruby's daughters received life-saving care as a result of the benevolent intervention of the doctors. But at the same time, doctors' management of "the gender issues," that is, their insistence on cosmetic genital surgeries and their failure to address issues related to the nonconforming behavior of her children, wreaked havoc in their lives.

"The Gender Issues"

The prominence of "the gender issues" in the life of Ruby and her children both do and do not distinguish their experience. Even for parents of children with no genital ambiguity, maternal work can involve complications around questions concerning gender. Training for social acceptance may require a mother to direct her daughter to behave at times more "like a girl" or teach her son to behave more "like a boy." At the same time, a parent may come to believe that a social script dictating a particular gender behavior is not appropriate for her child. Parents with convictions concerning the problematic nature of gender scripts may resist the imperative that encourages them to direct their children to behave according to the norms associated with a certain gender. For the most part, however, mothers generally harbor no doubts or anxieties about the "true sex" of their children. Absent such doubts or questions, mothers may experience less anxiety when their children fail to conform to particular lines of behavior. Unencumbered with doubts about her child's sex, a mother may shrug off her daughter's aversion to dolls. She needn't question whether such an aversion is a sign that her daughter isn't "really a girl" or wonder whether she "did the right thing in treating her as a girl." Anxiety that parents may feel if a daughter prefers trucks or a son prefers dolls is not concerned so much with their children's "sex" but with the possibility that their child will experience homosexual desire. The difference between the kind of "gender panic" manifested by parents afraid that their "apparently normal" girl or boy might be homosexual and that experienced by parents of children with ambiguous genitalia is the apparent tangibility of the diagnosis of intersexuality.[11]

Ruby's situation is complicated by such doubts concerning what she calls "the gender issues." Her husband's family responded with shame and criticism; her husband coped with the situation by withdrawing, first emotionally, then physically. More upsetting to her than even her family's shortcomings, however, was the alternating silence and denial she faced when she started asking doctors questions. "*Why*," she asked again and again, "do my girls behave this way? And what can I do to help them be more like girls?" In response to her questions, most of the doctors at the hospital had no answer. One impatiently cut her short: "They're girls. What's the problem?" The doctors' refusals to respond meaningfully to Ruby's questions may be symptomatic of doctors' own anxiety over whether they had made the right decisions in the management of Ruby's daughters. Whatever their motivation, the doctors here compound Ruby's vulnerability. Making every effort to fulfill her responsibilities to her daughters, she has had to rely on the recommendations of medical authorities who are themselves subjects of prevailing conceptions of sex and gender. When she seeks advice to address the consequences of the earlier recommendations, she is given to understand that her questions—questions that have arisen from her attentive connection to her children—are improper.

Ruby understood that her job as a mother was to help her girls grow up to get along in this world. Being a female and acting like a man wasn't going to get them far. When the girls had health problems associated with CAH, she could make sure that her questions were answered, and she could *do something*—she could monitor their cortisol levels or make sure they stayed hydrated. But when it came to the fact that her girls wouldn't play with "girls' toys" or really act "like girls," she was on her own. It is here, where Ruby deals with the gender roles and identities of her daughters, that support is conspicuously withheld, and her own ability to provide support is undermined.

It is only in retrospect that the "gender issues" began with the clitoridectomies performed when the girls were only a few months old. In Ruby's memory, there was no question that they would be performed. She and her husband were informed of the necessity for genital surgery in the same way a parent would be informed that a child's congenital heart defect would have to be corrected: The procedure was imperative for the healthy development of the child. The consent to corrective genital surgery was not a question, but a form that she and her husband signed along with all the others, consenting to the different procedures or administration of medicine their children required. It would be many years before her daughters would be able to articulate the effects of the surgeries, and thus many years before Ruby could understand the meaning of the consent she had offered.

Ruby credits the close relationship she now enjoys with her older daughter to hard work and the help of a therapist Ruby sought out after her divorce. Ruby's involvement in her daughter's life has meant that she can also be a resource to her daughter's close friend, another woman with CAH, whose mother never spoke to her about her condition. Things have not worked out so well with her younger daughter, who has found the maintenance of intimate relationships almost impossible. Despite Ruby's efforts, her relationship with her younger daughter has been strained for many years. Ruby is sympathetic. She understands that her daughter's physical pain and emotional isolation are constant reminders of the violation

she experienced in infancy and throughout childhood. But her daughter's anger
—undimmed by the years—is difficult for Ruby, too; her daughter's pain and distress are constant reminders of her role in inflicting that injury.

Trust and Domination

Trust is one of the factors crucial to the success of the relationship between a dependency worker and her charge. Kittay writes that the "charge must trust that the
dependency worker will be responsible to and respectful of her vulnerability and
will not abuse whatever authority and power has been vested in her to carry out
these responsibilities."[12] The fraying of trust between Ruby and her daughters is
not owing to any questionable intentions on Ruby's part. Rather, it is Ruby's own
vulnerability to her children's doctors that renders fragile, in turn, Ruby's relationship with her daughters. Her complicity in making decisions and maintaining
secrets that effected so much harm in the lives of her daughters drove a wedge between her and the daughters for whom, and about whom, she cares so deeply.
Ruby's children experienced pain, both momentary and enduring, physical and
emotional, as a result of decisions in which she participated. And yet, isolated by
the doctors, and herself subject to the secrecy of her children's treatment in which
she was forced to collude, Ruby's vulnerability as a dependency worker was exploited, and so exacerbated.

It is precisely because inequality characterizes the relationship between the dependency worker and her charge that trust is essential to the success of a dependency relationship. If trust that an abuse of power will not occur is essential to the
dependency relationship, the illegitimate exercise of power—domination—is
anathema to it.[13] At several points, Ruby's story speaks to the illegitimate exercise of power. Domination manifests itself in the physical scars on her daughters'
bodies; it reveals itself in her younger daughter's difficulty in forming intimate
relationships, and it is evident in the emotional rift between Ruby and her
younger daughter. At the same time, however, it is difficult to apply the term *domination* to a situation such as Ruby's. *Domination,* as Kittay uses it, is associated
with a willful agent of power, and while the illegitimate exercise of power has left
its mark, it is nonetheless difficult to locate the agent who left those marks. Ruby,
who went to such lengths to ensure her children's well-being, is an unlikely
"agent of domination." As Ruby tells it, the doctors, too, make for poor culprits:
Those recommending and performing genital surgeries do not intend harm; on the
contrary, it is their firm belief that genital surgeries are essential to the healthy
psychosexual development of a child born with ambiguous genitalia. Doctors
who ask that patients make themselves available to colleagues and medical residents for repeated examination by medical personnel do not mean for patients to
experience violation; rather, they understand themselves to be engaged in important educational work that advances medical progress. And yet, the injury suffered by Ruby's daughters, and the many others who have recently spoken out

against cosmetic genital surgeries, points to the exercise of power absent "moral legitimacy."[14]

Mary's Story

Twenty-five years after Ruby's first child was born, a young mother named Mary brought her twelve-year-old daughter, Jessica, to the pediatrician. The day before, Jessica had just come out of the shower after a ballet lesson when Mary noticed, out of the corner of her eye, a "growth" emerging from her daughter's labia. Mary had called the doctor, who agreed that Mary should bring Jessica in the following morning. Her daughter did not question why they would be going to the doctor. "Jessica was the type of child who never questioned me. She never spoke back. Never. Because she wanted to make me—us, her parents—happy, and not displease us."

That same day, Jessica's pediatrician sent her to a pediatric endocrinologist. A sonogram revealed that Jessica did not have a uterus, but undescended testes.[15]

The pediatric endocrinologist asked to speak with me alone. Jessica was in a different room. The doctor and I then sat and she explained to me that Jessica had XY chromosomes and Jessica would not be able to bear children. She also explained to me that this was something I should never, ever bring up with Jessica. I should never talk about it with Jessica. We should just take care of it as quickly as possible so that Jessica could live a normal life. I agreed to this because it was what she asked me to do. I was very young at the time. I was just in my late twenties.

Naturally I was shocked; I was stunned, I was saddened. I went home and told my husband, who had just come back from work. I told him all about it, what the pediatric endocrinologist said. I had never seen him cry before but he just broke down and sobbed in my arms. That's when it impacted me the most. . . . There were a lot of tears, a lot of feeling bad for Jessica, knowing that she couldn't have children naturally.

Mary was instructed to tell Jessica that "her ovaries hadn't developed properly and they would have to come out." Jessica was not told that her testes would be removed because doctors feared they would become cancerous. Nor was she informed of the clitorectomy[16] that would be performed at the same time.

Only a month later, Jessica was in the recovery room of the children's hospital. Mary remembers finding her daughter moaning in bed as she recovered from the anesthesia. She thought it was only from the pain, but Jessica has since told her that, having reached down, she realized that "a piece of her was gone." In the week that Jessica spent in the hospital, nothing was said about the clitorectomy. Doctors did inform her, however, that she would have to return to the hospital in a week to evaluate the effects of what they called "the plastic surgery."

Mary remembers that before the surgery, immediately after, and in the follow-up evaluation, "scores of male residents would come in to examine" her daughter. Mary had consented to the examinations because she knew that her daughter was being treated in a teaching hospital. It was not until years later, when Jessica had obtained her medical records and confronted her parents with what she had learned, that Mary would hear from her daughter's mouth, the terrible effects, not only of the surgery and the deception, but of the repeated examinations.

Looking back, it seems obvious to Mary that her daughter, who regarded her enlarged clitoris as perfectly normal, would have experienced the surgery and the examinations as painful violations. But if at the time she entertained such thoughts, she put them out of her mind. She remembers asking whether she should seek counseling for Jessica and in response was told the story of another girl with AIS who, as a teenager, had stolen a look at her records when the doctor was called out of the office. That girl, the doctors informed Mary, had had to be placed in a psychiatric institution as a result of learning "the truth." The surgery had taken care of the problem, Mary was told, and further discussion would only raise potentially damaging questions for Jessica. What was important was that Jessica look normal. If she looked normal, she would be able "to live her life as a normal girl."

When Mary speaks of the importance of the "normal appearance" of her daughter's genitals, it is difficult to discern whether her remarks reflect her own concerns or those of the doctors. Appearance, as opposed to sensation, is the governing criterion that determines whether genital surgery (and in some cases, a change in gender assignment) is indicated.[17] Perhaps it should not be surprising that parents of children with ambiguous genitalia follow the lead of doctors when it comes to making sense of a condition they have most likely encountered for the first time. Mary's response, as well as Ruby's, reflects the experiences of many other parents.[18] In focusing on genital appearance, rather than on the experience of the child, the mother fails to identify with her child, and in so doing, she puts both her child and her relationship to her child at risk.

Mary's story underscores one of the recurrent themes implicit in Ruby's narrative, namely, what might be described as a clouding of the dependency worker's "transparent self" as a result of a *failure of identification* with her charge. Kittay's discussion of the transparent self emphasizes the priority of the charge's needs over those of the dependency worker. The dependency worker as a dependency worker must defer her own needs in order to accommodate those of her charge.[19] The image of the "transparent self" also implies a capacity to recognize the other's needs through identification with the other. A mother of an infant can appreciate that hunger or a wet diaper would make one cross. Even if she does not directly know the particular discomfort, she can draw on her own experience to appreciate what her charge may experience. But in the case of children with genital ambiguity, it appears that a parent is forced to forsake this knowledge.

In a study conducted by psychologist Suzanne Kessler, college students were asked to imagine that they had been born with "clitoromegaly," a condition defined as having a clitoris larger than one centimeter at birth. In response to the question as to whether they would have wanted their parents to sanction clitoral surgery if the condition were not life-threatening, *93 percent* of the students reported that *they* would not have wanted their parents to agree to surgery:

Women predicted that having a large clitoris would not have had much of an impact on their peer relations and almost no impact on their relations with their parents. . . . [T]hey were more likely to want surgery to reduce a large nose, large ears, or large breasts than surgery to reduce a large clitoris.[20]

These findings, Kessler reflects, are not surprising, given that the respondents characterized genital sensation and the capacity for orgasm as "very important to the average woman, and the size of the clitoris as being not even 'somewhat important.'"[21] Men in the study were faced with a different dilemma, the one facing parents of boys with a "micropenis," a penis smaller than the putative standard of 2.5 centimeters at birth. Their question was whether to stay as male with a small penis or to be reassigned as female. More than half rejected the prospect of gender reassignment. But, according to Kessler,

> That percentage increases to almost all men if the surgery was described as reducing pleasurable sensitivity or orgasmic capability. Contrary to beliefs about male sexuality, the college men in this study did not think that having a micropenis would have had a major impact on their sexual relations, peer or parental relations, or self-esteem.[22]

This study confirms a kind of common sense that individuals are generally disinclined to compromise their erotic response for the sake of cosmetic enhancement. If asked if they themselves would be willing to subject themselves to cosmetic surgery, it is quite likely that parents would refuse. But when acting on behalf of their children, the majority of parents do opt for surgery.

In a separate study, Kessler and her team asked students to imagine that their child was born with ambiguous genitalia. Students in this study indicated they would make what Kessler describes as "more traditional choices." Students' rationales mirrored those of parents, which can now be found on new Internet bulletin boards devoted to parenting intersexed children: Students reported that they did not want their child to feel "different" and believed that early surgery would be less traumatizing than later surgery.[23] Like parents faced with these difficult decisions, students did not reflect on the possibility of lost sensation. It may be uncomfortable for parents (and even for those who are only imagining themselves as parents) to focus on the feeling in a child's genitals—it may sexualize the child in a way that causes discomfort to the parents. However, the case of children with ambiguous genitalia demands that parents take account of just those feelings in order to fulfill their obligations as dependency workers. To do that, parents require the assistance of the experts on whom they have come to rely when their own knowledge proves insufficient. Unfortunately, Kessler's team did not ask students participating in the first study what they would have done if faced with the decision of whether to consent to surgery for their children. If such questions had been included, it is possible that students in the first group would have been more disposed to identify with the children and to be more cautious about making cosmetic surgical decisions.

The juxtaposition of Kessler's studies suggests a conflict in the case of inter-sex between the needs of the individual child and the norms and expectations that govern society. A parent's obligation to her charge is complicated by the fact that socialization is also constitutive of her charge's needs. But socialization is not generally understood to be the dependency worker's primary obligation. In *Love's Labor*, Kittay writes that a "mother, acting in a manner compatible with the norms of maternal practice, does not force her child to sacrifice the child's own well-being for another's benefit. Such coercion is not commensurate with a maternal practice that remains true to the well-being of the child."[24] When parents such as Mary are presented with situations for which they can provide no context, and so are unable to make judgments concerning what is right for their children, they must rely on doctors to provide direction and advice. In place of the parent who has shared such a close relationship to her child, Mary becomes an agent of her daughter's violation. But parents like Mary who become agents of violation become, at the same time, objects of domination. Their relationship with their child is compromised, and the dependency worker is, as dependency worker, compromised, by virtue of her inability to identify with her charge. As is evident in her story, as well as that of Ruby, she was "led" by doctors to consent to actions that her child experienced as—and that now she has since acknowl-edged to be—coercive.

How are we to understand the doctors' attitudes? Why, for instance, do they jus-tify and endorse practices that privilege cosmetic appearance of genitals over the ca-pacity for sensation? Why do they see their own practices as justified and beneficial? In the next section, I provide an overview of the ways in which the medical estab-lishment has theorized and handled the condition of intersexed children.

II. MONEY'S THEORY

In Mary Cassatt's painting *Mother and Child*, a young girl, perhaps three or four years old, sits naked on the lap of her mother. One of the mother's hands rests lightly on her daughter's shoulder in a steadying gesture. The other hand holds a mirror to her daughter's face, which the girl's hands clasp awkwardly at the han-dle's lowest portion. Both faces turn toward the mirror as mother and daughter regard the effect of her mother's work. The mirror reflects the face of the child; her eyes look directly at the viewer.

One might read the portrait as an eloquent statement of an important dimension of maternal practice, namely, the role of the parent in the development of the child's identity. In holding the mirror to the child's face, supporting her as she reaches both hands to position it just so, the mother instructs her daughter in the ways of self-consciousness, that is, to see herself the way others see her.

Cassatt's painting is reproduced on the cover page of a 1970 article dealing with parents of children with ambiguous genitalia. It is an arresting image to introduce this, the first essay and, to date, the only research project dedicated to consideration of parents of intersexed children. "Divergent Ways of Coping with Hermaphrodite Children" presents two case studies of parents of intersexed children. These case studies are intended to elucidate challenges doctors face with respect to parents' acceptance of "the medical decision of sex assignment."[25] Understanding these challenges, the authors suggest, will help doctors help parents achieve "a feeling of complete conviction that they have either a son or a daughter."[26]

One family, the authors report, is white and upper middle class (the father is a "junior executive in a large company"). The other family is described as a large and uneducated family of Mexican descent (the father is a "migrant farm worker").[27] Both "Kitty West" and "Mary Torres," as the respective children are called, were born with genitalia that appeared more masculine than feminine. On learning that their children were girls and not boys, as they were first announced, both families responded with "extreme shock." Once informed of the situation, however, the parents' reactions diverged; it is the difference in their response that is of most interest to the authors.

The Wests, as the authors tell it, "wanted to understand the defect and have it corrected."[28] Mr. West found pride in the knowledge of their child's disorder; Mrs. West looks forward to the genital surgery, repeatedly asking how soon it can be performed.[29] The authors write approvingly of the gender-appropriate behavior the Wests display in interacting with their child and of the mother's reports of their one-and-half-year-old daughter's "flirtatiousness." The authors do concede that the question of whether any doubts or conflicts (e.g., over the parents' original wish to have a boy) "will complicate Kitty's eventual satisfactory sexual identity as a female is too early to tell."[30] The implication is that Kitty may become a lesbian due to the "conflicts and doubts" of her parents. Here the entanglement of "proper" gender, sex, and sexuality is particularly evident.[31]

The Torreses' response to the birth of their daughter differed markedly from that of the Wests'. Rather than join the doctors as partners in the treatment of their daughter, they were unsatisfied with the "medical assurance that according to the best medical knowledge the baby was a girl." That the physicians did not demonstrate perfect confidence in their own diagnosis "fit in with the parents' philosophy that there are many things which only God can know and perhaps the physicians made a mistake." In sum, the authors relate, the Torreses "coped with the intersex problem . . . by accepting the ambiguity of the situation and . . . actively implement[ed] it by giving the baby a neuter name (the name of a warlike tribe)."[32]

As the account of the case studies makes clear, the aim of "Divergent Ways of Coping with Hermaphrodite Children" is ultimately to foster in clinicians an appreciation of and sensitivity to cultural differences that can affect parents' acceptance of physician recommendations with respect to children's sex assignment. The Wests' "faith in medical science"—a product of their education and social milieu—indicates that they can be brought in as full partners in their child's treatment. The superstition harbored by the Torres family, on the other hand, disposes them to be suspicious of doctors' recommendations. The case study of the Torres family notes that Mary eventually does undergo cosmetic genital surgery. Had the doctors been absolutely certain of their diagnosis from the outset and conveyed that certainty in strong terms, perhaps Mary might not have had to wait until she was twelve to receive normalizing genital surgery. Had her parents not "accepted the ambiguity," perhaps she would have had a clearer gender identity than psychological tests indicate.[33]

The clear argument of Bing and Rudikoff's essay is this: For doctors to succeed in the work of sex assignment, as they promised to succeed in the case of the West family, cultural "differences" such as those that distinguish the Torres family from the West family must be taken into account. Rather than seek to understand how they might support parents in the "coping" they purport to address, the authors' aim appears to be much more narrowly confined to understanding how doctors can be most effective in overcoming obstacles (such as cultural "difference") in order to effect the surgical and social outcomes doctors have determined to be appropriate.

The medical protocols doctors employ in treating intersex children were first outlined by John Money, the psychologist credited with creating the framework for the management of intersexed infants. For Money, the origin of an individual's gender identity cannot be located in the innate characteristics that distinguish male from female. Gender identity is a function of socialization.[34] When parents dress the child announced to be a boy in blue and give him toys associated with masculine behavior, they are promoting his masculine sexual identity. For parents who unequivocally see their child as *either* male *or* female, social imperatives ensure that their comportment toward the child will result in an unambiguous gender identity. The problem with intersexed children, as Money saw it, was that ambiguous genitalia would promote doubt and confusion on the part of parents and so, on the child him- or herself.[35] Corrective genital surgery was then understood as necessary for the successful assimilation of the child into a world divided into men and women, boys and girls.

Almost forty years after Money's theories were first advanced, the rationale for the surgical assignment of gender remains largely unchanged. The Intersex Society of North America estimates that every day in this country, five children receive normalizing genital surgery.[36] That fact might not seem so remarkable, but for the revelation that the famous case that served as definitive proof of Money's theory has been revealed to be a sham. "The Case of John/Joan," or, as it may come to be known, "the true story of John/Joan," has been recounted everywhere from *Oprah* to NPR.[37] It is the story of a boy, an identical twin, who at the age of eight months was injured as doctors performed a routine circumcision. Under Money's counsel and supervision, "John" underwent sex change surgery and was reported to have been successfully raised as "Joan." A medical calamity was stunningly redeemed, and in 1972, just five years after the surgery, Money published, with his colleague Anke Ehrhardt, *Man and Woman, Boy and Girl*, the book that widely publicized the case and promoted a conception of gender as a product of "social construction."

But while the medical community and the general public—alerted by a story in *Time* magazine—were captivated by Money's tale of "the boy who became a girl," Joan's family was struggling to maintain the fiction that their daughter was a "normal" girl. While her twin brother recognized her as his sister, according to him, "she never acted the part. . . . When I say there was nothing feminine about Joan . . . I mean there was *nothing* feminine. She walked like a guy. She talked about guy things, didn't [care] about cleaning house, getting married, wearing makeup. . . . We both wanted to play with guys, build forts and have snowball fights and play army."[38] Joan's parents' reports are similar: from tearing at lacy dresses her mother made for her as a child to flushing down the toilet estrogen pills her father demanded she take at puberty, Joan displayed an intense resistance to taking up her assigned role as a girl. None of these details appeared in Money's book, however, or in subsequent follow-up reports that claimed that Joan's "behavior is so normally that of an active little girl, and so clearly different by contrast from the boyish ways of her twin brother, that it offers nothing to stimulate conjectures."[39] When she was fourteen and her father told her what had happened to her, Joan asked for a sex change. She took hormones, underwent mastectomy, had penile reconstruction, and called himself David. And what of the subsequent reports in the medical literature? Like so many children who have been the objects of studies of gender and sexual identity, Joan was "lost to follow-up" and no further reports of the case of Joan/John appeared in the literature.[40]

As presented by popular programs, the "problem" of the John/Joan case is the question that motivated Money's prolonged experiment, namely, whether gender is "natural" or "socially constructed." As Oprah tells it, the moral of the story is that "boys *will* be boys," that no amount of good intentions, surgical intervention, or social conditioning will change what is "biological fact." Despite the efforts made by Joan's parents, his teachers, the doctors at home in Canada who were treating him, or the team at Johns Hopkins to whom he and his family made annual visits, he simply would not be a girl.

As the details of Money's suppression of data are revealed, and as his refusals to comment on the case become more conspicuous with each call that he do so, the story also raises questions of a specifically ethical nature. But these are matters that are subordinated to the "truth" they reveal about sex. While, in popular discourse, the pendulum swings from "nurture" back to "nature," the management of intersex children—for which the John/Joan case served as cornerstone—remains intact, if not unchallenged.[41]

In her groundbreaking 1990 *Signs* article, Suzanne Kessler uncovers how the advancement of medical technology in the second half of the twentieth century allowed doctors to make determinations about an infant's "true sex" based on chromosomal and hormonal data.[42] Nevertheless, she writes,

Physicians who handle the cases of intersexed infants consider several factors be-
side biological ones in determining, assigning, and announcing the gender of a particular infant. Indeed, biological factors are often preempted in their deliberations
by such cultural factors as the "correct" length of the penis and the capacity of the
vagina.[43]

These concerns help to explain the preponderance of intersexed infants assigned female. As one doctor put it, "you can make a hole but you can't build
a pole,"[44] or at least you can't build a pole up to culturally acceptable specifications. While Kessler's observation might appear remarkable—doctors putting more stock in cultural understandings of gender than in "scientific"
determinations of sex—it appears less so when one takes into account the
enormous influence Money's theory of gender wielded, and continues to
wield, in the medical community. If, as he and his colleagues proposed, first in
1955, and then so sensationally in 1972 with the case of John/Joan, gender was
utterly pliable until the age of eighteen months, then it would follow that doctors could make sex determinations with impunity. Despite the fact of a clear
XY karyotype and the presence of testes, for example, an unusually small penis, or, in clinical terms, a "micropenis," could constitute grounds for clinical
castration and a female sex assignment. Likewise, if a female child is born
with a clitoris that is judged to be "too big," then "clitoral reduction" is indicated, based on the understanding that parents who are raising unambiguously
gendered children, must, as one physician put it, "go home and do their job as
child rearers with it very clear whether it's a boy or a girl."[45]

Whose Decision? Whose Choice?

Money and those who have followed him recognize that parents play a crucial
role in the healthy development of gender identity. But when it comes to making
decisions regarding their children's health, parents appear in the medical literature in the background, "stagehands"[46] to the "production" that features, in the
first act, the doctors with the children in their consulting rooms and surgical the-
aters, and in the second act, in what is explicitly marked (for the doctors at least)
as the children's convincing performance of gender.

That conception of intersex management is changing to some extent. In current
discussions, there is an increasing tendency to speak not of the "doctors' decisions," but rather of the "parents' decisions" to perform corrective genital surgery
and gender reassignment. A radio program produced by a Boston Public Radio
station featured the work of biologist Anne Fausto-Sterling, whose *Sexing the
Body* had just been published. A young surgeon called in to respond to Fausto-
Sterling's argument against corrective genital surgery to claim, "It's the *parents*
who want the surgery done." Another radio program produced by the BBC featured a woman who recounted the devastating effects of surgery to reduce the size

of her enlarged clitoris. On the heels of her testimony, a prominent surgeon explained, "This [ambiguous genitalia] is very distressing to the family, and surgery is available to make that appearance more acceptable."[47] These surgeons' statements are representative of the confusing attribution of "the decision" and "the choice" when speaking about the prospect of corrective genital surgery or gender reassignment.

Carol and Jim's Story

Even the most informed decisions reveal the ambivalent nature of consent and choice. Carol and Jim already had two children, Alex and Bobbie, when Sammy was born in the late 1990s. They were on their way to the hospital when they decided that their third child would be named Samuel or Samantha. They joke now about how their older children had unisex nicknames (short for Alexander and Barbara), but this was the first time that they had picked out a male name and its feminine equivalent. In retrospect Carol reflects that God had prepared them for what would happen.

In the birthing room, darkened for the mother's comfort, Sammy was pronounced a girl and nursed soon after birth. It was the middle of the night, and after an hour, when all seemed well, the doctor and birthing assistant were sent home. When Carol got up for the first time to use the bathroom, her husband joined the remaining medical resident to bathe the baby and conduct a more thorough exam. Both Jim and the resident noticed a "puffiness" in the baby's genital area, and together considered the possibility that Sammy was actually a boy. The resident told Jim that the swelling could be caused by any number of things, but that he would call the doctor back in. Jim should not tell Carol anything for the moment.

After some consultation, the doctor recommended discharging Carol and Jim so they could recover with Sammy at home. He was concerned that the genital swelling could be a sign of CAH, but, because Carol and Jim were experienced parents, he trusted them to keep a close eye on their baby for the next twenty-four hours and to go directly to the emergency room if the baby showed any signs of distress. In the meantime, a medical team would be assembled in the city children's hospital and they should bring Sammy in for tests. Carol remembers that when they began the tests,

They wouldn't tell us anything. It was all whispers and stuff like that. We had this feeling that they were leaning towards boy. They ordered an ultrasound and as the doctor did the ultrasound we both said, okay, "It's going to be a Samuel. It's going to be a Samuel," but then we heard them say, "Oh, there's the cervix."

Genetic tests revealed that Sammy had a rare "mosaic" chromosomal pattern, but with a predominance of X chromosomes. She had a vagina and uterus, as well as

a descended gonad that appeared to be composed of testicular tissue. It was removed for fear that it would develop a malignancy. The other, lodged in her abdomen, appeared to be an ovary, but contained no follicles.

Of those few days, Jim recounts,

*There was a lot of buzz going around. They were bringing in different interns and
everybody was poking in during different rounds at different times. You always
saw one of the doctors and somebody you hadn't seen before. So, we were like,
"Okay, this definitely isn't something normal because everybody wants to see and
come back and take a look." . . . They're kind of prepping us with words like "surgery" and "we're going to have to take that out." We knew they would have to do
some cutting sooner or later.*

Having been informed, in no uncertain terms, that their child was a girl, Carol and
Jim agreed to the removal of the remaining gonad in her abdomen, the reposi-
tioning of her urethra, and clitoral reduction.

Carol and Jim were not uninformed in these decisions. When the doctors began discussing surgery, Jim went on the Internet. The doctors at the hospital disapproved of Jim's pursuit of information; according to him, they "really tried to
steer you away from doing any research on your own. They were afraid that you
were going to uncover something that they didn't warn you about yet." When the
surgeon came and told them what he planned to do, Jim went back online and began a correspondence with a physician in Canada. He returned to the surgeon and
told him that he had decided that the surgery he had proposed was too experimental. The surgeon, according to Jim was "peeved," but relented, warning them
that he didn't want to wait "until puberty, because they're old enough to remember this." Carol and Jim believe that some of these decisions are properly
Sammy's, and when the time comes they will help her understand why the surgery to move her vagina and practice dilation are necessary.

Carol's and Jim's religious beliefs dictate that there are girls and boys, men and
women. There is nothing "in-between." They regard homosexuality as an un-
qualified wrong. Still, Carol wonders, remarking on the aggressive behavior of
their fearless and willful youngest child, so unlike her older siblings who are
"very much a girl and a boy," whether Sammy will grow up to desire women, to
feel more like a boy than the girl she is being raised to be. They watch Sammy
closely when she plays with dolls and trucks, but, just two years old, she prefers
the infamously gender-nonspecific Teletubbies. There are moments when Carol
wonders whether "they made the right decision," but most of the time expresses
confidence that the judgments she and her husband have made are sound.

Through it all, they retain their sense of humor. Carol and Jim joke that Bobbie
wanted a sister, but didn't get her order in fast enough. Jim, Carol reports with a
wry smile, wanted one of each. And Carol herself remembers that she always wondered, "What sort of people would give birth to a hermaphrodite? Oh, any sort of
people, really: Me."

III. DEPENDENCY WORKERS AND *HABITUS*

When Carol remembers asking, "What sort of people would give birth to a her-maphrodite?" she points to a shift that has occurred in her understanding of the world and the rules that govern it. Before the birth of her third child, she took for granted the clear division of the world into male and female. Now that she knows "the truth," that variation occurs, and occurs with some frequency, she has had to confront a tension between the settled expectations that had ordered her under-standing and her child's daily and insistent contradiction of those expectations.

Despite this contradiction, the expectations that organize Carol and Jim's world—what Bourdieu would call their *habitus*—remain largely intact. In the *Logic of Practice*, Bourdieu defines *habitus* as

systems of durable, transposable dispositions, structured structures predisposed to function as structuring structures, that is, as principles which generate and or-ganize practices and representations that can be objectively adapted to their out-comes without presupposing a conscious aiming at ends or an express mastery of the operations necessary in order to attain them.[48]

Habitus is only imprecisely understood in terms of "culture," the more or less fixed assumptions that ground a person's understanding of the world and her place within it. As Bourdieu describes it, this understanding is not, for the most part, a reflected or explicit understanding. But while Carol and Jim can no longer take for granted the "fact" of sexual difference, they continue to abide by its rules. A "structured structure," sexual difference itself "structures" the social order in which they move and make sense of the world. Carol and Jim maintain the secret of Sammy's mosaic chromosomal pattern from all but a few members of their im-mediate families because they know that others' ignorance or cruelty could harm Sammy. The rules that shape habitus dictate all too clearly what could happen if the secret were revealed. Carol and Jim, like Mary ten years before them, like Ruby almost thirty years earlier, maintain their silence for their child's protection.

But do they do so only for the children's sake? Bourdieu's analysis suggests that the habitus in which they move and make sense of the world, in turn, moves and makes sense of *them*, not only as men and women, but as parents. It is not only that the silence protects them from a kind of guilt by association: *"What sort of people would give birth to a hermaphrodite?"* But, as the doctors made clear to them all: What sort of *parents* would subject their child to life as a hermaph-rodite? The challenge for Carol and Jim, for Mary and for Ruby—the job of any parent—is not only to protect one's charge, but also to accommodate her to the world in which she lives. If, in the case of intersexed children, cosmetic genital surgery is presented to parents as a necessary adjustment, it is only too easy to understand why parents would consent to its performance.

For Kittay, the development of a "transparent self" provides dependency work-ers with an attunement, or identification, with their charges. But in the case of parents of intersexed children, this identification is discouraged. Parents are not given the chance to imagine their children's lives in any way except as in need of immediate correction. Despite the fact that doctors know, for instance, that later surgeries are less dangerous and more likely to produce desirable results—both with respect to appearance and the preservation of sensation—they nevertheless promote early surgery. Children, they claim, will experience less trauma if they are spared memories of the removal of gonads or the excision of phallic tissue. Doctors understate the eventual necessity of painful vaginal dilation in the case of the (majority of) children assigned female. The likely prospect of additional surgeries or other traumatic procedures in subsequent years generally also goes unmentioned, as does the option of delaying surgery until the child is older. If, as the experiences of the parents I interviewed suggest, decisions were not made *for* parents, they could be understood to have been made *through* them: Parents are not simple instruments of doctors' agendas; at the same time, their decisions cannot be regarded as products of an uncompromised agency. Similarly, doctors' failure to present a complete picture to parents may be seen, not as a conscious and deliberate effort to mislead parents for the sake of the maintenance of the binary structure of gender, but as a function of habitus, which functions, as Bourdieu understands it, to reproduce itself.

The very fact of intersex, that is, the material evidence that sex is not an either/or proposition, but rather exists on a continuum, poses a threat to the current construction of habitus—a threat that is managed by the prevention of the very possibility of posing questions about it:

> The *habitus* is a principle of the selective perception of indices tending to confirm and reinforce it rather than transform it, a matrix generating responses adapted in advance to all objective conditions identical to or homologous with the (past) conditions of its production; it adjusts itself to a probable future which it anticipates and helps to bring about because it reads it directly in the present of the presumed world, the only one it can even know.[49]

The dispositions that motivate the practices associated with corrective genital surgery must be very narrowly concerned with the reinforcement of "the present of the presumed world." Consider doctors' resistance to reconsidering standard practices despite the revelation of the true story of John/Joan and the increasing publication of critical narratives by intersexed adults. Consider the insistence with which doctors promote surgical "treatments" that are similar to many of the practices known in developing countries as "female circumcision" or clitorectomy.[50] In a recent statement, the American Academy of Pediatrics (AAP) declared that "[t]he birth of a child with ambiguous genitalia constitutes a social emergency."[51] If the AAP declines to elaborate on the nature of this emergency, it is perhaps because there is little question of the grave threat that the revelation of intersex poses to the existing social order.

The clouding of the transparent self in the case of parents of intersexed children is a function of habitus. Parents, unwilling to harm their children, nonetheless have a stake in its maintenance. At the same time, Kittay's analysis indicates the presence of an imperative—one that is itself a product of habitus—acting on the dependency worker to develop a transparent self capable of being attuned to what one's charge may experience, and further, to act for that charge in a way that respects and works to ensure the future agency of that child. While, as Kittay writes, many forms of dependency may be regarded as "natural" and "inevitable," the ways that dependency is regarded and understood, and the ways that dependency work is conceived, are neither natural nor inevitable. The normative force of Kittay's conception of the transparent self demonstrates how very embedded the concept is in habitus. But the habitus itself functions to cloud the transparent self. In the space of this contradiction, we may, or perhaps, following Kittay, we must ask: *What if* parents claimed their rights as dependency workers to secure the future autonomy of their children? *What if* parents opted to understand the decision to perform cosmetic genital surgery as the child's, that is, to forgo immediate corrective surgery? Understanding the management of intersex as a function of habitus suggests the radical potential of a dependency critique. If parents of intersexed children were to work to identify with their children as intersexed individuals, if doctors were to use their considerable authority to promote acceptance of genital variation instead of erasure, the prevailing habitus would undergo genuine transformation. Not only would such a positive identification lead to improved relationships between parents and children, it would also work against the conservative principles of habitus to effect social change.

NOTES

Without the generosity of the parents who agreed to speak with me, this chapter would not have been possible. While I cannot thank them by name, I am truly grateful to all who shared their stories with me. I owe a debt of thanks to Cheryl Chase, who encouraged my project and facilitated many of the meetings with parents. I thank Drs. Jorge Daaboul and William Reiner, who took precious time to speak with me about their work. I am also fortunate to be able to acknowledge the assistance of those who have taken such an interest in this project over the year I have been working on it. My heartfelt thanks to Carolyn Betensky, Deborah Cohen, Jennifer Di Toro, Eva Kittay, Karmen MacKendrick, Uma Narayan, and Gail Weiss. Finally, I acknowledge the College of Arts and Sciences and the Senate of American University, which provided funds and research time to pursue this project by granting me a Mellon Grant and a Research Fellowship.

1. See, e.g., essays by Martha Coventry, Howard Devore, D. Cameron, Kim, Tamara Alexander, Hale Hawbecker, and Angela Moreno in *Intersex in the Age of Ethics*, ed. Alice Domerat Dreger (Hagerstown, Md.: University Publishing Group, 1999), 71–82; 91–116; 137–140; Peter Hegarty and Cheryl Chase, "Intersex Activism, Feminism and Psychology: Opening a Dialogue on Theory, Research and Clinical Practice," *Feminism & Psychology* 10, no. 1 (2000): 117–32.

2. All uncited quotations are taken from transcripts of interviews conducted by the author.

3. Eva Feder Kittay, *Love's Labor: Essays on Women, Equality and Dependency* (New York: Routledge, 1999), x, 42. See also Martha Albertson Fineman, *The Neutered*

Mother, the Sexual Family and Other Twentieth Century Tragedies (New York: Routledge, 1995), 162.

4. The names of parents and their children have been changed to protect their privacy.
The parents from the seven families I interviewed live in nearly every region of the United
States, with the exception of one mother, who lives in a Westernized country outside the
United States.

5. Congenital Adrenal Hyperplasia (CAH) is a genetic condition associated with a de-
ficiency in the enzyme 21-hydroxylase, involved in making the steroid hormones cortisol
and aldosterone. Girls and boys with the "salt-losing variety" of CAH (such as Ruby's
daughters) require regular doses of the steroid cortisol, which they cannot produce on their
own, as well as of a salt-retaining hormone. Without such regular treatment, children will
experience crises similar to the one that brought both of Ruby's daughters so close to
death. Girls with CAH may have genital ambiguity, but boys do not. For discussion of the
variety of intersex conditions, as well as data concerning the frequency with which they
occur, see Anne Fausto-Sterling, *Sexing the Body: Gender Politics and the Construction of
Sexuality* (New York: Basic, 2000), 51–54. See also the website of the Intersex Society of
North America at www.isna.org.

6. Sara Ruddick, *Maternal Thinking* (New York: Beacon, 1989), cited in Kittay,
Love's Labor, 33.

7. Kittay, *Love's Labor*, 51.

8. Kittay, *Love's Labor*, 31. Original emphasis.

9. Kittay, *Love's Labor*, 44.

10. Kittay, *Love's Labor*, 45.

11. Perhaps for this reason, many parents of children with ambiguous genitalia, including many of those with girl children with Congenital Adrenal Hyperplasia, resist the association of the term *intersex* with their children (see postings at www.congenitaladrenalhy-
perplasia.org). As used in the medical literature, however, the term *intersex* designates any
"defect in the normal processes of sexual maturation that results in abnormality in . . . the
karyotype, the internal and external sexual organs, the gonads and the secondary sex characteristics which appear at puberty." See Sarah Creighton, "Surgery for Intersex," *Journal
of the Royal Society of Medicine*, 94 (May 2001): 218–20, 218. Resistance to the term *intersex* can also be understood as an effort, made by parents and by intersex individuals
alike, to deny their difference and "fit in" to the categories given by society. Bourdieu's
analysis, in the concluding section of this chapter, makes sense of this resistance.

12. Kittay, *Love's Labor*, 35.

13. Kittay, *Love's Labor*, 34.

14. Kittay, *Love's Labor*, 34.

15. Jessica had a form of Androgen Insensitivity Syndrome (AIS), a condition in which
a fetus with a normal (46XY) male karyotype is unable to absorb androgens in utero. In
its "complete" form, AIS would result in a child with typical feminine external genitalia
and undescended testicles. In its "partial" form, the body can absorb some androgens, and
at puberty an enlargement of the clitoris can result.

16. The use of the term *clitorectomy* is controversial. Western doctors today do not refer
to "clitorectomy," but instead to "clitoral recession," apparently to distinguish current practices from those that are now decades old. However, review of the older literature reveals
that concern for the retention of erotic sensation was not absent, as some practitioners now
suggest. In a chapter published in 1956, Hampson, Money, and Hampson write that "[p]ar-

tial amputation of an enlarged phallus in a girl is an operation approached with hesitation by many surgeons, in the fear that serious loss of sensitivity may ensue. Studies . . . indicate that these women have subsequently been erotically responsive and able to experience orgasm." See Joan G. Hampson, John Money, and John L. Hampson, "Hermaphrodism: Recommendations Concerning Case Management," *Journal of Clinical Endocrinology and Metabolism* 4 (1956): 547–56, 551.

Insistence on the more euphemistic term *clitoral recession* appears calculated not only to place distance between past and current practices, but also an effort to distinguish "medical" (beneficent, scientific, modern) practices from "cultural" (ignorant, primitive, uncivilized) practices that occur in "other countries." On interrogation, the distinction is credible neither linguistically nor practically. The suffix "-ectomy" simply means "to cut," not to completely excise. "Primitive" genital surgeries are not able to excise the clitoris in its entirety, because the structure is too deep and thereby inaccessible to the instruments used. Philosopher Diana Meyers proposes the term *genital cutting* to circumvent the euphemistic terminology used to characterize both "medical" and "cultural" practices. See Diana Tietjens Meyers, "Feminism and Women's Autonomy: The Challenge of Female Genital Cutting," *Metaphilosophy* 31, no. 5 (October 2000): 470.

17. See Suzanne J. Kessler, "The Medical Construction of Gender: Case Management of Intersexed Infants," *Signs: Journal of Women in Culture and Society* 16, no. 1 (1990): 18–21. Reproduced in *Lessons from the Intersexed* (New Brunswick, N.J.: Rutgers University Press, 1998), 25–27. It is also noteworthy that penises are deemed unworthy if they are not of sufficient length to penetrate a vagina. Surgery is also indicated if the position of the urinary meatus will not permit a boy to urinate in a standing position. Genital surgery is conducted on those assigned female with an eye not to performance, but to appearance. While neither is concerned with the sensate experience of the individuals, the emphasis on masculine "performance" (in sexual intercourse and in urination) and on feminine "appearance" is consonant with conventional conceptions of proper gender roles.

18. Of her examination of approximately one hundred letters written by mothers of children with ambiguous genitalia, Suzanne Kessler notes that parents' accounts of their children's surgery focus "disproportionately on how the genitals look rather than on what the child might be experiencing or how her genitals might function in the future" (Kessler, *Lessons from the Intersexed*, 98). The most recent accounts produced over the course of a year from a Web forum for parents of children with CAH (www.congenitaladrenalhyperplasia.org) manifest a similar concern with the appearance of the genitals, rather than with the experience of the child.

19. Kittay, *Love's Labor*, 51.

20. Kessler, *Lessons from the Intersexed*, 101. This prediction is borne out by the fact that there is no published evidence suggesting any "hazards, biological or otherwise, of having a large clitoris." While men with small penises have suffered some indignity, published studies have suggested that "[c]ontrary to conventional wisdom, it is not inevitable that such [men] must 'recognize that [they] are incomplete, physically defective and . . . must live apart.'" See Kenneth Kipnis and Milton Diamond, "Pediatric Ethics and the Surgical Assignment of Sex," in *Ethics in the Age of Intersex*, ed. Alice Domerat Dreger (Hagerstown, Md.: University Publishing Group, 1999), 181.

21. Kessler, *Lessons from the Intersexed*, 101–02.

22. Kessler, *Lessons from the Intersexed*, 103.

23. Kessler, *Lessons from the Intersexed*, 103.

24. Kittay, *Love's Labor*, 71.

25. Elizabeth Bing and Esselyn Rudikoff, "Divergent Ways of Coping with Hermaphrodite Children," *Medical Aspects of Human Sexuality* (December 1970): 77.

26. John Money, "Psychosexual Differentiation," in *Sex Research, New Developments*, ed. John Money (New York: Holdt, Rinehart and Winston, 1965), cited in Bing and Rudikoff, "Coping with Hermaphrodite Children," 77.

27. Bing and Rudikoff, "Coping with Hermaphrodite Children," 77.

28. Bing and Rudikoff, "Coping with Hermaphrodite Children," 80.

29. Bing and Rudikoff, "Coping with Hermaphrodite Children," 83.

30. Bing and Rudikoff, "Coping with Hermaphrodite Children," 88.

31. When doctors discuss gender reassignment with parents of intersexed children, anecdotal evidence suggests that doctors promote surgeries, in part, by invoking the specter of homosexuality. If the parents consent to the surgery, their children will be "proper" boys or girls, that is, they will be heterosexual boys and girls. Cheryl Chase has discussed the (unsubstantiated) assurances that doctors provide that the surgeries will result in happy men and women who will marry and have children (by adoption, if the intersex condition is associated with infertility) (see, e.g., Hegarty and Chase, "Intersex Activism," 126–27). See also Kessler's discussion of the heterosexual standard doctors employ in making assignment decisions in *Lessons from the Intersexed*, 26 (also in "Medical Construction," 20), and Fausto-Sterling, *Sexing the Body*, 71–73. As a threat (lest parents resist surgery) and as reassurance (to confirm the importance of the surgery), homosexuality figures prominently in the management of intersex.

32. Bing and Rudikoff, "Coping with Hermaphrodite Children," 80.

33. Bing and Rudikoff, "Coping with Hermaphrodite Children," 88.

34. This theory of gender socialization was initially regarded as promising by feminists such as Kessler and McKenna, who saw in it a way beyond repressive traditional beliefs about women's essential nature. See Suzanne J. Kessler and Wendy McKenna, *Gender: An Ethnomethodological Approach* (New York: Wiley-Interscience, 1978; Chicago: University of Chicago Press, 1985). Money's own recognition of this fact is reflected, as Cheryl Chase has observed (private conversation), in his tongue-in-cheek inclusion of an entry in the index of *Man and Woman, Boy and Girl* for "Woman's liberation, quotable material," which cites most of the contents of the book. See John Money and Anke A. Ehrhardt, *Man and Woman, Boy and Girl* (Baltimore, Md.: Johns Hopkins University Press, 1982), 310.

35. See, e.g., Money and Ehrhardt, *Man and Woman*, 16.

36. www.isna.org. Anne Fausto-Sterling estimates the frequency of the occurrence of intersex to be 1.7 percent of live births, though cautions that the number "should be taken as an order of magnitude estimate rather than a precise count" (Fausto-Sterling, *Sexing the Body*, 51).

37. See, e.g., "Why This Boy Was Raised as a Girl," *Oprah Winfrey Show*. Air date February 9, 2000. *Fresh Air* with Terry Gross. Air date February 16, 2000.

38. John Colapinto, "The True Story of John/Joan," *Rolling Stone*, December 11, 1997, 65–66. Original emphasis.

39. Quoted in Colapinto, "True Story," 70.

40. It was Milton Diamond, a biologist who had spent his entire career refuting Money's theories, who finally located the twin and publicized the story in an article published with one of the members of John's medical team in his native Canada. See Milton Diamond and Keith Sigmundson, "Sex Reassignment at Birth: Long-Term Review and Clinical Application," *Archives of Pediatric and Adolescent Medicine* 15, no. 11 (May 1997): 298–304.

41. In the wake of increasing skepticism concerning intersex management and explicit challenges to Money's theory (in addition to Diamond and Sigmundson, see, e.g., William Reiner, "To Be Male or Female: That Is the Question," *Archives of Pediatric and Adolescent Medicine* 151 (1997): 224–25; "Sex Assignment in the Neonate with Intersex or Inadequate Genitalia," *Archives of Pediatric and Adolescent Medicine* 151 (1997): 1044–45), Susan Bradley and colleagues in Canada report that a similar case of "ablatio penis" had the desired result: The child, a normal 46XY male at birth, currently identifies as female. Bradley and her colleagues report that, consonant with Money's theory, "the most plausible explanation of our patient's differentiation of a female gender identity is that the sex of rearing as a female . . . overrode any putative influences of a normal prenatal masculine sexual biology." The authors speculate that the gender identity of their patient differed from that of Money for two reasons. One, the decision to reassign the child happened much earlier than in "John's" case, and two, "that the parents of our patient, particularly the mother, had less ambivalence about the decision than the parents of [John]." See Susan J. Bradley, et al., "Experiment of Nurture: Ablatio Penis at 2 Months, Sex Reassignment at 7 Months, and a Psychosexual Follow-Up in Young Adulthood." *Pediatrics* 102, no. 1 (July 1998).

42. For an extended treatment of the history of "hermaphroditism," see Alice Dreger's *Hermaphrodites and the Medical Invention of Sex* (Cambridge, Mass.: Harvard University Press, 1999).

43. Suzanne Kessler, "The Medical Construction of Gender," 3; *Lessons from the Intersexed*, 12.

44. Quoted in Melissa Hendricks, "Is It a Boy or a Girl?" *Johns Hopkins Magazine* 46, no. 6 (November 1993): 10–16, 15.

45. Kessler, *Lessons from the Intersexed*, 16.

46. Frye, *Politics of Reality*, 38, cited in Kittay, *Love's Labor*, 38.

47. "The Science and Culture of Gender," May 24, 2000. *The Connection with Christopher Lydon,* broadcast on WBUR Boston, June, 2000. "Intersex Conditions" radio broadcast on the BBC December 11, 2001. Available from info1.shtml. See also Alice Dreger's discussion of the experience of Tod Chambers, a bioethicist consulting on a case of intersex who was informed by the attending surgeon that surgical correction of ambiguous genitalia was "really for the benefit of the parents." *ISNA News,* May 2001, 3. Available from www.isna.org.

48. Pierre Bourdieu, *The Logic of Practice* (Stanford, Calif.: Stanford University Press, 1990), 53.

49. Bourdieu, *Logic of Practice*, 64.

50. Indeed, these practices are prohibited by federal law in the United States. It would appear that 18 U.S.C. § 116, entitled, "Female Genital Mutilation" (1996), would apply to surgeries performed on intersexed children. The law states that "whoever knowingly circumcises, excises, or infibulates the whole or any part of the labia majora or labia minora or clitoris of another person who has not attained the age of 18 years shall be fined under this title or imprisoned not more than 5 years, or both." An exception is noted, however: "A surgical operation is not a violation of this section if the operation is . . . *necessary to the health of the person on whom it is performed,* and is performed by a person licensed in the place of its performance as a medical practitioner." In applying this exception, a subsection of the law clarifies that "no account shall be taken of the effect on the person on whom the operation is to be performed of any *belief on the part of that person, or any other person, that the operation is required as a matter of custom or ritual*" (emphases added). That the very conventions

of gender (as understood by Money and his colleagues) that explicitly motivate the surgeries could themselves be understood as "a matter of custom or ritual" is elided by the health exception written into the law.

51. American Academy of Pediatrics, "Evaluation of the Newborn with Developmental Anomalies of the External Genitalia," *Pediatrics* 106, no. 1 (July 2000): 138.

V

DEPENDENCY, SUBJECTIVITY, AND IDENTITY

14

Subjectivity as Responsivity: The Ethical Implications of Dependency

Kelly Oliver

DIALECTICS OF DEPENDENCE AND INDEPENDENCE

At least since Hegel's dialectical conception of subjectivity, philosophers have acknowledged, even insisted on, the subject's dependence upon others. The subject's sense of itself as an agent, its very subjectivity or self-consciousness, is dependent upon the subjectivity and agency of others. Hegel's famous metaphor of the onset of self-consciousness in the *Phenomenology of Spirit*, the struggle between lord and bondsman, postulates the dependence of subjectivity upon the recognition of the other: "Self-consciousness exists in and for itself when, and by the fact that, it so exists for another; that is, it exists only in being acknowledged."[1] The lord and the bondsman each seek recognition of their own self-consciousness through the self-consciousness of the other—they each want the other qua independent subject to recognize their independent subjectivity, too. As we know, this desire for recognition leads to a dialectic of alienation and otherness that oscillates between the subject and the other.

Within the Hegelian scenario, it is the bondsman who ultimately achieves self-conscious recognition by virtue of his willingness to risk his physical existence for the sake of his freedom and by virtue of his own work, his physical relationship to his environment. By risking his physical existence, he puts a stake in something beyond mere being and yet by that very move he also becomes conscious of his physical relationship to his environment. Through the fear of death, of not existing, the bondsman gets a perspective on his life as a whole. For Hegel, the bondsman's submission to the lord is crucial for his emerging self-consciousness. While the bondsman becomes independent through his work upon the physical environment and thereby gains his freedom, the lord becomes dependent upon the bondsman for his relation to the earth and thereby loses his freedom: "the lord, who has interposed the bondsman between it and himself, takes to himself only the dependent aspect of the thing and has the pure enjoyment of it. The aspect of its independence he leaves to the bondsman, who works on it."[2] So, although the bondsman is seen as dependent upon the lord, he can be independent because he works on the independence of the thing.

In the one case, the lord loses his freedom through his dependence upon dependent others (the bondsman and the earth), and in the other case, the bondsman gains his freedom from the other by his relationship with the earth through which he sees his own agency and subjectivity in his work on it. The lord makes the thing dependent on himself; it is a thing that exists for him. The lord annihilates the thing/object by making it his own. But since the bondsman merely works on it, the thing retains its independence; in fact, the bondsman's work proves the thing's independence—he appreciates that he cannot possess the thing, which continually requires his labor. The lord is lord over the thing and achieves (so he thinks) absolute negation of it.[3] The lord, it seems, is active and master of the thing, while bondsman is reduced to thingness.

Of course, the lord doesn't gain recognition through his mastery of the thing because the thing is not independent, and because it is a thing and not self-conscious. As a thing, it cannot recognize him. It is passive and not active.[4] For the bondsman, on the other hand, the thing remains independent and so, too, the bondsman is transformed into a truly independent consciousness because it is a "consciousness forced back into itself."[5] The bondsman sees his own negativity—his own transcendence of mere physical being—through the negativity involved in his relationship to the earth, "through his setting at nought the existing *shape* confronting him."[6] He sees the effects of his agency/subjectivity on the world and thereby sees that he is not merely a physical being or object but also a subject. For Hegel, subjectivity, then, is dependent upon the independence of the object. It is dependent upon a negativity that prevents the object from being assimilated into the subject. This is its independence and so the bondsman's independence.

In a sense, it is the bondsman's dependence upon the earth and his self-conscious recognition of this dependence—this closeness, this indebtedness—that separates him from the lord who is so far removed from the maintenance of his own physical existence that he no longer even realizes what it means to risk it. The bondsman's consciousness of his dependence upon the lord and upon the earth enables him to see their independence from him. It is through his dependence upon the earth and his work on it that he gains his independence from the lord and wins his freedom. Because the bondsman realizes that the earth upon which he works is independent from him—he does not master it or possess it, but works on it—he also realizes that he, too, is independent: "consciousness, *qua* worker, comes to see in the independent being [of the object] its *own* independence."[7] The bondsman's "formative activity" is crucial to his self-consciousness; it is through that activity and the forming and shaping of things that he sees his own agency. Yet the bondsman's independence and consciousness of himself as an agent do not come through possessing things or mastering them in the sense of dominating them or owning them.

Rather, the bondsman's formative activity necessitates a recognition of the thing's independence and the bondsman's inability to own it. If the bondsman's work is a form of mastery, it is only the form of self-mastery that comes from acknowledging what Hegel would call one's *negative* relationship to the earth—that is to say, acknowledging that the earth is not part of himself. Stepping away from Hegel's formulation, we could say that the bondsman overcomes his status as object or thing for the lord by recognizing the earth as an independent "agent" upon whom he depends for his existence and for his self-consciousness. The bondsman moves from thing or object to subject or agent through the reflection of his activity in the independence of the earth and lord.

How might this Hegelian dialectic of dependence-independence help us to formulate the meaning of dependence for subjectivity? What is the relationship between dependence and independence? What is the relationship between dependence and subjectivity? What are the ethical implications of this relationship? In this chapter, I take up these questions in an attempt to reconceive of the relationship between dependence-independence and subjectivity through concepts of responsivity and connection.

In the Hegelian scenario there is a dialectical relationship between dependence and independence; one cannot exist without the other. While independence is clearly the goal of the Hegelian dialectic, dependence is the only way to reach it. Indeed, as I suggested earlier, one way to interpret this Hegelian dialectic of dependence is to read independence as nothing more than the acknowledgment of one's dependence. True *independence* comes from recognizing that one is fundamentally dependent upon others—for Hegel's bondsman, the things and the lord, for us, our families, friends, neighbors, farmers, workers across the world, the earth, the air, the sun, and so on. Independence comes through the recognition of dependence on others who are themselves independent. Their independence is evidenced in the fact that they cannot be assimilated into me or my subjectivity— they are independent from me; they are other than me. This is Hegel's lord's mistake: He thinks that everything is his, belongs to him, is an extension of him. It is only by acknowledging that I cannot possess others or the earth, that they are independent of me, that I can become *independent* through the acknowledgment of my dependence upon them. Within this circular logic, dependence gives way to independence and vice versa. It is not just that the notions of independence and dependence are fundamentally dependent upon each other—which in itself makes dependence the primary relationship—but also that the notion of independence itself is based on the acknowledgment of the primacy of our dependence on others.

On Hegel's model, the lord loses his independence when he mistakes others and the world for parts of himself, existing for him, existing for his use or enjoyment only. Without any independent subjects to recognize him, he cannot become independent or self-conscious. Subjectivity depends upon recognizing the independence of the world and others. More than this, one's own independence requires acknowledging one's indebtedness to the world and others. I want to extend Hegel's analysis to suggest that this dependent foundation of subjectivity brings with it an ethical obligation to the world and others. Dependence is not a sign of a lack of freedom or a lack of agency; and independence is not total disconnection from others and the earth. Insofar as subjectivity is produced in, and sustained by, our relations to the world and others, an ethical obligation lies at the heart of subjectivity itself.

WITNESSING SUBJECTIVITY

Elsewhere, I have identified this ethical obligation at the heart of subjectivity with *witnessing*.[8] I use witnessing to describe the subject's absolute dependence on another or others for its very sense of itself as a subject and an agent. Acknowledging the witnessing structure of subjectivity means acknowledging that dependence. Like Hegel's bondsman who realizes himself through a recognition of his dependence upon independent others (the lord and the earth) whom he cannot possess even through his formative activity, the ethical subject as witnessing subjectivity acknowledges her dependence upon her addressee and interlocutor whom she cannot possess but upon whom she is absolutely dependent for her very subjectivity. This acknowledgment is the moment of ethical self-consciousness for the witnessing subject. It is the moment in which the subject realizes that an ethical obligation to others is built into the conditions of possibility for subjectivity.

I develop the notion of witnessing from Dori Laub's notion of an inner witness. From his work with Holocaust survivors, and being a survivor himself, Laub concludes that psychic survival depends on an addressable other, what he calls an "inner witness." The inner witness is produced and sustained by dialogic interaction with other people. It is dialogue with others that makes dialogue with oneself possible. In order to think, talk, act as an agent, the inner witness must be in place. This is to say that we learn to "talk to ourselves"— to think—by talking to others. Our experience is meaningful for us only if we can imagine that it is meaningful for others. And, our sense of what is meaningful, our sense of meaning itself, comes through our relationships with others. Meaning for oneself is possible through the internalization of meaning for others. Address and response are possible because the interpersonal dialogue is interiorized.

Having a sense of oneself as a subject and an agent requires that the structure of witnessing as the possibility of address and response has been set up through dialogic relations with others. The structure of witnessing not only makes it possible to relate to others but also to relate to oneself. In other words, self-reflection is the result of the structure of witness, which presupposes dialogic relations with others.

This structure of witnessing established in dialogic relationships is the structure of subjectivity. This structure of witnessing is the necessary condition for the addressability and response-ability inherent in subjectivity. On this account, subjectivity is the ability to address oneself to others combined with the ability to respond to others. One can only address oneself to oneself, or respond to oneself, if one has first addressed or been addressed by and responded to others. At its core, subjectivity is relational and formed and sustained by addressability (the ability to address others and be addressed by them) and response-ability (the ability to respond to others and oneself).

This witnessing structure is a necessary condition for assuming subjectivity or agency itself and for assuming a historical subject position. I mean to distinguish these by taking *subjectivity* to mean one's sense of oneself as an "I," as an agent, and *subject position* to mean one's position in society and history as developed through various social relationships. The structure of subjectivity is the structure that makes taking oneself as an agent or a self possible. I maintain that this structure, what I am calling a witnessing structure, is founded on the possibility of address and response; it is a fundamentally dialogic structure. Subject position, on the other hand, is not the very possibility of one's sense of oneself as an agent or an "I" per se, but the particular sense of one's kind of agency, so to speak, that comes through one's social position and historical context. While distinct, subject position and subjectivity are also intimately related. For example, if you are a black woman within a racist and sexist culture, then your subject position as oppressed could undermine your subjectivity, your sense of yourself as an agent. If you are a white man within a racist and sexist culture, then your subject position as privileged shores up your subjectivity and promotes your sense of yourself as an agent. If one's subject position is the sociohistorical position in which one finds oneself, and one's subjectivity is the structure of witnessing as infinite response-ability, then the inner witness is where subject position and subjectivity meet.

The inner witness operates as a negotiating voice between subject positions and subjectivity. If the inner witness is, on the one hand, the ability to address oneself or to be self-reflective in a way that is "learned" through addressing and being addressed by others, and also "learned" in a particular historical and social situation, then it is going to be both a prerequisite for a sense of agency per se and a governing factor in the particularities of and restrictions on that sense of agency. We internalize our relationships with others, which empowers us with a sense of our own agency, but can also leave us with a sense of the limitations of our own agency when we are in marginal or oppressed positions within the dominant culture. If we are in marginal or oppressed positions, then we can "learn" to see ourselves as limited or inferior agents, as helpless victims, mindless animals, infantile dependents, and so forth.

In addition to being formed within, and therefore affected by, the racist, sexist, and limited confines of dominant culture that also govern one's subject position, the inner witness is also a necessary part of the structure of subjectivity insofar as it sets up the possibility of response to others and oneself. Thus, there is a dialectical relationship between the structure of witnessing and one's subject position; external dialogues with others form one's sense of oneself—one's inner dialogues—and it is through those external dialogues that one first gets the sense of one's social position. On the one hand, if the inner witness is an incorporation of dialogic relations with others, of external witnesses, then its ability to create an enabling and empowering subject position is determined by the sociohistorical context of the dialogic relations with others.

To conceive of oneself as a subject is to have the ability to address oneself to another, real or imaginary, actual or potential. Subjectivity is, in fact, the result of, and depends upon, the process of witnessing—addressability and response-ability. It is the possibility of address and response that sustains psychic life and the subject's sense of its subjective agency. Oppression, domination, enslavement, and torture work to undermine and destroy the ability to respond and thereby undermine and destroy subjectivity. If the possibility of address is annihilated, then subjectivity is also annihilated. For Laub, part of his task as a psychoanalyst treating survivors is reconstructing the addressability that makes witnessing and subjectivity possible; he tries to restore the inner witness.

Subjectivity requires the possibility of a witness, and the witnessing at the heart of subjectivity brings with it responsibility. Subjectivity, in fact, is responsibility, response-ability, and ethical responsibility. It is the ability to respond and to be responded to. Subjectivity as the ability to respond is linked in its connection to ethical responsibility. Responsibility, then, has the double sense of opening up the ability to response—response-ability—and ethically obligating subjects to respond by virtue of their very subjectivity itself. Response-ability is the founding possibility of subjectivity and its most fundamental obligation. Reformulating Eva Kittay's analysis of relations of dependency, a subject who "refuses to support this bond absolves itself from its most fundamental obligation—its obligation to its founding possibility."[9]

If we are self-conscious subjects, and have subjectivity and agency by virtue of our dialogic relationships with others, then our freedom and subjectivity are not opposed to, but dependent on, others' freedom and subjectivity. Our subjectivity need not be bought through the enslavement of others. Rather, it is by virtue of others, by virtue of their response to us, that it is possible for us to respond to them. We have an obligation not only to respond, but also to respond in a way that opens up, rather than closes off, the possibility of response by others. This is what I take Emmanuel Levinas to mean when he says that we are responsible for the other's responsibility, that we always have one more responsibility.[10] We are responsible for the other's ability to respond. To serve subjectivity, and thereby humanity, we must be vigilant in our attempts to continually open and reopen the possibility of response. We have a responsibility to open ourselves to the responses that constitute us as subjects.

SUBJECTIVITY AS RESPONSIVITY

As human beings we depend on the ability to respond to others and to our environment. Our sensations, perceptions, emotions, and thoughts are responses to others and the environment. Psychologist J. J. Gibson maintains that we have perceptual systems that rely on coordinated information reception by different regions and organs in the body. For example, vision is dependent upon a basic orientation and responsiveness to the force of gravity, which is possible through the coordination of the responsiveness of hairs in the inner ear along with tactile sensations in the feet and other parts of the body. In order to see, we first have to orient ourselves and keep ourselves steady in relation to the force of gravity. Vision, touch, and basic orientation to the earth work together to produce sight.

In addition, all perception and sensation are the result of our receptivity to energy in our environment—electrical energy, chemical energy, thermal energy, mechanical energy, photic energy or light, magnetic energy, and so on. For example, vision, like other types of perception, is a response to energy, specifically differences in photic energy. Air, light, and various forms of energy are the mediums through which we experience the world. We are connected to the world through the circulation of energy that enables our perception, thought, language, and life itself. Indeed, we are conduits for energy of various sorts. Our relations to other people, like our relations to the environment, are constituted by the circulation and exchange of energy. With living beings, especially human beings, in addition to chemical energy, thermal energy, electric energy, and so forth, we exchange social energy.

The work of psychologists Andrew Meltzoff and Keith Moore has shown that already at birth, newborn infants respond to the facial and manual gestures of adults.[11] Their studies show that imitation of facial and manual gestures by infants is not the result of either conditioning or of innate releasing mechanisms;[12] rather it is the result of an inherent coordination between visual systems and motor systems that preexists any conditioning and suggests not only the infants' innate responsiveness to other people but also their innate ability to coordinate their responses to match those given to them. They hypothesize that "this imitation is mediated by a representational system that allows infants to unite within one common framework their own body transformations and those of others. According to this view, both visual and motor transformations of the body can be represented in common form and directly compared. Infants could thereby relate proprioceptive motor information about their own unseen body movements to their representation of the visually perceived model and create the match required . . . the proclivity to represent actions intermodally is the starting point of infant psychological development, not an end point reached after many months of postnatal development."[13]

Meltzoff and Moore's research suggests that infants are responsive to others from birth and that sociosomatic interpersonal interaction is innate, rather than acquired through any Lacanian mirror stage recognition. Primitive social interactions such as imitation are the result of complex sensory-perceptual systems that are inherently responsive. Shaun Gallagher and Meltzoff conclude that "recent studies of newborn imitation suggest that an experiential connection between self and others exists right from birth" that "is already an experience of pre-verbal communication in the language of gesture and action."[14] This research suggests an exchange of social energy from birth. Following Daniel Stern, we could interpret the imitation of facial and manual gestures between adults and infants as what he calls *affective attunement*, which suggests the circulation of affective energy between adult and infant.[15] Stern maintains that smiles and gestures exchanged between infants and adults produce affective attunement; they become attuned to each other's affects. Stern's research suggests that already at birth affective or psychic energy circulates between beings.

In a recent article entitled "Social Pressure," Teresa Brennan argues that what she calls *social pressure* operates like physical energy.[16] She suggests that social pressures are pressures to conform but also pressures exerted on the psyche in the same way that physical pressures are exerted on the body. She finds corroboration in Emile Durkheim's discussions of social energy, forces, and pressure. In his discussion of religious life, Durkheim identifies social energy as a sort of "electricity" generated when people are gathered together.[17] The experience of social electricity should be familiar to anyone who has attended a powerful religious service, a rock concert, a political rally, or even an aerobics class. The sum of collective energy is greater than its individual parts. This is why group experiences can be so powerful. This is also why we can feel energized by being part of a group. So, too, we can feel energized, or drained of energy, by interpersonal relations.

Durkheim's analysis of religious experience suggests that social energy operates as, or like, physical energy. He says "the heat or electricity that any object has received from outside can be transmitted to the surrounding milieu, and the mind readily accepts the possibility of that transmission. If religious forces are generally conceived of as external to the beings in which they reside, then there is no surprise in the extreme case with which religious forces radiate and diffuse."[18] Durkheim also proposes "the radiation of mental energy."[19] Just as our bodies radiate heat and electromagnetic energies, our psyches radiate affective energy. Just as thermal energy from our bodies can warm the bodies of others, affective energy from our psyches can affect the psyches of others.[20] In important ways, the psyche is a material biological phenomenon, a biosocial phenomenon.[21]

All human relationships are the result of the flow and circulation of energy, thermal energy, chemical energy, electrical energy, and social energy. Social energy includes affective energy, which can move between people. In our relationships, we constantly negotiate affective energy transfers. Just as we can train ourselves to be more attuned to photic, mechanical, or chemical energy in our environment, so, too, we can train ourselves to be more attuned to affective energy in our relationships. The art critic trains her eye to distinguish between subtle changes in photic energy or light. The musician trains her ear to distinguish between subtle changes in sound

waves or tone. The food or wine connoisseur trains her palate to distinguish between subtle changes in chemical energy or taste. So, too, some people, usually
women, are "trained" to be more attuned to changes in affective energy or mood.[22]

We are fundamentally connected to our environment and other people through
the circulation of energies that sustain us. The possibility of any perception or
sensation associated with subjectivity is the result of our *responsiveness* to the energy in our environment. Our dependence upon the energy in our environment
brings with it ethical obligations. Insofar as we *are* by virtue of our environment
and by virtue of relationships with other people, we have ethical obligations
rooted in the very possibility of subjectivity itself. We are obligated to respond to
our environment and other people in ways that open up, rather than close off, the
possibility of response.

Our means of existence becomes an ethical responsibility insofar as we are beholden to our environment and others. Our dependency upon our environment and
others obligates us as self-conscious subjects to respond in ways that sustain life.
Once we have the Hegelian realization that independence is the acknowledgment
of our own dependence, then we also realize that our dependence/independence
requires that we promote the health and well-being of others and our environment
in order to also sustain ourselves. As human beings, our sense of ourselves as subjects is dependent upon others. The response-ability inherent in the material world
becomes an ethical responsibility in the world of human subjectivity.

This ethical obligation is an obligation to life itself; human life is dependent
upon responsiveness—the ability to respond to the environment (a responsiveness
that we share with other animals, who, by the way, do not pollute it like we do),
and the ability to respond to other people (a responsiveness that makes us human
and distinguishes us from other animals, a responsiveness that brings with it an
ethical responsibility). Insofar as we are fundamentally dependent upon each other
for survival, and more than that, for what we might consider a particularly human
life, we have a fundamental obligation to sustain each other. More specifically, insofar as the ability to respond comes through relationships with other people, we
have an obligation to sustain this ability to respond. We have an ethical obligation
to sustain those who sustain us by becoming "connoisseurs" of human relationships and making ourselves aware of the subtleties in our relations with others.
Going beyond what I have read as Hegel's suggestion that the bondsman becomes
free by acknowledging his dependence on others, we not only have to acknowledge our dependence upon others, but also we have to attend to the effects of that
acknowledgment. I want to suggest that we have an ethical obligation to become
attuned to affective energy and our effects on others and the environment.

Living the responsibility to become attuned to our responses to the world and
other people, and to the energies that sustain us, is a type of loving attention. This
responsibility is the obligation to the fundamental possibility of responsiveness that
sustains us as embodied subjects. Responsiveness to the circulation of various
forms of energy, especially psychic and affective energy, enables subjectivity and

life itself. Just as the various parts of the body cannot function without the circulation of blood and oxygen, the psyche cannot function without the circulation of affective energy. Subjectivity itself is dependent upon the circulation of energy sustained through the process of witnessing. Witnessing is the heart of the circulation of energy that connects us, and obligates us, to each other. When response is cut off, the circulation of affective and psychic energies that sustains the process of witnessing, subjectivity, and life itself, is cut off. The spark of subjectivity is maintained by witnessing to our dependence on, and indebtedness to, others and our environment for our very subjectivity.

To be vigilant in our attempts to open up the circulation and flow of affective energy in all of our relationships becomes an ethical and social responsibility. For becoming a connoisseur of relationships means becoming attuned to the needs and situations of others and the earth. Therefore, attending to the responsiveness that makes subjectivity and life itself possible and trying to open and maintain the ability of others to respond require that we open ourselves to the needs and situations of others. Responding to others and vigilantly trying to open up the possibility of their response are impossible if we see others as existing for us. Indeed, if we see our own independence as the result of the enslavement or dependence of others, we not only deceive ourselves about the nature of independence and subjectivity, but also we destroy the possibility of ethical relationships. Therefore, the necessary responsiveness to others must not mean that we assimilate those needs or situations; thinking that we can do so puts us back in the exploitative and ultimately self-defeating position of Hegel's lord, and is counter to the ethical obligation inherent in subjectivity itself.

Levinas remarks that "to say that subjectivity begins in the person, that the person begins in freedom, that freedom is primary causality, is to blind oneself to the secret of the self and its relation to the past"—that is to say, to its relation to its very condition of possibility, which is the ability to respond.[23] Ultimately, ethics is impossible if we begin from the point of view of "independent" individuals bound only by external principles; the gap between individuals and those external principles is full of loopholes and rationalizations. Only if we begin by acknowledging our fundamental dependence on others can we find an ethical obligation internal to subjectivity itself.

Subjectivity is not the result of a war against all others. Rather, it is the result of a process of witnessing that connects us through the tissues of language, gestures, and care. Subjectivity is the result of a continual process of witnessing. Only by witnessing to the process of witnessing itself can we begin to reconstruct our relationships by imagining ourselves together; in the terms of the Hegelian dialectic of self-consciousness, only by acknowledging our dependence upon others and our environment do we become independent. Subjectivity, then, is not located in a subject who takes it away from his object or an other through some hostile struggle. Rather, subjectivity is the process of witnessing, of addressing oneself to others, of responding to the address from others. And, this witnessing structure at the heart of subjectivity makes us responsible for our actions and words and the consequences of them insofar as they open or close the possibility of response from others: Do they engender dialogue or silence others? But we are also responsible for our affects and psychic energy as they circulate through our relationships: Do they sustain others or do they poison them? We must learn to become attuned to the ways in which we affect others and the ways in which we can become more responsive to the needs and situations of others and thereby to our very responsibility to respond. We must become connoisseurs of the human relationships with others and with the earth.

NOTES

1. G. W. F. Hegel, *Phenomenology of Spirit*, trans. A. V. Miller (Oxford: Clarendon, 1977), 111.

2. Hegel, *Phenomenology*, 116.

3. Hegel, *Phenomenology*, 116.

4. Hegel, *Phenomenology*, 116–17.

5. Hegel, *Phenomenology*, 117.

6. Hegel, *Phenomenology*, 118.

7. Hegel, *Phenomenology*, 118.

8. See Kelly Oliver, *Witnessing: Beyond Recognition* (Minneapolis: University of Minnesota Press, 2000).

9. Eva Kittay, "Welfare, Dependency, and a Public Ethic of Care," *Social Justice* 25, no. 1, no. 71 (Spring 1998): 131.

10. See, e.g., Emmanuel Levinas, *Otherwise Than Being*, trans. Alphonso Lingis (Boston: Nijoff, 1991), 84; Emmanuel Levinas, *Ethics and Infinity*, trans. Richard Cohen (Pittsburgh, Pa.: Duquesne University Press, 1985), 99.

11. See Andrew Meltzoff and Keith Moore, "Newborn Infants Imitate Adult Facial Gestures," *Child Development* 54 (1983): 702–09; Andrew Meltzoff and Keith Moore, "Imitation of Facial and Manual Gestures by Human Neonates," *Science* 198 (1977): 75–78.

12. See Meltzoff and Moore, "Newborn Infants;" Meltzoff and Moore, "Imitation."

13. Meltzoff and Moore, "Newborn Infants," 708.

14. Shaun Gallagher and Andrew Meltzoff, "The Earliest Sense of Self and Others: Merleau-Ponty and Recent Developmental Studies," *Philosophical Psychology* 9 (1996): 212, 227.

15. See Daniel Stern, *The Interpersonal World of the Infant: A View from Psychoanalysis and Developmental Psychology* (New York: Basic, 1985). For a discussion of Stern and the notion of affective attunement, see Kelly Oliver, *Family Values, Subjects between Nature and Culture* (New York: Routledge, 1997).

16. See Teresa Brennan, "Social Pressure," *American Imago* 54, no. 3 (1997).

17. Emile Durkheim, *The Elementary Forms of Religious Life*, trans. Karen Fields (New York: Free Press, 1995), 217.

18. Durkheim, *The Elementary Forms*, 326–27.

19. Durkheim, *The Elementary Forms*, 210.

20. The work of psychologist Richard Restak suggests a type of psychic energy that moves between people. In one of his studies two people were connected to an EKG and, while having a conversation, their brain waves converged into the same pattern (see Restak 1984, 1984a, 1984b; cited in Teresa Brennan's *The Transmission of Affect*, forthcoming).

21. For more developed analysis of the psyche as a biosocial phenomenon, see Oliver, *Family Values*. See my discussion of the psyche as biosocial in the work of Julia Kristeva in the introduction to *The Portable Kristeva* (1998). See also Brennan, "Social Pressure."

22. Teresa Brennan argues that women are more likely to give what she calls directed attention to others; directed attention, she argues, is necessary for ego stability (1992).

23. Emmanuel Levinas, *Emmanuel Levinas: Basic Philosophical Writings*, ed. A. Peperzak, S. Critchley, and R. Bernasconi (Bloomington: Indiana University Press, 1996), 94.

15

"Race" and the Labor of Identity

Elizabeth V. Spelman

The description of racial identity as a "social construction" typically is offered as a challenge to the view that race is a biological feature (or a set of such features) present in every human being at birth and in virtue of which groups of humans are distinguishable from one another. On the social constructionist view, racial identity is not something one has in virtue of possessing some distinct and demarcated biological trait, but something one possesses in virtue of being subject to a process of radicalization, a branding—a "representational process whereby social significance is attached to certain biological (usually phenotypical) human features, on the basis of which those people possessing those characteristics are designated as a distinct collectivity" (Robert Miles, *Racism,* 71). The meaning of the various racial identities and the criteria for ascribing them to people are dictated not by what is discovered to be true about the constitution of human beings, but by the need or desire to sort humans for certain social and political ends, to make them markable for certain kinds of treatment and not others. Howard Winant has pointed to ways in which the social construction of racial categories is revealed in their being subject to "reconstitution" or to "constant rearticulation and reformulation . . . in respect to the changing historical contexts in which they are invoked" (*Racial Conditions: Politics, Theory, and Comparison,* 18, 115).

The term *social construction* suggests something that humans make and that by its very nature needs maintenance and repair—Winant's "reconstitution," "rearticulation," and "reformation" suggest—requires renovation, remodeling, refurbishing. (Toni Morrison recently has referred to the "struts and bolts" keeping up "The House That Race Built" ["Home," 11].) That such a construction is not literally a building, not something we can drive nails into or put on the market to sell, does not mean it is any less a product of human labor than they are, though our by now sometimes facile use of the notion of social construction tends to obscure that fact. In this brief chapter, I explore some aspects of the labor it takes to

334

construct and maintain racial identities as part of the social fabric of life in the United States (and elsewhere, too, but the focus here will be on the United States). As a partial but very provocative set of reflections on relations between whites and blacks suggests, a pernicious form of labor is exacted from blacks in order to keep that fabric from being rent. Although such work is also exacted from other nonwhite groups, in this brief space the task of exploring and exposing the nature of this work is better served by examining ways in which the demands for such labor have been made on one group in particular in a variety of contexts.

I

Historically, a not uncommon experience of blacks in the United States has been the demand that they acknowledge whiteness as being by its very nature superior to blackness. As writers such as James Baldwin and Judith Rollins remind us, this particular construction of the meaning of white and black racial identities remains alive and well into the latter part of the twentieth century. Both Baldwin and Rollins offer detailed descriptions of the labor it takes to keep this piece of the social fabric from falling into disrepair.

Drawing from both his sense of the history of race relations in the United States and the details of his own life, Baldwin suggests in *The Fire Next Time* that whatever changes in the meaning of whiteness there may have been historically, many whites have understood being white as not only distinct from but also superior to being black. Central to such whites' sense of themselves as white is the certainty that they "are in possession of some intrinsic value that black people need, or want" (127)—"intrinsic" in the sense that "God decreed it so" (40). But as Baldwin sees it, such certainty only thinly covers a kind of fear: for most whites in the United States, he claims, recognition of blacks as anything but inferior to whites is not possible on pain of "loss of their identity," an "upheaval in the universe" in which "heaven and earth are shaken to their foundations" (20). (Baldwin does not in any way suggest that this fear in whites depends on their socioeconomic status.) To try to ward off such an upheaval, whites build into the very meaning of whiteness—and thus also of blackness—what they fear may turn out to be false about whites and blacks. They make the matter of white superiority something about which no evidence can be probative either way. If whites are by their very nature superior, blacks by their very nature inferior ("God decreed it"), then these are not matters for proof or disproof. The white inability to recognize blacks as human beings (101) is something entirely different from an inability or failure to gather the appropriate evidence. Indeed, in warning non-Muslim blacks about the folly of becoming as committed to black superiority as whites are to white superiority, Baldwin comments on how this kind of belief functions: "I suddenly had a glimpse of what white people must go through at a dinner table when they are trying to prove that Negroes are not subhuman" (100). At the same time, he points out that even what appears to be the assertion of fundamental equality in fact "overwhelmingly corroborates the white man's sense of his own value" (127): "It is the Negro, of course, who is presumed to have become equal" (127).[1] What such an affirmation from whites means is, "You blacks are just as human as we are!"

Baldwin suggests that the idea that whites are by their very nature superior to blacks is not the result of deep metaphysical understanding of natural kinds or of careful attention to the empirical facts, but the produce of anxiety and self-delusion.[2] It functions to provide immunity from the possible onslaught of argument and evidence. Baldwin counsels his nephew that what whites believe about blacks, "as well as what they do and cause you to endure, does not testify to your inferiority but to their inhumanity and fear" (19)—fear that without such a guarantee of superiority, they will lose their identity.

The claim to innate white superiority, then, according to Baldwin, fails to command the acknowledgment and respect of those it is meant to cow into submission. The effort to secure independently of argument and evidence precisely what is feared can be taken away by argument and evidence is all too transparent. Moreover, the idea that whites are innately superior to blacks is treated by blacks such as Baldwin not as evidence of white superiority, but on the contrary as an invitation to pity those who embrace it. White people lack self-understanding; they "have had to believe for many years, and for innumerable reasons, that black men are inferior to white men" (19–20). In presuming that they have by nature a value that they are in a position to withhold or to grant to blacks, whites are depending on a value that "can scarcely be corroborated in any other way; there is certainly little enough in the white man's public or private life that one should desire to imitate" (127–28). Indeed, according to Baldwin, blacks in general have tended "to dismiss white people as the slightly mad victims of their own brainwashing" (137). At the same time blacks are fully aware that they cannot render such a dismissal with impunity in their everyday interactions with whites.

On several occasions in *The Fire Next Time,* Baldwin underscores his feeling of pity for whites rather than hatred of them. Given blacks' knowledge of whites, which Baldwin likens to the knowledge parents have of children (136), blacks should love whites rather than despise them. Baldwin believes that "it demands great spiritual resilience not to hate the hater whose foot is on your neck, and an even greater miracle of perception and charity not to teach your child to hate" (134). But blacks should love rather than hate not only because hatred toward whites simply reiterates white failures of humanity ("Whoever debases others is debasing himself"[113]), but also because whites desperately need the kind of love that "takes off the masks that we fear we cannot live without and know we cannot live within" (128). And because blacks will continue to be endangered as long as whites must live by the delusion of their superiority, "we, with love, shall force our brothers to see themselves as they are, to cease fleeing from reality and begin to change it" (21). Only this kind of love from blacks can free whites from their destructive anxiety, and until whites are free in this way, blacks cannot be free either (Baldwin here of course is nicely inverting the common phrase from the sixties about how no one is free until everyone is free, which was widely taken to mean that whites can't really be free unless blacks are).

In providing such counsel and direction to other blacks, Baldwin drives a stake into the heart of the idea of innate white superiority even while noting the ways in which blacks are supposed to affirm it (e.g., by greeting proclamations of equality with pleasure and gratitude). It is a notion forged of a desperate attempt to secure conceptually what it lacks empirically; it invites, indeed demands, a response of pity rather than worship or envy or desire to "be equal" to such "superior" beings; and the only solution, or anyway the best solution, to the problem of whites thinking they are by nature superior to blacks is for them to become subject to the ministrations of blacks' love—a love that does not leave whites as they are, but leads them into self-understanding and freedom from fear. The idea of innate white superiority is clear evidence of a kind of madness that can best be cured by those "inferior" blacks who have borne the brunt of such madness.

As James Baldwin sees it, then, the idea of innate white superiority is in several senses quite a piece of work. When he suggests that it would take a labor of love on the part of blacks to begin to unravel this piece of the U.S. social fabric, he is in effect urging blacks to engage in a different kind of labor than that exacted from them for centuries to keep it from unraveling. The nature of the latter kind of labor is illuminated in Judith Rollins's *Between Women: Domestics and Their Employers.*

In the early 1980s, Rollins completed a close study of the kind of work expected of black female domestics by their white female employers. In many cases, the black employees do not just clean house; intricately tied to the more obvious tasks they perform are required patterns of behavior and modes of appearance geared to attesting to the inequality of employer and domestic. The inequality the white employers want confirmed is not simply the delimited relative power of employer over employee in an unregulated and unprotected part of the labor market. What is supposed to be affirmed is an innate inequality (198), a distinction between persons of superior and persons of inferior human worth (203), of which the work relation is only a reflection. Though this inequality allegedly exists independently of any actual work arrangements, employers go out of their way to ensure that everything in the relation between employer and employee is to announce and reinforce this distinction in human worth (157, 162, 173, 180, 193, 194, 203).

In particular, the employers implicitly demand behavior on the part of their employees that expresses the employees' beliefs in their own natural inferiority and in their employers' natural superiority. Such arrangements can of course be used to try to reflect and reinforce notions of superiority and inferiority based on something other than race, as Rollins acknowledges and as workers in the service industry continue to attest.[3] But Rollins found that many white employers preferred dark-skinned (in her sample, black) over white domestic workers precisely in order to punctuate visually the difference between employer and employee.[4]

Focusing more finely on the nature of the superiority supposedly inherent in whiteness, Rollins enables us to see why insistence on its confirmation is so bizarre. Strictly speaking, there is nothing self-contradictory about the notion of something with which one is born and yet of which one needs confirmation. For example, someone might be born with a congenital disease, but she may not automatically be aware of it and for a variety of reasons may want to know whether she has it; for example, the availability of certain kinds of insurance may turn on confirmation or disconfirmation of such a condition. Similarly, we might wonder whether a property is inherent in something and come to confirm that it is—for example, the insolubility of cooper.

Rollins clarifies how the superiority said to inhere in whiteness is not anything like a discovery after the fact. When Rollins refers to the apparently never satisfied need of the white employer to confirm the relative positions of white employer and black employee, she is alerting us to the fact that if there is anything to be empirically confirmed rather than simply agreed to on demand, it is not the existence of innate differences between white and black, but the power of the employer to arrange relations between them in such a way as to preclude the very possibility of empirical disconfirmation. Everything in the behavior or attire demanded of the employee as a condition of continued employment is geared to underscore the alleged inequality of white and black. The kind of confirmation referred to in the examples in the preceding paragraph (finding out whether one has a congenital condition or whether copper is insoluble) is one in which it is an open question whether someone or something has a particular property. The kind of confirmation Rollins is talking about (here echoing Baldwin) is one about which there cannot possibly be such a question. It precludes confirmation in the empirical sense and demands confirmation in the sense of affirmation, agreement, or at the very least no obvious disagreement. What is demanded is not empirical proof that whites are superior specimens of humanity, but proof that black domestics believe this about whites.

Rollins helps us, then, to unravel several bizarre aspects to the notion of innate white superiority: (1) The kind of confirmation of white superiority exacted from black employees in social interactions with their white employers attests to the employers' unwillingness to countenance confirmation or disconfirmation of a more empirical nature. Indeed, the conditions of employment are geared to preclude the possibility of disconfirmation: "The domestic's 'place' is below her employer in every way (except, of course, in her capacity for prolonged physical labor). Any hint of competition with the employer must be avoided by the domestic's being clearly non-threatening in all ways, including her physical attractiveness" (201). Not only must there be no competition, no hint of the employee having capacities or relationships that suggest something other than her innate inferiority to her white employer, but there must also be no sign that she disagrees with the employer's assessment of their relative worth as human beings. The employees Rollins interviewed had no doubt about the importance of their appearing to share the employers' beliefs about white superiority and black inferiority (164), but equally no doubt that such beliefs were false. Their apparent acquiescence is the price they must pay to get and keep their jobs (189–90). (As Ellis Cose recently highlighted in *The Rage of a Privileged Class,* black lawyers, journalists, and other professionals are also expected to keep the warp and woof of white superiority from being damaged. Such expectation, of course, does not show up as part of their job description, but as an implicit condition of employment.[5])

(2) Because the kind of confirmation in question depends on what the black employees say and how they act, the white superiority being confirmed depends upon what is believed about whites by the very people those whites deem to be their inferiors. (3) Although the ability to exact such confirmation from blacks attests to the power of whites, its exercise reveals the very vulnerability it pretends not to have: it is power to get people to agree with you not because they believe what you say, but because it is too costly for them to disagree openly. (In this connection, no wonder Baldwin speaks about self-delusion: I know I have to make you agree, but I also take this agreement as a genuine expression of your belief.) (4) The nature of the confirmation of whites' belief in superiority suggests how ungrounded the belief is: it isn't really confirmation, but simply acclamation on demand.

II

Judith Rollins's analysis, like James Baldwin's, invites us to think seriously about the maintenance of the idea of white superiority and black inferiority as a kind of labor. The deference required of the black employees is not simply a condition of their employment as house cleaners. It is part of the larger sustained effort it takes to keep afloat the notions of innate white superiority and black inferiority—joint notions that have long been a piece of the social fabric of U.S. society. Because of that fabric, the whites Baldwin describes fear the overturning or the rending asunder of the world as they know it at the suggestion that whiteness does not carry with it any innate superiority to blackness. Not all parts of the social fabric are fabrications in the pejorative sense of being lying contrivances, but the notion of the innate superiority of whites and the innate inferiority of blacks surely is. Baldwin, no less than Rollins, reminds us of the labor of lies it takes to maintain this notion, and he insists that it would take the labor of love to undo it.

The words *work* and *labor* should not be understood as only metaphors here, though some common metaphors help us to understand the nature of this work. Think, for example, of the metaphor deployed in the idea—and a very common idea it is—of "the social fabric." The social fabric of our lives is not something that exists "in nature," independently of human beliefs, attitudes, behavior, language, gesture, and the many institutions that frame human interactions and survive the birth and death of particular human agents. Indeed, the metaphor suggests that we are bound together by something that we make, that needs maintenance, can be torn apart, and is subject to repair. That this fabric of our making is not literally a piece of cloth, not something we can hold in our hands or see on shelves in a shop, does not mean that it is not a product of human labor.

Baldwin and Rollins have brought to our attention a social construction (a metaphor with which we began) that—as attested to by the different historical and interpersonal contexts of which they write—continues to be part of the social fabric of U.S. society: the idea that there are distinct "races"—they have focused on white and black—and that one is by its very nature superior to the other as a specimen of humanity. Indeed, in the works of W. E. B. DuBois, David Roediger, Noel Ignatiev, and others, we can see how the alleged intrinsic superiority of being white has promised a refuge against the ravages of indignity brought on by attenuation of political freedom or the loss of acceptable work: whiteness attests to a kind of superiority as a human being that is impervious to the contingency of changes in economic, social, or political status.[6] At the same time, this superiority seems desperately in need of affirmation; in particular, as suggested by Baldwin's claim that "the power of the white world is threatened whenever a black man refuses to accept the white world's definition" (*The Fire Next Time,* 95), it requires affirmation from the allegedly inferior group. What kind of work does it take to keep this piece of the U.S. social fabric from being rent?

It is important here to distinguish this question form the questions broached in the rich literature on the distribution of jobs along racial lines. As is well known, one of the many functions of the notion of race has been to lubricate the conflation of the division of labor and the segmentation of the workforce: as job distribution in the United States and most elsewhere continues to show, the idea that there are different kinds of work matches up ever so nicely with the idea that there are different kinds of people and that they ought to do different kinds of work. For example, in the 1990s, white men were twice as likely as black men to be employed in managerial, administrative, or professional jobs, whereas black men were twice as likely as white men to be found in the service sector (William O'Hare et al., "African Americans in the 1990s," 52). Indeed, among the lessons from Judith Rollins's book is the continued push toward racial earmarking of domestic labor.

The focus of this chapter, however, is not the distribution of labor along racial lines, but rather the labor it takes to sustain a certain version of racial difference. What shall we call the labor it takes to construct, reproduce, and maintain the idea of distinct white and black racial identities and the natural superiority of one to the other?

One promising resource for spelling out the nature of such work comes from the growing body of literature on several forms of labor closely related to the kind in question. I am thinking in particular about the provision of services, about what has come to be called *shadow work,* and about the complex labor of social reproduction.

It is a commonplace in the 1990s to point to the expanding proportion of paid jobs around the globe that are not in agriculture, government, or the production of goods, but in the service sector—"jobs in which face-to-face or voice-to-voice interaction is a fundamental element of the work" (Cameron Lynne Macdonald and Carmen Sirianni, "The Service Society and the Changing Experience of

Work," 3). Familiar examples are order takers at fast-food restaurants, managers in delivery companies, secretaries, telemarketers—where the labor in question "no longer entails the assembly of a product but the creation and maintenance of a relationship" (Macdonald and Sirianni, "The Service Society," 5). Though such service is not palpable or tangible in the same way the production of goods is, it is recognized as work.

The term *shadow work* appears to have been coined by Ivan Illich in a book by that name to refer to work that is not recognized as being part of the economy, even though it is necessary to that economy (housework is his prime example). The term has come to be used more generally to designate work of any kind in any sector that is unpaid and usually invisible in part because of the terminology used in the labor market and the ways in which productivity is measured.[7] There are shadow aspects to many forms of service work. For example, as Rollins and others have pointed out, domestic workers often are expected to look and act in ways that prop up the ego and identity of their employers. Highly visible secretaries typically have to perform the not-so-visible (i.e., not-to-be-noted) functions of buffers and general smoother-overs (see Susan Eaton, "'The Customer Is Always Interesting': Unionized Harvard Clericals Renegotiate Work Relationships"). Like so much of the shadow work done at home, shadow work at the workplace is most noticeable when it is absent, even though when present it is not acknowledged as a recognizable part of the economy. Workers are not paid for it, but evaluations of their suitability for the job are likely to be highly influenced by judgments about how well they perform such functions.[8]

The work of social reproduction is "the creation and recreation of people as cultural and social, as well as physical, beings" (Evelyn Nakano Glenn, "From Servitude to Service Work: Historical Communities in the Racial Division of Paid Reproductive Labor," 117). It includes labor such as making sure food is on the table, providing and taking care of clothing and shelter, bringing up children, acculturating them, keeping relationships going (indeed, the love Baldwin says whites need from blacks is a kind of social reproductive work). It isn't necessarily work that is invisible and unpaid—food preparation can be waged or unwaged work in the household or waged work in a restaurant—though often it is, as for example in the socialization of children by adults or in the maintenance of ties with neighbors or merchants. Some aspects of social reproductive labor having to do with creating and maintaining relationships (and teaching others how to have them) are coming out of the shadows both at home and at the workplace.

Most of the literature about service, shadow, and reproductive labor focuses on the workplace and the home. Although the social fabric of which Baldwin and Rollins speak is woven into both workplace and home, it is not confined to those locations. The social fabric woven to guarantee innate white superiority is stronger than the microfabrics within the world of work or of home: even if one's superiority is not attested to in those places, one can somehow find refuge in one's whiteness. That is, the labor necessary for keeping afloat the notions of innate white superiority and black inferiority is also done, has to be done, outside what ordinarily counts as the workplace or the home. At the same time, Rollins describes the kind of shadow work within the workplace that helps to keep the larger social fabric from being rent. To the extent that the domestic worker is supposed to perform certain tasks and equally if not more importantly to "shore up her employer's sense of superiority by not reminding her of her reliance upon the worker,"[9] what she is doing not only happens to be, but must also remain invisible (Cameron Lynne Macdonald, "Shadow Mothers: Nannies, Au Pairs, and Invisible Work," 250). It would defeat the purpose of attesting to the superiority of the employer were it an acknowledged and officially paid for part of the employee's job to provide such affirmation. Black domestic workers are not paid for making sure this piece of the social fabric is not rent, but they are not paid unless they do the work of making sure it is not.

The kind of labor it takes to sustain the idea of innate white superiority appears to be like service work in several ways: it involves maintenance of relationships, not the production of objects; the relationships in question are not friendships or marriages or even formal contracts, but they proceed in accordance with certain protocols developed by one party to be followed by the other. However, unlike service work, this labor is unpaid and typically is exacted of people as a condition of paid labor in the service or other sectors.

This labor of racial identity also has elements of social reproductive work: it can, indeed, must, be found outside the workplace as well as inside it; what it reproduces is not bodies but ways of coding bodies as embodiments of natural types of humans: those superior by nature and those inferior by nature.

It is by its very nature shadow work: this work cannot be recognized as such, for the notion of innate white superiority cannot be sustained by a relationship if it is acknowledged that the point of the relationship is to create and maintain the notion.

So we can describe the work exacted of blacks to shore up the notion of innate white superiority as a kind of social reproductive shadow work.[10]

III

I have suggested a couple of approaches to making the case that we should regard what it takes to sustain the notion of innate white superiority and black inferiority as a kind of work. The first flows from thinking through the implications of the powerful metaphors of social fabric and social construction: the ideas and values in terms of which people are related are themselves the work of human creation, maintenance, and repair (and thus also subject to resistance and destruction). The second approach relies on taxonomies of work detailed in recent nuanced studies of labor suggesting that the work that goes into keeping afloat the idea of innate white superiority is a form of social reproductive shadow labor. I want now to suggest a third way of trying to capture and articulate the nature of such work.

Let's imagine for a moment what a job description would look like for the kind of work required of blacks to keep the notion of innate white superiority from being rent. The analyses of Baldwin and Rollins lead to a description along these lines:

NEEDED: Dark-skinned people to be identified as belonging to a group basically different from and innately inferior as human beings to white-skinned people. Must be willing to affirm or at least not deny such differences and to do so often enough to prevent any possible cracks in the picture of innate white superiority. Invisible menders especially welcome (i.e., those individuals who fix the rips that do appear in the racialized social fabric so that it looks as if they never had needed repair— indeed, as if they are not the kinds of things that are reparable or irreparable).[11] This is high-maintenance relationship.[12] Location: everywhere. Pay: no pay for this work, but doing it is a prerequisite for other jobs. Special qualifications: when answering this ad, make sure you act as if you never saw it.

(One way to compare demands implicitly made on blacks with those made on Latinos, Chicanos, Chinese Americans, and others is to imagine the details of such job descriptions for each group.)

What has stood in the way of being able to describe the notion of innate white superiority as the product of a kind of labor, and what is to be gained by doing so?

Several reasons why this labor would not immediately be noted as such have to do with the notion of social construction. The very familiarity of the phrase may make us disinclined to think about how much social constructions share in common with physical constructions, which we know need work: they are built, are subject to decay, and typically need maintenance and repair. A tendency to focus on the power and authority of scientific and legal institutions to define the meaning of the term *race* may keep us from looking at what is exacted of those conscripted to live out and give everyday content to such meanings. And the concept of shadow work may be a much-needed reminder that in many contexts, social constructions, especially those having to do with senses of individual or group identity, will collapse under their own weight if they are acknowledged as such.

Finally, what is to be gained by thinking about the idea of innate white superiority as something that requires labor?

(a) First, it invites us to ask what the investment might be in obscuring the need for and functioning of such labor. The recent literature on shadow work is quite instructive in this regard: it encourages us, for example, to wonder who gains from making it difficult to understand and appropriately value certain dimensions of clerical work[13] or to ask who gains from ignoring the function of housework in an economy that doesn't formally recognize it as work (Illich, *Shadow Work*, 1). So, too, we can ask: Who has what to gain from the failure to recognize or acknowledge the complex work of construction, maintenance, and repair required for that part of the social fabric into which the notion of innate white superiority is so tightly woven?

(b) In the hands of writers such as Baldwin and Rollins, we get to see the scaffolding that props up the never fully secured house of innate white superiority and the perverse ludicrousness of the construction. Having a sense of what it takes to sustain such scaffolding also offers a horrifying reminder of the burdens placed on those doing the work: the idea of innate white superiority and black inferiority is demeaning and degrading to blacks.[14] But the toll such an idea takes begins to show in fuller dimension when we see that it requires a kind of work on the part of blacks to sustain it: the house of innate white superiority threatens to topple in the absence of apparent black affirmation of it. That blacks are supposed to do work necessary to the maintenance and repair of innate white superiority is underscored by the massive resentment of and resistance to such demands. To exact such labor is like requiring someone to provide the kind of self-incriminating evidence that it is the business of the Fifth Amendment of the U.S. Constitution to prohibit.

(c) If maintaining the idea of innate white superiority and black inferiority is work, is there an accompanying economy in which it functions? Yes, a racial economy. In such an economy, there are different racial denominations, the values of which depend upon and always are relative to the values of the others (i.e., none has any value except relatively to the others). Some of the currency is white, and some of it is black.[15] To be white is to be the bearer of white currency, which by definition, by denomination, is worth more than black currency. (Because this racial economy exists in order to provide meaning for being white, to be black in its terms is to be the bearer of the devalued black currency; this racial economy has room for black identity only as a foil for white identity, not as anything that might be created more independently of the notion of higher-valued whiteness). You cannot use the social tender of white currency if you are black, for that would destroy the value of white currency. That is why it is so important for there to be— or rather for there to be thought to be—strict distinctions between the races: knowing which denomination is being used depends on knowing who is using it. That is also why under long-standing and still current political and social conditions, whites are born with a kind of racial capital blacks cannot possibly accumulate. As Cheryl Harris has argued, whiteness is something the ownership of which would become worthless were anyone able to acquire it ("Whiteness as Property").[16]

White hijackings of black currency fuel many dimensions of the economy in the larger sense—for example, in the entertainment and advertising industries—but black hijackings of white currency are rare. Indeed, the examples provided by Baldwin and Rollins point precisely to ways in which erosions of the distinction between white and black currency are prevented: whites do everything they can to keep the distinction between white and black clear and well defined.[17] But that is not quite accurate, for whites are also careful to ensure there's a difference between white hijackings of black currency and the dissolution of the distinction between white currency and black currency. Lucrative appropriations of black identity by whites are always partial in the sense that they count on audiences knowing that what is being offered is not black people or black experience, but a white version of something identified as black (an interesting reverse twist on treating blacks as black versions of white). In short, if Elvis had been black, he wouldn't have been Elvis, and his success depended on his audience's recognition of that fact.

Baldwin and Rollins provide rich descriptions of the rather desperate need of whites to have their whiteness and thereby their innate superiority affirmed. When we think about the workings of the racial economy we can see that such desperation expressed not only a psychological need to feel superior to others in order to have a sense of one's own identity and worth, but a desire to make sure one's racial endowment does not lose its value—not an irrational desire in those wishing to maximize the return on their investment in being white. It is not enough to have an economy in the ordinary sense and a workplace in the ordinary sense reflect and reinforce the notion of white superiority. The very meaning of being white or being black has to incorporate the idea of white superiority and black inferiority, for the currency must have value in every exchange in order to have value in any exchange: How valuable can it be if you are white in all situations, but it counts only in some? And—thinking about the power of James Baldwin's mockery of what he finds whites have to believe about blacks—how valuable can being white be if those you deem your natural inferiors don't want to be white and, in fact, come to pity people so desperate and deluded as to treat their whiteness as proof of innate superiority?

In the context of the kind of racial economy described by Baldwin and Rollins, whiteness is an *investment*—both in the archaic sense of a garment or outer layer and in the sense of something that promises returns. Indeed, putting the two senses together, whiteness is an investment in an investment. Investments (in the nonarchaic sense) depend upon goods maintaining or increasing in value. There is no point in being white unless in being tendered in the racial economy it can be recognized and bring rewards, including the refuge it promises when otherwise the chips are down. Blacks cannot benefit from this economy but are conscripted to do the work central to it both by embodying an identity necessary to the creation and meaning of white identity and by being in relationships with whites that are constructed to carry out the Sisyphean task of affirming innate white superiority (quite literally a form of affirmative action, the action of affirmation). What DuBois and most recently David Roediger have called the *wages of whiteness*—the privileges of being white or what I have referred to above as *white currency*—are the product of a highly exploitative form of social reproductive shadow work exacted of blacks.

To the extent that the racial economy prevails, the bearer of white currency has a built-in advantage over the bearer of black currency. So one way to gauge how thoroughly woven the racial economy is into the social fabric at any given time is to ask the following questions: Are blacks mistaken in thinking that (in the context of the larger society) if being black can't be made to count positively, it will count negatively? Are whites who wish to benefit from the sheer fact of their whiteness being illogical if they fear that (in the larger society) unless being black continues to count negatively, being white cannot continue to count positively? Careful answers to such questions have to be part of any assessment of affirmative action initiatives and hate speech regulations.

Finally and even more briefly: I have suggested that there is nothing more to white identity than the currency it has, the currency it *is,* in the racial economy.[18] As mentioned earlier, this does not of course mean that all there could possibly be to black identity is its denominational value in the racial economy. How struggles or debates among blacks over the meaning of black identity turn out will have profound implications for the question of whether any denominalization by "race" entails the kind of currency that constitutes what I have called the racial economy. If white identity in the context of racial economy requires labor of a deeply exploitative and degrading kind from blacks, then perhaps one test of any claim to "racial" identity is whether it, too, requires such labor from other "racial" groups.[19]

NOTES

This chapter originally appeared in *Racism and Philosophy,* edited by Susan E. Babbitt and Sue Campbell (Ithaca, N.Y.: Cornell University Press, 1999). Copyright © 1999 by Cornell University Press. Reprinted by permission of the publisher, Cornell University Press.

1. In a remark he soon regretted having made, historian Kenneth Stampp expressed his belief that "innately Negroes *are,* after all, only white men with black skins, nothing more, nothing less" (*The Peculiar Institution: Slavery in the Ante-Bellum South,* vii-viii).

2. Baldwin has no doubt about the tremendous political, social, and economic power whites in the United States wield. His analysis seems geared to showing how contrary to their own best self-interest the acquisition and deployment of such power is.

3. See, for example, Cameron Lynne Macdonald and Carmen Sirianni, eds. *Working in the Service Society.*

4. In this connection, students of Aristotle may recall his wish that visible characteristics of human beings reveal their given natures—it would be so much easier to pick out those who were meant "by nature" to be slaves (*Politics,* 1254b34–1255a2).

5. Cose (*The Rage of a Privileged Class*) recounts the endless occasions on which black professionals—many of whom are at the top of their professions—come up against the assumption on the part of their white coworkers (at every level in their organizations) that blacks really aren't, really can't be, the equal of whites. It is painfully clear to the blacks Cose interviewed what the consequences for them would be were they to bring attention to that assumption or try to do anything to undermine it. True, unlike the domestic workers Rollins got to know, black professionals aren't expected to wear clothing or engage in obvious forms of deferential behavior attesting to the natural superiority of whites (though their attire may need to be geared to combatting the presumption that they aren't as professional as their white coworkers). But the implicit sanctions against disturbing the presumption of white superiority are so heavy that the price of securing and keeping one's job typically includes not getting angry at the daily expressions of disbelief that blacks could have such jobs, let alone do them well. It is as if whites know that the presumption of white superiority sewn into the social fabric is always vulnerable to rending and ripping

and so they constantly reinforce the threads by means of what otherwise may appear to be gratuitous expressions of the assumptions that blacks couldn't possibly really belong there. They appear to count on blacks feeling caught in a double bind: if blacks don't complain about such treatment, there can't really be anything wrong with the social fabric (no matter that it is likely to include the assumption that what blacks want is to be the same as whites, in the sense Baldwin so richly derided, or the certainty that the corporation has no problem with racism). And if blacks do complain, their job—or certainly their enjoyment of many of its possible benefits—is likely to be on the line.

6. See W. E. B. DuBois, *Black Reconstruction in America, 1860–1880,* 17–31 and passim; David Roediger, *The Wages of Whiteness: Race and the Making of the American Working Class,* 12–13 and passim; Noel Ignatiev, *How the Irish Became White,* 96 and passim.

7. See Macdonald, "Shadow Mothers," 248; and Eaton, "The Customer," 306.

8. Some workers—for example, flight attendants—are explicitly employed to do what Arlie Russell Hochschild calls "emotional labor," producing emotions in themselves and in their customers that are deemed essential to the success of the enterprise (*The Managed Heart: Commercialization of Human Feeling,* 7 ff.)

9. This reminds us, as does Rollins's own analysis, that it is not only racial identity that requires labor.

10. For an enlightening discussion of some of the work whites are trained to do, see Lillian Smith, *Killers of the Dream.*

11. Invisible mending is offered by tailors for those who don't want their garments to show even the slightest sign of having been patched up.

12. This not uncommon expression has recently been elevated to the status of a book title: *High Maintenance Relationships: How to Handle Impossible People,* by Les Parrott III.

13. See, for example, Eaton, "The Customer," 297.

14. This idea is also, according to Baldwin, a sure sign of pitiful white self-delusion.

15. The racial economy is another place at which comparisons among African Americans, Japanese Americans, Chicanos, and others might fruitfully be explored.

16. For a review of some of the legal standards historically used to establish whiteness, see Harris, "Whiteness as Property." Naomi Zack has suggested that the formula for establishing whiteness amounts to this: white skin and no nonwhite forbears ("Race and Philosophic Meaning," 33). Or, as Ian F. Haney López puts it, whites are "those who are not non-white" (Haney López, *White By Law: The Legal Construction of Race,* 28).

17. As Ian Haney López has pointed out, many of the legal definitions of whiteness have involved anxious attempts to exclude people from parts of Japan, India, and Mexico (among other places) from naturalization and citizenship—another reason why full exploration of the meaning of whiteness must include more than a history of white–black relationships. See *White by Law,* especially 1–18, 49–77.

18. Hence, I would join Ian Haney López and others in wondering whether there could be any point to trying to redeem or look for the "positive" aspects of white identity. See Haney López, *White By Law,* especially 30–33, 183 ff.

19. Many thanks to Martha Minow, Larry Blum, Frances Smith Foster, Susan Babbitt, and Sue Campbell for very helpful criticism and comments.

16

Dependence on Place, Dependence in Place

Bonnie Mann

Should the emancipation and secularization of the modern age, which began with a turning-away, not necessarily from God, but from a god who was the Father of men in heaven, end with an even more fateful repudiation of an Earth who was the Mother of all living creatures under the sky? The Earth is the very quintessence of the human condition.

—Hannah Arendt

Hannah Arendt was not alone in noting that Euro-masculinist[1] cultures seem "possessed by a rebellion against the human condition,"[2] and particularly against our dependence on the Earth. At least since World War II, a small chorus of anxious voices has tried to remind us, with great urgency if not great success, of our forgetfulness that "we are tied to place undetachably and without reprieve."[3] Yet it is still rare for our inquiries into the nature of our relationship to the Earth we depend on to avoid the seemingly inevitable pressure of the subjective turn, the pressure to exchange this "free gift from nowhere . . . for something [we have] made [ourselves]."[4] When the Earth we depend on is exchanged for a "world" we create, we are left marveling again at the extraordinary accomplishing activity of a subject, but with no sense of the ground and condition for the possibility of such activity. We have, in opposing "Earth" to "world," fantasized a "world" freed from Earth, and this amounts to a grave misunderstanding of the world that we *have* made.

I am, to some extent, accepting Heidegger's distinction between Earth and world here, from "The Origin of the Work of Art,"[5] but my usage is closer to Hannah Arendt's more political contextualization and adaptation of Heidegger's distinction in *The Human Condition*. Here Arendt makes two important contributions. First, she sees the "battle" between Earth and world as a culturally and historically bound *orientation* that has accompanied Western philosophy since the Greeks, rather than as inevitable. Second, she emphasizes the role of the material *planet* Earth in Heidegger's rich but apparently more abstract notion. For Arendt the very planet we call Earth is "the quintessence of the human condition," even as how we live and understand our relation to the Earth in the broader sense becomes part of the human condition as well. Here there is already a distinction and a relation between a primary, irrevocable, and material dependence on the Earth, which is the "quintessence" of the human condition, and the conditions we create, that is, the way that quintessential condition is lived, altered, and built upon by the world-making activities of subjects. Arendt understands this relation better than Heidegger, because she both acknowledges that what is necessary in the relation is our dependence rather than "battle," and recasts the embattled nature of the relation as a kind of *disorientation* that can and must be corrected. This gives Arendt's account an urgency and relevance that is even more important today than when she wrote *The Human Condition* in 1958. Today, our exchange of Earth for world, and our quest for a strange emancipation from the Earth continues. These undermine our attempts to think of our relationship to the Earth in a way that is meaningful, and this at a time of unparalleled environmental destruction that makes the task of thinking this relationship more urgent every day.

This chapter is motivated by that urgency. I am working to articulate another understanding of the relation between Earth and world, not as a battle, though it easily becomes that, but as a morally charged relation of dependence. Here battle is one option among others, and the most depraved, but is the one we in the West have chosen, by and large. I begin with a brief examination of how the modern exchange of "Earth" for "world" persists after the postmodern turn in the notion of "performativity." This amounts to a retreat to the subjectivism of modernity, now absent the conceit of the sovereign subject. I employ the notion of *dependence*, which I borrow from Eva Kittay and extend to the relation between persons and the Earth, to resist this subjectivism. In the notion of dependence I hope to find "a knife sharp enough" to cut through the self-involved subjectivism that plagues us.[6] This necessitates a re-prioritization of place. While spatiality has received a good deal of renewed attention in postmodernity, Edward Casey is one of the first to prioritize place,[7] to call for "an outright geocentrism—or perhaps better, an engaged ecocentrism—[as] the most efficacious antidote to centuries of unself-questioning anthropocentrism and subjectivism."[8] I draw on his work to begin to spell out the consequences of facing and acknowledging our dependence on the Earth.

I take this dependence to be absolute. It is a kind of *relationship* to place, one that, properly faced, evokes both wonder and reverence. Wonder and reverence are the attitudes appropriate to our place here and give us the epistemological, moral, and political footing from which our world-building activity could be affirming of our relation to the Earth, rather than so suicidally destructive.

THE PERFORMATIVE AND THE DISCLOSIVE

One of the most persistent trends in modern philosophy since Descartes and perhaps its most original contribution to philosophy has been an exclusive concern with the self . . . an attempt to reduce all experiences with the world as well as with other human beings, to experiences between man and himself.

—Hannah Arendt

Even in postmodernity, we seem to always land ourselves, by whatever circuitous route, back in the lap of Immanuel Kant. In his crusade against the *Sturm und Drang's* tendencies toward pantheism, Kant was determined to exchange what he saw as a misplaced reverence for the natural world for reverence for human reason. We seem to have been infected with an overwhelming tendency to do the same. This is true of modernist realist accounts, where our reverence is turned toward the power of human intelligence and tools to really know, to possess fully, the secrets of the natural world, "as if we dispose of it from the outside."[9] It is true of the modern idealists and transcendentalists as well, whose fetishizing of the mental activity of subjects amounts to an abjection of the Earth, either by denying its existence, or bracketing the question of it, or collapsing its existence by whatever subtle sleight of hand, back into the self-aggrandizing "world-making" activity of some (simple or transcendental) subject. And perhaps surprisingly, it is true of the postmodernists, who finally decenter the subject, only to paradoxically recenter the *subjectivity* of the humbled subject through a fetishization of the power of language to make worlds of its own.

Indeed, two persistent confusions of modernism seem to have crossed over into postmodernity unscathed. The first is a confusion between what we call "Earth" and what we call "world," or perhaps better said, an inability to articulate the relation between the two. The second is a confusion about our relationship to Earth (which we replace with "world"), that constantly positions subjects as "world-makers," "authors," or "stewards," while never acknowledging our absolute and utter dependence in this relation. Both of these confusions, between Earth and world and between persons and place, I take to be symptomatic of the miscarriage of reverence that we who inhabit the postmodern have inherited from modernity.

By *miscarriage of reverence*, I mean to name a cultural transition that is perhaps most eloquently detailed in Kantian aesthetics, particularly in Kant's notion of the sublime. Here Kant narrates a confrontation between a rational (masculine) subject and the natural world in its might (dynamical sublime) and magnitude (mathematical sublime). In this story, the subject is at first humbled in the encounter, filled with awe and wonder. The first response to the might and magnitude of nature is a fearful reverence. Yet this moment of reverence for something that is external, humbling, and gendered female[10] is quickly exchanged for another sort of experience altogether. The confrontation with nature becomes a mere occasion for setting into motion a drama that is inward, self-aggrandizing, and triumphantly masculinist. The internalization of the drama involves the assignation of a feminine gender to the imagination, and of a masculine gender to reason, and the "breaking" of the imagination by reason.[11] The result is a reorientation of reverence, from the external to the internal, from the natural world to the subject, from the power of nature to the power of reason. In short, our reverence is *redirected from Earth to the self.*

So far from marking a transition from wonder to doubt, as Arendt supposed it did, the advent of what we call "modernism" marked a transition in the *orientation* of the Euro-masculine subject's wonder. The wonder of this awe-filled subject was *redirected*, through doubt, toward himself. And this newfound self-reverence seemed everywhere justified: in the progress of science and technology, in European empire building, in the accumulation of European wealth, and in the accomplishments of philosophy itself.

But if this is the subject who is criticized in postcolonialist and postmodernist writings, how is it that I can claim that the modernist miscarriage of reverence is carried over from the modern to the postmodern? There is nothing so irreverent as the postmodern attitude of skepticism toward the grandiose claims of the centered subject. This is the subject whose universalism has been undermined, whose grand narratives have been brought down to size, whose omnipotence has been exposed as a self-aggrandizing fiction, precisely through the deconstructive efforts of postmodernity. Yet it seems the very strategies that have been deployed to humble the modern subject, reinstantiate the accomplishing activity of that subject as the object of our wonder and admiration.

One way to clarify this reinstantiation is to look at the "performative" and "disclosive" in postmodernity. A postmodern reading of Kant emphasizes that sublime experience points to "that unpresentable Beyond that gives the lie to the totalizing claims of rational cognition."[12] The subject is humbled because "the incommensurability of reality to concept which is implied in the Kantian philosophy of the Sublime"[13] initiates the "discovery of the 'lack of reality' of reality, together with the invention of other realities."[14] This is why there has been such a flurry of interest in the sublime, since Lyotard recuperated the notion from Kant.

Yet this humbling is only a momentary effect of the sublime—this is the sublime's displeasure. We might just as well emphasize the other moment, that moment when something that seems at first to be *disclosed* to the subject in sublime experience, the givenness of the power of nature, discloses finally the pure *performative activity* of reason. This is the sublime's pleasure, when the subject recognizes that his reverence for nature has been misplaced, and reorients this reverence toward himself. This experience does involve a melting away of a sense of the externally real, but it also involves an experience of the "real" as precisely the internal accomplishing activity of the subject. And indeed, Lyotard recasts "seemingly non- or postreferential 'epistemology' in terms of linguistics, and in particular of theories of the performative."[15] So while the epistemological claims of the subject to know an external world that is *disclosed* are here detotalized, the *performative* activity of the subject becomes a kind of everything and everywhere, to be found in any apparently disclosive relation. To be sure, modern self-reverence is recast in the postmodern as *self-reference*, as the self-referentiality of texts, but the giddiness and exhilaration of the experience of finding the performative in the apparently disclosive amount to a kind of reverence in a sea of irreverence and remain every bit as focused on what subjects *do*, rather than on what they discover.

Fredric Jameson's discussion of the sculptures of Duane Hanson can serve to illustrate this point. Hanson's life-size polyester sculptures are on first glimpse lifelike. They are displayed in "real" settings. His *Museum Guard,* for example, is actually placed in the position a museum guard might occupy, and *Tourists II,* two stereotypically touristlike sculptures, are placed in a museum staring uncomprehendingly but importantly at a work of art. They are intended to be mistaken for the real thing. The experience created by making and then realizing this mistake is one of sublime intensity. These images, these signs, on Jameson's reading, have a "peculiar function" that

> lies in what Sartre would have called the derealization of the whole surrounding world of everyday reality. Your moment of doubt and hesitation as to the breath and warmth of these polyester figures, in other words, tends to return upon the real human beings moving about you in the museum and to transform them also for the briefest instant into so many dead and flesh-colored simulacra in their own right. The world thereby momentarily loses its depth and threatens to become a glossy skin, a stereoscopic illusion, a rush of filmic images without density. But is this now a terrifying or exhilarating experience?[16]

Both terrifying and exhilarating, I would argue; this experience is precisely that of "disclosivity" melting into "performativity," where something that seems at first to be not of human making, is discovered to be, essentially, a product, something *someone did*. Of course, this aesthetic experience is so effective precisely because it "points to" the "irreality" of living persons as well, the extent to which persons are *produced* in the *"chain of signification."* The experience certainly is humbling, since our perception of the real is destabilized, and the world around us is "derealized." But like Kant's sublime experience, our discomfort here gives way, on the one hand, to a kind of delight at the genius of the artist, that is, a kind of wonder at the accomplishing activity of a human subject. On the other hand, and even more significantly, it gives way to a wonder at the world of signs in which all of us are bound. This is the world of human making that *makes us*, that bestows social existence.[17]

While perhaps very appropriate to the world of art, there are consequences other than aesthetic delight when we repeat this experience in the face of *virtu-*

ally everything. When everything we confront in the external world gives rise to this melting away and delight at the self, Kantian self-reverence is reinstantiated in a kind of delirious postmodern register. We find ourselves everywhere. We are on the side of the subject to whom something is disclosed, and we are what is disclosed, because every act of "knowing" is an act of "making." *Disclosivity is really just performativity dissimulating.*

The consequences for our sense of place are here profound. Postmodernity has been very concerned to *locate* subjects, to recognize the *positionality* of subjects. Susan Bordo has perhaps recognized the subterfuge here most clearly, and again, the connections between the modern and postmodern are more revealing than their distinctions. "The Cartesian knower . . . being without a body, not only has 'no need of place' but actually is 'no place.'"[18] Yet the self of Cartesian consciousness becomes a kind of place, "'Myself' . . . is neither the public self, a social or familial identity, nor even the voice of personal conscience, belief, or commitment. It is an experiential 'space,' deeply interior."[19] As Casey puts it, "Within the machinations of this mental machine, place was reduced to what could be represented by icons, indices, or symbols: it became place-in-mind."[20] This interiority of the modern subject is turned inside out in postmodernity, where subjectivity does not inhabit the interior universe of individual subjects so much as it is the ocean we are swimming in. The entire world becomes a collective and textualized interiority, which is both made from and makes the performativity of each subject. Subjects engage here in textual play, a kind of "epistemological jouissance."[21] But as Bordo points out,

> This ideal [of ceaseless textual play] . . . although it arises out of a critique of modernist epistemological pretensions to represent reality adequately by achieving what Thomas Nagel has called the 'view from nowhere,' remains animated by its own fantasies of attaining an epistemological perspective free of the locatedness and limitations of embodied existence—a fantasy that I call a "dream of everywhere."[22]

Far from abandoning the modernist ideal of transcendence of place that created an interior universe of consciousness, the postmodern version simply exteriorizes and expands that universe, *in which* the now decentered and multiple subject engages in textual play. "Denial of the unity and stability of identity is one thing. The epistemological fantasy of becoming multiplicity—the dream of limitless multiple embodiments, allowing one to dance from place to place and self to self is another."[23] Without any limits between self and world, Bordo notes (or when the interiority of the subject becomes the exteriority of context, we might say), the postmodern subject is as placeless as the modern subject who was so concerned to wall up an interior consciousness over and against the world.

One need not dispute that there is much truth in this postmodern vision. We do live in significant and primary ways in what we build, whether technologically or linguistically. But is performativity *always* and *only* what is disclosed in our relationships with the worlds we make, the worlds that "world us" in Heidegger's terms? Only, I believe, if we are unwilling to fetishize our performative activity, particularly our capacities for language, will we have the wherewithal to *reorient* ourselves to what exceeds or *subtends* our prolific making.

It is only by asking an apparently naïve question that we are able to proceed. What enables all of this accomplishing activity, what enlivens the subject who is engaged in and by it? What is it that enlivens the body that speaks, that moment by moment, literally breath by breath, materially produces this body as a lived body to begin with? Philosophers have never taken seriously enough the all-too-commonplace reality that we have to breathe to think. Here I am presenting our relationship to the Earth in a very brute sense. I am reducing it, one might say, to its most basic and seemingly animalistic level, to that level where we don't make the world, but *it makes us*. Breath, heat/light, water, and food are all absolute necessities for philosophy, yet since the Ancients we have paid far too little attention to them, even though this seemingly mundane fact of human existence is the condition for the possibility of everything else. We don't make these four things (which correspond, of course, to the four elements of air, fire, water, and earth), though we may both cultivate and contaminate them. We *depend* on these gifts, irrevocably, absolutely, without choice or reprieve.

DEPENDENCE

> It was, after all, as a rejection of dependency on the feudal lord that Rousseau (echoing the sentiment of his day) declared the equality of men [*sic*]. But the deeper dependencies of infancy and early childhood, frail old age, disease and disability, do not vanish in a revolution. We have no lords to fight for this independence. So we have built fictions.
>
> —Eva Feder Kittay

> The independent individual is always a fictive creation of those men sufficiently privileged to shift the concern for dependence on to others.
>
> —Eva Feder Kittay

I admit to being rather smitten with Eva Kittay's work on dependence, which is saying a great deal, since I have a long-standing and almost lethal allergy to any sort of maternalism in feminist theory, and her work certainly comes out of this school. Yet Kittay's theory of dependence strikes me as in the very best tradition of feminist common sense. Starting with a simple and common aspect of the human condition, she proceeds to carefully and systematically dismantle the fetishization of independence in the Western political tradition. She manages this without essentializing women's relationship to mothering or caring, and without pretending that these relationships are gender-neutral. She insists, at the same time, that relationships in which persons depend on other persons for care are *essential* and *universal* relationships, and manages *this* claim without thereby depoliticizing such relations. On the contrary, Kittay is working to found feminist ethical and political claims on the bedrock of human dependency. Her work is germinal for feminist theories of epistemology, ethics, politics, and, I believe, for feminist environmentalism as well.

Kittay focuses on the most brute sorts of dependence—dependencies that are "inescapable," "inevitable," "determined neither by will nor desire," "unassailable facts," "unavoidable as birth and death," "a mark of our humanity"[24]—because only this kind of dependence provides "a knife sharp enough to cut through the fiction of our independence."[25] She is concerned with intersubjective dependence, the fact that dependents require care from other persons, and no one survives or thrives to become relatively *independent* without some minimal care from another.[26] Though influenced by maternalist ethics, Kittay's work cannot itself be said to be maternalist in the sense of ascribing a special epistemological vantage point, or moral insight to mothers. Her vision is far broader; she argues that the epistemological and moral footing to both know and fashion just social policies is in a *relationship* of dependence/care that *all of us* experience. It is more by virtue of having been mothered (and for Kittay, following Sara Ruddick, both men and women can mother), than by virtue of mothering, that we can know and do the right thing.

Several aspects of Kittay's work on dependence lend themselves to an articulation of the notion to the relationship between world and the Earth in a way that both acknowledges that this relation might become a battle and leaves open other possibilities. First, Kittay insists that relationships of dependence have a natural *priority* in relation to other kinds of human relationships. This priority has to do with the asymmetrical and nonreciprocal character of the relation, with the vulnerability of one person to another, with the inequality of power in the relation. Second, such relationships have immediate *moral* implications, including bestowing value on persons cared for, moral obligation on those in the position to care, and an equal entitlement to care on all persons in such relations. Third, the notion of dependence connects what we *are given* to what *we make* in a way that doesn't essentialize a conflict between them, but connects the human condition of dependence to political and social covenants. And fourth, there is a muted reference in Kittay's work to the *spiritual* implications of such relations. When we extend the notion of dependence to the relationship between persons and the Earth, all of these aspects remain important, though not simply analogous.

The priority of the relationship of dependence arises from its "ubiquity" in the human condition. "This relationship is ubiquitous in the human society and is as fundamental to our humanity as any property philosophers have invoked as distinctly human."[27] But in addition to the omnipresence of the most basic sorts of dependence in all cultures and at all times, it is also the condition for the possibility of all other human relations, since to come to a point of engaging in any relation, one must first be cared for. We can understand this priority as twofold. First, it is a *temporal* priority in the sense that everyone who achieves independence or interdependence is first dependent on another for care (and some people are always dependent). A relationship that is asymmetrical and nonreciprocal grounds more reciprocal relationships developmentally. Second, ongoing "independence," which is always a "relative independence" rather than absolute,[28] is purchased at a price.

> The world we know is one fashioned by the dreams of those who, by and large, consider themselves independent. Their self-understanding as independent persons is generally purchased at a price—one set so low and considered so inevitable that few have traditionally considered it pertinent to considerations of social justice. The purchase price of independence is a wife, a mother, a nursemaid, a nanny—a dependency worker.[29]

The very self-understanding that has founded Western conceits about independence requires the projection of necessary daily dependency work onto others. The independent political actor dissimulates; he keeps his dependency out of sight.

The very fabric of society is made up of what Kittay calls "nested dependencies." We can understand this in terms of the classic (today more mythical than real) situation of a young child in a relation of dependence to her mother; this relation is in turn "nested" in a relationship of dependency between these two and a breadwinner, who is himself "dependent" in relation to an employer, and so on. Though this classic situation is hardly in evidence anymore, dependency relations do seem to be nested in one another, as Kittay claims, more haphazardly but no less irrevocably than in the model of the nuclear family.

This insight seems to me to apply even more strongly to our dependence on the Earth, in which all such relationships are *ultimately* nested. Our dependency on the Earth does not shift and change over time like our intersubjective dependencies. We are moment to moment dependent in this more primary relation, cannot survive for more than a few minutes without the air and warmth the Earth "provides," for more than a few days without its water, for more than a few weeks without its food. The subject that was born in a fantasy of independence from *this* relationship dissimulates even more profoundly than the masculine breadwinner. This relation is the condition for the possibility for *any* intersubjective dependency relation or for any experience of relative independence. Moreover, it is a condition that follows the subject, moment by moment, place to place. It cannot be left behind at home like a dependency worker can.

Kittay is concerned to expose the ethical implications of dependency. "The relationship [of dependency] at its very crux, is a moral one, arising out of a claim of vulnerability on the part of the dependent on the one hand, and of a special positioning of the dependency worker to meet the need, on the other."[30] In morally charged moments, the needs of the dependent are prioritized over the needs of the dependency worker, and at such moments "this prioritization is absolute."[31]

A crucial distinction grounds Kittay's claim here, that between inequalities of power, and domination. Inequalities of power may result from domination certainly, but also from unequal capacities and from unequal situations (whether socially constructed or not). An inequality of power, the vulnerability of one person in relation to another, is precisely the morally charged situation that calls for a caring response. "Inequality of power is compatible with both justice and caring, if the relation does not become a relation of domination."[32] This is true whether or not the dependency relation is socially constructed, but Kittay does maintain that there are levels of coercion that void the claims of dependents to care. A "tyranny" of the caretaker by the dependent is a clear danger in some dependency relations. The dependent may "fail even to recognize the integrity of the other who exerts her labor on [her] behalf."[33] This said, the vulnerability of one person to another is ubiquitous in human relationships, as Kittay claims, and apart from situations of grave injustice, the moral claim these relations have on us seem to trump most others.

There is another aspect of the "claim" that these relations have on us that is even more general. Kittay uses an anecdote about her mother, who after serving food to the entire family would justify sitting down to eat herself by saying, "I, too, am some mother's child." Kittay turns this phrase, which could certainly be read as a particularly apt expression of the kind of self-effacing feminine virtue feminists criticize, into a study of how *caring* bestows *value*. There is a "fundamental connection between a mothering person and the fate of the individual she has mothered,"[34] Kittay claims, and this fundamental connection is recognized as a source of *entitlement* for the one who has received such care. In saying, "I, too, am some mother's child," one is claiming "I am due care," "I am worthy of this care," and "this worthiness is inalienable."[35] This establishes a new basis for moral claims, not in how persons are individuated or in terms of the properties they can be said to have, but in terms of the relationships of care in which they are bound. Because we are all "some mother's child," we can all claim the entitlement to care that this relation bestows.[36]

> That nothing can fully alienate the responsibility of others to recognize us as some mother's child resides in that feature of human existence that demands connection as a fundamental condition for human survival. . . . When we respect an individual as some mother's child, we honor the efforts of that mothering person and symbolically of all mothering persons. When we do not, not only are rights belonging to the abused individual violated, but the efforts of the mothering person are dishonored. The sanctity of the relation that makes possible all human connection *per se* is thereby disavowed.[37]

The moral situation we find ourselves in in relationship to the Earth is certainly not the same moral relation that we find ourselves in in relation to one another. We would have to anthropomorphize the Earth beyond all recognition to speak of the "obligations" that "she" has to us by virtue of our dependency on "her." But there are two aspects of Kittay's discussion of the moral implications of dependency that do seem relevant to a discussion of our dependence on the Earth. If, as Kittay claims, "dependency relations are the paradigmatic moral relations,"[38] then the dependency relation in which all others are nested must be the paradigm of paradigms. This relationship, too, is characterized by vulnerability, and as such is a moral relation (for us) at its very crux. Of course, in this case we are talking first about *our own* vulnerability, but it is precisely in this sort of experience that Kittay finds epistemological footing for moral claims. That we have chosen the path of "tyranny" over and against the Earth in this relationship, have "failed to recognize the integrity" of the Earth as separate from ourselves, have chosen to do battle with the Earth to the point of suicidal destruction of the environment, bespeaks an unfathomable *moral and epistemological* failure. Yet it is *possible* to know how to behave in the face of our vulnerability to the Earth; this very vulnerability is the vantage point from which we are called to right action.

This can be more clearly understood in terms of the second aspect of Kittay's discussion of the moral implications of dependency, which seems to me to be very relevant to our dependency on the Earth. Kittay's insight that dependency relations bestow value on dependents has implications for our relations with one another as all equally dependent on the Earth. "I, too, am given life by this Earth," might be a kind of environmentalist equivalent of Kittay's, "I, too, am some mother's child." Our inability to care for one another in our intersubjective relations (and here my "we" extends between nations and cultures) constitutes a second moral failure—but here we do not simply fail each other, we fail one another *in relation* to our dependency on the planet. We *dishonor* that relation as much as we dishonor one another.

That these moral failures are borne out in our social and political institutions is perhaps too obvious to require comment. "Questions of who takes on the responsibility of care, who does the hands-on care, who sees to it that the caring is done and done well, and who provides the support for the relationship of care and for both parties to the caring relationship—these are social and political questions. They are questions of social responsibility and political will."[39] Our failure to honor dependency relations in our social and political institutions is, on Kittay's reading, a failure to fulfill "the obligation of society to attend to relationships upon which all civic relationships depend." If dependents and those who care for them, and their *relationship*, are not protected and enabled by the social and political institutions we build, we have absolved ourselves of our "most fundamental obligation," the obligation to the "founding possibility" of society itself.[40] For Kittay, how we understand, how we *revere or disregard*, relations of dependency will determine a great deal about what kind of political institutions we build.

Of course, in our violence toward the natural world we turn away from an equally fundamental obligation, an obligation to the Earth that gives us life, moment by moment, breath by breath, while we build a world to live in. Like ourselves, *our world* is dependent on the Earth that sustains us. Furthermore, it is in this relation of dependence that "the political" becomes meaningful to begin with. In saying this, I'm claiming that this relationship is the ground or space on which domination is built, and struggles for liberation, equality, democracy, and so forth, are waged. How we understand, how we *revere or disregard* our relation to the planet will be key in every instance to how we engage political questions. This essential relationship between persons and the Earth gives the political a weight and depth, makes the political an urgent matter. If we understood our world-making to entail a fundamental obligation to protect and support our relation to the Earth, *which is its founding possibility*, what a different sort of world we would make!

Instead, fantasies of finally dominating the Earth permeate our social and political life. It seems to me that these circumstances bespeak not only a moral and political depravity, but a spiritual one as well. Though Kittay never explicitly evokes "the sacred" in her dependency critique, she seems to sense a violation of the sacred at the heart of our disregard for relations of dependence. When we are forgetful that an individual is "some mother's child," Kittay argues, "not only are the rights belonging to the abused individual violated, but the efforts of the mothering person are dishonored. The *sanctity* of the relation that makes possible all human connection *per se* is thereby disavowed."[41] Kittay moves here from the political (rights), to the moral (honor), to the spiritual (sanctity) in this short passage. A violation of this fundamental relationship is a violation at all three levels.

It is interesting to note that the historical moment that was marked by an extraordinary new fetishizing of independence or autonomy as the sine qua non of truly human life was equally marked by an exchange of the sacred for the "profane" products of human reason. If Kittay is correct in claiming that our inalienable entitlement to recognition as "some mother's child," "resides in that feature of human existence that demands connection as a fundamental condition for human survival,"[42] perhaps our very capacities for moral action and experience of the sacred reside in that feature of human existence that is our relationship of dependence to the Earth.

The word *reside* is important here, of course, evocative as it is of that very relationship. We not only depend on the Earth, we live here. It strikes me that the claim "I, too, am some mother's child" *locates* the specific person uttering the claim in a specific relation to another; it also locates her as a child among others, as equally a mother's child, crossing in one breath the border between the specific and the general, the one and the many. The utterance establishes a *place* for her in a vast world so populous with indifferent strangers, but she has this place *like others* have a place, or should have. By saying "I, too, am some mother's child," one claims, along with Kittay's mother, "I, too, have a place here at the table, which is my sacred right." To be "some mother's child" is to be some *place*, to be entitled to *place,* to take one's *place*, to be *im-placed*.

PERSONS AND PLACES

> There is no being except being in place. . . . To be a sentient bodily being at all
> is to be place-bound, bound to be in a place, bonded and bound therein.
>
> —Edward S. Casey

> When it comes to being ethical, there is no escaping the imperative of place.
>
> —Edward S. Casey

> A stance of ecocentrism does not, however, signify that the only genuinely eco-
> logical issue is whether we can save or preserve the land, especially wild land.
> We can and should and must do just this. But the more pressing question from
> a lococentric perspective is whether we will let the land save us.
>
> —Edward S. Casey

Edward S. Casey's *Getting Back into Place* is perhaps one of the first and most important postmodern redemption narratives. In this, it goes against the grain of the
postmodern, where we are, if nothing else, beyond redemption. For Casey, whose
work leads him into environmentalism, the deepest question is not whether we will
save the land, but "whether we will let *the land save us.*"[43] This is the motivating
question behind his complex narratives of place, the kind of attention to place that
may be capable of saving "those in a displaced, secular, and postmodern age who
lack any sense of a perduring place of collective self-belonging."[44] Indeed, in postmodernity we seem to be reaping the whirlwind of modern disregard for nature and
nature's gift of place. As Jameson put it, "postmodernism is what you have when the
modernization process is complete and nature is gone for good."[45] Jameson's reading of the postmodern is useful in order to understand what getting back into place
might *redeem us from.* For Jameson, the postmodern is fundamentally a repudiation
of depth, as characterized by "the emergence of a new kind of flatness or depthless-
ness, a new kind of superficiality in the most literal sense, [which is] perhaps the
supreme formal feature of all the postmodernisms."[46] This repudiation has focused
on at least four separate "depth models," including "the dialectical one of essence
and appearance . . . the Freudian model of latent and manifest . . . the existential
model of authenticity and inauthenticity . . . and most recently, the great semiotic opposition between signifier and signified."[47] All of these amount to an exchange of
depth for surface.

But what kind of place is a postmodern surface? What happens to the Earth in
a world of surfaces? Is the Earth itself another surface? We certainly say that we
live "on" the Earth, perhaps envisioning ourselves as in a child's drawing, pop-
up stick figures on a smooth, round, crayon-line planet. The surfaces we are left
with in postmodernism are not the "sensuous surfaces" of landscape;[48] such *deep*
surfaces have given way to the smooth flatness of a shopping-mall planet, where

"depth, the elusive basis of all dimensions, indeed the 'first dimension,' has been eliminated in favor of shallowness of affect and image, a flatness reinforced by glossy walls and sleek floors."[49] In Casey's terms, this amounts to an exchange of places for mere sites. Places, which are everywhere local and specific and rich in their specificity, are exchanged for sites, like shopping malls, everywhere alike and interchangeable. A site is certainly a kind of location, but it is a location emptied of depth, which is "a matter—perhaps even *the matter*—of place."[50] A depthless surface is devoid of both "life [and] place."[51] "A site is no place to be, much less to remain. It is not even worth a postmodern nomadic journey to get there. Once there, moreover, where are we?"[52] We are no place, dis-placed on the surface. We surface dwellers, it seems, live in a perpetual state of dis-orientation, on a mere planet, which is what the Earth becomes when it is no longer able to provide us with places. Even though our lack of orientation might engender postmodern excitement, terrifying and exhilarating as all sublime experience is, we are no less *mis-placed* for our giddiness.

This mis-placement is also an emptying out (individually, collectively). For Casey, placelessness gives rise to "a sense of unbearable emptiness."[53] And indeed, the postmodern subject has been emptied out, has him/herself become a mere site in the chain of signification,[54] even as signifying activity swallows up depth, both internal and external. When we are empty sites, mere occasions ourselves, the meaningfulness of our accomplishing activity, of our "world-making" collapses into mere discursive playfulness, into surface.

The point of Casey's work (and indeed Jameson's in another dimension), is to *get us back into place*, so that "we can resume the direction, and regain the depth of our individual and collective life once again—and know it for the first time."[55] Casey's implication, that we are dangerously off course, is reflected in the chorus of voices that have decried our *dis-orientation*, as a complex of Euro-American cultures, if not as a species, since World War II. But for Casey, it is the "insurrectional power of place"[56] itself that can counter the massive disorientation that characterizes postmodern life. By "getting back into place itself, back into the very idea, indeed the very experience, of place," we might "re-orient" ourselves in the most radical sense.

It is this notion of *reorientation* that is provocative in our consideration of dependency. If the Euro-masculinist abnegation and projection onto others of our dependence on the Earth is part of what has dis-placed, and thus dis-oriented us, then a reaffirmation of this relation might be the first step in an urgent *re*orientation.

Perhaps this is the time to note that I have been speaking all along of "the Earth," as if we really lived on/in the entire global sphere, rather than in the specific places *where we actually are*. Specific places are what we inhabit, never "the Earth" in some grander sense. Yet places are nested, like Kittay's dependencies, one in the other. This specific room where I write is in this flat, which in turn is in this 100-year-old house (which survived the two great earthquakes), in San

Francisco, in Northern California, and so forth. My invocation of dependency to name our relationship to the Earth is simply a shortcut for our dependency on the specific places, nested in one another, for which the Earth is simply the most encompassing horizon, the boundary that gives all of these places their own limit, and thus existence.

I mean to invoke "dependency" to name our relation to place at its most brutal and unforgiving, yet where we are perhaps most ungrateful and forgetful, our irrevocable dependence on air, heat/light, water, and food. But this relation is no mere biological imperative—certainly without these gifts we would die, and die as bodies die—but who has ever seen a *mere body* die? Who, indeed, has ever seen a *mere body* that was not already dead? Believing ourselves trapped within a prison of mortality, cursed to be bounded by flesh and blood, we have misunderstood that it is not only our biological life but our mental and spiritual life that are gifts of the planet. But this very "bounding" is what gives us existence in the fullest sense, is the condition for the possibility of *every aspect* of human existence, from the most primal biological functioning to the most developed spiritual practice.

Without focusing on dependency in the brute sense I am proposing here, Casey argues for the priority of place in a way that illuminates this multifaceted relation.[57] Attention to dependence, to this primary asymmetrical, nonreciprocal relation between persons and places strengthens the case Casey makes for the priority of place. At the same time, Casey's narrative of the many ways in which place is primary adds dimension to our study of dependence and lends depth to our description of the dependency *relation* between persons and places. Though Casey speaks on occasion of "the mutual enlivening of body and landscape,"[58] "the reciprocity of person and place,"[59] or "the mutual determination of person and place,"[60] the overwhelming focus of his work is on restoring a proper *priority* to place. "Orientation," he argues, "is given primarily by the places and not by my own body."[61] It is urgent that we "let the land take the lead,"[62] "let the Earth be the guiding force,"[63] because "*its* power, not ours in relation to it, is what is at stake."[64]

The priority of place in relation to performative activity is (at least) threefold. Places are phenomenologically prior (in the order of description), ontologically prior (in the order of being), and also "primary in the order of culture." Place is phenomenologically prior in that our implacement underlies our bodily experience and perception: places are "the pre-positions of our bodily lives, underlying every determinate bodily action or position, every static posture of our corpus, every coagulation of living experience in thought or word, sensation or memory, image or gesture."[65] Our very capacity to sense, perceive, describe is rooted in place. Places are ontologically prior. To exist at all is to be bounded or limited, to be bordered by place. This bordering or limiting is part of that very existence. If "there is no being except being in place,"[66] then it is because to be at all means to be limited by place, and "the limit of an existing thing is intrinsic to its being."[67] Place is primary in the order of culture, as well. "Just as every place is encultured, so every culture is implaced":[68] place is on the *inside* of culture as well as on the outside of culture, or under and around culture, which is always built in relation to place. Of course, another way of naming the priority of place in relation to us is to say *we depend on place*, phenomenologically, ontologically, and culturally. It is not difficult to see that these three aspects of place are actually *three modes of our dependence* on place.

One short passage reflects not only our multifaceted dependence on place, but how this dependence might *orient* us: "To be a sentient bodily being at all is to be place-bound, bound to be in a place, bonded and bound therein."[69] Casey's multiple senses of "bond/bound" are important here and carry us from an ontological priority, through a kind of telos, to a moral and ethical imperative, and to the human condition itself. First, we are place-*bound*, that is, dependent on place to provide a *boundary*, a limit to our existence. Second, we are *bound* to be in a place. As a condition of existence, "place-being is part of an entity's own-being;"[70] we are *purposively* bound to be there, we depend on place because it is part of who and what *we are* to be there. Our dependence on place means we are "bonded" by place, which for my purposes I would like to read as both "tied by affection or loyalty" and "obligated by a moral duty, a vow, or a promise." And finally, our dependence on place means we are "bound therein," embedded in place, through and through indebted to place.

Just as Kittay finds in intersubjective dependency relations an orientation that can inform our ethical choices, our social and political practice, we find in our relation of dependence on place an orientation that provides social, political, ethical, and spiritual direction. Casey hints at this connection when he remarks parenthetically that "anomie, a lack of social norms or values, often stems from atopia."[71] In reference to built places, Casey notes that the very activity of building or cultivation "localizes caring," that is, it gives caring a place. "We care about places as well as people," he writes, "so that we can say that *caring belongs to places*."[72] But this connection is precisely what we cannot take for granted, since we live in a world where the destruction of place, of the very ability of the Earth to provide us with places, seems to be on its way to becoming an absolute of the human condition. Perhaps in this case we would have to say, of the *inhuman* condition, since once places are gone, certainly humans will be gone as well. But if our intersubjective dependency is precisely the source of the moral call to care rather than to domination, then our dependency on the Earth is such a source as well. The importance of recuperating a sense of humility in the face of our dependence on the Earth is nothing less than the importance of recuperating a sense of what it means to be persons in place, that is, of our very humanity. In speaking of the indigenous people who have inhabited a particular place, Casey writes that "to inhabit a place in terms of the habitat and habitus is thus to re-inhabit it by living here on *preestablished terms* laid down long before the actual advent of current homesteaders."[73] But the "preestablished terms" are perhaps more clearly the ones that the very indigenous inhabitants seem to have been able, at least in many cases, to live *by and with,* rather than against. These are the terms that we, in what we call the "Western world," seem determined to live in rebellion against, no matter how suicidal and homicidal such a path ultimately proves to be. These are terms that are *disclosed to us* in the dependency relation, which is the condition for all other relations, and indeed for our very existence.

When Kant believed he looked into the mirror of nature only to see himself, perhaps he was right in one sense, and one sense only—nature *gives us* ourselves. But the Earth gives us to ourselves first *as children,* only later and only apparently as "independent" world-making adults. Our dependence on the Earth, which accompanies us through every experience, on every journey, moment by moment, is not something we make, even with our most powerful "performative" tool, language itself. When we say "Earth," as enculturated and enculturating as this speech is, still on the very inside of our speech is our breathing of the Earth's air, our being warmed by its heat, our drinking of its water, our eating of its food— all of which are prior to any saying of the Earth. On the inside of that utterance is the very enabling and enlivening relation of dependency on the Earth. This relation is not merely constructed in language, it enables language, it is the condition for the possibility of language, and thus *inhabits* language from the outset. The disclosive, at least here, discloses that the performative *would be nowhere at all* without place. The Earth is the very founding condition for the possibility of the worlds that we make.

Of course, we in the Euro-masculinist cultures of the West have misunderstood our dependence on the Earth as a kind of coercion and have responded by doing battle. We have not wanted to be "on nature's leading strings," so what we have made of our dependence is an ethical, social, and political disaster. We have failed the moral and political challenge of our *status as children* in relation to the Earth. This is, of course, a status that is not analogous to that of actual young people vis-à-vis their parents, because this moral relation demands care *from us* rather than simply for us. By this, I mean we have failed to respond in a situation of dependence with care, both for the Earth itself, and for one another. Anyone can claim, "I, too, am given life by this Earth," and this claim calls for an ethics and a politics of care that is both Earth-focused and intersubjective. Our response has been, instead, one of domination—against one another, but ultimately also against the Earth itself. This means that we have failed to protect the relationship that is the very founding condition of our capacities for care and of our world-making activity.

A profound miscarriage of reverence marks this failure. Kant failed to acknowledge that *the Earth has a claim on us* and instead treated the natural world as a mere site, a mere occasion for the dramas of reason. Though he claimed to be merely reversing a subreption by which nature had inspired such awe in "man," in fact the subreption was altogether the other way around. The "autonomy" that founds the self-reverence of the modern subject is both fraudulent and fictitious. And so is the fetishizing of performativity over and against disclosivity in postmodernity. The Earth has a claim on us, and this claim is on the very inside of our existence as subjects, of our capacities for language, and of the worlds that we make. The skeptical approach to the Earth, the doubt that *anything* is given, is a response that violates the sanctity of our relation to the Earth and that dishonors the Earth in the process. In saying this, I am saying that wonder, not doubt, and certainly not hostility, is the appropriate philosophical attitude in relation to *our relation* to the Earth. This wonder is called for in and by the very moment-to-moment sustenance, the moment-to-moment life-giving that is our dependence on the places the Earth provides us.

What Thoreau called "intelligence with the Earth"[74] is only possible on the basis of reverence for the Earth. Indeed, our *irreverence* toward the Earth has resulted in nothing less than environmental depravity. An "ethics and politics with the Earth" requires first a wonder-filled recognition of our utter and absolute dependence in relation to it.

NOTES

1. I use *Euro-masculinist,* much as I use the terms *West* or *Western.* These are political terms that describe the perpetrators of colonization and inheritors of the wealth and power accumulated during European colonization of much of the rest of the planet (which continues today). In this sense, neither are all women excluded from the descriptive scope of these terms, nor are all peoples of the geographic West included. All such terms are necessarily imprecise and inadequate, but neither can we do without them when discussing the grand themes of world history and thought that plague us globally. I choose *Euro-masculinist* because it points to both the economic and political dominance of Europe and (some) European-descended peoples and the masculinist frameworks in which this dominance was achieved and continues to be maintained.

2. Hannah Arendt, *The Human Condition* (Chicago: University of Chicago Press, 1958), 2.

3. Edward S. Casey, *Getting Back into Place: Toward a Renewed Understanding of the Place World* (Bloomington: Indiana University Press, 1993), xiii. These texts name the problem in various ways. Eliade speaks of the sacred and profane, Hannah Arendt of world-alienation, Weber and Berman of disenchantment, Susan Bordo of a "flight" from the feminine, Casey of "humanocentrism"—all are attempting in some way to name a fundamental transition in the relation of humans to the cosmos. To call this a transition from *reverence to self-reverence,* as I do here, is only to give a slightly different turn to these other formulations, but one that allows for a clear analogue between modern and postmodern philosophies. It is also to allow for a broad view of what is going on (as does Casey's "humanocentrism")—since it is not only subjectivist turns that centered human subjectivity but "realist" ones as well—the problem is not so much the epistemologies as the self-reverential position of the human knower in them.

4. Arendt, *Human Condition,* 2.

5. Martin Heidegger, "The Origin of the Work of Art," in *Poetry, Language and Thought,* trans. Albert Hofstadter (New York: Harper Colophon, 1971), 15–87.

6. The phrase "a knife sharp enough" is Kittay's; she uses it in an intersubjective context to try to "cut through" the myth of independence. Eva Feder Kittay, *Love's Labor: Essays on Women, Equality, and Dependency* (New York: Routledge, 1999), xiii.

7. Casey, *Getting Back into Place*, xi. Casey distinguishes space and place in this way: "The infinity and silence of space reflects its emptiness. They also signify the absence of place. For space as a vast vacuum does not allow for places, even though one might think that there would be plenty of room for them! In such space there are no places for particular things."

8. Casey, *Getting Back into Place*, 187.

9. Arendt, *Human Condition*, 262.

10. Immanuel Kant, *The Critique of Judgement,* trans. James Creed Meredith (Oxford: Clarendon, 1928). I am not so much accusing Kant of gendering nature here, explicitly, as I am pointing to a general and widespread cultural association of nature with the feminine, and reason with the masculine.

11. Kant's gendering of the imagination and reason simply follows the cultural associations mentioned previously. The imagination's association with the feminine is necessitated by its reliance on sense experience and consequent close association with nature. This gendering has been analyzed by feminist scholars such as Cornelia Klinger and is made explicit in Lyotard's reading of the Kantian sublime. Cornelia Klinger, "The Concepts of the Sublime and Beautiful in Kant and Lyotard," in *Feminist Interpretations of Immanuel Kant,* ed. Robin May Schott (University Park: Pennsylvania State University Press, 1997). Lyotard's extraordinary and seemingly exultant narrative on the Kantian sublime, which he refers to as "a family story," centers on a scene in which father (reason) rapes mother (imagination): "The sublime is the child of an unhappy encounter, that of the Idea with form. Unhappy because this Idea is unable to make concessions. The law (the father) is so authoritarian, so unconditional, and the regard the law requires so exclusive that he, the father, will do nothing to obtain consent, even through a delicious rivalry with the imagination. . . . He fertilizes the virgin who has devoted herself to forms, without regard for her favor. He demands regard only for himself, to the law and its realization. He has no need for a beautiful nature. He desperately needs an imagination that is violated, exceeded, exhausted. She will die in giving birth to the sublime. She will think she is dying [my translation]." Jean Francois Lyotard, "Das Interesse des Erhabene," in *Das Erhabene: Zwischen Grenzerfahrung und Grossenwahn,* ed. Christine Pries (Weinheim: VCH, 1989), 108–09.

12. Kirk Pillow, *Sublime Understanding: Aesthetic Reflection in Kant and Hegel* (Cambridge: MIT Press, 2000), 5–6.

13. Jean Francois Lyotard, *The Postmodern Condition: A Report on Knowledge,* trans. Geoff Bennington and Brian Massumi (Minneapolis: University of Minnesota Press, 1984), 79.

14. Lyotard, *Postmodern Condition,* 77.

15. Jameson in Lyotard, *Postmodern Condition,* ix.

16. Fredric Jameson, *Postmodernism or the Cultural Logic of Late Capitalism* (Durham, N.C.: Duke University Press, 1991), 32–34.

17. As Butler puts it, "Bound to seek recognition of its own existence in categories, terms, and names that are not of its own making the subject seeks the sign of its own existence outside itself, in a discourse that is at once dominant and indifferent." Judith Butler, *The Psychic Life of Power: Theories in Subjection* (Stanford, Calif.: Stanford University Press, 1997), 20.

18. Susan Bordo, *Feminist Interpretations of René Descartes* (University Park: Pennsylvania State University Press, 1999), 61.

19. Susan Bordo, *Feminist Interpretations*, 52.

20. Casey, *Getting Back into Place*, 312.

21. Susan R. Bordo, *Unbearable Weight: Feminism, Western Culture, and the Body* (Berkeley: University of California Press, 1993), 228.

22. Bordo, *Unbearable Weight*, 218.

23. Bordo, *Unbearable Weight*, 229.

24. Kittay, *Love's Labor*, 29.

25. Though a kind of brute dependence is presocial, how care for dependents is organized is deeply political, and many kinds of dependence are, at the root, political, such as the traditional dependence of men on women for the preparation of food and organizing of the household, for example, or the traditional dependence of women on men for income. Kittay, *Love's Labor*, xiii.

26. Kittay, *Love's Labor*, 1.

27. Kittay, *Love's Labor*, 25.

28. Kittay, *Love's Labor*, 184.

29. Kittay, *Love's Labor*, 183.

30. Kittay, *Love's Labor*, 35.

31. Kittay, *Love's Labor*, 52.

32. Kittay, *Love's Labor*, 34.

33. Kittay, *Love's Labor*, 35.

34. Kittay, *Love's Labor*, 24.

35. Kittay, *Love's Labor*, 68.

36. Kittay, *Love's Labor*, 27–28.

37. Kittay, *Love's Labor*, 69, emphasis added.

38. Kittay, *Love's Labor*, 71.

39. Kittay, *Love's Labor*, 1.

40. Kittay, *Love's Labor*, 130–31.

41. Kittay, *Love's Labor*, 69.

42. Kittay, *Love's Labor*, 69.

43. Casey, *Getting Back into Place*, 263, emphasis added.

44. Casey, *Getting Back into Place*, 309.

45. Jameson, *Postmodernism*, ix.

46. Jameson, *Postmodernism*, 9.

47. Jameson, *Postmodernism*, 12.

48. Casey, *Getting Back into Place*, 270.

49. Casey, *Getting Back into Place*, 269–70.

50. Casey, *Getting Back into Place*, 67.

51. Casey, *Getting Back into Place*, 269.

52. Casey, *Getting Back into Place*, 208.

53. Casey, *Getting Back into Place*, x.

54. As Butler writes, "The genealogy of the subject as a critical category . . . suggests that the subject, rather than be identified strictly with the individual, ought to be designated as a linguistic category, a *placeholder*, a structure in formation. Individuals come to *occupy the site* of the subject (the subject simultaneously *emerges as a 'site'* [Butler 1997, 11, emphasis added]).

55. Casey, *Getting Back into Place*, 314.

56. Casey, *Getting Back into Place*, 314.

57. In a fascinating passage on atmosphere in wild places, Casey does allude to this dependence: "As an inherent presence, atmosphere is invigorating and has as its most palpable expression the actual 'breath' of a living creature, though it is also at play as the air that penetrates and moves through inorganic substances. The overall effect is to alleviate and animate any given wildscape: to bestow upon it an *elan vital* that vivifies the whole scene and not just the literally alive being in it" (Casey, *Getting Back into Place*, 220).

58. Casey, *Getting Back into Place*, 29.

59. Casey, *Getting Back into Place*, 307.

60. Casey, *Getting Back into Place*, 308.

61. Casey, *Getting Back into Place*, 225.

62. Casey, *Getting Back into Place*, 260.

63. Casey, *Getting Back into Place*, 260.

64. Casey, *Getting Back into Place*, 264.

65. Casey, *Getting Back into Place*, 313.

66. Casey, *Getting Back into Place*, 313.

67. Casey, *Getting Back into Place*, 15.

68. Casey, *Getting Back into Place*, 31.

69. Casey, *Getting Back into Place*, 313.

70. Casey, *Getting Back into Place*, 16.

71. Casey, *Getting Back into Place*, xi.

72. Casey, *Getting Back into Place*, 175.

73. Casey, *Getting Back into Place*, 295, emphasis added.

74. Cited in Casey, *Getting Back into Place*, 245.

Index

About the Contributors

Diemut Grace Bubeck was senior lecturer in political theory at the London School of Economics, where she worked on feminist political theory, ethics, and Nietzsche. She published *Care, Gender, and Justice* (Clarendon Press, 1995) and numerous articles on the ethic of care and feminist theory. She now lives in Montreal and helps people to heal.

Ellen K. Feder is assistant professor in the Department of Philosophy and Religion at American University. She is editor, with Mary Rawlinson and Emily Zakin, of *Derrida and Feminism: Recasting the Question of Woman* (Routledge) and of a special issue of *Hypatia* on the "Family and Feminist Theory" with Eva Feder Kittay. She is currently at work on a monograph, *Disciplining the Family*.

Martha L.A. Fineman is the Dorothea S. Clarke professor of Feminist Jurisprudence at Cornell Law School. She is the author of *The Illusion of Equality: The Rhetoric and Reality of Divorce Reform* (University of Chicago Press, 1991) and *The Neutered Mother, the Sexual Family and Other Twentieth Century Tragedies* (Routledge, 1995), as well as numerous articles. Professor Fineman is also coeditor of *At the Boundaries of the Law: Feminism and Legal Theory* (Routledge, 1990); *The Public Nature of Private Violence* (Routledge, 1994); Mothers in Law (Columbia University Press, 1995); *Feminism, Media and the Law* (Oxford University Press, 1997); and *Feminism Confronts Homo Economicus* (Duke University Press, 2002).

Nancy Fraser is the Henry and Louise A. Loeb Professor of Politics and Philosophy at the Graduate Faculty of the New School for Social Research.

She is coeditor of *Constellations: An International Journal of Critical and Democratic Theory.* Her books include *Unruly Practices: Power, Discourse, and Gender in Contemporary Social Theory; Justice Interruptus: Critical Reflections on the "Postsocialist" Condition;* and *Adding Insult to Injury: Social Justice and the Politics of Recognition.* She has coauthored (with Seyla Benhabib, Judith Butler, and Drucilla Cornell) *Feminist Contentions: A Philosophical Exchange* and (with Axel Honneth) *Redistribution or Recognition? A Political-Philosophical Exchange.* Her current research is on globalization.

Diane Gibson is head of the Aged Care Unit of the Australian Institute of Health and Welfare. She is editor in chief of the *Australian Journal on Aging* and author of articles and books on social policy and feminism, including, most recently, *Aged Care: Old Policies, New Problems* (Cambridge University Press, 1998).

Robert E. Goodin is professor of social and political theory and philosophy in the Research School of Social Sciences, Australian National University. He is founding editor of *The Journal of Political Philosophy* and author of articles and books on political theory and public policy, including *Protecting the Vulnerable* (University of Chicago Press, 1985) and, most recently, *Reflective Democracy* (Oxford University Press, 2002).

Linda Gordon is professor of history at New York University, where she teaches courses on social movements and women's history. She is the author of books about family violence (*Heroes of Their Own Lives*) and welfare (*Pitied but Not Entitled*). Her most recent book, *The Great Arizona Orphan Abduction,* won the Bancroft prize for best book in U.S. history. An entirely revised and updated edition of her history of birth control politics, *The Moral Property of Women,* will be published late in 2002.

Eva Feder Kittay is professor of philosophy at the State University of New York, Stony Brook. Her most recent book is *Love's Labor: Essays on Women, Equality, and Dependency.* She has coedited special issues of *Hypatia* on "Feminism and Disability," and the "Family and Feminist Theory," as well as a special issue of *Social Theory and Practice* on "Embodied Values: Philosophy and Disabilities." Her previous books include *Women and Moral Theory; Metaphor: Its Cognitive Force and Linguistic Structure;* and *Frames, Fields, and Contrasts.* Her current work focuses on philosophical issues of disability.

Bonnie Mann is a longtime feminist activist and a Ph.D. candidate at the State University of New York, Stony Brook. Her dissertation, "Feminism and the Sublime," is an environmentalist and feminist critique of feminist post-modernism. She is a lecturer in philosophy at Sonoma State University in California.

Martha McCluskey is professor of law at the State University of New York at Buffalo. Her teaching and research interests include insurance law and policy, constitutional law, feminist legal theory, the welfare state, and regulatory law.

Martha C. Nussbaum is Ernst Freund Distinguished Service Professor of Law and Ethics at the University of Chicago, with appointments in the Philosophy Department, Law School, and Divinity School. She is on the board of the Center for Gender Studies and the Human Rights Program and is the coordinator of the New Center for Comparative Constitutionalism. She is the author of numerous books, the most recent of which are *Women and Human Development* (2000) and *Upheavals of Thought: The Intelligence of Emotions* (2001).

Kelly Oliver is professor of philosophy and women's studies at the State University of New York, Stony Brook. Her most recent books include *Noir Anxiety* (Minnesota, 2002), *Witnessing: Beyond Recognition* (Minnesota, 2001), and *Subjectivity without Subjects: From Abject Fathers to Desiring Mothers* (Rowman & Littlefield, 1998). She has also edited several anthologies, including *Enigmas: Essays on Sarah Kofman* (Cornell, 1999), *The Portable Kristeva* (Columbia, 1997), and *French Feminism Reader* (Rowman & Littlefield, 2000).

Dorothy E. Roberts holds the Kirkland and Ellis Chair at Northwestern University School of Law and is a faculty fellow of the Institute for Policy Research. She is a recipient of the 1998 Myers Center Award for the Study of Human Rights in North America. Her writings include *Killing the Black Body: Race, Reproduction, and the Meaning of Liberty* (Pantheon, 1997) and *Shattered Bonds: The Color of Child Welfare* (Basic, 2002). She serves as a consultant to the Center for Women Policy Studies and the Open Society Institute's Program on Reproductive Health and Rights, and as a member of the board of directors of the National Black Women's Health Project, the National Coalition for Child Protection Reform, and the Public Interest Law Center of New Jersey.

Ofelia Schutte is professor of women's studies and philosophy at the University of South Florida. Her areas of teaching and research are feminist theory, Latin American philosophy and social thought, philosophy of culture, and Continental European philosophy. She is the author of *Beyond Nihilism: Nietzsche without Masks*; *Cultural Identity and Social Liberation in Latin American Thought*; and numerous articles on feminist, Latin American, and Continental philosophy. Her current interests include all of the above, with a focus on theorizing Latin American, postcolonial, and transnational feminisms.

Elizabeth V. Spelman is professor of philosophy and the Barbara Richmond 1940 Professor in the Humanities at Smith College. The author of *Inessential Woman: Problems of Exclusion in Feminist Thought and Fruits of Sorrow: Framing Our Attention to Suffering*, she presently is at work on a book about the nature of repair.

Rickie Solinger is a historian and the author of *Beggars and Choosers: How the Politics of Choice Shapes Adoption, Abortion, and Welfare* (2001); *The Abortionist: A Woman against the Law* (1994); and *Wake Up Little Susie: Single Pregnancy and Race before Roe v. Wade* (1992, 2000). She is the editor of *Abortion Wars: A Half-Century of Struggle, 1950–2000* (1998) and coeditor, with Gwendolyn Mink, of *Welfare: A Documentary History of U.S. Policy and Politics* (forthcoming). She is currently writing a short history of reproductive politics in the United States and working on a book about the first welfare case ever heard by the U.S. Supreme Court.

Robin West is professor of law at Georgetown University Law Center, where she teaches legal philosophy, feminist legal theory, law and literature, torts, and contracts. She is the author of *Caring for Justice* (New York University Press, 1997), *Progressive Constitutionalism* (Duke University Press, 1994), and *Narrative, Authority and Law* (University of Michigan Press, 1993).

Iris Marion Young is professor of political science at the University of Chicago, where she is also affiliated with the Center for Gender Studies and the Human Rights Program. She is author of several books and many articles in political philosophy. Her most recent books are *Inclusion and Democracy* (Oxford University Press, 2000) and *Intersecting Voices: Dilemmas of Gender, Political Philosophy and Policy* (Princeton University Press, 1997). She has begun a project to conceptualize issues of political responsibility in the context of structural injustice.